PRINCIPLES FOR PEACE

Principles for Peace

Selections From Papal Documents

LEO XIII TO PIUS XII

Edited for the Bishops' Committee

on the Pope's Peace Points

By the Reverend Harry C. Koenig, S.T.D.,

Librarian, Saint Mary of the Lake Seminary,

Mundelein, Illinois

With a Preface

By the Most Reverend Samuel A. Stritch, D.D.,

Archbishop of Chicago

NATIONAL CATHOLIC WELFARE CONFERENCE

WASHINGTON

1943

10 500

To

Pius XII

with the prayer

that

"peace, the work of justice,"

may be realized

in our time.

PREFACE

We are looking forward to garnering the full fruits of the hardships and sacrifices of war in a lasting and just world peace. "It must not happen again" are the words on the tongue of the common man, as he goes into the armed services, sweats in war industries, accepts the deprivations which war imposes. Word goes out that war production must be increased at the cost of longer hours, more acres must be sowed with reduced farm labor, women in greater numbers must go into the factories. News of casualties comes, there are stories of heroic bravery, the strength of the enemy is not concealed, perhaps years will be needed before victory comes. With grim determination, resolved to do his full loyal part, the common man faces hardships and sacrifices, whispering to himself: "It must not happen again." Once before since the turn of the century he engaged in war to outlaw war and to bring security to the nations. Something happened in the aftermath. He is not sure of just what did happen. Things which should have been done were not done, and things which should not have been done were done. He was disappointed. The seeds of the greatest war in history were allowed to germinate and grow. Somebody, something failed him. This time the common man is determined as he tells himself over and over: "It must not, it cannot happen again." And we have a duty to see to it that he is not disappointed again. This time we must make a peace which will give lasting security to all nations and peoples. It is hard to contemplate what would be the consequences of a failure at the peace-table when victory comes. There is the resolution in all of us: "It must not happen again."

The Axis Powers offer a peace—a sham peace. With immoral propaganda they deluded and deceived many thousands of men into accepting their proposals. When their propaganda failed, they employed brute force to impose their wills on more thousands of unwilling, undeceived human beings. Even in their own countries great numbers are looking to us and not to them for a good peace. There is no hope of peace from the Axis Powers. They made much of national inequalities and the sorry state of the "have not" nations. Yet so great an authority as Pope Pius XII early after the first aggressions of the Axis Powers wrote: "The international problems involved were by no means insoluble." Whatever were the problems pressing on some nations, they could have been solved without war. Despite all efforts to preserve peace, the Nazi Party went to war. It did not conceal its objective of setting up by force a new world order in which a single nation would dominate and the other nations would be mere tributaries to its wealth and power. In this vaunted world order social and historic realities were forgotten, the moral law scoffed and even in the bosom of the privileged nation human rights denied. Let any student in full calmness and impartiality examine the proposal of the Axis and study the philosophy which inspires it, and he will be compelled to conclude that it holds no promise of world peace. We cannot look therefore to the Axis Powers for a contribution to the lasting and just world peace which honest men are looking forward to with the victory of our arms.

Our own country has proclaimed its war objectives—the defense of the four freedoms and the making of them the basis for neighborly international collaboration. This is the language of honest peacemakers. We recognize the rights of other nations, large and small, strong and weak. We have no ambition to dominate the world. Every nation has its own individuality, its own cultural inheritance. We shall not attempt to impose our political institutions on other nations. We do believe however that there is a necessary common denominator in all national institutions and that is the recognition of basic native human rights under the moral law, and we intend to use our full international influence to securing men everywhere in their native rights. History has bestowed on us a great, grave world responsibility. We shall be a mighty force at the peace-table. Men everywhere are looking to us to give them a good peace. We dare not fail. Even in the midst of war we are trying to make the plan of a peace which will offer lasting security. To us men look for a genuine peace and we must leave no stone unturned to give it to them when victory comes to our arms.

It is easy to say that we want a good peace. There is no doubt about our sincerity and our purpose. The hard thing will be to formulate the good peace. Good will alone is not enough. There must be a deep understanding of the ills which afflict our world, a right evaluation of the problems of nations and peoples, a frank admission of past mistakes, a willingness to sacrifice seeming national advantages beyond even the limit of justice. Antecedent to all this there must be a deep humility in the nations, particularly the powerful nations, a humility which is inconsistent with sordid national interests and frees the mind to discover reality in its full proportions. In the long story of the nations there have been many indefensible injustices and some of them cannot be righted fully at this time without added injustices. A willingness to forget historic hatreds and prejudices in the interest of a true peace must inspire the peace-makers. The task will be difficult but it is not impossible and it must be done.

There are certain facts, truths and principles which must guide the peace-makers. In such an undertaking it is imperative that right principles be clearly understood and undeviatingly followed. Failure in the past was due in no little measure to the weakness of substituting expediency for principle. It is not realistic, but fanciful, to depart from ageless truth. True, we are living in a world of men and must never forget human equations, and for that very reason we must keep our eyes always on true human values and not allow ourselves to drift into the unreal dreams of ideologies which obliterate these values. Nowhere do we find a clearer statement of the truths, facts and principles which are postulates in the making of a good peace than in the Statements of the Popes of our times. These Pontiffs, from Leo XIII to Pius XII, have stood above parties and apart from nationalisms, and yet nobody questions their knowledge of their times. Courageously they have pointed to sorry aberrations and unfalteringly they have indicated the path which leads to peace. When their warnings were not heeded, they did not desist in their admonitions and condemnations and pleadings. In the light of events the warnings of these Popes now read like the language of prophecy. We need these Statements on peace and the conditions for peace. Unfortunately they are scattered through many letters, allocutions, addresses and messages.

To meet a real need, scholars under the sponsorship of The Bishops' Committee on the Pope's Peace Points have gathered them together and now offer them to the public in a single volume. Here we shall find carefully indexed these Statements which are a clear exposition of truths, facts and principles for the making of a good peace. Some may be disappointed in finding that these Statements are not detailed specific applications of principles to particular political problems of our times. They forget that the Church recognizes and defends the independence and sovereignty of the State in its own sphere and that the Popes do not enter the domain of statesmen. They are the witnesses of religious and moral truth. Peace involves this truth and the Popes have spoken within their own sphere, leaving to statesmen to add what is purely social, purely political. And yet it must not be understood that the Popes have merely enunciated abstract moral principles which have to do with peace. Courageously they have taught these principles in the language of the changing experiences of nations and individuals. These Statements offer a practical guide for the peace-makers who will seek to give the world a lasting and just peace.

Pope Pius XII on Christmas Eve offered to the nations his Five-Point Peace Plan. This plan delineates in broad outline a good peace. Great interest has been shown in it throughout the world and it has been imbedded in the studies of serious, able students and in the pronouncements of many groups on the peace. Much of what is in it is a statement of the moral law for international life, and its proposals for international security are fully consonant with the dictates of justice and national sovereignty. Christian truth permeates it, and it may be called the Christian plan for peace. To understand it, something more than a reading of the text is necessary. It calls back to the many Statements of the Popes on peace for a proper interpretation. These Statements strongly defend native human rights, assert the dignity of man, inculcate the social derivations from human personality, defend against racists and tribalists the unity of the human race, vindicate the moral law in all human relations, social, political and international, denounce the usurpation by the State of authority to dominate all human behavior under the tyrannical claim that it is the sole source of all rights, call for the freedom and dignity of the family, and postulate Christian brotherhood in our dealing with all peoples. They point out the errors in political systems which threaten tyranny and oppression. When the Pope's Peace Plan is read and studied in the light of these Statements, it is clear that it offers to statesmen a safe guide in formulating the peace in justice and charity which we are demanding as the fruits of our victory. Our own peace aims, which are enunciated only in large outline, are complemented and supplemented by the papal plan. Not only is there no contradiction between our aims and the papal plan, but that plan comprehends our aims and gives them the weight of sound philosophy and moral right. It is hoped that this volume will be a distinct contribution to the making and enduring of a good world peace.

✠ Samuel A. Stritch,
 Archbishop of Chicago,
 Chairman, Bishops' Committee on the
 Pope's Peace Points.

CONTENTS

INTRODUCTION

At some future hour, known now only to God, a group of statesmen will take their places around a conference table and hammer out a treaty designed to settle the staggering problems of a world torn apart by years of bitter war. When that hour strikes, what role will the pope play in forging that instrument which will decisively determine the character of the post-war world?

Will the pope remain a complete outsider, a mere bystander? In the Peace of Paris at the end of the last war, Benedict XV, by explicit provision of the secret Treaty of London, was deliberately excluded from having any voice in the peace settlement. The Treaty of Versailles, with all its short-sighted ineptness, can be laid squarely at the doorstep of self-sufficient secular statesmanship. Will the mind of the men of Versailles live again at the end of the present conflict? Or will their disastrous failure to achieve a lasting peace so chasten the leaders of the world that in the coming peace settlement the unique competence and vision and disinterestedness of the pope will be allowed to help mould a document wiser than that signed in the Hall of Mirrors in 1919?

Today these questions come to the lips not only of Catholics—some three hundred million strong, in every nation under heaven—but of all men of good will, men who are fired with a determination that this time no avenue will remain unexplored in the quest for a peace that will end forever the horror and bloodshed under which mankind has groaned these many years.

Fourteen years ago Pius XI defined the stand which the Papacy itself will take toward participating in the conference. In the Lateran Treaty of 1929 he wrote: "The Holy See declares that it wishes to remain and will remain extraneous to all temporal disputes between nations, and to national congresses convoked for the settlement of such disputes, unless the contending parties make a joint appeal to its mission of peace; nevertheless, it reserves the right in every case to exercise its moral and spiritual power." In broad principle, then, the stand of the papacy is clear: the pope will play only that part which victors and vanquished assign him. But precisely what will that part be?

To anyone sincerely concerned with the establishment of a just and lasting peace, it is inconceivable that the peacemakers will spurn the invaluable contribution which the pope can make toward the settlement of the deep problems that lie at the roots of modern political and social disorder. For the past sixty-five years the Church has been uninterruptedly blessed with magnificent leadership almost without parallel in its history. During these years five great men have sat on the throne of Peter and each has tried with the assistance of Almighty God and the best minds in Christendom to plan the construction of an order based on justice and charity.

These popes were not untried in the field of statesmanship. They came to the papacy experienced in the intricate problems of contemporary Europe. Leo XIII was a career diplomat and had served as Nuncio to Belgium; Benedict XV was secretary to the Nuncio to Spain, and for many years assistant secretary of state; Pius XI was Nuncio to Poland during the trying reconstruction period at the close of the last war; and the present Holy Father, Pius XII, has spent the entire forty-odd years of his priesthood in the diplomatic service of the Church.

During the years of their pontificates they enjoyed avenues of information that have no counterpart among secular governments. The pope is, indeed, served by a highly capable diplomatic force all over the world; but far beyond that, he is the spiritual father of three hundred million Catholics who come to him for guidance; he is the trusted confidant of countless bishops and priests who minister to his flocks. No one else in the world is in as advantageous a position to feel the pulse of mankind as is the Holy Father. Among rulers he is unique in that his viewpoint is as broad as the world itself, charged as he is before God with the welfare not of one nation, or a group of nations, but of all nations. Victor, vanquished, great nation, tiny principality, soldier, civilian, statesman, citizen, Englishman, Italian, German, Frenchman, American, Russian—all look to him as their father in Christ, and his is the responsibility before God of thinking, planning, caring for all, irrespective of nation or language or class.

To harvest the accumulated wisdom of these past sixty-five years during which each of the five popes was deeply concerned with the problem of peace; to make the riches of that wisdom available to the English-speaking world; to reveal to all men the incalculable help the popes can offer in the making of a lasting peace—these are the aims of this book. Within its covers lies the mature thought of the five popes on the issues which, unsolved, have turned Europe into a vast mire of blood and devastation. The book aims to make the principles for the solution of those problems accessible to all concerned with building a new and better world.

This is not a book for the faint-hearted. Dealing for the most part with general principles rather than with concrete situations, it sometimes makes hard, slow reading. Most of the documents are given only in part, since the complete text would require a book of unmanageable proportions. Translated from Latin or one of the modern European languages, some of the selections still retain traces of the original idiom which may seem strange to one who is accustomed to the terseness and directness of English; a more perfect rendition into English would have required more time than was available. Nevertheless, the inherent value of the doctrine itself and the realization of the unthinkable calamity in store for a world that refuses to find a solution for the problems herein analyzed will more than encourage the sincere student to bear with the hardships involved in reading the text.

As the reader becomes more thoroughly acquainted with these documents and appreciates more and more the skill, the confidence with which the popes attack the issues involved in the establishment of an enduring peace, the conviction will deepen that herein the popes, as pastors of souls, are dealing with matters entirely within the scope of their authority. The pope's province is, of course, not politics; neither is it diplomacy, nor international relations, nor economics—as such. His province is faith and morals. But only the most shallow of minds would refuse to admit deep moral implications in the issues that today disturb the tranquillity of society. Problems that in one generation led to the slaughter of eight and a half million men, to impoverishment, suffering, and hatred without precedent in history, and that less than a quarter of a century afterwards flared up anew with consequences which will probably be much more catastrophic—these problems fall squarely within the jurisdiction of the pope as spiritual and moral leader. And any hollow accusation that the pope in outlining a peace program is interfering in a sphere foreign to his office cannot stand up under analysis.

There are four general characteristics of the peace documents that merit the reader's attention.

First, there is the broad sweep, the all-embracing nature of the solution offered by the popes. The many languages from which the documents were translated help to emphasize the universality of the papal peace proposals. The pope is planning not for one nation, not for any favored group of nations, but for all the wide world. The documents themselves are the most eloquent refutation of any charge that the pope is not genuinely neutral and impartial, that he forgets that he is the common father of all belligerents. On the other hand, the pages that follow illustrate strikingly the pope's solicitude for those nations that are the victims of injustice. There is no hesitation on his part in springing to the defense of any nation that has been unjustly invaded or attacked, no timidity in castigating the perpetrator of evil, no matter who he may be. More than once the popes have explicitly condemned aggressor nations.

It is not merely "peace in our time" that the popes desire, but peace for all time. It is not merely order that the popes work for, nor merely the absence of war; it is deep, lasting, internal peace founded on Christian charity and justice. The papal principles aim not merely at a more stable political order, a more equitable economic order; they aim at a thoroughly Christian human order. Their program is not merely an assortment of isolated, unconnected suggestions for reform; it is a completely integrated program of political, social, economic principles based on natural law and Christian revelation. It is a radical program; it goes down deep to the roots of modern disorder. The popes will not rest satisfied merely with a surface redistribution of territory, a "working agreement" among nations; the popes call for a change deep in the hearts of men if there is to be any lasting peace.

Secondly, the reader will be impressed by the essential unity, the continuity of the pronouncements made by all five popes. It would be inaccurate to think of a distinct peace plan of Leo XIII, or one of Benedict XV, or one of Pius XII. As Archbishop Stritch has said recently, there is one papal peace plan, a plan of all popes. Through the doctrines and pronouncements of the five popes there runs an unmistakable oneness in principle, a reiteration of the same basic tenets. Linked with this essential unity, however, is a gradual development, a greater clarification and unfolding, a growth as the principles come to be applied to new issues. The more complete industrialization of modern society, the startling advance of technical science in the past sixty-five years, the invention of the airplane and its ever-increasing use as a weapon of warfare, the adoption of new military tactics, the historical evolution of individual nations—these factors raise new moral issues; and the intimate contact of the papacy with the realities of the ever-changing world scene is reflected in the new problems attacked by later popes.

A hasty glance at the index in the back of the book will reveal how well the popes have remained abreast of the times. It will help, too, in making the reader realize the timeliness of the problems treated in these pages. These men did not live with their eyes turned back toward the Middle Ages; their concerns were the issues of the hour. "May an invading airplane force bomb a city? May poison gas ever be used as an instrument of warfare? To what degree is sabotage, boycotting, licit? May one nation apply sanctions against another? Is there an obligation on the part of a nation to join an international organization such as the League of Nations, should such an organization be founded at the end of the present war? What are the obligations of a victor nation in occupying conquered territory? Should reparations be exacted from aggressor nations?" These are but a few of the many perplexing questions upon which the popes speak out in this volume.

Thirdly, the popes with superhuman vision and accuracy recognized long years in advance the conflicts that would inevitably arise if dangerous injustices, inequalities, points of friction were not eliminated. It is difficult for the reader not to pause occasionally to speculate on what a different course modern history would have taken if the nations of Europe had given the papal suggestions the attention which they deserved. If, for instance, the social reforms suggested by Leo XIII had been achieved, would the Socialism of the nineteenth century have spawned the Communist monster of today? If the peace proposals of Benedict XV had been used as the basis of the Peace of Paris rather than the selfish nationalism of the men of Versailles, would the world have gone to war a second time? If Pius XI's early warnings about the dangers inherent in the totalitarian doctrines of Communism, Fascism, and Nazism had been heeded and steps had been taken to correct the evils that made the growth of these menaces almost inevitable, would our generation have witnessed such outrages to human dignity as blood purges and concentration camps? If the rulers of nations had cooperated with the valiant diplomatic efforts of Pius XII during the spring and summer of 1939 and had agreed to solve their problems around a conference table rather than out on a battlefield, would not the crisis of our age be today much closer to a solution instead of having grown more acute through four years of warfare?

With these thoughts in mind, one cannot but pause to wonder how the statesmen of Europe can possibly spurn again the voice of the pope as he outlines a structure for the new Christian order in Europe. The tragic consequences of such a course of action are unthinkable.

Fourthly, there runs through papal teaching on peace a note of optimism, of hope. In days when so many masters in Israel are throwing up their hands in despair and pronouncing the chaos utterly hopeless, it is indeed consoling to find someone who has the grasp of the situation and the authority that belongs only to the pope, and yet who is confident that the problems are capable of solution if only adequate remedies are applied without stint or delay.

Yes, say the popes, the problems are staggering; the obstacles are mountainous. But, they say, we can yet save the day if only we are sufficiently wise, sufficiently Christian, sufficiently courageous, sufficiently trustful in Divine Providence to apply the means at our disposal toward an immediate unraveling of the problems that have created our modern crisis.

Along with clarifying the principles for peace these documents tell an inspiring story of long years of earnest effort on the part of the popes to stave off threatened wars, to alleviate the suffering of the wounded and imprisoned during wartime, to locate civilians separated from their families in the confusion of battle. The popes are not mere doctrinaires whose contributions to peace never pass beyond the realm of ideas; they search for opportunity to practice the principles of justice and mercy which they preach to others. No one can read the history of papal arbitration and mediation that emerges from this volume without realizing the hard-headed wisdom displayed by the papacy in settling international disputes. Bismarck, certainly no friend of the Holy See, was yet shrewd enough and unprejudiced enough to recognize the unique qualifications of the pope as arbiter, and asked Leo XIII in 1885 to arbitrate the quarrel between Germany and Spain over the Caroline Islands in the Pacific. The willing acceptance of the pope's decision in this and in similar instances stamps the papacy as an ideal instrument of arbitration—an historical fact which the statesmen of our day might well bear in mind for the future when problems will inevitably arise and clamor for a solution which only arbitration or mediation can offer.

Besides the documents of which the popes themselves were author, the editor has included those letters which were issued officially by the papal secretary of state. The intimate association of the cardinal secretary with the pope seemed adequate warrant for considering these documents truly papal and an integral part of the papal plan although originally they appeared over the signature of the secretary of state.

Although no effort was spared to collect all the documents, the collection still remains somewhat incomplete. Throughout the compilation of the book the editor felt the restrictions imposed by war. He was limited to the resources of American libraries. During these last months it has grown increasingly difficult to obtain issues of the *Acta Apostolicae Sedis* and the *Osservatore Romano*. In spite of all these limitations, however, to publish whatever was available and hence to make the papal peace plan accessible now when it is needed so desperately seemed a much wiser policy than to wait till a later day when possibly the collection of documents might have been more nearly complete.

In an endeavor to present the papal doctrine on peace in all its fullness, the editor has also included many documents in which the popes take up problems which are not so obviously related to peace, such as the nature and extent of human rights, the problems of social and economic reform, the internal constitution of states. At first glance some of these problems might seem outside the scope of a volume on peace; on closer analysis, however, the irrelevance will prove only superficial. The papal program, we have said, is a radical program; and the popes in elucidating, for instance, the nature of human rights were aiming directly at the heart of modern disorder: the denial of man's inherent dignity and inviolable rights as son of God and brother of Christ. This error was the source from which much of the social chaos of the past proceeded; it lies today at the core of the totalitarian ideologies, whether of the Communist, Nazi, or Fascist variety. A clarification of the rights of man is an integral part of the papal peace plan, for this doctrine is the foundation upon which any rational, Christian plan for reconstruction can be built.

More apparent, probably, will be the reason for including the popes' program for social and economic reform. Pius XII, in the motto of his pontificate, *Pax opus justitiae,* emphasizes the necessary connection between the attainment of justice and the achievement of peace; peace demands the rooting out of injustice not only among nations but between the social classes within the nation itself. In a radio address to the Catholics of Spain on April 16, 1939, Pius XII reaffirmed a conviction many times expressed by his predecessors when he said that social reform was indispensable to enduring peace. "We especially exhort the rulers and the pastors of Catholic Spain," he said, "to illumine the minds of those led astray . . . putting before them the principles of individual and social justice contained in the Holy Gospel and in the doctrine of the Church, without which the peace and prosperity of nations, however powerful, cannot endure."

In selecting the material the editor tried to include documents concerning as many countries as possible, to emphasize not only the world-wide range of the popes' fatherly solicitude, but also their understanding of the problems that face modern man in every quarter of the globe. Neither the pastoral mission of the popes nor their grasp of current issues tolerates any frontiers. These pages reveal a mind and heart in touch with the suffering of mankind from Finland in the Baltic across the world to sub-equatorial New Zealand, from the Republic of Chile in the Andes of South America back to Poland and Russia. We cannot too often stress this unique catholicity of outlook on the part of the papacy. It springs from a vision as universal as the light of the sun.

The book is composed of five parts, each part presenting the pronouncements of one of the five popes. The five pontificates and the messages of each pope are arranged in chronological order. Each of the selections is headed by a brief phrase, the words with which the complete document begins in the original text. This is the traditional practice used to designate papal writings, and has been followed throughout the volume, the only exceptions being those instances, particularly among the more recent papal statements, when it was impossible to obtain the original document. Before the actual text the editor has given a brief summary of its contents in English, that the reader might learn in a glance the matter of which the pronouncement treats.

The documents are, of course, not given in full; of necessity only the pertinent passages of each could be included. Omissions have been indicated by periods, three for the omission of less than a paragraph, six for a paragraph or more. The English versions have been gathered from many sources; they are not all of the same quality. Whenever a translation was borrowed from the work of another author, the source is indicated. Lack of reference to a source is indication that the translation given herein is original. Much more time might have been spent in polishing the language of the translations, since not a few of them bear traces of the original idiom; however, the urgency of getting the papal doctrine into the hands of men now when it can do the most good rendered further improvement impossible. The editor has compared the various translations with the original and presents these as faithful and, in his opinion, the best available at the moment. It is the hope of the Bishops' Committee to publish a second volume in which the original documents will be placed in the hands of scholars.

The heart of the papal plan, the *sine qua non* for its success is a spirit of Christian cooperation; no plan for peace, no matter how wise or sublime, can ever pass into the realm of reality unless nations are willing to cooperate with other nations, groups with other groups, men with their fellow men. If the cooperation given the editor in the task of compiling this book could be taken as a gauge of that spirit among men today, the days of enduring peace would not be far off. Of necessity he called on the kindness of many friends in collecting and translating these documents and in preparing them for publication. The generosity with which all contributed their services has been most heartening. The list of those to whom he stands in debt is too long to allow personal mention of each name; there are some names, however, that must be singled out for special acknowledgment.

The first debt of gratitude is owed to His Excellency, Archbishop Stritch of Chicago, Chairman of the Bishops' Committee on the Pope's Peace Points. A life-long student of the papal encyclicals, Archbishop Stritch saw the need for this book; it was at his suggestion that the editor took up the task of compiling it. Together with the Most Reverend James Ryan, Bishop of Omaha, and the Most Reverend Aloysius Muench, Bishop of Fargo, his colleagues on the Committee, Archbishop Stritch is responsible for the publication of *Principles for Peace*.

A special word of thanks is due to the Catholic Association for International Peace, particularly to the Reverend Raymond Mc-Gowan and to Miss Catherine Schaefer who generously made all the resources of the Association's files available. For most of the original English translations the editor is indebted to Dr. Martin R. P. McGuire of the Catholic University of America and to his associates, the Reverend John Gavigan, O.S.A., of Villanova College, the Reverend Hermengeld Dressler, O.F.M., of Saint Joseph's College, Sister M. Dominic Ramaccioti, S.S.N.D., Dean of the College of Notre Dame of Maryland, Sister Jerome Keeler, O.S.B., of the College of Mount Saint Scholastica, Dr. Alessandro S. Crisafulli of the Catholic University of America, and Dr. Regina Soria of the College of Notre Dame of Maryland. The Right Reverend Monsignor Francis J. Haas of the Catholic University of America kindly consented to the use of his translations of *Rerum Novarum* and *Quadragesimo Anno*.

In the task of preparing the book for print the editor received invaluable help from the Reverend Joseph B. Lux, D.D., and Miss Eileen O'Hayer of the *Extension Magazine,* from the Right Right Reverend Monsignor•Thomas J. McDonnell, National Director of the Society for the Propagation of the Faith, the Reverend Austin Schmidt, S.J., of the Loyola University Press, the Reverend Michael O'Connell, C.M., of De Paul University, the Reverend John J. Wright, S.T.D., of Saint John's Seminary, Brighton, Massachusetts, and Miss Kathryn Harrold of the *Catholic Historical Review*. The latest 1942 numbers of the *Acta Apostolicae Sedis* were made available through the kindness of the Reverend Jerome D. Hannan, J.C.D., of the Catholic University of America. In the work of research the edition was helped considerably by the Reverend Joseph Christ and the Reverend Cletus O'Donnell.

Another factor that lightened the work of the editor was the kindness and interest shown by his fellow librarians throughout the United States, particularly at the Library of Congress, the Catholic University of America, Harvard University, the University of Notre

Dame, the Boston Public Library, and Marygrove College.

Finally, to the Rector, the Faculty, and the students of Saint Mary of the Lake Seminary, the editor expresses his heartfelt gratitude. Only their loyal and persevering cooperation made the publication of this book possible.

Sincere appreciation is expressed to the following publishers for granting permission to quote from their publications. Benziger Brothers: *The Great Encyclical Letters of Pope Leo XIII; The Life and Acts of Pope Leo XIII,* by Joseph E. Keller. Central Bureau Press: *Directives for Catholic Action,* by James D. Loeffler. John Figgord: *Benedict XV, the Pope of Peace,* by Henry E. G. Rope. Franciscan Herald Press: *Rome Hath Spoken.* Harcourt, Brace & Co.: *The Pope Speaks.* B. Herder Co.: *The Encyclicals of Pius XI.* The Macmillan Co.: *The Peace Conference at the Hague,* by Frederick W. Holls. John C. Winston Co.: *Pope Leo XIII,* by Bernard O'Reilly. The America Press, the Catholic Association for International Peace and the Catholic Truth Society of England have generously cooperated by giving authorization to use their many publications. To the following periodicals and newspapers we are also indebted: *American Ecclesiastical Review; Australasian Catholic Record; Catholic Action; Catholic Herald* (London); *The Catholic Messenger* (Davenport); *The Catholic University Bulletin; Dublin Review; English Catholic Newsletter; Irish Ecclesiastical Record; National Catholic Welfare Conference News Service; The New World* (Chicago); *The Sword of the Spirit Bulletin; The Tablet* (London).

PART ONE

LEO XIII

1878-1903

INTRODUCTION

A TALL, ascetic-looking nobleman of profound scholarship and forty-odd years' experience in diplomacy and administration, a penetrating student of his own times, at home in the field of social theory as well as in philosophy and literature, brilliant, vigorous, sympathetic yet uncompromising — this was Gioacchino Vincenzo Cardinal Pecci, who in 1878 came to the Chair of Peter after the stormy pontificate of Pius IX.

Born in Carpineto on March 2, 1810, the future Leo XIII had been schooled by the Jesuits first at Viterbo, later at the Roman College. On the completion of his studies at the Sapienza and the Pontificia Accademia dei Nobili Ecclesiastici, he was ordained in 1837 and launched on a diplomatic career that took him to Benevento in the Kingdom of Naples as papal governor in 1838, to Perugia as Apostolic Delegate in 1841, to Brussels as Nuncio with the dignity of archbishop in 1843. Recalled from Brussels in 1846, he was appointed Bishop of Perugia, where he remained for thirty-one years. Created cardinal in 1853, he came to Rome as Camerlengo in 1877, and was elected pope on February 20, 1878.

At Leo's accession the voice of the pope carried little weight in the courts and universities of Europe, caught up in the aftermath of the French Revolution and nineteenth century liberalism. Resolutely, Leo set out to effect a rapprochement, pursuing a bold policy of energetic initiative to bring the saving force of Christianity to bear on the critical problems raised by a century of revolution. In diplomacy, in scholarship, in social reform his success was brilliant.

Diplomat *par excellence,* Leo happily witnessed the end of Bismarck's *Kulturkampf* against the Church in Germany, the re-establishment of diplomatic relations with the Czar of Russia, a growing friendliness with England and the United States. The fears of French Catholics in supporting a republican form of government, he ended decisively in 1891 by advocating openly the *Ralliement* policy, a rallying of French Catholics to the legitimate republican government. Twice he was asked to arbitrate international disputes, and was invited by Nicholas II of Russia to participate in the First Hague Conference.

In 1880 his encyclical *Aeterni Patris* restored to Catholic schools the *philosophia perennis* of Thomas Aquinas. In 1881 he opened the doors of the hitherto secret Vatican archives to scholars of every creed and nation. "Go back as far as you can," he told historians. "We are not afraid of the publication of documents." Christian archaeology, Scripture, the writings of Dante won countless new devotees through Leo's encouragement.

A life-long interest in the cause of the exploited workingman was crowned by his magnificent defense of labor, *Rerum Novarum,* issued in 1891, a document proclaimed as the *Magna Charta* of labor, earning for its author the title, "Pope of the Workingman."

Leo's death on July 20, 1903, after twenty-five years in the papacy, found the prestige of Peter greater than it had been in generations.

DOCUMENTS

ENCYCLICAL *Inscrutabili Dei* ON THE EVILS OF SOCIETY.[1]

> *The endless sources of disagreement, whence arise civil strife, ruthless war and bloodshed, have their cause chiefly in the fact that the authority of the Church has been despised and set aside.*

April 21, 1878

1. . . . . . . For, from the very beginning of Our Pontificate, the sad sight has presented itself to Us of the evils by which the human race is oppressed on every side: the widespread subversion of the primary truths on which, as on its foundations, human society is based; the obstinacy of mind that will not brook any authority however lawful; the endless sources of disagreement, whence arrive civil strife, and ruthless war and bloodshed; the contempt of law which moulds characters and is the shield of righteousness; the insatiable craving for things perishable, with complete forgetfulness of things eternal, leading up to the desperate madness whereby so many wretched beings, in all directions, scruple not to lay violent hands upon themselves; the reckless mismanagement, waste, and misappropriation of the public funds; the shamelessness of those who, full of treachery, make semblance of being champions of country, of freedom, and every kind of right; in fine, the deadly kind of plague which infects society in its inmost recesses, allowing it no respite and foreboding ever fresh disturbances and final disaster.

2. Now, the source of these evils lies chiefly, We are convinced, in this, that the holy and venerable authority of the Church, which in God's name rules mankind, upholding and defending all lawful authority, has been despised and set aside. The enemies of public order, being fully aware of this, have thought nothing better suited to destroy the foundations of society than to make an unflagging attack upon the Church of God, to bring her into discredit and odium by spreading infamous calumnies, and accusing her of being

---

[1] Translation from *The Great Encyclical Letters of Pope Leo XIII*, pp. 9-16. Original Latin, *A.S.S.*, v. 10, pp. 585-589 (1878).

opposed to genuine progress. They labor to weaken her influence and power by wounds daily inflicted, and to overthrow the authority of the Bishop of Rome, in whom the abiding and unchangeable principles of right and good find their earthly guardian and champion. . . .

3. It is perfectly clear and evident, Venerable Brothers, that the very notion of civilization is a fiction of the brain if it rest not on the abiding principles of truth and the unchanging laws of virtue and justice, and if unfeigned love knit not together the wills of men, and gently control the interchange and the character of their mutual service. Now, who would make bold to deny that the Church, by spreading the Gospel throughout the nations, has brought the light of truth amongst people utterly savage and steeped in foul superstition, and has quickened them alike to recognize the Divine Author of nature and duly to respect themselves? Further, who will deny that the Church has done away with the curse of slavery and restored men to the original dignity of their noble nature; and—by uplifting the standard of Redemption in all quarters of the globe, by introducing, or shielding under her protection, the sciences and arts, by founding and taking into her keeping excellent charitable institutions which provide relief for ills of every kind—has throughout the world, in private or in public life, civilized the human race, freed it from degradation, and with all care trained it to a way of living such as befits the dignity and the hopes of man? And if any one of sound mind compare the age in which We live, so hostile to religion and to the Church of Christ, with those happy times when the Church was revered as a mother by the nations, beyond all question he will see that Our epoch is rushing wildly along the straight road to destruction; while in those times which most abounded in excellent institutions, peaceful life, wealth, and prosperity the people showed themselves most obedient to the Church's rule and laws. Therefore, if the many blessings We have mentioned, due to the agency and saving help of the Church, are the true and worthy outcome of civilization, the Church of Christ, far from being alien to or neglectful of progress, has a just claim to all men's praise as its nurse, its mistress and its mother.

4. Furthermore, that kind of civilization which conflicts with the doctrines and laws of holy Church is nothing but a worthless

imitation and a meaningless name. Of this, those peoples on whom the Gospel light has never shone afford ample proof, since in their mode of life a shadowy semblance only of civilization is discoverable, while its true and solid blessings have never been possessed. Undoubtedly that cannot by any means be accounted the perfection of civilized life which sets all legitimate authority boldly at defiance; nor can that be regarded as liberty which, shamefully and by the vilest means, spreading false principles, and freely indulging the sensual gratification of lustful desires, claims impunity for all crime and misdemeanor, and thwarts the goodly influence of the worthiest citizens of whatsoever class. Delusive, perverse and misleading as are these principles, they cannot possibly have any inherent power to perfect the human race and fill it with blessing, for *sin maketh nations miserable.*[2] Such principles, as a matter of course, must hurry nations, corrupted in mind and heart, into every kind of infamy, weaken all right order, and thus, sooner or later, bring the standing and peace of the State to the very brink of ruin.

5. Again, if We consider the achievements of the See of Rome, what can be more wicked than to deny how much and how well the Roman Bishops have served civilized society at large? For Our Predecessors, to provide for the peoples' good, encountered struggles of every kind, endured to the utmost burdensome toils, and never hesitated to expose themselves to most dangerous trials. With eyes fixed on heaven, they neither bowed down their head before the threats of the wicked, nor allowed themselves to be led by flattery or bribes into unworthy compliance. This Apostolic Chair it was that gathered and held together the crumbling remains of the old order of things; this was the kindly light by whose help the culture of Christian times shone far and wide; this was an anchor of safety in the fierce storms by which the human race has been convulsed; this was the sacred bond of union that linked together nations distant in region and differing in character; in short, this was a common center from which was sought instruction in faith and religion, no less than guidance and advice for the maintenance of peace and the functions of practical life. In very truth it is the glory of the Supreme Pontiffs that they steadfastly set themselves up as a wall and a bulwark to save human society from falling back into its former superstition and barbarism.

[2] *Proverbs*, XIV, 34.

6. Would that this healing authority had never been slighted or set aside! Assuredly neither would the civil power have lost that venerable and sacred glory, the lustrous gift of religion, which alone renders the state of subjection noble and worthy of man; nor would so many revolutions and wars have been fomented to ravage the world with desolation and bloodshed; nor would kingdoms, once so flourishing, but now fallen from the height of prosperity, lie crushed beneath the weight of every kind of calamity. . . .

7. . . . At the same time We address Ourselves to princes and chief rulers of the nations, and earnestly beseech them in the august name of the most high God, not to refuse the Church's aid, proffered them in a season of such need, but with united and friendly aims to join themselves to her as the source of authority and salvation, and to attach themselves to her more and more in the bonds of hearty love and devotedness. God grant that—seeing the truth of Our words and considering within themselves that the teaching of Christ is, as Augustine used to say, "a great blessing to the State, if obeyed," [3] and that their own peace and safety, as well as that of their people, is bound up with the safety of the Church and the reverence due to her—they may give their whole thought and care to mitigating the evils by which the Church and its visible Head are harassed, and so it may at last come to pass that the peoples whom they govern may enter on the way of justice and peace, and rejoice in a happy era of prosperity and glory. . . . . . .

LETTER *Da Grave Sventura* TO CARDINAL LORENZO NINA, NEW SECRETARY OF STATE.[4]

In the darkest periods of history the Church was the only refuge where the nations found peace and safety.

August 27, 1878

8. . . . . . . We said that the chief reason of this great moral ruin was the openly proclaimed separation and the attempted apostasy of the society of our day from Christ and His Church, which alone has the power to repair all the evils of society. In the noonday light of facts We then showed that the Church founded by Christ to

---

[3] *Epistola* 138 (or 5) *ad Marcellinum* n. 15 in Migne, *P.L.*, v. 33, c. 532.
[4] Translation from O'Reilly, *Life of Leo XIII*, pp. 337-338. Original Italian, *A.S.S.*, v. 11, pp. 274-276 (1878).

renovate the world, from her first appearance in it began to give it great comfort by her superhuman virtue; that in the darkest and most destructive periods the Church was the only beacon light which made the road of life safe to the nations, the only refuge where they found peace and safety.

9. From this it was easy to conclude that if in past ages the Church was able to bestow upon the world such signal benefits, she can also do it most certainly at present; that the Church, as every Catholic believes, being ever animated by the Spirit of Christ—Who promised her His unfailing assistance—was by Him established teacher of truth and guardian of a holy and faultless law; and that, being such, she possesses at this day all the force necessary to resist the intellectual and moral decay which sickens society, and to restore the latter to health.

10. And inasmuch as unprincipled foes, in order to bring her into disrepute and to draw on her the enmity of the world, continue to propagate against her the gravest calumnies, We endeavored from the beginning to dissipate these prejudices and to expose these falsehoods, resting assured that the nations, when they come to know the Church as she is in reality, and in her own beneficent nature, will everywhere willingly return to her bosom.

11. Urged by this purpose, We resolved also to make Our voice heard to those who rule the nations, inviting them earnestly not to reject, in these times of pressing need, the strong support which the Church offers them. And under the impulse of Our apostolic charity, We addressed Ourselves even to those who are not bound to Us by the tie of the Catholic religion, desiring, as We did, that their subjects also should experience the kindly influence of that divine institution.

12. You are well aware, my Lord Cardinal, that in following out this impulse of Our heart We addressed Ourselves also to the mighty emperor of the illustrious German nation—a nation which demanded Our special attention on account of the hard conditions there imposed on Catholics. Our words, *inspired solely by the desire to see religious peace restored to Germany,* were favorably received by the emperor and had the good effect to lead to friendly negotiations. In these Our purpose was, not to rest satisfied with a simple suspension of hostilities, but, removing every obstacle in the way, *to come to a true, solid and lasting peace.*

13. The importance of this aim was justly appreciated by those who hold in their hands the destinies of that empire, and this will lead them, as We sincerely trust, to join hands with Us in attaining it. The Church assuredly would rejoice to see peace brought back to that great nation; but the empire itself would not rejoice less that, consciences being appeased, the sons of the Catholic Church would be found still—what they had at other times proved themselves to be—the most faithful and the most generous of subjects. . . . . . .

LETTER *Solatio Nobis* TO ARCHBISHOP MELCHERS OF COLOGNE.[5]

The Pope is striving to obtain the blessings and the fruits of a lasting peace for the German people.

December 24, 1878

14. . . . . . . For you well know, Venerable Brother, that We entertain the most intimate conviction—a conviction which We have often expressed and publicly declared—that the cause of the dangers which threaten society is to be sought principally in the fact that the authority of the Church is on all sides intercepted, and prevented from exercising its salutary influence for the public good, and that its liberty is so fettered that it is scarcely allowed to provide for the private necessities and welfare of individuals. And this persuasion is generated in Our mind not only by the knowledge which We have of the nature and powerful influence of the Church, but also by unquestionable historical proofs from which it is manifest that the condition of civil society is then most prosperous when the Church enjoys full liberty of action, and that whenever she is shackled by restrictions, those principles and doctrines which tend to the fall and dissolution of all human society begin to prevail.

15. Since, then, this has been long Our settled opinion, it was natural that, from the very beginning of Our Pontificate, We should strive to call back princes and people to peace and friendship with the Church. And to you, Venerable Brother, it is certainly well known that We have for some time directed Our efforts to the end that the noble nation of the Germans may see the end of its

[5] Translation from Keller, *The Life and Acts of Pope Leo XIII*, pp. 343-345. Original Latin, *A.S.S.*, v. 11, pp. 321-323 (1878).

dissensions and obtain the blessings and fruits of a lasting peace without injury to the rights of the Church; and We think that you also know that, as far as We are concerned, We have neglected no means of arriving at an end so noble and so worthy of Our solicitude. But whether that which We have undertaken and are striving to effect will at last be prosperously accomplished He knows from Whom comes everything that is good, and Who has implanted in Us so ardent a desire and longing for peace.

16. But whatever may be the ultimate issue, resigning Ourselves to the Divine Will, but animated by the same desire, We will persevere in the arduous task committed to Us, so long as life shall endure. For so great a duty can not lawfully be postponed or neglected, while, by the perverted teaching of perfidious men, who have thrown off all restraint of law, religious, political and social order is threatened with destruction. We should hold Ourselves to be neglecting the duty of Our apostolic ministry if We did not offer to human society, in this most dangerous crisis of its existence, the efficacious remedies which the Church provides....And that this work of salvation undertaken by Us may be more perfectly and speedily accomplished, We call upon you, Venerable Brother, and the illustrious bishops of your country, to strive together with Us, with united desires and efforts, that the faithful committed to your charge may show themselves more and more docile to the teachings of the Church, and may more exactly observe the prescriptions of the divine law, so that *the communication of their faith may be more manifest in the acknowledgment of every good work, which is in them in Christ Jesus.*[6] Thence will result that moderation and that obedience to laws (not repugnant to the faith and duty of a Catholic) by which they will show themselves worthy to receive the blessings of peace and to enjoy its happy fruits. But you are perfectly aware, Venerable Brother, that Our endeavors in so grave a matter will be altogether vain, unless We have the blessing and help of God. . . . Wherefore we must pour forth before Him fervent supplications and prayers, earnestly beseeching Him to enlighten His Vicar on earth and the bishops. . . . . . .

---

[6] *Philemon*, v. 6.

ENCYCLICAL *Quod Apostolici Muneris* ON SOCIALISM, COM-
MUNISM AND NIHILISM.[7]

> *Neither peace nor tranquillity remains in private or*
> *public life where the subversive doctrines of Socialism,*
> *Communism or Nihilism are taught.*

December 28, 1878

17. . . . . . . You are aware, Venerable Brethren, that the warfare raised against the Church by the reformers in the sixteenth century still continues and tends to this end, that by the denial of all
revelation and the suppression of the supernatural order, the reason
of man may run riot in its own conceits. This error, which unjustly
derives its name from reason, flatters the pride of man, loosens the
reins to all his passions, and thus it has deceived many minds, whilst
it has made deep ravages on civil society. Hence it comes that, by
a new sort of impiety, unknown to the pagans, States constitute
themselves independently of God or of the order which He has
established. Public authority is declared to derive neither its principle nor its power from God, but from the multitude, which,
believing itself free from all divine sanction, obeys no laws but
such as its own caprice has dictated. Supernatural truth being rejected as contrary to reason, the Creator and Redeemer of the
human race is ignored and banished from the universities, the
lyceums and schools, as also from the whole economy of human
life. The rewards and punishments of a future and eternal life are
forgotten in the pursuit of present pleasure. With these doctrines
widely spread, and this extreme license of thought and action extended everywhere, it is not surprising that men of the lowest order,
weary of the poverty of their home or of their little workshop,
should yearn to seize upon the dwellings and possessions of the
rich; that there remains neither peace nor tranquillity in private or
public life, and that society is brought to the brink of destruction. . . . . . .

18. . . . If, however, at times it happens that public power is
exercised by princes rashly and beyond bound, the Catholic doctrine
does not allow subjects to rebel against a ruler by private authority,
lest the peaceful order be more and more disturbed and society

[7] Translation from Keller, *The Life and Acts of Pope Leo XIII*, pp. 348-352. Original
Latin, *A.S.S.*, v. 11, pp. 370-373 (1878).

suffer greater detriment. And when things have come to such a pass that no other hope of safety appears, it teaches that a speedy remedy is to be sought from God by the merit of Christian forbearance and by fervent supplications. But if the ordinances of legislators and princes sanction or command what is contrary to the divine or the natural law, then the dignity of the Christian name, our duty, and the apostolic precept proclaim that *we must obey God rather than men.*[8] . . . . . .

LETTER *Ea Prosperitatis Omina* TO EMPEROR ALEXANDER OF RUSSIA.[9]

The Catholic religion is ever striving to bring peace and harmony between subjects and rulers in all countries.

April 12, 1880

19. Sire: All the prosperity which, through Our cardinal pronuncio in Vienna, We wished your Imperial Majesty on the occasion of the twenty-fifth anniversary of your accession to the throne, We now wish anew in this letter, praying from Our heart that the King of kings and Lord of lords may fulfill Our prayers.

20. We cannot, however, forbear to profit by this opportunity to appeal to your Majesty, beseeching you to bestow your thoughts and attention on the cruel condition of the Catholics belonging to your vast empire. Their state fills Us with unceasing pain and anxiety. The deep zeal which moves Us, in the discharge of Our office of Supreme Pastor of the Church, to provide for the spiritual needs of these faithful Catholics, should, it seems to Us, impel your Majesty, in the midst of so many political revolutions, of so many convulsions produced by greedy human passions, to grant to the Catholic Church such liberty as would assuredly create peace, beget fidelity and bind to your person the trusting hearts of your subjects.

21. Your Majesty's sense of justice and right moves Us to hope that We can both bring about an accord entirely to Our mutual satisfaction. For your Majesty cannot be ignorant of the fact that

[8] *Acts,* V, 29.
[9] Translation from O'Reilly, *Life of Leo XIII,* pp. 373-374. Original Latin, *Leonis XIII Pontificis Maximi Acta,* v. 2, pp. 61-62 (1882).

the Catholic religion deems it her duty everywhere to spread the spirit of peace and to labor to preserve the tranquillity of kingdoms and peoples. . . .

LETTER *Perlectae a Nobis* TO CARDINAL GUIBERT, ARCHBISHOP OF PARIS.[10]

The Church, in all its dealings with governments, has only one purpose in mind, to preserve Christianity.

October 22, 1880

22. . . . . . . It is not to be supposed that the Catholic Church either blames or condemns any form of government, and the institutions established by the Church for the general good can prosper, whether the administration of the State be entrusted to the power and justice of an individual or of several. And as, amid political vicissitudes and changes, it is necessary that the Apostolic See continue to treat of affairs with those who govern, it has in view but a single thing, namely, to safeguard Christian interests; but to infringe on the *rights of sovereignty,* no matter who those may be who exercise it, the Holy See never does and never can desire. Nor is it to be doubted that people ought to obey governments in everything that is not contrary to justice; the maintenance of order that is the foundation of the public good requires this. But it must not therefore be concluded that this obedience implies approval of whatever injustice there might be in the State's constitution and administration. . . . . . .

ENCYCLICAL *Diuturnum* ON THE ORIGIN OF CIVIL POWER.[11]

Leo XIII teaches what Catholic doctrine demands of the State and of the citizen for the maintenance of public order and peace.

June 29, 1881

23. . . . . . . These perils to commonwealths, which are before Our eyes, fill Us with grave anxiety, when We behold the security

[10] Translation from Furey, *Life of Leo XIII and History of His Pontificate,* p. 199. Original Latin, *A.S.S.,* v. 13, p. 196 (1880).
[11] Translation from *The Tablet,* v. 58, pp. 109-111 (July 16, 1881). Original Latin, *A.S.S.,* v. 14, pp. 3-14 (1881).

of princes and the tranquillity of empires, together with the safety of nations, put in peril almost from hour to hour. Nevertheless, the Divine power of the Christian religion has given birth to excellent principles of stability and order for the State, while at the same time it has penetrated into the customs and institutions of States. And of this power not the least nor last fruit is a just and wise proportion of mutual rights and duties in both princes and peoples. For in the precepts and examples of Christ Our Lord there is a wonderful force for restraining in their duty as much those who obey as those who rule, and for keeping between them that agreement which is most according to nature, and that, so to say, concord of wills, from which arises a course of administration which is tranquil and free from all disturbance. Wherefore, being, by the favor of God, intrusted with the government of the Catholic Church, and made the Guardian and the Interpreter of the doctrines of Christ, We judge that it belongs to Our jurisdiction, Venerable Brethren, publicly to set forth that which Catholic truth demands of every one in this sphere of duty; from which also it is made clear by what way and by what means measures may be taken for the public safety in so critical a state of affairs. . . . . . .

24. There is no question here respecting forms of government, for there is no reason why the Church should not approve of the chief power being held by one man or by more, provided only it be just, and that it tend to the common advantage. Wherefore, so long as justice be respected, the people are not hindered from choosing for themselves that form of government which suits best either their own disposition, or the institutions and customs of their ancestors. . . . . . .

25. But from the time when the civil society of men, raised from the ruins of the Roman Empire, gave hope of its future Christian greatness, the Roman Pontiffs by the institution of *The Holy Empire,* consecrated the political power in a wonderful manner. Greatly, indeed, was the authority of rulers ennobled; and it is not to be doubted that what was then instituted would always have been a very great gain, both to ecclesiastical and civil society, if princes and peoples had ever looked to the same object as the Church. And, indeed, tranquillity and a sufficient prosperity lasted so long as there was a friendly agreement between these two powers. If the people were turbulent, the Church was at once the mediator

for peace; and recalling all to their duty, she subdued the more lawless passions partly by kindness and partly by authority. So, if, in ruling, princes erred in their government, she would go to them and, putting before them the rights, needs and lawful wants of their people, would urge them to equity, mercy and kindness. Whence it was often brought about that the dangers of civil wars and of tumults were stayed. . . . . . .

26. To princes and other rulers of the State We have offered the protection of religion, and We have exhorted the people to make abundant use of the great benefits which the Church supplies. Our present object is to make princes understand that that protection which is stronger than any is again offered to them; and We earnestly exhort them in our Lord to defend religion, and to consult the interest of their States by giving that liberty to the Church which cannot be taken away without injury and ruin to the commonwealth. The Church of Christ indeed cannot be an object of suspicion to rulers, nor of hatred to the people; for it urges rulers to follow justice, and in nothing to decline from their duty; while at the same time it strengthens and in many ways supports their authority. All things that are of a civil nature the Church acknowledges and declares to be under the power and authority of the ruler: and in those things the judgment of which belongs, for different reasons, both to the sacred and to the civil power, the Church wishes that there should be harmony between the two so that injurious contests may be avoided. As to what regards the people, the Church has been established for the salvation of all men and has ever loved them as a mother. For the Church it is which by the exercise of its charity has given gentleness to the minds of men, kindness to their manners, and justice to their laws; and, never opposed to honest liberty, she has always detested a tyrant's rule. This custom which the Church has ever had of deserving well of mankind is notably expressed by St. Augustine when he says: "The Church teaches Kings to study the welfare of their people and people to submit to their Kings, showing what is due to all: and that to all is due charity and to no one injustice."[12] For these reasons, Venerable Brethren, your work will be most useful and salutary if you employ with Us every industry and effort which God has given to you in averting the dangers and evils of human society. Strive with

[12] *De moribus Ecclesiae*, bk. 1, ch. 30 in Migne, *P.L.*, v. 32, cc. 1336-1337.

all possible care to make men understand and show forth in their lives what the Catholic Church teaches on government and the duty of obedience. Let the people be frequently urged by your authority and teaching to fly from the forbidden sects, to abhor all conspiracy, to have nothing to do with sedition, and let them understand that they who, for God's sake, obey their rulers render a reasonable service and a generous obedience. And as it is God *who gives safety to Kings*[13] grants to the people *to rest in the beauty of peace and in the tabernacles of confidence and in wealthy repose,*[14] it is to Him that we must pray, beseeching Him to incline all minds to uprightness and truth, to calm angry passions, to restore the long-wished-for tranquillity to the world. . . . . . .

ENCYCLICAL *Etsi Nos* ON CONDITIONS IN ITALY.[15]

Without Christian morality liberty becomes license; and turbulence and disorder plague the State.

February 15, 1882

27. . . . . . . If Christianity has been to all nations their strongest safeguard, the guardian of their laws and the protectress of all justice; if it has held in check blind and rash cupidity, and promoted all that is right, praiseworthy, and great; if it has bound together in complete and lasting harmony the different orders of the commonwealth and the various members of the State; if it has done this for other nations, then in still more abundant measure has it conferred these benefits on Italy. There are many, far too many, so perverse as to repeat that the Church is an obstacle to the welfare and the development of the State, and to set down the Roman Pontificate as inimical to the prosperity and the greatness of Italy. The truth is that Italy owes it to the Roman Pontiffs that her glory has gone abroad to distant peoples, that she has sustained the repeated attacks of barbarians, that she has repulsed the dreaded Turk, that she has so long preserved in so many things her just and lawful liberties, and enriched her cities with so many immortal works of art. And it is not the least of the services of

---

[13] *Psalms,* CXLIII, 10.
[14] *Isaias,* XXXII, 18.
[15] Translation from *The Dublin Review,* 3rd Series, v. 7, pp. 463-464 (April, 1882). Original Latin, *A.S.S.,* v. 14, pp. 338-340 (1882).

the Popes that the various provinces of Italy, differing as they do in character and in customs, have been kept united by a common faith and a common religion, and free from the most fatal of all sources of discord. In many times of danger and calamity Italy would have been nigh unto perishing had it not been for the Popes. And, if not prevented by human perversity, the Roman Pontificate will be as great a blessing to her in the future as it has been in the past. The beneficent power of Catholicism is immutable and perpetual because it is inherent and essential. As the Catholic religion knows no limits of space or time, when the interests of souls are concerned, so is it everywhere and at every moment prepared to further the well-being of States and peoples.

28.   When these good things depart, evil things take their place; for those who reject the teachings of Christianity, whatever they may say themselves, are the enemies of the commonwealth. Their doctrines tend directly to dangerous popular excitement and to unrestrained license and cupidity. In matters of knowledge and science, they repudiate the divine light of faith; and without faith men, as a rule, err grievously, and are blind to the truth, and with difficulty escape the degradations of materialism. In matters of morality they reject the everlasting and unchangeable rule of right, and despise God, the supreme Giver of laws and Avenger of wrong; and thus morality has no foundation or sanction, and each man's will becomes his law. In public affairs, their boasted liberty quickly becomes license, and where there is license there are turbulence and disorder, the worst plagues of the State.

29.   Never have cities and states been reduced to such a condition of horror and of misery as when such men and such teachings have for a time prevailed. Did not recent experience afford us examples, it would be utterly incredible that men should ever go to such lengths of wickedness, of audacity, and of fury as we have witnessed, and should rush wildly into the excesses of fire and blood whilst insulting the name of liberty with their lips. If Italy has not so far been subjected to such horrors, it is, first of all, the effect of the singular mercy of God, and it is owing, secondly, to the fact that the large majority of Italians are still earnest Catholics, and so beyond the power of these pernicious teachings. But once the safeguard of religion were broken down, Italy would suffer as other great peoples have suffered. . . . . . .

LETTER *Benevolentiae Caritas* TO THE BISHOPS OF IRELAND.[16]

> *Men have a right to claim the lawful redress of their wrongs; but a nation's welfare cannot be procured by dishonor and crime.*

August 1, 1882

30. The kindly affection which We cherish toward Irishmen, and which seems to increase with their present sufferings, forces Us to follow the course of events in your island with the deep concern of a fatherly heart. From their consideration, however, We derive more of anxiety than of comfort, seeing that the condition of the people is not what We wish it to be, one of peace and prosperity.

31. There still remain many sources of grievance; conflicting party passions incite many persons to violent courses; some even have stained themselves with fearful murders, as if a nation's welfare could be procured by dishonor and crime!

32. This state of things is to you as well as to Us a cause of serious alarm, as We had evidence of ere now, and as We have just noticed by the resolutions adopted in your meeting at Dublin. Fearful as you were for the salvation of your people, you have clearly shown them what they have to refrain from in the present critical conjuncture and in the very midst of the national struggle.

33. In this you have discharged the duty imposed alike by your episcopal office and your love of country. At no time do a people more need the advice of their bishops than when, carried away by some powerful passion, they see before them deceptive prospects of bettering their condition. It is when impelled to commit what is criminal and disgraceful that the multitude need the voice and the hand of the bishop to keep them back from doing wrong, and to recall them by timely exhortation to moderation and self-control. Most timely, therefore, was your advice to your people, reminding them of the Saviour's injunction, *Seek ye first the kingdom of God and His justice.*[17] For all Christians are therein commanded to keep their thoughts fixed, in their ordinary conduct as well as in their political acts, on the goal of their eternal salvation, and to hold all things subordinate to their duty to God.

[16] Translation from O'Reilly, *Life of Leo XIII*, pp. 426-429. Original Latin, *A.S.S.*, v. 15, pp. 97-99 (1882).

[17] *Matthew*, VI, 33.

34. If Irishmen will only keep to these rules of conduct they will be free to seek to rise from the state of misery into which they have fallen. They surely have a right to claim the lawful redress of their wrongs. For no one can maintain *that Irishmen cannot do what it is lawful for all other peoples to do.*

35. Nevertheless even the public welfare must be regulated by the principles of honesty and righteousness. It is a matter for serious thought that the most righteous cause is dishonored by being promoted by iniquitous means. Justice is inconsistent not only with all violence, but especially so with any participation in the deeds of unlawful societies, which, under the fair pretext of righting wrong, bring all communities to the verge of ruin. Just as Our Predecessors have taught that all right-minded men should carefully shun these dark associations, even so you have added your timely admonition to the same effect. . . . . . .

36. . . . As We have already declared to you, We trust still that the government will conclude to grant satisfaction to the just claims of Irishmen. This We are led to believe from their acquaintance with the true state of things and from their statesmanlike wisdom; for there can be no question that on the safety of Ireland depends the tranquillity of the whole empire.

37. Meanwhile, sustained by this hope, We shall lose no opportunity of helping the Irish people by Our advice, pouring forth to God for them prayers filled with the warmest zeal and love, beseeching God to look down with kindness on a nation made illustrious by the practice of so many virtues, to appease the present storm of political passion, and to reward them at length with peace and prosperity. . . .

ENCYCLICAL *Cum Multa* ON CONDITIONS IN SPAIN.[18]

The fundamental principle of concord in the State as well as in the Church is obedience to lawful authority.

December 8, 1882

38. . . . . . . It is, then, right to look on religion, and whatever is connected by any particular bond with it, as belonging to a higher

[18] Translation from *The Tablet*, v. 61, pp. 9-10 (January 6, 1883). Original Latin, *A.S.S.*, v. 15, pp. 243-246 (1882).

order. Hence, in the vicissitudes of human affairs, and even in the very revolutions in States, religion, which is the supreme good, should remain intact; for it embraces all times and all places. Men of opposite parties, though differing in all else, should be agreed unanimously in this: that in the State the Catholic religion should be preserved in all its integrity. To this noble and indispensable aim, all who love the Catholic religion ought, as if bound by a compact, to direct all their efforts; they should be somewhat silent about their various political opinions, which they are, however, at' perfect liberty to ventilate in their proper place: for the Church is far from condemning such matters, when they are not opposed to religion or justice; apart and removed from all the turmoil of strife, she carries on her work of fostering the common weal, and of cherishing all men with the love of a mother, those particularly whose faith and piety are greatest.

39. The fundamental principle of this concord of which We speak is at once the same in religion and in every rightly constituted State; it is obedience to the lawful authority which orders, forbids, directs, legislates, and thus establishes harmonious union amid the diverse minds of men. We shall here have to repeat some well-known truths, which, however, ought not to be the subjects of mere speculative knowledge, but should become rules applicable to the practice of life.

40. Now, even as the Roman Pontiff is the Teacher and Prince of the Universal Church, so likewise are bishops the rulers and chiefs of the churches that have been duly intrusted to them. Each has within his own jurisdiction the power of leading, supporting, or correcting, and generally of deciding in such matters as may seem to affect religion. . . . We see, therefore, that bishops should have paid to them that respect which the eminence of their charge exacts, and receive in all matters within their office a perfect obedience.

41. In face of the passions that at this moment are troubling the minds of so many in Spain, We exhort, nay, We conjure, all Spaniards to recall this so important duty and to fulfill it with all zeal. Let those especially who are of the clergy, and whose words and example exercise such potent influence, scrupulously apply themselves to observe moderation and obedience. For be it known to them that their toil in the fulfillment of their duties will be most profitable to themselves and efficacious to their neighbor,

when they follow in full submission the guidance of him who is placed over them as head of the diocese. Assuredly it is not conduct consonant with the duties of the priesthood to give oneself up so entirely to the rivalries of parties as to appear more busy with the things of men than with those of God. . . .

42. We deem those associations peculiarly fitted to aid them in this work which are, so to speak, the auxiliary forces destined to support the interests of the Catholic religion; and We approve, therefore, their object and the energy they display; We ardently desire that they may increase in number and in zeal, and that from day to day their fruits may be more abundant. But since the object of such societies is the defense and encouragement of Catholic interests, and as it is the bishops who, each in their proper diocese, have to watch over those interests, it naturally follows that they should be controlled by their bishops, and should set great value on their authority and commands. In the next place they should with equal care apply themselves to preserving union, first, because on the agreement of men's wills all the power and influence of any human society depends; and next, because in the societies of which We speak that mutual charity should especially be found which necessarily accompanies good works and is the characteristic trait of those whom Christian discipline has moulded. Now as it may easily happen that the members may differ on politics, they should recall to themselves the aim of all Catholic associations, and thereby prevent political partisanship from disturbing their cordial unity. . . .

43. Lastly, it is most important that those who defend the interests of religion in the Press, and particularly in the daily papers, should take up the same attitude. We are aware of the objects they strive to attain and the intentions with which they have entered the arena, and We cannot but concede to them well-earned praise for their good service to the Catholic religion. But so lofty, so noble, is the cause to which they have devoted themselves, that it exacts from the defenders of truth and justice a rigorous observance of numerous duties which they must not fail to fulfill; and in seeking to accomplish some of these, the others must not be neglected. The admonitions, therefore, which We have given to associations, We likewise give to writers; We exhort them to remove all dissensions by their gentleness and moderation, and to

preserve concord amongst themselves and in the people, for the influence of writers is great on either side. But nothing can be more opposed to concord than biting words, rash judgments, or perfidious insinuations, and everything of this kind should be shunned with the greatest care and held in the utmost abhorrence. A discussion in which are concerned the sacred rights of the Church and the doctrines of the Catholic religion should not be acrimonious, but calm and temperate; it is weight of reasoning, and not violence and bitterness of language, which must win victory for the Catholic writer.

44.   These rules of conduct will be, in Our judgment, of great use in removing the causes which impede perfect concord. It will be your task, Beloved Sons, Venerable Brethren, to explain Our thoughts to the people and to endeavor to the utmost of your power to make all conform their lives to the rules We have here laid down. . . . . . .

ENCYCLICAL *Nobilissima Gallorum Gens* TO THE BISHOPS OF FRANCE.[19]

> *The State and the Church are two perfect societies and,
> as such, can and should work together in perfect har-
> mony and peace.*

February 8, 1884

45.   . . . . . . As there are on earth two principal societies, the one civil, the proximate end of which is the temporal and worldly good of the human race; the other religious, whose office it is to lead mankind to that true, heavenly and everlasting happiness for which we are created; so these are twin powers, both subordinate to the eternal law of nature, and each working for its own ends in matters concerning its own order and domain. But when anything has to be settled which for different reasons and in a different way concerns both powers, necessity and public utility demand that an agreement shall be effected between them, without which an uncertain and unstable condition of things will be the result, totally inconsistent with the peace either of

---

[19] Translation from *The Tablet,* v. 63, p. 242 (February 16, 1884). Original Latin, *A.S.S.,* v. 16, pp. 244-245 (1906, Reprint ed.).

Church or State. When, therefore, a solemn public compact has been made between the sacred and the civil power, then it is as much the interest of the State as it is just that the compact should remain inviolate; because, as each power has services to render to the other, a certain and reciprocal advantage is enjoyed and conferred by each.

46. In France, at the beginning of this century, after the previous public commotions and terrors had subsided, the rulers themselves understood that they could not more effectually relieve the State, wearied with so many ruins, than by the restoration of the Catholic religion. In anticipation of future advantages, Our Predecessor, Pius VII, spontaneously acceded to the desire of the First Consul, and acted as indulgently as was consistent with his duty. And when an agreement was reached as regarded the principal points, the bases were laid, and a safe course marked out for the restoration and gradual establishment of religion. Many prudent regulations, indeed, were made at that and at subsequent times for the safety and honor of the Church. And great were the advantages derived therefrom, which were all the more to be valued in consequence of the state of prostration and oppression into which religion had been brought in France. With the restoration of public dignity to religion, Christian institutions manifestly revived; and it was wonderful what an increase of civil prosperity was the result. For when the State had scarcely emerged from the tempestuous waves and was anxiously looking for firm foundations on which to base tranquillity and public order, it found the very thing which it desired opportunely offered to it by the Catholic Church, so that it was apparent that the idea of effecting an agreement with the latter was the outcome of a prudent mind and a true regard for the people's welfare. Wherefore, if there were no other reasons for it, the same motive which led to the work of pacification being undertaken, ought now to operate for its maintenance. For—now that the desire of innovation has been enkindled everywhere, and in the existing uncertainty as to the future—to sow fresh seeds of discord between the two powers, and by the interposition of obstacles to fetter or delay the beneficial action of the Church, would be a course void of wisdom and full of peril. . . . . . .

ENCYCLICAL *Humanum Genus* ON FREEMASONRY.[20]

Against false accusations, the Pope teaches that the State and Church together can promote public order and tranquillity.

April 20, 1884

47. . . . . . . The Church, if she directs men to render obedience chiefly and above all to God, the sovereign Lord, is wrongly and falsely believed either to be envious of the civil power or to arrogate to herself something of the rights of sovereigns. On the contrary, she teaches that what is rightly due to the civil power must be rendered to it with a conviction and consciousness of duty. In teaching that from God Himself comes the right of ruling, she adds a great dignity to civil authority, and no small help towards obtaining the obedience and good-will of the citizens. The friend of peace and sustainer of concord, she embraces all with maternal love; and, intent only upon giving help to moral man, she teaches that to justice must be joined clemency, equity to authority, and moderation to law-giving; that no one's right must be violated; that order and public tranquillity are to be maintained; and that the poverty of those who are in need is, as far as possible, to be relieved by public and private charity. . . . . . .

PROPOSAL OF HIS HOLINESS, LEO XIII, MEDIATOR IN THE QUESTION OF THE CAROLINE ARCHIPELAGO AND THE PALAOS.[21]

Leo XIII presents an acceptable solution for this dispute.

October 22, 1885

48. The discovery made by Spain, in the sixteenth century, of the islands forming the archipelago of the Carolines and the Palaos, and the series of acts accomplished in these same islands by the Spanish Government for the benefit of the natives, have created, in the conviction of the said government and of the nation, a title of sovereignty, founded upon the principles of international law which are quoted and obeyed in our days in similar cases.

[20] Translation from *The Great Encyclical Letters of Pope Leo XIII,* pp. 100-101. Original Latin, *A.S.S.,* v. 16, p. 429 (1906, reprint ed.).

[21] Translation from Talbot, *Pope Leo XIII; His Life and Letters,* pp. 362-363. Original French, Müller, *Das Friedenswerk der Kirche,* pp. 325-326.

49. And, in fact, when we consider the sum of the above-mentioned acts, the authenticity of which is confirmed by various documents in the archives of Propaganda, we cannot mistake the beneficent course of Spain in regard to these islanders. It is, moreover, to be observed that no other government has exercised a like action towards them. This explains what must be kept in mind, — the constant tradition and conviction of the Spanish people in respect to that sovereignty, — a tradition and a conviction which were manifested two months ago, with an ardor and an animosity capable of compromising for an instant the internal peace of two friendly governments and their mutual relations.

50. On the other hand, Germany, as well as England, declared expressly in 1875 to the Spanish Government, that she did not recognize the sovereignty of Spain over these islands. The Imperial Government holds that it is the effectual occupation of a territory which constitutes the origin of the right of sovereignty over it, and that such occupation has never been realized by Spain in the case of the Carolines. It has acted in conformity with that principle in the Island of Yap; and in this the Mediator is happy to recognize, as the Spanish Government has also done, the loyalty of the Imperial Government.

51. In consequence, and in order that this divergence of views between the two States may be no obstacle to an honorable arrangement, the Mediator, having weighed all things, proposes that the new arrangement should adopt the formulas of the protocol relating to the Archipelago of Jolo, signed at Madrid on the 7th of March last, by the representatives of Great Britain, of Germany and of Spain; and that the following points be observed:

(1) Affirmation of the sovereignty of Spain over the Carolines and the Palaos.

(2) The Spanish Government, in order to render this sovereignty effectual, undertakes to establish as quickly as possible, in the archipelago in question, a regular administration, with a sufficient force to guarantee order and the rights acquired.

(3) Spain offers to Germany full and entire liberty of commerce, of navigation, and of fishery within the islands, as also the right of establishing a naval and a coaling station.

(4) Spain also assures to Germany the liberty of plantation within the islands, and of the foundation of agricultural establish-

ments upon the same footing as that of undertakings by Spanish subjects.

ENCYCLICAL *Immortale Dei* ON THE CHRISTIAN CONSTITUTION OF STATES.[22]

All public power proceeds from God and, therefore, a State from which religion is banished can never be well regulated.

November 1, 1885

52. . . . . . . It is not difficult to determine what would be the form and character of the State were it governed according to the principles of Christian philosophy. Man's natural instinct moves him to live in civil society, for he cannot, if dwelling apart, provide himself with the necessary requirements of life, nor procure the means of developing his mental and moral faculties. Hence, it is divinely ordained that he should lead his life — be it family, social, or civil — with his fellowmen, amongst whom alone his several wants can be adequately supplied. But as no society can hold together unless some one be over all, directing all to strive earnestly for the common good, every civilized community must have a ruling authority, and this authority, no less than society itself, has its source in nature, and has, consequently, God for its Author. Hence, it follows that all public power must proceed from God: for God alone is the true and supreme Lord of the world. Everything, without exception, must be subject to Him, and must serve Him, so that whosoever holds the right to govern, holds it from one sole and single Source, namely God, the Sovereign Ruler of all. *There is no power but from God.*[23]

53. The right to rule is not necessarily, however, bound up with any special mode of government. It may take this or that form, provided only that it be of a nature to insure the general welfare. But whatever be the nature of the government, rulers must ever bear in mind that God is the paramount Ruler of the world, and must set Him before themselves as their exemplar and law in the administration of the State. For, in things visible, God

[22] Translation from *The Catholic Mind*, v. 34, n. 21, pp. 426-448 (November 8, 1936).
Original Latin, *A.S.S.*, v. 18, pp. 162-179 (1885).
[23] *Romans*, XIII, 1.

has fashioned secondary causes in which His divine action can in some wise be discerned, leading up to the end to which the course of the world is ever tending. In like manner in civil society, God has always willed that there should be a ruling authority, and that they who are invested with it should reflect the divine power and providence in some measure over the human race.

54. They, therefore, who rule should rule with even-handed justice, not as masters, but rather as fathers, for the rule of God over man is most just, and is tempered always with a father's kindness. Government should moreover be administered for the well-being of the citizens, because they who govern others possess authority solely for the welfare of the State. Furthermore, the civil power must not be subservient to the advantage of any one individual, or of some few persons; inasmuch as it was established for the common good of all. But if those who are in authority rule unjustly, if they govern overbearingly or arrogantly, and if their measures prove hurtful to the people, they must remember that the Almighty will one day bring them to account, the more strictly in proportion to the sacredness of their office and pre-eminence of their dignity. *The mighty shall be mightily tormented*.[24] Then truly will the majesty of the law meet with the dutiful and willing homage of the people, when they are convinced that their rulers hold authority from God, and feel that it is a matter of justice and duty to obey them, and to show them reverence and fealty, united to a love not unlike that which children show their parents. *Let every soul be subject to higher powers*.[25] To despise legitimate authority, in whomsoever vested, is unlawful, as a rebellion against the Divine Will; and whoever resists that rushes wilfully to destruction. *He that resisteth the power resisteth the ordinance of God, and they that resist, purchase to themselves damnation*.[26] To cast aside obedience and by popular violence to incite to revolt, is, therefore, treason, not against man only, but against God. . . . . . .

55. It is a public crime to act as though there were no God. So, too, is it a sin in the State not to have care for religion, as a something beyond its scope, or as of no practical benefit; or out of many forms of religion to adopt that one which chimes in with the

---

[24] *Wisdom*, VI, 7.
[25] *Romans*, XIII, 1.
[26] *Romans*, XIII, 2.

fancy; for we are bound absolutely to worship God in that way
which He has shown to be His will. All who rule, therefore,
should hold in honor the holy Name of God, and one of their chief
duties must be to favor religion, to protect it, to shield it under
the credit and sanction of the laws, and neither to organize nor
enact any measures that may compromise its safety. This is the
bounden duty of rulers to the people over whom they rule: for one
and all we are destined, by our birth and adoption, to enjoy, when
this frail and fleeting life is ended, a supreme and final good in
heaven, and to the attainment of this every endeavor should be
directed. Since, then, upon this depends the full and perfect happiness of mankind, the securing of this end should be, of all imagin-
able interests, the most urgent. Hence, civil society, established for
the common welfare, should not only safeguard the well-being of
the community, but have also at heart the interests of its individual
members, in such mode as not in any way to hinder, but in every
manner to render as easy as may be, the possession of that highest
and unchangeable good for which all should seek. Wherefore, for
this purpose, care must especially be taken to preserve unharmed
and unimpeded the religion whereof the practice is the link con-
necting man with his God. . . . . . .

56. The Almighty, therefore, has appointed the charge of the
human race between two powers, the ecclesiastical and the divine,
the one being set over divine, and the other over human things.
Each in its kind is supreme, each has fixed limits within which it
is contained, limits which are defined by the nature and special
object of the province of each, so that there is, we may say, an orbit
traced out within which the action of each is brought into play by
its own native right.

57. . . . There must, accordingly, exist, between these two powers, a certain orderly connection, which may be compared to the
union of the soul and body in man. The nature and scope of that
connection can be determined only, as We have laid down, by
having regard to the nature of each power, and by taking account
of the relative excellence and nobleness of their purpose. One of
the two has for its proximate and chief object the well-being of
this mortal life; the other the everlasting joys of heaven. Whatever,
therefore, in things human is of a sacred character, whatever belongs either of its own nature or by reason of the end to which it

is referred, to the salvation of souls, or to the worship of God, is subject to the power and judgment of the Church. Whatever is to be ranged under the civil and political order is rightly subject to the civil authority. Jesus Christ has Himself given command that what is Cæsar's is to be rendered to Cæsar, and that what belongs to God is to be rendered to God.

58. There are, nevertheless, occasions when another method of concord is available, for the sake of peace and liberty: We mean when rulers of the State and the Roman Pontiff come to an understanding touching some special matter. At such times the Church gives signal proof of her motherly love by showing the greatest possible kindliness and indulgence. . . . . . .

59. . . . To exclude the Church, founded by God Himself, from the business of life, from the power of making laws, from the training of youth, from domestic society, is a grave and fatal error. A State from which religion is banished can never be well regulated; and already perhaps more than is desirable is known of the nature and tendency of the so-called *civil* philosophy of life and morals. The Church of Christ is the true and sole teacher of virtue and guardian of morals. She it is who preserves in their purity the principles from which duties flow, and by setting forth most urgent reasons for virtuous life, bids us not only to turn away from wicked deeds, but even to curb all movements of the mind that are opposed to reason; even though they be not carried out in action.

60. To wish the Church to be subject to the civil power in the exercise of her duty is a great folly and a sheer injustice. Whenever this is the case, order is disturbed, for things natural are put above things supernatural; the many benefits which the Church, if free to act, would confer on society are either prevented or at least lessened in number; and a way is prepared for enmities and contentions between the two powers; with how evil result to both the issue of events has taught us only too frequently. . . . . . .

61. In the same way the Church cannot approve of that liberty which begets a contempt of the most sacred laws of God, and casts off the obedience due to lawful authority, for this is not liberty so much as license, and is most correctly styled by St. Augustine the "liberty of self-ruin,"[27] and by the Apostle, St. Peter, the *cloak for*

[27] *Epistola CV ad Donatistas,* c. II, n. 9 in Migne *P.L.,* v. 33, c. 399.

malice.[28] Indeed, since it is opposed to reason, it is a true slavery, *for whosoever committeth sin is the servant of sin.*[29] On the other hand, that liberty is truly genuine, and to be sought after, which in regard to the individual does not allow men to be the slaves of error and of passion, the worst of all masters; which, too, in public administration guides the citizens in wisdom and provides for them increased means of well-being; and which, further, protects the State from foreign interference.

62. This honorable liberty, alone worthy of human beings, the Church approves most highly and has never slackened her endeavor to preserve, strong and unchanged, among nations. And in truth whatever in the State is of chief avail for the common welfare; whatever has been usefully established to curb the license of rulers who are opposed to the true interests of the people, or to prevent governments from unwarrantably interfering in municipal or family affairs; — whatever tends to uphold the honor, manhood and equal rights of individual citizens; — of all these things, as the monuments of past ages bear witness, the Catholic Church has always been the originator, the promoter, or the guardian. Ever, therefore, consistent with herself, while on the one hand she rejects that exorbitant liberty which in individuals and in nations ends in license or in thraldom, on the other hand, she willingly and most gladly welcomes whatever improvements the age brings forth, if these really secure the prosperity of life here below, which is as it were a stage in the journey to the life that will know no ending. . . . . . .

63. All this, though so reasonable and full of counsel, finds little favor nowadays, when States not only refuse to conform to the rules of Christian wisdom, but seem even anxious to recede from them further and further on each successive day. Nevertheless, since truth when brought to light is wont, of its own nature, to spread itself far and wide, and gradually take possession of the minds of men, We, moved by the great and holy duty of Our Apostolic mission to all nations, speak, as We are bound to do, with freedom. Our eyes are not closed to the spirit of the times. We repudiate not the assured and useful improvements of our age, but devoutly wish affairs of State to take a safer course than they are

[28] I *Peter*, II, 16.
[29] *John*, VIII, 34.

now taking, and to rest on a more firm foundation without injury to the true freedom of the people. For the best parent and guardian of liberty amongst men is truth. *The truth shall make you free.*[30] . . . . . .

64. But in matters merely political, as for instance the best form of government, and this or that system of administration, a difference of opinion is lawful. Those, therefore, whose piety is in other respects known, and whose minds are ready to accept in all obedience the decrees of the Apostolic See, cannot in justice be accounted as bad men because they disagree as to subjects We have mentioned; and still graver wrong will be done them, if — as We have more than once perceived with regret — they are accused of violating, or of wavering in, the Catholic Faith.

65. Let this be well borne in mind by all who are in the habit of publishing their opinions, and above all by journalists. In the endeavor to secure interests of the highest order there is no room for intestine strife or party rivalries, since all should aim with one mind and purpose to make safe that which is the common object of all — the maintenance of Religion and of the State.

66. If, therefore, there have hitherto been dissensions, let them henceforth be gladly buried in oblivion. If rash or injurious acts have been committed, whoever may have been at fault, let mutual charity make amends, and let the past be redeemed by a special submission of all to the Apostolic See.

67. In this way Catholics will attain two most excellent results: they will become helpers to the Church in preserving and propagating Christian wisdom; and they will confer the greatest benefit on civil society, the safety of which is exceedingly imperiled by evil teachings and bad passions. This, Venerable Brethren, is what We have thought it Our duty to expound to all nations of the Catholic world touching the Christian constitution of States and the duties of individual citizens.

[30] *John,* VIII, 32.

LETTER *Cum de Carolinis Insulis* TO PRINCE BISMARCK OF
GERMANY.[31]

*The dispute concerning the Caroline Islands has been
settled according to the solution proposed by Leo XIII.*

December 31, 1885

68. The dispute arising in regard to the Caroline Islands having been happily ended on the conditions laid down by Us, We
have expressed Our joy thereat to His Majesty, the German Emperor, and We wish now to renew to Your Highness Our expression of the same sentiment; for it was you who proposed that the
solution of this conflict be submitted to Us. We are pleased to
acknowledge, in conformity with the truth, that it was in a large
part due to your constant zeal that the difficulties met with in the
settlement of this affair could have been overcome; for, from beginning to end, you never ceased to second Our efforts by entering
into Our views. So We now hasten to show you Our gratitude
for having so effectively contributed to furnishing Us with a most
favorable opportunity for exercising so exalted a ministry in the
interest of harmony. History, it is true, tells us that this task is not
new to the Holy See, but it is a long time since such a proposal was
made to it, though there is scarcely any function more in harmony
with the spirit and nature of the Roman Papacy. Free from all
prejudices, you have looked at the situation rather from the standpoint of truth than from that of the opinions and inclinations of
others, and you have not hesitated to place your confidence in Our
impartiality. By acting thus you have obtained the approval of all
men whose thoughts are not dominated by their prejudices—especially that of Catholics throughout the whole world, who ought to
be deeply touched by the honor done to their Father, their chief
Pastor. Your political sagacity, as the whole world acknowledged,
has contributed vastly to the formation of the great and powerful
German empire, and it is natural that that empire's solidity and
prosperity, based on strength and durable well-being, be the first
object of your efforts; but it cannot by any means have escaped your
clear-sightedness how many means are at the disposal of the power
with which We are vested, for the maintenance of political and

[31] Translation from Furey, *Life of Leo XIII and History of His Pontificate*, pp. 220-222.
Original Latin, *A.S.S.*, v. 18, p. 417 (1885).

social order, especially if this power enjoys unshackled its full liberty of action. Permit Us, then, to anticipate events in spirit, and to regard what has been done as a pledge of what the future will bring. So that you may have from now a testimony of Our esteem, We name you a knight of the Order of Christ, the insignia of which order will be sent to you along with this letter.

LETTER *Jampridem* TO THE BISHOPS OF PRUSSIA.[32]

The Pope is willing to co-operate with secular rulers but he must insist upon the recognition of the rights of the Church.

January 6, 1886

69. . . . . . . The desire which We have had and still have to re-establish concord and peace on a solid basis is so great that We have not failed to inform rulers that We are ready to comply with their will in so far as the divine laws and the duty of conscience permit. And what is more, We have not hesitated to give clear proof of this intention; and it is Our firm purpose not to neglect to do anything in the future which may contribute to the re-establishing and strengthening of concord.

70. However, in order that Our desire and hope may be realized, special care must be taken that the public laws be purged of all that is contrary to Catholic discipline in whatever pertains chiefly and more closely to the piety of the faithful. There must likewise be a repeal of whatever hampers the proper freedom of bishops in governing their churches according to the divinely established ordinances and in training the youth in seminaries according to the prescriptions of canon law. For though We are animated by a sincere desire for peace, still We may not dare do anything that is contrary to what has been divinely established and ordained, for the defense of which, if need be, We are ready, after the example of Our Predecessors, to endure the greatest hardships. . . . . . .

---

[32] Original Latin, *A.S.S.,* v. 18, pp. 388-389 (1886).

ALLOCUTION *Etsi Res* TO THE COLLEGE OF CARDINALS.[33]

*Leo XIII explains his decision in the controversy be-
tween Spain and Germany over possession of the Caroline Islands.*

January 15, 1886

71. Even though the affair which We have decided to treat is
now a matter of public knowledge, nevertheless, since it is connected with the public good of nations and has renewed a custom
that is very honorable to the Apostolic See, and one which for a
long time has been interrupted, We judge it proper to make reference about it to you here and in Our own person.

72. Last September, when the Emperor of Germany and the
King of Spain together had asked Us to be the arbitrator in the
dispute over the Caroline Islands, We gladly accepted the office
thus entrusted to Us because We hoped thereby to serve the cause
of peace and humanity. We, therefore, examined and weighed in
the balance of an impartial and equitable judgment the arguments
of both litigants, and then We submitted to them certain propositions as a basis of mutual agreement, which We hoped would
prove acceptable to them.

73. Spain brought forward many reasons in support of her
right to that distant portion of Micronesia. She was the first nation
whose ships had reached those shores—a fact acknowledged by the
most distinguished geographers. The very name of Carolines
attested the Spanish title. Besides, the kings of Spain had more
than once sent thither apostolic men as missionaries, and of this
the records of the Roman Pontificate afford confirmatory proof;
for there exists a letter of Our Predecessor, Clement XI, to Philip V,
written in 1706, praising this prince for having equipped and furnished a vessel to convey missionaries to the Carolines. In it the
Pontiff also exhorts the king to continue to help propagate the
Christian name and procure the salvation of multitudes of human
beings.

74. The same Pontiff also wrote to Louis XIV, beseeching him
not to hinder in any way the carrying out of an enterprise so happily begun by his grandson. Again, Philip V fixed an annual

[33] Original Latin, *A.S.S.*, v. 18, pp. 309-311 (1886).

33

sum of two thousand crowns to be set apart for the support of these missions. Furthermore, no nation but the Spanish ever did anything to bring the light of the Gospel to these islands. And, finally, whatever information we possess of the manner of living and customs of the natives has been furnished by the missionaries.

75. From this series of facts, viewed especially in the light of the international jurisprudence then in vigor, it is evident that the right of Spain to the Caroline Islands is fairly established. For if any claim to sovereignty can be derived from the labor of civilizing a barbarous country, this claim must be highest in favor of such as endeavor to reclaim barbarians from pagan superstition to the Gospel morality, inasmuch as in true religion are to be found all the most powerful civilizing forces. On this principle were often founded the rights of sovereignty; and this was the case, for instance, of several islands in the ocean, of which not a few bear names given them by the Christian religion.

76. Seeing, therefore, that a constant and well-founded public opinion conceded to Spain the sovereignty over the Carolines, it is not surprising that when the late dispute began about their possession the whole Spanish nation was stirred with such excitement as to threaten not only the internal peace of the kingdom, but to imperil its relations with a friendly power.

77. To the arguments brought forward by Spain, Germany on her side opposed others also based on the law of nations—that residence on land is necessary to possession: that, taking into account the facts of recent history, the law of nations sanctions as legitimate the claim to ownership of territory when the claimant occupies and uses it; that where the territory is not so occupied and used the land is accounted as having no owner. Wherefore, considering the fact that the Carolines had not during a century and a half been occupied by Spain, these islands should have been adjudged the property of the first person taking possession of them. In addition to these reasons it was alleged that some such dispute as the present having arisen in the year 1875, both Germany and Great Britain affirmed they did not at all acknowledge the sovereignty of Spain over the Carolines.

78. In this divergence of opinions We took into account the respective rights and interests of the two contending nations, and confidently submitted a plan which We thought well fitted for

bringing about a peaceful settlement of the difficulty. We were guided solely in this by Our own sense of equity, and, as you are aware, both parties willingly accepted Our proposal.

79. Thus was accomplished an event which the present currents of public opinion forbade Us to look forward to. Providence willed that two illustrious nations should do homage to the supreme authority in the Church by asking it to fulfill an office so much in keeping with its nature, to preserve by its action the threatened peace and harmony between them. This is the fruit of that salutary and beneficent influence which God has attached to the power of the Supreme Pontiffs. Superior to the envious jealousy of its enemies, and more mighty than the prevailing iniquity of the age, it is subject neither to destruction nor to change.

80. From all this, too, it becomes manifest how grievous an evil are the wars waged against the Apostolic See and the lessening of its rightful liberty. For thereby it is not merely justice and religion that are made to suffer, but the public good itself, since in the present critical and changeful condition of public affairs the Roman Pontificate would confer far greater benefits on the world if, with perfect freedom and rights unimpaired, it could devote all its energies to promoting, without hindrance, the salvation of the human race. . . .

ENCYCLICAL LETTER *Quod Multum* TO THE BISHOPS OF HUNGARY.[34]

The firmest foundation for peace in any nation is the Catholic religion.

August 22, 1886

81. . . . . . . Certainly it has never been more necessary than at present to understand and to be convinced thoroughly not only of the great opportunity but of the absolute necessity of the Catholic religion for peace and public welfare. Daily experience reveals to Us to what an extremity those who are accustomed to respect no authority and who tolerate no limits to their own desires would reduce the State. No one is unaware, in these days, of what they intend, and by what means and with what determination they

---

[34] Original Latin, *A.S.S.,* v. 19, pp. 99-100 (1886).

strive to accomplish these things. The greatest empires and the most flourishing republics are at the present time assailed by these groups of men united by a common purpose and by similar methods of action so that the public tranquillity is constantly menaced by some kind of peril. In order to combat such an onslaught of evil, the salutary counsel of strengthening the authority of the magistrates and of increasing the rigor of the laws has been given in some countries. And yet to avoid the terrors of Socialism, a very excellent and truly efficacious means, without which the fear of punishment will have little effect, is to inspire in the citizens a deep religious spirit and to inculcate in them a respect for and a love of the Church. The Church is the sacred guardian of religion, the parent and the teacher of the purity of customs and of all the virtues which spring from religion as their source. Whoever religiously and wholeheartedly follows the precepts of the Gospel shall by that very fact remain far from the shadow of Socialism. Even as religion commands men to worship and to fear God, so also it orders them to submit to and to obey lawful authority; it forbids anyone to take part in sedition; it prescribes respect for the goods and the rights of others; it commands those who are rich to come to the aid of the multitudes. It surrounds the poor with the resources of charity; it brings sweet consolations to the unfortunate by inspiring in them a hope for immeasurable and immortal goods which will be greater than those from the deprivation of which they have suffered so harshly and for such a long time. . . . . . .

LETTER *Quamvis Animi* TO CARDINAL RAMPOLLA, SECRETARY OF STATE.[35]

Mere private practice of religion is not enough to establish a lasting peace.

June 15, 1887

82. . . . . . . But without the Church the common good will simply never be realized; without her salutary influence, which can safely guide minds to truth and strengthen souls to virtue and to bearing every difficulty, neither the severity of laws, nor punishments meted out by human justice, nor armed force itself will be

---

[35] Original Latin, *A.S.S.*, v. 20, pp. 7-19 (1887).

sufficient to avert the present crisis, much less to rebuild society upon its natural and solid foundations.

83. Firmly convinced of this We consider it Our duty to carry out this work of the common good already begun by spreading the precepts of the holy Gospel, by winning over once more to the Church and her hierarchy the minds of all, and finally by acquiring for both a fuller freedom, that they may be able to carry out in the world with abundant success a most useful mission which they have received from God. . . . . . .

84. But to come to the point of really establishing lasting peace, it is not enough, as in other matters, to make provision for some private need of religion, to mitigate or abolish hostile laws, to impede, to avert some measures enacted contrary to Our interests which they may perchance enforce, but it is necessary besides, nay even of first and foremost importance, that the position of the Supreme Head of the Church, which many years ago through violence and injustice became positively unworthy of him and incompatible with the Apostolic office, be established as is fitting and becoming. Wherefore, in a previous allocution, We were careful to set up the rights and dignity of the Apostolic See as the very first foundation stone of this reconciliation and to demand for Ourselves that condition in which the Roman Pontiff would be subject to no one and would enjoy complete freedom, not merely a mocking semblance of it. . . . . . .

85. In very truth, if it be borne in mind that the war waged against the sovereignty of the Roman Pontiffs has always had the enemies of the Church as its instigators, and in these latter times bands of conspirators and public enemies, whose purpose in overthrowing the temporal dominion has been to open a way for attacking and destroying the spiritual power itself of the Popes, this very fact clearly proves that the royal sovereignty of the Popes is still, in the plans of Divine Providence, a means for the peaceful exercise of their Apostolic authority since it effectively safeguards their autonomy and liberty. . . . . . .

86. Here where the Roman Pontiff usually lives, and rules, teaches, and commands, it is particularly necessary that he be established in such a position of autonomy that his freedom be not in the least hindered by anyone, and that it be clear to all that he is positively free, so that the faithful who are scattered through-

out the world may with confidence and security manifest the faith and obedience they owe him on account of his sacred office. Let this be brought about not by that kind of agreement which changes and is altered under every circumstance, but by one which is of its very nature firm and lasting. Without any fear of hindrances which may perchance be put in the way, here more than anywhere else the full development of Catholic life, the solemnity of divine worship, regard for the laws of the Church and their public observance must be possible, and likewise the peaceful and legal existence and life of all pious works which have been established by the Catholic Church. . . . . . .

87. On the other hand, it is not difficult to foresee possible events, as a result of which the status of the Roman Pontiff may become worse, whether indeed through the successful attempts of rebels and those men who make no pretense whatever of hiding their feelings against the Vicar of Christ, or on account of the varying fortunes and countless complications which may turn out to his detriment. . . . . . .

LETTER *In Plurimis* TO THE BISHOPS OF BRAZIL.[36]

The Bishops of Brazil are commended for helping to rid their country of slavery. The newly freed slaves are exhorted to maintain peaceful relations with their former masters.

May 5, 1888

88. . . . . . . And now, Venerable Brethren, Our thoughts and letters desire to turn to you that We may again announce to you and again share with you the exceeding joy which We feel on account of the determinations which have been publicly entered into in that empire with regard to slavery. If indeed it seemed to Us a good, happy, and propitious event, that it was provided and insisted upon by law that whoever were still in the condition of slaves ought to be admitted to the status and rights of free men, so also it confirms and increases Our hope of future acts which will be the cause of joy, both in civil and religious matters. Thus the

[36] Translation from *The Tablet*, v. 71, pp. 876-877 (June 2, 1888). Original Latin, *A.S.S.*, v. 20, pp. 557-558 (1888).

name of the Empire of Brazil will be justly held in honor and
praise among the most civilized nations, and the name of its august
Emperor will likewise be esteemed whose excellent speech is on
record, that he desired nothing more ardently than that every
vestige of slavery should be speedily obliterated from his territories.
But truly, until those precepts of the laws are carried into effect,
earnestly endeavor, We beseech you, by all means, and press on
as much as possible the accomplishment of this affair, which no
light difficulties hinder. Through your means let it be brought
to pass that masters and slaves may mutually agree with the highest
goodwill and best good faith, nor let there be any transgression of
clemency or justice, but whatever things have to be carried out let
all be done lawfully, temperately, and in a Christian manner;
it is, however, chiefly to be wished that this may be prosperously
accomplished, which all desire, that slavery may be banished and
blotted out without any injury to divine or human rights, with
no agitation of the State, and so with the solid benefit of the slaves
themselves, for whose sake it is undertaken. To each one of these,
whether they have already been made free or are about to become
so, We address with a pastoral intention and fatherly mind a few
salutary cautions culled from the words of the great Apostle of the
Gentiles. Let them, then, endeavor piously and constantly to
retain a grateful memory and feeling towards those by whose
counsel and exertion they were set at liberty. Let them never show
themselves unworthy of so great a gift nor ever confound liberty
with license; but let them use it as becomes well-ordered citizens
for the industry of an active life, for the benefit and advantage both
of their family and of the State. To respect and increase the dignity
of their princes, to obey the magistrates, to be obedient to the laws,
these and similar duties let them diligently fulfill, under the influence, not so much of fear as of religion; let them also restrain and
keep in subjection envy of another's wealth or position, which
unfortunately daily distresses so many of those in inferior positions,
and presents so many incitements of rebellion against security of
order and peace. Content with their state and lot, let them think
nothing dearer, let them desire nothing more ardently than the good
things of the heavenly kingdom by whose grace they have been
brought to the light and redeemed by Christ. . . . . . .

39

ENCYCLICAL *Libertas Praestantissimum* ON HUMAN LIBERTY.[37]

*The Pope writes on the true nature of human liberty
and explains how this concept has been corrupted in
modern times. Now the peace of the world is threatened by false notions of human liberty.*

June 20, 1888

89. . . . . . . What has been said of the liberty of individuals is
no less applicable to them when considered as bound together in
civil society. For, what reason and the natural law do for individuals, that *human law,* promulgated for their good, does for the
citizens of States. Of the laws enacted by men, some are concerned
with what is good or bad by its very nature; and they command
men to follow after what is right and to shun what is wrong,
adding at the same time a suitable sanction. But such laws by no
means derive their origin from civil society; because just as civil
society did not create human nature, so neither can it be said to
be the author of the good which befits human nature, or of the
evil which is contrary to it. Laws come before men live together
in society, and have their origin in the natural, and consequently
in the eternal, law. The precepts, therefore, of the natural law,
contained bodily in the laws of men, have not merely the force of
human law, but they possess that higher and more august sanction
which belongs to the law of nature and the eternal law. And within
the sphere of this kind of laws, the duty of the civil legislator is,
mainly, to keep the community in obedience by the adoption of a
common discipline and by putting restraint upon refractory and
viciously inclined men, so that, deterred from evil, they may turn
to what is good, or at any rate may avoid causing trouble and disturbance to the State. Now there are other enactments of the civil
authority, which do not follow directly, but somewhat remotely,
from the natural law, and decide many points which the law of
nature treats only in a general and indefinite way. For instance,
though nature commands all to contribute to the public peace and
prosperity, still whatever belongs to the manner and circumstances,
and conditions under which such service is to be rendered must
be determined by the wisdom of men and not by nature herself.

[37] Translation from *The Great Encyclical Letters of Pope Leo XIII,* pp. 141-162.
Original Latin, *A.S.S.,* v. 20, pp. 597-613 (1888).

It is in the constitution of these particular rules of life, suggested by reason and prudence, and put forth by competent authority, that human law, properly so called, consists, binding all citizens to work together for the attainment of the common end proposed to the community, and forbidding them to depart from this end; and in so far as human law is in conformity with the dictates of nature, leading to what is good, and deterring from evil.

90. From this it is manifest that the eternal law of God is the sole standard and rule of human liberty, not only in each individual man, but also in the community and civil society which men constitute when united. Therefore, the true liberty of human society does not consist in every man doing what he pleases, for this would simply end in turmoil and confusion, and bring on the overthrow of the State; but rather in this, that through the injunctions of the civil law all may more easily conform to the prescriptions of the eternal law. Likewise, the liberty of those who are in authority does not consist in the power to lay unreasonable and capricious commands upon their subjects, which would equally be criminal and would lead to the ruin of the commonwealth; but the binding force of human laws is in this, that they are to be regarded as applications of the eternal law, and incapable of sanctioning anything which is not contained in the eternal law, as in the principle of all law. . . . . . .

91. Therefore, the nature of human liberty, however it be considered, whether in individuals or in society, whether in those who command or in those who obey, supposes the necessity of obedience to some supreme and eternal law, which is no other than the authority of God, commanding good and forbidding evil. And so far from this most just authority of God over men diminishing, or even destroying, their liberty, it protects and perfects it, for the real perfection of all creatures is found in the prosecution and attainment of their respective ends; but the supreme end to which human liberty must aspire is God.

92. These precepts of the truest and highest teaching, made known to us by the light of reason itself, the Church, instructed by the example and doctrine of her divine Author, has ever propagated and asserted; for she has ever made them the measure of her office and of her teaching to the Christian nations. As to morals, the laws of the Gospel not only immeasurably surpass the

wisdom of the heathen, but are an invitation and an introduction to a state of holiness unknown to the ancients; and, bringing man nearer to God, they make him at once the possessor of a more perfect liberty. Thus the powerful influence of the Church has ever been manifested in the custody and protection of the civil and political liberty of the people. The enumeration of its merits in this respect does not belong to our present purpose. It is sufficient to recall the fact that slavery, that old reproach of the heathen nations, was mainly abolished by the beneficent efforts of the Church. The impartiality of law and the true brotherhood of man were first asserted by Jesus Christ; and His Apostles re-echoed His voice when they declared that in future there was to be neither Jew, nor Gentile, nor Barbarian, nor Scythian, but all were brothers in Christ. So powerful, so conspicuous in this respect, is the influence of the Church, that experience abundantly testifies how savage customs are no longer possible in any land where she has once set her foot; but that gentleness speedily takes the place of cruelty, and the light of truth quickly dispels the darkness of barbarism. Nor has the Church been less lavish in the benefits she has conferred on civilized nations in every age, either by resisting the tyranny of the wicked, or by protecting the innocent and helpless from injury; or finally by using her influence in the support of any form of government which commended itself to the citizens at home, because of its justice, or was feared by their enemies without, because of its power.

93. Moreover, the highest duty is to respect authority, and obediently to submit to just law; and by this the members of a community are effectually protected from the wrongdoing of evil men. Lawful power is from God, *and whosoever resisteth authority resisteth the ordinance of God;*[38] wherefore obedience is greatly ennobled when subjected to an authority which is the most just and supreme of all. But where the power to command is wanting, or where a law is enacted contrary to reason, or to the eternal law, or to some ordinance of God, obedience is unlawful, lest, while obeying man, we become disobedient to God. Thus, an effectual barrier being opposed to tyranny, the authority in the State will not have all its own way, but the interests and rights of all will be safeguarded—the rights of individuals, of domestic society, and

---

[38] *Romans,* XIII, 2.

of all the members of the commonwealth; all being free to live
according to law and right reason; and in this, as We have shown,
true liberty really consists.

94. . . . . . . For, once ascribe to human reason the only authority to decide what is true and what is good, and the real distinction between good and evil is destroyed; honor and dishonor differ
not in their nature, but in the opinion and judgment of each one;
pleasure is the measure of what is lawful; and, given a code of
morality which can have little or no power to restrain or quiet the
unruly propensities of man, a way is naturally opened to universal
corruption. With reference also to public affairs: authority is
severed from the true and natural principle whence it derives all
its efficacy for the common good; and the law determining what
it is right to do and avoid doing is at the mercy of a majority.
Now this is simply a road leading straight to tyranny. The empire
of God over man and civil society once repudiated, it follows that
religion, as a public institution, can have no claim to exist, and that
everything that belongs to religion will be treated with complete
indifference. Furthermore, with ambitious designs on sovereignty,
tumult and sedition will be common amongst the people; and when
duty and conscience cease to appeal to them, there will be nothing
to hold them back but force, which of itself alone is powerless to
keep their covetousness in check. Of this we have almost daily
evidence in the conflict with *Socialists* and members of other
seditious societies, who labor unceasingly to bring about revolution.
It is for those, then, who are capable of forming a just estimate
of things to decide whether such doctrines promote that true liberty
which alone is worthy of man, or rather pervert and destroy it.

95. . . . . . . Religion, of its essence, is wonderfully helpful
to the State. For, since it derives the prime origin of all power
directly from God Himself, with grave authority it charges rulers
to be mindful of their duty, to govern without injustice or severity,
to rule their people kindly and with almost paternal charity; it
admonishes subjects to be obedient to lawful authority, as to the
ministers of God; and it binds them to their rulers, not merely by
obedience, but by reverence and affection, forbidding all seditions
and venturesome enterprises calculated to disturb public order and
tranquillity, and cause greater restrictions to be put upon the liberty
of the people. We need not mention how greatly religion conduces

43

to pure morals, and pure morals to liberty. Reason shows, and history confirms the fact, that the higher the morality of States, the greater are the liberty and wealth and power which they enjoy.

96. We must now consider briefly *liberty of speech,* and liberty of the Press. It is hardly necessary to say that there can be no such right as this, if it be not used in moderation, and if it pass beyond the bounds and end of all true liberty. For right is a moral power which—as We have before said and must again and again repeat—it is absurd to suppose that nature has accorded indifferently to truth and falsehood, to justice and injustice. Men have a right freely and prudently to propagate throughout the State what things soever are true and honorable, so that as many as possible may possess them; but lying opinions, than which no mental plague is greater, and vices which corrupt the heart and moral life, should be diligently repressed by public authority, lest they insidiously work the ruin of the State. The excesses of an unbridled intellect, which unfailingly end in the oppression of the untutored multitude, are no less rightly controlled by the authority of the law than are the injuries inflicted by violence upon the weak. And this all the more surely, because by far the greater part of the community is either absolutely unable, or able only with great difficulty, to escape from illusions and deceitful subtleties, especially such as flatter the passions. If unbridled license of speech and of writing be granted to all, nothing will remain sacred and inviolate; even the highest and truest mandates of nature, justly held to be the common and noblest heritage of the human race, will not be spared. Thus, truth being gradually obscured by darkness, pernicious and manifold error, as too often happens, will easily prevail. Thus, too, license will gain what liberty loses; for liberty will ever be more free and secure, in proportion as license is kept in fuller restraint. In regard, however, to all matters of opinion which God leaves to man's free discussion, full liberty of thought and of speech is naturally within the right of every one; for such liberty never leads men to suppress the truth, but often to discover it and make it known.

97. A like judgment must be passed upon what is called *liberty of teaching.* There can be no doubt that truth alone should imbue the minds of men; for in it are found the well-being, the end, and the perfection of every intelligent nature; and, therefore, nothing but truth should be taught both to the ignorant and to the edu-

cated, so as to bring knowledge to those who have it not, and to preserve it in those who possess it. For this reason it is plainly the duty of all who teach to banish error from the mind, and by sure safeguards to close the entry to all false convictions. From this it follows, as is evident, that the liberty of which We have been speaking, is greatly opposed to reason, and tends absolutely to pervert men's minds, inasmuch as it claims for itself the right of teaching whatever it pleases—a liberty which the State cannot grant without failing in its duty. And the more so, because the authority of teachers has great weight with their hearers, who can rarely decide for themselves as to the truth or falsehood of the instruction given to them.

98. . . . . . . Unless it be otherwise determined, by reason of some exceptional condition of things, it is expedient to take part in the administration of public affairs. And the Church approves of every one devoting his services to the common good, and doing all that he can for the defense, preservation and prosperity of his country.

99. Neither does the Church condemn those who, if it can be done without violation of justice, wish to make their country independent of any foreign or despotic power. Nor does she blame those who wish to assign to the State the power of self-government, and to its citizens the greatest possible measure of prosperity. The Church has always most faithfully fostered civil liberty, and this was seen especially in Italy, in the municipal prosperity, and wealth, and glory, which were obtained at a time when the salutary power of the Church had spread, without opposition, to all parts of the State. . . . . . .

LETTER *Saepe Nos* TO THE BISHOPS OF IRELAND.[39]

The Pope desires to see Ireland free again but he deplores the use of violence to obtain this freedom.

June 24, 1888

100. . . . . . . The condition of Ireland affects Us more than anyone, and We desire nothing more anxiously than to see the Irish

[39] Translation from Furey, *Life of Leo XIII and History of His Pontificate*, pp. 168-169. Original Latin, *A.S.S.*, v. 21, pp. 4-5 (1888).

at last, after having secured the peace and just prosperity they have
merited, breathe freedom once again. We have never disputed
their right to seek to better their condition; but can anyone be
permitted to have recourse to crime as a means? Far from it; for,
with the irruption of the passions and party political interests, good
and evil are mingled in the same cause. We are constantly called
upon to distinguish what is honorable from what is not so, and
to turn Catholics away from everything that the rule of Christian
morality does not approve. . . .

101. . . . Our office forbade Us to tolerate that so many Catholics, whose salvation is especially entrusted to Us, should follow
a dangerous and slippery path, better calculated to destroy everything than to assuage misfortune. The question must be looked
at, then, in accordance with truth; and Ireland should recognize
in that very decree Our love for her and Our desire that she prosper, because nothing is more fatal to a cause, no matter how just it
may be, than that it be defended by violence and injustice. . . . . . .

LETTER *Exeunte Jam Anno* TO THE CATHOLICS OF THE WHOLE
WORLD.[40]

The Pope prays for real peace, the peace of order.

December 25, 1888

102. . . . . . . You see, O Lord, how the winds blow from
every quarter and how the sea swells in its violently throbbing
waves. Command the winds and the waves, We beseech You Who
alone can do it. Give to mankind the real peace which the world
cannot give, the peace of order. Let men, through Your grace and
acting on Your impulse, return to the order wished for, by making
live again as they ought piety towards God, justice and charity
towards our neighbor, temperance in regard to themselves, subduing
the passions by reason. May Thy Kingdom come, and may those
also who by vain toil seek far from You truth and salvation understand that they must submit to and obey You. Your laws are
permeated with equity and paternal kindness, and You Yourself
give us the power to live up to them with ease. Man's life on earth

---

[40] Translation from Furey, *Life of Leo XIII and History of His Pontificate*, p. 276.
Original Latin, *A.S.S.*, v. 21, p. 334 (1888).

is a struggle, but "You take that struggle into account and help man to triumph; You raise him up when he falls, and You crown him in his victory."[41] . . . . . .

ALLOCUTION *Nostis Errorem* TO THE COLLEGE OF CARDINALS.[42]

Peace has its foundation in justice and charity and the Church has always promoted the practice of these two virtues.

February 11, 1889

103. . . . . . . And there is yet another consideration why the present is a most fitting opportunity. If ever there was a time when peace was unanimously desired by the world it is surely to-day, when words of peace, rest, and repose are on all lips. The sovereign princes and all those who in Europe guide public affairs declare that all they desire, that the one object of their aims, is to make sure of peace, and herein they speak with the full consent of all classes of society, for the hatred the nations have of war is daily more clearly shown. This hatred is a most proper one, for if war is sometimes necessary, it always brings in its train very many miseries. But how much more calamitous would it not be to-day, when the number of soldiers is so great, the progress of the military art so highly developed, and the number of instruments of destruction so multiplied? Whenever We let Our thoughts rest on this, We feel Ourself filled more and more with charity for the Christian peoples, and We cannot keep from trembling for the dangers which threaten them. There is, therefore, nothing of more importance than to remove from Europe the danger of war, and all that is done with that object deserves to be considered as a contribution to the public safety.

104. But the wish does not do much to render peace assured, and the mere desire for peace is not a sufficient guarantee. Again, the vast number of soldiers and the stupendous armaments may for a while prevent an enemy attacking, but they can never secure a sure and lasting peace. Moreover, armaments which are a menace are fitter rather to hasten than retard a conflict; they fill the mind

---

[41] *Cf.* St. Augustine, *In psalmum 32*, in Migne, *P.L.*, v. 36, c. 279.
[42] Translation from *The Tablet*, v. 73, pp. 281-282 (February 23, 1889). Original Latin, *A.S.S.*, v. 21, pp. 386-388 (1889).

with disquietude for the future, and among other drawbacks they have this, that they impose such burdens upon the nations that it is doubtful if war would not be more bearable.

105. Wherefore We must seek for peace some basis more sound and more in accordance with nature; for if nature does not forbid one to defend one's rights by force, she does not permit that force should become the efficient cause of right. Since peace is based upon good order, it follows that, for empires as well as for individuals, concord should have her principal foundation in justice and charity.

106. To commit no wrong against another, to respect the sanctity of another's rights, to practice mutual trust and good will, these are indeed the unchanging and most lasting bonds of peace, whose virtue is such that she stifles even the germs of hatred and jealousy.

107. But God has made His Church guardian and mother of the two virtues of which We speak, on which account she has had and will have nothing closer to her heart than to uphold, to spread and to protect the laws of justice and charity. For this purpose she has overrun all parts of the earth; and all the world knows that, having tamed the barbarian races by inspiring them with love of justice, she has led them from the ferocity of their warlike habits to the practice of the arts of peace and civilization. To the little and to the great, to those who obey and to those who command, she alike imposes the duty of observing justice and of attacking no one wrongfully. It is the Church who, in spite of distance, in spite of the differences of races, has joined together all peoples by friendship and brotherly charity. Mindful ever of the laws and the example of her Divine Founder, Who desired to be called the King of Peace, and Whose birth was even announced in heavenly canticles of peace, she wishes men to rest in the beauty of peace, and she ceases not from praying to obtain of God that He will preserve the lives and the fortunes of the nations from the risks of war. As often as it was necessary, and as the circumstances permitted, she has labored with all her heart, by interposing her authority, to re-establish concord and the peace of States.

108. These considerations and motives, most great and most holy, inspire Our actions, Venerable Brethren, and We obey them. Whatever events the future may bring forth, whatever may be the

judgments or the actions of men, We shall always act in accordance with this rule, and from it We are convinced We shall never depart. In any case, if We cannot otherwise contribute to the preservation of peace, We shall still have this resource, which no one can take from Us, that We shall continue to have recourse to Him Who can recall the mind of man whence, and send it whither, He wills; and We shall earnestly beseech Him that, all fear of war being removed, and the regular order of things being, by His mercy, restored, He may grant Europe to rest upon true and firm foundations. . . . . . .

ENCYCLICAL *Sapientiae Christianae* ON THE CHIEF DUTIES OF CHRISTIANS AS CITIZENS.[43]

The citizen owes obedience both to God and to his country but in cases of conflict between these two powers he must obey God rather than men.

January 10, 1890

109. . . . . . . But the man who has embraced the Christian faith, as in duty bound, is by that very fact a subject of the Church as one of the children born of her, and becomes a member of that greatest and holiest body, which it is the special charge of the Roman Pontiff to rule with supreme power, under its Invisible Head, Jesus Christ.

110. Now, if the natural law enjoins us to love devotedly and to defend the country in which we had birth, and in which we were brought up, so that every good citizen hesitates not to face death for his native land, very much more is it the urgent duty of Christians to be ever quickened by like feelings toward the Church. For the Church is the holy city of the living God, born of God Himself, and by Him built up and established. Upon this earth indeed she accomplishes her pilgrimage, but by instructing and guiding men, she summons them to eternal happiness. We are bound, then, to love dearly the country whence we have received the means of enjoyment this mortal life affords, but we have a much more urgent obligation to love, with ardent love, the Church to

---

[43] Translation from *The Great Encyclical Letters of Pope Leo XIII*, pp. 183-186. Original Latin, *A.S.S.*, v. 22, pp. 387-389 (1889-1890).

which we owe the life of the soul, a life that will endure forever. For fitting it is to prefer the good of the soul to the well-being of the body, inasmuch as duties toward God are of a far more hallowed character than those toward men.

111. Moreover, if we would judge aright, the supernatural love for the Church and the natural love of our own country proceed from the same eternal principle, since God Himself is their Author and originating Cause. Consequently, it follows that between the duties they respectively enjoin, neither can come into collision with the other. We can, certainly, and should love ourselves, bear ourselves kindly towards our fellow men, nourish affection for the State and the governing powers; but at the same time we can and must cherish towards the Church a feeling of filial piety, and love God with the deepest love of which we are capable. The order of precedence of these duties is, however, at times, either under stress of public calamities, or through the perverse will of men, inverted. For instances occur where the State seems to require from men as subjects one thing, and religion, from men as Christians, quite another; and this in reality without any other ground, than that the rulers of the State either hold the sacred power of the Church of no account, or endeavor to subject it to their own will. Hence arises a conflict, and an occasion, through such conflict, of virtue being put to the proof. The two powers are confronted and urge their behests in a contrary sense; to obey both is wholly impossible. *No man can serve two masters,*[44] for to please the one amounts to contemning the other.

112. As to which should be preferred no one ought to hesitate for an instant. It is a high crime indeed to withdraw allegiance from God in order to please men; an act of consummate wickedness to break the laws of Jesus Christ, in order to yield obedience to earthly rulers, or, under pretext of keeping the civil law, to ignore the rights of the Church; *we ought to obey God rather than men.*[45] This answer, which of old Peter and the other Apostles were used to give the civil authorities who enjoined unrighteous things, we must, in like circumstances, give always and without hesitation. No better citizen is there, whether in time of peace or war, than the Christian who is mindful of his duty; but such a one should

[44] *Matthew*, VI, 24.
[45] *Acts*, V, 29.

be ready to suffer all things, even death itself, rather than abandon the cause of God or of the Church.

113. Hence they who blame, and call by the name of sedition, this steadfastness of attitude in the choice of duty, have not rightly apprehended the force and nature of true law. . . .

114. Hallowed, therefore, in the minds of Christians is the very idea of public authority, in which they recognize some likeness and symbol as it were of the divine Majesty, even when it is exercised by one unworthy. A just and due reverence to the laws abides in them, not from force and threats, but from a consciousness of duty; *for God hath not given us the spirit of fear.*[46]

115. But if the laws of the State are manifestly at variance with the divine law, containing enactments hurtful to the Church, or conveying injunctions adverse to the duties imposed by religion, or if they violate in the person of the Supreme Pontiff, the authority of Jesus Christ, then truly, to resist becomes a positive duty, to obey, a crime; a crime, moreover, combined with misdemeanor against the State itself, inasmuch as every offense leveled against religion is also a sin against the State. . . .

116. Wherefore, to love both countries, that of earth below and that of heaven above, yet in such mode that the love of our heavenly surpass the love of our earthly home, and that human laws be never set above the divine law, is the essential duty of Christians, and the fountain-head, so to say, from which all other duties spring. . . . . . .

LETTER *Quum Grata* TO CHARLES CHESNELONG, PRESIDENT OF THE 19TH ASSEMBLY OF THE CATHOLICS OF FRANCE.[47]

The Pope exhorts the Assembly to execute its resolutions in peace and concord.

June 14, 1890

117. . . . . . . It is now needful that the unanimity and wisdom which are displayed in your resolutions should be equalled by the energy and the concord which you should show in their performance. We have every reason to expect it, for all that you have hitherto done fills Us with glad hopes for the future. You have

[46] II *Timothy*, I, 7.
[47] Translation from *The Tablet*, v. 76, p. 52 (July 12, 1890). Original Latin, *Acta Leonis XIII*, v. 10, p. 153.

increased Our hope by your protest that your love for the common
Mother of the faithful, the Holy Church, is not lessened by your
love of country. You need have no fear that your duties to your
country are likely to be lessened by your devotion to the Church.
The Founder and Master of both, Who is God, has sweetly disposed all things that the good which you do to safeguard the honor
of the Church may bring forth on the country of which you are a
citizen the most abundant fruits of salvation.

ENCYCLICAL *Rerum Novarum* ON THE CONDITION OF WORKERS.[48]

*Leo XIII enunciates the principles that must govern
peaceful relations between capital and labor.*

May 15, 1891

118. Once the passion for revolutionary change was aroused—
a passion long disturbing governments—it was bound to follow
sooner or later that eagerness for change would pass from the
political sphere over into the related field of economics. In fact, new
developments in industry, new techniques striking out on new paths,
changed relations of employer and employee, abounding wealth
among a very small number and destitution among the masses,
increased self-reliance on the part of workers as well as a closer bond
of union with one another, and, in addition to all this, a decline in
morals have caused conflict to break forth. The momentous nature
of the questions involved in this conflict is evident from the fact
that it keeps men's minds in anxious expectation, occupying the
talents of the learned, the discussions of the wise and experienced,
the assemblies of the people, the judgment of lawmakers, and the
deliberations of rulers, so that now no topic more strongly holds
men's interests.

119. Therefore, Venerable Brethren, with the cause of the
Church and the common welfare before Us, We have thought it
advisable, following Our custom on other occasions when We issued
to you the Encyclicals *On Political Power, On Human Liberty, On
the Christian Constitution of States,* and others of similar nature,
which seemed opportune to refute erroneous opinions, that We

---

[48] Translation from *Two Basic Social Encyclicals.* Original Latin, *A.A.S.,* v. 23, pp.
641-670 (1891).

ought to do the same now, and for the same reasons, *On the Condition of Workers*. We have on occasion touched more than once upon this subject. In this Encyclical, however, consciousness of Our Apostolic office admonishes Us to treat the entire question thoroughly, in order that the principles may stand out in clear light, and the conflict may thereby be brought to an end as required by truth and equity.

120. The problem is difficult to resolve and is not free from dangers. It is hard indeed to fix the boundaries of the rights and duties within which the rich and the proletariat—those who furnish material things and those who furnish work—ought to be restricted in relation to each other. The controversy is truly dangerous, for in various places it is being twisted by turbulent and crafty men to pervert judgment as to truth and seditiously to incite the masses.

121. In any event, We see clearly, and all are agreed that the poor must be speedily and fittingly cared for, since the great majority of them live undeservedly in miserable and wretched conditions. After the old trade guilds had been destroyed in the last century, and no protection was substituted in their place, and when public institutions and legislation had cast off traditional religious teaching, it gradually came about that the present age handed over the workers, each alone and defenseless, to the inhumanity of employers and the unbridled greed of competitors. A devouring usury, although often condemned by the Church, but practiced nevertheless under another form by avaricious and grasping men, has increased the evil; and in addition the whole process of production as well as trade in every kind of goods has been brought almost entirely under the power of a few, so that a very few rich and exceedingly rich men have laid a yoke almost of slavery on the unnumbered masses of non-owning workers.

122. To cure this evil, the Socialists, exciting the envy of the poor toward the rich, contend that it is necessary to do away with private possession of goods and in its place to make the goods of individuals common to all, and that the men who preside over a municipality or who direct the entire State should act as administrators of these goods. They hold that, by such a transfer of private goods from private individuals to the community, they can cure the present evil through dividing wealth and benefits equally among the citizens. But their program is so unsuited for terminating the con-

flict that it actually injures the workers themselves. Moreover, it is highly unjust, because it violates the rights of lawful owners, perverts the functions of the State, and throws governments into utter confusion.

123. Clearly the essential reason why those who engage in any gainful occupation undertake labor, and at the same time the end to which workers immediately look, is to procure property for themselves and to retain it by individual right as theirs and as their very own. When the worker places his energy and his labor at the disposal of another, he does so for the purpose of getting the means necessary for livelihood. He seeks in return for the work done, accordingly, a true and full right not only to demand his wage but to dispose of it as he sees fit. Therefore, if he saves something by restricting expenditures and invests his savings in a piece of land in order to keep the fruit of his thrift more safe, a holding of this kind is certainly nothing else than his wage under a different form; and on this account land which the worker thus buys is necessarily under his full control as much as the wage which he earned by his labor. But, as is obvious, it is clearly in this that the ownership of movable and immovable goods consists. Therefore, inasmuch as the Socialists seek to transfer the goods of private persons to the community at large, they make the lot of all wage earners worse, because in abolishing the freedom to dispose of wages they take away from them by this very act the hope and the opportunity of increasing their property and of securing advantages for themselves.

124. But, what is of more vital concern, they propose a remedy openly in conflict with justice, inasmuch as nature confers on man the right to possess things privately as his own. . . . . .

125. Rightly, therefore, the human race as a whole, moved in no wise by the dissenting opinions of a few, and observing nature carefully, has found in the law of nature itself the basis of the distribution of goods, and, by the practice of all ages, has consecrated private possession as something best adapted to man's nature and to peaceful and tranquil living together. Now civil laws, which, when just, derive their power from the natural law itself, confirm and, even by the use of force, protect this right of which We speak. And this same right has been sanctioned by the authority of the divine law, which forbids us most strictly even to desire what belongs to another. *Thou shalt not covet thy neighbor's wife, nor*

his house, nor his field, nor his maid-servant, nor his ox, nor his ass,
nor anything that is his.[49]

126. Rights of this kind which reside in individuals are seen
to have much greater validity when viewed as fitted into and connected with the obligations of human beings in family life.

127. There is no question that in choosing a state of life it is
within the power and discretion of individuals to prefer the one or
the other state, either to follow the counsel of Jesus Christ regarding
virginity or to bind oneself in marriage. No law of man can abolish
the natural and primeval right of marriage, or in any way set aside
the chief purpose of matrimony established in the beginning by the
authority of God: *Increase and multiply.*[50] Behold, therefore, the
family, or rather the society of the household, a very small society
indeed, but a true one, and older than any polity! For that reason
it must have certain rights and duties of its own entirely independent of the State. Thus, right of ownership, which We have
shown to be bestowed on individual persons by nature, must be
assigned to man in his capacity as head of a family. Nay rather,
this right is all the stronger, since the human person in family life
embraces much more.

128. It is a most sacred law of nature that the father of a family
see that his offspring are provided with all the necessities of life,
and nature even prompts him to desire to provide and to furnish
his children, who, in fact reflect and in a sense continue his person,
with the means of decently protecting themselves against harsh
fortune in the uncertainties of life. He can do this surely in no
other way than by owning fruitful goods to transmit by inheritance
to his children. As already noted, the family, like the State, is by
the same token a society in the strictest sense of the term, and it is
governed by its own proper authority, namely, by that of the father.
Wherefore, assuming, of course, that those limits be observed which
are fixed by its immediate purpose, the family assuredly possesses
rights, at least equal with those of civil society, in respect to choosing
and employing the things necessary for its protection and its just
liberty. We say "at least equal" because, inasmuch as domestic living
together is prior both in thought and in fact to uniting into a polity,
it follows that its rights and duties are also prior and more in con-

[49] *Deuteronomy*, V, 21.
[50] *Genesis*, I, 28.

55

formity with nature. But if citizens, if families, after becoming participants in common life and society, were to experience injury in a commonwealth instead of help, impairment of their rights instead of protection, society would be something to be repudiated rather than to be sought for.

129. To desire, therefore, that the civil power should enter arbitrarily into the privacy of homes is a great and pernicious error. If a family perchance is in such extreme difficulty and is so completely without plans that it is entirely unable to help itself, it is right that the distress be remedied by public aid, for each individual family is a part of the community. Similarly, if anywhere there is a grave violation of mutual rights within the family walls, public authority shall restore to each his right: for this is not usurping the rights of citizens, but protecting and confirming them with just and due care. Those in charge of public affairs, however, must stop here: nature does not permit them to go beyond these limits. Paternal authority is such that it can be neither abolished nor absorbed by the State, because it has the same origin in common with that of man's own life. "Children are a part of their father," and, as it were, a kind of extension of the father's person; and, strictly speaking, not through themselves, but through the medium of the family society in which they are begotten, they enter into and participate in civil society. And for the very reason that children "are by nature part of their father . . . before they have the use of free will, they are kept under the care of their parents." [51] Inasmuch as the Socialists, therefore, disregard care by parents and in its place introduce care by the State, they act *against natural justice* and dissolve the structure of the home.

130. And apart from the injustice involved, it is also only too evident what turmoil and disorder would obtain among all classes; and what a harsh and odious enslavement of citizens would result! The door would be open to mutual envy, detraction and dissension. If incentives to ingenuity and skill in individual persons were to be abolished, the very fountains of wealth would necessarily dry up; and the equality conjured up by the Socialist imagination would, in reality, be nothing but uniform wretchedness and meanness for one and all, without distinction.

131. From all these considerations, it is perceived that the fun-

[51] St. Thomas, *Summa Theologica,* 2a 2ae, Q.x, art. 12.

damental principle of Socialism which would make all possessions public property is to be utterly rejected because it injures the very ones whom it seeks to help, contravenes the natural rights of individual persons, and throws the functions of the State and public peace into confusion. Let it be regarded, therefore, as established that in seeking help for the masses this principle before all is to be considered as basic, namely, that private ownership must be preserved inviolate. With this understood, We shall explain whence the desired remedy is to be sought.

132. We approach the subject with confidence and surely by Our right, for the question under consideration is certainly one for which no satisfactory solution will be found unless religion and the Church have been called upon to aid. Moreover, since the safeguarding of religion and all things within the jurisdiction of the Church is especially Our stewardship, silence on Our part might be regarded as failure in Our duty.

133. Assuredly, a question as formidable as this requires the attention and effort of others as well, namely, the heads of the State, employers and the rich, and, finally, those in whose behalf efforts are being made, the workers themselves. Yet without hesitation We affirm that if the Church is disregarded, human striving will be in vain. Manifestly, it is the Church which draws from the Gospel the teachings through which the struggle can be composed entirely or, after its bitterness is removed, can certainly become more tempered. It is the Church, again, that strives not only to instruct the mind but to regulate by her precepts the life and morals of individuals, that ameliorates the condition of the workers through her numerous and beneficent institutions, and that wishes and aims to have the thought and energy of all classes of society united to this end, that the interests of the workers be protected as fully as possible. And to accomplish this purpose she holds that the laws and the authority of the State, within reasonable limits, ought to be employed.

134. Therefore, let it be laid down in the first place that a condition of human existence must be borne with, namely, that in civil society the lowest cannot be made equal with the highest. Socialists, of course, agitate the contrary, but all struggling against nature is vain. There are truly very great and very many natural differences among men. Neither the talents, nor the skill, nor the

health, nor the capacities of all are the same, and unequal fortune
follows of itself upon necessary inequality in respect to these en-
dowments. And clearly this condition of things is adapted to benefit
both individuals and the community; for to carry on its affairs
community life requires varied aptitudes and diverse services, and
to perform these diverse services men are impelled most by differences in individual property holdings. So far as bodily labor is
concerned, man even before the Fall was not destined to be wholly
idle; but certainly what his will at that time would have freely
embraced to his soul's delight, necessity afterwards forced him to
accept, with a feeling of irksomeness for the expiation of his guilt.
*Cursed be the earth in thy work: in thy labor thou shalt eat of it
all the days of thy life.*[52] Likewise, there is to be no end on earth
of other hardships, for the evil consequences of sin are hard, trying,
and bitter to bear, and will necessarily accompany men even to
the end of life. Therefore, to suffer and endure is human, and
although men may strive in all possible ways, they will never be
able by any power or art wholly to banish such tribulations from
human life. If any claim they can do this, if they promise the poor
in their misery a life free from all sorrow and vexation and filled
with repose and perpetual pleasures, they actually impose upon
these people and perpetrate a fraud which will ultimately lead to
evils greater than the present. The best course is to view human
affairs as they are and, as We have stated, at the same time to seek
appropriate relief for these troubles elsewhere.

135. It is a capital evil with respect to the question We are
discussing to take for granted that the one class of society is of itself
hostile to the others, as if nature had set rich and poor against each
other to fight fiercely in implacable war. This is so abhorrent to
reason and truth that the exact opposite is true; for just as in the
human body the different members harmonize with one another,
whence arises that disposition of parts and proportion in the human figure rightly called symmetry, so likewise nature has commanded in the case of the State that the two classes mentioned
should agree harmoniously and should properly form equally balanced counterparts to each other. Each needs the other completely:
neither capital can do without labor, nor labor without capital.
Concord begets beauty and order in things. Conversely, from per-

---

[52] *Genesis*, III, 17.

petual strife there must arise disorder accompanied by bestial
cruelty. But for putting an end to conflict and for cutting away
its very roots, there is wondrous and multiple power in Christian
institutions. And first and foremost, the entire body of religious
teaching and practice, of which the Church is the interpreter and
guardian, can pre-eminently bring together and unite the rich and
the poor by recalling these two classes of society to their mutual
duties, and in particular to those duties which derive from justice.
Among these duties the following concern the poor and the workers: To perform entirely and conscientiously whatever work has
been voluntarily and equitably agreed upon; not in any way to
injure the property or to harm the person of employers; in protecting their own interests, to refrain from violence and never to
engage in rioting; not to associate with vicious men who craftily
hold out exaggerated hopes and make huge promises, a course
usually ending in vain regrets and in the destruction of wealth.
The following duties, on the other hand, concern rich men and
employers: workers are not to be treated as slaves; justice demands
that the dignity of human personality be respected in them, ennobled as it has been through what we call the Christian character.
If we hearken to natural reason and to Christian philosophy, gainful occupations are not a mark of shame to man, but rather of
respect, as they provide him with an honorable means of supporting
life. It is shameful and inhuman, however, to use men as things
for gain and to put no more value on them than what they are
worth in muscle and energy. Likewise, it is enjoined that the
religious interests and the spiritual well-being of the workers receive proper consideration. Wherefore, it is the duty of employers
to see that the worker is free for adequate periods to attend to his
religious obligations; not to expose anyone to corrupting influences
or the enticements of sin; and in no way to alienate him from care
for his family and the practice of thrift. Likewise, more work is
not to be imposed than strength can endure, nor that kind of work
which is unsuited to a worker's age or sex. Among the most important duties of employers the principal one is to give every
worker what is justly due him. Assuredly, to establish a rule of
pay in accord with justice, many factors must be taken into account. But, in general, the rich and employers should remember
that no laws, either human or divine, permit them for their own

profit to oppress the needy and the wretched or to seek gain from
another's want. To defraud anyone of the wage due him is a great
crime that calls down avenging wrath from heaven. *Behold, the
wages of the laborers . . . which have been kept back by you unjustly, cry out: and their cry has entered into the ears of the Lord
of Hosts.*[53] Finally, the rich must religiously avoid harming in any
way the savings of the workers either by coercion, or by fraud, or
by the arts of usury; and the more for this reason, that the workers
are not sufficiently protected against injustices and violence, and
their property, being so meagre, ought to be regarded as all the
more sacred. Could not the observance alone of the foregoing laws
remove the bitterness and the causes of conflict?

136. But the Church, with Jesus Christ as her Teacher and
Leader, seeks greater things than this; namely, by commanding
something more perfect, she aims at joining the two social classes
to each other in closest neighborliness and friendship. We cannot
understand and evaluate mortal things rightly unless the mind
reflects upon the other life, the life which is immortal. If this
other life indeed were taken away, the form and true notion of
the right would immediately perish; nay, this entire world would
become an enigma insoluble to man. Therefore, what we learn
from nature itself as our teacher is also a Christian dogma and on it
the whole system and structure of religion rests, as it were, on
its main foundation; namely, that, when we have left this life,
only then shall we truly begin to live. God has not created man
for the fragile and transitory things of this world, but for heaven
and eternity, and He has ordained the earth as a place of exile,
not as our permanent home. Whether you abound in, or whether
you lack, riches and all the other things which are called good, is
of no importance in relation to eternal happiness. But how you
use them, that is truly of utmost importance. Jesus Christ by His
"plentiful redemption" has by no means taken away the various
tribulations with which mortal life is interwoven, but has so clearly
transformed them into incentives to virtue and sources of merit
that no mortal can attain eternal reward unless he follow the
blood-stained footsteps of Jesus Christ. *If we endure, we shall also
reign with Him.*[54] By the labors and sufferings which He volun-

[53] *James*, V, 4.
[54] II *Timothy*, II, 12.

tarily accepted, He has wondrously lightened the burden of suffering and labor, and not only by His example but also by His grace and by holding before us the hope of eternal reward, He has made endurance of sorrows easier: *for our present light affliction, which is for the moment, prepares for us an eternal weight of glory that is beyond all measure.*[55]

137.   Therefore, the well-to-do are admonished that wealth does not give surcease of sorrow, and that wealth is of no avail unto the happiness of eternal life but is rather a hindrance;[56] that the threats[57] pronounced by Jesus Christ, so unusual coming from Him, ought to cause the rich to fear; and that on one day the strictest account for the use of wealth must be rendered to God as Judge. On the use of wealth we have the excellent and extremely weighty teaching, which, although found in a rudimentary stage in pagan philosophy, the Church has handed down in a completely developed form and causes to be observed not only in theory but in every-day life. The foundation of this teaching rests on this, that the just ownership of money is distinct from the just use of money. To own goods privately, as We saw above, is a right natural to man, and to exercise this right, especially in life in society, is not only lawful, but clearly necessary. "It is lawful for man to own his own things. It is even necessary for human life." [58] But if the question be asked: How ought man use his possessions? the Church replies without hesitation: "As to this point, man ought not regard external goods as his own, but as common so that, in fact, a person should readily share them when he sees others in need. Wherefore the Apostle says: *Charge the rich of this world . . . to give readily, to share with others."* [59] No one, certainly, is obliged to assist others out of what is required for his own necessary use or for that of his family, or even to give to others what he himself needs to maintain his station in life becomingly and decently: "No one is obliged to live unbecomingly." [60] But when the demands of necessity and propriety have been sufficiently met, it is a duty to give to the poor out of that which remains. *Give that which re-*

[55] II *Corinthians,* IV, 17.
[56] *Matthew,* XIX, 23-24.
[57] *Luke,* VI, 24-25.
[58] St. Thomas, *Summa Theologica,* 2a 2ae, Q. lxvi, art. 2.
[59] *Ibid.,* 2a 2ae, Q. lxv, art. 2.
[60] *Ibid.,* 2a 2ae, Q. xxxii, art. 6.

mains as alms.[61] These are duties not of justice, except in cases of extreme need, but of Christian charity, which obviously cannot be enforced by legal action. But the laws and judgments of men yield precedence to the law and judgment of Christ the Lord, Who in many ways urges the practice of alms-giving: *It is more blessed to give than to receive,*[62] and Who will judge a kindness done or denied to the poor as done or denied to Himself. *As long as you did it for one of these, the least of My brethren you did it for Me.*[63] The substance of all this is the following: whoever has received from the bounty of God a greater share of goods, whether corporeal and external, or of the soul, has received them for this purpose, namely, that he employ them for his own perfection and, likewise, as a servant of Divine Providence, for the benefit of others. "Therefore, he that hath talent, let him constantly see to it that he be not silent; he that hath an abundance of goods, let him be on the watch that he grow not slothful in the generosity of mercy; he that hath a trade whereby he supports himself, let him be especially eager to share with his neighbor the use and benefit thereof."[64]

138. Those who lack fortune's goods are taught by the Church that, before God as Judge, poverty is no disgrace, and that no one should be ashamed because he makes his living by toil. And Jesus Christ has confirmed this by fact and by deed, Who for the salvation of men, *being rich, became poor;*[65] and although He was the Son of God and God Himself, yet He willed to seem and to be thought the son of a carpenter; nay, He even did not disdain to spend a great part of His life at the work of a carpenter. *Is not this the carpenter, the Son of Mary?*[66] Those who contemplate this Divine example will more easily understand these truths: true dignity and excellence in men resides in moral living, that is, in virtue; virtue is the common inheritance of man, attainable equally by the humblest and the mightiest, by the rich and the poor; and the reward of eternal happiness will follow upon virtue and merit alone, regardless of the person in whom they may be found. Nay, rather the favor of God Himself seems to incline more

[61] *Luke*, XI, 41.
[62] *Acts*, XX, 35.
[63] *Matthew*, XXV, 40.
[64] St. Gregory the Great, *In Evangelium, Homilia* IX, n. 7.
[65] II *Corinthians*, VIII, 9.
[66] *Mark*, VI, 3.

toward the unfortunate as a class; for Jesus Christ calls the poor[67] blessed, and He invites most lovingly all who are in labor or sorrow[68] to come to Him for solace, embracing with special love the lowly and those harassed by injustice. At the realization of these things the proud spirit of the rich is easily brought down, and the downcast heart of the afflicted is lifted up; the former are moved toward kindness, the latter, toward reasonableness in their demands. Thus the distance between the classes which pride seeks is reduced, and it will easily be brought to pass that the two classes, with hands clasped in friendship, will be united in heart.

139. Yet, if they obey Christian teachings, not merely friendship but brotherly love also will bind them to each other. They will feel and understand that all men indeed have been created by God, their Common Father; that all strive for the same object of good, which is God Himself, Who alone can communicate to both men and angels perfect and absolute happiness; that all equally have been redeemed by the grace of Jesus Christ and restored to the dignity of the sons of God, so that they are clearly united by the bonds of brotherhood not only with one another but also with Christ the Lord, the firstborn among many brethren; and further, that the goods of nature and the gifts of divine grace belong in common and without distinction to all human kind, and that no one, unless he is unworthy, will be deprived of the inheritance of heaven. *But if we are sons, we are also heirs: heirs indeed of God and joint heirs with Christ.*[69] Such is the economy of duties and rights according to Christian philosophy. Would it not seem that all conflict would soon cease wherever this economy were to prevail in civil society? . . . . . .

140. Wherefore, if human society is to be healed, only a return to Christian life and institutions will heal it. In the case of decaying societies, they are most correctly advised that, if they wish to be regenerated, they must be recalled to their origins. For the perfection of all associations is this, namely, to work for and to attain the purpose for which they were formed, so that all social actions should be inspired by the same principle which brought the society itself into being. Wherefore, turning away from the original pur-

[67] *Matthew*, V, 3.
[68] *Matthew*, XI, 28.
[69] *Romans*, VIII, 17.

pose is corruption, while going back to this purpose is recovery. And just as we affirm this as unquestionably true of the entire body of the commonwealth, in like manner we affirm it of that order of citizens who sustain life by labor and who constitute the vast majority of society.

141. But it must not be supposed that the Church so concentrates her energies on caring for souls as to overlook things which pertain to mortal and earthly life. As regards the non-owning workers specifically, she desires and strives that they rise from their most wretched state and enjoy better conditions. And to achieve this result she makes no small contribution by the very fact that she calls men to and trains them in virtue. For when Christian morals are completely observed, they yield of themselves a certain measure of prosperity to material existence, because they win the favor of God, the Source and Fountain of all goods; because they restrain the twin plagues of life—excessive desire for wealth and thirst[70] for pleasure—which too often make man wretched amidst the very abundance of riches; and because finally, Christian morals make men content with a moderate livelihood and make them supplement income by thrift, removing them far from the vices which swallow up both modest sums and huge fortunes, and dissipate splendid inheritances.

142. But, in addition, the Church provides directly for the well-being of the non-owning workers by instituting and promoting activities which she knows to be suitable to relieve their distress. Nay, even in the field of works of mercy, she has always so excelled that she is highly praised by her very enemies. The force of mutual charity among the first Christians was such that the wealthier very often divested themselves of their riches to aid others; wherefore: *Nor was there anyone among them in want.*[71] To the deacons, an order founded expressly for this purpose, the Apostles assigned the duty of dispensing alms daily; and the Apostle, Paul, although burdened with the care of all the churches, did not hesitate to spend himself on toilsome journeys in order to bring alms personally to the poorer Christians. Monies of this kind, contributed voluntarily by the Christians in every assembly, Tertullian calls "piety's deposit fund," because they were expended "to support

[70] I *Timothy*, VI, 10.
[71] *Acts*, IV, 34.

and bury poor people, to supply the wants of orphan boys and girls without means of support, of aged household servants, and of such, too, as had suffered shipwreck."[72]

143. Thence, gradually there came into existence that patrimony which the Church has guarded with religious care as the property of the poor. Nay, even disregarding the feeling of shame associated with begging, she provided aid for the wretched poor. For, as the Common Parent of rich and poor, with charity everywhere stimulated to the highest degree, she founded religious societies and numerous other useful bodies, so that, with the aid which these furnished, there was scarcely any form of human misery that went uncared for. And yet many today go so far as to condemn the Church, as the ancient pagans once did, for such outstanding charity, and would substitute in lieu thereof a system of benevolence established by the laws of the State. But no human devices can ever be found to supplant Christian charity, which gives itself entirely for the benefit of others. This virtue belongs to the Church alone, for, unless it is derived from the Most Sacred Heart of Jesus, it is in no wise a virtue; and whosoever departs from the Church wanders far from Christ.

144. But there can be no question that, to attain Our purpose, those helps also which are within the power of men are necessary. Absolutely all who are concerned with the matter must, according to their capacity, bend their efforts to this same end and work for it. And this activity has a certain likeness to Divine Providence governing the world; for generally we see effects flow from the concert of all the elements upon which as causes these effects depend. But it is now in order to inquire what portion of the remedy should be expected from the State. By State here We understand not the form of government which this or that people has, but rather that form which right reason in accordance with nature requires and the teachings of Divine Wisdom approve, matters that We have explained specifically in Our Encyclical *On the Christian Constitution of States.*

145. Therefore, those governing the State ought primarily to devote themselves to the service of individual groups and of the whole commonwealth, and through the entire scheme of laws and institutions to cause both public and individual well-being to de-

[72] *Apologia Secunda,* XXXIX.

velop spontaneously out of the very structure and administration of the State. For this is the duty of wise statesmanship and the essential office of those in charge of the State. Now, States are made prosperous especially by wholesome morality, properly ordered family life, protection of religion and justice, moderate imposition and equitable distribution of public burdens, progressive development of industry and trade, thriving agriculture, and by all other things of this nature, which, the more actively they are promoted, the better and happier the life of the citizens is destined to be. Therefore, by virtue of these things, it is within the competence of the rulers of the State that, as they benefit other groups, they also improve in particular the condition of the workers. Furthermore, they do this with full right and without laying themselves open to any charge of unwarranted interference. For the State is bound by the very law of its office to serve the common interest. And the richer the benefits which come from this general providence on the part of the State, the less necessary it will be to experiment with other measures for the well-being of workers.

146. This ought to be considered, as it touches the question more deeply; namely, that the State has one basic purpose for existence, which embraces in common the highest and the lowest of its members. Non-owning workers are unquestionably citizens by nature in virtue of the same right as the rich; that is, true and vital parts whence, through the medium of families, the body of the State is constituted; and it hardly need be added that they are by far the greatest number in every urban area. Since it would be quite absurd to look out for one portion of the citizens and to neglect another, it follows that public authority ought to exercise due care in safe-guarding the well-being and the interests of non-owning workers. Unless this is done, justice, which commands that everyone be given his own, will be violated. Wherefore St. Thomas says wisely: "Even as part and whole are in a certain way the same, so, too, that which pertains to the whole, pertains in a certain way to the part also." [73] Consequently, among the numerous and weighty duties of rulers who would serve their people well, this is first and foremost: namely, that they protect equitably each and every class of citizens, maintaining inviolate that justice especially which is called *distributive*.

[73] *Summa Theologica,* 2a 2ae, Q. lxi, art. 1 *ad* 2.

147. Although all citizens, without exception, are obliged to contribute something to the sum-total of common goods, some share of which naturally goes back to individuals, yet all can by no means contribute the same amount and in equal degree. Whatever the vicissitudes that occur in the forms of government, there will always be those differences in the condition of citizens without which society could neither exist nor be conceived. It is altogether necessary that there be some who dedicate themselves to the service of the State, who make laws, who dispense justice, and, finally, by whose counsel and authority civil and military affairs are administered. These men, as is clear, play the chief role in the State, and among every people are to be regarded as occupying first place, because they work for the common good most directly and pre-eminently. On the other hand, those engaged in some calling benefit the State, but not in the same way as the men just mentioned, nor by performing the same duties; yet they, too, in a high degree, although less directly, serve the public weal. Assuredly, since social good must be of such a character that men through its acquisition are made better, it must necessarily be founded chiefly on virtue. Nevertheless, an abundance of corporeal and external goods is likewise a characteristic of a well constituted State, "the use of which goods is necessary for the practice of virtue."[74] To produce these goods the labor of the workers, whether they expend their skill and strength on farms or in factories, is most efficacious and necessary. Nay, in this respect, their energy and effectiveness are so important that it is incontestable that the wealth of nations originates from no other source than from the labor of workers. Equity, therefore, commands that public authority show proper concern for the worker so that from what he contributes to the common good he may receive what will enable him, housed, clothed and secure, to live his life without hardship. Whence, it follows that all those measures ought to be favored which seem in any way capable of benefiting the condition of workers. Such solicitude is so far from injuring anyone, that it is destined rather to benefit all, because it is of absolute interest to the State that those citizens should not be miserable in every respect from whom such necessary goods proceed.

148. It is not right, as We have said, for either the citizen or

[74] St. Thomas, *De Regimine Principum*, I, c. 15.

the family to be absorbed by the State; it is proper that the individual and the family should be permitted to retain their freedom of action, so far as this is possible without jeopardizing the common good and without injuring anyone. Nevertheless, those who govern must see to it that they protect the community and its constituent parts: the community, because nature has entrusted its safeguarding to the sovereign power in the State to such an extent that the protection of the public welfare is not only the supreme law, but is the entire cause and reason for sovereignty; and the constituent parts, because philosophy and Christian faith agree that the administration of the State has from nature as its purpose, not the benefit of those to whom it has been entrusted, but the benefit of those who have been entrusted to it. And since the power of governing comes from God and is a participation, as it were, in His supreme sovereignty, it ought to be administered according to the example of the Divine power, which looks with paternal care to the welfare of individual creatures as well as to that of all creation. If, therefore, any injury has been done to or threatens either the common good or the interest of individual groups, which injury cannot in any other way be repaired or prevented, it is necessary for public authority to intervene.

149. It is vitally important to public as well as to private welfare that there be peace and good order; likewise, that the whole regime of family life be directed according to the ordinances of God and the principles of nature, that religion be observed and cultivated, that sound morals flourish in private and public life, that justice be kept sacred and that no one be wronged with impunity by another, and that strong citizens grow up, capable of supporting, and, if necessary, of protecting the State. Wherefore, if at any time disorder should threaten because of strikes or concerted stoppages of work, if the natural bonds of family life should be relaxed among the poor, if religion among the workers should be outraged by failure to provide sufficient opportunity for performing religious duties, if in factories danger should assail the integrity of morals through the mixing of the sexes or other pernicious incitements to sin, or if the employer class should oppress the working class with unjust burdens or should degrade them with conditions inimical to human personality or to human dignity, if health should be injured by immoderate work and such as is not

suited to sex or age—in all these cases, the power and authority of
the law, but of course within certain limits, manifestly ought to be
employed. And these limits are determined by the same reason
which demands the aid of the law, that is, the law ought not undertake more, nor ought it go farther, than the remedy of evils or the
removal of danger requires.

150. Rights indeed, by whomsoever possessed, must be religiously protected; and public authority, in warding off injuries and
punishing wrongs, ought to see to it that individuals may have
and hold what belongs to them. In protecting the rights of private
individuals, however, special consideration must be given to the
weak and the poor. For the nation, as it were, of the rich, is guarded
by its own defenses and is in less need of governmental protection, whereas the suffering multitude, without the means to protect
itself, relies especially on the protection of the State. Wherefore,
since wage workers are numbered among the great mass of the
needy, the State must include them under its special care and foresight.

151. But it will be well to touch here expressly on certain
matters of special importance. The capital point is this, that private
property ought to be safeguarded by the sovereign power of the
State and through the bulwark of its laws. And especially, in view
of such a great flaming up of passion at the present time, the masses
ought to be kept within the bounds of their moral obligations. For,
while justice does not oppose our striving for better things, on the
other hand, it does forbid anyone to take from another what is his
and, in the name of a certain absurd equality, to seize forcibly the
property of others; nor does the interest of the common good itself
permit this. Certainly, the great majority of working people prefer
to secure better conditions by honest toil, without doing wrong to
anyone. Nevertheless, not a few individuals are found who, imbued
with evil ideas and eager for revolution, use every means to stir up
disorder and incite to violence. The authority of the State, therefore,
should intervene and, by putting restraint upon such disturbers,
protect the morals of workers from their corrupting arts and lawful
owners from the danger of spoliation.

152. Labor which is too long and too hard and the belief that
pay is inadequate not infrequently give workers cause to strike and
become voluntarily idle. This evil, which is frequent and serious,

ought to be remedied by public authority, because such interruption of work inflicts damage not only upon employers and upon the workers themselves, but also injures trade and commerce and the general interests of the State, and, since it is usually not far removed from violence and rioting, it very frequently jeopardizes public peace. In this matter it is more effective and salutary that the authority of the law anticipate and completely prevent the evil from breaking out by removing early the causes from which it would seem that conflict between employers and workers is bound to arise.

153. And in like manner, in the case of the worker, there are many things which the power of the State should protect; and, first of all, the goods of his soul. For however good and desirable mortal life be, yet it is not the ultimate goal for which we are born, but a road only and a means for perfecting, through knowledge of truth and love of good, the life of the soul. The soul bears the express image and likeness of God, and there resides in it that sovereignty through the medium of which man has been bidden to rule all created nature below him and to make all lands and all seas serve his interests. *Fill the earth and subdue it, and rule over the fishes of the sea and the fowls of the air and all living creatures that move upon the earth.*[75] In this respect all men are equal, and there is no difference between rich and poor, between masters and servants, between rulers and subjects: *For there is the same Lord of all.*[76] No one may with impunity outrage the dignity of man, which God Himself treats with great reverence, nor impede his course to that level of perfection which accords with eternal life in heaven. Nay, more, in this connection a man cannot even by his own free choice allow himself to be treated in a way inconsistent with his nature, and voluntarily put his soul in slavery; for there is no question here of rights belonging to man, but of duties owed to God, which are to be religiously observed. . . . . . .

154. Now as concerns the protection of corporeal and physical goods, the oppressed workers, above all, ought to be liberated from the savagery of greedy men, who inordinately use human beings as things for gain. Assuredly, neither justice nor humanity can countenance the exaction of so much work that the spirit is dulled

[75] *Genesis*, I, 28.
[76] *Romans*, X, 12.

from excessive toil and that along with it the body sinks crushed from exhaustion. The working energy of a man, like his entire nature, is circumscribed by definite limits beyond which it cannot go. It is developed indeed by exercise and use, but only on condition that a man cease from work at regular intervals and rest. With respect to daily work, therefore, care ought to be taken not to extend it beyond the hours that human strength warrants. The length of rest intervals ought to be decided on the basis of the varying nature of the work, of the circumstances of time and place, and of the physical condition of the workers themselves. Since the labor of those who quarry stone from the earth, or who mine iron, copper, and other underground materials, is much more severe and harmful to health, the working period for such men ought to be correspondingly shortened. The seasons of the year also must be taken into account; for often a given kind of work is easy to endure in one season but cannot be endured at all in another, or not without the greatest difficulty.

155. Finally, it is not right to demand of a woman or a child what a strong adult man is capable of doing or would be willing to do. Nay, as regards children, special care ought to be taken that the factory does not get hold of them before age has sufficiently matured their physical, intellectual and moral powers. For budding strength in childhood, like greening verdure in spring, is crushed by premature harsh treatment; and under such circumstances all education of the child must needs be foregone. Certain occupations likewise are less fitted for women, who are intended by nature for the work of the home—work indeed which especially protects modesty in women and accords by nature with the education of children and the well-being of the family. Let it be the rule everywhere that workers be given as much leisure as will compensate for the energy consumed by toil, for rest from work is necessary to restore strength consumed by use. In every obligation which is mutually contracted between employers and workers, this condition, either written or tacit, is always present: that both kinds of rest be provided for; nor would it be equitable to make an agreement otherwise, because no one has the right to demand of, or to make an agreement with anyone to neglect those duties which bind a man to God or to himself.

156. We shall now touch upon a matter of very great impor-

tance, and one which must be correctly understood in order to avoid falling into error on one side or the other. We are told that free consent fixes the amount of a wage; that, therefore, the employer, after paying the wage agreed to, would seem to have discharged his obligation and not to owe anything more; that only then would injustice be done if either the employer should refuse to pay the whole amount of the wage, or the worker should refuse to perform all the work to which he had committed himself; and that in these cases, but in no others, is it proper for the public authority to intervene to safeguard the rights of each party.

157. An impartial judge would not assent readily or without reservation to this reasoning, because it is not complete in all respects: one factor to be considered, and one of the greatest importance, is missing. To work is to expend one's energy for the purpose of securing the things necessary for the various needs of life and especially for its preservation. *In the sweat of thy face shalt thou eat bread*.[77] Accordingly, in man labor has two marks, as it were, implanted by nature so that it is truly *personal*, because work energy inheres in the person and belongs completely to him by whom it is expended and for whose use it is destined by nature; and, secondly, that it is *necessary*, because man has need of the fruit of his labors to preserve his life, and nature itself, which must be most strictly obeyed, commands him to preserve it. If labor should be considered only under the aspect that it is personal, there is no doubt that it would be entirely in the worker's power to set the amount of the agreed wage at too low a figure. For inasmuch as he performs work by his own free will, he can also by his own free will be satisfied with either a paltry wage for his work or even with none at all. But this matter must be judged far differently, if with the factor of *personality* we combine the factor of *necessity*, from which indeed the former is separable in thought but not in reality. In fact, to preserve one's life is a duty common to all individuals, and to neglect this duty is a crime. Hence, arises necessarily the right of securing things to sustain life, and only a wage earned by his labor gives a poor man the means to acquire these things.

158. Let it be granted, then, that worker and employer may enter freely into agreements and, in particular, concerning the

[77] *Genesis*, III, 1.

amount of the wage; yet there is always underlying such agreements an element of natural justice, and one greater and more ancient than the free consent of contracting parties; namely, that the wage shall not be less than enough to support a worker who is thrifty and upright. If, compelled by necessity or moved by fear of a worse evil, a worker accepts a harder condition, which although against his will he must accept because the employer or contractor imposes it, he certainly submits to force, against which justice cries out in protest.

159. But in these and similar questions, such as the number of hours of work in each kind of occupation and the health safeguards to be provided, particularly in factories, it will be better, in order to avoid unwarranted governmental intervention, especially since circumstances of business, seasons and places are so varied, that decision be reserved to the organization of which We are about to speak below, or else to pursue another course whereby the interests of the workers may be adequately safeguarded—the State, if the occasion demands, to furnish help and protection.

160. If a worker receives a wage sufficiently large to enable him to provide comfortably for himself, his wife and his children, he will, if prudent, gladly strive to practice thrift; and the result will be, as nature itself seems to counsel, that after expenditures are deducted there will remain something over and above through which he can come into the possession of a little wealth. We have seen, in fact, that the whole question under consideration cannot be settled effectually unless it is assumed and established as a principle, that the right of private property must be regarded as sacred. Wherefore, the law ought to favor this right and, so far as it can, see that the largest possible number among the masses of the population prefer to own property.

161. If this is done, excellent benefits will follow, foremost among which will surely be a more equitable division of goods. For the violence of public disorder has divided cities into two classes of citizens, with an immense gulf lying between them. On the one side is a faction exceedingly powerful because exceedingly rich. Since it alone has under its control every kind of work and business, it diverts to its own advantage and interest all production sources of wealth and exerts no little power in the administration itself of the State. On the other side are the needy and helpless

masses with minds inflamed and always ready for disorder. But if the productive activity of the multitude can be stimulated by the hope of acquiring some property in land, it will gradually come to pass that, with the difference between extreme wealth and extreme penury removed, one class will become neighbor to the other. Moreover, there will surely be a greater abundance of the things which the earth produces. For when men know they are working on what belongs to them, they work with far greater eagerness and diligence. Nay, in a word, they learn to love the land cultivated by their own hands, whence they look not only for food but for some measure of abundance for themselves and their dependents. All can see how much this willing eagerness contributes to an abundance of produce and the wealth of a nation. Hence, in the third place, will flow the benefit that men can easily be kept from leaving the country in which they have been born and bred; for they would not exchange their native country for a foreign land if their native country furnished them sufficient means of living. But these advantages can be attained only if private wealth is not drained away by crushing taxes of every kind. For since the right of possessing goods privately has been conferred not by man's law, but by nature, public authority cannot abolish it, but can only control its exercise and bring it into conformity with the common-weal. Public authority, therefore, would act unjustly and inhumanly, if in the name of taxes it should appropriate from the property of private individuals more than is equitable.

162. Finally, employers and workers themselves can accomplish much in this matter, manifestly through those institutions by the help of which the poor are opportunely assisted and the two classes of society are brought closer to each other. Under this category come associations for giving mutual aid; various agencies established by the foresight of private persons to care for the worker and likewise for his dependent wife and children in the event that an accident, sickness, or death befalls him; and foundations to care for boys and girls, for adolescents, and for the aged.

163. But associations of workers occupy first place, and they include within their circle nearly all the rest. The beneficent achievements of the guilds of artisans among our ancestors have long been well known. Truly, they yielded noteworthy advantages not only to artisans, but, as many monuments bear witness, brought glory

and progress to the arts themselves. In our present age of greater culture, with its new customs and ways of living, and with the increased number of things required by daily life, it is most clearly necessary that workers' associations be adapted to meet the present need. It is gratifying that societies of this kind, composed either of workers alone or of workers and employers together, are being formed everywhere, and it is truly to be desired that they grow in number and in active vigor. Although We have spoken of them more than once, it seems well to show in this place that they are highly opportune and are formed by their own right, and, likewise, to show how they should be organized and what they should do.

164. Inadequacy of his own strength, learned from experience, impels and urges a man to enlist the help of others. Such is the teaching of Holy Scripture: *It is better, therefore, that two should be together, than one: for they have the advantage of their society. If one fall he shall be supported by the other; woe to him that is alone, for when he falleth he hath none to lift him up.*[78] And this also: *A brother that is helped by his brother, is like a strong city.*[79] Just as man is drawn by this natural propensity into civil union and association, so also he seeks with his fellow citizens to form other societies, admittedly small and not perfect, but societies nonetheless.

165. Between these latter and the large society of the State, there is, because of their different immediate purposes, a very great distinction. The end of civil society concerns absolutely all members of this society, since the end of civil society is centered in the common good, in which latter, one and all in due proportion have a right to participate. Wherefore, this society is called *public,* because through it "men share with one another in establishing a commonwealth."[80] On the other hand, societies which are formed, so to speak, within its bosom are considered *private* and are such because their immediate object is private advantage, appertaining to those alone who are thus associated together. "Now a private society is one which is formed to carry out some private business, as when two or three enter into association for the purpose of engaging together in trade."[81]

[78] *Ecclesiastes,* IV, 9-10.
[79] *Proverbs,* XVIII, 19.
[80] St. Thomas, *Contra Impugnantes Dei Cultum et Religionem,* C. II, 8.
[81] *Ibid.*

166. Although private societies exist within the State and are, as it were, so many parts of it, still it is not within the authority of the State universally and *per se* to forbid them to exist as such. For man is permitted by a right of nature to form private societies; the State, on the other hand, has been instituted to protect and not to destroy natural right, and if it should forbid its citizens to enter into associations, it would clearly do something contradictory to itself because both the State itself and private associations are begotten of one and the same principle: namely, that men are by nature inclined to associate. Occasionally there are times when it is proper for the laws to oppose associations of this kind, that is, if they professedly seek after any objective which is clearly at variance with good morals, with justice, or with the welfare of the State. Indeed, in these cases the public power shall justly prevent such associations from forming and shall also justly dissolve those already formed. Nevertheless, it must use the greatest precaution lest it appear to infringe on the rights of its citizens, and lest, under the pretext of public benefit, it enact any measure that sound reason would not support. For laws are to be obeyed only insofar as they conform with right reason and thus with the eternal law of God.[82]

167. Here come to Our mind for consideration the various confraternities, societies, and religious Orders which the authority of the Church and the piety of Christians have brought into being; and history down to our own times speaks of the wonderful benefit they have been to the human race. Since societies of this character, even if judged in the light of reason alone, have been formed for an honest purpose, it is clear that they have been formed in accordance with natural right. But in whatever respect they concern religion, they are properly subject to the Church alone. Therefore, those in charge of the State cannot in justice arrogate to themselves any right over them or assume their administration to themselves. Rather it is the office of the State to respect, to conserve, and, as occasion may require, to protect them from injustice. Yet we have seen something entirely different being done, especially at the present time. In many places, the State has violated associations of

---

[82] "Human law has the essential nature of law only insofar as it is in accordance with right reason, and thus manifestly it derives from the eternal law. But insofar as it deviates from reason, it is called unjust law, and so it does not have the essential nature of law, but rather a kind of violence." St. Thomas, *Summa Theologica,* 1a 2ae, Q. xciii, art. 3, *ad* 2.

this kind, and in fact with manifold injury, since it has put them in the bonds of the civil law, has divested them of their lawful right to be considered legal persons, and has robbed them of their property. In this property the Church possessed her rights and individual association members possessed theirs, as did also the persons who donated this property for a designated purpose as well as those for whose benefit and relief it had been donated. Consequently, We cannot refrain from deploring such vicious and unjust acts of robbery, and so much the more because We see the road being closed to Catholic associations, which are law-abiding and in every respect useful, at the very time when it is being decreed that most assuredly men are permitted by law to form associations, and at the very time when this freedom is being lavishly granted in actual fact to men urging a course of conduct pernicious at once to religion and to the State.

168. Certainly, the number of associations of almost every possible kind, especially of associations of workers, is now far greater than ever before. This is not the place to inquire whence many of them originate, what object they have, or how they proceed. But the opinion is, and it is one confirmed by a good deal of evidence, that they are largely under the control of secret leaders and that these same leaders apply principles which are in harmony with neither Christianity nor the welfare of States, and that, after having possession of all available work, they contrive that those who refuse to join with them will be forced by want to pay the penalty. Under these circumstances, workers who are Christians must choose one of two things: either to join associations in which it is greatly to be feared that there is danger to religion, or to form their own associations and unite their forces in such a way that they may be able manfully to free themselves from such unjust and intolerable oppression. Can they who refuse to place man's highest good in imminent jeopardy hesitate to affirm that the second course is by all means to be followed?

169. Many of our Faith are indeed to be highly commended, who, having rightly perceived what the times require of them, are experimenting and striving to discover how by honest means they can raise the non-owning working class to higher living levels. They have championed their cause and are endeavoring to increase the prosperity of both families and individuals, and at the same

time to regulate justly the mutual obligations which rest upon
workers and employers and to foster and strengthen in both consciousness of duty and observance of the precepts of the Gospel—
precepts, in truth, which hold man back from excess and prevent
him from over-stepping the bounds of moderation and, in the midst
of the widest divergences among persons and things, maintain
harmony in the State. For this reason, we see eminent men meeting together frequently to exchange ideas, to combine their forces,
and to deliberate on the most expedient programs of action. Others
are endeavoring to unite the various kinds of workers in suitable
associations, are assisting them with advice and money, and making
plans to prevent a lack of honest and profitable work. The bishops
are giving encouragement and bestowing support; and under their
authority and auspices many from the ranks of the clergy, both
regular and diocesan, are showing zealous care for all that pertains
to the spiritual improvement of the members of these associations.
Finally, there are not wanting Catholics of great wealth, yet voluntary sharers, as it were, in the lot of the wage workers, who by
their own generous contributions are striving to found and extend
associations through which the worker is readily enabled to obtain
from his toil not only immediate benefits, but also assurance of
honorable retirement in the future. How much good such manifold and enthusiastic activity has contributed to the benefit of all
is too well-known to make discussion necessary. From all this, We
have taken auguries of good hope for the future, provided that
societies of this kind continually grow and that they are founded
with wise organization. Let the State protect these lawfully associated bodies of citizens; let it not, however, interfere with their
private concerns and order of life; for vital activity is set in motion
by an inner principle, and it is very easily destroyed, as We know,
by intrusion from without.

170. Unquestionably, wise direction and organization are essential to these associations in order that in their activities there be
unity of purpose and concord of wills. Furthermore, if citizens
have free right to associate, as in fact they do, they also must have
the right freely to adopt the organization and the rules which they
judge most appropriate to achieve their purpose. We do not feel
that the precise character in all details which the aforementioned
direction and organization of associations ought to have can be

determined by fast and fixed rules, since this is a matter to be decided rather in the light of the temperament of each people, of experiment and practice, of the nature and character of the work, of the extent of trade and commerce, and of other circumstances of a material and temporal kind, all of which must be carefully considered. In summary, let this be laid down as a general and constant law: workers' associations ought to be so constituted and so governed as to furnish the most suitable and most convenient means to attain the object proposed, which consists in this, that the individual members of the association secure, so far as is possible, an increase in the goods of body, of soul, and of property. It is clear, however, that moral and religious perfection ought to be regarded as their principal goal, and that their social organization as such ought above all to be directed completely by this goal. For otherwise they would degenerate in nature and would be little better than those associations in which no account is ordinarily taken of religion. Besides, what would it profit a worker to secure through an association an abundance of goods, if his soul through lack of its proper food should run the risk of perishing? *What doth it profit a man, if he gain the whole world, but suffer the loss of his own soul?*[83] . . . . . .

171. When the regulations of associations are founded upon religion, the way is easy toward establishing the mutual relations of the members so that peaceful living together and prosperity will result. Offices in the associations are to be distributed properly in accordance with the common interest, and in such a way, moreover, that wide difference in these offices may not create discord. It is of special importance that obligations be apportioned wisely and be clearly defined, to the end that no one is done an injustice. Let the funds be disbursed equitably in such way that the amount of benefit to be paid out to members is fixed beforehand in accordance with individual needs, and let the rights and duties of employers be properly adjusted to the rights and duties of workers. If any one in these two groups feels that he has been injured in any way, nothing is more to be desired than that prudent and upright men of the same body be available, and that the association regulations themselves prescribe that the dispute be settled according to the decision of these men. It must also be specially provided

[83] *Matthew*, XVI, 26.

that the worker at no time be without sufficient work, and that the monies paid into the treasury of the association furnish the means of assisting individual members in need, not only during sudden and unforeseen changes in industry, but also whenever anyone is stricken by sickness, by old age, or by misfortune.

172. Through these regulations, provided they are readily accepted, the interests and welfare of the poor will be adequately cared for. Associations of Catholics, moreover, will undoubtedly be of great importance in promoting prosperity in the State. Through past events we can, without temerity, foresee the future. Age presses hard upon age, but there are wondrous similarities in history, governed as it is by the Providence of God, Who guides and directs the continuity and the chain of events in accordance with that purpose which He set before Himself in creating the human race. In the early ages, when the Church was in her youth, We know that the reproach was hurled at the Christians that the great majority of them lived by precarious alms or by toil. Yet, although destitute of wealth and power, they succeeded in winning the good will of the rich and the protection of the mighty. All could see that they were energetic, industrious, peace-loving, and exemplarily devoted to the practice of justice and especially of charity. In the presence of life and conduct such as this, all prejudice vanished, the taunting voices of the malevolent were silenced, and the falsehoods of inveterate superstition yielded little by little to Christian truth.

173. The condition of workers is a subject of bitter controversy at the present time; and whether this controversy is resolved in accordance with reason or otherwise, it is, in either event, of utmost importance to the State. Now Christian workers will readily resolve it in accordance with reason, if, united in associations and under wise leaders, they enter upon the path which their fathers and their ancestors followed to their own best welfare as well as to that of the State. For, no matter how strong the power of prejudice and passion in man, yet, unless perversity of will has deadened the sense of the right and just, the good-will of citizens is certain to be more freely inclined toward those whom they learn to know as industrious and temperate, and who clearly place justice before profit and conscientious observance of duty before all else. . . .

174. These, Venerable Brethren, are the persons, and this is the procedure to be employed in dealing with this most difficult ques-

tion. Everyone according to his position ought to gird himself for the task, and indeed as speedily as possible, lest, by delaying the remedy, the evil, which is already of vast dimensions, become incurable. Let those in charge of States make use of the provision afforded by laws and institutions; let the rich and employers be mindful of their duties; let the workers, whose cause is at stake, press their claims with reason. And since religion alone, as We said in the beginning, can remove the evil, root and branch, let all reflect upon this: first and foremost, Christian morals must be reestablished, without which even the weapons of prudence, which are considered especially effective, will be of no avail to secure well-being.

175. So far as the Church is concerned, at no time and in no manner will she permit her efforts to be wanting, and she will contribute all the more help in proportion as she has more freedom of action. Let this be understood in particular by those whose duty it is to promote the public welfare. Let the members of the Sacred Ministry exert all their strength of mind and all their diligence, and, Venerable Brethren, under the guidance of your authority and example, let them not cease to impress upon men of all ranks the principles of Christian living as found in the Gospel; by all means in their power let them strive for the well-being of peoples; and especially let them aim both to preserve in themselves and to arouse in others, in the highest equally as well as in the lowest, the mistress and queen of the virtues, Charity. . . . . . .

ENCYCLICAL *Au Milieu des Sollicitudes* TO THE CHURCH IN FRANCE.[84]

> The Pope analyzes the relations between the Church and the State in France. There can be no internal peace in the State unless religion be protected.

February 16, 1892

176. . . . . . . Now We deem it opportune, nay, even necessary, once again to raise Our voice entreating still more earnestly, We shall not say Catholics only, but all upright and intelligent French-

[84] Translation from *The Great Encyclical Letters of Pope Leo XIII*, pp. 250-259. Original French, *A.S.S.* v. 24, pp. 519-526 (1892).

men, utterly to disregard all germs of political strife in order to devote their efforts solely to the pacification of their country. All understand the value of this pacification; all continue to desire it more and more. And We who crave it more than any one, since We represent on earth the God of peace,[85] urge by these present Letters all righteous souls, all generous hearts, to assist Us in making it stable and fruitful.

177. First of all, let us take as a starting-point a well-known truth admitted by all men of good sense and loudly proclaimed by the history of all peoples; namely, that religion, and religion only, can create the social bond; that it alone maintains the peace of a nation on a solid foundation. When different families, without giving up the rights and duties of domestic society, unite under the inspiration of nature, in order to constitute themselves members of another larger family circle called civil society, their object is not only to find therein the means of providing for their material welfare, but, above all, to draw thence the boon of moral improvement. Otherwise society would rise but little above the level of an aggregation of beings devoid of reason, and whose whole life would consist in the satisfaction of sensual instincts. Moreover, without this moral improvement it would be difficult to demonstrate that civil society was an advantage rather than a detriment to man, as man.

178. Now, morality, in man, by the mere fact that it should establish harmony among so many dissimilar rights and duties, since it enters as an element into every human act, necessarily supposes God, and with God, religion, that sacred bond whose privilege is to unite, anteriorly to all other bonds, man to God. Indeed, the idea of morality signifies, above all, an order of dependence in regard to truth which is the light of the mind; in regard to good which is the object of the will; and without truth and good there is no morality worthy of the name. And what is the principal and essential Truth, that from which all truth is derived? It is God. What, therefore, is the supreme Good from which all other good proceeds? God. Finally, who is the Creator and Guardian of our reason, our will, our whole being, as well as the end of our life? God; always God. Since, therefore, religion is the interior and exterior expression of the dependence which, in justice, we owe

---

[85] Cf. I Corinthians, XIV, 33.

to God, there follows a grave obligation. All citizens are bound
to unite in maintaining in the nation true religious sentiment, and
to defend it in case of need, if ever, despite the protestations of
nature and of history, an atheistical school should set about banishing God from society, thereby surely annihilating the moral sense
even in the depths of the human conscience. Among men who have
not lost all notion of integrity there can exist no difference of
opinion on this point. . . . . . .

179. Various political governments have succeeded one another
in France during the last century, each having its own distinctive
form: the Empire, the Monarchy, and the Republic. By giving
oneself up to abstractions, one could at length conclude which is
the best of these forms, considered in themselves; and in all truth
it may be affirmed that each of them is good, provided it lead
straight to its end—that is to say, to the common good for which
social authority is constituted; and finally, it may be added that,
from a relative point of view, such and such a form of government
may be preferable because of being better adapted to the character
and customs of such or such a nation. In this order of speculative
ideas, Catholics, like all other citizens, are free to prefer one form
of government to another precisely because no one of these social
forms is, in itself, opposed to the principles of sound reason nor to
the maxims of Christian doctrine. . . . . . .

180. However, here it must be carefully observed that whatever be the form of civil power in a nation, it cannot be considered
so definitive as to have the right to remain immutable, even though
such were the intention of those who, in the beginning, determined
it. . . . But, in regard to purely human societies, it is an oft-repeated
historical fact that time, that great transformer of all things here
below, operates great changes in their political institutions. On
some occasions it limits itself to modifying something in the form
of the established government; or, again, it will go so far as to
substitute other forms for the primitive ones—forms totally different, even as regards the mode of transmitting sovereign power.

181. And how are these political changes of which We speak
produced? They sometimes follow in the wake of violent crises,
too often of a bloody character, in the midst of which pre-existing
governments totally disappear; then anarchy holds sway, and soon
public order is shaken to its very foundations and finally over-

thrown. From that time onward a *social need* obtrudes itself upon the nation; it must provide for itself without delay. Is it not its privilege—or, better still, its duty—to defend itself against a state of affairs troubling it so deeply, and to re-establish public peace in the tranquillity of order? Now, this social need justifies the creation and the existence of new governments, whatever form they take; since, in the hypothesis wherein we reason, these new governments are a requisite to public order, all public order being impossible without a government. Thence it follows that, in similar junctures, all the novelty is limited to the political form of civil power, or to its mode of transmission; it in no wise affects the power considered in itself. This continues to be immutable and worthy of respect, as, considered in its nature, it is constituted to provide for the common good, the supreme end which gives human society its origin. To put it otherwise, in all hypotheses, civil power, considered as such, is from God, always from God: *For there is no power but from God.*[86]

182. Consequently, when new governments representing this immutable power are constituted, their acceptance is not only permissible but even obligatory, being imposed by the need of the social good which has made and which upholds them. This is all the more imperative because an insurrection stirs up hatred among citizens, provokes civil war, and may throw a nation into chaos and anarchy, and this great duty of respect and dependence will endure as long as the exigencies of the common good shall demand it, since this good is, after God, the first and last law in society.

183. Thus the wisdom of the Church explains itself in the maintenance of her relations with the numerous governments which have succeeded one another in France in less than a century, each change causing violent shocks. Such a line of conduct would be the surest and most salutary for all Frenchmen in their civil relations with the Republic, which is the actual government of their nation. Far be it from them to encourage the political dissensions which divide them; all their efforts should be combined to preserve and elevate the moral greatness of their native land.

184. But a difficulty presents itself. "This Republic," it is said, "is animated by such anti-Christian sentiments that honest men, Catholics particularly, could not conscientiously accept it." This,

[86] *Romans*, XIII, 1.

more than anything else, has given rise to dissensions, and, in fact, aggravated them. . . . These regrettable differences would have been avoided if the very considerable distinction between *constituted power* and *legislation* had been carefully kept in view. In so much does legislation differ from political power and its form, that, under a system of government most excellent in form, legislation could be detestable; while quite the opposite, under a régime most imperfect in form, might be found excellent legislation. It were an easy task to prove this truth, history in hand, but what would be the use? All are convinced of it. And who, better than the Church, is in position to know it—she who has striven to maintain habitual relations with all political governments? Assuredly she, better than any other power, could tell the consolation or sorrow occasioned her by the laws of the various governments by which nations have been ruled from the Roman Empire down to the present.

185. If the distinction just established has its major importance, it is likewise manifestly reasonable: legislation is the work of men invested with power, and who, in fact, govern the nation; therefore, it follows that, practically, the quality of the laws depends more upon the quality of these men than upon the form of power. The laws will be good or bad accordingly as the minds of the legislators are imbued with good or bad principles, and as they allow themselves to be guided by political prudence or by passion. . . . . . .

ALLOCUTION *Molti e Segnalati* TO THE COLLEGE OF CARDINALS.[87]

In human society peace is the daughter of justice.

December 23, 1893

186. Without doubt, the benefits for which We render thanks to the loving Providence of God are many and remarkable, and We are happy, Lord Cardinal, that the Sacred College also renders thanks and praise to the Lord with Us, as Our praise and Our thanks alone would be insufficient return for such an abundance of mercy. It is the Hand of God that keeps Us safe in Our advanced years, which gives Us the great consolation of seeing alive in the people the devotion to the Apostolic See, and guides Us without fear through the cares of a ministry that even in less difficult times

[87] Original Italian, *Acta Leonis Papae XIII*, v. 5, pp. 227-228.

and circumstances might have proved exceedingly heavy for Our shoulders.

187. In the meantime, determined as We are to accomplish to the limit of Our strength Our heavy duties, We would ask for nothing more eagerly than that which you, Lord Cardinal, have wished Us just now: to be permitted to be, as many of Our Predecessors have been, real ministers and bearers of peace to Europe and to the world. . . . It is indeed true, that by the nature of Our office, We are partisans and abettors of peace; because peace, both in the individual and in human society, is the daughter of justice, and justice derives life from faith: *Justus ex fide vivit.*[88] Indeed, the highest Christian priesthood being the incorruptible guardian of faith and the supreme vindicator of all justice, is by consequence an apostolate of unification and peace. Give free reins to this apostolate which derives its mission from above; receive without suspicion the message that it brings; let it penetrate the conscience of the citizen, of the family, and of the government of the States, and you will behold the tranquillity of order, that supreme aspiration and supreme need of the people. . . . The moral reason of the present troublous times is to be found particularly in the weakening of religious beliefs. When the human mind loses sight of heaven, and keeps the eye pinned to earth, then uniting charity disappears, and dividing selfishness prevails. Hence the dark discords hidden under lying appearances, rivalries, and mad ambitions; the growing unrest in every social class, the hungry desire for revolution which springs up everywhere, bringing about disorder and strife. Under such conditions, peoples and nations instinctively feel a need for peace and search for it ardently, but true peace is nowhere to be found, because for too long a time they have forgotten Him Who alone can give it.

188. Should we not, then, hope for a religious revival, forerunner of happier days? Indeed we should, and strongly, because Jesus Christ never forsakes mankind whom He has redeemed. As the Spirit of God, on the first day of creation, moved over the new waters and made them fruitful, so at the moment designed by His mercy will that Spirit descend on humankind and will revive, by its virtue and the work of the Church, the spent or scarcely living germ of Divine Faith.

[88] *Romans*, I, 17.

189. With this sweet hope in Our heart, We welcome the good wishes which the Sacred College has expressed to Us through its worthy Dean. And as a just exchange, in the august and beautiful solemnities of these days, We shall pray the Divine Child to bestow abundantly upon the Sacred College His heavenly graces. Meanwhile, as a token of fatherly love, We bestow on it, on the Bishops, on the various Prelates, and on all those present Our Apostolic Blessing.

ENCYCLICAL *Caritatis* TO THE CATHOLICS OF POLAND.[89]

The Pope states the doctrine of the Church on the duties of citizens and rulers of States.

March 19, 1894

190. . . . . . . On the other hand, the Church does not teach and prescribe anything that is injurious or contrary to the majesty of princes or to the happiness or progress of peoples; nay, rather, from the treasury of Christian wisdom she is constantly drawing what may be of the greatest possible advantage to them. Among the truths which she teaches, it is proper to mention the following: those who possess power bear among men the image of the Divine Power of Providence; their command must be just and imitate that of God, be tempered by a paternal kindness, and tend solely to the welfare of the State; they will one day have to render an account to God, their Judge, an account so much the more serious the higher their dignity. As for those who are under the dependence of authority, they are bound to observe respect and fidelity towards princes as exercising towards God His authority through the intermediation of men; they must obey them, not only from fear of chastisement, but also from conscience,[90] pray for them and give thanks in their behalf,[91] religiously respect the order of the State, abstain from the plots of men of disorder and from adhesion to secret societies; they must commit no seditious act, but must assist with all their efforts in maintaining peace in justice. . . . . . .

[89] Translation from Furey, *Life of Leo XIII and History of His Pontificate*, p. 244. Original Latin, *A.S.S.*, v. .26, p. 525 (1894).
[90] *Cf. Romans*, XIII, 5.
[91] *Cf.* I *Timothy*, II, 1.

APOSTOLIC LETTER *Praeclara Gratulationis* TO ALL RULERS AND PEOPLES.[92]

If governments and States are restored to the unity of the faith, peace and security will return to the world.

June 20, 1894

191. . . . . . . Were this twofold danger averted, and government and States restored to the unity of faith, it is wonderful what efficacious remedies for evils and abundant store of benefits would ensue. We will touch upon the principal ones.

192. The first regards the dignity and office of the Church. She would receive that honor which is her due and she would go on her way, free from envy and strong in her liberty, as the minister of Gospel truth and grace to the notable welfare of States. For as she has been given by God as a teacher and guide to the human race, she can contribute assistance which is peculiarly adapted to direct even the most radical transformations of time to the common good, to solve the most complicated questions, and to promote uprightness and justice, which are the most solid foundations of the commonwealth. Moreover, there would be a marked increase of union among the nations, a thing most desirable to ward off the horrors of war.

193. We behold the condition of Europe. For many years past peace has been rather an appearance than a reality. Possessed with mutual suspicions, almost all the nations are vying with one another in equipping themselves with military armaments. Inexperienced youths are removed from parental direction and control, to be thrown amid the dangers of the soldier's life; robust young men are taken from agriculture or ennobling studies or trade or the arts to be put under arms. Hence the treasures of States are exhausted by the enormous expenditure, the national resources are frittered away, and private fortunes impaired; and this, as it were, armed peace, which now prevails, cannot last much longer. Can this be the normal condition of human society? Yet we cannot escape from this situation, and obtain true peace, except by the aid of

---

[92] Translation from *The Great Encyclical Letters of Pope Leo XIII*, pp. 315-316. Original Latin, *A.S.S.*, v. 26, p. 714 (1894).

Jesus Christ. For to repress ambition and covetousness and envy—
the chief instigators of war—nothing is more fitted than the Christian virtues and, in particular, the virtue of justice; for, by its exercise, both the law of nations and the faith of treaties may be maintained inviolate, and the bonds of brotherhood continue unbroken,
if men are but convinced that *justice exalteth a nation.*[93] As in its
external relations, so in the internal life of the State itself, the
Christian virtues will provide a guarantee of the commonweal much
more sure and far stronger than any which law or armies can afford.
For there is no one who does not see that the dangers to public
security and order are daily on the increase, since seditious societies
continue to conspire for the overthrow and ruin of States, as the
frequency of their atrocious outrages testifies. . . . . . .

ENCYCLICAL *Jucunda Semper Expectatione* ON THE HOLY ROSARY.[94]

*To safeguard the peace of Christian society, prayer is
necessary and the Rosary is especially adapted for this
kind of prayer.*

September 8, 1894

194. . . . . . . But the Rosary, if rightly considered, will be
found to have in itself special virtues, whether for producing and
continuing a state of recollection, or for touching the conscience
for its healing, or for lifting up the soul. As all men know, it is
composed of two parts, distinct but inseparable—the meditation of
the Mysteries and the recitation of the prayers. It is thus a kind
of prayer that requires not only some raising of the soul to God,
but also a particular and explicit attention, so that by reflection
upon the things to be contemplated, impulses and resolutions may
follow for the reformation and sanctification of life.

195. Those same things are, in fact, the most important and
the most admirable of Christianity, the things through which the
world was renewed and filled with the fruits of truth, justice
and peace. And it is remarkable how well adapted to every kind
of mind, however unskilled, is the manner in which these things

[93] *Proverbs,* XIV, 34.
[94] Translation from *The Tablet,* v. 84, p. 498 (September 29, 1894). Original Latin,
A.S.S., v. 27, pp. 181-182 (1894-95).

are proposed to us in the Rosary. They are proposed less as truths or doctrines to be speculated upon than as present facts to be seen and perceived. . . .

196. . . . At the present day—and on this We have already touched—there is a signal necessity of special help from heaven, particularly manifest in the many tribulations suffered by the Church as to her liberties and her rights, as also in the perils whereby the prosperity and peace of Christian society are fundamentally threatened. So it is that it belongs to Our office to assert once again that We place the best of Our hopes in the holy Rosary, inasmuch as more than any other means it can impetrate from God the succor which We need. . . . . . .

LETTER *Tres Puissant Negus* TO KING MENELIK OF ABYSSINIA.[95]

The Pope asks mercy for the Italian prisoners.

May 11, 1896

197. . . . It has pleased You on a former occasion spontaneously to salute the beginning of Our Pontificate, and ten years later, upon the occasion of Our sacerdotal jubilee, You offered Us a new testimonial of Your courtesy. These proofs of good will filled Our heart with joy; they do honor to Your heart. So, it is to Your heart of a monarch and a Christian that We address Our words today in order to urge You to perform an act of sovereign generosity. Victory has left numerous prisoners in Your hands. They are vigorous young men and worthy of respect, who, in the flower of their manhood and at the dawn of the finest hopes, have been snatched from their families and their homeland. Their captivity neither augments the measure of Your power, nor the extent of Your prestige; but the longer it lasts the more poignant is the grief in the souls of thousands of mothers and innocent wives. For Our part, filled with the holy mission which Our Lord Jesus Christ has entrusted to Us and which extends to all Christian nations, We love them as sons. Therefore, deign to heed the request which We make with a father's heart, in the name of the Divine Trinity, in the name of the Blessed Virgin, in the name of all that You hold most dear in this world; be pleased to grant them their liberty

[95] Original French, *L'Osservatore Romano* (November 14, 1896).

without delay. Most powerful Negus Negesti, do not refuse to show Yourself magnanimous before the eyes of the nations. Inscribe this glorious page in the annals of Your reign! After all, what are the merciless rights of war alongside of the rights and duties of human fraternity? God will give You a very rich reward, for He is the Father of mercy! Thousands of voices will be raised in chorus to bless You, and Ours will be the first to be heard. . . .

LETTER OF CARDINAL RAMPOLLA, SECRETARY OF STATE, TO THE SEVENTH WORLD PEACE CONGRESS AT BUDAPEST.[96]

The Pope as the Head of the Church has a special obligation to promote peace.

December 15, 1896

198. The homage rendered the Holy Father by the World Peace Congress, recently held in Budapest, and of which you were the spokesman, pleased him exceedingly. He readily recognized this expression of confidence as a public testimony of respect for the high office of peace with which the Head of the Church is vested. As a matter of fact, it was the most outstanding duty of the chief Prince of the Church, who has at all times placed his authority and influence in the service of civilization and of concord among peoples, to bring the world under the influence of justice and peace, and to unite all nations, as in a single family, by the bonds of Christian brotherhood. The Pope who today rules the Church has of his own initiative put his heart and soul to this extraordinary Christian and beneficent work, and he will not cease to devote his solicitude and efforts to this work in the future. He is strengthened in this intention by the conviction, of which men are becoming more and more conscious, that the foundations on which civil society rests are performance of all duties and respect for all rights, that the law of reason succeeds the law of force, and that a new era of true civilization will facilitate for the human family the fulfillment of their chief duties. . . .

---

[96] Original German, Müller, *Das Friedenswerk der Kirche,* pp. 344-345.

LETTER *Spesse Volte* TO THE CATHOLIC CLERGY AND LAITY OF
ITALY.[97]

*The Catholic religion, which teaches justice and honor,
is the enemy of disorder and insurrection.*

August 5, 1898

199. . . . . . . We did not fail to raise Our voice against these
serious and repeated attacks. We complained of them on account
of our holy Religion, exposed to the greatest dangers; We complained of them also—and We say this with all the sincerity of
Our heart—on account of our country, because Religion is the
source of prosperity and greatness for the nation and the principal
foundation of every well-regulated society. And, in fact, when the
religious sentiment, which elevates and ennobles the soul and deeply
impresses upon it the ideas of justice and honor, is weakened, man
declines and abandons himself to savage instincts and material
interests; whence follow, as a logical result, rancors, divisions,
depravity, conflicts and disturbance of order, for which evils sure
and sufficient remedies are not to be found either in the severity
of the laws, or the harshness of the tribunals, or the use of armed
force itself. To this natural and intrinsic connection between religious decadence and the development of insurrection and disorder,
We have often called the attention of those with whom rests the
formidable responsibility of power, pointing out in public documents addressed to the Italian people the progress of Socialism
and anarchy and the endless evils to which they exposed the
nation. . . . . . .

200. But then took place the painful occurrences which, accompanied by tumults and the shedding of citizens' blood, brought
disaster to several districts in Italy. No one suffered more in mind
or was more disturbed than We at this sad sight. We thought,
however, that at the beginning of these outbreaks and these struggles between brethren, those who have the direction of public affairs
would recognize the unhappy but natural fruit of the evil seed
scattered so widely, and for such a long time scattered with impunity, throughout the whole peninsula; We thought that, going
back from the effects to the causes, and profiting by the bitter

[97] Translation from *The American Ecclesiastical Review*, v. 19, pp. 392-397 (1898).
Original Italian, *A.S.S.*, v. 31, pp. 129-133 (1898-1899).

lessons received, they would return to the Christian standards of social order by which nations are restored, if they are not allowed to perish, and that, therefore, they would hold in honor the principles of justice, probity and religion to which are to be mainly attributed even the material welfare of the people. We thought at least that in looking for the authors and accomplices of these outbreaks they would seek them amongst those who oppose Catholic teaching, and, through naturalism and scientific and political materialism, stir up every kind of inordinate cupidity amongst those who, under cover of sectarian gatherings, conceal evil designs and take up arms against order and the security of society. And indeed there were not wanting even in the camp of the enemy some elevated and impartial minds who understood and had the praiseworthy courage to proclaim publicly the true cause of the lamentable disorders. . . . . . .

201. The Italian Catholics, by virtue of the immutable and well-known principles of their Religion, eschew all conspiracy and rebellion against the public authorities, to which they render due tribute. Their conduct in the past, to which all impartial men can render honorable testimony, is a guarantee of their conduct in the future, and this ought to be sufficient to assure them the justice and liberty to which all peaceful citizens have a right. More than this, being, owing to the doctrine they profess, the strongest supporters of order, they are entitled to respect, and if virtue and merit were adequately appreciated, they would also have a right to the regard and gratitude of those at the head of public affairs. . . . . . .

FIRST DIPLOMATIC NOTE OF CARDINAL RAMPOLLA, SECRETARY OF
   STATE, TO COUNT MOURAVIEV, SECRETARY OF FOREIGN AFFAIRS
   FOR RUSSIA.[98]

*Peace cannot be established if it does not rest on the
foundation of Christian public law.*

September 15, 1898

202. . . . The noble initiative of His Majesty corresponds to one of the most ardent wishes of the Sovereign Pontiff. The Pope holds that peace cannot possibly be established if it does not rest

[98] Original French, *Revue des Deux-Mondes*, v. 154, p. 593 sqq.

on the foundation of Christian public law, from which comes the concord of princes among themselves and of peoples with their princes.

203. In order that mutual mistrust, and the reciprocal motives of offense and defense which have led the nations of our day to develop their armaments, should cease, and in order that a spirit of peace, spreading throughout the universe, should lead nations to regard one another as brothers, Christian justice must have full vigor in the world, the maxims of the Gospel must again be held in honor, and the difficult art of governing peoples must have as its principal element that fear of God which is the beginning of wisdom.

204. Men have wished to regulate the relations among nations by a new law founded on utilitarian interests, on the predominance of force, on the success of accomplished deeds, and on other theories which are the negation of the eternal and immutable principles of justice. This is the capital error which has brought Europe to a state of disaster.

205. Against such a baneful system, the Holy See has not ceased to raise its voice in order to arouse the attention of princes and peoples. Already, during the Middle Ages, by means of the happy unity of Christendom, the voice of the Roman Pontiffs found everywhere easy access; it succeeded by the force of its authority alone to conciliate princes and peoples, to put an end to quarrels by words of arbitration, to defend the weak against the unjust oppression of the strong, to prevent war, and to save Christian civilization.

206. Today again, although the conditions of the world are changed, the Pope does not cease to use his moral power with a constant solicitude, in order to fill the minds of peoples with the Christian idea of justice and of love, to recall nations to the reciprocal duties of brotherhood, to inculcate respect for the authority established by God for the good of peoples, and to oppose to the law of might the might of law, in conformity with the principles of the Gospel. . . . . . .

SECOND DIPLOMATIC NOTE OF CARDINAL RAMPOLLA, SECRETARY OF STATE, TO COUNT MOURAVIEV, SECRETARY OF FOREIGN AFFAIRS FOR RUSSIA.[99]

Mediation and arbitration, not force, are the solution for international disputes.

February 10, 1899

207. . . . . . . There is lacking in the international consortium of nations a system of legal and moral means proper to determine, to make good the right of each. There only remains, then, immediate recourse to force. The result is the rivalry of nations in the development of their military power. . . .

208. . . . In view of such an unfortunate state of things, the institution of mediation and arbitration appears to be the most opportune remedy; it corresponds in all respects to the aspirations of the Holy See. Perhaps—and this will be better brought out in the discussions of the Conference—perhaps we cannot hope that arbitration, obligatory by its very nature, can become in all circumstances the object of unanimous acceptance and assent. An institution of mediation, invested with authority, clothed with all the necessary moral prestige, fortified with the indispensable guarantees of competence and impartiality, in no way restraining the liberty of the litigating parties, would be less exposed to meet obstacles.[100]

209. . . . At the same time, the Holy See expresses the most ardent wish that in the councils of the powers the principle of mediation and of arbitration may find a favorable welcome and may be applied as widely as possible. It gives its keenest sympathy to such a proposal and it declares that it is always disposed to co-operate most willingly in order that such a proposal may have a favorable issue. For it is convinced that, if an effective international accord could be realized, the latter would have a most happy effect in the interests of civilization. . . . . . .

---

[99] Original French, *Revue des Deux-Mondes*, v. 154, pp. 597-598 (1899).
[100] Such an institution was the permanent International Court of Arbitration of The Hague.

Discourse *Rivedere Qui Oggi* to the College of Cardinals.[101]

*History clearly teaches how often the Popes have
worked for peace among nations.*

April 11, 1899

210. Gladly Our thoughts, Lord Cardinal, turn to the fact[102]
which you have just mentioned, which We Ourselves have anticipated by desire and which comes now as a ray of sunlight to console
the decline of the century. To make rarer and less bloody the
terrible play of arms, and thus to prepare the way for a more tranquil social life is such an enterprise that it will make illustrious in
the history of civilization him who had sufficient intelligence and
courage to take the initiative in it. Thus, from the very beginning,
We have greeted this plan with that eagerness of will which befits
him who has the supreme task of promoting and disseminating on
earth the peaceful influence of the Gospel. We do not cease to
pray that this noble enterprise may result in complete and universal
success. Heaven grant that this first step may lead to the experiment of resolving disputes among nations by means of purely moral
and persuasive measures.

211. What could be more ardently wished for and desired by
the Church, mother of nations, the natural enemy of violence and
bloodshed, who could not happily fulfill her sacred rites without
dispelling by her prayers the scourge of war? The spirit of the
Church is a spirit of humanity, of sweetness, of concord, of universal
charity. Her mission, like that of Christ, is peaceful and peace-
making by nature because she has for her object the reconciliation
of man with God. Hence, results the efficacy of the religious power
to translate into actuality true peace among men, not only in the
realm of conscience, which it does every day, but also in the public
and social order, by reason always of the liberty of action granted to
her; an action, which, when it has intervened directly in the great
affairs of the world, has never been exerted without producing some
public benefit.

212. It suffices to recall how many times it has been given to
the Roman Pontiffs to put a stop to oppressions, to dispel wars, to
obtain truces, agreements, treaties of peace. They have been moved

---

[101] Original Italian, *Civiltà Cattolica*, ser. 17, v. 6, pp. 354-355 (April 24, 1899).
[102] The International Peace Conference being held at The Hague.

by the realization of their exalted office, by the driving force of their spiritual fatherhood, which unites brothers and saves them. Woe to the civilization of nations if the papal authority had not hastened in certain crises to curb the inhuman instincts of tyranny and conquest, by claiming in law and in fact the natural supremacy of reason over force. Thus speak the indissolubly united names of Alexander III and Legnano, of St. Ghislieri (family name of Pope St. Pius V) and Lepanto.

213. Such is the intrinsic virtue of the religious power. Contradictions and pressure may be able, here and there, to hinder the effects; but in itself it lives immutable and indefectible. So that, whatever may be the fortune of the times, the Church of God will follow her course with serenity, always doing good. Her gaze is towards heaven, but her action embraces heaven and earth because all things have been united in Christ, the things of heaven as those of earth. That is why the promise of a true and lasting prosperity by purely human means would be a vain illusion. It would even be regression and ruin to try to deprive civilization of the breath of Christianity which gives life and form to it and which alone can preserve for it the solidity of existence and the fruitfulness of results.

ENCYCLICAL *Annum Sacrum* ON THE CONSECRATION OF MANKIND TO THE SACRED HEART.[103]

> *To insure peace between nations there must be a closer bond between religion and civil society.*

May 25, 1899

214. . . . . . . This world-wide and solemn testimony of allegiance and piety is especially appropriate to Jesus Christ, Who is the Head and Supreme Lord of the race. His empire extends not only over Catholic nations and those who, having been duly washed in the waters of holy baptism, belong of right to the Church, although erroneous opinions keep them astray, or dissent from her teaching cuts them off from her care; it comprises also all those who are

---

[103] Translation from *The Holy Ghost and the Sacred Heart* (Catholic Truth Society of England Pamphlet), pp. 24-29. Original Latin, *A.S.S.*, v. 31, pp. 647-650 (1898-1899).

deprived of the Christian Faith, so that the whole human race is most truly under the power of Jesus Christ. . . . . . .

215. Such an act of consecration, since it can establish or draw tighter the bonds which naturally connect public affairs with God, gives to States a hope of better things. In these latter times especially, a policy has been followed which has resulted in a sort of wall being raised between the Church and civil society. In the constitution and administration of States the authority of sacred and divine law is utterly disregarded, with a view to the exclusion of religion from having any constant part in public life. This policy almost tends to the removal of the Christian Faith from our midst, and, if that were possible, to the banishment of God Himself from the earth. When men's minds are raised to such a height of insolent pride, what wonder is it that the greater part of the human race should have fallen into such disquiet of mind and be buffeted by waves so rough that no one is suffered to be free from anxiety and peril? When religion is once discarded it follows of necessity that the surest foundations of the public welfare must give way, whilst God, to inflict on His enemies the punishment they so richly deserve, has left them the prey of their own evil desires, so that they . . . wear themselves out by excess of liberty.

216. Hence that abundance of evils which have now for a long time settled upon the world, and which pressingly call upon us to seek for help from Him by Whose strength alone they can be driven away. Who can He be but Jesus Christ, the only begotten Son of God? *For there is no other name under heaven given to men whereby we must be saved.*[104] We must have recourse to Him Who is the Way, the Truth and the Life. We have gone astray and we must return to the right path: darkness has overshadowed our minds, and the gloom must be dispelled by the light of truth: death has seized upon us, and we must lay hold of life. It will at length be possible that our many wounds be healed and all justice spring forth again with the hope of restored authority; that the splendors of peace be renewed, and swords and arms drop from the hand when all men shall acknowledge the empire of Christ and willingly obey His word, and *every tongue shall confess that Our Lord Jesus Christ is in the glory of God the Father.*[105] . . . . . .

[104] *Acts,* IV, 12.
[105] *Philippians,* II, 11.

LETTER *Nous Ne Pouvons* TO QUEEN WILHELMINA OF HOLLAND.[106]

The Popes always have and always will work for peace among the nations.

May 29, 1899

217. We cannot but find agreeable the letter by which Your Majesty, in announcing to Us the meeting of the Conference for Peace[107] in Your capital, did Us the courtesy to request Our moral support for that assembly. We hasten to express Our keen sympathy for the august initiator of the Conference,[108] and for Your Majesty, who extended to it such spontaneous and noble hospitality, and for the eminently moral and beneficent object toward which the labors already begun are tending.

218. We consider that it comes especially within Our province not only to lend Our moral support to such enterprises, but to co-operate actively in them, for the object in question is supremely noble in its nature and intimately bound up with Our August Ministry, which, through the Divine Founder of the Church, and in virtue of traditions of many secular instances, has been invested with the highest possible mission, that of being a mediator of peace. In fact, the authority of the Supreme Pontiff goes beyond the boundaries of nations; it embraces all peoples, to the end of federating them in the true peace of the Gospel. His action to promote the general good of humanity rises above the special interests which the chiefs of the various States have in view, and, better than any one else, his authority knows how to incline toward concord peoples of diverse nature and character. History itself bears witness to all that has been done, by the influence of Our Predecessors, to soften the inexorable laws of war, to arrest bloody conflicts when controversies have arisen between princes, to terminate peacefully even the most acute differences between nations, to vindicate courageously the rights of the weak against the pretensions of the strong. Even unto Us, notwithstanding the abnormal condition to which We are at present reduced, it has been given to put an end

[106] Translation from Holls, *The Peace Conference at The Hague,* pp. 339-340. Original French, *A.S.S.,* v. 32, pp. 65-67 (1900).
[107] The First Peace Conference at The Hague.
[108] The Czar Nicholas II of Russia.

to grave differences between great nations such as Germany and Spain,[109] and this very day We hope to be able soon to establish concord between two nations of South America[110] which have submitted their controversy to Our arbitration.

219. In spite of obstacles which may arise, We shall continue, since it rests with Us to fulfill that traditional mission, without seeking any other object than the public weal, without envying any glory but that of serving the sacred cause of Christian civilization. . . . . . .

ENCYCLICAL *Depuis le Jour* ON ECCLESIASTICAL EDUCATION IN FRANCE.[111]

> *Priests must teach the salutary principles of religion which furnish the only solution for the crisis.*

September 8, 1899

220. . . . . . . The present times are evil; the future is still more gloomy and menacing, and seems to herald the approach of a redoubtable crisis and social upheaval. It behooves us, then, as We have said on many occasions, to honor the salutary principles of Religion, as well as those of justice, charity, respect and duty. It is for us to imbue men's souls with these principles—and especially those souls which have become captive to infidelity or disturbed by destroying passions, to bring about the reign of the grace and peace of our Divine Redeemer, Who is the Light and the Resurrection and the Life, and in Him to unite all men, notwithstanding the inevitable social distinctions which divide them. Yet, now more than ever, is there need of the help and devotedness of exemplary priests, full of faith, discretion and zeal, who, taking inspiration from the gentleness and energy of Jesus Christ, Whose true ambassadors they are . . . to announce with a courageous and inexhaustible patience the eternal truths which are seldom fruitless of virtue in men's souls. . . . . . .

---

[109] The dispute over the Caroline Islands in 1885.
[110] The difficulty of establishing a boundary between Haiti and Santo Domingo.
[111] Translation from *The Catholic University Bulletin*, v. 5, p. 501 (1899). Original French, *A.S.S.*, v. 32, p. 213 (1900).

ALLOCUTION *Auspicandae Celebritatis* TO THE COLLEGE OF
CARDINALS.[112]

*Leo XIII regrets the exclusion of the Holy See from the
International Peace Conference at The Hague.*

December 14, 1899

221. . . . . . . Meanwhile, the year nearing its end brought
forth another setback combined with injury to the Apostolic See,
and one condemned by the universal agreement of men who judge
justly, which We could not tolerate in silence; We refer to the conference of legates of the highest rulers at The Hague. At the
suggestion of the august Czar of Russia, there was to be a consultation about establishing more firmly the peace of empires and
about restricting both the frequency and cruelty of wars. What
could be more deserving of the support of the Pontiff? In truth,
to contend for justice, to bring about peace, to prevent quarrels,
is divinely fixed in the Roman Pontificate; all previous ages have
recognized this both in judgment and in practice. That Our Predecessors have frequently performed these functions to the great
advantage of Christian nations is too well-known to need mention.

222. In fact, even from the beginning, the help of Our authority had been spontaneously sought for that undertaking at once
so fruitful and so noble; even then, it was desired, and for the most
part opinions were inclined to give Us a place in The Hague
Conference. One voice out of all dissented, and indeed it continued stubborn in its dissent as long as it aroused opposition against
Us: the voice of those very men, I say, who have exposed the
supreme ruler of the Church to their power by their capture of
the City. What hostility should We not fear from such men, when
they do not hesitate in the sight of Europe to offer violence to the
sanctity of the laws and the duties which proceed spontaneously
from the Apostolic Office? Nevertheless, of whatever sort future
times may be, they shall find Us, with God's help, neither conniving
nor fearful. . . . . . .

[112] Original Latin, *A.S.S.*, v. 32, pp. 322-323 (1900).

ALLOCUTION *C'Incamminiamo* TO THE COLLEGE OF CARDINALS.[113]

The Pope asks all to pray for a speedy end to the war in South Africa.

March 2, 1900

223. . . . . . . For the rest, it will not appear foreign to the nature of today's celebrations to invite you, as We do, to join with Us in the holy union of a prayer for a purpose altogether conformed to the dictates of that evangelical love which knows neither distance of place nor difference of race. Let us all unitedly supplicate the Lord that He deign to look with pity on the bloody duel which has been fought for months on the African land, and that He permit it not to continue further. They are all His sons and our brothers who suffer in the difficult trial of the anxieties and engagements of war. May the blessed God look upon them with a fatherly eye, extinguish their wrath, and lead their hearts to sentiments of reciprocal moderation and agreement, so that they may come, as soon as possible, to a loyal and solid friendship consecrated by the mutual kiss of peace and of justice. . . .

ENCYCLICAL *Tametsi* ON JESUS CHRIST, OUR REDEEMER.[114]

If Christ is forgotten or excluded from civil society, the peace and security of States will be completely undermined.

November 1, 1900

224. . . . . . . When Jesus had blotted out the handwriting which was contrary to us, and fastened it to the cross, the wrath of heaven was immediately appeased; the disordered and erring race of man had the bonds of their ancient slavery loosed, the Will of God was reconciled to them, grace restored, the way to eternal happiness opened, and the title to possess and the means of attaining it both given back. Then, as though awakened from a long-lingering and deadly lethargy, man beheld the light of truth so long desired, but for generations sought in vain; he recognized, in

---

[113] Translation from *The Tablet,* v. 95, p. 374 (March 10, 1900). Original Italian, *Civiltá Cattolica,* ser. 17, v. 9, pp. 738-739 (1900).
[114] Translation from *The Great Encyclical Letters of Pope Leo XIII,* pp. 465-476. Original Latin, *A.S.S.,* v. 33, pp. 275-284 (1900-1901).

particular, that he was born for much higher and more splendid things than the frail and fleeting objects of sense, to which he had formerly confined his thoughts and pursuits, and that this was in fine the constitution and supreme law of human life, and the end to which all must tend, that as we came from God so we should one day return to Him. From this beginning and on this foundation consciousness of human dignity was restored and lived again; the sense of a common brotherhood took possession of men's hearts; their rights and duties in consequence were perfected or established anew and virtues beyond the imagination or conception of ancient philosophy were revived. So men's purposes, tenor of life, and characters were changed, and the knowledge of the Redeemer having spread far and wide, and His power having penetrated into the very life-blood of nations, expelling their ignorance and their ancient vices, a marvelous transformation took place, which, originating in Christian civilization, utterly changed the face of the earth. . . . . . .

225. Besides, to suffer and to bear is the lot of humanity. Man can no more construct for himself a life free from pain and replete with every happiness than he can annul the counsels of his divine Creator, Who has willed that the consequences of our fault should remain in perpetuity. It is proper, therefore, not to look for an end of pain upon the earth, but to strengthen our mind to bear pain which, in fact, educates us to the attainment of the greatest of all good things for which we hope. For it is not to wealth and luxury, nor to worldly honors and powers that Christ has promised eternal happiness in heaven, but to patient suffering and tears, to the desire of justice and to cleanness of heart. . . . . . .

226. The case of governments is much the same as that of the individual; they also must run into fatal issues, if they depart from *the Way*. The Creator and Redeemer of human nature, the Son of God, is King and Lord of the world, and holds absolute sovereignty over men, both as individuals and as members of society. *He hath given to Him power and honor and dominion, and all peoples, tribes, and languages shall serve Him.*[115] *Yet am I established King by Him. . . . . . I will give Thee the nations for Thine inheritance, and the ends of the earth for Thy possession.*[116] There-

[115] *Daniel*, VII, 14.
[116] *Psalms*, II, 6, 8.

fore, the law of Christ ought to hold sway in human society, and in communities so far as to be the teacher and guide of public no less than private life. This being divinely appointed and provided, no one may resist with impunity, and it fares ill with any commonwealth in which Christian institutions are not allowed their proper place. Let Jesus be excluded, and human reason is left without its greatest protection and illumination; the very notion is easily lost of the end for which God created human society, to wit: that by help of their civil union the citizens should attain their natural good, but nevertheless in a way not to conflict with that highest and most perfect and enduring good which is above nature. Their minds busy with a hundred confused projects, rulers and subjects alike travel a devious road; bereft, as they are, of safe guidance and fixed principle. . . . . . .

227. . . . How little that kind of virtue which despises faith avails in the end, and what sort of fruit it brings forth, we see only too plainly. Why is it that with so much zeal displayed for establishing and augmenting the commonwealth, nations still have to labor and yet in so many and such important matters fare worse and worse every day? They say indeed that civil society is self-dependent, that it can go on happily without the protection of Christian institutions, that by its own unaided energies it can reach its goal. Hence, they prefer to have public affairs conducted on a secular basis, so that in civil discipline and public life there are always fewer and fewer traces discernible of the old religious spirit. They do not see what they are doing. Take away the supremacy of God, Who judges right and wrong; and law necessarily loses its paramount authority, while at the same time justice is undermined, these two being the strongest and most essential bonds of social union. In the same way, when the hope and expectation of immortality are gone, it is only human to seek greedily after perishable things, and everyone will try, in proportion to his power, to clutch a larger share of them. Hence spring jealousies, envies, hatreds; the most iniquitous plots to overthrow all power and mad schemes of universal ruin are formed. There is no peace abroad, nor security at home, and social life is made hideous by crime.

228. In such strife of passions, in such impending perils, we must either look for utter ruin, or some effective remedy must be found without delay. To restrain evil-doers, to soften the manners

of our populations, to deter them from committing crimes by legislative intervention, is right and necessary; but that is by no means all. The healing of the nations goes deeper; a mightier influence must be invoked than human endeavor, one that may touch the conscience and reawaken the sense of duty, the same influence that has once already delivered from destruction a world overwhelmed with far greater evils.

229. Do away with the obstacles to the spirit of Christianity; revive and make it strong in the State, and the State will be recreated. The strife between high and low will at once be appeased, and each will observe with mutual respect the rights of the other. If they listen to Christ, the prosperous and the unfortunate will both alike remember their duty; the one will feel that they must keep justice and charity, if they would be saved; the other that they must show temperance and moderation. Domestic society will have been solidly established under a salutary fear of the divine commands and prohibitions; and so likewise in society at large, the precepts of the natural law will prevail, which tells us that it is right to respect lawful authority, and to obey the laws, to do no seditious act nor contrive anything by unlawful association. Thus, when Christian law exerts its power without being thwarted in any way, naturally and without effort the order of society is maintained as constituted by divine Providence, and prosperity and public safety are secured. The security of the State demands that we should be brought back to Him from Whom we ought never to have departed, to Him Who is the Way, the Truth and the Life, not as individuals merely, but as human society through all its extent. Christ our Lord must be reinstated as the Ruler of human society. It belongs to Him, as do all its members. All the elements of the commonwealth; legal commands and prohibitions, popular institutions, schools, marriage, home life, the workshop and the palace, all must be made to come to that Fountain and imbibe the life that comes from Him. No one should fail to see that on this largely depends the civilization of nations, which is so eagerly sought, but which is nourished and augmented not so much by bodily comforts and conveniences, as by what belongs to the soul, viz., commendable lives and the cultivation of virtue. . . . . . .

LETTER *Reputantibus* TO THE BISHOPS OF BOHEMIA AND MORAVIA.[117]

Although nations and peoples may differ in race and in language, they are one in Christ.

August 20, 1901

230. . . . . . . Certainly the keeping of one's native tongue, if it be restricted with certain bounds, does not deserve blame; yet what holds with regard to other rights of private individuals must be considered to hold here also lest the public good of the commonwealth suffer harm from their exercise. . . . . . .

231. And so, Venerable Brethren, We vehemently desire and urge that the faithful entrusted to each of you, even though they be different in origin and language, nevertheless retain that relationship of soul which is by far the most noble; and which is begotten of communion of faith and of the same sacred rites. For as many as are baptized in Christ have the one Lord and the one Faith; and, therefore, they are one body and one spirit as they are called in one hope of their calling.[118] . . .

232. Therefore, this relationship of soul which comes from Christ is to be inculcated assiduously among the faithful, and is to be extolled with all zeal. "The brotherhood of Christ indeed is greater than that of blood; for brotherhood of blood shows a likeness of body only, but the brotherhood of Christ shows a oneness of heart and soul, as it is written:[119] *There was one heart and one soul in the multitude of believers.*"[120]

233. Under the circumstances, it is necessary that members of the sacred clergy precede others by their example. For in addition to the fact that it is not in keeping with their office to become involved in dissensions of this kind, if they are in places inhabited by men of different race and different language, they will easily, unless they abstain from all appearance of contention, become hateful and offensive to both parties, and nothing is more detrimental to the exercise of their sacred office than this. The faithful

[117] Original Latin, *A.S.S.,* v. 34, pp. 321-322 (1902).
[118] Cf. *Ephesians* IV, 4.
[119] Sermon of St. Maximus found among St. Augustine's *Works;* cf. Migne, *P.L.,* v. 39, c. 1937.
[120] *Acts,* IV, 32.

should know through actual experience that the ministers of the Church value only the eternal interests of souls and do not desire at all the things that are their own, but only the things that are of Jesus Christ. . . . . . .

LETTER *Pervenuti* IN WHICH LEO XIII REVIEWS HIS PONTIFICATE.[121]

As nations continue to repudiate Christian principles, war becomes more certain.

March 19, 1902

234. . . . . . . Consequent upon the repudiation of those Christian principles which had contributed so efficaciously to unite the nations in the bonds of brotherhood and to bring all humanity into one great family, there has arisen little by little, in the international order, a system of jealous egoism, in consequence of which the nations now watch each other, if not with hate, at least with the suspicion of rivals. Hence, in their great undertakings they lose sight of the lofty principles of morality and justice and forget the protection which the feeble and oppressed have a right to demand.

235. In the desire by which they are actuated to increase their national riches, they regard only the opportunity which circumstances afford, the advantages of successful enterprises, and the tempting bait of an accomplished fact, sure that no one will trouble them in the name of right or the respect which right can claim. Such are the fatal principles which have consecrated material power as the supreme law of the world, and to them is to be imputed the limitless increase of military establishments and that armed peace which in many respects is equivalent to a disastrous war. This lamentable confusion in the realm of ideas has produced restlessness among the people, outbreaks and the general spirit of rebellion. From these have sprung the frequent popular agitations and disorders of our times which are only the preludes of much more terrible disorders in the future. . . . . . .

---

[121] Translation from *American Ecclesiastical Review*, v. 26, p. 690 (June, 1902). Original Italian, *A.S.S.*, v. 34, pp. 519-520 (1902).

ENCYCLICAL *Mirae Caritatis* ON THE HOLY EUCHARIST.[122]

It is because men and nations fail to practice Christian charity that dissensions and wars arise.

May 28, 1902

236. . . . . . . Indeed, it is greatly to be desired that those men would rightly esteem and would make due provision for life everlasting whose industry or talents or rank have put it in their power to shape the course of human events. But, alas! we see with sorrow that such men too often proudly flatter themselves that they have conferred upon this world, as it were, a fresh lease of life and prosperity, inasmuch as by their own energetic action they are urging it on to the race for wealth, to a struggle for the possession of commodities which minister to the love of comfort and display. And yet, whithersoever we turn, we see that human society, if it be estranged from God, instead of enjoying that peace in its possessions for which it had sought, is shaken and tossed like one who is in the agony and heat of fever; for while it anxiously strives for prosperity, and trusts to it alone, it is pursuing an object that ever escapes it, clinging to one that ever eludes the grasp. For as men and States alike necessarily have their being from God, so they can do nothing good except in God through Jesus Christ, through Whom every best and choicest gift has ever proceeded and proceeds. But the source and chief of all these gifts is the venerable Eucharist, which not only nourishes and sustains that life, the desire whereof demands our most strenuous efforts, but also enhances beyond measure that dignity of man of which in these days we hear so much. . . . . . .

237. Furthermore, if anyone will diligently examine into the causes of the evils of our day, he will find that they arise from this, that as charity towards God has grown cold, the mutual charity of men among themselves has likewise cooled. Men have forgotten that they are children of God and brethren in Jesus Christ; they care for nothing except their own individual interests; the interests and the rights of others they not only make light of, but often attack and invade.

238. Hence, frequent disturbances and strifes between class and

---

[122] Translation from *The Great Encyclical Letters of Pope Leo XIII*, pp. 522-529. Original Latin, *A.S.S.*, v. 34, pp. 644-649 (1902).

class: arrogance, oppression, fraud on the part of the more powerful:
misery, envy and turbulence among the poor. These are evils for
which it is in vain to seek a remedy in legislation, in threats of
penalties to be incurred, or in any other device of merely human
prudence. Our chief care and endeavor ought to be, according to
the admonitions which We have more than once given at considerable length, to secure the union of classes in a mutual interchange
of dutiful services, a union which, having its origin in God, shall
issue in deeds that reflect the true spirit of Jesus Christ and a
genuine charity. This charity Christ brought into the world; with
it He would have all hearts on fire. For it alone is capable of
affording to soul and body alike, even in this life, a foretaste of
blessedness; since it restrains man's inordinate self-love, and puts
a check on avarice, which *is the root of all evil*.[123] And whereas
it is right to uphold all the claims of justice as between the various
classes of society, nevertheless, it is only with the efficacious aid of
charity, which tempers justice, that the *equality* which St. Paul commended,[124] and which is so salutary for human society, can be
established and maintained. . . . All of which is confirmed by the
declaration of the Council of Trent that Christ left the Eucharist
in His Church "as a symbol of that unity and charity whereby He
would have all Christians mutually joined and united . . . a symbol of that one body of which He is Himself the Head, and to
which He would have us, as members, attached by the closest bonds
of faith, hope, and charity."[125]

[123] I *Timothy*, VI, 10.
[124] II *Corinthians*, VIII, 14.
[125] *Council of Trent*, Session XIII, *De Eucharistia*, c. II.

PART TWO

PIUS X

1903-1914

INTRODUCTION

"To restore all things in Christ" was the lofty ambition of Giuseppe Melchior Cardinal Sarto, Patriarch of Venice, when as Pius X on August 4, 1903, he succeeded Leo XIII in the papacy. In origin, experience, temperament he differed greatly from the aristocratic diplomat who had preceded him; yet Pius X's pontificate, concentrating more on the internal reform of the Church, greatly enhanced the new power and influence the papacy had attained under Leo.

Born at Riese in the province of Venice on June 2, 1835, the son of a postman, he attended the seminary at Padua, and was ordained on September 15, 1858. After doing parish work at Tombolo, Salzano and Treviso, he was appointed canon of the cathedral in 1875, then rector of the seminary, chancellor and vicar general of the diocese, and in 1884 was appointed Bishop of Mantua, a diocese that had been without a bishop for ten years because of difficulties with the Italian government. His zeal in reforming Mantua caught the attention of Leo XIII, and in 1893 Bishop Sarto was made Cardinal Patriarch of Venice, although he was unable to take possession of his diocese for eighteen months because of opposition from the government. Ten years later, in the conclave of 1903, he was elected pope after Austria had vetoed the election of Cardinal Rampolla.

"A country pastor on the papal throne," one writer calls Pius X, since most of his life had been bound up exclusively in pastoral work among the common people. A priest of unusual sanctity, of surpassing simplicity and gentleness, Pius X kept himself aloof from diplomacy and international relations, concentrating more on the directly spiritual apostolate of souls. The keynote of his reign was the spiritual reform of the Church; and almost every phase of Catholic life felt his influence.

Served throughout his pontificate by a devoted Secretary of State, Cardinal Merry del Val, Pius X accomplished much in his eleven years. In 1903 he issued a famous *Motu Proprio* on Church music, restoring Gregorian Chant to its primitive preeminent position. In 1904 he set up a commission to codify Church law. He shortened and simplified the Roman breviary, reorganized seminaries, rearranged the Roman congregations. The rising heresy of Modernism he decisively crushed within the Church by a series of letters and decrees in 1907. In 1909 he founded the Biblical Institute in Rome to train experts in the field of Scripture studies.

The early days of his pontificate witnessed a growing anti-Catholic spirit in the policies of the French government, culminating in the "Law of Separation" of 1905, by which Church property was confiscated, and many of the clergy and religious were exiled. He relaxed the more severe restrictions made by Pius IX and Leo XIII against Catholic participation in Italian politics.

The last days of his pontificate were saddened by the outbreak of the World War. A long, tender letter sent by Pius to the aged Emperor Franz Josef was intercepted en route and never reached its destination. Pius X died on August 20, 1914. World-wide affirmation of his sanctity prompted the recent introduction of his cause at Rome.

DOCUMENTS

ENCYCLICAL *E Supremi Apostolatus* ON THE RESTORATION OF
ALL THINGS IN CHRIST.[1]

Peace without God is an absurdity.

October 4, 1903

239. . . . . . . For, Venerable Brethren, who can avoid being
appalled and afflicted when he beholds, in the midst of a progress
in civilization which is justly extolled, the greater part of mankind
fighting among themselves so savagely as to make it seem as though
strife were universal? The desire for peace is certainly harbored
in every breast, and there is no one who does not ardently invoke
it. But to want peace without God is an absurdity, seeing that
where God is absent thence, too, justice flies, and when justice is
taken away it is vain to cherish the hope of peace. *And the work
of justice shall be peace.*[2] There are many, we are well aware, who,
in yearning for peace, that is to say, the tranquillity of order, band
themselves into societies and parties which they style parties of
order. Hope and labor lost! For there is but one party of order
capable of restoring peace in the midst of all this turmoil, and that
is the party of God. It is this party, therefore, that we must advance,
and to it attract as many as possible, if we are really urged by the
love of peace. . . . . . .

ALLOCUTION *Amplissimum Coetum* TO THE COLLEGE OF
CARDINALS.[3]

> *The Holy See acts as arbitrator in the boundary dispute
> between Brazil, Peru and Bolivia.*

March 27, 1905

240. . . . . . . Meanwhile, Venerable Brethren, Our soul is still
cast into sorrow by the terrible war as a result of which the furthest

---

[1] Translation from *The American Catholic Quarterly Review*, v. 29, p. 13 (January,
1904). Original Latin, *A.S.S.*, v. 36, pp. 132-133 (1903-1904).
[2] *Isaias*, XXXII, 17.
[3] Original Latin, *A.S.S.*, v. 37, p. 560 (1904-1905).

shores of the Orient have long been saddened by slaughter, fire and bloodshed. How many things there move Us to tears! Holding on this earth the place of Him Who is the Author and Conciliator of peace, We earnestly beg God in a spirit of humility that He in His kindness may grant to princes and people plans leading to peace. So many and such great evils consume the human race everywhere that there is no need that it be troubled also by the clash of arms and the strife of war!

241. How much ought to be conceded on all sides to the desire for peace, has recently and happily been experienced by the rulers of Brazil, Peru and Bolivia. For when controversies had arisen regarding the determination and government of boundaries between the United States of Brazil and the two other nations, that is to say, Peru and Bolivia, their long standing harmony seemed to be endangered. But their governments, adopting a wise and most salutary plan, decided that the dispute should be terminated by the arbitration of others. Since in this situation they considered very wisely that the duty of guarding peace is natural to and innate in the Roman Pontificate, by common consent they made the Nuncio of the Apostolic See president of the board by whose votes the affair was to be decided. While We with joyful mind communicate this news to you, Venerable Brethren, it is Our pleasure to give thanks publicly to the rulers of the said nations for having wished to show such an honor to Us and to the Chair of St. Peter. . . . . . .

ENCYCLICAL *Il Fermo Proposito* ON CATHOLIC ACTION IN ITALY.[4]

> *If the Christian ideal were realized, peace and concord would reign. It is the duty of Catholic Action to work toward this ideal.*

June 11, 1905

242. . . . . . . The Church, while preaching Jesus crucified, Who was a stumbling-block and folly to the world,[5] has been the first inspirer and promoter of civilization. She has spread it wherever her Apostles have preached, preserving and perfecting

---

[4] Translation from *The Pope and the People*, pp. 190-198. Original Italian, *A.S.S.*, v. 37, pp. 745-761 (1904-1905).
[5] I *Corinthians*, I, 23.

what was good in ancient pagan civilization, rescuing from barbarism and raising to a form of civilized society the new peoples who took refuge in her maternal bosom, and giving to the whole of human society, little by little, no doubt, but with a sure and ever onward march, that characteristic stamp, which it still everywhere preserves. The civilization of the world is Christian civilization; the more frankly Christian it is, so much is it more true, more lasting, and more productive of precious fruit; the more it withdraws from the Christian ideal, so much the feebler is it, to the great detriment of society.

243. Thus, by the intrinsic force of things, the Church becomes again in fact the guardian and protector of Christian civilization. This truth was recognized and admitted in former times; it even formed the immovable foundation of civil legislation. On it rested the relations of Church and States, the public recognition of the authority of the Church in all matters relating in any way to conscience, the subordination of all State laws to the divine laws of the Gospel, the harmony of the two powers, civil and ecclesiastical, for procuring the temporal well-being of the nations without injury to their eternal welfare.

244. It is unnecessary to tell you what prosperity and happiness, what peace and concord, what respectful submission to authority, and what excellent government would be established and maintained in the world if the perfect ideal of Christian civilization could be everywhere realized. But, given the continual warfare of the flesh with the spirit, of darkness with light, of Satan with God, we cannot hope for so great a good, at least in its full measure. Hence, against the peaceful conquests of the Church arose unceasing attacks, the more deplorable and fatal as human society tends more to govern itself by principles opposed to the Christian ideal, and to separate itself wholly from God. . . . . . .

245. *To restore all things in Christ* has ever been the Church's motto, and it is specially Ours, in the perilous times in which we live. To restore all things, not in any fashion, but in Christ; *that are in heaven, and on earth, in Him*,[6] adds the Apostle; to restore in Christ not only what directly depends on the divine mission of the Church to conduct souls to God, but also, as We have explained, that which flows spontaneously from this divine mission, viz.,

---

[6] *Ephesians*, I, 10.

Christian civilization in each and every one of the elements which compose it.

246. To dwell only on this last part of the desired restoration, you see well what support is given to the Church by those chosen bands of Catholics whose aim is to unite all their forces in order to combat anti-Christian civilization by every just and lawful means, and to repair in every way the grievous disorders which flow from it; to reinstate Jesus Christ in the family, the school and society; to re-establish the principle that human authority represents that of God; to take intimately to heart the interests of the people, especially those of the working and agricultural classes, not only by the inculcation of religion, the only true source of comfort in the sorrows of life, but also by striving to dry their tears, to soothe their sufferings, and by wise measures to improve their economic condition; to endeavor, consequently, to make public laws conformable to justice, to amend or suppress those which are not so; finally, with a true Catholic spirit, to defend and support the rights of God in everything, and the no less sacred rights of the Church.

247. All these works, of which Catholic laymen are the principal supporters and promoters, and whose form varies according to the special needs of each nation, and the particular circumstances of each country, constitute what is generally known by a distinctive, and surely a very noble name: *Catholic Action* or *Action of Catholics*. This has always come to the aid of the Church, and the Church has always welcomed and blessed it, although it has acted in various ways in accordance with the age. . . . . . .

248. Further, in order that Catholic Action may be effectual on all points, it is not enough that it be adapted to actual social needs only; it ought also to be invigorated by all the practical methods furnished at the present day by progress in social and economic studies, by experience already gained elsewhere, by the condition of civil society, and even by the public life of States. Otherwise there will be a risk of groping for a long time for new and hazardous things, while good and safe ones are ready to hand, and have been already well tried; or again, there will be the danger of proposing institutions and methods suitable, perhaps, in former times, but not understood by people of the present day; or finally, there will be the danger of stopping half-way by not using, in the measure in which they are granted, those rights of citizenship which

modern constitutions offer to all, and, therefore, also to Catholics.

249. We dwell on this last point, for it is certain that the present constitution of States offers to all without distinction the power of influencing public opinion, and Catholics, while recognizing the obligations imposed by the law of God and the precepts of the Church, may with safe conscience enjoy this liberty, and prove themselves capable, as much as, and even more than others, of co-operating in the material and civil well-being of the people, thus acquiring that authority and respect which may make it even possible for them to defend and promote a higher good, namely, that of the soul.

250. These civil rights are many and various, going as far as a direct share in the political life of the country by representing the people in the legislature. . . . This makes it incumbent on all Catholics to prepare themselves prudently and seriously for political life in case they should be called to it. . . .

251. Lastly, in order to renew and increase in all Catholic undertakings the necessary enthusiasm, to give to their promoters and members an opportunity of seeing and becoming acquainted with each other, to draw ever more closely the bonds of brotherly love, to enkindle in one another a more burning zeal for efficient action, and to provide for the better establishment and spread of the same works, a wonderful help will be found in the meeting from time to time, according to the rules already given by the Holy See, of general or local Congresses of Italian Catholics; and they ought to be a solemn manifestation of Catholic faith, and a common festival of harmony and peace. . . . . . .

LETTER *Poloniae Populum* TO THE BISHOPS OF RUSSIAN POLAND.[7]

Catholics must stand on the side of peace and order.

December 3, 1905

252. . . . . . . The most Holy Religion of Christ demands that we never allow ourselves to be carried away by disturbances of passion, but rather that a sound mind govern them and compel them to submit to control. Wherefore, all Catholics are forbidden to belong to factional groups which run counter to the law of God.

[7] Original Latin, *A.S.S.*, v. 38, pp. 324-325 (1906).

Nor surely does it free them from guilt, the fact that they do this for human advantages. For again Catholic doctrine warns us that the gains of eternal goods ought to be preferred to all the fleeting advantages of this life, according to the Lord's words: *For what does it profit a man, if he gain the whole world, but suffer the loss of his own soul?*[8]

253. With this established as a foundation, so to speak, another principle follows: in the midst of the movements and changes by which the Russian Empire is now being disturbed, and at the same time that part of Poland which is subject to the same empire, Catholics must constantly stand on the side of peace and order.

254. In this situation it should help all to remember what Our Predecessor of happy memory wrote to you on March 19, 1894: "They who are subject to power ought constantly to observe reverence and loyalty toward their princes, as though to God exercising His rule through man, and obey them: *not only for wrath, but also for conscience' sake*,[9] and on their behalf offer *supplications, prayers, intercessions and thanksgivings*,[10] they should keep holy the discipline of the State, abstain from the machinations and factions of the wicked, and do nothing seditiously, and do everything to preserve tranquil peace in justice."[11]

255. In order that Catholics may not only love this tranquillity of peace and pray ardently for it, but also, as is their duty, hasten to bring it to realization and, when obtained, preserve it in safety, it is absolutely necessary that, following the examples of the turbulent, they enter into societies and groups wherein with united plan and effort they may fight efficaciously for religion and country. . . . . . .

---

[8] *Matthew*, XVI, 26.
[9] *Romans*, XIII, 5.
[10] I *Timothy*, II, 1-2.
[11] Encyclical *Caritatis* of March 19, 1894. Cf. *A.S.S.*, v. 26, p. 525 (1893-1894), and *supra* n. 190.

ENCYCLICAL *Vehementer Nos* ON THE FRENCH SEPARATION LAW.[12]

Reciprocal security of nations depends mainly on the inviolable fidelity and the sacred respect with which they observe their treaties.

February 11, 1906

256. . . . . . . The Concordat[13] entered upon by the Sovereign Pontiff and the French Government was, like all treaties of the same kind concluded between States, a bilateral contract binding on both parties to it. The Roman Pontiff on the one side and the head of the French nation on the other solemnly stipulated both for themselves and their successors to maintain inviolate the pact they signed. Hence, the same rule applied to the Concordat as to all international treaties, viz., the law of nations, which prescribes that it could not be in any way annulled by one alone of the contracting parties. The Holy See has always observed with scrupulous fidelity the engagements it has made, and it has always required the same fidelity from the State. This is a truth which no impartial judge can deny. Yet to-day the State, by its sole authority, abrogates the solemn pact it signed. Thus it violates its sworn promise. To break with the Church, to free itself from her friendship, it has stopped at nothing, and has not hesitated to outrage the Apostolic See by this violation of the law of nations, and to disturb the social and political order itself—for the reciprocal security of nations in their relations with one another depends mainly on the inviolable fidelity and the sacred respect with which they observe their treaties.

257. . . . . . . Besides the injury it inflicts on the interests of the Church, the new law[14] is destined to be most disastrous to your country. For there can be no doubt but that it lamentably destroys union and concord. And yet without such union and concord no nation can live long or prosper. Especially in the present state of Europe, the maintenance of perfect harmony must be the most ardent wish of everybody in France who loves his country and has its salvation at heart. As for Us, following the example of Our

[12] Translation from *The American Catholic Quarterly Review*, v. 31, pp. 212-217 (April, 1906). Original Latin, *A.S.S.*, v. 39, pp. 6-12 (1906).
[13] Concordat of 1801 between Pius VII and Napoleon I.
[14] The Law of Separation between Church and State of 1905.

Predecessor and inheriting from him a special predilection for your nation, We have not confined Ourself to striving for the preservation of all the rights of the religion of your forefathers, but with that fraternal peace of which religion is certainly the strongest bond, ever before Our eyes, We have always endeavored to promote unity among you. We cannot, therefore, without the keenest sorrow, observe that the French Government has just done a deed which inflames, on religious grounds, passions already too dangerously excited, and which, therefore, seems to be calculated to plunge the whole country into disorder. . . . . . .

ENCYCLICAL *Gravissimo Officii Munere* FORBIDDING FRENCH ASSOCIATIONS OF WORSHIP.[15]

In difficulties between the Church and the State the Pope forbids seditions and violence but demands firmness in defense of their natural rights.

August 10, 1906

258. . . . . . . Therefore, if they desire to show Us their submission and their devotion, let the Catholic men of France struggle for the Church in accordance with the directions We have already given them—that is to say, with perseverance and energy, and yet without acting in a seditious and violent manner. It is not by violence, but by firmness, that, fortifying themselves in their good right as within a citadel, they will succeed in breaking the obstinacy of their enemies. Let them well understand, as We have said and as We repeat, that their efforts will be useless unless they unite in a perfect understanding for the defense of religion. As they now know Our verdict[16] on the subject of this nefarious law, they should wholeheartedly conform to it, and whatever the opinions of some or others of them may have been hitherto during the discussion of the question, We entreat all that no one shall permit

[15] Translation from the *Catholic University Bulletin,* v. 12, pp. 537-538 (Oct., 1906). Original Latin, *A.S.S.,* v. 39, pp. 389-390 (1906).

[16] The Pope forbade French Catholics to form the associations of worship which were required by the Law of Separation. These associations would have placed control of ecclesiastical affairs and church property exclusively in the hands of the laity. Later the Law of Separation was amended so that the formation of these associations was not necessary.

himself to wound anyone whomsoever on the pretext that his own way of seeing is the best. What can be done by concord of will and union of forces, let them learn from their adversaries, and just as the latter were able to impose on the nation the stigma of this criminal law, so Our people will be able to eliminate and remove it. . . . . . .

Letter of Cardinal Merry del Val, Secretary of State, to the President of the 15th World Peace Conference in Milan.[17]

The Pope is deeply interested in all peace movements throughout the world.

November 3, 1906

259. The Holy Father, through His Eminence, the Archbishop of Milan, has answered in sympathetic words the respectful greetings sent him by many delegates to the 15th World Peace Congress. This frank expression of sincere sentiments occasioned that noble-minded letter that you forwarded to His Holiness in the name of the illustrious convention at Milan over which you presided last September. His Holiness received this tribute of honor with deep gratitude, because it was directed rather to the exalted dignity with which he is vested, than to his own person. It acknowledges the high office of peace that God has entrusted to the Head of the Catholic Church.

260. History proves that the Popes have always endeavored to fulfill this office. The present Pontiff was happy that the opportunity was granted him, without his taking the initiative, to carry out this mandate. He presided, through one of his representatives, over a peace court of arbitration to which three American republics committed their differences so that they might avoid war.

261. One can understand, therefore, the interest with which the Holy Father, Pius X, follows the endeavors of the international peace associations, as well as his ardent wish to see these efforts crowned with success. The assurance of this interest and this wish may possibly help to increase that lively zeal which inspires you and your colleagues. It is my honor, therefore, to submit to you, in

[17] Original German, Müller, *Das Friedenswerk der Kirche,* pp. 345-346.

this regard, the above-mentioned clear and definite explanations. At the same time the Sovereign Pontiff expresses the hope that the great idea that inspires you may be duly esteemed, both in avoiding and circumventing the danger of war, and in lessening the terror when this danger can no longer be averted. . . . . . .

ALLOCUTION *Nous Vous Remercions* TO THE FRENCH PILGRIMS ON THE OCCASION OF THE BEATIFICATION OF JOAN OF ARC.[18]

Catholicism fosters a proper love of one's country.

April 19, 1909

262. . . . . . . Venerable Brethren and Beloved Children, because you preach and practice the teachings of the Church without human respect and in obedience to your conscience, you have had to suffer all sorts of insults, you are pointed out for public scorn, you are branded as enemies of your country! Have courage, and throw back in the face of your accusers this vile calumny which opens in your Catholic hearts a wound so deep that it can only be pardoned with the help of divine grace. There is not, in fact, any more undeserving outrage to your honor and your Faith, for if Catholicism were an enemy of one's native land, it would no longer be a divine religion.

263. Yes, your country is worthy not only of love but of predilection, whose sacred name awakens in your minds the dearest memories and thrills all the fibers of your soul, this common land which has been your cradle and to which the bonds of blood and that other more noble community of affections and traditions attach you. But this love of the native soil, these bonds of patriotic brotherhood, which are common to all countries, are stronger when the terrestrial country remains indissolubly united to that other country, the Catholic Church, which knows neither differences of language nor the barriers of mountains and seas, which embraces both the visible world and that beyond the grave.

264. This grace, if it is also possessed by other nations, belongs especially to you, very dear sons of France, to you who have so much at heart the love of your country, because it is united with the Church of which you are the defenders. . . . . . .

[18] Original French, *A.A.S.*, v. 1, pp. 408-409 (May 15, 1909).

LETTER *Libenter abs Te* TO ARCHBISHOP FALCONIO, APOSTOLIC
DELEGATE TO THE UNITED STATES.[19]

The Pope praises the Carnegie Endowment for International Peace on the occasion of its foundation.

June 11, 1911

265. With gladness We have learned from you that in the United States of America learned men, under the patronage of a group whose influence with the people is very great, are busily engaged in making studies the purpose of which is the preservation of the benefits of peace for all nations. To compose differences, to restrain the outbreak of hostilities, to prevent the dangers of war, to remove even the anxieties of so-called armed peace is, indeed, most praiseworthy, and any effort in this cause, even though it may not immediately or wholly accomplish its purpose, manifests, nevertheless, a zeal which cannot but redound to the credit of its authors and be of benefit to the States.

266. This is especially true at the present day, when vast armies, instrumentalities most destructive to human life, and the advanced state of military science portend wars which must be a source of fear even to the most powerful rulers.

267. Wherefore, We most heartily commend the work already begun, which should be approved by all good men and especially by Us, holding as We do, the supreme pontificate of the Church and representing Him Who is both the God and the Prince of Peace; and We most gladly lend the weight of Our authority to those who are striving to realize this most beneficent purpose.

268. For We do not doubt that the same distinguished men who possess so much ability and such wisdom in affairs of State will construct in behalf of a struggling age a royal road for the nations leading to peace and conciliation in accordance with the laws of justice and charity, which should be sacredly observed by all. For, inasmuch as peace consists in order, who will vainly think that it can be established unless he strives with all the force within him that due respect be everywhere given to those virtues which are the principles of order and its firmest foundation?

269. As for the remaining aspects of the matter, We recall to

[19] Translation from Schaefer, *A Papal Peace Mosaic*, pp. 14-15. Original Latin, *A.A.S.*, v. 3, pp. 473-474 (September 30, 1911).

mind the example of so many of Our illustrious Predecessors, who, when the condition of the times permitted, rendered, in this very matter also, the most signal service to the cause of humanity and to the stability of governments; but since the present age allows Us to aid in this cause only by pious prayers to God, We, therefore, most earnestly pray God, Who knows the hearts of men and inclines them as He wills, that He may be gracious to those who are furthering peace among the peoples, and may grant to the nations which, with united purposes, are laboring to this end, that the destruction of war and its disasters being averted, they may at length find repose in the beauty of peace. . . . . . .

Telegram of Cardinal Merry del Val, Secretary of State, to Archbishop Mora y del Rio of Mexico City.[20]

The Holy Father asks the Mexican Catholics to encourage the present peace movement in their country.

May 9, 1914

270. The Holy Father, Pius X, inspired by the paternal affection which he cherishes for Mexico and preoccupied with the supreme interests of your dearly beloved nation, desires most earnestly that the generous initiative of the three South American conferences for peace may meet with efficacious support from Mexican Catholics for the public tranquillity and prosperity of their country. It would be a great satisfaction for the Holy Father if these sentiments and wishes were communicated to His Excellency, the President, and all influential persons in the Mexican Republic.

Allocution *Ex Quo Postremum* to the College of Cardinals.[21]

Peace depends not only on statesmen but also upon the people who must have a profound sense of justice and charity.

May 25, 1914

271. . . . And yet, thanks to God's mercy, We are not without timely consolations. Such a consolation was the centenary celebra-

---

[20] Original Italian, *Civiltà Cattolica,* 1914, v. 3, p. 110.
[21] Original Latin, *A.A.S.,* v. 6, p. 254 (May 28, 1914).

tion last year of the peace and unhampered liberty secured for the Church, after so long a period of trials and tribulations, by the edict of Constantine the Great. During those months the continual demonstrations of filial devotion, so admirable and memorable, could not but greatly encourage Us; in them the Catholic world zealously strengthened its own faith and before troubled humanity held up the Cross of Christ as the only source of peace and salvation.

272. To-day more than ever they seek for peace, and indeed we see classes of citizens, races, nations fighting among themselves, and from the enmities ever becoming more intense among them we see break out sudden fearful wars. True, there are clever and distinguished statesmen who put before themselves the good of nations and indeed of human society, and seek by common agreement for the means of arresting the harm that comes from the strife of classes and the slaughters of war, and of securing within and without their borders the benefits of peace. These, without doubt, are excellent endeavors, but their counsels will bear little fruit, unless at the same time they can ensure that the precepts of justice and Christian charity are deeply rooted in souls. To-day peace or war in society and in the State do not depend so much on the governors as on the multitudes. Deprived of the light of truth revealed by God, unused to the discipline of the laws of Christ, what wonder if the multitudes, the prey of blind passions, rush to their common ruin, instigated by clever agitators who seek nothing but their own advantage? . . . . . .

EXHORTATION *Dum Europa Fere Omnis* TO THE CATHOLICS OF THE WHOLE WORLD.[22]

On the outbreak of the World War the Pope asks all Catholics to pray for peace.

August 2, 1914

273. While nearly all Europe is being dragged into the whirlpool of a most deadly war, of whose dangers, bloodshed and consequences no one can think without feeling oppressed with sorrow and alarm, We, too, cannot but be anxious and feel Our soul rent

[22] Translation from Schaefer, *A Papal Peace Mosaic*, pp. 16-17. Original Latin, *A.A.S* v. 6, p. 373 (August 3, 1914).

by the most bitter grief for the safety and for the lives of so many citizens and so many peoples for whose welfare We are supremely solicitous.

274. Amid this tremendous upheaval and danger We deeply feel and realize that Our fatherly charity and Our Apostolic Ministry demand of Us that We direct men's minds upward to Him from Whom alone help can come, to Christ, the Prince of Peace, and man's all-powerful Mediator with God. Therefore, We do exhort the Catholics of the whole world to turn, full of confidence, to His throne of grace and mercy, and let the clergy lead the way by their example and by appointing special prayers in their respective parishes, under the orders of the bishops, that God may be moved to pity and may remove as soon as possible the disastrous torch of war and inspire the supreme rulers of the nations with thoughts of peace and not of affliction.

PART THREE

BENEDICT XV

1914-1922

INTRODUCTION

THE OUTBREAK of the World War in 1914, involving millions of Catholics on both sides of the conflict, created an extremely delicate position for the Vicar of Christ, the Common Father of all. Under such circumstances, it was indeed fortunate that the saintly Pius X was succeeded by Giacomo Cardinal della Chiesa, Archbishop of Bologna, a veteran diplomat, keenly aware of the difficulties of his position.

The background of Benedict XV bears many resemblances to that of Leo XIII. Born in Genoa on November 21, 1854, della Chiesa was the son of a marquis, and it was at the suggestion of his father that he took up the study of law, obtaining the doctorate at the Royal University in 1875. Turning toward the priesthood, he enrolled at the Capranica College and the Gregorian University in Rome, and was ordained in 1878. After finishing his training for a diplomatic career at the Pontificia Accademia dei Nobili Ecclesiastici, in 1883 he was selected to go to Madrid as personal secretary to the newly-appointed Nuncio to Spain, Monsignor Rampolla. In 1887, when Leo XIII recalled Rampolla to make him Secretary of State, della Chiesa returned to Rome to work in the secretariate. After serving as Under-Secretary of State from 1901, he was appointed Archbishop of Bologna on December 16, 1907. He was created cardinal in May, 1914, and less than four months afterward was elected pope.

A tiny figure of unprepossessing appearance, Benedict XV had few consolations during the eight years of his pontificate; yet his dignity, his courage and firmness, in the face of bitter criticism and suspicion, won the tardy admiration of the world. Two principles of action guided him throughout the four years of the war: to maintain strict neutrality toward both belligerents and to promote peace by every available means. Assisted by an unusually gifted Secretary of State, Cardinal Gasparri, he explored every avenue for bringing about an early cessation of hostilities. Encouraged by the friendly reception given to his legate, Monsignor Pacelli, by the German Emperor, Benedict offered both Powers a basis for opening peace negotiations in 1917, but it was rejected.

Through the co-operation of neutral Switzerland, Benedict was instrumental in exchanging countless war prisoners on both sides and helped to promote better hospitalization for the wounded. Through his intercession, bereaved families of missing soldiers received definite information about the fate of their relatives.

After the war, the pope was excluded from participating in the peace settlement due to the Treaty of London, a secret arrangement made by Italy with Great Britain, France and Russia before Italy entered the struggle in 1915.

During Benedict's reign, diplomatic relations were renewed with France, and initiated with England, Holland, Finland, Poland, Czechoslovakia and Latvia.

An attack of influenza resulted in his death on January 22, 1922, and very soon he was completely forgotten. It is one of the ironies of history that it has taken another World War to reveal Benedict's accomplishments in their true historical perspective.

DOCUMENTS

EXHORTATION *Ubi Primum* TO THE CATHOLICS OF THE WHOLE WORLD.[1]

The Sovereign Pontiff is determined to neglect nothing to hasten the end of the war.

September 8, 1914

275. . . . But when We look from the height of this Apostolic See toward the Lord's flock committed to Our care, We are filled with horror and inexpressible grief by the sight of this war through which so great a part of Europe is reddened with Christian blood, devastated by fire and sword. From the Good Shepherd, Jesus Christ, Whose place We hold in the government of the Church, We have this very duty, that We embrace with the bowels of paternal love all the lambs and sheep of His flock. Inasmuch, then, as from the example of the Lord Himself, We must be—as indeed We are—ready to give even Our life itself for their salvation, We are firmly and deliberately determined to leave nothing that is in Our power undone to hasten the end of so great a calamity. Now, therefore—even before We address Encyclical Letters to all the bishops, as is the established custom of the Roman Pontiffs at the beginning of their Apostolate—We cannot refrain from repeating the last words of Our most saintly Predecessor, Pius X, worthy of immortal memory, spoken on his death-bed at the first thunder of war, out of his Apostolic solicitude and love of the human race. Wherefore, while We Ourselves will be suppliant before God with eyes and hands raised to Heaven, We exhort and pray all children of the Church, particularly those in Holy Orders, as Our Predecessor exhorted and urged them, that they insistently, in all ways possible, whether privately in humble prayer or publicly with solemn supplications, implore God, the Arbiter and Sovereign Master of all things, that mindful of His pity He may put away this scourge of His wrath with which He exacts of the people

[1] Translation from *The Tablet*, v. 124, pp. 435-436 (October 3, 1914). Original Latin, *A.A.S.*, v. 6, pp. 501-502 (September 17, 1914).

penance for their sins. And may you be assisted and protected
in your common prayers by the Virgin Mother of God whose most
blessed Nativity, celebrated this very day, has shone out like a
dawn-light of peace on an afflicted world—the Virgin who was to
give birth to Him in Whom the Eternal Father willed to reconcile
all things, *making peace through the blood of His cross, both as
to the things on earth and the things that are in heaven.*[2]

276. But We urgently implore and conjure those who rule the
affairs of peoples, that they now turn their minds to forget all
their own discords for the sake of the salvation of human society;
that they consider that already there is enough misery and trouble
in the life of men, that it should not be rendered for a long time
more miserable and troubled; that they be satisfied with the ruin
wrought, the human blood already shed; that they initiate councils
of peace and reconcile themselves; for thus will they truly deserve
well of God and of their own peoples, and will be benefactors of
the civil society of the nations. And for Us who see grave troubles
in the terrible disorganization of all things at this the very beginning of Our Apostolic Office, let them know that they will be doing
a thing most pleasing to Us and one which from all Our heart
We desire.

LETTER *C'Est avec un Intérêt* TO CARDINAL LUÇON, ARCH-
BISHOP OF RHEIMS.[3]

> *The Pope laments the spiritual and material damages
> of the war.*

October 16, 1914

277. . . . If it is a deep sorrow for Us that We have from the
beginning of Our Pontificate had to witness the sad events of the
present time, it is equally distressing to Us to have heard from you
a sorrowful echo, and to have to write to you for the first time in
circumstances and for reasons so little comforting. We have not
failed to follow with special attention the news of the grave events
of which Rheims, your episcopal see, has lately been the scene.
We are grateful to you for having given Us a detailed account of

---

[2] *Colossians,* I, 20.
[3] Translation from *The Tablet,* v. 124, p. 724 (November 28, 1914). Original French,
A.A.S., v. 6, p. 541 (November 9, 1914).

the facts set forth in all their exactitude. Be assured of the part We take in the deep sorrow caused you by the sight of so many evils, and by the thought of the dire consequences of the war from the point of view of religion and art, and also from the material point of view to your sorely tried diocese. . . .

LETTER *Gratum Equidem* TO CARDINAL VON HARTMANN, ARCH-BISHOP OF COLOGNE.[4]

The Holy Father is gratified to learn that French priests, prisoners of war, will be treated as officers.[5]

October 18, 1914

278. We have received from you the very welcome news that His Majesty, the German Emperor, acceding to your request, has determined that all French priests among the French soldiers now held as prisoners of war in Germany shall be treated strictly as officers. In this bitter time, when We see nearly all Europe laid waste by fire and sword and reddened with the blood of Christians, and when the terrible spectacle of this whole war fills Our mind with an indescribable sickness of heart, the news which you have recently given Us has afforded Us great consolation. For from this news We have seen with what zealous love your heart is enkindled towards those who are bound to you by the bond of the priesthood.

279. This, too, is Our firm conviction, that your great charity will embrace not only French clerics who are captives, but, so far as can be, all others, without distinction of religion or nationality, who are detained within your boundaries, and those especially who are afflicted with sickness or wounds, in order that their sufferings and ills may be alleviated and that provision may be made for their spiritual welfare. The duty of such charity, as is clearly evident, is common to all men; in a special way, however, is that duty incumbent upon the ministers of God and all other religious persons. Wherefore, We are confident that all indeed who glory in the name of Christian, particularly, however, Catholic bishops and priests, will imitate your shining example not in Germany only but in all other regions also where refugees, captives, and especially sick and wounded men are consumed with grief. . . .

[4] Original Latin, *A.A.S.*, v. 6, p. 542 (November 9, 1914).
[5] Priests were drafted into the French army as common soldiers.

ENCYCLICAL *Ad Beatissimi* ON WORLD WAR I.[6]

The bloody conflict produces deep sorrow in the heart of the Common Father of all nations. He analyzes the basic causes of the war and issues an earnest appeal for peace.

November 1, 1914

280. . . . . . . As soon, therefore, as We had looked, from the height of the Apostolic dignity, upon the direction in which human affairs were going, and had seen the lamentable state of civil society, We were filled with bitter sorrow. For how could it be that We, the Common Father of all, should not be pierced to the heart by the spectacle of Europe and the world—a spectacle perhaps the darkest and saddest in all human history? It seems as if the days foretold by Christ had indeed come: *You shall hear of wars and rumors of wars. For nation shall rise against nation, and kingdom against kingdom.*[7] The dread image of war overshadows the world, and absorbs nearly every thought. The strongest and wealthiest nations are in conflict. What wonder, then, that, furnished as they are with the latest weapons devised by military science, their struggle is causing enormous slaughter. There is no end to the ruin, no end to the deaths; each day sees the earth flowing with fresh blood, and covered with dead and wounded. Who would think that the nations, thus armed against each other, are all descended from one ancestor, share the same nature, belong to the same human family? Who could realize that they are brethren, children of the same Father in heaven? And while the mighty hosts are contending in the fury of combat, cities, families, individuals are being oppressed by those evils and miseries which follow at the heels of war; day by day the numbers increase of widows and orphans; the paths of commerce are blocked; the fields are left untilled; the arts are at a standstill; the rich are made poor, the poor still more destitute, all are made to mourn.

281. Shocked by so great evils, We have held it to be Our duty, at the very beginning of Our Supreme Pontificate, and as the first act of Our Apostolic Ministry, to take up and repeat the last

[6] Official English version, *A.A.S.,* v. 6, pp. 647-660 (November 25, 1914). Official Latin version, *A.A.S.,* v. 6, pp. 565-581 (November 18, 1914).
[7] *Matthew,* XXIV, 6-7.

words that fell from the lips of Our Predecessor — a Pontiff of illustrious and so holy memory; and, therefore, We earnestly beseech princes and rulers that, moved by the sight of so many tears, so much blood already shed, they delay not to bring back to their peoples the life-giving blessings of peace. When the divine Redeemer first appeared upon earth, the glad tidings were sung by angels' voice, so now, may God in His mercy grant that, at the beginning of Our labor as Christ's Vicar, the same voice be heard proclaiming: *Peace on earth to men of good will.*[8] We beg of those who hold in their hands the destinies of peoples, to give heed to that voice. If their rights have been violated, they can certainly find other ways and other means of obtaining a remedy; to these, laying aside the weapons of war, let them have recourse in sincerity of conscience, and good will. With no view to Our own self-interest do We speak thus, but in charity toward them and toward all nations. Let them not suffer Our voice of father and friend to pass away unheeded.

282. But it is not only the murderous struggle now going on that is ruining the nations, and filling Us with anxious alarm. There is another dreadful evil, which goes deep down in modern society, an evil that inspires fear in the minds of thoughtful men, because while it has already caused, and is threatening still to cause immense mischief to nations, it must also be recognized as the true source of the present deplorable conflict. Truly, as soon as the rules and dictates of Christian wisdom, which are the assured basis of stability and peace, came to be disregarded in the ordering of public life, the very structure of the State began to be shaken to its fall; and there has also ensued so great a change of thought and conduct, that, unless God comes to the rescue, the dissolution of human society itself would seem to be at hand. The more prominent disorders are these: the lack of mutual love among men; disregard for authority; unjust quarrels between the various classes; material prosperity become the absorbing object of human endeavor, as though there were nothing higher and better to be gained. These We regard as the four chief causes why the world is so terribly shaken. We must labor earnestly, therefore, by putting in practice Christian principles, to remove such disorders from our midst, if indeed we have at heart the common peace and welfare.

[8] *Luke*, II, 14.

283.   When Jesus Christ came from heaven for the very purpose of restoring the Kingdom of Peace, which had been ruined by the envy of Satan, He chose no other foundation for it than that of brotherly love. Hence those words of His so often repeated: *A new commandment I give unto you, that you love one another;*[9] *This is my commandment, that you love one another;*[10] *These things I command you, that you love one another;*[11] as though the whole scope and purpose of His coming were to make men love each other. To stimulate us to this love, what motives has He not set before us? He bids us to lift up our eyes to heaven: *For one is your Father, Who is in heaven.*[12] Setting aside every difference of race, of language and of interest, He puts the selfsame prayer on the lips of all: *Our Father Who art in heaven;*[13] He even teaches that the heavenly Father in bestowing nature's gifts, is not swayed by our deserving: *Who maketh His sun to rise upon the good and bad, and raineth upon the just and the unjust.*[14] He further declares that we are all brethren: *But all you are brethren;*[15] and brethren of Himself: *That he might be the first-born amongst many brethren.*[16] Then, what ought most powerfully to urge us to brotherly love, even towards those whom our natural pride would lead us to despise, He went so far as to identify Himself with the meanest of men, in whom He wished us to recognize His own personal dignity: *As long as you did it to one of these My least brethren, you did it to Me.*[17] What more? At the close of His life, He earnestly besought of the Father, that all who should believe in Him might be made one by the bond of charity: *As Thou Father in Me and I in Thee.*[18] Lastly, when hanging on the Cross, He poured out His blood upon us all, so that, as if compacted and joined together in one body, mutual love should be found amongst us, just as mutual sympathy is found amongst the members of the same body.

[9] *John*, XIII, 34.
[10] *John*, XV, 12.
[11] *John*, XV, 17.
[12] *Matthew*, XXIII, 9.
[13] *Matthew*, VI, 9.
[14] *Matthew*, V, 45.
[15] *Matthew*, XXIII, 8.
[16] *Romans*, VIII, 29.
[17] *Matthew*, XXV, 40.
[18] *John*, XVII, 21.

284. But in these times the conduct of men is far different. Never perhaps was human brotherhood more preached than now; nay, it is pretended that, without any help from the teaching of the Gospel, or from the work of Christ and the Church, the spirit of brotherhood has been one of the highest creations of modern civilization. Yet the truth is, that men never acted towards each other in less brotherly fashion than now. Race hatreds are becoming almost a frenzy; nation is divided from nation more by enmity and jealousy than by geographical position; in the same city, within the same walls, the different ranks are on fire with mutual envy; all take as their supreme law their own self-interest.

285. You see, Venerable Brethren, how necessary it is that no effort should be spared to bring back among men the power of the charity of Christ. This shall be Our constant endeavor, the chosen task of Our Pontificate; to this We exhort you to attend. Let us not grow weary of teaching and practicing the injunction of the Apostle, St. John: *That we love one another.*[19] Doubtless there are numerous benevolent institutions now doing useful and valuable work, but they do not prove to be of real benefit, unless they help in promoting a true love of God and our neighbor; without this they are worth nothing, for: *He that loveth not, abideth in death.*[20]

286. We have said that another cause of social disorder lies in this, that authority is generally disregarded. For as soon as human authority began to emancipate itself from God, the Creator and Master of the universe, and to seek its origin in man's free choice, the bonds between superiors and subjects were relaxed so that now they would almost seem not to exist. An unbridled spirit of independence, joined with pride, has gradually permeated everywhere, not sparing even the family, where nature itself discloses authority in the clearest light; what is more to be deplored, the evil has even reached the sanctuary. Hence, the contempt for law; hence, the insubordination of the masses; hence, the petulant criticism of the commands of authority; hence, the continual attempts to break its power; hence, the monstrous deeds of those who, making profession of anarchy, have no respect either for the property or the lives of others.

287. In the presence of this perversity of thought and deed—a

[19] I *John*, III, 23.
[20] I *John*, III, 14.

perversity destructive of all human society—We, to whom has been committed the guardianship of divine Truth, cannot be silent; and We admonish all of that doctrine which cannot be changed by man's will: *There is no power but from God; and those that are, are ordained of God.*[21] All power, therefore, whether of the sovereign or of subordinate authorities, comes from God. Wherefore St. Paul teaches the duty of obeying, not in any way, but for conscience' sake, those who have the rule over us, except when what is commanded is against the law of God: *Wherefore be subject of necessity, not only for wrath, but also for conscience' sake.*[22] In agreement with this are the words of the Prince of the Apostles: *Be ye subject, therefore, to every human creature for God's sake: whether it be to the king as excelling, or to governors as sent by Him.*[23] From this doctrine the same Apostle of the Gentiles draws the conclusion, that whoever is a rebel against lawful human authority, is a rebel against God, and prepares for himself eternal punishment: *Therefore, he that resisteth the power, resisteth the ordinance of God. And they that resist, purchase to themselves damnation.*[24]

288. Let princes and rulers of the peoples bear this in mind and bethink themselves whether it be wise and salutary that public authority should divorce itself from the holy Religion of Jesus Christ, in which it may find so powerful a support. Let them seriously consider whether it be politically wise to banish from public instruction the teaching of the Gospel and of the Church. Experience teaches only too well that where religion is absent public authority falls. It generally happens to States as it happened to our first parent after his failure in his duty to God. As in him, scarcely had the will been rebel to God when the passions broke loose and rebelled against the will; so, too, whenever those who have the rule over peoples disdain the authority of God, the peoples in their turn are prompt to hold lightly the authority of man. Certainly there remains the usual expedient of suppressing rebellion by violence; but where is the gain? Violence may subdue the body, it cannot conquer the will.

289. The double element of cohesion in the body social, that is,

[21] *Romans*, XIII, 1.
[22] *Romans*, XIII, 5.
[23] I *Peter*, II, 13-14.
[24] *Romans*, XIII, 2.

the union of the members among themselves by mutual charity, and the union of the members with the head by obedience to authority, being thus destroyed or weakened, what wonder, Venerable Brethren, that modern society should show itself as divided into two opposing forces struggling against each other fiercely, and without truce? Over against those who have happened to receive, or have industriously earned a certain amount of wealth, there are ranged a number of the indigent and of workers, inflamed with ill will, because, possessing the same human nature as those better off, they do not enjoy equal fortune. When once they have been deluded by the sophistries of demagogues, to whom they generally show themselves most submissive, who shall persuade them that, because men have equality of nature, it does not follow that they must have equality of rank in social life, but that each holds that position which, not frustrated by circumstances, he has gained for himself? When, therefore, the poor assail the rich, as though these had appropriated to themselves what belongs to others, they are acting not only against justice and charity, but even against reason, particularly because they themselves might better their own position by force of honorable labor.

290. It would be superfluous to point out the consequences, disastrous alike to individuals and to the community, that flow from this class hatred. We all know and deplore those frequent strikes by which the whole of public life, even in its most necessary activities, is suddenly checked; and then the riotous outbreaks in which recourse is frequently had to arms, and this followed by bloodshed.

291. We will not now repeat the arguments that show the untenableness of Socialism and similar errors. This has been done with supreme wisdom by Our Predecessor, Leo XIII, in his memorable Encyclicals; but We appeal to you, Venerable Brethren, to use your endeavors that that authoritative teaching be not forgotten; that by means of Catholic associations and congresses, of sermons and the Catholic Press, it be adequately explained and enforced, as circumstances may require. But, above all, and We do not hesitate to repeat it, let us make it our care, using every argument supplied by the Gospel, by reason and by public or private good, to stimulate all men to mutual brotherly love in accordance with the divine law of charity. This brotherly love does not set itself to sweep away all differences of rank and condition—this is no

more possible than it is possible in a living body that all the members should have the same place and function—but it has power to make those of a higher rank act toward those of a lower, not only with justice, as is indeed imperative, but also with good-will, and kindness, and consideration; and it makes those of a lower rank to be glad at the prosperity of others, and to have confidence in their readiness to help; just as in the same family the younger trust to the care and protection of the elder.

292. The evils We have just been deploring find their cause, Venerable Brethren, in a deeper root, and unless the good use their efforts to destroy it, We shall look in vain for the realization of Our desire for a solid and lasting peace among men. What that root is, the Apostle tells us: *The desire of money is the root of all evils.*[25] And to this root are indeed attributable all the evils now afflicting the world. When Godless schools, moulding as wax the tender hearts of the young, when an unscrupulous Press, continually playing upon the inexperienced minds of the multitude, when those other agencies that form public opinion, have succeeded in propagating the deadly error that man ought not to look for a happy eternity; that it is only here that happiness is to be found, in the riches, the honors, the pleasures of this life; it is not surprising that men, with their inextinguishable desire of happiness, should attack what stands in the way of that happiness with all the impelling force of their desire. But since earthly goods are unequally divided, and since it is the office of the State to prevent individuals seizing at their own will what belongs to others, it has come about that hatred has been engendered against the public authority, that envy of the more fortunate has taken hold of the less fortunate, and that the different classes of fellow-citizens are in open antagonism—those who have not, striving by every means to obtain, and the others, striving to keep what they have and to increase it.

293. Foreseeing these things, Christ our Lord, in the divine Sermon on the Mount, thought it good to explain what are man's true beatitudes even here on earth, and so to lay the foundations, as it were, of Christian philosophy. Men far removed from the Faith have yet seen in this teaching a supreme wisdom, and the most perfect form of religious and moral doctrine; and indeed, all agree that before Christ, Who is Truth itself, no one ever spoke

[25] I *Timothy,* VI, 10.

of these things as He has spoken, with such dignity, such power, and so exalted a sentiment of love.

,294. Now the deep and underlying thought of this divine philosophy is that the good things of this life have only the appearance without the reality of good, and so cannot bestow true happiness. In the truth of God's word, riches and pleasure are so far from bringing true happiness, that to secure true happiness we must rather renounce these things for the love of God. *Blessed are ye poor . . . Blessed are ye that weep now . . . Blessed shall you be when men shall hate you, and shall separate you, and shall reproach you, and cast out your name as evil.*[26] That is to say, if we bear patiently, as we ought, the sorrows, hardships and miseries of this life, we open for ourselves a way to the possession of those true and imperishable goods, *which God hath prepared for those who love Him.*[27] But this important teaching of the Faith is neglected by too many, and by not a few is altogether forgotten. It is for you, Venerable Brethren, to make this teaching live again amongst men; without it men and communities of men will never find peace. We urge, therefore, all who are suffering under any kind of hardship, not to keep their eyes fixed on earth, which is but a place of exile, but to lift them up to heaven, whither we are tending; for *we have not here a lasting city, but we seek one that is to come.*[28] In times of adversity, with which God tries the steadiness of their service, let them often reflect on the greatness of the reward when they have come victorious out of the struggle: *For that which is at present momentary and light of our tribulation, worketh for us above measure exceedingly an eternal weight of glory.*[29] Lastly, it should be one of your chief cares, Venerable Brethren, with all zeal and energy to make faith in the supernatural live again amongst men, and with faith the pursuit, the desire and the hope of what is eternal; for this work We ask the co-operation not only of the clergy, but of all those Catholics who, banded together in various societies, are laboring for God's honor and man's true good. The more this faith grows amongst men the more will the feverish pursuit of earthly vanities cease, and as charity grows strong, social conflicts and tumults will gradually die away.

[26] *Luke*, VI, 20-22.
[27] I *Corinthians*, II, 9.
[28] *Hebrews*, XIII, 14.
[29] II *Corinthians*, IV, 17.

295. . . . . . . And now, Venerable Brethren, at the close of this letter, Our mind goes back spontaneously to the thought of peace with which We began; We pray with unceasing prayer for the good of men and of the Church that this disastrous war may cease; for the good of men, so that by the bringing back of peace they may go forward on the path of true progress; for the good of Christ's Church, that it may be left unhindered to bear help and salvation to every part of the world. Too long has the Church been curtailed of its necessary freedom of action, ever since the Head of the Church, the Supreme Pontiff, began to lack that defense of his freedom which the Providence of God had raised up during the course of centuries. The loss of that protection has inevitably caused no light anxiety in the Catholic body; for all the children of the Roman Pontiff, whether near or living afar, have a right not to be left in doubt concerning the possession by their common Father of a true and undeniable freedom in the exercise of his Apostolic Ministry.

296. While We pray for the speedy return of peace to the world, We also pray that an end be put to the abnormal state in which the Head of the Church is placed—a state which in many ways is an impediment to the common tranquillity. Our Predecessors have protested, not from self-interest, but from a sense of sacred duty, against this state of things; those protests We renew, and for the same reason—to protect the rights and dignity of the Apostolic See.

297. It remains for us, Venerable Brethren, to lift up our voices in prayer to God, in Whose hands are the hearts of princes, and of all responsible for the continuance of the scourges now afflicting us, and to cry in the name of all mankind: *Give peace, O Lord, in our days.* And may He, who said of Himself: *I am the Lord . . . I make peace,*[30] be moved by our prayers, and speedily still the tempest now tossing civil and religious society. And may the Blessed Virgin be mercifully at hand to assist us—she who bore the Prince of Peace; may she regard and protect with a mother's love Us in Our lowliness, Our Pontificate, the Church, and with the Church the souls of all men redeemed by the divine Blood of her Son. . . .

[30] *Isaias,* XLV, 6-7.

LETTER *Ex Quo Pontificatum* TO ARCHBISHOP DOBRECIC OF ANTIVARI.[31]

The Pope exhorts Archbishop Dobrecic to care for the spiritual and material needs of the prisoners in his archdiocese.

November 8, 1914

298. Ever since We were raised to the Pontificate We have tried, according to the measure of Our forces, to bring about some alleviation of the troubles produced by this enormous war. With this aim We, as you know, recently sent to Our beloved son, Cardinal Felix von Hartmann, Archbishop of Cologne, a letter, in which We not only paid him a tribute of praise for having asked and obtained from the Emperor of Germany that the French priests made prisoners should be treated according to their dignity, but further warmly exhorted him to procure that all prisoners, without distinction of religion, nationality, or condition, and especially the sick and wounded among them, should be treated according to all the dictates of charity. And now We also wish that you do the same with all your strength, seeing that there opens before you, Venerable Brother, a field not dissimilar in which you may exercise your pity. Following, then, the charity of Christ, Who *went about doing good and healing all,*[32] exert yourself with all love to help those soldiers who are being held as prisoners of war near you, and especially those who, by reason of the wounds they have received, or their broken health, have the best claim on the greater part of your solicitude. We have, indeed, no doubt but that those at the head of affairs in your kingdom, following the law of nations and at the same time the voice of humanity, are disposed to treat with clemency and kindness those most unfortunate men, and when you, Venerable Brother, add your efforts to theirs, far better provision will be made for the grievous necessities of the case. In order that this desirable end may be achieved, and as a pledge of heavenly favors and a proof of Our affection, We impart the Apostolic Benediction to you, to your clergy and to your people.

---

[31] Translation from *The Tablet,* v. 124, p. 703 (November 21, 1914). Original Latin, *A.A.S.,* v. 6, p. 546 (November 9, 1914).
[32] *Acts,* X, 38.

LETTER OF CARDINAL GASPARRI, SECRETARY OF STATE, TO CAR-
DINAL AMETTE, ARCHBISHOP OF PARIS, AND CARDINAL BOURNE,
ARCHBISHOP OF WESTMINSTER.[33]

Negotiations for a truce on Christmas.[34]

November 26, 1914

299.   The Holy Father intends to ask the leaders of the belligerent States to suspend hostilities at least throughout the day of next
December 25, the Feast of Christmas, as an act of faith and of
Christian piety towards Our Lord Jesus Christ, come into the world
to give glory to God and to bring peace to men.

300.   As is quite natural, before formulating such a demand,
His Holiness is desirous of knowing just in what way such a
proposal would be received by each and every one of the respective
Governments. Consequently, with regard to your country, I would
be grateful to Your Eminence if you would find out, by whatever
confidential way your tact may suggest, if and to what extent the
Government would be willing to accept this noble proposal of the
Holy Father, with the understanding, of course, that it would be
accepted by all the other States. . . .

LETTER *Cum de Fidelibus* TO CARDINAL MERCIER, ARCHBISHOP
OF MALINES.[35]

*The compassion of the Holy Father for those suffering
in Belgium.*

December 8, 1914

301.   The fatherly solicitude which We feel for all the faithful
whom Divine Providence has entrusted to Our care, causes Us to

---

[33] Original French, *L'Opera della Santa Sede*, p. 31.
[34] This was "a project that met with sympathy 'in principle' from Great Britain, Belgium and Germany, but refusal from France (for alleged military reasons) and
from Russia (objecting the different date of the Orthodox Christmas and distrust
of Germany)." Cited from Rope, *Benedict XV, the Pope of Peace*, p. 70.
[35] Translation from *The Tablet*, v. 125, p. 42 (January 9, 1915). Original Latin,
A.A.S., v. 6, pp. 668-669 (December 9, 1914). Similar documents, not included in
this book, concerning Belgium are: Letter of Cardinal Gasparri to the Apostolic
Nuncio, December 10, 1914 (*L'Opera della Santa Sede*, p. 198). Letter of Cardinal
Gasparri to Countess Felice De Merode, June 7, 1915 (*op. cit.*, p. 208). Letter of
Cardinal Gasparri to the Apostolic Nuncio, August 17, 1915 (*op. cit.*, p. 212). Letter of Cardinal Gasparri to the Belgian Minister, December 20, 1915 (*op. cit.*, p.
221). Letter of Cardinal Gasparri to the Duchess of Vendome, December 20, 1915
(*op. cit.*, p. 222).

share their griefs even more fully than their joys. Could We, then, fail to be moved by keenest sorrow at the sight of the Belgian nation, which We so dearly love, reduced by a most cruel and most disastrous war to this lamentable state.

302. We behold the King and his august family, the members of the Government, the chief persons of the country, bishops, priests, and whole people enduring evils which must fill with pity all gentle hearts, and which Our own soul, in the fervor of parental love, must be the first to compassionate. Thus, under the burden of this distress and this mourning, We call in Our prayers for an end to such misfortunes. May the God of mercy hasten the day! Meanwhile We strive to mitigate, as far as in Us lies, this excessive suffering. Therefore, the step taken by Our dear son, Cardinal Hartmann, Archbishop of Cologne, at whose request it was arranged that French or Belgian priests detained in Germany should have the treatment of officers, gave Us great satisfaction, and We have expressed Our thanks to him for his action.

303. As regards Belgium, We have been informed that the faithful of that nation, so sorely tried, did not neglect, in their piety, to turn towards Us their thoughts, and that even under the blow of so many calamities they proposed to gather this year, as in all preceding years, the offerings of St. Peter, which supply the necessities of the Apostolic See. This truly incomparable proof of piety and of attachment filled Us with admiration; We accept it with all the affection that is due from a grateful heart; but having regard to the painful position in which Our dear children are placed, We cannot bring Ourselves to favor the fulfillment of that project, noble though it is. If any alms are to be gathered, Our wish is that the money should be entirely devoted to the succor of the Belgian people, who are as illustrious by reason of their nobility and their piety as they are today worthy of all sympathy. Amid the difficulties and anxieties of the present hour We would remind the sons who are so dear to Us that the *Arm of God is not shortened, that He is ever able to save, that His Ear is not deaf to prayer.*[36]

304. Let the hope of Divine aid increase with the approach of the festival of Christmas and of the mysteries that celebrate the birth of our Lord, and recall that peace which God proclaimed to mankind by His angels. May the souls of the suffering and afflicted

[36] *Isaias,* LIX, 1.

find comfort and consolation in the assurance of the paternal tenderness that prompts Our prayers. Yes, may God take pity upon the Belgian people, and grant them the abundance of all good. As a pledge of these prayers and good wishes, We now grant to all, and in the first place to you, Our dear son, the Apostolic Benediction.

DECREE OF MONSIGNOR PACELLI, SECRETARY OF THE SACRED CONGREGATION OF EXTRAORDINARY ECCLESIASTICAL AFFAIRS.[37]

The Bishops and the clergy are exhorted to care for the spiritual and material welfare of war prisoners in their countries.

December 21, 1914

305. Our Holy Father, Benedict XV, by Divine Providence Pope, sharing keenly in the trials of the unhappy and most numerous prisoners of war, and in the anxieties which weigh upon so many families left entirely without news of those dear to them, and desiring to render all the aid and comfort he possibly can to both classes, on the report of the Secretary of the S. Congregation of Extraordinary Ecclesiastical Affairs, confident that on the one hand, the episcopate and clergy will give generous and exact effect to his prescriptions, and that, on the other, the civil Governments will render valid and efficacious co-operation to his humane and merciful undertaking, prescribes:

(1) The Most Reverend Ordinaries of the dioceses in which the prisoners are shall designate immediately one or more priests, according to necessity, possessing a sufficient knowledge of the prisoners' languages, and should there be none such in their own dioceses, shall ask them of other Most Reverend Ordinaries, who shall solicitously hasten to supply them.

(2) These priests shall with all zeal seek the spiritual and material welfare of the prisoners, doing everything in their power to comfort and assist them in the various and often painful necessities in which they are.

(3) Especially, the priests shall ascertain whether the prisoners entrusted to their care have written or in some way sent news of

---

[37] Translation from *Rome*, v. 17, p. 162 (April 3, 1915). Original Latin, *A.A.S.*, v. 6, pp. 710-711 (December 30, 1914).

themselves to their families, and if not shall persuade them to do so at once, at least by post cards.

(4)   When prisoners are unable, either through illiteracy, or sickness, or for any other reason, to correspond in this way with their families, the priests themselves, shall charitably undertake to do so for them and in their name, and at the same time do what they can to ensure the safe delivery of the correspondence.

CARDINAL GASPARRI, SECRETARY OF STATE, TRANSMITS THE DECREE OF THE SACRED CONGREGATION OF EXTRAORDINARY ECCLESIASTICAL AFFAIRS TO ALL THE CARDINALS.[38]

In the spiritual and corporal care of prisoners, no distinction of religion, nationality or language should be made.

December 22, 1914

306.   The August Pontiff, Benedict XV, greatly afflicted by the evils caused everywhere by the present enormous war, has been graciously pleased to turn once more his benevolent and affectionate attention to the prisoners of war and, in his fatherly charity, to provide in some way for their spiritual and corporal welfare, issued yesterday through the S. Congregation of Extraordinary Ecclesiastical Affairs a decree some copies of which I hasten to transmit to Your Eminence.[39] . . . . . .

307.   I think it needless to add that in speaking of prisoners in the decree His Holiness wishes that no distinction be made either of religion, nationality or language, but if Your Eminence should deem it opportune, kindly, when transmitting the decree to the different bishops, make known to them the Holy Father's intention, so that the good work of the priests indicated in the decree may include all the unfortunate prisoners with the same embrace of the charity of Jesus Christ. . . .

[38] Translation from *Rome*, v. 16, p. 88 (December 26, 1914). Original Italian, Müller, *Das Friedenswerk der Kirche*, p. 428.
[39] A paragraph of the original Italian, which has no special importance, was not translated by the editor of *Rome*.

ALLOCUTION *Di Accogliere* TO THE COLLEGE OF CARDINALS.[40]

Despite many disappointments, Benedict XV will continue to work for peace.

December 24, 1914

308. . . . . . . We could not forget that We were come to continue the work of Jesus Christ, Prince of Peace, described in the prophecies as He in Whose days should come at last the sun of justice and the abundance of peace. Remembering, then, Our more than human mission both in public and private, We left no way untried that the counsel, the desire, the necessity of peace should be fully recognized. It was indeed with this scope that there came to Our mind the proposal to pierce this darkness of warring death with at least a ray, one single ray, of the Divine sun of peace, and We thought of suggesting to the fighting nations a truce, short indeed and limited, for Christmas, nourishing the hope that while We could not dissipate the black gloom of war, it might be given Us at least to bring one healing balm to the wounds it inflicts. Ah, the dear hope that We had cherished of consoling so many mothers and so many wives with the certainty that in the few hours consecrated to the memory of the Divine Birthday their dear ones would not have fallen under the enemy's lead; ah, the dear illusion that We held of giving once more to the world at least a taste of that peaceful quiet which for so many months now it has not known! Our Christian initiative was not, however, crowned with happy success. Still, We are not discouraged by this, and We intend to put forth every effort to hasten the end of the unparalleled scourge, or at least to alleviate its miserable consequences.

309. It seems to Us that the Divine Spirit says to Us as once to the Prophet: *Clama ne cesses,*[41] *Clama ne cesses,* and We have cried, not without hope of success, for the exchange of prisoners rendered unfit for further military service. *Clama ne cesses,* and We have asked that to the poor prisoners of war should be given priests who know their language, to bring them those comforts of which they have need, and at the same time offer themselves as willing intermediaries between them and their families who

[40] Translation from Schaefer, *A Papal Peace Mosaic,* pp. 19-20. Original Italian, *A.A.S.,* v. 6, pp. 695-696 (December 30, 1914).
[41] *Isaias,* LVIII, 1.

might be worn out and afflicted by lack of news. *Clama ne cesses,* and We praise the reverend pastors and single individuals who have determined to promote or multiply public or private prayers to do sweet violence to the Most Sacred Heart of Jesus to obtain that an end may come to the terrible scourge which now grips and throttles such a great part of the world.

310. Ah! may the fratricidal weapons fall to the ground! Already they are too bloodstained: let them at last fall! And may the hands of those who have had to wield them return to the labors of industry and commerce, to the works of civilization and peace. Ah! may at least today the rulers and the peoples hear the angelic voice which announces the superhuman gift of the King Who is born, "the Gift of Peace," and themselves too, by works of justice, faith and clemency show that "Good Will" which is laid down by God as the condition for the enjoyment of the peace. . . . . . .

LETTER OF CARDINAL GASPARRI, SECRETARY OF STATE, TO CARDINAL SEVIN, ARCHBISHOP OF LYONS.[42]

The Holy See remains officially neutral in regard to the war.

December 24, 1914

311. I have received the letter which Your Eminence has done me the honor to send me on November 10, and I hastened to present it to the Holy Father. The Sovereign Pontiff also could not help feeling the same unpleasant impression on reading the second part of this missive, and he charges me to make known to you the pain it has caused him. Your Eminence is not unaware that from the beginning of the present war the Holy See, embracing with the same solicitude the pastors and the faithful of the Universal Church, set itself to observe, and has constantly observed, the strictest and most absolute impartiality towards the different belligerent nations, and has peremptorily enjoined it on the Catholic Press, and especially that of Rome. I can assure you that this direction and these counsels of the Holy See, both by the *Osservatore Romano,* which is immediately under its direction, and by

---

[42] Translation from *The Tablet,* v. 125, p. 20 (January 2, 1915). We have been unable to locate the original of this letter.

the *Corriere d'Italia,* the principal organ of the Società Editrice, have been scrupulously followed. Meanwhile, we are ready to communicate to Your Eminence all the documents you may desire proving this affirmation. Your Eminence will dispense me from citing the provincial papers which escape the immediate superintendence of the Holy See, and the responsibility for which can in no way be attributed to it. But with regard to these, too, I can assure you that they have not failed to abide by the above-mentioned directions, especially after some few instances in which they have been reminded of their duty. As for the assertion that prelates in Rome have not paid heed to the recommendations of the Holy See, this is not in harmony with the truth, and it would be very difficult for Your Eminence to give us the name of a single prelate who has published anything hostile to France. But we know the source of the calumnies which are diffused in France, and to which, it is painful to have to admit, too much faith is given even by Catholics themselves. His Holiness earnestly desires Your Eminence to give the widest possible publicity to this letter in order to enlighten and instruct the public mind and Catholic opinion, and to dissipate the calumnies and biased news which have been circulated in the past, or may be circulated in the future, as to the attitude of the Holy See in the present grave contingencies.

TELEGRAM OF BENEDICT XV TO THEIR MAJESTIES, THE SOVEREIGNS OF AUSTRIA-HUNGARY, BAVARIA, BELGIUM, GERMANY, ENGLAND, RUSSIA AND SERBIA.[43]

The Pope asks the sovereigns of the belligerent nations to exchange war prisoners incapable of further military service.

December 31, 1914

312. Confident in the feelings of Christian charity which animate Your Majesty, We pray that it may please Your Majesty to

---

[43] Original French, *L'Opera della Santa Sede,* p. 42. Similar appeals for exchange of prisoners incapable of military service, not included in this volume, are: Telegram of Benedict XV to Mohammed V, Emperor of Turkey, December 31, 1914 (*L'Opera della Santa Sede,* p. 45). Telegram of Benedict XV to Nicholas I, King of Montenegro, January 1, 1915 (*op. cit.,* p. 46). Telegram of Benedict XV to M. Raymond Poincaré, President of France, January 4, 1915 (*op. cit.,* p. 46). Telegram of Benedict XV to Yoshihito, Emperor of Japan, January 9, 1915 (*op. cit.,* p. 47). Letter of Cardinal Gasparri, Secretary of State, to the Ambassador of Austria-Hungary, December 21, 1914 (*op. cit.,* p. 48).

close this fatal year and to begin well the new by an act of sovereign generosity, in receiving Our proposal that the belligerent nations exchange prisoners incapable of further military service.

DECREE *La Santità di N. Signore* OF CARDINAL GASPARRI, SECRETARY OF STATE.[44]

The Holy Father composes a special prayer for peace.

January 10, 1915

313. His Holiness, our sovereign Lord, Pope Benedict XV, in deep affliction at the sight of a war which destroys thousands of young lives, brings misery to families and cities, and rushes flourishing nations to the brink of ruin, yet bearing in mind that Almighty God, Whose prerogative it is to heal by chastisement and through pardon to preserve, is moved by the prayers which spring from contrite and humble hearts, desires ardently that above the clang of arms may be heard the voice of Faith, Hope and Charity, alone capable of welding together the hearts of men in one mind and one spirit. Therefore, while he exhorts the clergy and the faithful of the whole world to works of mortification and piety in expiation for the sins by which we have called down upon ourselves the just wrath of God, the Holy Father has ordained that throughout the Catholic Church solemn prayers shall be offered in order to obtain from the mercy of Almighty God the peace which all desire. . . . . . .

314. *The Special Prayer Ordered by the Pope Is as Follows:*

Dismayed by the horrors of a war which is bringing ruin to peoples and nations, we turn, O Jesus, to Thy most loving Heart as to our last hope. O God of Mercy, with tears we invoke Thee to end this fearful scourge; O King of Peace, we humbly implore the peace for which we long. From Thy Sacred Heart, Thou didst shed forth over the world divine Charity, so that discord might end and love alone might reign among men. During Thy life on earth Thy Heart beat with tender compassion for the sorrows of men; in this hour made terrible with burning hate, with

[44] Authentic English version, *A.A.S.,* v. 7, pp. 12-14 (January 15, 1915). Original Italian, *A.A.S.,* v. 7, pp. 8-10 (January 15, 1915).

bloodshed and with slaughter, once more may Thy Divine Heart be moved to pity. Pity the countless mothers in anguish for the fate of their sons; pity the numberless families now bereaved of their fathers; pity Europe over which broods such havoc and disaster. Do Thou inspire rulers and peoples with counsels of meekness; do Thou heal the discords that tear the nations asunder; Thou Who didst shed Thy Precious Blood that they might live as brothers, bring men together once more in loving harmony. And as once before to the cry of the Apostle, Peter: *Save us, Lord, we perish,*[45] Thou didst answer with words of mercy and didst still the raging waves, so now deign to hear our trustful prayer, and give back to the world peace and tranquillity. And do thou, O most holy Virgin, as in other times of sore distress, be now our help, our protection and our safeguard. Amen.

LETTER OF CARDINAL GASPARRI, SECRETARY OF STATE, TO THE AMBASSADORS OF AUSTRIA-HUNGARY, BAVARIA, BELGIUM, ENGLAND, PRUSSIA AND RUSSIA.[46]

The Pope requests all belligerent nations to free captured civilians unfit for military service.

January 11, 1915

315. The undersigned Cardinal Secretary of State has the honor of informing His Excellency . . . that the Holy See, recognizing

---

[45] *Matthew,* VIII, 25.

[46] Original French, *L'Opera della Santa Sede,* p. 50. Similar documents, not included in this book, concerning exchange of civilians between the belligerents are: Letter of Cardinal Gasparri to the Minister of England, January 13, 1915 (*L'Opera della Santa Sede,* p. 52). Letter of Cardinal Gasparri to the Minister of Russia, February 18, 1915 (*op. cit.,* p. 56). Letter of Cardinal Gasparri to the Minister of Prussia, February 22, 1915 (*op. cit.,* p. 57). Letter of Cardinal Gasparri to the Minister of Prussia, March 2, 1915 (*op. cit.,* p. 58). Letter of Cardinal Gasparri to the Minister of England, March 2, 1915 (*op. cit.,* p. 59). Letter of Cardinal Gasparri to the Minister of England, March 6, 1915 (*op. cit.,* p. 60). Letter of Cardinal Gasparri to the Minister of England, May 1, 1915 (*op. cit.,* p. 61). Letter of Cardinal Gasparri to the Minister of Prussia, May 6, 1915 (*op. cit.,* p. 62). Letter of Cardinal Gasparri to the Minister of England, May 30, 1915 (*op. cit.,* pp. 64-65). Letter of Cardinal Gasparri to the Minister of Prussia, July 3, 1915 (*op. cit.,* p. 65). Telegram of Cardinal Gasparri to the Minister of Prussia, August 9, 1915 (*op. cit.,* p. 69). Letter of Cardinal Gasparri to the Minister of Prussia, August 25, 1915 (*op. cit.,* pp. 70-71). There are many similar documents given in the book, *L'Opera della Santa Sede,* but these few will suffice to illustrate the indefatigable activity of the Vatican regarding the exchange of civilians.

the favorable reception given to its first proposal in favor of military prisoners, is confident that the benevolence of the sovereigns and the chiefs of State will wish to extend it equally to detained civilians. To this end, the Holy See asks each and every belligerent nation to grant the following categories of interned civilians freedom to return to their own country, save a few exceptions which each Government may believe necessary:

(1) All women and young girls.

(2) All children and young people under the age of seventeen years.

(3) All adults over the age of fifty-five years.

(4) All adults who have not passed the age of fifty-five years but who are:

    a) doctors or surgeons,

    b) priests,

    c) known to be unfit for military service either through sickness or for any other reason.

LETTER OF CARDINAL GASPARRI, SECRETARY OF STATE, TO REV. J. T. ROCHE, PRIEST OF THE ROCKFORD DIOCESE.[47]

Benedict XV wishes the American Catholic Press to co-operate in promoting a Christian peace.

January 18, 1915

316. There will still be vividly fresh in the soul of Your Reverence the sweet impression, produced by the sovereign benevolence, with which the Holy Father, a few days ago, vouchsafed to receive you in private audience and to accede to the desire manifested by you for a few encouraging words for the Catholic Press of the United States at the opening of the new year.

317. This greeting, which Your Reverence has had the singular good fortune to hear from the very lips of the August Pontiff and which I, by the venerable charge entrusted to me by His Holiness,

---

[47] Translation from *Rome*, v. 17, pp. 43-44 (January 23, 1915). We have been unable to locate the original of this document. Rev. Joseph Thomas Roche, a priest of the Rockford, Ill. (U.S.A.) diocese, was the correspondent of several Catholic journals in this country. Knowing that the Catholic Press of the United States heartily seconded the peace efforts of Benedict XV, he asked the Pope to give the Catholic Press a few words of encouragement at the beginning of the new year. This letter, written by Cardinal Gasparri, was the answer to his request.

have today the pleasure of presenting to you, may be summarized in the expression of those sentiments of charity and peace, of which Benedict XV, faithful to his Apostolic mission, has made me the mouthpiece.

318. Father of all the faithful, supreme and loving head of all mankind, the Pontiff deplores the misfortunes wrought by this fearful struggle and, not being able to quench at once the fire which is devouring the blinded brethren, feels in his heart all the pain of the orphans, the widows, the mothers, the families made desolate; he hears the lamentations of the prisoners, the groans of the wounded and he, first of all, bears on his shoulders the sorrows of the whole human race.

319. But all this tribulation, far from discouraging, stimulates and renders fruitful the charitable action of the August Pontiff, who does not cease to try in every way to bring comfort to the afflicted.

320. And if on this earth so many difficulties oppose themselves to the work of the Angel of Charity, he raises suppliant hands to heaven and he earnestly desires that the eyes of all the faithful be turned to heaven, praying that the God of Mercy, the Prince of Peace, may renew in men's hearts the sentiments of fraternal charity and inspire in rulers an efficacious desire for peace.

ALLOCUTION *Convocare Vos* TO THE COLLEGE OF CARDINALS.[48]

> *The Pope is disappointed at the prolongation of the war. He scores every violation of justice and condemns all unnecessary violence.*

January 22, 1915

321. ...... But at the outset, Venerable Brethren, in seeing you assembled here who by the special bond which unites you to Us have so close a part in Our thoughts and solicitudes, We cannot refrain from again telling you of the anguish which, as you know, weighs so heavily upon Our heart. Alas, month follows month without a gleam of even a distant hope that we shall soon see the end of this fatal war, this awful massacre. If We have not been able

[48] Translation from *The Tablet*, v. 125, pp. 156-157 (January 30, 1915). Original Latin, *A.A.S.*, v. 7, pp. 33-36 (January 22, 1915).

to hasten the end of this dreadful scourge, We have at least been able to alleviate its deplorable consequences. We have, as you are aware, done all that was in Our power up till now, and We shall not fail to use Our efforts in the future as long as it may be necessary.

322. To do more to-day is not in the power given Us by Our Apostolic charge. To proclaim that for no reason is it allowable to injure justice is assuredly a duty that belongs to the Sovereign Pontiff, who is the divinely authorized supreme interpreter of the eternal law. And that We proclaim without waste of words, denouncing all injustice on whatever side it has been committed. But it would be neither proper nor useful to entangle the pontifical authority in the disputes between the belligerents.

323. It is, for every thinking man, abundantly clear that in this frightful conflict the Holy See, whilst unceasingly watching it with the closest attention, must preserve the most absolute neutrality. The Roman Pontiff, as, on the one hand, the Vicar of Jesus Christ Who died for all and each, and on the other, as the Common Father of Catholics, must embrace all the combatants in the same sentiment of charity. He has on both the belligerent sides a great number of sons for whose salvation he must have an equal solicitude. He must accordingly consider not the special interests which divide them, but the common bond of faith that makes them brothers. Any other attitude on his part not only would not assist the cause of peace, but would, what is worse, create a lack of sympathy with and hatred against religion and expose the tranquillity and internal concord of the Church to grave disturbances.

324. But, whilst not inclining to either party in the struggle, We occupy Ourselves equally on behalf of both; and at the same time We follow with anxiety and anguish the awful phases of this war and even fear that sometimes the violence of attack exceeded all measure. We are struck with the respectful attachment to the Common Father of the faithful; an example of which is seen in regard to Our beloved people of Belgium in the letter which We recently addressed to the Cardinal Archbishop of Malines.

325. And We here make an appeal to the humanity of those who have crossed the frontiers of adversary nations and beseech them not to devastate invaded regions more than is strictly required by the necessities of military occupation, and what is of even greater importance, not to wound without real necessity the in-

habitants in what they hold most dear, their sacred temples, the ministers of God, the rights of religion and of faith. We fully understand how hard it is for those whose country is occupied by the enemy to find themselves forced under the yoke of the foreigner, but We would not have the ardent desire of recovering their independence induce them to disturb the maintenance of public order and so seriously aggravate their own position.

326. For the rest, Venerable Brethren, we ought not, in the midst of the great and heavy sorrows which press upon us, to lose courage; the darker the future seems, the greater should be the confidence with which *we approach the throne of grace to obtain mercy and find grace in seasonable aid.*[49]

327. We must, therefore, as We have already ordered, address instant and humble prayers to the Lord Who is the Master and Sovereign Arbiter of human affairs and Who alone can, as He thinks best, direct the wills of man. We do not think that peace departed from the world without the Will of God. The nations which have placed all their thoughts on the things of this world are permitted by God to punish each other by slaughter for the disrespect and negligence with which they have treated Him, and other happenings befall to compel men to humble themselves *under the mighty Hand of God.*[50]

328. Of such a sort is the catastrophe of these last days, the horrible devastation of which we all know. And that is the reason, since prayer in common is the most pleasing to God and the most fruitful, that We call upon all men of good will to propitiate the Divine mercy, by personal prayer, and, above all, by taking part in the public prayers in the churches. In order that an immense chorus of suppliant voices may rise to heaven, We have prescribed two solemn ceremonies of expiation, one for the Catholics of Europe on February 7, and the other for the rest of the Catholic world on March 21. We have decided to assist at the first in St. Peter's, and We are sure that you, Venerable Brethren, will not fail to take part in it along with Us.

329. May the Blessed Virgin, the Help of Christians, hearken to and strengthen the prayers of the Church. May her intercession obtain from her Divine Son that men's minds may return to the

---

[49] *Hebrews,* IV, 16.
[50] I *Peter,* V, 6.

worship of the truth, their souls to that of justice, and may the peace of Christ return to the world and establish its dwelling amongst men. . . .

LETTER *Opinionem Quam Habebamus* TO ARCHBISHOP LIKOWSKI OF GNESEN.[51]

The Holy Father laments the miserable condition of Poland.

February 1, 1915

330. . . . And what you have related to Us in the aforesaid letters concerning the miseries of Poland is indeed such that, although it had already been otherwise ascertained by Us, it has nevertheless filled Our heart with no common sadness.

331. For, as We have long known that the illustrious citizens of Poland have always been firm in their adhesion both to the Church of God and to this Apostolic See, We have indeed extended to them, as is fitting, Our benevolence and love. For this reason, as joy and sadness are shared in common by father and sons, in no wise can it be that We, surrounded with griefs and difficulties, are not affected by the greatest sorrow owing to the calamities whereby, during this most cruel war, the inhabitants of Poland are so shockingly tortured. And, whilst We turn Our mind and heart to them with paternal charity, how many tears start to Our eyes! All these things so vehemently stir Our inmost and secret feelings, that We feel the charity of the Father toward children so grievously harassed, increased in the highest degree. Therefore, to the eternal Author of all consolations We commend exceedingly the citizens of Poland, to Us indeed most dear, and We earnestly beseech Him at length to restrain the fury of war and propitiously and with good-will to grant the peace most earnestly desired and the choicest fruits of peace. These Our desires may God regard and prosper and may He in His highest clemency be pleased to turn to good for the Poles whatsoever evils they have suffered and are still suffering. But do you, Venerable Brother, and the other Bishops of Poland, continue to do what pastoral love can devise

---

[51] Translation from *Rome*, v. 17, pp. 140-141 (March 20, 1915). Original Latin, *A.A.S.*, v. 7, pp. 91-92 (February 27, 1915).

and to display all solicitude and care for each one of your flock; and strive with all your strength by your aid to mitigate the sufferings of your children, to alleviate their sorrows, to dry their tears. And We are led to cherish good hopes that, by the intercession of the Blessed Virgin, patroness of Poland, the God of all prosperity will open to the Poles and benignantly pour out upon them the treasures of His gifts. May these be guaranteed and secured by the Apostolic Benediction which . . . We impart very lovingly in the Lord.

LETTER *Quod Erat* TO BISHOP HEYLEN OF NAMUR.[52]

Deep papal sympathy for Belgium.

February 4, 1915

332. What We have already known about the sad state to which, in general, the Belgian hopes and Belgian affairs have been miserably reduced by the terrible and bitter war, has been confirmed by your recent official letters in connection with a specific case, namely the diocese of Namur, so dear to Us. What you have told Us, though, is enough to afflict anyone with the greatest sorrow. What, then, shall be said of Our feelings, of Us who carry the burden of fatherhood, and by that fact feel worry and care for the well-being and care of Our children? But if the pity and love of a parent brings much comfort to the children who are suffering, then there is reason for you and your flock to be comforted and consoled; for We have been, and do not cease to be, sharers of all the hardships and difficulties by which We see you so grievously oppressed, and We extend to you Our special good will and love. Consequently, nothing would be more preferable to Us than finally to see the end of so great, so terrible a scourge. Therefore, We earnestly commend to God, Who alone is omnipotent, all these sons of Ours who mourn, especially the citizens of the distinguished Belgian nation, fervently praying that with His grace the day of that most desired peace may soon begin to break, and that He in His mercy will deign propitiously to give the ripest and best fruit of peace especially to you who have endured so much. . . .

---

[52] Original Latin, *L'Opera della Santa Sede,* pp. 176-177.

LETTER OF CARDINAL GASPARRI, SECRETARY OF STATE, TO GUS-
TAVE ADOR, PRESIDENT OF THE RED CROSS.[53]

*The Holy Father praises and congratulates the Red
Cross.*

February 19, 1915

333. Amid the bitter pains which afflict the heart of the August
Pontiff, dismayed at the desolating spectacle presented by the
present enormous war, one thing has given him precious encouragement: the knowledge that in his apostolic work, aimed at diminishing the immensity of the ruins caused by the war, or at least
mitigating its disastrous effects by assuaging the sorrow of families,
of the wounded, of the prisoners, he has had, and continues to
have, the collaboration of an elect band of persons, especially abroad
in free Switzerland, who are helping him faithfully and even
anticipating him in his yearnings of Christian charity. To this
band, instinct with a splendid spirit of Christian brotherhood and
most noble pity, the Red Cross of Geneva, so worthily presided
over by you, is proud to belong, and, therefore, to you and to the
Red Cross go with good right the gratitude of numberless unhappy
ones, and the congratulations and praises of the August Pontiff.
His Holiness hopes to have you always as his co-operator in works
of charity, and trusts that you will ever continue to dedicate, with
generosity and confidence, all your beneficent activity to the cause
of the afflicted. And the Lord, Who counts every tear of suffering
that has been pitifully dried, will not fail to reward every charitable
undertaking with His choicest blessings.

LETTER OF CARDINAL GASPARRI, SECRETARY OF STATE, TO HENRY
SIENKIEWICZ, PRESIDENT OF THE GENERAL COMMITTEE OF
RELIEF FOR WAR VICTIMS IN POLAND.[54]

An offering to relieve the distress in Poland.

March 12, 1915

334. The August Pontiff, instead of sending the usual tele-
graphic reply, has charged me to let you know of the feelings of

[53] Translation from *The Tablet*, v. 125, p. 375 (March 6, 1915). Original Italian,
Civiltà Cattolica, 1915, v. 2, p. 498 (May 8, 1915).
[54] Translation from *Rome*, v. 17, pp. 169-170 (April 10, 1915). Original Italian,
L'Opera della Santa Sede, pp. 200-201.

gratitude and fatherly affection produced in him by the reading of the telegram, so full of devotion, of the General Relief Committee for the victims of the war in Poland. You know how deep the Holy Father's grief is at the terrifying spectacle of the awful slaughter and ruins which are the consequences of the present war. As Vicar of that merciful God Who has infinitely loved all men and given for all the price of His Blood, he suffers from the pains of all the combatants and is in mourning for all the families. His affection goes out to all his children without distinction and, as he said at the last Consistory, his heart is especially touched at the thought of the pain of all those sons of his who are most grievously tried by this horrible catastrophe. I can assure you truly that your Committee, by relieving the victims of the war in Poland and thus carrying on a work eminently charitable and merciful, has profoundly moved the fatherly heart of the August Pontiff.

335. In his beloved sons of Poland he sees not only a people plunged in terror and desolation, but he recognizes and loves in them children especially affectionate and generous, who are devoted to the Holy See to the point of sacrifice. Hence, as His Holiness has already given a proof of his interest in Catholic Belgium by sending it a letter of encouragement with his personal offering and that of the Sacred College, so now he is especially glad to be able to confer the same privileges on his well-beloved people of Poland, by sending a similar offering in his own august name and in that of his College, together with an autograph letter to relieve their distress and to comfort them in their anguish. And now His Holiness congratulates your Relief Committee on the truly charitable work which is relieving the miseries of his most beloved children of Catholic Poland, and in token of his fatherly affection he bestows with all his heart the Apostolic Blessing on all the Polish nation, on all who assist it, and especially on you and on the members of the Committee.

DECREE *Annuendo alla Pia Domanda* ISSUED BY CARDINAL GASPARRI, SECRETARY OF STATE.[55]

The Pope authorizes another day of prayer for peace.

March 15, 1915

336. Our Most Holy Lord, Pope Benedict XV, assenting to the pious request of many of the faithful and particularly of the Priests Adorers of Italy, who, moved by devotion towards the Most Holy Eucharist and also by the desire of concurring by repeated prayers in obtaining from the Divine Mercy the grace of peace, have implored authorization to be empowered to repeat in the churches of Europe, on the 21st of the current month of March, the sacred functions ordered by His Holiness, for that day, in the dioceses outside of Europe, has been graciously pleased to acquiesce in the above mentioned request, according right willingly the authorization requested to all those who wish freely to avail of it, and granting a plenary indulgence to all those who, having confessed and communicated, shall assist at the sacred functions or shall pray for some time in the presence of the Blessed Sacrament exposed for the adoration of the faithful.

LETTER *Certiores Quotidie* TO CARDINAL GIBBONS, ARCHBISHOP OF BALTIMORE.[56]

The Holy Father thanks him for the alms offered the Mexican victims of the civil war.

March 17, 1915

337. We are in constant receipt of information about the efforts that Catholics, and especially the Catholics of the United States of America, are making under the guidance of the venerable bishops, to carry out Our wishes and to alleviate the sorrow and distress which for so long have been the heavy portion of many of Our brethren in Catholic Mexico, a country sorely harassed by revolu-

---

[55] Translation from *Rome*, v. 17, pp. 189-190 (April 17, 1915). Original Italian, *A.A.S.*, v. 7, p. 138 (March 15, 1915).

[56] Translation from *America*, v. 13, p. 42 (April 24, 1915). Original Latin, *A.A.S.*, v. 7, pp. 168-169 (April 20, 1915).

tion. And in particular We are not unaware of the widespread, active charity, which has manifested itself in so many ways: through assistance given by the Press and by public meetings, by subscriptions and collections, and the inauguration of good works of all kinds. Different men have helped on the cause in various ways, some by lending to it the prestige of their high position as citizens, others by giving it financial assistance, and still others—and to these We call especial attention—by devoting to it their best qualities of head and heart; but in every case the motive power of their action has been charity. This has made it possible to shelter and afford assistance to the exiled bishops, priests and religious of both sexes, and has given Us the great consolation of seeing the young Mexican aspirants to the priesthood, notwithstanding their poverty, continuing their education in the seminaries. The result is that here in Europe all are beginning to recognize that the love, care and protection thus shown the exiles, are among the most beautiful characteristics of Christian and civil life in America. . . . . . .

ALLOCUTION *C'Est avec Couleurs Bien Sombres* TO M. VAN DEN HEUVEL, MINISTER OF BELGIUM TO THE HOLY SEE.[57]

> *The Pope expresses compassion for Belgium.*

March 17, 1915

338. In very sombre colors, *M. le Ministre,* you have depicted for Us the situation of your country. We, too, on receiving the letter of His Majesty, the King of the Belgians, accrediting you as his Envoy Extraordinary and Minister Plenipotentiary to the Holy See, are thinking of the misfortunes which have struck your noble country in these recent times. This sad memory constrains Us to repeat the sentiments which We have expressed directly to the Cardinal Archbishop of Malines and on the solemn occasion of the last Consistory. At the present moment We are glad to welcome you to Rome, *M. le Ministre,* but We cannot do so without expressing the deep affliction which rends Our heart since the beginning

---

[57] Translation from *The Tablet,* v. 125, p. 441 (April 3, 1915). We have been unable to locate the original of this allocution; the *Osservatore Romano,* March 18, 1915, carries an account of this audience but gives no direct quotations.

of Our Pontificate. Still, We think that the Belgians should not forget that after the storm comes the sunshine, with comfort for those who dwell here below. We desire for Our beloved children of Belgium that it may soon be given to them to hail the fair sun of peace on the horizon of their country. We even wish We were not obliged to confine Ourself to mere desires. But for the moment We ask the people of Belgium not to doubt the affection which We love to cherish for them. This affection inspires Us when We assure the new Minister of Belgium of the welcome he will always find from Us in the fulfillment of his mission to strengthen the good relations which exist between his Government and the Holy See. Meanwhile We beg him to convey to his August Sovereign the expression of Our friendly sentiments, and to accept for himself the assurance of the satisfaction given Us by the selection of a personage who, having been Minister of Justice and Professor of Law at the University of Louvain, cannot but be inspired by love of justice and truth.

LETTER OF CARDINAL GASPARRI, SECRETARY OF STATE, TO CARDINAL MERCIER, ARCHBISHOP OF MALINES.[58]

Moved by the misfortunes of Belgium, the Holy Father sends an offering to help the war victims.

April 6, 1915

339. From the beginning of his Pontificate, His Holiness, Benedict XV, looking out over the whole world, fixed his gaze chiefly on Europe, convulsed by this horrible war, and especially on Belgium, where he followed the painful events that have taken place there. Deeply moved by the misfortunes of this noble and generous nation, all the more dear to his heart in that it has remained faithful to the Church and the Holy See, and desiring to contribute to the relief of the sufferings of your dearly-beloved people, the Holy Father was most desirous to send the offering of his charity and of his august poverty. Never ceasing to send up the most ardent prayers to heaven to obtain from the God of Mercies the end of the terrible scourge of war, the Holy Father conjured Him especially to

[58] Translation from *The Tablet*, v. 125, pp. 535-536 (April 24, 1915). Original French, *L'Opera della Santa Sede*, pp. 202-203.

relieve the sorrows of your dear people, and wishing to give them a new proof of benevolence and love, His Holiness has decided to join to his prayers the offering of his fatherly charity, charging me to send you, notwithstanding the present painful conditions of the Holy See, the sum of twenty-five thousand francs, which I am glad to be able to enclose in the present letter. He cherishes the hope that the example of the Father of the faithful will be generously followed by his numerous children, and that the offering of their charity, united with their prayers, will contribute to mitigate the sufferings of their brethren in Belgium. The Sovereign Pontiff has been glad to learn that numerous Relief Committees for Belgium have been founded, and have obtained consoling results, and he hopes that they will continue to develop a salutary activity and that all will willingly respond to their urgent appeals. As a pledge of heavenly favors and of his most special predilection, His Holiness, with all the effusion of his heart, accords a special blessing to Your Eminence, to the episcopate, and to the clergy and people of Belgium, blessing at the same time all who come to their assistance.

LETTER OF CARDINAL GASPARRI, SECRETARY OF STATE, TO BISHOP SAPIEHA OF CRACOW.[59]

The Holy Father contributes alms for the suffering people of Poland.

April 9, 1915

340. The misery in which languish all the people of Poland, who more than others have had to suffer, and are suffering, the sad consequences of the war, has long since filled with immense sorrow the fatherly heart of the August Pontiff, and moved him to show by a personal offering and an autograph letter all the grief of his soul and all his fatherly predilection. But the later information that continues to arrive is so painfully grave that the Holy

[59] Translation from *The Tablet*, v. 125, pp. 372-373 (September 18, 1915). Original Italian, *L'Opera della Santa Sede*, pp. 203-205. Similar documents, not included in this book, concerning relief given to Poland are: Letter of Cardinal Gasparri to Bishop Sapieha of Cracow, March 24, 1915 (*L'Opera della Santa Sede*, p. 202). Letter of Cardinal Gasparri to H. Sienkiewicz, President of the Relief Commission for Poland, February 5, 1916 (*op. cit.*, p. 227). Letter of Cardinal Gasparri to H. Sienkiewicz, February 16, 1916 (*op. cit.*, p. 227). Letter of Cardinal Gasparri to H. Sienkiewicz, March 14, 1916 (*op. cit.*, p. 228).

Father cannot but hasten again to the aid of the unhappy Poles, with the utmost desire to mitigate in some way their immense sufferings. Hence, His Holiness, while he never ceases to offer up prayers to the Most High that the beneficent beams of peace may again shine on the world, at the same time turns his most ardent hopes and his fervent prayers to the special benefit of the whole Polish people, that generous people who, by ancient tradition, are so devoted to the Holy See, and who are now being so sorely tried by the greatest misfortunes. Hence, together with his good wishes and prayers, His Holiness is eager to send a new and tangible proof of his interest in all Poland, belonging to the Austrian, German and Russian Empires. And in view of the urgency of the need, His Holiness, intending to address himself to all the Polish episcopate, has charged me to send Your Lordship, with whom the Holy See can most easily communicate, the enclosed sum of twenty-five thousand crowns, an amount which is, of course, altogether disproportionate to the grave necessities of Poland, but which is a clear proof of the most special solicitude which the Vicar of Jesus Christ, in his august poverty, more accentuated than ever at this terrible hour, cherishes for the whole of Poland. In communicating to Your Lordship, and through you to the other Bishops of Poland, the comforting assurance of the special prayers of the Holy Father, and in sending you at the same time this offering of his charity, which you and the other Bishops of all Poland will kindly distribute, together with words of comfort and hope, where the need is most urgent, I am glad to add that His Holiness would see with satisfaction all the Bishops of Austrian, German, and Russian Poland address a brotherly invitation to all Catholics to nave them as co-operators and imitators of the Common Father of the Faithful in his prayers and in his offering The woes of Poland can now be alleviated only by the universal succor of the peoples, and the Holy Father trusts that all his children, responding to the invitation of the Polish episcopate, will vie with one another in harkening to the appeal and in alleviating by their united prayers and their united offerings the calamities of that noble people. And in this hope the August Pontiff, Vicar of that merciful God who has been pleased to count as done to Himself what is done for those in affliction and misery, in invoking upon all beloved Poland an abundance of heavenly comfort and of fraternal charitable offerings, imparts with all the affection of his heart a special Apostolic Blessing to all who, by their prayers and their offerings, show themselves as merciful benefactors. . . .

DECREE *Mossa dal Pio Desiderio* OF CARDINAL GASPARRI, SECRETARY OF STATE.[60]

Prayers for peace shall be recited during the May Devotions.

April 9, 1915

341. His Holiness, Pope Benedict XV, moved by the pious desire ever the more to increase devotion to the Most Holy Virgin, to whom is consecrated the month of May, and animated also by the comforting confidence that, by means of the powerful intercession of the Mother of God, who amongst her other titles is likewise adorned with that most noble title of *Queen of Peace,* the end of the present most distressing war can be secured at the earliest possible moment, has decreed that in the whole Catholic world be recited every day, during the sacred May Devotions, the prayer for peace, composed by His Holiness himself, to which prayer the Holy Father has been graciously pleased to attach an indulgence of 300 days to be gained *once a day,* and a plenary indulgence to be gained in customary form of the Church by those of the faithful who for not less than 20 days will have taken part in the recital of the same prayer.

LETTER OF CARDINAL GASPARRI, SECRETARY OF STATE, TO CARDINAL AMETTE, ARCHBISHOP OF PARIS.[61]

The Holy Father has tried to mitigate the disastrous consequences of the war without distinctions of nationality, party or religion.

April 23, 1915

342. You know what a painful effect the heart of the Holy Father has experienced from the disasters caused by the terrible war which is spreading its ruins all over Europe, nor are you unaware that

[60] Translation from *Rome,* v. 17, p. 190 (April 17, 1915). Original Italian, *A.A.S.,* v. 7, p. 193 (April 20, 1915).
[61] Translation from *Rome,* v. 17, pp. 224-225 (May 8, 1915). Original French, *A.A.S.,* v. 7, pp. 249-250 (May 21, 1915).

His Holiness has made every effort in his power to mitigate its disastrous consequences without considering any distinctions of party, nationality, or religion. Still it is natural that the solicitude of the Father of all the faithful be exercised especially for those of his children who show most warmly their respect and affection for him.

343. Among these, particular mention is due to the children of France, the children of that nation which with just reason came to be called the "Eldest Daughter of the Church" which has ever given splendid proofs of its generosity towards Catholic works, and especially towards the Missions, and which at this moment, and for months past, and from one end to the other of its territory, in the army as well as in the ambulances, in the hospitals and even in the smallest villages, presents splendid demonstrations of faith and piety that greatly console the Holy Father.

344. Hence, His Holiness, amid all the great evils of the hour, has with good reason felt himself drawn with particular sympathy towards certain portions of the French people which have been tried more severely than the others by the scourge of war—so much so that, notwithstanding the charitable efforts of the nation and the world, they are in great need of material and moral assistance. Most deeply touched by their sufferings the Supreme Pontiff, while never ceasing to offer up to the Most High his prayers and supplications to obtain the termination of this era of bloodshed, fervently entreats the Divine Bounty to grant help and comfort in their sorrows to the most sorely afflicted portions of the French people.

345. To these hopes and prayers the Holy Father desires to add a tangible proof of the affectionate interest he takes in the unfortunate people. His Holiness has, therefore, charged me to send Your Eminence by this letter, that it may be used for their relief, the sum of forty thousand francs: an offering small indeed when compared with the extent of the disasters, but one which will at least manifestly show the fatherly affection which the Vicar of Christ, in his august poverty, rendered more acute by the difficulties of the present times, wishes to testify to France, his dearly beloved daughter.

346. And as we have learned that on the Sunday and Monday of next Pentecost there is to be a great collection organized by a committee, which has been constituted with your concurrence, on

behalf of the occupied districts, the Holy Father hopes his own act of liberality may serve as a prelude to the generosity of all the French in favor of an initiative so Christian and so patriotic. The August Pontiff, happy in the thought that he will thus have as co-operators in charity, prayer and contributions all his beloved children of France united under the guidance of their venerated Bishops, invokes upon them with all his heart a rich reward in heaven. . . .

LETTER OF CARDINAL GASPARRI, SECRETARY OF STATE, TO BISHOP SCHULTE OF PADERBORN.[62]

The German clergy are praised for treating their war prisoners as brothers in Jesus Christ.

April 29, 1915

347. Your Excellency, it is my pleasure to answer your letter of April first, in which you informed me of the charitable work accomplished by you in behalf of the war prisoners, with the precious co-operation of your clergy. In this connection you informed me that numerous persons of good will are continually working in the office created for that purpose, devoting themselves with an admirable spirit of self-sacrifice to the task of bringing relief to the prisoners and their families; doing this all the more cheerfully because they realize that they are carrying on the beneficent work initiated by the Holy Father, and all the more commendably, because they are succoring enemies, whom true evangelical charity makes them regard as brothers in Jesus Christ, without distinctions of nationality and religion.

348. It affords me great pleasure, Your Excellency, to assure you once more that His Holiness looks with the highest approval upon your intelligent and merciful work. Such activity finds a worthy parallel in the eagerness shown by the other reverend prelates of Germany in behalf of war and civilian prisoners, and in particular in the work undertaken for the relief of the imprisoned French clergymen by Cardinal von Hartmann, work for which he merited the solemn praise of His Holiness in the letter of October eighteenth of the past year.[63]

[62] Original Italian, *A.A.S.*, v. 7, pp. 224-225 (May 6, 1915).
[63] See *supra* n. 278.

349. It is, therefore, the wish of the Holy Father that Your Excellency and all those who, with exquisite sense of Christian charity, are striving and will continue to strive to co-operate with him, receive the expression of his sovereign approval and praise. In the meanwhile, to encourage even more their holy fervor, he again bestows upon you and all your associates, the Apostolic Blessing, as a sign of particular benevolence. . . .

LETTER *Communes Litteras* TO THE BAVARIAN BISHOPS.[64]

> *An exhortation to the faithful of Germany to be instant*
> *in prayer for peace.*

May 3, 1915

350. The common letter which you, recently assembled together, have addressed to Us, We have most gladly read, both because of the expression of your dutifulness and affection, which is indeed very gratifying to Us, and because of the hope of better things which it announces to Us; of which, as you write, the widespread revival of popular piety in your dioceses also affords promise. May it indeed come to pass that, with God's assistance, even the calamities of this frightful war may co-operate unto good; and this, needless to say, will come to pass the more fruitfully, in proportion as your charity is the more vigilant. Meanwhile you have acted very wisely, as, in obedience to Our wishes, you have exhorted the faithful of your dioceses, to be instant in prayer in the existing grievous circumstances; for, as you know, the assiduous supplication of the just man availeth much: and We trust that it will come to pass that God, supplicated by common prayer, will fulfill the general desires, so bestowing the desired gifts of peace, that the nations of afflicted Europe may as long as possible enjoy its plenitude. Meanwhile, may the Apostolic Benediction, which as a token of Our benevolence We very lovingly in the Lord bestow on all of you, Our Beloved Son and Venerable Brethren, and on the clergy and people committed to each one of you, be a harbinger of the divine favors. . . .

---

[64] Translation from *Rome,* v. 17, pp. 293-294 (June 19, 1915). Original Latin, *A.A.S.,* v. 7, p. 259 (June 1, 1915).

LETTER OF CARDINAL GASPARRI, SECRETARY OF STATE, TO
M. SCHOLLAERT, PRESIDENT OF THE HOUSE OF REPRESENTA-
TIVES IN BELGIUM.[65]

*The Pope promises that the Vatican Library will donate
its duplicate books and its own publications to help
rebuild the destroyed Louvain Library.*

May 8, 1915

351. The Holy Father has duly received the letter of the 15
April last, whereby Your Excellency, as member of the General
Council of the University of Louvain, solicits the support of the
Holy See for the reconstruction of the Library of the University.

352. It affords me pleasure to announce to you that, always
deeply interested in everything that concerns the well-being of his
dear children of Belgium and desiring that the belligerents in the
course of the struggle be careful to safeguard the scientific and literary treasures of every people, the Sovereign Pontiff will be very
happy to contribute, by every means in his power, towards the
reconstruction of that famous Library which contained such precious
literary treasures, of the greatest advantage to the intellectual culture and civilization of Belgium and of the whole world.

353. In order to encourage and favor from now onward an
enterprise so laudable, His Holiness has been pleased to order that
there be destined thereto not only the publications of the Vatican
Library but also all the works therein disposable, without prejudice
to other ways in which the Holy Father, who has it so much at
heart to follow in this the noble traditions of his Predecessors, may
be able later on to assist so excellent a work, and thus manifest his
zeal for the increase of the sciences and the preservation of the
literary patrimony of humanity.

354. At present I deem it opportune to advise Your Excellency
that you will at once receive the catalog of the above mentioned
works, and that they will be forwarded as soon as circumstances
permit. . . .

[65] Translation from *Rome,* v. 18, p. 56 (July 31, 1915). Original French, *L'Opera
della Santa Sede,* p. 207.

LETTER OF CARDINAL GASPARRI, SECRETARY OF STATE, TO CARDINAL AMETTE, ARCHBISHOP OF PARIS.[66]

Cardinal reports on negotiations with the Swiss Government to give hospital care to the wounded of the belligerent powers.

May 14, 1915

355. The Sovereign Pontiff, Benedict XV, always occupied with lessening, as much as he is able, the sad consequences of the war, wishes in particular to lighten the burden of the prisoners of war. Thus, he is impressed by the desire expressed by the French Government that the Helvetic Republic, already so renowned for her traditional hospitality and for the important part which she has taken in the exchange of invalid prisoners, receive on her soil wounded or sick prisoners of war.

356. To this end the Holy Father has sent a trustworthy person to His Excellency, the President of the Swiss Confederation, who has graciously consented to this humanitarian endeavor, informing the Holy See that the Federal Government is disposed to hospitalize, at a definite place on its territory, a considerable number of

---

[66] Original French, *L'Opera della Santa Sede*, pp. 99-100. Similar documents, not included in this book, concerning the hospitalization of sick and wounded prisoners are: Letter of Cardinal Gasparri to Cardinal Amette, April 3, 1915 (*L'Opera della Santa Sede*, p. 95). Letter of Cardinal Gasparri to the Ambassador of Austria-Hungary, May 14, 1915 (*op. cit.*, p. 96-97). Letter of Cardinal Gasparri to the Ministers of Belgium and England, May 14, 1915 (*op. cit.*, pp. 98-99). Letter of Cardinal Gasparri to the Minister of Prussia, June 7, 1915 (*op. cit.*, pp. 102-103). Letter of Cardinal Gasparri to the Minister of Prussia, June 16, 1915 (*op. cit.*, p. 103). Letter of Cardinal Gasparri to the Minister of Prussia, July 31, 1915 (*op. cit.*, pp. 105-106). Telegram of Cardinal Gasparri to the Minister of Prussia, January 29, 1916 (*op. cit.*, pp. 106-107). Telegram of Cardinal Gasparri to the Bishop of Coira, January 26, 1916 (*op. cit.*, p. 107). Letter of Cardinal Gasparri to the Minister of England, July 21, 1916 (*op. cit.*, p. 109). Letter of Cardinal Gasparri to the Minister of Russia, January 7, 1916 (*op. cit.*, p. 111). Letter of Cardinal Gasparri to the Minister of Russia, February 14, 1916 (*op. cit.*, p. 112). Letter of Cardinal Gasparri to the Minister of Prussia, June 7, 1916 (*op. cit.*, pp. 112-113). Letter of Cardinal Gasparri to the Chargé d'Affaires of Russia, June 9, 1916 (*op. cit.*, pp. 113-114). Letter of Cardinal Gasparri to Msgr. Marchetti-Selvaggiani, July 13, 1916 (*op. cit.*, p. 117). Letter of Cardinal Gasparri to the Chargé d'Affaires of Russia, July 23, 1916 (*op. cit.*, pp. 117-118). Letter of Cardinal Gasparri to Cardinal von Hartmann, Archbishop of Cologne, May 19, 1916 (*op. cit.*, pp. 118-119). Letter of Cardinal Gasparri to Cardinal Amette, July 4, 1916 (*op. cit.*, p. 121). Letter of Cardinal Gasparri to the Pro-Apostolic Nuncio in Vienna, July 8, 1916 (*op. cit.*, p. 122). Letter of Cardinal Gasparri to the Chargé d'Affaires of Russia, July 8, 1916 (*op. cit.*, p. 123).

Franco-Anglo-Belgian wounded or sick prisoners; and, at another location, an equal number of Austro-German prisoners who are in the same condition. The Swiss Government will be able to begin by accepting 10,000 prisoners from each side, without undue difficulty.

357. The major lines of this project will be the following:

(1) Each Government is responsible to the Swiss Government for the amount of all the expenses occasioned by the prisoners of its nation.

(2) The Swiss Government will assume the responsibility of guarding the prisoners entrusted to her; at the same time, France and her allies on the one hand, Germany, Austro-Hungary and Turkey on the other, must do everything in their power, in the case of the escape of one of their prisoner-subjects, to return him to the guard of the Federal Government.

(3) Those men who have recovered will be sent back to the Government which originally interned them as prisoners.

(4) They will successively provide for the replacement of the dead and of those men who have recovered.

As to the other phases of the project, they will be determined by the Swiss, in agreement with the various belligerents.

358. Such is the whole of the project which I have the honor of communicating to Your Eminence, praying you to acquaint the French Government in the way you may think best with this knowledge, in order that we may know how the latter will receive an official proposal by the Holy See on this matter.

359. The Russian, Serbian, Montenegrin prisoners held in Germany, in Austria, or in Turkey, as also the Austro-German or Turkish prisoners held in Russia, Serbia, Montenegro, not being able to be hospitalized in Switzerland, will be the object of later solicitude on the part of the Holy See; and to this end I shall not fail to enter into discussions with the respective Governments. . . .

LETTER *Era Nostro Proposito* TO CARDINAL S. VANNUTELLI, DEAN OF THE SACRED COLLEGE.[67]

The appeals for peace go unheeded; now Italy enters the war.

May 25, 1915

360. . . . . . . But as Our words cannot be addressed to all the Sacred College together, We think well to make them known to you, Lord Cardinal, with the intention in this way of speaking to the individual members of the venerable body of which you are the worthy Dean. In Our first Encyclical, moved by the supreme desire to see ended the horrible slaughter which is dishonoring Europe, We exhorted the Governments of the belligerent nations that, considering all the tears and all the blood that had been so far shed, they should make haste to give back to their peoples the life-giving benefits of peace: "We beg of those who hold in their hands the destinies of peoples," We said, "to give heed to that voice. If their rights have been violated, they can certainly find other ways and other means of obtaining a remedy; to these, laying aside the weapons of war, let them have recourse in sincerity of conscience, and good-will. With no view to Our own self-interest do We speak thus, but in charity toward them and toward all nations. Let them not suffer Our voice of father and friend to pass away unheeded." But, We say it with a heart broken with sorrow, the voice of the friend and the father was not listened to; the war continues to ensanguine Europe, and not even do men recoil from means of attack, on land and on sea, contrary to the laws of humanity and to international law. And, as if that were not enough, the terrible conflagration has extended also to Our beloved Italy, giving ground, alas, to fear for her also that sequel of tears and disasters which is wont to follow every war even when fortunate. While Our heart bleeds at the sight of so many misfortunes, We have not desisted from endeavoring to alleviate and diminish, as far as is possible for Us, the most unhappy consequences of the war. We give thanks to God for having crowned with happy success the efforts We have made to obtain from the belligerent nations the exchange of the prisoners of war unfit for

[67] Translation from *The Tablet*, v. 125, p. 770 (June 12, 1915). Original Italian, *A.A.S.*, v. 7, pp. 253-255 (June 1, 1915).

further military service. In addition to that We have recently also exerted Ourself on behalf of wounded or invalided prisoners of war not wholly unfit for military service, in order to render their lot less grave and to facilitate their cure. But the needs of the soul, so much superior to those of the body, have above all engaged Our fatherly attention. To this end We have furnished the military chaplains with the most ample faculties, authorizing them to avail themselves for the celebration of Mass and for the assistance of the dying of privileges which can be conceded only in the most exceptional circumstances. Those faculties and these privileges We intend to be used not only by the priests now called to render service as chaplains in the Italian army but also by all priests who find themselves under any title whatever in the ranks of the said army. And We conjure them all by the bowels of the charity of Jesus Christ to show themselves worthy of so holy a mission and to spare no care and no labor so that the soldiers may not be lacking in the arduous fight of the unspeakable comforts of religion. Painful is the hour, and terrible is the moment through which we are passing; but *sursum corda*. More frequent and more fervent be the prayers we send up to Him in whose hands are the destinies of nations. Let us all turn with confidence to the afflicted and Immaculate Heart of Mary, the most gentle Mother of Jesus and our Mother, that she, by her powerful intercession, may obtain from her Divine Son the speedy disappearance of the scourge of war and the return of peace and tranquillity. . . . . . .

Letter of Cardinal Gasparri, Secretary of State, to the Minister of Prussia.[68]

The English government consents to treat the captured crews of submarines just like other war prisoners.

July 3, 1915

361. The Holy See has learned, with profound satisfaction, that the Government of His Britannic Majesty has agreed to treat the commanders and crews of German submarines like other prisoners of war, and that, therefore, the Imperial German Government has

[68] Original Italian, *Civiltà Cattolica*, 1918, v. 2, p. 307 (May 10, 1918).

consented, for its part, to render to all English officer prisoners the treatment which they formerly received.

362. Since the rumored method of treating German submarine prisoners by England has been the sole motive of the German Government for withdrawing its consent, already given because of the intervention of the Holy See, to the exchange of civilian prisoners who, regardless of their age, are incapable of military service, the Holy See now hopes that, this obstacle having been removed, the German Government will consent without delay to carry out the aforementioned exchange of civilian prisoners.

LETTER OF CARDINAL GASPARRI, SECRETARY OF STATE, TO J. VAN DEN HEUVEL, BELGIAN MINISTER TO THE VATICAN.[69]

He rejects M. Latapie's interpretations of the Holy Father's views on the war.[70] He explains precisely the Pope's ideas, and lists a number of pertinent documents.

July 6, 1915

363. I have not failed to give my best attention to the memorandum which Your Excellency handed to me with your note of June 30, and I now have the honor of communicating to you the observations which it has suggested to me. As Your Excellency is fully aware, the Holy See recognizes no authority in M. Latapie's account. As I have already declared in my interview with the representative of the *Corriere d'Italia,* he has in no passage of his article reproduced exactly the real views of the Holy Father; in several he has completely misrepresented them, and some others are pure inventions. If the Holy Father denies all value to M. Latapie's narrative, it is clear that this rejection applies all the more strongly to what he may have said since upon the same subject.

364. It cannot escape Your Excellency's keen penetration that the thought of the Holy Father ought to be looked for in his public and official acts, and not in publications or accounts given by

---

[69] Translation from *The Tablet,* v. 126, pp. 137-138 (July 31, 1915). Original French, Arnaud, *Benoît XV et le Conflit Européen,* v. 2, pp. 210-215.

[70] M. Latapie, a correspondent of the French newspaper, *Liberté,* published on June 22 what purported to be an interview with Benedict XV. M. Latapie actually interviewed the Holy Father but his newspaper accounts entirely misrepresented the Pope's mind. Cf. Rope, *Benedict XV, the Pope of Peace,* pp. 85-86.

individuals; political passion often causes what is said to be misunderstood, and this, passed on from mouth to mouth, ends by
taking on fantastic proportions.

365. This general observation should of itself constitute a complete reply to the reflections contained in the memorandum. But
out of my special regard for Your Excellency, I have no difficulty
in discussing in detail the various points raised in it.

366. (I) As regards the neutrality of Belgium, I must assure
Your Excellency in the most categorical manner that the Holy
Father did not give M. Latapie the reply which he has dared to
imagine and state in his article.

367. The truth on the matter is as follows:—

The German Chancellor, Herr von Bethmann-Hollweg, openly
declared on August 4, 1914, in Parliament, that in invading Belgian
territory, Germany was violating the neutrality of Belgium contrary to international law. As a general rule, in present conflicts,
one party brings forward an accusation which the other denies;
and the Holy See, not being able to throw light upon it by an
inquiry, finds it impossible to pronounce on the matter. But, in
this case, the German Chancellor himself recognized that the invasion of Belgium was a violation of neutrality contrary to international law, though he pleaded its justification by military
necessity. Hence the invasion of Belgium was directly included in
the words of the Allocution in the Consistory of January 22, by
which the Pope utterly condemned all injustices by whichever side
and with whatever motive committed. It is true that since then
Germany has published certain documents of the Belgian Head-
quarters Staff, by which she seeks to show that Belgium had, before
the war, failed in her duty as a neutral, and that, consequently,
her neutrality at the moment of invasion was no longer in existence.
It is not for the Holy See to decide this historical question, and its
solution is not necessary, seeing that even if the German view were
admitted, it would not alter the fact that Germany, on the Chancellor's own admission, invaded Belgium with the consciousness
of thereby violating her neutrality, and so of committing an injustice. This is sufficient for it to be considered that such action
is directly included in the Pope's Allocution.

368. (II) Concerning Cardinal Mercier, M. Latapie puts into
the mouth of the Holy Father these words: — "I shall astonish

you, but Cardinal Mercier was never put under arrest; he can go about his diocese as he desires." Had M. Latapie wished to be exact, he should have put the matter somewhat as follows:—

369. Cardinal Mercier has not, as a matter of fact, been arrested in the strict sense of the word. The Holy See was led to understand that he had, and accordingly hastened to protest by an official note to the Prussian Minister on January 10. But since then it has learned that this protest could not be sustained as to an arrest of Cardinal Mercier in the strict sense of the word.

370. Was the Cardinal at least detained, confined, or under guard in his palace? On the morning of January 4, Herr von Strempel, aide-de-camp of the Governor-General of Brussels, brought Cardinal Mercier a letter from him, with orders to wait for a reply. Quite rightly, the Cardinal preferred to postpone his reply till evening, in order to have time for consideration. Notwithstanding the pressing but courteous invitation made to him by the Cardinal to leave and return for the reply, the officer remained on the ground floor of the archiepiscopal palace, and kept his motorcar in the courtyard. Towards lunch-time he went into the town. Then, returning in the afternoon, he took the letter of reply and went off. That is more or less what happened. If it be wished to call that detention or confinement, the Holy See has no objection to make; but this is certain, that the Holy See, on being informed of what had occurred, did not fail to make its observations to the Prussian Minister.

371. It is undeniable that Cardinal Mercier has not always been treated with the respect due to a Prince of the Church, and has not always been allowed the liberty to which he had a right for the exercise of his episcopal ministry. On each occasion, the Holy See, which is the jealous guardian of the honor and rights of the episcopate, and especially of the Sacred College, has been instant in drawing the attention of the German Government to the matter, in the way best fitted to the circumstances, and the more so in this case of a Cardinal so learned and holy as the Archbishop of Malines.

372. In this connection it is opportune to recall that on the morning of January 3, which was a Sunday, a telegram came from the Government, requesting Cardinal Mercier not to go in the afternoon to Antwerp, where he was to preside at a religious cere-

mony in the cathedral. His Eminence had already decided not to go to Antwerp, but quite rightly regarded the message he had received as an invasion of the liberty of his pastoral ministry. To the remonstrances of the Holy See, the Minister of Prussia replied that the invitation or prohibition was grounded on reasons of public order arising out of the special circumstances of the moment.

373. It is to be noted that if all the Bishops of Belgium, outside the zone of war, were free to go about their dioceses, Cardinal Mercier had, on account of his high dignity, actually obtained a permit for that purpose even outside his own diocese, except in certain places designated as being within the zone of military operations, and for which all, members of the diplomatic corps included, must have a special permit. This permission having been taken away from him, the Holy See expostulated with the German Government, which immediately restored to the Cardinal the privilege to go about freely which he had previously enjoyed.

374. And here it will not be irrelevant to recall that the Holy See has interested itself actively in the lot of the suffragans of the Cardinal, the Bishops of Belgium. Without unduly extending the limits of this explanation, it will suffice to say that the Apostolic Nunciature protested to the Governor-General against the bad treatment of which the Bishops of Tournai and Namur were the object. After the taking of Antwerp, it demanded special protection both for the Cardinal and the Bishops of Ghent and Bruges; and on several occasions the *personnel* of the Nunciature went to different towns to visit the Bishops and see if they stood in need of anything. These visits helped to gain for the Bishop of Namur, as also for the Bishop of Liége and his Vicars-General, permission to go about freely in their dioceses, to gain an order for the evacuation of the diocesan seminary of Tournai by the military ambulance, and to obtain other important advantages which for the sake of brevity we refrain from enumerating.

375. (III) Lastly, as regards the shooting of priests, the destruction of churches and of buildings devoted to learning, and the sufferings of the Belgian people, the Holy See, far from remaining indifferent, has not only deplored such acts, but what is much more to the point, has employed every means to prevent or at least mitigate them.

376. Amongst the many documents and acts which could be

quoted to prove the constant solicitude of the Holy See on this matter, I will only here mention the following:—

(1) A Letter of the Holy Father to Cardinal Mercier of December 8, 1914, in which the Holy Father, lamenting the sad condition of the Belgian nation, and praising their intention to collect Peter's Pence as usual, allocates the money so obtained for the needs of these unhappy people.

(2) The Consistorial Allocution of January 22, in which the Holy Father appealed to the sentiments of humanity of those who invaded enemies' country and besought them to abstain from needless devastation of the invaded territory, and what is more important, from wounding the sentiments of the people in what they held most dear—their sacred temples, the ministers of God, the rights of religion and faith.

(3) Another Letter of the Holy Father of January 23, 1915, to Cardinal Mercier (and keenly appreciated by and very pleasing to him), in which His Holiness expresses to him his lively interest in his person, and his grief at the lack of respect shown to him and the restrictions placed upon his liberty.

(4) A Letter of His Holiness on February 4, 1915, to Mgr. Thomas Louis Heylen, Bishop of Namur, in which the August Pontiff, affirming his paternal good-will for his beloved Belgian children, laments the misfortunes with which they are afflicted.

(5) A Letter of the Cardinal Secretary of State to Cardinal Mercier of April 6, 1915, in which he transmits an offering from the Holy Father of 25,000 lire for the relief of the suffering of the Belgian people, and invites the Catholics of the whole world to follow his example. This invitation the Cardinal Secretary of State specially extended to the United States in his congratulations to Cardinal Gibbons, Archbishop of Baltimore, on having accepted the honorary presidency of the Belgian Committee there formed, and in his wishes that the faithful of the great Republic would contribute generously to the fund.

(6) A Letter of the Cardinal Secretary of State of May 8, 1915, to the General Council of the Catholic University of Louvain for the reconstruction of the University, in which the Holy See publicly expressed its desire that the belligerents, in the heat of strife, would do all they could to safeguard the literary and scientific treasures of the nations.

(7) A Letter of June 16, 1915, in which the Secretary of State conveys the blessing of the Holy Father to the League for the Restoration of Worship in Belgium, and recommends the work to the Catholics of the whole world, and sends, as a mark of His Holiness' paternal interest, an offering of 10,000 lire.

(8) In addition to all this, the Holy See has done all it could, both directly and through the Nunciatures of Brussels and Munich, to exert its influence on behalf of religious, priests, and people of Belgium.

377. For truly, the faith and virtues of the Belgian clergy and people have always marked them for the paternal affection of the Holy Father, who has keenly felt their sorrows, as he proclaimed in his Consistorial Allocution of January 22. And the August Pontiff hopes, as he told Your Excellency when you presented your credentials on March 17, that his beloved sons of Belgium may soon be able to hail the bright sun of peace on the horizon of their country. He would wish not to have to confine himself to mere prayers, but for the moment he calls upon Belgians not to doubt the goodwill with which he loves to surround them. . . .

LETTER *Nous Avons Reçu* TO CARDINAL AMETTE, ARCHBISHOP OF PARIS.[71]

His Holiness repudiates the Latapie article.

July 11, 1915

378. We have received the letter you addressed to Us on June 25 on the subject of the well-known article published by M. Latapie in the *Liberté*. As you know, We refuse all authority to the interview. M. Latapie has, in his article, reproduced neither Our thought nor Our words, and he published it without any revision or authorization on Our part, despite the promise he made.

379. For the rest, it cannot have escaped your perspicacity that Our true thought must be derived from the public and official acts of the Holy See, and not from individual accounts of conversations with Us. Political passion or individual prejudices often put a gloss on the words heard, and, passing from mouth to mouth, these take on fantastic proportions.

---

[71] Translation from *The Tablet*, v. 126, p. 116 (July 24, 1915). Original French, Arnaud, *Benoît XV, et le Conflit Européen*, v. 2, pp. 216-217.

380. To Our declaration, which itself constitutes a conclusive reply to your letter and to the many inaccurate comments which have appeared, especially in the Press, you may give what publicity you think fit.

381. In order the better to enlighten your knowledge on the various points touched upon in M. Latapie's letter, We have given instructions that there shall be sent with Our letter the declaration made by Our Cardinal Secretary of State to the *Corriere d'Italia,* and also the letters addressed by the Cardinal Secretary to the British Minister and Belgian Minister of dates July 1 and 6 respectively. . . .

382. With the certainty that this exposé is of a nature further to assure Our beloved children of France of the constant solicitude of Our heart in their regard, and in the hope of having fully satisfied your desire, We grant, with all Our heart, to you and to the faithful Our Apostolic Benediction.

LETTER OF CARDINAL GASPARRI, SECRETARY OF STATE, TO BISHOP SCÓZZOLI OF RIMINI.[72]

The Pope demands respect for international law.

July 12, 1915

383. The anxiety which, in your letter of the 30th of June, Your Lordship, as a watchful and loving pastor, expressed on behalf of your faithful grievously visited or threatened by the horrors of the war, is not only shared by the other Bishops of the Adriatic coast who, exposed to the same serious dangers, have hastened to place their troubles before the Common Father, but also finds a profound echo in the heart of the August Pontiff, who feels even more deeply all the sadness of human misfortunes. From the very beginning of his troubled Pontificate His Holiness has had no other thought than to arrest the terrible conflict raging in Europe or at least to mitigate its fearful consequences, and no sooner did he see this beloved country also invaded by war than he looked with loving anxiety toward those of his children nearest to him—anxiety all the keener for the closeness of the ties which unite their lot with

---

[72] Translation from *Rome,* v. 18, p. 39 (July 24, 1915). Original Italian, *L'Opera della Santa Sede,* pp. 39-40.

that of the Successors of St. Peter and for the glory of the monuments of religion and art built on that privileged soil. So, faithful to his mission of sovereign charity, and deeply moved by the trials undergone first of all after the outbreak of hostilities by the cities of the Adriatic coast, His Holiness did not delay a moment to make known to His Majesty, the Apostolic Emperor and King, and to the Imperial and Royal Government of Austria-Hungary his keen desire that the present unhappy war should be conducted in conformity with international laws and the principles of humanity, and that in consequence open and undefended cities, artistic monuments and sacred temples should be respected, particularly the Sanctuary of Loreto, glory and guardian of the Marches, Italy and the world.

384. If the Holy Father's noble wish has not been able to be carried fully into effect at present, will Your Lordship please be assured that the charity of the Vicar of Jesus Christ does not limit itself to one step only. Indeed I am in a position to assure you that in the future it will never cease, in the firm hope that the desolating cloud which hangs over the heads of the beloved children of those dioceses may pass away, to give place to the serene atmosphere of tranquil life and, by God's will, to change into the glory of peace. And may peace be hastened by the prayers and penitence of the priests and faithful, particularly in those same dioceses, on which His Holiness with paternal benevolence invokes every celestial comfort, imparting from his heart the Apostolic Benediction.

EXHORTATION *Allorchè Fummo* TO THE BELLIGERENT PEOPLES AND TO THEIR LEADERS.[73]

After a year of war the Pope invites the warring nations to end the conflict and to make a just peace.

July 28, 1915

385. When We, though all unworthy, were called to succeed on the Apostolic Throne the meek Pius X, whose life of holiness and well-doing was cut short by grief at the fratricidal struggle that had just burst forth in Europe, We, too, on turning a fearful

[73] Official English translation, *A.A.S.*, v. 7, pp. 375-377. Original Italian, *A.A.S.*, v. 7, pp. 365-368 (July 31, 1915).

glance on the blood-stained battlefields, felt the anguish of a father, who sees his homestead devastated and in ruins before the fury of the hurricane. And thinking with unspeakable regret of Our young sons, who were being mown down by death in thousands, We opened Our heart, enlarged by the charity of Christ, to all the crushing sorrow of the mothers, and of the wives made widows before their time, and to all the inconsolable laments of the little ones, too early bereft of a father's care. Sharing in the anxious fears of innumerable families, and fully conscious of the imperative duties imposed upon Us by the sublime mission of peace and of love, entrusted to Our care in days of so much sadness, We conceived at once the firm purpose of consecrating all Our energy and all Our power to the reconciling of the peoples at war: indeed, We made it a solemn promise to Our Divine Saviour, Who willed to make all men brothers at the cost of His Blood.

386. And Our first words, as the Chief Shepherd of Souls, addressed to the nations and their rulers, were words of peace and of love. But Our advice, affectionate and insistent as that of a father and a friend, remained unheard. Our grief was aggravated, but Our purpose was unshaken; We turned, therefore, in all confidence to the Almighty, Who holds in His Hands the minds and hearts of subjects, as of Kings, begging of Him the cessation of the unprecedented scourge. We wished to associate all the faithful in Our fervent and humble prayer, and to make it the more efficacious, We arranged that it should be accompanied by works of Christian penance. But today, on the anniversary of the outbreak of the tremendous conflict, more intense is the desire of Our heart for the speedy conclusion of the war; still louder is Our fatherly cry for peace. May this cry, prevailing over the dreadful clash of arms, reach unto the peoples who are now at war, and unto their rulers, inclining both to milder and more serene views.

387. In the holy name of God, in the name of our heavenly Father and Lord, by the Blessed Blood of Jesus, Price of man's redemption, We conjure you, whom Divine Providence has placed over the nations at war, to put an end at last to this horrible slaughter, which for a whole year has dishonored Europe. It is the blood of brothers that is being poured out on land and sea. The most beautiful regions of Europe, this garden of the world, are sown with corpses and with ruin: there, where but a short time ago

flourished the industry of manufactures and the fruitful labor of
the fields, now thunders fearfully the cannon, and in its destructive
fury it spares neither village nor city, but spreads everywhere havoc
and death. You bear before God and man the tremendous responsibility of peace and war; give ear to Our prayer, to the fatherly
voice of the Vicar of the Eternal and Supreme Judge, to Whom
you must render an account as well of your public undertakings,
as of your own individual deeds.

388. The abounding wealth, with which God, the Creator, has
enriched the lands that are subject to you, allow you to go on
with the struggle; but at what cost? Let the thousands of young
lives quenched every day on the fields of battle make answer:
answer, the ruins of so many towns and villages, of so many monuments raised by the piety and genius of your ancestors. And the
bitter tears shed in the secrecy of home, or at the foot of altars where
suppliants beseech—do not these also repeat that the price of the
long drawn-out struggle is great—too great?

389. Nor let it be said that the immense conflict cannot be
settled without the violence of war. Lay aside your mutual purpose of destruction; remember that nations do not die; humbled
and oppressed, they chafe under the yoke imposed upon them,
preparing a renewal of the combat, and passing down from generation to generation a mournful heritage of hatred and revenge.

390. Why not from this moment weigh with serene mind the
rights and lawful aspirations of the peoples? Why not initiate with
a good will an exchange of views, directly or indirectly, with the
object of holding in due account, within the limits of possibility,
those rights and aspirations, and thus succeed in putting an end
to the monstrous struggle, as has been done under other similar
circumstances? Blessed be he who will first raise the olive-branch,
and hold out his right hand to the enemy with an offer of reasonable terms of peace. The equilibrium of the world, and the prosperity and assured tranquillity of nations rest upon mutual
benevolence and respect for the rights and the dignity of others,
much more than upon hosts of armed men and the 'ring of
formidable fortresses.

391. This is the cry of peace which breaks forth from Our heart
with added vehemence on this mournful day; and We invite all,
whosoever are the friends of peace the world over, to give Us a

helping hand in order to hasten the termination of the war, which for a long year has changed Europe into one vast battlefield. May the merciful Jesus, through the intercession of His Sorrowful Mother, grant that at last, after so horrible a storm, the dawn of peace may break, placid and radiant, an image of His own Divine Countenance. May hymns of thanksgiving soon rise to the Most High, the Giver of all good things, for the accomplished reconciliation of the States; may the peoples, bound in bonds of brotherly love, return to the peaceful rivalry of studies, of arts, of industries, and, with the empire of right re-established, may they resolve from now henceforth to entrust the settlement of their differences, not to the sword's edge, but to reasons of equity and justice, pondered with due calm and deliberation. This will be their most splendid and glorious conquest!

392. In loving trust that the tree of peace may soon return to rejoice the world with such desirable fruits, We impart the Apostolic Benediction to all who make up the mystical flock confided to Us, and also for those, who do not yet belong to the Church of Rome, We pray the Lord to draw them close to Us in the bonds of perfect charity.

LETTER *Au Milieu de Vos Angoisses* TO CARDINAL LUÇON, ARCHBISHOP OF RHEIMS.[74]

The Pope prays for the days of peace when the destroyed city of Rheims can be rebuilt.

August 1, 1915

393. . . . . . . And now, dear Son, We feel the need of reminding you of Our desire that days of peace and happiness will not be slow in rising upon your dear country, and in particular upon your diocese so sorely tried; that you may soon have the consolation of seeing your ruins rebuilt and prosperity and joy reborn in the midst of your beloved people. . . .

---

[74] Original French, *Actes de Benoit XV*, I, p. 87.

LETTER *Testem Vestrae in Nos* TO THE BISHOPS OF LOMBARDY.[75]

The Pope purposes to continue his work for peace.

August 15, 1915

394. Testimony of your homage to Us, We have received the letter, which you addressed to Us some days ago, when you held the annual conference at Milan. Therein undoubtedly you recall things that are sad; but amidst such a clash of arms and so many and such protracted sorrows, We fully understand that there can scarcely be anyone who does not continually ponder these things, who does not in daily conversation mention these things, because of which life has been for a long time past lived in continual solicitude. What We have done to secure peace and to lessen the calamities of the war, We have done urged by the charity of Christ; and under the same guidance We are resolved to continue what We have begun, so that the peoples so very numerous, having had such rich experience of the maternal providence of the Church, may, again recovering their senses, love its protection and guidance exceedingly. . . .

LETTER *Officiosissimis Litteris* TO THE SWISS BISHOPS.[76]

The Pope suffers with the afflicted war victims.

August 17, 1915

395. . . . With the afflicted We are afflicted, and because of them We are oppressed with cares and wearied with labors and immersed in anxious solicitude day and night. Whatsoever measures charity suggests or each day presents for restoring peace and for diminishing the hardships of the war, these, as you well know, We proceed to make trial of, confiding for the most part in Him Who ever assists good designs.

396. More than once, Venerable Brethren, and not indeed un-willingly, have We turned Our thoughts, amidst so great a clash of arms, to the Swiss peoples, and with you We have clearly per-

[75] Translation from *Rome*, v. 18, p. 195 (October 16, 1915). Original Latin, *A.A.S.*, v. 7, p. 458 (October 6, 1915).
[76] Translation from *Rome*, v. 18, pp. 136-137 (September 18, 1915). Original Latin, *A.A.S.*, v. 7, p. 434 (September 4, 1915).

ceived and understood how much they owe, in regard to the peace preserved, to the Divine benignity in the first instance, and also to the prudence of their Swiss rulers . . . We acknowledge how highly rated amongst you and amongst your citizens are the designs and undertakings of Our paternal solicitude. . . .

LETTER OF CARDINAL GASPARRI, SECRETARY OF STATE, TO BISHOP KOPPES OF LUXEMBOURG.[77]

Cardinal Gasparri sends 10,000 francs for relief.

August 17, 1915

397. I have the honor to inform Your Excellency that the Holy Father, in a burning desire to hasten to the aid of as many as feel the consequences of this frightful war, has expressed a desire to be informed about the present situation of the Grand Duchy of Luxembourg, especially in the matter of means of sustenance.

398. Having learned to his sorrow how Luxembourg, if possibly not in the same proportions as the other unfortunate countries involved in the war, suffered its disastrous consequences, he has decided to turn to it his paternal and solicitous concern, and to help its wretched condition as much as it is within his power.

399. Indeed while he hoped and unceasingly hopes for the end of this most sorrowful misfortune, and while he raises to the Most High fervent prayers of hope, His Holiness has deigned to grant to Luxembourg, as a proof of his fatherly and special interest, the sum of ten thousand francs, and he has commissioned me to send it to Your Excellency, as the authority best fitted, in the present circumstances of the country, to receive the aforesaid assistance and to distribute it with a real knowledge of the needs.

400. Such an offering is certainly not proportioned to the needs of that country, yet I am sure that Your Excellency will fittingly appreciate it, after considering the exceptional restrictions under which the Holy See labors because of the distressing consequences of the war. . . .

[77] Original Italian, *L'Opera della Santa Sede*, pp. 212-213. Other documents, not included in this book, concerning relief work in Luxembourg, are: Letter of Cardinal Gasparri to the Apostolic Nuncio in Belgium, January 28, 1915 (*L'Opera della Santa Sede*, pp. 209-210). Letter of Cardinal Gasparri to the Apostolic Nuncio in Belgium, August 17, 1915 (*op. cit.*, p. 212).

LETTER OF CARDINAL GASPARRI, SECRETARY OF STATE, TO THE
REPRESENTATIVES OF THE FOREIGN NATIONS ACCREDITED TO THE
HOLY SEE.[78]

*Cardinal Gasparri expresses the Holy Father's desire
that all war prisoners should rest on Sundays.*

August 23, 1915

401. In his persevering solicitude to procure all possible alleviation of the lot of war prisoners, the Holy Father is concerned over
information to the effect that they are forced to labor the entire
week without any day of rest. Hence, he has thought it opportune
to address an ardent appeal to the Governments of the belligerent
nations so that, inspired with sentiments of religion and humanity,
they may agree in establishing in all places, without exception,
wherever prisoners are to be found, the absolute observance of
the Sunday rest.

402. In conformity with the instructions of the Sovereign Pontiff,
the undersigned Cardinal Secretary of State makes known this
desire of His Holiness to Your Excellency, and appeals most
urgently to your noble and intelligent assistance, in order to obtain
from your Government . . . the desired agreement to the proposi-
tion formulated above. . . .

LETTER *Haerent Animo* TO CARDINAL CSERNOCH, ARCHBISHOP
OF STRIGONIA.[79]

*The faithful look to the Holy See as the first source
of peace.*

August 30, 1915

403. Writing to Us, who bewail the bitter lamentations and
tears both of those who are dying in the war and of those who

---

[78] Original French, *L'Opera della Santa Sede,* p. 124. Similar documents, not included
in this book, concerning Sunday rest for war prisoners, are: Letter of Cardinal
Gasparri to the Apostolic Delegate in Constantinople, August 23, 1915 (*L'Opera
della Santa Sede,* pp. 124-125). Letter of Cardinal Gasparri to the Cardinal Archbishop of Paris, September 24, 1915 (*op. cit.,* p. 127). Letter of Cardinal Gasparri
to the Ministers of Belgium, England and Russia and to the Delegate of Serbia,
October 28, 1915 (*op. cit.,* p. 132). Letter of Cardinal Gasparri to the Apostolic
Nuncio in Vienna, October 29, 1915 (*op. cit.,* pp. 132-133). Letter of Cardinal
Gasparri to the Apostolic Nuncio in Bavaria, October 29, 1915 (*op. cit.,* p. 133).
[79] Translation from *Rome,* v. 18, p. 195 (October 23, 1915). Original Latin, *A.A.S.,*
v. 7, p. 459 (October 6, 1915).

mourn their loss, these things which you recall linger in the mind: and for that reason We have even very recently sought to recommend to and urge upon kings and peoples alike peace, the work of justice. You indeed add, Our Beloved Son, that these offices of paternal charity have so stimulated for you and yours the desire of peace that, with expectant minds, you look to this Apostolic See as to the Orient from which the first light of the so long looked for peace shall at length shine upon the peoples: God grant that, as wished for, this may happen as speedily as possible! As meanwhile Our every hope is in God, We have, as you well know, exhorted the faithful to confident and humble prayer to Him, to admonish them, in the first place, that the best recommendation of those who pray is found in virtues and example in keeping with the Christian profession. . . .

LETTER *Fuldae* TO CARDINAL VON HARTMANN, ARCHBISHOP OF COLOGNE.[80]

Catholics are exhorted to devote themselves to the restoration of peace.

September 6, 1915

404. . . . . . . Amidst the billows which buffet the nations, by whose tempestuous fury We behold the most flourishing States of Europe thrown into disorder and almost rent asunder, you easily understand, Our Beloved Son and Venerable Brother, Our state of mind owing to the daily slaughter of so many men and the calamities of so many peoples. The graver these things become with the lapse of time, We also note, the more ardent the desire for peace becomes amongst all. But We should very much wish that all these desires should amongst all pursue that royal road which, in charity, patient and benign, lies open to peace; from this road would they indeed wander far, who would deem it allowable for them by word or writing so to find fault with the Catholics of another nation that, provoking one another, as the Apostle says, envying one another, they would add new fuel to those feelings of wrath whose flames they are bound to extinguish with

---

[80] Translation from *Rome*, v. 18, p. 196 (October 23, 1915). Original Latin, *A.A.S.*, v. 7, pp. 460-461 (October 6, 1915).

kindness of judgment and gentleness of mind. Wherefore, whilst with all longing We desire peace—and a peace indeed such as is needed by justice and is consonant with the dignity of the peoples— We exhort Catholics, doing nothing through a spirit of contention, to devote themselves severally, with Christian brotherly love, to the restoration of peace. . . .

LETTER *Di Altissimo Pregio* TO FATHER BECCI, O.P., DIRECTOR OF THE ASSOCIATION OF THE PERPETUAL ROSARY IN ITALY.[81]

There is need of insistent and incessant prayer for peace.

September 18, 1915

405. From Our earliest years We have ever held in highest honor, as bringing happiness and holiness to individuals, to families, to society, the mystic Crown which the Christian people with inspired words of veneration and affection places every day on the royal head of the Mother of God. And now that through Divine Providence We have been raised to the Apostolic throne from which height there is a wider view of human needs, while their remedy is seen more clearly, We realize more keenly the need of Christian prayers, and We see that among all, that of the Rosary is more than ever necessary, for not only is it turned to her through whom it pleased God that all grace should come to us, but it bears the impression, more than any other, of the universal character of collective and domestic prayer.

406. . . . . . . The sadness of the grave time in which we live, the increasing weakness of spirit, the need, too long felt, of bringing back to the convulsed nations the blessings of the peace they have banished—show with the clearness innate in the teachings of God that to-day more than ever there is need of insistent and incessant prayer to conjure of Divine Compassion that we may be given a truce in the terrible course of avenging justice.

407. After such an outpouring of blood, which has not softened but has increased hatred among brothers, the Month of the Rosary comes ardently desired and propitious for humble prayers to the Mother of Pity and Queen of Peace. Therefore, it is Our desire

---

[81] Translation from *The Tablet*, v. 126, pp. 500-501 (October 16, 1915). Original Italian, *Civiltà Cattolica*, 1915, v. 4, pp. 239-240 (October 6, 1915).

that in the coming month of October in every sacred function devoted to the recital of the Holy Rosary there should be added some
special prayer for peace. So let all those pray who treasure the
devotion of the Rosary. Day and night let them raise their arms
to heaven, imploring pardon, brotherhood, peace. And as once
when their leader raised his arms in prayer the chosen people
conquered, so to-day may the Father of the faithful conquer, in his
unfailing prayer for peace, supported by the arms of the suppliant
band of those who treasure the devotion of Mary.

LETTER *Plane Videmus Te* TO BISHOP BERTRAM OF BRESLAU.[82]

The evils of war must not diminish the ardor of charity.

October 10, 1915

408. We clearly see that you are laboring like a good soldier
of Christ. For scarcely a year having elapsed since your episcopate
at Breslau began, although the vicissitudes of the time which are so
grave make in the highest degree a call upon your solicitude and your
attention, and the need for rendering assistance is so grave and so
urgent, you think of convening a meeting of the seniors amongst
your clergy, so that by common counsel you may the better provide
for the general good of your diocese. This zeal of yours, Venerable
Brother, has seemed to Us to promise the more joyous results because it has not been dissociated from a wise choice of the matters
to be dealt with at the meeting. Indeed you seem to have omitted
nothing which the times demand for the fruitful government of
your diocese: nothing which might contribute to strengthen and
defend Catholic discipline; nothing which would stimulate the
mind to the daily study of piety.

409. From this, then, you understand with what glad expectation and how heartily We, by earnest prayer, as you say that you
desire, implore the assistance of heaven for your designs and undertakings. And since you also beg of Us to foster, by paternal exhortation, a clear understanding and a persevering will in those who
amongst you are wholly devoting themselves to alleviating and
diminishing the calamities of the war, know likewise that you have

---

[82] Translation from *Rome*, v. 18, p. 243 (November 20, 1915). Original Latin,
A.A.S., v. 7, p. 475 (October 27, 1915).

easily obtained that from Us: in such wise, however, that instead of exhortation it is a pleasure for Us to bestow the most ample commendation and praise on the same, and in the first place on the clergy and on the religious of both sexes. For We prefer to employ these rewards and encouragements as regards those who have displayed so many and such great examples of Christian charity as you yourself mention in your letter. Owing to the prolongation of the war and its resulting misfortunes which are daily becoming more grave, the ardor of a charity so abundant and so active, so far from decreasing in fervor should rather become more and more inflamed; for there is nothing arduous which is not to be expected from those whose love of country is fostered by the hope of an enduring reward in the better life. May the Apostolic Benediction, which very lovingly in the Lord We bestow on you, Venerable Brother, and on your clergy and people, be a pledge of the divine favors and a token of Our benevolence. . . .

LETTER OF CARDINAL GASPARRI, SECRETARY OF STATE, TO THE DUCHESS OF VENDÔME.[83]

The Pope gives 30,000 francs to Belgium.

October 31, 1915

410. In the letter which the Sovereign Pontiff, Benedict XV, deigned to address to Your Royal Highness on the fourth of last September, His Holiness informed you of the decision which the Bishops of Spain had taken to send to the Holy See the results of collections made and offerings received in their dioceses in favor of the belligerent nations, and he assured you at the same time that he would be guided, in the apportionment of these offerings, by his paternal love for Belgium.

411. Now that these offerings have been received by the Holy See, His Holiness has charged me with the task of sending you the greater part of these offerings—30,000 francs. It is most agreeable for me to execute this august mission to Your Highness, and to be able to renew in this manner the testimony of the special solicitude of the Sovereign Pontiff for Belgium, so sorely tried at present. . . .

[83] Original French, *L'Opera della Santa Sede,* pp. 220-221.

ALLOCUTION *Nostis Profecto* TO THE COLLEGE OF CARDINALS.[84]

Only through an honest exchange of ideas, clearly stated
and carefully considered, can a just peace be made.

December 6, 1915

412. . . . . . . Immense ruins have been accumulating for full
sixteen months: the desire for peace increases in every heart and
families innumerable sigh for peace with tears. We Ourself have
used every means that could in any way hasten peace and settle
discords—nevertheless, this fatal war continues still by land and sea,
and now, too, is bringing utter ruin on poor Armenia. The Letter
which We directed to the fighting peoples and their rulers on the
anniversary of the outbreak of the war, though received indeed
with reverence, still did not produce the happy effects which were
expected of it.

413. Vicar on earth of Him Who is the *King of Peace* and
Prince of Peace, We cannot but be ever more deeply moved by the
misery of so many of Our children, and ever lift Our arms in
supplication to the God of Mercies, praying with all Our heart that
He may deign at last to put an end with His might to this bloody
conflict. And while We endeavor to alleviate its sad consequences,
as far as lies in Our power, by the opportune provisions which are
well known to you, We feel Ourself urged by Our Apostolic
Office to teach once again the one and only means which can lead
without delay to the extinction of the awful conflagration. To prepare the way for peace, the peace which is ardently desired by all
humanity, a peace that is just, lasting, and not profitable to only
one of the fighting parties, the way which can truly lead to a happy
result is that which has already been tried and found good in similar
circumstances, and which We pointed out in that same Letter: that
is to say, that in an exchange of ideas, directly or indirectly, there
should be definitely and clearly put forward and duly weighed, with
good-will and serene conscience, the aspirations of each one, eliminating all that is unjust and impossible and taking count of all
that is just and possible, with any arrangement and compensation
that may be needful. Naturally, as is the case in all human con-

---

[84] Translation from *Rome,* v. 18, pp. 281-282 (December 11, 1915). Original Latin,
    A.A.S., v. 7, pp. 510-512 (December 9, 1915).

troversies which are settled by the contending parties themselves, it is absolutely necessary that on one side and the other of the belligerents there should be concession on some point and renunciation of some hoped for gain; and each should make such concessions willingly, even if it entail some sacrifice, in order not to assume before God and men the enormous responsibility of the continuation of a carnage which is without example, and which, if prolonged still further, might well be for Europe the beginning of the decadence of that degree of civil prosperity to which the Christian religion had raised it.

414. These are the feelings in Our mind regarding the war, considered in relation to the peoples who find themselves unhappily embroiled in it. If, further, we consider the inconveniences which the European conflict has brought in its train for the Catholic cause and the Apostolic See, it is evident to all how serious they are and how harmful to the dignity of the Roman Pontiff. More than once already, following in the footsteps of Our Predecessors, We have lamented that the situation of the Roman Pontiff was such as not to grant him the use of that full liberty which is absolutely necessary to him for the government of the Church. But who is there who does not see that this has become far more evident in the present circumstances? Certainly those who are governing Italy have not lacked the good intention to eliminate the inconveniences, but that very thing shows clearly that the situation of the Roman Pontiff depends on the civil powers and that, with a change of men and circumstances, it also can be changed and made more difficult. No man of sense can affirm that a situation which is so uncertain and so subject to the will of others is indeed that which is suitable for the Apostolic See. Neither was it possible, through the very force of things, to prevent the occurrence of several inconveniences of evident gravity. Not to speak of others, We limit Ourself to calling attention to the fact that some of the Ambassadors or Ministers accredited to Us by their Sovereigns were constrained to go away in order to safeguard their personal dignity and the prerogatives of their office, which means, for the Holy See, the curtailment of a right proper and native to it and the weakening of a necessary guarantee, as well as the deprivation of the ordinary and by far the most suitable means it is accustomed to use for conducting affairs with foreign governments. And in this regard

We have to point out with regret how on the other fighting side it has even been possible that there should arise the suspicion that We, through the necessity of things, in conducting affairs which concern peoples at war, allow Ourself now to be directed and guided only by the suggestions of those who can make their voices heard by Us. And what can be said of the increased difficulty of communications between Us and the Catholic world, which makes it so hard for Us to form the complete and exact judgment of events which indeed would be so useful to Us?

415. We think, Venerable Brothers, that what We have said up to now will suffice to show you how Our grief grows from day to day, since while this holocaust of men, worthy of more barbarous ages, grows fearfully, at the same time the situation of the Apostolic See becomes worse. We are certain that, as you share in the cares and anxieties which the Apostolic Office lays on Us, so you participate in this Our double affliction. . . . . . .

LETTER *Communem Vestram* TO THE BISHOPS OF GALICIA.[85]

He comforts them in the trials of war.

December 10, 1915

416. Your common letter is recommended to Us by that expression of devotion and homage, which We know that not only the bishops of Catholic Poland, but the clergy and people also, have been exemplary in tendering. But do not think, Venerable Brothers, that We wish to yield to you in love. For an old and quite singular charity toward your nation resides in Our heart; and how wonderfully it is now increased even by those manifold and grave calamities whereby, owing to this war, We see you almost overwhelmed. To these latter We have, as you know, turned Our paternal consideration, grieving for one thing only, that Our favors have not gone as far as have gone the desires of a heart the most loving. Never, however, do We omit to pray God Who is rich in mercy so to be present with you, Venerable Brethren, and with all Poland, as to temper the bitterness of these days and to fulfill all your lawful desires. . . .

[85] Translation from *Rome*, v. 19, p. 52 (January 29, 1916). Original Latin, *A.A.S.*, v. 7, pp. 591-592 (December 31, 1915).

LETTER *Et Horrida Doletis* TO CARDINAL CSERNOCH, ARCH-
BISHOP OF STRIGONIA, AND TO THE OTHER ARCHBISHOPS AND
BISHOPS OF HUNGARY.[86]

The Catholics of Hungary promise to pray for peace.

December 12, 1915

417. You both bewail the sorrows of this war and carefully
recall what We, urged by the charity of Christ, have done to lessen
and mitigate its calamities; and you promise every day to recommend more earnestly to God by devout prayer the common desires
for peace. In your letter and courtesies there is nothing wanting
of those things which the devotion of the most loving brothers
could desire; and these We both accept with gratitude and with
like exchange of affection repay, bestowing very lovingly in the
Lord on all of you, Our Beloved Son and Venerable Brothers, and
on the flocks, over whom your care and zeal keep guard, the
Apostolic Benediction, a pledge of heavenly gifts and a testimony
of Our benevolence.

ALLOCUTION *È Pur Troppo Vero* TO THE COLLEGE OF CAR-
DINALS.[87]

Prayer is the only hope for peace.

December 24, 1915

418. It is only too true that a cloud of sadness darkens, this
year, the happy celebration of the Nativity; and you, Lord Cardinal,
expressing in the name of the Sacred College the thoughts inspired
by this joyous anniversary, have not been able to suppress in your
words the note of the general mourning. We are confronted to-day
again with the savage spectacle of human slaughter; and if, last
year, We deplored the extent, the ferocity, and all the results of
this tremendous conflict, We must to-day mourn over the wider
spread, the greater pertinacity, the excess, which, with their terrible
consequences, have turned the world to an ossuary and a hospital,

---

[86] Translation from *Rome*, v. 19, p. 64 (February 5, 1916). Original Latin, *A.A.S.*,
v. 7, p. 593 (December 31, 1915).
[87] Translation from *The Tablet*, v. 127, pp. 6-7 (January 1, 1916). Original Italian,
Civiltà Cattolica, 1916, v. 1, pp. 212-214 (January 8, 1916).

and the progress of human civilization to an anti-Christian retrogression.

419. All this notwithstanding, you, Lord Cardinal, raising your eyes to the higher regions of faith, have found in this festivity a motive of good wishes for Our person, of consolation for the afflicted, of hope for the future of mankind. Grateful for your homage, thankful for the noble expression of your good will, We join earnestly and with fatherly accord in the aspirations of the Sacred College toward a time to come that shall prove less fatal for the Pontiff, for the Church, for civilization. And We accept the expression of that hope all the more joyfully in that We read therein not only a comforting increase of filial affection, but also the need of more intense and urgent prayer and supplication, upraised in the midst of tumult by the whole Sacred College—keenly aware of the extremity of our common need—to Him Who alone is able to quell the tempest. These prayers, We declare to you with full sincerity, give Us more comfort than any other testimony of your devotion.

420. And oh! how many times in the months past of Our Pontificate, months made so weary by the long delay of any sign of cessation in this human conflict, has Our heart sought refuge in prayer as in the only hope of safety! If God does not give succor, what is there that We can do? In truth, there is nothing.

421. Called to the government of the Church in the most terrible days in all history, We fondly hoped that the love of the father might not prove altogether unfruitful for his unhappy sons. But oh! vain hope! During all the sixteen months of this effort of Our love We have seen it to be almost entirely sterile. That voice of Ours, obedient to the precept, *Clama, ne cesses,* We intended should never hold its peace until it should find an echo in softened human hearts; but too often has it fallen into vacancy, a voice *clamantis in deserto.* And what of that good, of those ideals, which We loved to think We might be the means of furthering in the civil and the religious commonwealth? Far otherwise! Every wish, every hope, every project has been shattered. Indeed here also We have been compelled to confess Ourself powerless.

422. Yet Our faith is all unshaken. Hearkening to those divine words whereby in like straits Our Lord Jesus Christ showed His followers that way in which now more than ever we, too, need to

be guided, We cherish at heart, as the Apostle of the Gentiles cherished it, one great hope against all human hope. *In spem contra spem,* and in God, in God alone, do We put Our whole trust, invincibly sustained by the omnipotent promise contained in that serene reproof, *Modicae fidei, quare dubitasti?* He, let us be certain, will glorify His Name, saving us *ex hac hora,* even if for a time He reply, as the heavens replied to the words of Jesus, with lightnings and thunder, and if for a time He repeat, *Nunc judicium est mundi.*

423. This faith, alive in Our heart every day of the year, is stronger and more certain when a dear anniversary brings vividly to Our thoughts the reassuring sight of that which took place in the cave of Bethlehem. For Us it is not a vain record, an empty recollection, but a real and true renewal of the ineffable Mystery, and thus a source of hope infallible; for here is a return of that date when—even the barbaric pagan world being at peace—the King of Peace Himself came among men in the most peaceful of all forms. Oh, with what good cause may We now rehearse, even in the distraction of the present hour, the words of Pope St. Leo, *Neque enim fas est locum esse tristitiae ubi natalis est vitae!*

424. The sight of Christ, born for us, is made complete, moreover, by the sight of Mary, in whom the faith of believers and the love of sons recognize, not only Mediatrix of Peace, but also Mediatrix between rebellious man and merciful God. She is the *aurora pacis rutilans* across the darkness of this world. She fails not in her plea to her Son, albeit *nondum venerit hora ejus.* And she who has not failed to plead for suffering mankind in the hour of peril will surely hasten to meet our supplications, Mother of so many orphans, Advocate for us all in our tremendous ruin.

425. Therefore, with this great purpose, not less than with the intention of guiding Christian thought and Christian faith to the prevailing ministry of the Mother of God, We, echoing the sigh of many of Our children far and near, permit that to the Litany of Loreto be added the invocation, "Queen of Peace." Will Mary, who is queen not of wars and slaughter, but of the kingdom of peace, disappoint the trust and the prayers of her faithful children? Will she, in the most blessed night when, fulfilling prophecies and promises of happy and golden days, she gave us the Celestial Babe who is the Author of all peace, not smile upon the prayers of chil-

dren called by the episcopate and by Ourself to the holy Eucharistic Table to honor this most beloved festival? When man has hardened his own heart, and his hates have overrun the earth; when fire and sword are raging, and when the world rings with the sound of weeping and the noise of arms; when human reason is found at fault, and all civilized rights are scattered like thistledown, faith and history alike point us to the one succor, to the omnipotence of prayer, to the Mediatrix, to Mary. In all security and trust we cry, *Regina pacis, ora pro nobis.*

426. It is this confidence that inspires Us in returning the message of the Sacred College and in wishing you, Lord Cardinal, and all your eminent colleagues a speedy and an ample possession of the fruits of that peace which We hope to obtain through the intercession of the Virgin. Oh, may this blessed Jesus, Who at the prayer of His Mother did the first of His miracles, accept to-day once more the intercession of the heavenly Mediatrix, and comfort His Christian family with that abundance of graces, a pledge whereof We desire to give by this Apostolic Benediction. We here bestow it with fatherly affection upon the Sacred College, upon the bishops and prelates here present, and upon all, clergy and laity, who have proved to Us that dear sons are not far in heart from the father in the hour of mourning and of grief.

LETTER OF CARDINAL GASPARRI, SECRETARY OF STATE, TO THE MINISTER OF RUSSIA.[88]

Cardinal Gasparri sends money to be distributed to the German prisoners in Russia.

December 25, 1915

427. At the invitation of and following upon the appeal of the German Bishops, collections have been made in all their dioceses in behalf of the prisoners who are interned there.

428. Certainly in these offerings the German Catholics have not been able to forget their fellow countrymen who are captives

---

[88] Original French, *L'Opera della Santa Sede,* p. 225. Similar documents, not included in this book, concerning relief for Germany, are: Letter of Cardinal Gasparri to the Apostolic Nuncio in Bavaria, July 21, 1915 (*L'Opera della Santa Sede,* p. 216). Letter of Cardinal Gasparri to Bishop Bludau of Warmia, September 11, 1915 (*op. cit.,* pp. 218-219). Letter of Cardinal Gasparri to Bishop Cieplak of Mohilew, December 21, 1915 (*op. cit.,* pp. 224-225).

in Russia. And so I have the honor and the pleasure of sending to Your Excellency the enclosed sum of 28,800 Italian lire destined for the relief of all German prisoners who are interned in Russia, without distinction of religion.

429. Begging Your Excellency to see, with your customary kindness, that the aforesaid sum reaches His Lordship, John Baptist Cieplak, Suffragan Bishop of Mohilew, together with my letter which accompanies this communication, I offer you my anticipated thanks, and I beg Your Excellency to accept the assurance of my highest esteem.

LETTER OF CARDINAL GASPARRI, SECRETARY OF STATE, TO THE MOST REVEREND STEPHEN SOTER ORTYNSKY, BISHOP OF THE RUTHENIAN CATHOLICS IN THE UNITED STATES.[89]

Cardinal Gasparri tells of papal solicitude for the suffering Ruthenian Catholics.

January 29, 1916

430. The Holy Father has received from His Eminence, Cardinal Falconio, the letter wherein Your Excellency implored the intervention of the Holy See in behalf of the Ruthenians so harshly tried by the war, and the three thousand lire which Your Excellency and Your faithful have offered for Peter's Pence.

431. His Holiness, who entertains a special and most ardent affection for the Ruthenian Catholics, has vouchsafed to accept with pleasure the aforesaid offering. He has shown paternal gratification with the zeal with which Your Excellency and the faithful entrusted to your care undertook the collection of funds necessary for alleviating the miseries and the sufferings of their brethren in Europe. So, in order to console Your Excellency and your flock and in order that your flock may be further stimulated in its chosen work of truly fraternal Christian charity, the Holy Father has ordered me to inform Your Excellency that the Holy See, anticipating the requests now submitted to her, has not hesitated to do everything in her power to come to the aid of her suffering Ruthenian children.

432. In fact, through the agency of the Cardinal Apostolic Pro-

[89] Original Italian, *L'Opera della Santa Sede*, p. 226.

Nuncio of Vienna, she has already distributed ten thousand crowns in behalf of those Ruthenians who have been more sharply hit by the vicissitudes of the war. In itself, this is only a small amount; but, in view of the current economic conditions and of the countless staggering necessities which she has to take care of especially in the present circumstances, the sum is large.

433. The Holy See did not fail to take an active and eager interest in the lot of Msgr. Szeptysky, the Greek-Ruthenian Archbishop of Leopolis. She interceded for him repeatedly and sought in vain to get him a permit to go to Canada to exercise his ministry among the faithful of his rite residing there.

434. Besides this, she has not missed an opportunity to remonstrate against the war-time occupation by non-Catholics of churches belonging to the Ruthenian Catholics. Lastly, she has provided spiritual assistance for the faithful of this rite who are refugees from Galicia and Bucovina and are now scattered throughout the Austrian Empire, assigning them as Apostolic Administrator the Most Reverend Father Platonide Filas, Provincial of the Basilian Order in Galicia. . . . . . .

CARDINAL GASPARRI, SECRETARY OF STATE, REPLIES TO THE PETITION OF THE AMERICAN JEWISH COMMITTEE OF NEW YORK.[90]

The principles of the natural law must be observed in the case of the Jews as well as of all others.

February 9, 1916

435. The Supreme Pontiff has with interest taken cognizance of the letter you have been pleased to address to him, dated December 30, 1915. In the name of three million Israelite citizens of the United States of America, you turn to His Holiness to complain in general of the ill-treatment your co-religionists in various countries complain they are exposed to, and at the same time you beg him to intervene· "with the weight of his supreme moral and spiritual power, for the purpose of putting an end at last to these

---

[90] Translation from *The Tablet*, v. 127, p. 565 (April 29, 1916). Original Italian, *Civiltà Cattolica,* 1916, v. 2, pp. 358-359 (April 28, 1916). This petition of the American Jewish Committee besought the Holy Father to use his great moral and spiritual influence in behalf of the Jews of Poland, who were suffering unnecessary cruelties due to the war.

sufferings by an act of that humanity to which the Holy Father is so passionately devoted." The Supreme Pontiff is not in a position to pronounce on the specific facts mentioned in the memorandum attached to your letter; but, on principle, as Head of the Catholic Church, which, faithful to its divine doctrine and to its most glorious traditions, considers all men as brothers and teaches them to love one another, he never ceases to inculcate among individuals, as well as among peoples, the observance of the principles of the natural law and to condemn everything which violates them. This law must be observed and respected in the case of the children of Israel, as well as of all others, because it would not be conformable to justice or to religion itself to derogate from it solely on account of divergence of religious confessions. The Supreme Pontiff at this moment feels in his fatherly heart, torn by the spectacle of the present horrible war, more painfully than ever the necessity for all men of remembering that they are brothers, and that their salvation lies in their return to the law of love which is the law of the Gospel. Hence, he desires to interest with himself in this noble purpose all those who, especially by reason of the sacred attributions of their pastoral ministry, are in a position to render efficacious help in attaining this important result. Meanwhile His Holiness rejoices in the harmony which reigns in the United States in the civil relations between the members of the various religious confessions, and which contributes so powerfully to the peaceful prosperity of your great country. His Holiness prays God that peace may at last return for the happiness of that humanity of which, as you have with good reason said, His Holiness is always the loving guardian. . . .

LETTER OF CARDINAL GASPARRI, SECRETARY OF STATE, TO ARCH-
BISHOP MORGANTI OF RAVENNA.[91]

The Holy Father protests against the bombing of open
and undefended cities.

February 17, 1916

436. I have not failed to make known to the August Pontiff the accurate report sent to me by Your Grace on the 14th of this

[91] Translation from *The Tablet*, v. 127, p. 309 (March 4, 1916). Original Italian,
L'Opera della Santa Sede, p. 41.

month, concerning the recent bombardment of your city by enemy aviators. This fresh incursion has not only brought grief to many families and to a whole city, but has caused keen sorrow to the heart of the Holy Father, who feels deep sympathy for the innocent victims, and at the same time is afflicted for the dangers and damages which your famous monuments have incurred. His Holiness, as vigilant guardian of the supreme interests of religion, of history and of the arts, has not failed to repeat his paternal and insistent recommendations to the Imperial and Royal Austro-Hungarian Government that the war be conducted in conformity with the recognized principles, by virtue of which open and undefended cities are to be respected, and the monuments and churches which form their precious treasure are to be safeguarded from all harm. The Holy Father would have liked to do more: he would have desired that in the Italo-Austrian War the throwing of bombs from areoplanes should have been suppressed altogether, and if it has not been possible to attain this noble aim, I can assure Your Grace that this has not been at all due to want of warm interest on the part of the Common Father of all the faithful, but to reasons which I shall be able to explain orally to Your Grace when the opportunity offers. Kindly make known in the name of the Holy Father all the affectionate condolence which His Holiness cherishes for the unhappy families of the poor victims and the fervent prayers which His Holiness offers up for the deceased. . . .

LETTER *Al Tremendo Conflitto* TO CARDINAL POMPILI, VICAR OF ROME.[92]

The Pope asks the faithful to offer prayers, sacrifices and alms during Lent for the return of peace.

March 4, 1916

437.   To the tremendous conflict now rending Europe asunder, We, as the universal Shepherd of Souls, cannot, without failing in the duty imposed upon Us by the sublime mission of peace and love entrusted to Us by God, remain indifferent, nor can We witness it in silence. Thus, from the earliest days of Our pontificate,

[92] Translation from *The Tablet*, v. 127, p. 335 (March 11, 1916). Original Italian, *A.A.S.*, v. 8, pp. 58-60 (March 4, 1916).

in the anguish of Our heart before this cruel spectacle, We urged repeatedly Our exhortations and Our counsels upon the contending nations, in order to induce them to lay down their arms, and to settle their dissensions, according to the requirements of human dignity, by pacific consultation. Throwing Ourself as it were among the belligerents, as a father might do between sons at strife, We have entreated them, in the name of that God Who is Himself Love Infinite, to renounce the purpose of mutual destruction, to declare clearly once for all, whether directly or indirectly, what are the aims and objects of each nation, bearing in mind, as far as is just and practicable, the several national aspirations, but accepting, where need is, for the sake of equal good in the general commonwealth of nations, whatever sacrifice of self-love or selfish interest may be demanded. That was, that is, the only way to calm this monstrous conflict according to the dictates of justice, and to reach a peace profitable not to one alone of the contending parties, but to all, and thus a peace equitable and lasting.

438. It is too true that Our paternal counsels have hitherto been unheeded, and the war with all its horrors rages on. Nevertheless, Lord Cardinal, We may not, We must not, be silent. It is not permitted to a father whose sons are in deadly conflict, to cease, because they resist his entreaty and reject his tears, from calling upon them. You are aware, however, that if Our repeated cry for peace has been ineffectual, it has not been without a soothing echo deep in the hearts of the people of the belligerent countries, and indeed of the whole world, and has aroused an acute and instant desire for the speedy ending of this sanguinary strife. Therefore, it is not possible for Us to abstain from raising Our voice yet once more against a war which seems to Us to be the suicide of civilized Europe. We must not cease, when occasion serves, from pointing to any means whatsoever that may be within reach, in the hope of attaining to the much-desired end.

439. And occasion is provided Us to-day by certain religious women, who have informed Us of their intention of joining in spiritual union for prayer and self-denial, with the hope of obtaining from the infinite mercy of God the withdrawal of this scourge. Such a project could not but be most acceptable to Us, who have ever insisted upon diligent prayer and Christian penance as the only refuge for Our own heart and for every human heart in the

time of this horrible fratricidal war, and as the one effectual means for obtaining from God the peace for which We sigh. We have, therefore, blessed this enterprise with all the warmth of Our fatherly heart, and We give it public praise, wishing that all the faithful may make it their own. We trust that not only in Rome, but in the whole of Italy and in the belligerent countries, Catholic families, especially in the time consecrated by the Church to Christian penance, will withdraw themselves from worldly shows and amusements, and join in such an increase of fervent prayer and of the practice of Christian mortification as may commend to Our Lord the desires of His children, and express at such a time as this the longing of every honest heart. We make a special appeal to all women who are mothers, wives, daughters, sisters of combatants, and whose tender and gentle souls, more truly than those of any others, feel the extent and the calamity of the present terrific war, so that their example and their sweet influence in the home may induce all members of their families to raise to God in this "acceptable time" and in this "day of salvation" one urgent and continuous prayer, and to lay at the foot of His heavenly throne an offering of voluntary sacrifices that shall turn aside the most just anger of God. It would be greatly pleasing to Us that such families among all combatant nations should unite in this undertaking on the day that is held sacred to the sublime Sacrifice of Him Who was God and Man, and who by His own suffering drew together in brotherhood all the sons of Adam; that they should, in those hours made eternally memorable by His infinite love, beseech of Him, through the intercession of the suffering but unconquered Mother, Queen of Martyrs, the grace to endure with fortitude and Christian resignation the anguish of loss brought about by the war, and that they should implore of His mercy the end of this long and terrible trial.

440. And since through almsgiving sins are expiated and heaven is propitiated, We desire that each family should offer, in proportion to its possessions, the alms of charity in favor of the poor and the afflicted, so dear to Jesus, our Redeemer, and more particularly for the relief of the unhappy children of those fallen in this horrible war.

441. In the hope, finally, that to this enterprise of Christian piety may be gathered—urged thereto by human compassion, and yet more strongly by the supernatural charity that must unite the

children of one Heavenly Father—the families also of neutral States, We bestow upon you, Lord Cardinal, and upon all these Catholic women and their families, Our Apostolic Benediction.

DISPATCH SENT BY CARDINAL GASPARRI, SECRETARY OF STATE, TO THE CARDINAL APOSTOLIC PRO-NUNCIO IN VIENNA.[93]

The Holy Father sends relief to the Serbian people.

March 13, 1916

442. The Holy Father, grieved by the extremely sad plight of the Serbian people, has vouchsafed to send to them a charitable subsidy of ten thousand lire. Will Your Eminence be so good as to distribute this sum in behalf of the aforesaid people in the name of His Holiness? Do it in whatever way Your Eminence thinks best. . . . . . .

DISPATCH SENT BY CARDINAL GASPARRI, SECRETARY OF STATE, TO THE CARDINAL APOSTOLIC PRO-NUNCIO IN BAVARIA.[94]

The Pope sends relief to the suffering people of Lithuania.

March 13, 1916

443. The Holy Father, upon learning of the sad conditions in which the inhabitants of Lithuania are now living, has vouchsafed to send them a charitable subsidy of ten thousand lire. Will Your Eminence be so good as to distribute this sum in behalf of the Lithuanian people in the name of His Holiness? Do it in whatever way Your Eminence thinks best. . . . . . .

NOTE OF THE CARDINAL SECRETARY OF STATE TO THE ENGLISH MINISTER TO THE VATICAN.[95]

Benedict XV asks permission of the British Government for the transportation of food from America to the starving inhabitants of Poland.

March 24, 1916

444. We are well acquainted with the generous work undertaken in favor of Belgium by the *American Commission for Relief*

[93] Original Italian, *L'Opera della Santa Sede*, p. 228.
[94] Original Italian, *L'Opera della Santa Sede*, p. 229.
[95] Original French, *L'Opera della Santa Sede*, p. 138.

in Belgium, with the mutual consent of England and Germany. The noteworthy services rendered by this Committee and which it still continues to render to the Belgian people in the present distressing circumstances are matters of public knowledge.

445. No less sad is the present situation in Poland, where the extreme penury of food supplies of absolute necessity exposes the civilian population of this country to the most terrible sufferings. That is why the Polish hierarchy and the *General Committee for Aid to War-Victims in Poland* have addressed the most insistent and moving pleas to the Holy See so that the Holy Father is extremely anxious of intervening in some way in favor of this unfortunate nation.

446. The Sovereign Pontiff, whose heart is open to all unfortunates, has not been able to remain deaf to the pleas of his sons, the inhabitants of this very noble country. Consequently, he has deigned to charge the undersigned Cardinal Secretary of State to make an ardent appeal, through the gracious intermediation of Your Excellency, to the Government of His Britannic Majesty, confident that the latter, inspired by his lofty sentiments of humanity, will presently allow, as has been so successfully done with regard to Belgium, the purchase and transportation from America to Poland of all that is necessary for the subsistence of these people. . . .

LETTER OF CARDINAL GASPARRI, SECRETARY OF STATE, TO THE BISHOPS OF ITALY.[96]

He urges them to visit the Austro-Hungarian prisoners in their dioceses.

March 31, 1916

447. His Holiness, with burning and unceasing concern, desires, as much as circumstances permit, to soothe the wounds and the sufferings caused by this horrible war. Hence, he has a fatherly interest in the poor Austro-Hungarian prisoners detained in Italy and wishes to reach them with an august word of comfort.

448. Therefore, supposing that in these dioceses there may be quartered groups of captured prisoners, the Holy Father entrusts to Your Eminence (and to Your Excellencies) the charitable mis-

[96] Original Italian, *L'Opera della Santa Sede,* pp. 240-241.

sion to visit them in his name in order to comfort them and to make manifest to them the affectionate solicitude of his heart.

449. His Holiness asks that, after you have fulfilled this pontifical mission, you will send me a short account to submit to His Holiness about the material and moral conditions of the prisoners. . . .

LETTER OF CARDINAL GASPARRI, SECRETARY OF STATE, TO BISHOP LONGHIN OF TREVISO[97]

The Holy Father protests against the airplane bombing of Treviso.

April 26, 1916

450. His Holiness, who has raised his august voice more than once against the use which is being made in this horrible war of means of offense so harmful to the pacific and innocent part of the belligerent nations, deplores that his fatherly exhortations find the hearts of his children hardened, and are broken against the dominant calculations of this terrible conflict. Sharing, then, in the bitter grief of your beloved city, and especially in the affliction which fills the heart of its bishop, His Holiness sorrowfully laments the unhappy victims who have been hurled into eternity in such a tragic way, and for them he prays God for that peace which the world cannot give, offering at the same time words of comfort and hope for the poor wounded, for whom he implores from heaven the recovery they desire and that strength which only the Christian can know amid the most sorrowful trials. . . .

LETTER *Epistola Quam Mediolani* TO CARDINAL FERRARI OF MILAN AND TO THE BISHOPS OF LOMBARDY.[98]

The practice of Christian social action must prepare the way for a lasting peace.

May 22, 1916

451. The letter which you sent Us when you were recently gathered at Milan not only carried your words and wishes but ex-

[97] Translation from *The Tablet*, v. 127, pp. 597-598 (May 6, 1916). We have been unable to locate the original of this document.
[98] Original Latin, *A.A.S.*, v. 8, p. 261 (August 1, 1916).

pressed your mind in such a way that it showed that you were most united with Us in zeal and obedience and every kind of duty. Your wishes are the wishes of peace, and you write that you will beg this peace from God so that with the auspices and help of the Apostolic See it may as soon as possible be consecrated by the kiss of justice and charity. There is scarcely anything which in the midst of such troubled affairs may be more hoped for by those who are dominated by the related love of religion and country; and be assured that you will act with very great wisdom if, as is your plan, you with particular care embrace social action in a Christian way. For even now the masses must be won over to it; our forces must be united and strengthened by the discipline of religion in such a way that Catholics themselves may be able to enjoy with greater security the benefits of peace when it has been won. . . .

LETTER OF CARDINAL GASPARRI, SECRETARY OF STATE, IN RESPONSE TO A MESSAGE FROM A GROUP OF INFLUENTIAL DANISH WOMEN.[99]

The papacy has always championed the cause of peace.

June, 1916

452. Our Holy Father, Pope Benedict XV, has been deeply touched by the sentiments so nobly expressed in your collective letter of March 20 last. You have been moved at the thought of the anxieties and heart sorrows of the August Pontiff before the immensity of the catastrophies of the terrible war. You express your gratitude to the Pope, God's minister of peace, for having seized every opportunity to plead the cause of the pacification of the world by a peace founded on justice and right. It is with reason that you recall the secular role of the Roman Pontiff, mediator between peoples, born defender of just causes, guardian of morality, law and civilization. As Universal Pastor of Souls the Pope has received in deposit the evangelical doctrine of peace and justice, and history bears eloquent testimony to the sovereign prestige, to the moderating and pacifying action of the Papacy along the ages.

453. So, too, Our Holy Father, Pope Benedict XV, has assumed with a great heart this traditional role and obeying that precept

---

[99] Translation from *Rome,* v. 19, p. 302 (June 24, 1916). Unfortunately we have been unable to find the original text of this letter nor do we know its exact date.

of the Bible, *Clama ne cesses,*[100] he desires to render possible a peace which may solve with equity and wisdom the formidable complexity of problems which have been raised up in the world. While guiding souls towards their heavenly home he considers it a duty of his charge to work and pray that quarrels, hatred and sanguinary rivalries may cease and peace and concord be restored to the city of nations.

454. Making myself the interpreter of the gratitude of His Holiness for your action so generously and so loftily inspired I beg you to accept the expression of my devoted sentiments. . . .

LETTER OF CARDINAL GASPARRI, SECRETARY OF STATE, TO CARDINAL VON HARTMANN, ARCHBISHOP OF COLOGNE.[101]

Transfer of French children into Germany protested.

June 7, 1916

455. According to certain reports recently communicated to the Holy See, the Imperial German Authorities of the occupied regions of France are supposed to have deported into Germany during these last few months various groups of young people of both sexes mixed together, with no regard for the norms of justice and morality, thus causing grief to parents and the whole people.

456. Even though the Holy See has no proof of such a fact, which would be a very serious accusation against the administration of these same Authorities, yet desiring to possess some more positive facts with which to respond to the above mentioned informers, I . . . beg you to gather precise news of this matter and kindly to send it to me. . . .

DECREE OF CARDINAL GASPARRI, SECRETARY OF STATE.[102]

European children are asked to receive Communion for the Holy Father's intention—i.e., peace.

June 26, 1916

457. His Holiness, Benedict XV, by Divine Providence Pope, who has greatly at heart the devout and rigorous observance of the

---

[100] *Isaias,* LVIII, 1.
[101] Original Italian, *L'Opera della Santa Sede,* p. 250.
[102] Translation from *The Tablet,* v. 128, p. 49 (July 8, 1916). Original Latin, *A.A.S.,* v. 8, p. 217 (July 7, 1916).

Decrees, *Sacra Tridentina Synodus* and *Quam Singulari,* of his Predecessor, Pius X, of happy memory, on the report of me, the undersigned Secretary of State, has been pleased to ordain, on the approach of the second anniversary of the great calamity, as follows:— All the Ordinaries of places in Europe are to provide with all solicitude that on July 30th this year, which falls on a Sunday, in all the churches and oratories under their respective jurisdiction, the children of both sexes shall, in the most solemn form possible, approach the Holy Table for the intention of the Holy Father. . . .

LETTER *Pietatis in Nos* TO ARCHBISHOP CONAN OF PORT-AU-PRINCE AND TO THE OTHER BISHOPS OF HAITI.[103]

> *The Bishops of Haiti have appreciated the papal efforts for peace.*

July 4, 1916

458. In your letter which you sent to Us after a recent assembly, We see, as it were, an expressed image of your filial devotion toward the Holy See. We understand how We stand with you, for you are striving to guard and to strengthen the bonds of friendship which bind Us; you gratefully recall the charity We have expended upon you and your nation; and you acknowledge what We did in Apostolic solicitude to promote peace and to remove the terrors of war. . . . . . .

ADDRESS *Era Ben Giusto* TO THE CHILDREN OF ROME.[104]

> *The Holy Father places unbounded trust in their prayers for peace.*

July 30, 1916

459. It is indeed both just and natural that to the appeal sent out by Us to all the children of Europe that on this day, the anniversary of an unhappy event, they should approach the Holy Eucharistic Table both in great numbers and with great fervor, the children of this Our Rome should be the first to correspond.

---

[103] Original Latin, *A.A.S.,* v. 8, p. 308 (September 1, 1916).
[104] Translation from *The Tablet,* v. 128, p. 216 (August 12, 1916). Original Italian, *Civiltà Cattolica,* 1916, v. 3, pp. 395-396 (August 10, 1916).

Nearest to the heart of the Vicar of Christ, they see his needs from close at hand, they best know his aspirations, his sorrows; born citizens of Rome they feel, even at their tender age, the pulsations of that heart of the world, the Papal See; descendants of their glorious ancestors in our Faith, they have in their veins the blood of Tarcisius, which lifts their hearts to the Sacrament of the Altar in which lives all reason of their faith and of their life as Romans. So We are grateful to you, Lord Cardinal, for having given Us the pleasure of being able to see this elect and numerous band of children who from the Altar and Table of the invisible God have come to Us, who perpetuate visibly the Authority and the Person of Christ; and We see them here, breathing sincerity and love, bringing to Us their simple hearts still warm with divine affection; We hear them open in salutation to Us their pure young lips, still resonant with that supreme prayer which We desired should accompany the universal Communion.

460. Often have We asked Ourselves, sadly, if perchance the life which human society is today living, far indeed from the field of battle but not far from the consequent horrors of the war, is not utterly out of keeping with the spirit of Christian mortification which is so imperiously suggested by the conditions of the times. And, indeed, We have had to reply that the desolation, which a second time, according to the words of Scripture, is laying desolate every land, does not appear depicted on men's faces; and, indeed, notwithstanding calls to recollection and penitence arising from so many disasters, grown-up people cannot separate themselves from the pleasures of modern life.

461. Trembling, therefore, for the salvation of the human race, but yet not despairing of the pity of Him Who made the peoples so that they could be healed, We take refuge in the thought and hope that it may please the infinite goodness of the Divine Father to consider not so much the penitence of the adults as the innocence of the little ones. So We have turned to you, children, who just as you hold all the affection of your parents, you assuage their sufferings, you are their future, so you hold, too, the very special affection of the Father of the faithful; you sweeten his bitternesses, in you lie his hopes. . . . . . .

LETTER OF CARDINAL GASPARRI, SECRETARY OF STATE, TO THE
DIPLOMATIC REPRESENTATIVES ATTACHED TO THE HOLY SEE.[105]

*Energetic protest against the confiscation of the Palazzo
di Venezia, the residence of the Austrian Ambassador
to the Vatican.*

August 30, 1916

462. The undersigned, Secretary of State of His Holiness, begs
to call the attention of Your Excellency to the Decree by which the
Italian Government has established that on the date of publication
of said Decree (August 25, 1916) the Palazzo di Venezia, in Rome,
becomes the property of the State. The polemics on the subject
which had appeared in the Press by license of the said Government
during the preceding days were an indication of the imminence of
this serious determination, inasmuch as, although the Government
could have checked them, it did not do so. Only on August 26,
at about ten o'clock in the morning, was the information brought
—on behalf of the Italian Government—to the Holy Father, and
he has lost no time in expressing his disapproval of the fact already
accomplished. The Holy See does not intend at the present moment to consider whether the motives given in the Decree are sufficient to justify the taking possession of the Palazzo di Venezia, either
in respect to moral law or international right. Similarly, the Holy
See abstains from any consideration as to whether that taking possession is prudent, as it might provoke grave reprisals on the part
of the adversary, and as to whether it is to be regarded as a political
act of a nature to increase or diminish the good name and prestige
of Italy before peaceful and impartial men of any country and
before history. But the Holy See cannot fail to point out the violation of its most sacred rights resulting from this measure.

463. The Palazzo di Venezia is in fact the habitual residence
of the Ambassador of His Imperial and Royal Apostolic Majesty to
the Holy See, and his actual absence does not take from the palace
this character, inasmuch as it is only temporary, and caused simply
by the abnormal circumstances due to the war. . . .

[105] Translation from *The Tablet*, v. 128, pp. 505-506 (October 14, 1916). Original
Italian, *Civiltà Cattolica*, 1916, v. 4, pp. 237-238 (October 13, 1916).

LETTER *Commisso Divinitus Nobis* TO CARDINAL BÉGIN, ARCH-
BISHOP OF QUEBEC, AND TO THE OTHER BISHOPS OF CANADA.[106]

*The Pope urgently recommends mutual concord
among the faithful in Canada.*

September 8, 1916

464. The office divinely entrusted to Us of feeding the Lord's
flock strongly impels Us to endeavor with all Our strength to compose any differences among the children of the Church which en-
danger peace and union among them. For what could be more
hurtful to the Catholic name, or what more foreign to the divine
precepts and to the principles of the Church than that factions
should exist among the faithful of Christ? . . .

465. Wherefore, Venerable Brothers, We are very deeply concerned by the disputes which have been raging for some years back
among the Catholics of your country, whose faith and piety in other
respects is a matter of common knowledge. That these disputes
are daily becoming more acute and that they are publicly known,
We learn in numerous and sure ways, as well as from what you
have told Us.

466. The cause of the trouble is evident. Among the Catholics
of Canada some are descended from the French and use the French
language, others though descended from various nationalities use
English, and this has produced disputes and contentions among
them. . . . . . .

467. Would that all these points were being debated calmly and
peaceably! But, as though the cause of nationality or religion were
at stake, they are agitated with such bitterness in newspapers and
periodicals, in books and pamphlets, in private conversations and in
public speeches, that opinions have grown more and more inflamed
and excited, and the dissension between both sides is becoming
daily more irremediable.

468. To provide suitable remedies for this great inconvenience,
We are pleased to communicate Our design to you, Venerable
Brothers, whom We know to be most closely united to Us. Take
it for certain that you will be acting in accordance with Our dearest

[106] Translation from *Rome,* v. 20, pp. 239-241 (November 18, 1916). Original Latin,
A.A.S., v. 8, pp. 389-393 (November 3, 1916).

wishes if you put forth every effort to restore, with the gifts of peace and charity, harmony and union among the faithful entrusted to your charge. . . .

469. And if the faithful in your country are divided in opinion by reason of race and nationality, and "the vessels of flesh are straightened," it is necessary, so Augustine argues, that "the spaces of charity be widened."[107] And if it is not possible to reach an agreement on all points according to what is good and fair and by means of the law of charity alone, there are those in the Church, placed by the Holy Ghost, to judge and whose decisions the faithful ought to obey if they wish to be of Christ and not to be regarded as the heathen and the publican.

470. To settle, therefore, the controversies which exist among Canadian Catholics on the rights of the two languages and their use in the churches and the Catholic schools, is a matter belonging to the bishops, and especially to those who are at the head of dioceses in which the dispute is most warmly carried on. Hence, We exhort them to meet together, to consider and weigh carefully this most important subject, and, having in view only the cause of Christ and the salvation of souls, to lay down and decree such decisions as shall seem just and opportune. Should it happen, for any reason, that the question cannot be settled and finished by their sentence, they are to bring it before this Apostolic See, which will so solve the case according to the law of justice and charity that the faithful may for the future observe peace and mutual affection, as becometh saints.

471. In the meanwhile, newspapers and periodicals which glory in the name of Catholic must not foster discord among the faithful or anticipate the judgment of the Church; those who write for them will be acting in a manner worthy of their profession by remaining patiently and modestly silent, and by dedicating themselves to the work of soothing animosities. Let the faithful also refrain from treating this question in public meetings, in speeches, and in Catholic gatherings; for otherwise it is almost inevitable that speakers will be carried away by party zeal and only add new fuel to flames already burning so fiercely.

472. What We prescribe for all in a fatherly spirit, the clergy will remember that they should be the first to follow. For since

[107] *Sermon* LXIX, in Migne, *P.L.,* v. 38, c. 440.

priests ought to become and to be from the heart the pattern of the flock, it is evidently unbecoming for them to allow themselves to be tossed about by such storms of rivalry and animosity. Hence, We exhort them most affectionately to excel the rest of the people, in moderation and kindness, in reverence for the bishops especially in all things relating to justice and ecclesiastical discipline and on which the Church decides of its own right. It will certainly be for the spiritual good and the concord of Catholics of both languages if all the priests know the two languages. Hence, We were wonderfully pleased when We learned that in some seminaries it has been made the rule that the clerics learn to speak both French and English—an example which We would wish to be followed by the others. Meanwhile let the priests engaged in the Sacred Ministry endeavor to acquire skill and practice in both languages, and setting aside all animosity use one or the other as the needs of the faithful require. . . . . . .

473. For the rest, Venerable Brothers, We have such reliance on your faithfulness and skill, and We know you to be so mindful of your office and so solicitous about the account you must render before the Divine Judge, that We take it for certain that you will leave nothing undone which may help to remove the harm and to restore peace. Give all your thought and care, therefore, to ensure that *all may be one* and *be consummated in one,* as the Divine Master taught and prayed shortly before seeking death on the cross for us. . . . . . .

LETTER *Legentes Vestram* TO THE GERMAN BISHOPS.[108]

The Pope urges the practice of Christian charity during the war.

September 8, 1916

474. . . . For indeed, while Our heart still bleeds at the sight of this long and cruel slaughter of Our children, Our grief is the more increased at seeing how Our incessant appeals for peace have given rise to unworthy suspicions among some people, and have provoked expressions of discontent among others, almost as if Our

[108] Translation from *The Tablet*, v. 128, p. 538 (October 21, 1916). Original Latin, *A.A.S.*, v. 8, pp. 356-357 (October 5, 1916).

exhortations were not prompted by a wish for the public good, but by some design for Our own interests, or as if We wished that the war might finish in a peace not founded on the principles of equity and justice. Truly, if passion had not clouded understanding, this thing could not be obscure—this thing which in itself is supremely evident—that the Supreme Pontiff, Vicar of the King of Peace and Father of all Christians, cannot, through his high duty of conscience, counsel, suggest, teach aught else but peace; and that in doing so He does not favor the cause of *any men,* but of *humanity,* and that especially in a war so murderous that, if anyone could shorten it even for a single day, he would deserve the gratitude of the human race.

475. Waiting meanwhile for the peace which We invoke, We shall continue to alleviate, at least in part, by every possible means, the awful load of misery, the unhappy consequence of the war. And it is in this field of charity that We see you distinguishing yourselves with works of enlightened zeal both in federating all the Catholic societies in Germany devoted to charity in order to bring more ready and efficacious succor to the innumerable miseries of the unfortunate, and in establishing those beneficent undertakings in Paderborn which have the scope of improving the conditions of all the prisoners in the Empire. Wherefore, while We praise this effort of Christian charity, We, in that, are praising both the unfailing kindness of the Bishop and clergy of Paderborn and the liberality of all the Catholics of Germany. But in truth to-day the highest duty of charity (which you are doing, and in which We exhort you to persevere), is this:—That each man should strive to again make brothers the peoples whom the war has divided, not making hatred more acute, but softening it little by little in mutual works of pity.

476. So, almost naturally, the way will be prepared for the peace which is, in the aspirations of every honest man, a peace which will be the more lasting in that it will have roots deep down in men's hearts. Cease not, then, to implore, as you are doing, the divine aid with new expiatory prayers and by calling the children frequently to the Eucharistic Table, for none can estimate the value before the Lord of humble and suppliant prayers, especially when they are strengthened by penance and innocence. . . . . . .

LETTER *Singulare Tuum* TO CARDINAL VON BETTINGER, ARCH-
BISHOP OF MUNICH.[109]

> *Nothing is more befitting the Apostolic See than to
> labor for peace.*

September 10, 1916

477. The exceptional ardor of your piety and obedience towards
Us shines forth from the most friendly letter which you have sent
to Us on the second anniversary of Our Pontificate. For We learn
not only that the grief which We feel from this bitterness of the
times is common to Us with you, but that you also are laboring
likewise to lessen it in Us. You write that, although We were not
able to bring about peace, We have striven up to the present to
mitigate so great and such varied sorrows of war. This We certainly have tried to do with all Our strength during the past two
years, and nothing, furthermore, is more fitting to Apostolic duty.
If We have accomplished anything in this work, all is to be attributed to the favor of God. No despair is now to be felt about common safety, especially if we properly use as our intercessor with
God His own great Mother, whom recently We have ordered all
Christians to invoke as "Queen of Peace." Bavaria should do this
with even greater zeal, as We have recently declared her its special
patron. . . .

LETTER *I Nuovi Motivi* TO ARCHBISHOP LA FONTAINE OF
VENICE.[110]

> *Benedict XV deplores the bombing of Venice.*

September 16, 1916

478. The new cause for sorrow over the unhappy lot of Venice
moves Us to a new expression of sympathy. Carrying out in your
letter of the 13th inst., your intention of letting the Head of the
Church share in the vicissitudes, already truly unhappy, of your
Patriarchate, you tell Us of the air raid of the previous night over
your city, so dear to Our heart and so precious for religion, history

---

[109] Original Latin, *A.A.S.*, v. 8, p. 394 (November 3, 1916).
[110] Translation from *The Tablet*, v. 128, p. 438 (September 30, 1916). Original
Italian, *Civiltà Cattolica*, 1916, v. 4, p. 102 (September 30, 1916).

and art, and you give Us notice that the church of SS. John and Paul has not escaped damage but that, fortunately, it is not irreparable. The new disaster, preceded only a few days before by the fall of a bomb quite close to the façade of St. Mark's—a bomb which Providence did not allow to remain of unhappy memory—brings back to Our mind the disaster of the church of Santa Maria Formosa, which, in its turn, re-opens in Our heart the bitter wound of the church of the Scalzi. Indeed, the paternal solicitude, which, as you know, We have not failed to interpose in order to prevent such disasters, has not had the effect which Our heart so keenly hoped. So, as it is not given Us to ward off the heavy blows from the heads of Our children, We, without seeking into the reasons, must limit Ourself to deploring once again this new kind of calamity, which for Us is not the least grave among the consequences of the war. Meanwhile, We take pleasure in assuring the beloved Venetians that as We are with them in all their sufferings, so We are and shall be near them with sympathy, comfort, and with help, too, according to Our power, and We pray earnestly to the Lord that He may put an end to their troubles which are a grievous sorrow to all. . . .

LETTER OF CARDINAL GASPARRI, SECRETARY OF STATE, TO CARDINAL GUSMINI, ARCHBISHOP OF BOLOGNA.[111]

Mankind is not yet worthy of peace.

September 25, 1916

479. More than thirty thousand boys and girls of the city and archdiocese of Bologna have signed their names in the precious album which Your Eminence had the noble and delicate thought of lately presenting at the Throne of the August Pontiff, offering him the devout homage, which the beloved sons of St. Petronius have rendered to the Holy Father, by approaching in great numbers the Eucharistic Banquet of Peace on Sunday, the 30th of last July, when, at the invitation of the Pontiff, all their little brethren in other churches, cities and districts at the same hour and with the same intention advanced to the same Table.

[111] Translation from *Rome*, v. 20, pp. 168-169 (October 6, 1916). Original Italian, *Civiltà Cattolica*, 1916, v. 4, pp. 234-235 (October 13, 1916).

480. On that day, memorable for the whole world, while innocence on earth, receiving into virgin hearts the flesh of the Immaculate Lamb, were united in mystic wedlock with innocence in heaven, multitudes of angels, as in the cave of Bethlehem of old, repeated the glad tidings of peace. But mankind, forgetful of love and blinded by sin, was not yet worthy of peace, and the close of a second year of hatred and slaughter was followed, alas, by the still sadder dawn of a third year of war.

481. This was a fresh wound reserved for the sorrowing heart of His Holiness, but it has found a very sweet balm in the comfort which his little angel consolers, the children of the whole world and especially of your archdiocese, have piously afforded him by the offering of their Communions and their prayers.

482. The prayer of children, who have become the living and real temple of Jesus, ascends like fragrant incense to the Throne of the Most High, and if it cannot be spread thence over this barren vale, like mystic dew, to restore peace and benediction, it is still destined for that most lofty end of assuaging the sorrows which surround the Vicar of Christ, with whose fervent and constant aspirations it is in harmony.

483. Such has been, in reality, the beneficent fruit of the homage of the children of the archdiocese of Bologna, and His Holiness has been happy to welcome it, all the more so as He has been able to run over the signatures contained in the imposing volume and recollect, in the great majority of the names, the boys and girls who have received from his hands the sacred chrism of the soldiers of Christ.

484. To each one of them, therefore, and to their households, as well as to the good priests who carefully prepared them to approach worthily the Heavenly Banquet, His Holiness wishes to express, through Your Eminence, his sovereign and ever paternal satisfaction, and he desires moreover, in return for their filial homage, to wish them that profound peace of soul and that special protection of God, which are the symbol and source of every higher prosperity.

485. Of this peace and of this protection the Apostolic Benediction will be an affectionate pledge, which the August Pontiff, with all fatherly benevolence, has deigned to impart to Your Eminence, to the clergy and people of the archdiocese, and especially to the

beloved children, reserved in the wishes of the Supreme Pastor for
the vision of a most happy existence. . . . . . .

LETTER *Pietà Profonda* TO CARDINAL GIBBONS, ARCHBISHOP OF BALTIMORE.[112]

American children are exhorted to contribute alms for
the starving Belgian youth.

October 28, 1916

486. Profound compassion of a father has again moved Our
heart, when We read an important letter recently sent to Us by the
distinguished chairman[113] of the praiseworthy Commission for Relief in Belgium, describing in few words yet showing proof of
most terrible reality, the pitiable situation of numerous Belgian
children who, during two sad years, have been suffering from the
lack of that proper nourishment necessary to sustain the tender
existence of budding childhood. In most moving terms the chairman has described how so many desolate families, after having
given everything humanly possible to give, now find themselves
with nothing left with which to appease the hunger of their little
ones.

487. He has made Us see, almost as if they were passing before
these very eyes, dimmed with tears, the long file, continuously
increasing, of Belgian infants waiting for their daily distribution
of bread; unhappy little ones whose bodies, emaciated by lack of
proper nutrition, bear not infrequently the impress of some deadly
sickness brought about by their failure to receive the food which
children of their age require. . . .

488. In this emergency the worthy chairman has turned his
thought and his heart to the millions of children of your happy,
noble America, who, in the abundance with which they are now
surrounded, could they be given an exact idea of the pitiable and
unfortunate condition of their little fellow-creatures in Belgium
. . . would not hesitate a moment to co-operate heartily in accordance with some prearranged plan, to come promptly to the relief of
these needy Belgian babies.

[112] Translation from *America*, v. 16, p. 218 (December 16, 1916). Original Italian,
  A.A.S., v. 9, pp. 10-11 (January 10, 1917).
[113] Mr. Herbert C. Hoover.

489. In view of this condition of affairs, We have considered the work indicated so humanitarian and so holy that, in prompt compliance with the appeal addressed to Us . . . We have decided to approve and recommend it, as We hereby do indorse it most heartily by these words to you, My Lord Cardinal, and, through you, to the illustrious members of the American Episcopate, to the clergy and to every generous heart; but particularly to those children of America upon whom is based every hope of success for the plan devised by this beneficent institution.

490. Neither do We doubt, in truth, that the happy children of America, without distinction of faith or of class, at this approach of another winter . . . will vie, in their innocent pride, with each other to be able to extend to their little brothers and sisters of the Belgian nation, even though across the immense ocean, the helping hand and the offerings of that charity which knows no distance. The words of our Divine Redeemer, *As long as you did it to one of these My least brethren, you did it to Me,*[114] so appropriately brought to mind in these circumstances, are a sure pledge of heavenly pleasure and reward; while We feel likewise, how greatly are ennobled, even in the eyes of the world in this period of atrocious fratricidal carnage, the people of more fortunate lands by the performance of true and loving deeds and by the pouring of a little balm upon the wounds of those less fortunate. . . . . . .

TELEGRAM OF CARDINAL GASPARRI, SECRETARY OF STATE, TO BISHOP PELLIZZO OF PADUA.[115]

The bombing of open cities is condemned.

November, 1916

491. The Holy Father, deploring and condemning aerial bombardments of inoffensive open towns, by whomsoever they be perpetrated, sends for the families in your city who have just been visited by so great a misfortune, the sum of 10,000 lire, and comforts you and your diocesans with the Apostolic Benediction.

[114] *Matthew*, XXV, 40.
[115] Translation from *Rome*, v. 20, p. 237 (November 18, 1916). We have been unable to find the original text of this message. *L'Osservatore Romano*, November 16, 1916, carries an editorial entitled: *"L'opera e la parola del Papa contro i bombardamenti aerei,"* in which a few words from this telegram are cited.

LETTER OF CARDINAL GASPARRI, SECRETARY OF STATE, TO CAR-
DINAL MERCIER, ARCHBISHOP OF MALINES.[116]

*The Holy Father endeavors to persuade the German
Government to return Belgian youths deported into the
Reich.*

November 29, 1916

492. The Holy Father has received the letter of Your Eminence,
dated the 12th of this month, with the accompanying documents
concerning the deportation of Belgian youths into Germany.

493. The August Pontiff, in whose paternal heart all the sorrows of his beloved Belgian people find a profound echo, has ordered me to inform Your Eminence that he has already interceded
most earnestly with the Imperial German Government in favor
of those populations so sorely tried, and will do all in his power
to bring about a cessation of the aforesaid deportations and the
return of the young men, already sent far away from their country,
into the bosom of their afflicted families. His Holiness has also
given me the agreeable charge of transmitting to Your Eminence
and the faithful of Belgium his very special Blessing. . . .

ALLOCUTION *Quandoquidem* TO THE COLLEGE OF CARDINALS.[117]

*Prosperity and peace reign where the observance of law
flourishes.*

December 4, 1916

494. . . . . . . It is a well-known fact in every human society,
and in the international domain itself, that where observance of law
flourishes, prosperity and peace reign; while, on the other hand,
when the authority of the law is neglected or depised and discord
and caprice prevail, all public and private right is thrown into confusion. This is confirmed, were confirmation needed, in a most
striking way by what is happening today. The horrible madness
of the conflict which is devastating Europe shows too clearly to
what slaughter and ruin disrespect for the supreme laws, which

[116] Original Italian, *Civiltà Cattolica*, 1917, v. 1, p. 348 (January 27, 1917).
[117] Translation from Schaefer, *A Papal Peace Mosaic*, pp. 27-28. Original Latin, *A.A.S.*,
v. 8, pp. 467-468 (December 9, 1916).

regulate the mutual relations of States, may lead. In this general convulsion of peoples, we behold the desecration of sacred things, and the vile treatment meted out to ministers of worship, even those of high dignity, although inviolable by divine law and by the law of nations; numerous peaceable citizens are taken away from their homes, amid the tears of mothers, wives, children; open cities and undefended populations are being molested, especially by aerial raids; everywhere, by land and sea, such misdeeds are perpetrated as fill the soul with horror and anguish. While deploring this mass of evils, and while again condemning the injustices that are committed in this war, wherever and by whomsoever perpetrated, We fondly entertain the hope, confiding in God for its accomplishment, that as with the promulgation of the new Code a happier and more tranquil era will, as We trust, dawn for the Church; so, too, may States soon enjoy the blessings of long expected peace, founded on reverence for right and justice, and bringing to all nations, once more united by the bonds of friendship, an abundance of all prosperity. . . . . . .

ALLOCUTION *Ancora Una Volta* TO THE COLLEGE OF CARDINALS.[118]

Christmas appeal for peace.

December 24, 1916

495. . . . . . . How, indeed, could Our children aspire with Us to peace, to that just and lasting peace which is to put an end to the horrors of the present war, if no conditioned good has ever been attained without fulfillment of the condition, and the *pax hominibus bonæ voluntatis* rings out to-day as a conditional promise neither more nor less than when it echoed for the first time round the crib of the newly-born Redeemer. Time and again during the fearful course of the horrible storm which devastates so large a part of the world, while reading the petitions of mothers, wives, fathers, children, and measuring with the eye and the heart the social and domestic ruins of the immense cataclysm, We have thought of the tears shed by Jesus at the sight of Jerusalem, sinful, unbelieving, wayward. But

[118] Translation from Schaefer, *A Papal Peace Mosaic,* pp. 28-29. Original Italian, *Civiltà Cattolica,* 1917, v. 1, pp. 10-12 (December 28, 1916).

more than the tears, eloquent as they are, it is the sorrowful words of Our Lord that terrify Us most: *Hadst thou but known the things that are to thy peace, but now they are hidden from thine eyes, because thou hast not known the time of thy visitation.*[119] Oh! let the world know now, amid the angelic singing and the sweet attraction of the Babe of Peace, the things which are for its peace; let those who wield powers second the voice of this illustrious Senate to arrest the course of the destruction of the peoples; let the nations reflect that the Church, by the light of the Faith and through the assistance of Him Who is the Way, the Truth and the Life, sees, nay, sees much farther than the eyes of human frailty; let the contending parties yield at last to the repeated admonitions and prayers of the Father of the Christian family.

ALLOCUTION *Degnamente Fin* TO THE ROMAN NOBILITY.[120]

Peace will not return until men make reparation to Divine Justice for their iniquity.

January 5, 1917

496. . . . . . . We keep fixed in mind the thought that, just as this dreadful scourge of war was roused by the iniquities of mankind, neither can it abate before men have rendered to Divine Justice due reparation for their iniquities. The manifold and varied practice of charity carried on by you, O beloved sons, proves that you are just as apprehensive of the calamity as We are, and just as confident in the efficacy of the remedy: wherefore it is but Our duty to confirm you in this loving trust, in order that the labors of your charity be multiplied more and more, and that they may secure the desired result. To charity let there be united, in turn, the care of making ready the ways of peace by means of a better adjustment of men's hearts. Let that which was the prey of disorder come back to uprightness: let him who wandered along the crooked byway retake the straight road. And, since it is necessary that every example descend from higher up, so also should the incitement to virtue start with the Patricians and with the Nobles of Rome. . . . . . .

[119] *Luke*, XIX, 42-44.
[120] Original Italian, *Civiltà Cattolica*, 1917, v. 1, p. 227 (January 19, 1917).

LETTER *Communi Vestra Epistola* TO THE BISHOPS OF HUN-GARY.[121]

Attempts to establish peace must now be redoubled.

January 10, 1917

497. . . . . . . As regards the calamitous conditions so gener-ally prevalent, We clearly see that your views agree with Ours and the same care which torments Us, keeps you also vehemently anxious. Hence, it naturally results that you both grieve at the length of the war and beg from God the longed-for peace, with desire more ardent and prayer more instant as the day is longer delayed. And matters indeed have come to this that counsels must be matured and attempts redoubled for the procuring of peace. May those, in whose hands are the destinies of so many peoples, quickly discover and courageously follow the *way of peace!* . . .

LETTER OF CARDINAL GASPARRI, SECRETARY OF STATE, TO BISHOP KAREVIC OF SAMOGIZIA (NOW KAUNAS).[122]

The Holy Father authorizes a collection for the war-stricken Lithuanians.

February 10, 1917

498. The Holy Father was painfully aware that, in the violence of the European conflict, the most pitiful fate had befallen the Lithuanian people, so that the flourishing country and the rich cities of that stricken land are today reduced to poverty and ruins.

499. But what shocked the compassionate heart of our Com-mon Father even more was the message sent by the Central Lithu-anian Committee to the effect that the charity of their brothers in the whole world, which has already been conspicuous towards so many war-victims and particularly towards the Belgians and the Poles, has not yet reached the hapless inhabitants of noble Lithu-ania who have been languishing so long in privation and sorrow.

500. Deeply sensitive to the groans of so many of his sons, who have the worthy claim of having always remained faithful to re-ligion and to the Church, the August Pontiff does not cease to offer

---

[121] Translation from *Rome*, v. 21, p. 5 (January, 1917). Original Latin, *A.A.S.*, v. 9, p. 81 (February 1, 1917).
[122] Original Italian, *A.A.S.*, v. 9, pp. 155-156 (March 1, 1917).

special and fervent prayers that the comforting effects of Divine Mercy may the sooner descend upon them.

501. Meanwhile, wishing to contribute personally, in the measure permitted by his present difficulties and the ever-increasing number of urgent obligations, in order to relieve the lot of the suffering Lithuanians, His Holiness has deigned to assign for their benefit the enclosed sum of twenty thousand francs, thereby indicating, if not wealth, at least the love of the Father of the poor.

502. Knowing well, however, from the hard experience of no less than thirty months of war, how necessary it is that for the relief of the Lithuanian population, a world-wide contribution be sent by all those who have not yet been subjected to the painful ordeal of war, even though they have felt the repercussions of the huge conflict, the Holy Father has deigned, as he formerly did in the case of the Polish people, to authorize Your Excellency and the other Lithuanian Bishops to invite the Bishops of the entire world to set a holyday of the current year (such as the Sunday within the Octave of the Ascension) on which in all Catholic churches there will be public prayers and a collection of funds for the relief of the poor Lithuanians.

503. The August Pontiff is confident that the charity of all those who feel the bonds of Christian brotherhood will meet his paternal appeal with a generosity proportionate to your misfortunes, and he trusts that the fruits of the merciful alms will afford to your desolate multitudes lasting economic help no less than moral comfort. . . . . . .

LETTER OF CARDINAL GASPARRI, SECRETARY OF STATE, TO M. VAN DEN HEUVEL, BELGIAN AMBASSADOR TO THE HOLY SEE.[123]

Cardinal Gasparri presents the answer of Count Hertling, Foreign Minister of Bavaria, concerning the deportation of Belgian laborers into Germany.

March 30, 1917

504. The undersigned Cardinal Secretary of State of His Holiness hastens with pleasure to communicate to Your Excellency the following note which Count Hertling, President of the Council of

[123] Original Italian, *Civiltà Cattolica,* 1917, v. 2, pp. 221-222 (April 13, 1917).

Ministers and Foreign Minister of the Kingdom of Bavaria, has recently sent to Monsignor Aversa, Apostolic Nuncio in Munich:

505. "In reply to the esteemed note of the 26th of last month, I have the honor to make known to Your Excellency that the solicitude which the Holy See manifested for a satisfactory solution of the question of the Belgian workers has not been without results.

506. "According to very reliable information, which I have recently received from Berlin, the competent authorities are disposed, first of all, to abstain from all further forced deportation of workers from Belgium into Germany, and to allow the return to their country of all those who, through some possible error, were unjustly deported. I am especially pleased that in this way is fulfilled the desire of His Holiness, the Pope, so often made known to me by Your Excellency and which I have taken care to communicate most earnestly to the Authority of the Reich. . . ."

LETTER *Il 27 Aprile* 1915 TO CARDINAL GASPARRI, SECRETARY OF STATE.[124]

Peace must be sought from Jesus Christ by frequent prayers through the intercession of the Blessed Virgin.

May 5, 1917

507. . . . . . . We were encouraged at that time by the vivid and serene hope that the Divine Redeemer would prepare all souls to receive Our paternal invitation to peace which We were preparing to address, in His August Name, to the belligerent peoples and their leaders, on the first anniversary of the breaking out of the present terrible war. The ardor with which Christian families and even the soldiers of the various fighting armies offered to Christ on that day the homage of loving submission which is so acceptable to His Divine Sacred Heart, increased Our hope and encouraged Us to raise higher Our paternal cry for peace.

508. We pointed out to the people then the only way to conciliate their dissensions—in a way honorable and favorable to all— and, tracing the foundations on which the future order of States would have to rest in order to be enduring, We conjured them, in the name of God and of humanity, to abandon their designs for

[124] Original Italian, *A.A.S.*, v. 9, pp. 265-266 (June 1, 1917).

mutual destruction and to come to a just and equitable accord.

509. But Our troubled voice, calling for the cessation of the cruel war, the suicide of Europe, remained unheeded that day and later! It seemed that the dark tide of hatred gathering strength among the belligerent nations rose even higher, and that the war, sweeping other countries into its frightful vortex, increased its slaughter and destruction.

510. Nevertheless, Our faith did not fail! You, my Lord Cardinal, who have lived and are still living with Us in the anxious expectation of the longed-for peace, well know this. In the unspeakable torture of Our soul and amidst the most bitter tears shed on account of the atrocious evils which have been heaped upon the warring peoples by this horrible tempest, We like to hope that the auspicious day is not now far distant when all men, sons of the same Heavenly Father, will again look upon one another as brothers. The sufferings of the peoples, which have become almost intolerable, have rendered the general desire for peace more acute and intense. May the Divine Redeemer, in the infinite goodness of His Heart, bring about that, in the hearts of the rulers also, mildness may prevail, and that, conscious of their own responsibility before God and humanity, they may no longer resist the voice of the peoples begging for peace!

511. Therefore, there ascends to Christ, especially in the month dedicated to His Sacred Heart, prayers more frequent, humble and confident, from the whole unhappy human family, imploring of Him the cessation of the terrible scourge. . . . And since all the graces which God deigns to bestow in pity upon men are dispensed through Mary, We urge that in this terrible hour, the trusting petitions of her most afflicted children be directed to her! . . . . . .

LETTER *Communem Vestram Epistolam* TO ARCHBISHOP ROSSI OF CAGLIARI AND TO THE OTHER BISHOPS OF SARDINIA.[125]

The war has deprived many parishes of their pastors.

May 8, 1917

512. . . . . . . The last part of your letter refers Us to those clerics whom more holy functions and higher aspirations have

[125] Original Latin, *A.A.S.*, v. 9, p. 326 (July 2, 1917).

long ago withdrawn to a more noble camp. We have the same
opinion as yourselves and We frequently turn over silently in Our
mind and with great sadness what you relate with sorrow. We
fear, and not rashly, that the hearts of those men may be soiled
with human dust whose virtue ought first to shine before all others.
And vehemently and solicitously, We turn Our thought particularly
to those parishes without number which, because of the removal of
their pastors, have no priest to impart the nourishment of holy
doctrine and administer the Sacraments. Oh, that even these adversities may work together unto good! . . .

LETTER *Epistola Vestra* TO CARDINAL FERRARI, ARCHBISHOP OF
MILAN, AND TO THE OTHER BISHOPS OF LOMBARDY.[126]

> *The Bishops must explain to their flocks the efforts the
> Holy See has undertaken for peace.*

May 12, 1917

513. . . . . . . So far as We are concerned, We think that the
attitude and mind with which We regard these adversities of the
times, what We give to the present, what promise We make to the
future, is made clear from what We have often said and done when
time and necessity seemed to demand. However that may be, your
cares must be bent in this direction, to this your labors must be
especially directed, that, whatever the Apostolic See performs either
to lessen the calamities of war or to bring about peace, all may
know this and esteem it as just. For the result will be that the truth
will recall men to better plans. . . .

LETTER OF CARDINAL GASPARRI, SECRETARY OF STATE, IN RE-
SPONSE TO AN APPEAL FOR PEACE FROM THE SWISS CHRISTIAN
SOCIAL ORGANIZATIONS.[127]

> *The Swiss are praised for their marvelous charity dur-
> ing the war.*

July 25, 1917

514. Childlike reverence marked the letter which the convention
of the Christian Social Labor Organizations of Switzerland,

[126] Original Latin, *A.A.S.*, v. 9, p. 327 (July 2, 1917).
[127] Original German, Müller, *Das Friedenswerk der Kirche*, pp. 462-463.

gathered at Zurich, sent to the Holy Father. Through it they presented him a solemn testimony of their loyalty, gratitude and love.

515. Besides the merit of the letter as an acknowledgment of the gratitude of true and loyal sons, these lofty and noble words of the Swiss workers seemed, to the Holy Father, to have the characteristics of an impressive invitation from a fortunate island to the countless poor shipwrecked souls who are hopelessly battling the surging waves of a monstrous war, that has now rocked the human family for three years and swallows up its most hopeful members.

516. To these poor shipwrecked is offered the plank of safety; and the longed-for shore of peace comes into sight. This is the sincere and absolute return to God of both individual and social, private and public life. It is the recognition of the supreme authority of Him, Whose teaching never changes, because it is Truth itself, Whose reign has gloriously withstood the centuries, because it is a clear embodiment of Love and Wisdom, Whose power, diffusing peace and benevolence, because it is the power of God, of Love and Peace itself, reaches from one end of the earth to the other.

517. The reading of the letter of devotedness awakened in the heart of the Holy Father sentiments of tender love with feelings of lively gratitude. These occasioned his ardent wish that no one might remain deaf to the convincing voice of Swiss Catholic labor, just as no one has rejected the fraternal hand of the Swiss people, as it was extended to all, to assuage their painful fears, and to heal their sick and wounded in its own hospitable land.

518. May the august Queen of Peace, unceasingly implored by the suppliant voices of her children, hear the sighs of all those who suffer and love; may she, in motherly solicitude, settle the rending conflicts, after the consuming flames of hate have been permanently extinguished in human society; may she soon bring the refreshing dew and consoling dawn of peace, so ardently desired. In these sentiments His Holiness renews his thanks to the Swiss laborers and bestows on them with paternal benevolence the desired Apostolic Blessing.

EXHORTATION *Dès le Début* TO THE BELLIGERENT PEOPLES AND
TO THEIR LEADERS.[128]

Benedict XV submits concrete proposals for peace.

August 1, 1917

519. Since the beginning of Our Pontificate, in the midst of the horrors of the terrible war which has burst upon Europe, We have considered three things among others:

To maintain an absolute impartiality towards all belligerents, as becomes him who is the Common Father, and who loves all his children with an equal affection;

To endeavor continually to do the utmost good to all without distinction of persons, nationality or religion, in accordance not only with the universal law of charity, but also with the supreme spiritual duty laid upon Us by Christ; and

Finally, as is demanded by Our pacific mission to omit nothing, as far as in Our power lies, to contribute to hasten the end of this calamity by trying to bring the peoples and their leaders to more moderate resolutions in the discussion of means that will secure a "just and lasting peace."

520. Whoever has followed Our work during these three sorrowful years that have just ended has been able easily to recognize, that, as We remained ever faithful to Our resolution of absolute impartiality and Our work of well-doing, so, We have not ceased to exhort the belligerent peoples and Governments to become once again brothers, even though publicity was not given to all that We have done in order to attain this noble end.

521. Toward the end of the first year of war We addressed to the nations who are at grips the most earnest exhortations, and, further, We indicated the road to be followed in order to reach a peace which would be stable and honorable for all. Unhappily, Our appeal was not heard and the war continued desperately for another two years with all its horrors.

522. It became even more cruel, and spread upon the face of the earth, upon the sea, and even into the sky; and on defenseless cities, on tranquil villages, on their innocent populations, were seen to descend desolation and death.

---

[128] Translation from Eppstein, *The Catholic Tradition of the Law of Nations*, pp. 215-218. Original French, *A.A.S.*, v. 9, pp. 417-420 (September 1, 1917).

523. And now anyone can imagine how the sufferings of all would be multiplied and aggravated if yet more months, or worse still, more years, were to be added to this blood-stained time. Must the civilized world be nothing more than a field of death, and shall Europe, so glorious and flourishing, rush to the abyss, as if dragged by some universal madness, and lend a hand in her own destruction?

524. In a situation of so much anguish, in presence of so terribly serious a situation, We—who have no private political aim, who listen not to the suggestions or interests of any of the belligerents, but are influenced only by the sentiment of Our supreme duty as the Father of the faithful, by the solicitations of Our children who beg for Our intervention and Our mediatory word, and for the voice of humanity and reason—now again throw out a cry for peace, and We renew Our pressing appeal to those who hold in their hands the destinies of nations.

525. But that We may no longer limit Ourselves to general terms, as circumstances counseled Us in the past, We desire now to put forward some more concrete and practical propositions, and invite the Governments of the belligerents to come to some agreement on the following points, which seem to offer the bases of a just and lasting peace, though leaving to them the duty of adjusting and completing them: First of all, the fundamental point must be that the moral force of right shall be substituted for the material force of arms; thence must follow a just agreement of all for the simultaneous and reciprocal diminution of armaments, in accordance with rules and guarantees to be established hereafter, in a measure sufficient and necessary for the maintenance of public order in each State; next, as a substitute for armies, the institution of arbitration, with its high peace-making function, subject to regulations to be agreed on and sanctions to be determined against the State which should refuse either to submit international questions to arbitration or to accept its decision.

526. Once the supremacy of right is thus established, let all obstacles to the free intercourse of people be swept aside, in assuring, by means of rules, to be fixed in the same way, the true liberty of and common rights over the sea, which on the one hand would eliminate numerous causes of conflict, and, on the other, would open to all new sources of prosperity and progress.

527. As to the damage to be made good and the cost of the war, We see no other way of solving the question but to lay down, as a general principle, an entire and reciprocal condonation, justified moreover by the immense benefits which will accrue from disarmament—the more so as the continuation of such carnage solely for economic reasons would be inconceivable. If in certain cases there are, on the other hand, particular reasons, let them be weighed justly and equitably.

528. But these peaceful agreements, with the immense advantages which flow from them, are not possible without the reciprocal restitution of territories at the moment occupied—consequently, on the part of Germany, a total evacuation of Belgium, with a guarantee of her complete political, military and economic independence, as against any other Power whatever; similar evacuation of French territory; on the part of other belligerent Powers a similar restitution of the German Colonies.

529. As regards territorial questions — as, for instance, those pending between Italy and Austria, and between Germany and France—there is ground for hope that in view of the immense advantages of a permanent peace with disarmament, the disputants would feel disposed to examine them in a conciliatory spirit, giving due weight, within the limits of justice and feasibility, as We have said previously, to the aspirations of the populations, and, on occasion, bringing their particular interests into harmony with the general welfare of the great community of mankind.

530. The same spirit of equity and justice must direct the examination of the remaining territorial and political questions, and particularly those which concern Armenia, the Balkan States, and the territories which form part of the former kingdom of Poland, which in particular, by reason of her noble historical traditions and the sufferings endured, specially during the present war, has a just claim on the sympathies of all nations.

531. Such are the principal foundations on which We believe that the future reorganization of the peoples must be built. They are of a nature to make impossible the return of similar conflicts, and to prepare the solution of the economic question, which is so important for the material well-being of all the belligerent States.

532. In laying these proposals before you, who at this tragic hour are guiding the destinies of the belligerent nations, We are

animated by a sweet hope—that of seeing them accepted, and thus of witnessing the speedy end of the terrible struggle which more and more seems to be a useless slaughter. The whole world, on the other hand, recognizes that on one side as well as on the other the honor of their arms has been amply vindicated.

533. Lend an ear, therefore, to Our prayers; accept the paternal invitation which We address to you in the name of the Divine Redeemer, the Prince of Peace. Reflect on your very grave responsibility before God and before men; on your decision depend the repose and joy of unnumbered families, the lives of thousands of young men, the happiness, in a word, of the peoples, to secure whose welfare is your absolute duty.

534. May God inspire you with a decision in harmony with His most holy will. Heaven grant that in meriting the applause of your contemporaries you may assure to yourselves, in the sight of future generations, the noble name of peace-makers. For Us, in close communion in prayer and penitence with all the faithful souls who are sighing for peace, We implore for you from the Divine Spirit enlightenment and counsel.

LETTER *Graves inter Amaritudines* TO CARDINAL VON HART-MANN, ARCHBISHOP OF COLOGNE, AND TO THE OTHER ARCH-BISHOPS AND BISHOPS ATTENDING THE MEETING AT FULDA.[129]

The German Bishops offered the Pope their felicitations for his intervention in behalf of peace.

September 7, 1917

535. . . . And in the first place it pleased you, Beloved Son and Venerable Brethren, to give approval to Our letters by which We vehemently urged the leaders of the peoples waging war to put aside arms and to discuss and enter upon a just and lasting peace, and at the same time you promised that with all your power and especially by your prayers and the prayers of your faithful you would aid Us in Our attempts at peace . . . We rejoice at the same time when We notice that this slight gift has furnished you with a cause of pouring forth prayers to God that He may bestow upon Us the oil of consolation and strength to alleviate the wounds of

---

[129] Original Latin, *A.A.S.*, v. 9, pp. 485-486 (October 1, 1917).

Our heart and give Us courage in adversity. You will easily perceive from what source We expect the greatest consolation in these times. Wherefore, proceed together with your peoples by penance and prayers to lessen the Divine Wrath and to pray with Us that Almighty God may hasten to send down at length from heaven upon the whole world swallowed up in a monstrous war, as though in a whirlpool of fire and blood, a snowy dove bearing the olive branch in her mouth. . . .

LETTER OF CARDINAL GASPARRI, SECRETARY OF STATE, TO BISHOP DE GIBERGUES OF VALENCE.[130]

Cardinal Gasparri explains how the papal peace proposal of August 1 applies to France.

September 10, 1917

536. . . . . . . In considering the various points which the Holy Father regards as the main conditions of the peace which he desires to be just and lasting, it certainly is not France that can consider herself as hardly treated by the first and second, which concern mutual and simultaneous disarmament, and as a consequence the establishment of a court of compulsory arbitration and of the freedom of the seas.

537. As to the compensation for the damage done and the cost of the war, the Holy Father, in the third point, proposes reciprocal condonation as a general principle, adding, however, that if in certain cases there are special reasons in the way of it (as in the case of Belgium), they must be considered with justice and equity. Your Excellency must certainly remember that M. Ribot, in accord with the Provisory Government of Russia, has admitted that in the eventual peace conferences there must be no demand for a war indemnity; but he reserved for France the right of demanding compensation for the damage caused by the ill-feeling of military commanders without any military necessity. Conceived as it was in general terms, the Papal Note does not stand in the way of compensation for such damage being included in the exception above mentioned. But even apart from the enormous difficulty of esti-

[130] Translation from *The Tablet*, v. 130, p. 459 (September 27, 1917). Original French, *Documentation Catholique*, v. 32, cc. 1334-1335 (December 29, 1934).

mating on the various sectors the damage needlessly caused by the fault of the military commanders, it is for France to determine if it will be worth her while, even on the supposition that she will be victorious, to prolong the war for even a year in order to demand reparation for such damage of the enemy, taking into account the losses in money and the still greater losses in men, and the heaps of ruins which the war would leave in Belgium and in the occupied districts in France.

538. In his fourth point, the Holy Father means that the French territory now in the occupation of the German armies shall be immediately and completely evacuated. That certainly cannot be displeasing to France, which for more than three years has been shedding the best blood of her sons without having achieved the liberation of those districts. And lastly, in his fifth point, the Holy Father does not, and could not, propose any solution of the question of Alsace-Lorraine. But he expresses a wish that France and Germany may examine it in a conciliatory disposition, and have regard, so far as may be just and possible, to the aspirations of the people concerned. It is, therefore, hard to see how such desires and hopes could be offensive to French patriotism; on the contrary, if this question, which is the apple of discord between two great nations, could be solved peaceably and in a way satisfactory to both parties (and no one will say that this is impossible), would it not be better, not only for Germany and France, but for all mankind? It is, then, clear that while the Papal Note is on many points favorable to France, it is offensive in none, which encourages the hope that when the first hasty impression has passed, France will give the Papal Note a fairer and more favorable appreciation.

LETTER *Redditæ Sunt Nobis* TO THE BISHOPS OF SWITZERLAND.[131]

His Holiness praises the Swiss for their abundant charity during the war.

September 10, 1917

539. Your common letters have been given to Us, and when We read them We felt that your love towards Us was being in-

---

[131] Original Latin, *A.A.S.*, v. 9, p. 486 (October 1, 1917).

creased, that your former intentions of pleasing Us were being strengthened more and more, and finally that even greater hope was being nourished that in the future so many of Our unhappy sons in Christ would receive by Our aid and industry a harvest of benefits. In thanking Us for the manifold care which during the whole war We have given captive soldiers, it has pleased you to call Switzerland, which is free from slaughter, "an isle of peace," truly a beautiful appellation and one most deserved.

540. We prefer to call your hospitable land "a most beautiful theatre of charity," and We bestow this same praise all the more willingly because We know that the kindly virtue of the Swiss people has made itself a companion to Our paternal charity. . . . . . .

LETTER OF CARDINAL GASPARRI, SECRETARY OF STATE, TO LLOYD GEORGE, PRIME MINISTER OF ENGLAND.[132]

To have international peace there must be a simultaneous and reciprocal suppression of compulsory military service.

September 28, 1917

541. . . . . . . As for the reciprocal and simultaneous disarmament universally desired, a true earnest of peace and prosperity, the Holy Father, out of deference to the belligerent Powers, did not intend in his letter to indicate the means for effecting and maintaining this, preferring to leave the determination of such means to the Powers themselves; but he considers that the only practical and easy way of effecting this is the following: a pact among civilized nations, including non-belligerents, requiring the simultaneous and reciprocal suppression of compulsory military service; the institution of a tribunal of arbitration to decide international controversies; and the imposition of a general boycott as a sanction against any nation that might attempt to re-establish obligatory military service, or might refuse to submit an international question to arbitration or to accept the decision thereon.

542. Omitting other considerations, the recent example of England and of America proves that voluntary military service certainly

[132] Original Italian, *Civiltà Cattolica*, 1919, v. 3, p. 439 (October 4, 1919).

gives the forces necessary for the maintenance of public order, although it does not supply the enormous armies which modern war requires. Therefore, once obligatory military service has been suppressed by common accord and voluntary service introduced in its stead, we would have, without any disturbance of public order, almost automatically a complete disarmament, with all the benefits directly consequent thereon: a lasting international peace (as far as that is possible in this world), and the restoration of sound finances in the various nations in as short a time as possible, without speaking of other advantages which need not be enumerated, since they are readily foreseen. Compulsory military service has been the true cause of so many evils for more than a century; in its simultaneous and reciprocal suppression lies the true remedy. And since, once suppressed, it could not, even in the actual constitution of the Central Empires, be re-established without a law of Parliament approving it (an improbable approbation for many reasons), we would have not only the word of rulers, but even the guarantee of peoples, as requested in recent documents by persons of authority. . . .

LETTER OF CARDINAL GASPARRI, SECRETARY OF STATE, TO ARCHBISHOP CHESNELONG OF SENS.[133]

He clarifies and elaborates the various proposals of the August 1 peace note.

October 7, 1917

543. . . . . . . Your Grace will have seen my letter to the Bishop of Valence,[134] which gives expression to the astonishment which I have experienced at the generally hostile attitude of the French Press in regard to the Papal Note. In that letter I have demonstrated (what was plain from a perusal of the document of the Pope) that none of the points indicated by the Holy Father, as bases of a just and lasting peace, could be wounding to French patriotism. Nay, some of those points are clearly favorable to France; and so much so that if any nation is favored in the Papal

---

[133] Translation from *The Tablet*, v. 130, pp. 574-575 (November 3, 1917). Original French, La Briere, *La Patrie et la Paix*, pp. 154-159.

[134] See *supra* n. 536.

Letter it is not Germany or Austria, but France and Belgium. My surprise and astonishment were, therefore, very great.

544. The Papal document has been represented as inspired by the Central Empires, and especially by Austria. But this assertion is completely false. The declarations of the Holy See and those of the German Chancellor, the replies of the Central Empires, the opposition of the Pan-Germanist and conservative Press of Germany place this point beyond a doubt; and I may add that, owing to a wholly involuntary delay in its transmission, the Emperor of Austria and his Government were the last to receive the text of the Papal Letter.

545. The genesis of the letter was, besides, very simple—so simple that there is no need to have recourse to the idea of any foreign inspiration at all. From the declarations made by the statesmen and parliaments of the belligerent Powers, the Holy See had noted with the liveliest satisfaction that on certain fundamental points there was substantial agreement; and it accordingly brought these different points together and invited the Powers themselves to define and complete them, and to examine them in a spirit of conciliation, taking into account as far as possible the aspirations of the peoples concerned. There you have the whole purport and purpose of the Pope's Letter of August 1.

546. Thus, for example, nearly all the belligerents — Russia, France, England, Germany and Austria — had declared that peace should be concluded without indemnities. Russia, Germany and Austria made no distinction between the cost of the war and the damage wrought by the war, indicating by this that compensation for the damage would not be demanded. M. Ribot was the only one who declared that in future negotiations for peace France reserved to herself the right to claim compensation for the damage caused upon her territory unnecessarily and by the fault of the military authorities. It is for this reason that in the third point of the Papal Appeal the Holy See proposes that there should be, as a general rule, reciprocal condonation of the cost and damage of the war; but it added that *if in any cases there were special reasons against this, those reasons should be weighed with justice and equity.* Stated in such general terms, this proposal does not exclude the reservations put forward by M. Ribot; and France remains free to judge whether, in the hypothesis of her being vic-

torious, it is worth her while to prolong the war, even for a year, in order to exact from Germany compensation for the damage of which she has been guilty.

547. Again, it has been said that the Holy Father, in his capacity of supreme judge of morality and justice, ought in the first place to have declared which side was wrong and which was right. This is a strange criticism, forsooth! In the interest of mankind the Holy Father, in his Letter, assumes the office of *mediator,* and does all that is possible to persuade the belligerent nations, each of which claims to have right on its side, to lay down their arms, to enter into conversation and to become reconciled. Now, is it, I would ask, the part of a mediator to decide which of the parties concerned is wrong and which is right? If he sought to settle this question, is it likely that he would attain the object he proposes, which is that of getting the parties to enter on the path of reconciliation and peace?

548. Moreover, and here I pass over some other points of less importance, it has been objected that the proposals of the Holy Father are not all capable of being realized. And it has been particularly pointed out that reciprocal and simultaneous disarmament must be placed in the rank of the aspirations destined to remain without effect. But disarmament is desired by all without exception, as the only means of removing the danger of war, remedying the financial difficulties of the nations concerned, and of avoiding the social convulsions which are, unless it comes about, only too easy to foresee. As soon, however, as it becomes a question of the way in which this disarmament is to be effected and maintained, agreement ceases. I have no hesitation in acknowledging frankly that none of the systems so far put forward is really practicable. And yet there is such a practicable system.

549. The Holy See, in its Appeal of August 1, did not, out of deference for the heads of the belligerent nations, think it well to point to it, preferring to leave to them the task of deciding on it. But, for itself, the practical system and one which is, besides, easily applied, given a little good-will, would be something of this sort: the suppression, by common accord among civilized nations, of compulsory military service; the constitution of a Court of Arbitration, as was mentioned in the Pope's Appeal, for the solution of international questions; and lastly, for the prevention of infrac-

tions and as a penalty, the establishment of a universal *boycott* against the nation which should seek to set up compulsory military service, or should refuse either to submit an international question to the Court of Arbitration or to accept its decision.

550.   Lord Robert Cecil has himself, in one of his speeches, fully recognized the practical efficacy of such a penalty. And indeed, not to mention other considerations, the recent example of England and America is evidence in favor of the adoption of this system. England and America had voluntary service, but in order to take an effective part in the present war, they have been obliged to have recourse to conscription. This shows that voluntary service provided the men necessary for maintenance of public order (and is not public order maintained in England and America as well as, if not better than, in other countries?), but it was not able to furnish the enormous armies needed in modern warfare. So then, by the suppression, by common agreement, among civilized nations of compulsory service and its replacement by voluntary service, disarmament, with all the happy consequences indicated above, would be brought about automatically and without any perturbation of public order.

551.   For more than a century conscription has been the real cause of a multitude of evils afflicting society, for which a simultaneous and reciprocal suppression of it will be the true remedy. And once suppressed, conscription should not be able to be re-established except by special law, for which even under the existing constitution in the Central Empires, the approval of Parliament would be necessary, and that would be very improbable for many reasons, and especially owing to the sad experience of the present war. Thus we should come to have, for the maintenance of the agreement arrived at, just what is so much desired—the guarantee of the peoples themselves. If, on the other hand, the right of peace or war were reserved to the people by way of referendum or at least to Parliament, peace between nations would be assured, at least so far as is possible in this world.

LETTER *Tanta Nos Mole* TO CARDINAL CSERNOCH, ARCHBISHOP OF STRIGONIA, AND TO THE OTHER BISHOPS OF HUNGARY.[135]

The motives behind the papal intervention for peace.

December 3, 1917

552. . . . Particularly, however, do We embrace the clear meaning of your gratitude that We recently suggested reconciliation and peace to the rulers of peoples contending with one another; all the more, because that proof of paternal love which had suggested itself to Us by the consciousness of Our Apostolic duty, by commiseration for common troubles, by love of justice and right no less than by love of public tranquillity, We have seen called into unworthy suspicion by certain men of prejudiced opinions. Through the activity of most wicked factions there is thus stirred up daily more and more against the clergy the blind rashness of multitudes so that We can now use that expression of the Apostle: *We are reviled, and we bless; we are persecuted, and we suffer it; we are blasphemed, and we entreat.*[136] Nevertheless, relying on divine aid, We wish to continue constantly to perform the duties of Our office. In the meantime, let us not cease, by our humble and suppliant prayer, to beg God that He Himself may ultimately deign in His mercy to grant that peace which the world cannot give. . . .

LETTER *Gratias Vobis* TO THE ARCHBISHOPS AND BISHOPS OF BAVARIA.[137]

His Holiness grieves that the papal message of peace has been misunderstood.

December 5, 1917

553. We thank you from Our heart for your common letter of homage whereby at the beginning of the meeting at Friesing you gave testimony of your supreme obedience and fidelity toward Us. For this was no common pleasure, or rather it was a consolation to Us, a consolation which indeed you see that We greatly need in these bitter times. For to the other anxieties and cares which

---

[135] Original Latin, *A.A.S.*, v. 10, p. 14 (January 2, 1918).
[136] I *Corinthians*, IV, 12-13.
[137] Original Latin, *A.A.S.*, v. 10, p. 15 (January 2, 1918).

afflict Our soul by the length of this terrible war there is added
this, namely, that Our exhortation to restore peace, which in truth
sprang from no other motive than from a sincere desire of public
good, not only had an effect that We hoped for least of all but
even was twisted against Us by wicked men into a cause for public
hatred against Us although it was a proof of Our love. In this
matter We do not so much complain at the injustice visited upon
Us—for We ought to be always ready to bear insults for the name
of Jesus—as We grieve at the loss of so many souls. Relying, however, on the help of Jesus Christ, Who will never be wanting to
His Church, and imploring from Him an end of such great evils,
let us, with supreme effort, continue to strive that in the bosom of
the Church holiness of morals and discipline may flourish more
and more. . . .

ALLOCUTION *A Lei, Signor Cardinale* TO THE COLLEGE OF CAR-
DINALS.[138]

*The Pope laments that the belligerent nations have
refused to consider his peace proposals.*

December 24, 1917

554. . . . . . . By now accustomed to celebrate, by the Divine
Will, with joy tempered by sadness, the most sweet recurrence of
the holy feast, We were preparing to give voice to the sorrows
of the father and the anguish of the shepherd, in this fourth war-
time celebration of the anniversary of the Birth of Our Lord
Jesus Christ.

555. Alas! How many souls We saw in sorrow because of the
present day, how many in fear and darkness because of the morrow!
As guardian of the Fold that only a false shepherd could bear to
see fall to destruction, We felt, like Paul, a keen sorrow when
all Our endeavors to effect a reconciliation among the peoples had
failed. We were grieved particularly, that the invitation addressed
by Us to the chiefs of the belligerent peoples had gone unheeded—
not because personal gratification had been denied Us, but because the peace of nations had been delayed.

556. From the most authoritative circles there had been an-

---

[138] Original Italian, *Civiltà Cattolica*, 1918, v. 1, pp. 15-17 (December 28, 1917).

nounced some essential principles of discussion that could have been used as a basis for a common understanding. We had gathered these points simply to invite the heads of the belligerent States to make them the object of their particular attention, with the sole purpose of obtaining more quickly the realization of that wish that lies secret and stifled in the hearts of all. However, when We saw that We were either unheeded or looked upon with suspicion, We could not fail to perceive in Ourselves the *signum cui contradicetur*.[139] We were comforted by the hope that Our invitation to peace, since it was not one that looked for immediate effects, might perhaps be likened to the kernel of wheat of which our Divine Master says, *Unless the grain of wheat falling into the ground die, itself remaineth alone; but if it die, it bringeth forth much fruit.*[140] Above all, We were comforted by the knowledge that it is Our right and obligation to pursue in the world the peace-making mission of Jesus Christ. No obstacle and no danger appeared strong enough to make Us break Our resolution to do Our duty and to exercise the right that belongs to the representative of the Prince of Peace.

557. But We cannot deny that on witnessing the deadly struggles of nations that were once flourishing but were now being driven to the extremes of mutual destruction, and fearing that the suicide of European civilization was drawing nearer and nearer, We asked in sorrow, "When, and how, will this horrible tragedy end?" . . . Opportunely have you spoken, Lord Cardinal, and We applaud the fitness of your advice, according to which you look upon the present conflict in the light of Faith, and from that Faith you derive the firm conviction that the present calamities will not come to an end until men return to God.

558. But in order that the comfort which We are pleased to derive from the Christmas greetings of the Sacred College, expressed by their Most Eminent Dean, be a messenger of better days, We shall not limit Ourselves merely to acknowledge the affirmed importance of a return to God, but, with the most earnest and heartfelt longing, We desire to hasten the hour of the salutary return of contemporary society to the school of the Gospel. "When the blind of today shall see, and the deaf shall hear, when every

139 *Luke*, II, 34.
140 *John*, XII, 24-25.

deviation shall be righted and every roughness smoothed," when, in other words, man and society shall go back to God, then—and only then—*shall all flesh see the salvation of God—videbit omnis caro salutare Dei*[141] and to the poor and to the suffering shall the good tidings of peace be announced. Oh! the great lesson that the Church repeats to us with the words of the liturgy for these holy days! . . . . . .

559. And to return to God it would be sufficient to go to Bethlehem with the single-heartedness of the shepherds; it would suffice to hearken to the voice of heaven's messenger above the Crib of the Divine. Oh! Peace of Christ, dear to every age that possessed you, how much dearer should you be to our age which lost you for so long a time! . . . But the Peace announced by the angels at Bethlehem countenances neither hatred nor vengeance, cupidity nor slaughter . . . it is the voice of meekness and forgiveness. . . . It is a promise, indeed, it is a reward announced to *men of good will.* Oh! Let this never be forgotten by those who see in the annual recurrence of the Christmas celebration an invitation to return to the Lord by way of Bethlehem! . . . . . .

LETTER *Natalis Trecentesimi* TO MOTHER ANGELA OF OUR LADY, SUPERIOR GENERAL OF THE URSULINES.[142]

Laxity of morals increases with the progress of the war.

December 27, 1917

560. It is indeed fitting that the solemn celebration of the three-hundredth anniversary of the foundation of the Religious Order of the Visitation take place in these tempestuous times. It is evident that the cause of so many evils is to be placed especially in this fact that too many people have publicly and privately abandoned those Christian precepts and practices which are the very foundations of States. For a long time now, but especially since the change in French policy, the effort was that the beneficent authority of the Church, gradually restricted to a narrower field, should finally lose all influence in human society. Moreover, there has been a determined effort to remove womanhood from the maternal care and

---

[141] *Luke,* III, 6.
[142] Original Latin, *A.A.S.,* v. 10, p. 57 (February 1, 1918).

protection of the Church. Woman has indeed marvelous powers, either for good or for bad, upon the fortunes of the human race; for if she openly departs from the path of virtue, all training both by the family and by the State is easily destroyed. And so one can see that when religion has been removed, women have been taught to lay aside all modesty and piety. One can see, too, that there are many women who, devoting themselves too much to pursuits foreign to their nature, have acquired manners of acting which are utterly masculine; and that these same women, deserting their duties in the home for which they were created, rashly throw themselves into the midst of life's struggle. This is the source of that deplorable perversity of morals which the license of the war itself has unbelievably increased and widely propagated. As far as has been in your power you have opposed this perversion of right standards by properly educating girls in Christian wisdom; and with God's help your results in this work have been great and outstanding. . . .

LETTER *Annua Pietatis Vestrae* TO CARDINAL GUSMINI, ARCHBISHOP OF BOLOGNA.[143]

> *Without God's help, men cannot restore order in the world.*

December 29, 1917

561. The annual expression of your filial devotion, which you sent to Us with happy wishes, comes to Us, not indeed as joyful as it might have been, considering the sorrowful times, but nevertheless as most pleasing and gratifying, since it comes from those whom We know to be closely united to Us by ties of long standing. Responding to your kindness with that paternal love which We have for you and which is at the same time known to you, We ask the Divine Infant to pour forth His gifts upon you, especially the perfection of them all—peace—which at His birth He brought to all men. For anyone can have this peace in his soul, even in the most difficult circumstances. Would that the nations of the world would settle this terrible conflict and would become sharers of that peace as soon as possible! Yes, men can of their

[143] Original Latin, *A.A.S.*, v. 10, pp. 58-59 (February 1, 1918).

own power throw the whole world into disorder and destroy everything; but they cannot rebuild again and set things in order unless
God helps them. Therefore, since peace must be sought from
heaven, We must continue to pray for it in all Our supplications,
even though Our frequent exhortations to men have thus far been
of no avail. Just as you do, We shall constantly commend Our
prayers to the patronage of the Blessed Virgin. From her the world
received peace with Christ; under her guidance may it return to
the possession of that peace which it has so unfortunately lost. . . .

ADDRESS *In Ogni Periodo* TO THE ROMAN NOBILITY.[144]

The Pope condemns injustice wherever it appears.

January 5, 1918

562. . . . . . . This year, however, We have a special reason
to be pleased with the good wishes of the Roman Patriciate and
Nobility. In this very instant We have heard the worthy representative of this high rank echo Our words, inviting all peoples
to return to God, in order to hasten the end of the tremendous
calamity which has afflicted the world for more than three years.
When in this very hall We sent forth that invitation to the nations
to return to God, We wished especially that the great ones of the
world should be the first to answer the appeal, because it is for
them to go before the little ones with the light of good example.
To-day the Roman Patriciate and Nobility have come to Us, and,
celebrating, through the voice of a common interpreter, the civilization brought by Christ, recognize with Us that the world must
return to Christ to enjoy the benefits of that civilization. . . .

563. The joy of Our soul is increased by the certainty that each
one of you, dearly beloved sons, wishes to run in the way which
Christian society must follow to return to Christ. This is a way of
justice and of love. But We have already remarked your zeal for
justice in the words with which, alluding to the sorrowful events
which have lately afflicted our country, you have condemned
methods of war which are not in conformity with the dictates of
the law of nations. In this also you have associated yourselves

[144] Translation from *The Tablet*, v. 131, p. 81 (January 19, 1918). Original Italian,
L'Osservatore Romano, January 6, 1918.

with Us, who, faithful to Our program of condemning injustice wherever it appears, have even recently raised Our voice against a form of war which, waged on undefended cities, whilst it does not obtain results of military value, can make, and indeed has made, victims amongst non-combatants, and can and has damaged the sacred inheritance of religion and of art, making national hatred and lust for vengeance even more keen. We hope that the love of justice will follow you also in every other phase of private and public life, and will confirm you in the resolution to render unto God that which is due to Him, and to your neighbor that which you would wish for yourselves. . . . . . .

LETTER *Conspirantibus Adversus* TO THE AUSTRIAN BISHOPS.[145]

The Pope endeavors not only to alleviate the cruel tragedies of the war but also to hasten its end.

February 2, 1918

564. . . . It is a very opportune consolation to Us that you approve greatly Our manner of action with regard to this calamity of war. And indeed it was fitting both to Our Apostolic office and to Our charity that We would strive with all Our strength not only to alleviate great sorrows but also to urge and to hasten the end of this slaughter of Our children. But if this profession of your gratitude delights Us, how much, on the other hand, does malevolence pain Us! You know that some went so far that, rejecting Our exhortation to peace, they placed the blame for the evils which followed upon that proof of paternal love. However, We in this case as in all others which belong to Our office are motivated by religious duty, not by the approval of men: and placing all Our hope in Jesus Christ, Who will never abandon His Church, there is no reason why We should be moved by these difficulties. And so while the war lasts, let Us continue—the only thing that is left—to lighten in some measure so great a burden of troubles and griefs by the various offices of Christian charity; and, in the meantime, by Our prayers to strive, along with you and with all good men, finally to call down peace, the companion of justice, from heaven, whence eventually it must be expected. . . .

[145] Original Latin, *A.A.S.*, v. 10, p. 90 (March 1, 1918).

Discourse to Delegates from Finland.[146]

*Before the Holy See all nations, large or small, have
equal rights.*

March 2, 1918

565. True to its tradition to recognize the same rights for small
nations as for the large ones, the Holy See will be happy to establish
immediate friendly relations with the government of Finland.

Letter of Cardinal Gasparri, Secretary of State, to M. Denys Cochin.[147]

*Cardinal Gasparri tries to clear up French misunder-
standings concerning the effort of the Holy See to prevent the deportation of Frenchmen into Germany.*

March 16, 1918

566. I have duly received your letter of February 22,[148] in which
you reply to mine of February 18. The sole object of my letter was
to put a stop to the deportations, and with that object I forwarded
to you Germany's proposals concerning them. If you think that
these proposals compromised a principle, and were, therefore, un-
acceptable, even with reservations on the principle, you have only
a very simple course to take—not to accept them.

567. You say that the Holy See has no word of reprobation
for the deportations. Are you quite sure of that? Do you know
the documents that are in the archives of the Secretary of State?
As to seeing in my letter any affirmation that Alsace-Lorraine is
German, that is going altogether too far. When you wrote your
letter you had plainly lost your customary command of your pen,
so please allow me to consider your letter as not having been
received.

---

[146] Original Italian, *Osservatore Romano* (March 3, 1918). German translation from
Lama, *Papst und Kurie*, p. 430.
[147] Translation from *The Tablet*, v. 131, pp. 490-491 (April 13, 1918). Italian translation from the French original, which we have been unable to find, *Civiltà
Cattolica*, 1918, v. 2, p. 173 (April 12, 1918).
[148] M. Denys labored under the misapprehension that the proposals offered by Germany
were made by the Holy See.

LETTER *In Maximis* TO ARCHBISHOP KAKOWSKI OF WARSAW.[149]

*To help in the reconstruction of Poland the Pope sends
Achille Ratti as Apostolic Visitor.*

April 25, 1918

568. In the midst of the great difficulties and anxieties that
weigh upon Us, brought on by this murderous war that is daily
increasing in violence, as with new fire added to existing flames,
the merciful goodness of God permits Us to enjoy at intervals
some consolation which strengthens within Us the hope that when
once this huge accumulation of miseries shall have disappeared,
things will turn out in such wise as to benefit the Catholic Religion
and the eternal salvation of men. Thus it was that We derived
no little joy of heart from the letter which you addressed to Us
on the 11th of December last; for after giving the fullest expression of your love and reverence for Us, you went on to tell Us of
the very weighty deliberations you had held in the council of
bishops convened that very day in Warsaw, with a view to establishing on a new basis the Catholic cause in the territory of Poland.

569. Certainly no one, much less Ourself, could entertain
any doubt as to your very close union with Us, since it is a fact
of common knowledge that ever and uninterruptedly, through
whatever difficult circumstances may have prevailed, you have per-
severed in communion with the Apostolic See. But We set a greater
value upon this more recent expression of your devoted attachment
to Us for this reason, that it comes opportunely at a juncture when
a more widespread increase of political freedom and a full and
entire liberty to practice the Faith of their ancestors seem to be
dawning for the Catholics of Poland.

570. You are undertaking a highly important and difficult work,
and it demands that you set aside every division of opinion and
bring all your powers to bear upon it; if thus your minds are in
agreement, the result can only be that, with God's help, the benefits
to religion will correspond in abundance to the harmony of your
action.

571. In order to give a public and unmistakable testimony of
the special care and benevolence We bear towards you and the

---

[149] Original Latin, *Actes de Benoît XV*, v. 1, pp. 191-193.

task that now engages you, as also to receive the expressions of good-will in Our behalf of which you have made profession, We have resolved to send to you as Our personal representative, Our beloved son, Achille Ratti, Prothonotary Apostolic and Prefect of the Apostolic Vatican Library. To him as Apostolic Visitor will pertain matters strictly ecclesiastical; We charge him, that is to say, with the task of examining into what advice, what powers, what remedies the Catholic structure needs in your midst; and in making such regulations for it as will seem best under the circumstances, he is to be your associate and fellow counselor. Holding, therefore, this appointment as intermediary between the Apostolic See and the bishops of Poland, he will with greater ease make known to Us your desires and communicate to you Our decisions; the result of this arrangement will undoubtedly be that the new order of things which you have begun to create will be put into effect in perfect harmony with Our ideas and your own as well.

572. There is no need, assuredly to recommend to you a man whom his personal piety, his zeal for religion, his practical experience in affairs and his universally known learning more than sufficiently recommend; this, though, We desire you to know: that Our confidence in this admirable man is such that We are convinced that his labors will prove of very great benefit to your episcopal sees. Since, however, human counsels are of no avail unless they be seconded by the grace of the omnipotent God, We beseech Him with earnest prayers to enlighten and direct your minds with the gifts of His heavenly wisdom. . . .

MOTU PROPRIO—*Quartus Jam Annus.*[150]

> *All priests must celebrate Holy Mass on June 29 for the speedy end of the war.*

May 9, 1918

573. Already the fourth year is drawing to its close since the moment when, soon after the European conflagration had broken out, We took up the burden of the Supreme Pontificate; and in all this space of time since, the fury of war, instead of decreasing, has

[150] Translation from *The Tablet*, v. 131, p. 658 (May 18, 1918). Original Latin, *A.A.S.*, v. 10, pp. 225-227 (June 1, 1918).

gained continually in strength, the anguish of Our heart has had no rest before the terrible evils which have been accumulating. Following this tragic sequel of events, not only have We shared in the sufferings of all, even to being able to say with St. Paul: *Who is weak, and I am not weak? Who is made to stumble, and I am not inflamed?*[151]; but further, as far as has been possible to Us, We have omitted nothing which consciousness of the Apostolic duty dictated or the charity of Christ suggested to Us. And now the condition in which We find Ourself is such that it recalls that of King Josaphat when in his anguish he exclaimed: *Lord, God of our Fathers, Thou art God in heaven, and rulest over all kingdoms and nations; in Thy hand is strength and power, and no one can resist Thee . . . we will cry to Thee in our afflictions, and Thou wilt hear and save us. . . . O our God . . . as we know not what to do, we can only turn our eyes to Thee.*[152]

574. Therefore, *laying all Our anxiety in the Hands of God,*[153] Who rules the hearts of men and the course of events, from Him alone "Who heals whilst punishing, and forgiving saves," We await the end of this terrible scourge, that He may soon give back His peace to the world and restore the reign of charity and justice among men.

575. But, before all, must be appeased the just wrath of God, caused by the spread of perversity in sin. Humble and suppliant prayer, offered with perseverance and trust, will contribute much to this end; but more efficacious still in obtaining Divine Mercy is the Holy Sacrifice of the Mass, in which we offer to our Heavenly Father Him *Who gave Himself in redemption for all,*[154] and *lives still to intercede for us.*[155]

576. And the Church is right in ordaining that pastors of souls shall celebrate on fixed days for the needs of the Christian people when this loving Mother wishes to invoke the mercies of God on the needs of her children. And what need can be to-day more urgent than this in which all are comprised—that tranquillity and true brotherhood between peoples may reign again?

577. It seems, therefore, most opportune to Us to invite to that

[151] II *Corinthians,* XI, 29.
[152] II *Paralipomenon,* XX, 6-12.
[153] I *Peter,* V, 7.
[154] I *Timothy,* II, 6.
[155] *Hebrews,* VII, 25.

end all pastors to celebrate together with Us on a solemn occasion; and, therefore, by this *Motu proprio* We ordain that on June 29, Feast of the holy Apostles, Peter and Paul, help and patrons of Christendom, all priests who are under the obligation of celebrating *pro populo* shall offer the Holy Sacrifice for this Our intention, and furthermore let all other priests of both branches of the clergy know that they will be doing an act most pleasing to Us if they also, celebrating on that day, will unite their intention to Ours. Thus will the whole Catholic priesthood, in union with the Vicar of Christ, offer on every altar of the world the Host of propitiation and love, and by doing violence together to the Heart of God, will strengthen the hope that at length that for which all people long may be realized: *Justice and peace have kissed.*[156]

LETTER *Maximas inter Horum* TO CARDINAL FERRARI, ARCH-
BISHOP OF MILAN, AND TO THE OTHER BISHOPS OF LOM-
BARDY.[157]

> *The papal peace efforts have been scandalously misin-
> terpreted by the enemies of the Church.*

May 22, 1918

578. In the profound sorrows of the present time, the collective letter which you sent Us on the 25th of April last has brought Us no small comfort. In your meeting, as those responsible for the government of the Church in the province of Lombardy, you at once felt that "the Father could not be absent from a meeting of the brethren;" therefore, with ardent affection you called for Us to be present in your midst, confirming with most noble words your union with and attachment to Us, which are all the stronger "in that in the present upheaval of society the enemies of religion are attacking the supreme authority of Jesus Christ entrusted to him whom God constituted teacher and upholder of justice."

579. Over and above the unutterable horrors of this war which is without precedent, and threatens to drag poor Europe down into the abyss, much grief is caused Us by the insidious and crafty campaign of calumny and hatred against Our person and Our work,

---

[156] *Psalms,* LXXXIV, 11.
[157] Translation from *The Tablet,* v. 131, p. 800 (June 22, 1918). Original Latin, *A.A.S.,* v. 10, pp. 273-275 (July 1, 1918).

while We could conscientiously say to the human race, bathed in its own blood, in the words of sacred Scripture:—*What is there that I ought to do more to my vineyard, that I have not done to it?*[158]

580. After the outbreak of this conflagration, which for the good of all We wished could have been averted, as far as was in Our power We missed no opportunity of doing or attempting anything that might soften and mitigate the terrible consequences. More than once, and especially in the Consistorial Allocution at the beginning of 1915, and again more explicitly in the other of December 4 in the following year, We reproved, as again now We reprove, every kind of violation of right wherever it may be perpetrated. In addition to that, with exhortations, public prayers, expiatory functions, with proposals for a just and lasting peace, We studied to bring nearer the end of this awful slaughter. In spite of that, Beloved Son and Venerable Brothers, you know well the crazy and absurd calumnies which, under many and varied forms, publicly and secretly, by word of mouth and in writing, are being spread everywhere. In the country and the villages, where sorrow is deepest, and on that account more deserving of regard and respect, it is being said that We desired the war; in the cities, on the other hand, it is spread about that We desire peace, but an unjust peace which would be an advantage only to one of the belligerent groups. And Our words are so twisted, Our thoughts and intentions so suspected, Our silence with regard to this or that misdeed is so scandalously misinterpreted, as if in such a state of uncertainty, and when passion is so fiercely aroused, it were easy or even possible to inflict single condemnations on single facts which, by a condemnation pronounced by Us in virtue of a general all-embracing principle, have, every one of them, already been reproved, and surely with fairer judgment.

581. But this campaign of hatred is not confined to Ourself and Our work. The gravest injury is done also to most highly deserving priests and illustrious bishops in casting doubt on their loyalty to their country; by the lowest devices of persecutors and informers, attempts are made to take them by surprise, to defame them and bring them into the courts. And so, at the very moment when Italy should have so much need of peace and concord among all citizens, the enemies of religion, actually taking advantage of this unhappy

[158] *Isaias*, V, 4.

time, are striving to stir up the ignorant and simple multitude against this Seat of truth and justice, against the clergy, against the Catholics, sowing the seeds of discord among the different social classes.

582. But though this perverse campaign causes Us deepest sorrow, still it does not surprise Us or discourage Us; much less does it enfeeble Us. Far from it. Called by the hidden counsels of Divine Providence to govern the Church, We have profound feeling of Our duty to defend its sanctity and safeguard its honor. And, therefore, against this diffusion of calumnies and hatred We, too, together with you, Beloved Son and Venerable Brethren, protest anew with the voice of Our Divine Ministry, and We denounce it before the conscience, not only of the faithful, but of all honest men. . . . . . .

LETTER *Litteris Apostolicis* TO CARDINAL BÉGIN, ARCHBISHOP OF QUEBEC, AND TO THE OTHER ARCHBISHOPS AND BISHOPS OF CANADA.[159]

> *All language controversies should be solved in the spirit of charity.*

June 7, 1918

583. In Our Apostolic letter, *Commisso Divinitus,*[160] which We sent you on September 8, 1916, We earnestly exhorted the clergy and Catholic people of your country that they should lay aside all contentions and quarrels which have arisen either by reason of race or from diversity of languages. At the same time We urged that if controversies should thereafter occur from these causes they should be restricted as charity requires, as it becomes saints careful to serve the unity of the spirit in the bond of peace. . . . . . .

584. Now the time has come to address Our words to all Our brethren, the bishops of the Dominion of Canada, and to repeat to them from the depths of Our soul the exhortation which We gave two years since: that they *be of one heart and of one mind* and that there may be no division among them by reason either of racial origin or of speech. For one and the same Spirit *set them to rule the Church of God,* the Spirit of unity and of peace. Thus

---

[159] Translation from Eppstein, *The Catholic Tradition of the Law of Nations,* p. 388.
       Original Latin, *A.A.S.,* v. 10, pp. 440-441 (November 2, 1918).
[160] See *supra* n. 464.

will it be right for you, *being made a pattern of the flock from the heart,*[161] with greater authority and efficacity, Venerable Brethren, to order your priests (and We enjoin that this order be strictly given) both to observe spiritual concord amongst themselves and strive by word and example to have it preserved by the faithful. To which end We desire again and again to recommend what in earlier Apostolic letters We have recommended, "that all the priests should seek to acquire the habit of speaking competently each of the two languages, English and French, and casting all prejudices aside, should use now one, now the other to meet the needs of the faithful." . . . . . .

LETTER *Gratissimum Hibernis* TO CARDINAL LOGUE, ARCHBISHOP OF ARMAGH, AND TO THE OTHER ARCHBISHOPS AND BISHOPS OF IRELAND.[162]

> The Pope realizes that his efforts for peace will be appreciated by fair-minded men after the war.

July 26, 1918

585. . . . . . . Appropriately you recall what We have done from the very beginning of Our Pontificate, with the help of God, toward lessening the sorrows of this cruel war and hastening its end. Indeed, paying no attention to those attacks and that contumely, We shall persevere in Our efforts for human society, for We well know that Our advice and Our acts will be approved by all fair-minded men as instinct with justice and charity when affairs and minds have been tranquillized. . . . . . .

LETTER *Pro Vestro* TO BISHOP STAMMLER OF BASLE AND TO THE OTHER BISHOPS OF SWITZERLAND.[163]

> The Swiss Bishops are congratulated for their zeal in behalf of the captives.

October 13, 1918

586. . . . As regards the pleasing news which you have given Us regarding those captives, who, at Our request, are kept along

---

[161] I *Peter,* V, 3.
[162] Translation from *Irish Ecclesiastical Record,* ser. 5, v. 12, p. 338 (October, 1918).
     Original Latin, *Irish Ecclesiastical Record,* ser. 5, v. 12, p. 337 (October, 1918).
[163] Original Latin, *A.A.S.,* v. 10, p. 448 (November 2, 1918).

the Swiss border because of their health, We are grateful to you in return, Venerable Brethren, who, spurred on by the love of Christ, have always been accustomed zealously to help Us to alleviate their suffering. We pray that God may reward you by an abundance of His gifts. . . .

LETTER *Nel Grave Periodo* TO ARCHBISHOP KAKOWSKI OF WAR-SAW.[164]

Benedict XV wishes to see Poland restored to full independence.

October 15, 1918

587. In the grave crisis which is passing over Europe, We cannot resist the promptings of Our affection to send to you and to the noble Polish nation a word of comfort and hope. History has recorded in letters of gold what Poland has done for Christianity and for European civilization; but, alas, it also has to record the evil with which Europe has repaid its merits. After having violently despoiled it of political independence, it has endeavored in certain quarters to deprive it of its Catholic Faith and its very nationality; but with admirable resistance, the Poles have known how to preserve both one and the other, and today, after surviving an oppression of more than a century, *Polonia semper fidelis* is more active than ever.

588. The Holy See, which loved Poland at the height of its glory, loves it still more, if that be possible, in the depths of its misfortunes, even as a mother's love for her children increases with their increasing unhappiness. We cannot but recall that the only one, during the dismemberment of Poland, who set himself to maintain, though in the event without success, the nationality and independence of Poland, was Pope Clement XIV, of happy memory, who wrote to all the Catholic sovereigns in the strongest of terms. It is well also to record the fact that, during the long years of Polish martyrdom, while others merely watched in silence the oppressor's exercise of brutal force, Our Predecessors, Gregory XVI and Pius IX, lifted their voices in vigorous protest in behalf of the oppressed.

---

[164] Translation from *America*, v. 20, p. 356 (January 18, 1919). Original Italian, *Civiltà Cattolica*, 1918, v. 4, p. 430 (November 29, 1918).

When the story of the Catholic Church in Poland during the eighteenth century is published, with the authentic documents in Our archives, and We hope it will appear soon, more light will be thrown on the indescribable sufferings of the Polish people and the unceasing, truly maternal solicitude of the Holy See to render them assistance.

589. But, infinite thanks be to the Lord, the dawn of the resurrection of Poland is at last appearing. It is Our ardent desire that it may be restored to its full independence at the earliest possible date, and that it may take its place in the congress of nations and continue its history as a civil and Christian nation; and it is Our fond hope that at the same time all the other nations, non-Catholic nations included, that have hitherto been subject to Russia, may be allowed to decide their own lot and develop and prosper according to their native genius and their own individual resources.

590. In the hope of seeing the realization of these wishes of Ours in the near future, We desire, in addition to the provision We have recently made for an enlarged and more adequate establishment of the Catholic hierarchy in that land, to give to you, Venerable Brother, and through you to the Polish people, a further and more solemn proof of Our good-will and confidence; and to this end it is Our purpose, at the first Consistory which the Lord shall grant Us to hold, to elevate you to the cardinalate. . . . . . .

LETTER *Animus Tuus* TO CARDINAL BÉGIN, ARCHBISHOP OF QUEBEC.[165]

The Pope in urging peace makes no distinction among the belligerents.

October 16, 1918

591. . . . This fury of arms had already broken out in Europe when We were elevated to the Supreme Pontificate: and since it was not allowed to Us to limit that outbreak, much less to repress it, We began to try the one thing that remained, namely, to lessen the misfortunes connected with this great evil so far as We were able. Hence, Our various plans and charitable services for lessening miseries and distress.

[165] Original Latin, *A.A.S.,* v. 10, p. 449 (November 2, 1918).

592. In enumerating these services you rightly affirm that We, in performing them, have made no distinction among the belligerents. In accordance with that same design, which would be salutary for all nations, to the end that slaughter and destruction might be terminated, We, as often as seemed proper, have urged peace, and a peace in harmony with justice. You have supported Our position in an outstanding manner, being grieved that the voice and exhortation of a Father was neglected, then in particular when he had proposed those points which alone seemed capable of securing a settlement of hostilities. Indeed, We were taken aback that Our charity was answered in this way; for who would believe that what had proceeded from Us as a duty of Our love to reconcile men with one another would be turned against Us and become a matter of public hatred? Although in this affair the wickedness of certain men who bitterly accused Us to the public of favoritism for one side or the other, is not so much to be wondered at as the rashness of many who gave credence to a most ridiculous charge.

593. Now We most joyfully learn from your letter that this fickleness of judgment is in no wise to be reprehended in the case of Canadian Catholics of both tongues, who have always with one mind and voice agreed with Us about this war. . . .

LETTER OF CARDINAL GASPARRI, SECRETARY OF STATE, TO CARDINAL VON HARTMANN, ARCHBISHOP OF COLOGNE.[166]

Peace deliberations must be approached in good will.

November 6, 1918

594. The letter sent by Your Eminence, in the name of the bishops who are accustomed to gather annually at Fulda, awakened the most profound compassion in the heart of the Holy Father. In it you related vividly the sufferings of the German people in this dreadful war and begged him to use his influence in behalf of the German fatherland, which you saw threatened in its very existence.

595. Inspired by that love that draws him especially to his troubled and suffering children, the Holy Father well understands

---

[166] German text from Lama, *Papst und Kurie,* p. 5. Lama's reference to the *Osservatore Romano,* December 6, 1918, is a mistake because we have searched in vain through the November and December issues for this letter.

and feels the full bitterness of the sorrow that fills Your Eminence and your zealous colleagues. From the depth of his heart he implores the Lord God to give you consolation and strength.

596. During the war the Holy Father did not cease to deplore injustices and cruelties, no matter which side committed them. He did not tire in imploring the warring sides to abandon their intentions of destroying one another and to turn instead to charity and mercy. Thus, too, in the present overwhelming events, he has repeatedly turned to the leader of a large warring State and adjured him by the Precious Blood of Jesus Christ, Saviour of the world, to approach the armistice proposal and peace deliberations in good will, so that a peace, just and honorable for all, might ensue. May the Almighty bless these efforts; may He in His boundless mercy soon grant the hard-tried people of Germany the good fortune of a just and lasting peace. As security there is the Apostolic Blessing which His Holiness grants all the German dioceses and their Venerable Shepherds. . . .

LETTER *Dopo gli Ultimi* TO CARDINAL GASPARRI, SECRETARY OF STATE.[167]

*The Pope rejoices in the Austrian-Italian peace nego-
tiations.*

November 8, 1918

597. After the last fortunate successes of the Italian arms, the enemies of this Apostolic See, firm in their determination to use to its detriment happy as well as unhappy events, have endeavored, and are still endeavoring, to excite against it Italian public opinion which is rejoicing in the victory attained, as if forsooth the Supreme Pontiff was in his heart displeased thereat. You, Lord Cardinal, through daily intercourse, are well aware of Our sentiments, as also of the practice and teaching of the Church in similar circumstances. In the letter of August 1, 1917, to the rulers of the different belligerent Powers, We expressed the hope, which, indeed, was repeated later on other occasions, that the territorial questions between Austria and Italy might find a solution in conformity with

---

[167] Translation from *The Tablet*, v. 132, p. 579 (November 23, 1918). Original Italian, *A.A.S.,* v. 10, pp. 478-479 (December 5, 1918).

the just aspirations of the peoples; and recently We have given instructions to Our Nuncio at Vienna to establish friendly relations with the different nationalities of the Austro-Hungarian Empire which have constituted themselves into independent States. In fact, the Church, a perfect society, which has for its one and only aim the sanctification of men in all times and all countries, while it adapts itself to different forms of government, so it accepts without any difficulty the legitimate territorial and political variations of the peoples. We believe that if these judgments and appreciations of Ours were more generally known, no person of good sense would persist in attributing to Us a regret for which there is no foundation. But We cannot deny that a cloud still disturbs the calmness of Our mind because hostilities have not yet ceased everywhere, and the clash of arms still gives rise in many places to anxiety and fear. But We hope that it will not be long before the happy dawn of peace which has arisen also over Our beloved country rejoices the other warring peoples, and We foretaste the sweetness of that day, now not far off, in which charity will return to reign amongst men, and universal concord will unite the nations in a league fruitful of good. Meanwhile We are glad to confirm to you, Lord Cardinal, Our special benevolence, a new pledge of which shall be the Apostolic Benediction which We impart to you with deep and very special affection.

ENCYCLICAL *Quod Jam Diu* ON THE FUTURE PEACE CONFERENCE.[168]

Catholics are requested to pray for the coming peace conference that from it a just and lasting peace may result.

December 1, 1918

598. That which the entire world has so long sighed for, what Christianity implored with so much fervent prayer, and what We, the interpreter of the sorrow of all, with the heart of a father, continually kept asking for, has come in a moment. The clang of arms has ceased at last. It is true that peace has not yet formally

[168] Translation from *The Catholic Mind*, v. 17, pp. 67-68 (February 8, 1919). Original Latin, *A.A.S.*, v. 10, pp. 473-474 (December 5, 1918).

put an end to the war. However, with the armistice, which has meantime suspended carnage and devastation by land, sea and air, the road to peace is fortunately clear.

599. In order to explain such a sudden event several causes might be adduced. But if we want to seek the principal cause, we absolutely must look to Him Who governs all occurrences, Who, led to mercy by the continual prayers of the good, granted humanity to withdraw from so many struggles and so many causes of anguish. Therefore, while giving thanks to the goodness of the Lord, we rejoice at the many imposing demonstrations of piety that have been held throughout the Catholic world for the purpose.

600. Now it remains to us to beg of Divine Clemency that the great favor granted to us may have its crowning success. Within a short time the delegates of the several nations will unite in solemn congress for the purpose of giving to the world a just and lasting peace. They will accordingly have to come to decisions of such grave importance and of so complex a nature as were never before taken by any human assembly.

601. It is, then, not necessary to point out how imperative it is that they receive light from above in order to execute properly their mandate. And since there is question of decisions that concern the weal of all humanity to the highest degree, without any doubt all Catholics, who are in conscience bound to favor order and the progress of civilization, have the obligation of invoking the Divine aid for those who take part in the Peace Conference. We wish this duty to be remembered by all Catholics. Therefore, Venerable Brothers, in order that the fruit of the approaching congress may be that great gift of heaven, which is true peace founded upon the Christian principles of justice, it will be your care to announce public prayers in each parish of your respective dioceses in that form which you will consider timely, to implore for it the *light of the Heavenly Father*.

602. As far as We Ourselves are concerned, representing, however unworthily, Jesus Christ, the *King of Peace,* We shall use all the influence of Our Apostolic Ministry so that the decisions that may be arrived at for the purpose of perpetuating tranquillity, good order and concord in the world may be accepted and faithfully followed everywhere by Catholics. . . .

ALLOCUTION *È la Quinta Volta* TO THE COLLEGE OF CARDI-
NALS.[169]

*Benedict XV prays that God's blessing be upon the
Versailles Peace Conference.*

December 24, 1918

603. This is the fifth time that the happy recurrence of the
Christmas solemnity has united about Us the distinguished circle
of the Sacred College, but it is in reality the first in which We
are able to accept from it with joy the best wishes of the season.

604. Our soul is no longer wrung with bitterness and anxiety
over a sad condition of affairs which was so opposed to that message of peace and of love proper to this sweet feast. Lord Cardinal,
with what sublimity and nicety of language, so familiar to your
lips, have you offered to Us in the name of the Sacred College,
a wish which seems more fitting at the present time than any
other and which certainly corresponds better than any other to
the sentiments of Our soul.

605. With the liveliest pleasure have We indeed received your
augury that there may be multiplied always the fruits of that
spiritual fatherhood which, in a special way, We possess from God,
*from Whom all fatherhood in heaven and on earth receives its
name,*[170] and which desires to imitate, as far as is possible, the
inexhaustible charity and continual beneficence of God. We are
grateful to the Most Eminent Dean of the Sacred College for having
pointed out in this fatherhood of Ours the prime font of the activity
We have exercised during the days of the great scourge which has
finally ceased only a short time ago, and with all sincerity We
offer to him and to his Most Eminent colleagues the return of good
wishes and prayers, in testimony also of Our gratitude for the
delicate reference which has just been made to Our sorrows and to
Our cares of a private and domestic nature.[171]

606. Upon the heights of the Vatican there have come, alas,
the sorrowing cries of these years of war; there have come the
groans of the victims of the daily slaughter; there have come the dis-

[169] Original Italian, *Civiltà Cattolica*, 1919, v. 1, pp. 63-67 (December 28, 1918).
[170] *Ephesians*, III, 15.
[71] Benedict XV refers to the death of his brother, Marquis Giovanni Antonio della
Chiesa on December 9.

tressing pleas that the end of the horrible conflict be not long delayed. And may the Lord be praised that He gave Us the power of being a father and of acting as one, and that more than once He made Our weakness the instrument of His merciful power.

607. Hence it was that We longed for and frequently obtained the mitigation of those sorrows which found their echo in Our paternal heart; hence it was that with the urging as well as the restraint of a father, We deplored and condemned the excesses of brutal hate, leaving open, however, at the same time the way to a further examination in accord with the ever certain duties of Our compassionate fatherhood; hence it was also that We directed Our forces and Our suggestions to hasten the dawn of peace by recalling the principles of the unchanging and eternal Justice of Christ, the supreme Law-giver of civil society, and the Source, not of possible repression but rather of the complete restoration of every right.

608. That fatherhood which was the norm in Our counsels, in Our condemnations, in Our judgments and in Our good works of the past, the same guides Us also in Our conduct of the present hour. Oh, while We embrace all Our children, tired at length of conflict and of slaughter, Our thoughts fly to that great conference of the nations[172] assembled for the noble purpose of securing peace to the world. And, nourishing in Our breast the warmest interest in the happy outcome of the arduous tasks set before the illustrious assembly, We wish with all Our heart that above its sessions may hover that spirit of which We are the custodian, and to this sublime intention We dedicate all Our longings and all the support of Our fatherly heart.

609. But since every best grace and every perfect gift comes down from the Father of lights alone, from the Vatican Hill we shall every day invoke the assistance of that celestial light upon the historic congress—imitating Moses who, for the sake of his people, ascended the mountain and prayed with outstretched arms during the momentous time of battle. With heart and arms raised to the Divine Majesty, that ancient leader guided his dear people to triumphant success; will not Our prayers, then, hasten the noonday of that peace whose radiant dawn We now hail? But Our arms, like those of Moses, are weary and heavy, and they would

---

[172] The Conference at Versailles.

falter were they not sustained by those sons who, according to the plan of Divine Providence, are like the staff by which the father is supported. Hence, just as Aaron and Hur ascended the mountain with Moses and upheld the arms of their leader on either side, *stayed up his hands on both sides,*[173] so We have bid the Christian world to come to Our aid by ordering that in accord with the circumstances of the various localities, united prayers of propitiation be raised to heaven for this most momentous of congresses. In the midst of, and participating in these prayers, according to His unfailing promise, will be the Divine Head of the Church Himself, who will contribute to their success that same force which the hands of his disciples secured to the extended arms of Moses.

610. However, prayer is not the only means by which We intend that Our fatherhood should be manifested at the present time. For to it We join Our entreaties toward hastening both the assembling and the happy conclusion of the peace congress; We join to it the desire by which, not content with showing Our fatherly interest in the great event, We express again the hope that the deliberations of the congress will consider not only the restoration of order, but also the renewal of those humane sentiments which make it pleasant to dwell in harmony with our brethren and even to sacrifice ourselves for them. Above all, to prayer which is the most noteworthy form which Our fatherhood takes at the present hour, We join the firm resolve to secure to the just deliberations of the world congress the support of Our influence among the faithful, so that just as We have children everywhere, so also everywhere may be facilitated through the help of Our fatherhood, the observance of those decisions which may be made to give to the world a just and lasting peace.

611. But the announcement of this resolve of Ours, as well as of what ought to be carried out in the future, already makes it clear that, if in the past and the present We have held Our fatherhood as the norm of Our activities, We do not intend to seek elsewhere for Our future directives. We have been a father in the past; We are a father in the present; and We shall be a father in the future as long as life remains to Us, looking always, as the rule and guide of Our work, to that fatherhood which God has confided to Us,

[173] *Exodus,* XVII, 12.

and which is all-embracing like that of which it is a participated likeness.

612. Now this fatherhood of Ours makes Us rejoice exceedingly over the good which We hope will come from peace restored, and strongly urges Us to secure by every means its protection and increase. The dreadful tempest which has passed over the earth has left behind it very sad traces of its havoc. But it is even more to be feared that it has left in the hearts of men distressing vestiges of ancient rancors, unwholesome germs of discord, of revenge, and of ungenerous reprisals. The very ardors of war, and the burning desire—noble in its origin—of defending one's country, inflame the soul with an indignation, however just it be in its beginnings, which, in its final consequences, can too easily lead to excess by not stifling but rather strengthening with new life the ancient seeds of social discord which it should desire to be remedied in justice. Will not that be the work of a father which We shall, in order to secure the just and lasting peace which We have always extolled, direct toward repairing the moral evils of the war not less than the material havoc of the dreadful scourge? It will be the work of a father to remove the dangers of fresh disturbances of order— such as might quickly arise from hatreds and intense national aspirations. Oh, fortunate will be Our age, if it shall behold the kiss of justice and of peace accompanied by the spirit of charity, since only the law of love joins in a marvelous union the children of the same father, and forms of men of good-will one real family. Fear, want, material force—oh, how experience has shown this to us in lessons of blood—are not only inadequate bonds, but also unworthy of human society. Social unity to be reasonable must be founded on natural benevolence; to be Christian it must be ennobled by the charity of Christ.

613. To make this charity flourish once more in the midst of nations, We shall, therefore, direct Our desires and Our fatherly care, in order that it may be evident that Our fatherhood, which has remained constant in the past and is steadfast in the present, shall likewise continue unfailing in the future.

614. It pleases Us to hope that Our efforts can become the echo of those deliberations which very soon will be undertaken by the peace congress toward which turn at present the aspirations of

all hearts. But in the task of restoring society, just as We are able to count upon the wisdom and advice of the Senate of the Church, so also We are confident of finding docile and generous helpers in all those who desire to promote Catholic Action. The care and instruction of children, the protection and prudent direction of working-men, the opportune advice and suggestion given to the well-to-do to use properly their riches and authority—here is the field in which for the future the task of a father should be principally exercised; and here it is where the Father hopes to have his sons as helpers in order to reap together with them abundant fruits of true Catholic Action. . . . . . .

ALLOCUTION *Antequam Ordinem* TO THE COLLEGE OF CAR-
DINALS.[174]

> *Benedict XV is especially concerned over the suffering Eastern Peoples.*

March 10, 1919

615. . . . . . . As long as the terrible war lasted We made every effort in Our power to alleviate the immense miseries by which the peoples living in the territories of Russia, the Balkans and Turkey were oppressed. For We saw there an entire people massacred, almost exterminated, crowds of poor wretches leaving their homes, taking refuge in the mountains and falling victims to hardship and famine; in other places Christian communities scattered, priests driven out or imprisoned, churches, monasteries, schools, hospices converted to profane uses, ecclesiastical and private property brought to ruin and destruction. All that was in Our power We did to remedy these evils without any distinction of nationality or religion. Our anxiety was, above all, for the Armenians and the inhabitants of Syria and the Lebanon, as those whom We had seen most often persecuted by deportations, exposed to the tortures of hunger, and even slaughtered *en masse*.

616. And, therefore, on behalf of the Armenians in general and in particular those condemned to death or in any need of Our help, personally and repeatedly We appealed to the Emperor

---

[174] Translation from *The Tablet*, v. 133, pp. 353-354 (March 22, 1919). Original Latin, *A.A.S.*, v. 11, pp. 99-101 (March 12, 1919).

of the Ottomans or urgently put their case before those sovereigns who seemed to Us to have most influence over him. We succeeded thus, by Divine aid, in preventing massacres in several places and in saving many lives. Moved by compassion for the many orphans of Armenia, We opened a refuge for them in Constantinople. As regards Syria and the Lebanon, in order to prevent horrors which were feared and to provide food for the inhabitants there, We appealed for the intervention and help of various Governments. All sufferers in the Orient, in fact, We endeavored to help with the material and moral means in Our power, assisted in Our task by the zeal of Our representatives. And even now that the armistice has come and the clash of war has ceased, Our anxiety is still keen on behalf of the Christians of the Orient. For serious political upheavals and rekindled struggles of nationalities are hindering there the normal development of civil and religious life, especially among the subject peoples of the Russian Empire, where the proclamation of religious liberty had aroused such hopes of a better future. In the other parts of the Orient, too, there appears before Our eyes the sad spectacle of missions dispersed, Christian communities robbed of churches and pastors, peoples in prey of political convulsions fighting among themselves for the first necessaries of life.

617. But there is one matter on which We are most specially anxious, and that is the fate of the Holy Places, on account of the special dignity and importance for which they are so venerated by every Christian. Who can ever tell the full story of all the efforts of Our Predecessors to free them from the dominion of infidels, the heroic deeds and the blood shed by the Christians of the West through the centuries? And now that, amid the rejoicing of all good men, they have finally returned into the hands of the Christians, Our anxiety is most keen as to the decisions which the Peace Congress at Paris is soon to take concerning them. For surely it would be a terrible grief for Us and for all the Christian faithful if infidels were placed in a privileged and prominent position; much more if those most holy sanctuaries of the Christian religion were given into the charge of non-Christians. . . .

618. . . . Helpless, deprived of all they have, those poor souls are stretching out to Us suppliant arms, imploring not only food and clothing but the rebuilding of their churches, the re-opening of their schools, the restoration of their missions. To this end We

have for Our part already set aside a certain sum, and most willingly would We give more if the present poverty of the Holy See allowed. But it is Our intention to excite the interest of the bishops of the whole Catholic world that they may take to heart such a noble and holy cause, arousing among all the faithful that sense of active charity which their ancestors always showed toward their brethren of the Orient. . . . . . .

LETTER *Eure Eminenz* TO CARDINAL VON HARTMANN, ARCHBISHOP OF COLOGNE.[175]

> *The Pope labors to effect the return of the German war prisoners.*

March 10, 1919

619. Your Eminence has related to Us in moving words the sufferings of numerous families who, while they see war prisoners of foreign nations joyfully leaving Germany, are themselves tortured by the fearful uncertainty concerning the time when they will again embrace their dear ones, whose help and consolation they need the more, as the times become more woeful.

620. Your Eminence knows with what unceasing care We have attempted to dry so many tears in this war. You will, therefore, readily understand how heavily these pains and sufferings also redound in Our paternal heart, and how happy We would be if We would succeed in securing redress.

621. Last November, after the signing of the armistice, Our Cardinal Secretary of State took steps with several States of the Allies on behalf of the German war prisoners, namely, the sick and the wounded. The following month he repeated, always in Our name, his efforts in the most loving manner, to improve the condition of many unfortunate ones and to assure them more spiritual help through German priests. We turned Our attention sympathetically, too, to the prisoners who are nearer to Us, and asked the bishops of the Italian dioceses and the army bishops to give these all possible care.

622. On a festive occasion a little later, We expressed to a noted

---

[175] German text from Lama, *Papst und Kurie,* pp. 114-115.

person[176] Our ardent desire to see the hundreds and thousands of German prisoners who had endured the sufferings of imprisonment for a long time, brought back to their own firesides. We had the satisfaction of hearing that this person fully shared Our loving wishes and was inclined to support them. Since then the Cardinal Secretary of State has issued an urgent appeal to one of the allied States to win its interest for this thoroughly charitable and humane work, and We are still awaiting an answer.

623. May the good and merciful God bless these efforts which We shall continue unceasingly with that zeal and love which Our divine mission and sincere sympathy for those unhappy souls inspire in Us. May the King of Peace grant to the many sorrowing families the first precious fruits that they had hoped for in this so ardently desired peace.

LETTER *Multiplices Quidem* TO CARDINAL CSERNOCH, ARCH-BISHOP OF STRIGONIA.[177]

The Vatican is deeply concerned over the critical situation in Hungary.

March 12, 1919

624. Many anxieties have been brought to Us by so cruel and so long a war; but nothing makes Us more anxious and solicitous than the fact that the disturbances resulting therefrom have overflowed not only into civil society but even into the religious affairs of nations. Particularly, however, are We concerned over the great misfortunes of those peoples who made up the Austro-Hungarian Empire, and who are now each striving after that form of government which corresponds to the wishes of individual nations. For since an important part of the flock divinely entrusted to Us is contained in these peoples, and a part which has always been outstanding for its faith and great devotion towards this Apostolic See, it is easy to understand that We are concerned in a special way that religion among them suffer no harm. We sincerely hope that all those men who govern those States, while they are anxious to

[176] This was Woodrow Wilson, President of the United States, who had an audience with Benedict XV on January 4, 1919.
[177] Original Latin, *A.A.S.,* v. 11, p. 122 (April 1, 1919).

establish peace and prosperity for their peoples, will see to it that they preserve intact the rights and laws of the Church, if they truly wish the foundations of justice in civil society and of the public good to stand safe and sound. Now, nobody is unaware how much the Apostolic See has at heart the internal peace and good of nations and how ready it always is to lend its aid to accomplish this. Even more, to achieve this end better, it is accustomed to enter into mutual unions or relations with the legitimate rulers of States who have signified that they have the same desire themselves. . . .

TELEGRAM OF CARDINAL GASPARRI, SECRETARY OF STATE, TO LENIN, FOUNDER OF THE UNION OF SOVIET RUSSIA.[178]

The Holy See pleads for the persecuted Orthodox.

March 12, 1919

625. . . . The Holy Father adjures you to give strict orders that the servants of every religion be respected. Humanity and religion will be grateful to you.

LETTER *C'Est avec la Plus Vive Complaisance* TO CARDINAL MERCIER AND TO THE BISHOPS OF BELGIUM.[179]

The Pope has special sympathy and compassion for the people of Belgium.

April 3, 1919

626. . . . . . . Your letter recalls the long series of calamities which have fallen upon your well-beloved country, the unfortunate consequences of which are still being experienced. With great delicacy of heart you recall also Our solemn protestations against the injustices and violations of law committed with regard to Belgium, as well as Our efforts to alleviate such great sufferings, and you stress especially your unfailing confidence in Our action.

627. This confidence, certainly, was not without foundation. As a matter of fact, while being animated with that universal charity which binds Us to all Our children overwhelmed with affliction and sorrow, that charity which has its source in the very

[178] German text from Lama, *Papst und Kurie*, p. 368.
[179] Original French, *Documentation Catholique*, v. 1, pp. 647-648 (June 21, 1919).

Heart of Our Saviour Jesus Christ, We could not help regarding your people with a special sympathy and experiencing for them a particular compassion.

628. While We are using all Our power to bring some relief to the sufferings of so many unfortunate sons, We have never ceased striving to the end that full political, military and economic independence be restored to your dear nation, and that the losses she has sustained be repaired.

629. We are fully conscious of having done for Belgium and for her people all that was possible for Us to do, all that the radiating Charity of Christ and the most tender paternal affection could suggest. Nevertheless, Venerable Brethren, it is consoling for Us to hear you say again that you have never doubted your Father, not even in most critical moments. . . . . . .

ENCYCLICAL *In Hac Tanta* ON THE TWELFTH CENTENARY OF ST. BONIFACE, APOSTLE OF GERMANY.[180]

Christian charity alone will be able to heal the wounds remaining from the war.

May 14, 1919

630. While the great weight of calamities and troubles which in these most bitter times oppresses Us beyond measure from every side, *besides those outer things, there is my daily pressing anxiety, the care of all the churches*,[181] to use the words of the Apostle, We have recently followed with greater solicitude and more anxious care, Beloved Son and Venerable Brethren, the sudden calamities and most disturbing public events which have occurred among your nation and neighboring nations and which still hold our minds in suspense in expectation of what is to come. . . . . . .

631. Yet We add this, Beloved Son and Venerable Brethren— although We know that this is known to all of you—that this wonderful charity of Boniface, which was not contained by the boundaries of Germany alone, embraced absolutely all nations, though they were most hostile to one another; just as with even greater love, according to the order of virtue, the Apostle of Ger-

---

[180] Original Latin, *A.A.S.*, v. 11, pp. 209-220 (June 2, 1919).
[181] II *Corinthians*, XI, 28.

many embraced the neighboring nation of the Franks, of whom he was likewise the most prudent reformer, and his own countrymen "born of the race and stock of the Angles." To the Angles he, as a member of the same race, a legate of the Church Universal, and a servant of the Apostolic See, commended the propagation of the Catholic Faith . . . among the Saxon peoples, who were born of the very same race. Finally he commended that "unity and community of love" were to be guarded in a most charitable way.[182]

632. Since in truth charity is—to use as Our own once more the words of the same writer whom We have quoted above—"the origin and end of all good things, let us place our end in it,"[183] Beloved Son and Venerable Brethren. This, therefore, We beg in every way, that in this disturbed society of mankind, when the rights, laws, worship, and the memory itself of Almighty God and His Church have been restored, Christian charity may blossom once more, and, putting an end to raging wars and hatred and to divisions, schisms and errors that creep in on every side, may unite peoples with one another by a stronger bond than the passing agreements of men, primarily by the unity of faith and the tie of ancient connections or rather by kinship with this Holy See, which Christ our Lord willed to be the established foundation of His family on earth and to be consecrated by the virtues, the wisdom, and the labors of so many saints, and finally by the very blood of martyrs like your Boniface.

633. When this harmony of faith and union of wills have been restored throughout the world, We shall be seen also to claim by a certain right of Ours from the whole Christian people, what Pope Clement, moved by the knowledge of the Roman Primacy and the sacred authority of the Apostolic See, even from the first century wrote in a special way to the Corinthians: "You will give us delight and joy if, obeying what we have written by the Holy Ghost, you root out the wicked passion of your jealousy according to the exhortation which we have made in this letter about peace and concord."[184] . . . . . .

---

[182] St. Boniface, *Epistolæ*, XXXVI in Migne, *P.L.*, v. 89, c. 735.
[183] *Ibid.*
[184] St. Clement of Rome, *Epistola ad Corinthios*, n. 63 in Rouet de Journel, *Enchiridion Patristicum* (5th ed., 1922), p. 10.

LETTER OF CARDINAL GASPARRI, SECRETARY OF STATE, TO CARDINAL PIFFL, ARCHBISHOP OF VIENNA.[185]

*The Holy See will not fail to do all that can possibly
be done to bring about a just and lasting peace.*

July 3, 1919

634. . . . Thinking only of the good of all peoples, His Holiness was confident that the peace settlement would mean the end of the unholy hatred of men and would bring to the whole world a new era of true brotherly love and community spirit, imperturbable calm and genuine welfare. I can assure Your Eminence, your Venerable Brethren in the episcopate and all who expect the Holy Father to intervene in the matter of the conditions of peace, that the Holy See has already taken steps in this direction and will not fail to do all that can possibly be done. . . .

ALLOCUTION *Nobis Quidem* TO THE COLLEGE OF CARDINALS.[186]

*His Holiness asks for assurance that the Versailles
Treaty will protect the rights and interests of the
Catholic Missions.*

July 3, 1919

635. . . . . . . Now to pass over other matters here which pertain not merely to the Orient, but to the entire Christian world, We will not be silent that We have been in anxiety about the Catholic Missions. When We were informed that some measures were being considered at the Versailles Peace Conference by which the right of preaching the Gospel did not seem to be safeguarded, We confidently asked the members of the conference to give their serious attention to this matter. We also sent as Our representative a worthy prelate of the Roman Curia to protect these same rights to the utmost. It is a pleasure to say here that those men satisfied in large measure Our demands after they considered them with open minds. Consequently, We are led to hope that the same men will follow a like fairness of mind in putting into action the decisions which they have made in this regard, a matter which is of

---

[185] German text from Lama, *Papst und Kurie*, p. 101.
[186] Original Latin, *A.A.S.*, v. 11, p. 259 (July 4, 1919).

importance not only to the Catholic Religion but also to civil society and culture. And since hostilities have finally come to an end, We suppliantly invoke Divine Mercy to regard this Our prayer, that the blockade be lifted on account of which a countless multitude is suffering famine and the direst want of everything, that as many as are yet prisoners of war be set free as soon as possible, that finally men and nations, till now enemies, be again united in the bonds of Christian charity, without which, We do not cease to insist, every peace conference will be in vain. . . . . . .

LETTER *Diuturni* TO THE BISHOPS OF GERMANY.[187]

Every effort must be made to relieve the misery of post-war Germany.

July 15, 1919

636. The day has at last arrived which marks for your nation the end of the long and most distressing war; with the signing of the Treaty of Peace an end has been put finally to the blockade which made so many victims, specially and above all among those who in point of fact were taking no part in the war. We, who as the Universal Father have at heart the belligerents on both sides and tried by every means in Our power to put an end to the terrible conflagration or to mitigate its consequences, give the Almighty thanks for this boon together with you and all your nation. It should be your care now to repair as soon as possible the immense harm produced amongst you by the war, and inasmuch as nothing can be so useful to that end as the work of the Catholic Church, assisted by Divine Grace, We have thought fit to send you this letter. And first of all, in order that there may not come to pass in Germany public disturbances which would bring on your nation and indeed on Europe the ruin which is overcoming other nations, every effort must be made that the populations may not lack food. To that end, Venerable Brethren, by means of the parish priests and such other ecclesiastics as are in the closest touch with the people, you should strongly urge the faithful in country districts not to refuse the inhabitants of the cities who are

---

[187] Translation from *The Tablet*, v. 134, p. 149 (August 2, 1919). Original Latin, *A.A.S.*, v. 11, pp. 305-306 (August 1, 1919).

suffering hunger as much food as they themselves can manage to
do without. In these hard times, that duty is laid on them strictly
by the law of charity which, if it embraces all, including enemies,
wishes that we should specially love our fellow countrymen. And,
in addition, We feel confident that all who belong to civilized
nations, and in particular the Catholics among them, will hasten
to help the populations which they know are reduced to extremities,
doing so not so much on account of the dangers threatening society
as from their membership in the family of mankind itself and
under the impulse of Christian charity. Indeed, we should all call
to mind what the Apostle, St. John, teaches: *He who has the goods
of this world and sees his brother in need and closes his heart to
him, how does the love of God abide in him? My dear children,
let us not love in word, neither with the tongue, but in deed and in
truth.*[188] In the second place, Venerable Brethren, each one of you
should use all the authority of his sacred office to heal the spiritual
wounds which the war either inflicted on your nation or made
more sore.

637. It is specially necessary to eliminate every feeling of hatred
either towards foreigners with whom the nation was at war or
towards fellow-citizens of other parties, and in the place of hatred
put the brotherly love which is of Christ, which knows no barrier
or limit or strife of class. And We repeat here the hope We expressed at the last Consistory, that "men and peoples may be again
united in Christian charity, because if that is lacking every Peace
Treaty will be vain." We feel sure that you, Venerable Brethren,
as good pastors and ministers of peace and charity, will engage all
your care and energy in this task and will not cease to ask pity
of the Lord, together with your clergy and your flocks. For Us,
Our help will never fail you in these terrible times for your country, because Our heart of a father turns with greater pity towards
Our children who are suffering most, following the example of the
loving Redeemer Who, taking pity on the sufferings of a great
multitude, spoke these memorable words: *I have compassion on
the crowd.*[189] Meanwhile . . . upon you, Venerable Brethren, and
upon all those entrusted to your pastoral care We impart . . . the
Apostolic Benediction.

[188] I *John,* III, 17-18.
[189] *Mark,* VIII, 2.

LETTER OF CARDINAL GASPARRI, SECRETARY OF STATE, TO ARCH-
BISHOP MUNDELEIN OF CHICAGO AND THE CATHOLIC CENTRAL
VEREIN OF AMERICA.[190]

*America must help to relieve the distress in post-war
Germany.*

July 18, 1919

638. The information has come to the Holy Father that the
Central Verein, after the long interruption caused by the war, will
soon meet again in the city of Chicago. This information has been
received with the greatest satisfaction by the Sovereign Pontiff, who
is well acquainted with the splendid merits of its work. . . . And
now that the Central Verein takes up its labors anew, the Sovereign
Pontiff desires to pay it the tribute of praise it has well earned by
the work it has so successfully accomplished in the past, and also to
send to its members his fatherly greetings as a harbinger of an even
happier future.

639. His Holiness has no doubt whatever that such a bright
future is in store for them, because of those remarkable qualities
which the German-Americans have given proof of on every occasion, and particularly during the recent war. While keeping alive
the love they bore for the land of their fathers, yet this has not
hindered them from doing their full duty towards their adopted
country, and nobly indeed have they responded to its different calls,
pouring out for it lavishly, their money, their service and their lives.

640. But now that the war has at last come to an end, there is
offered an even more promising field for their beneficent zeal. It
is, alas, only too true that this cruel war which has so completely
divided the human race into two opposite camps, has left behind
it a trail of hate among the nations. And yet the world cannot
possibly enjoy the blessed fruits of peace for any length of time
unless that hatred be entirely blotted out and all the nations be
brought together again in the sweet bonds of Christian brotherhood.

641. To bring this about the Catholics in a more particular
manner must lend themselves, since they are already closely united
in the Mystical Body of Jesus Christ, and should, therefore, constantly give others an example of Christian charity. And in accom-

[190] Original English, *The New World* (Chicago diocesan newspaper), September 19,
1919.

plishing this result, the work of the German Catholics in the United States, who being united by the closest ties to both lately warring races, ought to be particularly successful.

642. Consequently, the Holy Father, to whose heart there is nothing dearer than the real reconciliation of the nations, and who has already addressed himself on this subject to the Bishops of Germany, now appeals to you in order that you, too, may co-operate in such a noble mission. Moreover, knowing the dreadful conditions under which our brethren in Germany are now living, the Sovereign Pontiff implores you most fervently to lend them every assistance, material as well as moral, and in the quickest and most effective way, especially facilitating the early resumption of commerce and all those benefits that naturally follow in its wake. To this invitation the Holy Father feels certain that not only you will gladly respond, but all the children of your generous country without any distinction whatever, for surely they will be mindful of the great services their fellow citizens of German birth and descent have rendered their country during this war. In this way they will become real benefactors of the human race and draw upon their own nation Almighty God's choicest blessing. . . .

LETTER *Amor Ille* TO CARDINAL AMETTE, ARCHBISHOP OF PARIS.[191]

Christians must love their enemies.

October 7, 1919

643. . . . . . . While the most Sacred Heart of Jesus, therefore, shows in a sensible manner His boundless love for His children, who too often, alas, are forgetful, at the same time it reminds us of this great duty whereby we ought to love God above all things and our neighbor as ourselves.

644. Moreover, the love of neighbors, which is stronger the more it is concerned with those nearest us, extends to all men, even to our enemies, since we all are united to one another by the bond of brotherhood, inasmuch as we are sons of the same God and have been redeemed by the same Blood of Jesus Christ: *You have heard that it hath been said, Thou shalt love thy neighbor, and hate thy*

[191] Original Latin, *A.A.S.*, v. 11, p. 413 (November 3, 1919).

enemy. But I say to you, Love your enemies: do good to them that hate you: and pray for them that persecute and calumniate you: that you may be the children of your Father, Who is in heaven.[192] This Our Lord and Master has commanded, thus the Apostles with one voice, and especially that herald of love, St. John, have handed down, and this has been followed in practice, we know, by all who have conducted their lives in accordance with the wisdom of the Gospel.

645.   We know, of course, that a precept of this kind made by Christ our Lord does not please the world, and this is so to such a degree that the world interprets perversely the counsels of those who affirm and defend its sanctity and repays them with all calumnies. So it was done with Jesus Christ; nor will it ever be otherwise if anyone preaches forgetfulness of injuries and love towards those who have done evil to us and have attacked our country. But the displeasure of the wicked ought not retard anyone from following and inculcating such a weighty precept of the Gospel, upon which especially the tranquillity of human association and the condition of States depend. . . . . . .

LETTER OF CARDINAL GASPARRI, SECRETARY OF STATE, TO CARDINAL BOURNE, ARCHBISHOP OF WESTMINSTER.[193]

The suffering victims of Central Europe are a cause of anxiety to Benedict XV.

October 29, 1919

646.   I lost no time in informing the Holy Father that the Westminster Catholic Federation, presided over by Your Eminence, had formed the truly noble and charitable plan of an appeal to the entire world to lighten the distress in which large numbers of the inhabitants of Central Europe are languishing—a distress which bears most gravely and cruelly upon little children.

647.   The cessation of hostilities has brought only inadequate relief to these unfortunates, and in some regions it has even increased the hardships which make existence impossible. The information sent to the Holy See from different quarters shows,

[192] *Matthew*, V, 43-45.
[193] Original English, *The Tablet*, v. 134, p. 722 (November 29, 1919).

among other things, that many dwellers in large towns have become utterly enfeebled through their enormous and increasing difficulties, and that every day long files of sufferers can be seen outside the premises of charitable societies waiting to receive a miserable ration. The reports of medical men abound with heartrending descriptions of the pitiable state of the children in orphanages and free schools, "emaciated little creatures, without exception too small for their age, among whom rickets are becoming more and more serious, while a peculiarly deadly tuberculosis makes rapid strides."

648. All this fills the heart of the August Pontiff with profound pity, for amidst the ills bred by the war, those of which childhood is the victim are worthy of the greatest compassion. It is, indeed, a mournful sight to behold these little beings, whose eyes have hardly opened to the light, bearing in their faces and in their glances the signs of decay and of a premature sadness born of long-drawn grief, instead of the frank lightheartedness proper to their age.

649. Your Eminence, therefore, can easily picture how greatly the Holy Father is consoled by the knowledge of this generous project, and with what warmth he praises and encourages all those who stretch forth their hands to help those innocents and to furnish them with those things which their parents are not able to provide. But who can remain indifferent face to face with the sufferings of these hapless ones? Are they not the tender flower of humanity for whom the Redeemer of the world has shown a surpassing love and care? . . . . . .

ENCYCLICAL *Paterno Jam Diu* ON CHRISTIAN CHARITY FOR THE CHILDREN OF CENTRAL EUROPE.[194]

The bishops of the entire world are asked to collect funds for the starving children of Central Europe.

November 24, 1919

650. It was the expectation and hope of Our paternal heart that, once the terrible conflict was ended, and the spirit of Christian char-

---

[194] Translation from *The Tablet*, v. 134, p. 741 (December 6, 1919). Original Latin, *A.A.S.*, v. 11, pp. 437-439 (December 1, 1919).

ity restored, the regions desolated by famine and misery, especially in Central Europe, might little by little improve their condition, thanks to the united efforts of all good men. But this Our hope has not been realized by events. As a matter of fact, information reaches Us from all sides that those populous regions are deprived of food and clothing to a degree beyond all imagination, so that a most lamentable decay of health is the result among the less hardy, and especially among the children. This their misfortune afflicts Our heart all the more as they are altogether innocent and even ignorant of the sanguinary conflict which has desolated almost the whole world; and, moreover, they represent the germs of the future generations, which cannot but feel the effects of their debilitation.

651. Nevertheless, Our distress has been somewhat relieved by learning that men of good will have banded themselves in societies in order to "save the children." We have not hesitated to approve and confirm with Our authority, as was fitting, this noble plan. Indeed, it corresponds with the grave duty of affection which We feel towards that tender age which is most dear to Our Divine Redeemer, and which has least strength to bear and suffer ills. In fact, We had done this formerly. You will remember that at no distant date We endeavored with all Our means to succor the little children in Belgium who were in extremity of hunger and of misery, and recommend them to the public charity of Catholics. The generosity of the latter was such that in great part it was owing to it that it was possible to provide for the necessities of so many innocent children and to preserve their life and health. In fact, as soon as We had addressed Our exhortation for this noble purpose to the Episcopate of the United States of America, Our desires were generously met by the widest correspondence. We record this happy result to-day, not only to pay the tribute of Our praise to men worthy of being remembered in the annals of Christian charity, but also by Our voice and authority to invite the bishops of the whole world to take steps in order to carry into effect Our proposal, and for this purpose to employ all their prestige with their flocks. With the approach of the season of Christmas, commemorating the birth of Our Lord Jesus Christ, Our thoughts spontaneously fly to the poor little children, especially in Central Europe, who are most cruelly feeling the wants of the necessities of life; and We embrace this tender age with all the more solicitude inasmuch as it

279

more exactly recalls the image of the Divine Infant, suffering, for love of men in the cave at Bethlehem, the rigor of winter and the want of all things. No other circumstance could be more opportune than this to induce Us to solicit for innocent children the charity and pity of Christians and of all who do not despair of the salvation of the human race.

652. Wherefore, Venerable Brethren, with the purpose of attaining in your respective dioceses the object of which We have spoken, We direct that on next December 28, the feast of the Holy Innocents, you should order public prayers and gather the alms of the faithful. In order to help on a larger scale so many poor children in this most noble competition of charity, in addition to money it will be necessary to gather food, medicines and clothing, all of which are so greatly wanting in these regions. We need not delay in explaining how such offerings may be conveniently divided and forwarded to their destination. This task may be confided to the committees which have been formed for this object, and may provide for it in any manner whatsoever.

653. Finally, We trust that the exhortation which, moved by duty of that universal fatherhood which God has confided to Us, We have made, although addressed principally to Catholics, may be benevolently listened to by all who have the sentiments of humanity. Moreover, in order to afford an example to others, notwithstanding the continual requests for help which reach Us from all sides, We have determined, to the extent of Our means, to contribute to the relief of these poor children the sum of 100,000 lire. . . . . . .

LETTER *Celeberrima Evenisse Sollemnia* TO CARDINAL BELLO, ARCHBISHOP OF LISBON, AND TO THE OTHER ARCHBISHOPS AND BISHOPS OF PORTUGAL.[195]

> *For the peace of their nation, the faithful must be subject to those who are in legitimate authority.*

December 18, 1919

654. We were indeed very glad to hear that the solemnities were very well attended which took place recently in honor of

---

[195] Original Latin, *A.A.S.*, v. 12, pp. 32-33 (February 2, 1920).

Blessed Nonius Alvares at Lisbon, and that very many of you took part in them. For thus taking advantage of the excellent opportunity you not only took counsel over the state of affairs with one another, in order to set forth a joint program for your flocks in matters which pertain to Religion and State, but you also learned from the Apostolic Nuncio Our opinion in this most serious matter. Nevertheless, Venerable Brethren, on account of Our special love for the most noble Portuguese nation We wish to speak to you paternally. First of all We cherish a well-founded hope that all—whether clergy or laity, whose sincere love of country is certainly most clearly established—will be second to none in re-establishing peace and good-will among their fellow citizens. For since the Church, as is evident, must neither be responsible to political parties, nor serve political interests, it is, therefore, her duty to urge the faithful to obey those who are in authority, whatever be the constitution of the State. For on this depends the common good, which is certainly, according to God's plan, the first law of the State, as Our Predecessor of happy memory, Leo XIII, clearly set forth in his Encyclical, *Au Milieu des Sollicitudes,* of February 16, 1892.[196] Moreover, writing to the Cardinals of France on the 3rd of May of the same year, he stated that it was a Christian's duty faithfully to submit to the authority which is actually in power. Following, therefore, the teaching and practice of the Church, which has always been accustomed to be on friendly terms with States of whatever constitution, and which has recently restored relations with the Republic of Portugal, let Catholics, with a clear conscience, submit also to this civil authority as it is now constituted, and for the common good of Religion and State let them willingly accept public offices if they are conferred. We make these exhortations all the more willingly because, from what has been reported to Us, We are confident that the Portuguese authorities will uphold the complete freedom of the Church and the exercise of her sacred rights that she may there most profitably carry out her divine commission. It will be your task, Venerable Brethren, together with the clergy to urge the faithful from time to time that, considering Mother Church more important than worldly interests and political parties, they strive by all means to protect her rights with united strength. For thus they will greatly contribute to the increase and prosperity

[196] Cf. *supra* n. 176.

of their native Portugal, that she may successfully continue to carry out the most glorious task she has received from Divine Providence especially in spreading the Faith and civilization throughout the vast extent of her colonies. . . .

ALLOCUTION *Il Linguaggio* TO THE COLLEGE OF CARDINALS.[197]

A fair penalty, not destruction, may be imposed upon conquered peoples.

December 24, 1919

655. . . . . . . Far, however, from being afraid for the future of individuals and of society, We subscribe to the wish of the Sacred College, desiring that, first of all, the spirit of faith be revived in individuals and in society, and that both one and the other may then enjoy the fruits of that peace which is the daughter of a true life of faith.

656. The Apostle, Saint Paul, after having taught the Romans that *the Kingdom of God is not meat and drink; but justice, and peace, and joy in the Holy Ghost,* used to draw from his teaching this conclusion: *Let us do, therefore, that which is useful to peace: itaque quae pacis sunt sectemur.*[198] We, also, have recently co-operated, within the limited measure of Our strength, in the extension of the Kingdom of God by furthering the propagation of the Faith throughout the whole world.

657. . . . Hence, having taken care to revive the spirit of faith by calling to mind the nativity of our Lord Jesus Christ, in order that it be vouchsafed to individuals and to society to enjoy more copiously the fruits of that peace which faith alone can give, We also, with St. Paul, must remind them of the obligation of doing all which helps to maintain that ineffable good: *itaque quae pacis sunt sectemur.*

658. Because *pacis sunt,* our acts of homage and of obedience to divine and human laws, which acts, in a direct or indirect way, recognize the supreme dominion of God over creation, are useful to peace; because *pacis sunt,* the mortifications and the penances, with which the senses are subjected to the spirit, help to promote

[197] Original Italian, *La Civiltà Cattolica*, 1920, v. 1, pp. 73-74.
[198] *Romans*, XIV, 17-19.

peace; because *pacis sunt,* the kindness which in our words and acts we employ towards our brethren, even at the price of self love, helps to promote peace.

659. And if we pass from the consideration of the good of the individual to that of society, we ought once again to repeat the exhortation of St. Paul: *itaque quae pacis sunt sectemur.*

660. *Pacis sunt* the public act by which it is acknowledged that from neither schools, nor from courtrooms, nor from public assemblies must God, Who is not only the Lord of the individual but of society, be ostracized; *pacis sunt* the work and care devoted to establish the alliance of peoples on the foundation of justice; *pacis sunt* the decisions and sentences which impose upon conquered peoples a fair penalty, but not destruction. . . . . . .

LETTER *Par l'Intermédiaire* TO MR. HERBERT HOOVER, THE AMERICAN COMMISSIONER OF SUPPLIES FOR EUROPE.[199]

Hoover's relief work is highly praised.

January 9, 1920

661. Through Our dear son, the Cardinal Archbishop of Baltimore, We have received further news of the really admirable and providential work that you are continuing to carry out to alleviate the serious and complex troubles from which Europe is suffering in the matter of food supplies. Such beneficent work will undoubtedly ensure for you a very high place in the annals of Christian charity, and, so to speak, a unique title to the gratitude of the peoples; and it fills Our heart with sincere pleasure and lively consolation when We think of the immense good that it is bringing to the multitude of suffering people in this desolated Europe. Especially, We have learned, you are concentrating your attention and anxious care on the little children. We still retain a vivid recollection of what you did to help the unfortunate children of Belgium at a moment when they were dying through the lack of the food their young lives required. We spoke then from Our heart, encouraging your generous initiative. We can do no less now, the more so in that it is not a question of the lives of the children of one

---

[199] Translation from *The Tablet,* v. 135, pp. 223-224 (February 14, 1920). Original French, *A.A.S.,* v. 12, pp. 35-36 (February 2, 1920).

nation only, but, from what We hear, of three millions of children belonging to different States of Europe. Moved by the charity of Jesus Christ, therefore, and feeling the love that He felt for the children, We most heartily recommend the work which you are doing to all American citizens, without distinction of faith or party, feeling sure that they who have always opened their hearts to every noble initiative will respond with enthusiasm to this appeal. The more so in that We are happy to see that in your work there is no place for resentment or particularism of any sort, it aims at helping all suffering children, in preference the children of the enemies of yesterday who are undergoing the worst sufferings. We, as you know, were moved by these same high sentiments when We turned to the bishops of the whole world, urging them to rouse the charity of the faithful to help the children of Central Europe on Holy Innocents' Day, and when We gladly approved the work of the "Save the Children Fund" of London, which had taken a similar initiative. We have no doubt at all that with God's aid all these efforts will have the happiest results, but, on the other hand, We think that success would be more easily attained if all the initiatives were to come together in a common understanding. With all Our heart We wish the greatest success to your generous effort, and We fervently pray that God may grant you the most precious reward.

ENCYCLICAL *Pacem Dei Munus Pulcherrimum* ON PEACE AND CHRISTIAN RECONCILIATION.[200]

Unless Christian charity and justice are practiced by the nations, the peace treaty will be in vain.

May 23, 1920

662. Peace, the beautiful gift of God, the name of which, as St. Augustine says, is the sweetest word to our hearing and the best and most desirable possession;[201] peace, which was for more than four years implored by the ardent wishes of all good peoples, by the prayers of pious souls and the tears of mothers, begins at

---

[200] Translation from Eppstein, *The Catholic Tradition of the Law of Nations*, pp. 236-242. Original Latin, *A.A.S.*, v. 12, pp. 209-218 (June 1, 1920).
[201] *De Civitate Dei*, bk. XIX, ch. 11 in Migne, *P.L.*, v. 41, c. 637.

last to shine upon the nations. At this We are indeed the happiest of all, and heartily do We rejoice. But this joy of Our paternal heart is disturbed by many bitter anxieties, for if in most places peace is in some sort established and treaties are signed, the germs of former enmities remain; and you well know, Venerable Brethren, that there can be no stable peace or lasting treaties, though made after long and difficult negotiations and duly signed, unless there be a return of mutual charity to appease hate and banish enmity. This, then, Venerable Brethren, is the anxious and dangerous question upon which We wish to dwell and to put forward recommendations to be brought home to your people.

663. For Ourselves, since We were raised by the hidden designs of God to this Chair, We have never ceased to do everything in Our power from the very beginning of the war that all the nations of the world might resume cordial relations as soon as possible. To that end We never ceased to pray, to repeat exhortations, to propose ways of arrangement, to try every means, in fact, to open by divine aid a path to a just, honorable, and lasting peace; and at the same time We exercised all Our paternal care to alleviate everywhere that terrible load of sorrow and disaster of every sort by which the immense tragedy was accompanied.

664. And now, just as from the beginning of Our troubled pontificate the charity of Jesus Christ led Us to work both for the return of peace and to alleviate the horrors of the war, so now that comparative peace has been concluded, this same charity urges Us to exhort all the children of the Church, and all mankind, to clear their hearts of bitterness, and give place to mutual love and concord.

665. There is no need from Us of long proof to show that society would incur the risk of great loss if, while peace is signed, latent hostility and enmity were to continue among the nations. There is no need to mention the loss of all that maintains and fosters civil life, such as commerce and industry, art and literature, which flourish only when the nations are at peace. But, what is even more important, grave harm would accrue to the form and essence of the Christian life, which consists essentially in charity and the preaching of which is called the Gospel of peace.[202]

666. You know well, and We have frequently reminded you of it, that nothing was so often and so carefully inculcated on His

[202] *Ephesians*, VI, 15.

285

disciples by Jesus Christ as this precept of mutual charity, as the one which contains all others. Christ called it the new commandment, His very own, and desired that it should be the sign of Christians by which they might be distinguished from all others; and on the eve of His death it was His last testament to His disciples to love one another and thus try to imitate the ineffable unity of the three Divine Persons in the Trinity. *That they may be one as we also are one . . . that they may be made perfect in one.*[203]

667. The Apostles, following in the steps of the Divine Master, and conforming to His word and commands, were unceasing in their exhortation to the faithful: *Before all things have a constant mutual charity among yourselves.*[204] *But above all these things have charity which is the bond of perfection.*[205] *Dearly beloved, let us love one another, for charity is of God.*[206] Our brethren of the first Christian ages faithfully observed these commands of Jesus Christ and the Apostles. They belonged to different and rival nations, yet they willingly forgot their causes of quarrel and lived in perfect concord, and such a union of hearts was in striking contrast with the deadly enmities by which human society was then consumed.

668. What has already been said in favor of charity holds good for the inculcation of the pardoning of injuries which is no less solemnly commanded by the Lord: *But I say to you, love your enemies; do good to them that hate you; pray for those that persecute and calumniate you, that you may be the children of your Father Who is in heaven, Who maketh His sun to rise upon the good and bad.*[207] Hence, that terribly severe warning of the Apostle, St. John: *Whosoever hateth his brother is a murderer. And you know that no murderer hath eternal life abiding in himself.*[208]

669. Our Lord Jesus Christ, in teaching us how to pray to God, makes us say that we wish for pardon as we forgive others: *Forgive us our trespasses as we forgive them that trespass against us.*[209] And if the observance of this law is sometimes hard and difficult, we have not only the timely assistance of the grace of Our Divine Redeemer, but also His example to help us to overcome the diffi-

[203] *John*, XVII, 22-23.
[204] I *Peter*, IV, 8.
[205] *Colossians*, III, 14.
[206] I *John*, IV, 7.
[207] *Matthew*, V, 44-45.
[208] I *John*, III, 15.
[209] *Matthew*, VI, 12.

culty. For as He hung on the Cross He thus excused before His Father those who so unjustly and wickedly tortured Him: *Father, forgive them, for they know not what they do.*[210] We, then, who should be the first to imitate the pity and loving kindness of Jesus Christ, Whose Vicar, without any merit of Our own, We are; with all Our heart, and following His example, We forgive all Our enemies who knowingly or unknowingly have heaped and are still heaping on Our person and Our work every sort of vituperation, and We embrace all in Our charity and benevolence and neglect no opportunity to do them all the good in Our power. That is indeed what Christians worthy of the name ought to do toward those who during the war have done them wrong.

670. Christian charity ought not to be content with not hating our enemies and loving them as brothers; it also demands that we treat them with kindness, following the rule of the Divine Master who *went about doing good and healing all that were oppressed by the devil,*[211] and finished His mortal life, the course of which was marked by good deeds, by shedding His blood for them. So said St. John: *In this we have known the charity of God, because He hath laid down His life for us, and we ought to lay down our lives for the brethren. He that hath the substance of this world and shall see his brother in need and shall shut up his bowels from him: how doth the charity of God abide in him? My little children, let us not love in word nor by tongue, but in deed and in truth.*[212]

671. Never indeed was there a time when we should "stretch the bounds of charity" more than in these days of universal suffering and sorrow; never perhaps as to-day has humanity so needed that universal beneficence which springs from the love of others, and is full of sacrifice and zeal. For if we look around where the fury of the war has been let loose we see immense regions utterly desolate, uncultivated and abandoned; multitudes reduced to want of food, clothing and shelter; innumerable widows and orphans reft of everything, and an incredible number of enfeebled beings, particularly children and young people, who carry on their bodies the ravages of this atrocious war.

672. When one regards all these miseries by which the human

[210] *Luke,* XXIII, 34.
[211] *Acts,* X, 38.
[212] I *John,* III, 16-18.

race is stricken one inevitably thinks of the traveler in the Gospel,[213] who, going down from Jerusalem to Jericho, fell among thieves, who robbed him, and covered him with wounds and left him half dead. The two cases are very similar; and as to the traveler there came the good Samaritan, full of compassion, who bound up his wounds, pouring in oil and wine, took him to an inn, and undertook all care for him, so, too, is it necessary that Jesus, of Whom the Samaritan was the figure, should lay His Hands upon the wounds of society.

673. This work, this duty the Church claims as her own as heir and guardian of the spirit of Jesus Christ—the Church whose entire existence is a marvelously varied tissue of all kinds of good deeds, the Church, that "real mother of Christians in the full sense of the word, who has such tenderness of love and charity for her neighbor that she can offer the best remedies for the different evils which afflict souls on account of their sins." That is why she "treats and teaches children with tenderness, young people with firmness, old people with great calm, taking account of not only the age but also the condition of soul of each."[214] It would be difficult to exaggerate the effect of this many-sided Christian beneficence in softening the heart and thus facilitating the return of tranquillity to the nations.

674. Therefore, Venerable Brethren, We pray you and exhort you in the mercy and charity of Jesus Christ, strive with all zeal and diligence not only to urge the faithful entrusted to your care to abandon hatred and to pardon offenses; but—and what is more immediately practical—to promote all those works of Christian benevolence which bring aid to the needy, comfort to the afflicted, and protection to the weak, and to give opportune and appropriate assistance of every kind to all who have suffered from the war. It is Our especial wish that you should exhort your priests, as the ministers of peace, to be assiduous in urging this love of one's neighbor and even of enemies which is the essence of the Christian life and by *being all things to all men*[215] and giving an example to others, wage war everywhere on enmity and hatred, thus doing a thing most agreeable to the loving Heart of Jesus and to him

---

[213] *Luke*, X, 30 *sq.*
[214] St. Augustine, *De Moribus Ecclesiae Catholicae*, bk. I, ch. 30, in Migne, *P.L.*, v. 32, c. 1336.
[215] I *Corinthians*, IX, 22.

who, however unworthy, holds His place on earth. In this connection Catholic writers and journalists should be invited to clothe
themselves *as elect of God, holy and beloved, with pity and kindness.*[216] Let them show this charity in their writings by abstaining
not only from false and groundless accusations, but also from all
intemperance and bitterness of language, all of which is contrary
to the law of Christ and does but reopen sores as yet unhealed,
seeing that the slightest touch is a serious irritant to a heart whose
wounds are recent.

675. All that We have said here to individuals about the duty
of charity We wish to say also to the peoples who have been delivered from the burden of a long war, in order that, when every
cause of disagreement has been, as far as possible, removed—and
without prejudice to the rights of justice—they may resume friendly
relations among themselves. The Gospel has not one law of charity
for individuals and another for States and nations, which are indeed
but collections of individuals. The war being now over, people seem
called to a general reconciliation not only from motives of charity,
but from necessity; the nations are naturally drawn together by
the need they have of one another, and by the bond of mutual
good-will, bonds which are to-day strengthened by the development
of civilization and the marvelous increase of communication.

676. Truly, as We have already said, this Apostolic See has
never wearied of teaching during the war such pardon of offenses
and the fraternal reconciliation of the peoples, in conformity with
the most holy law of Jesus Christ, and in agreement with the needs
of civil life and human intercourse; nor did it allow that amid
dissension and hate these moral principles should be forgotten.
With all the more reason, then, now that the Treaties of Peace are
signed, does it proclaim these principles as, for example, it did a
short time ago in the Letter to the Bishops of Germany,[217] and in
that addressed to the Archbishop of Paris.[218]

677. And this concord between civilized nations is maintained
and fostered by the modern custom of visits and meetings at which
the heads of States and princes are accustomed to treat of matters
of special importance. So, then, considering the changed circum-

[216] *Colossians*, III, 12.
[217] Apostolic Letter *Diuturni*, July 15, 1919. See *supra* nn. 636-637.
[218] Letter *Amor Ille*, October 7, 1919. See *supra* nn. 643-645.

stances of the times and the dangerous trend of events, and in order to encourage this concord, We would not be unwilling to relax in some measure the severity of the conditions justly laid down by Our Predecessors, when the civil power of the Apostolic See was overthrown, against the official visits of the heads of Catholic States to Rome. But at the same time We formally declare that this concession, which seems counseled or rather demanded by the grave circumstances in which to-day society is placed, must not be interpreted as a tacit renunciation of its sacrosanct rights by the Apostolic See, as if it acquiesced in the unlawful situation in which it is placed. Rather do We seize this opportunity to renew for the same reasons the protests which Our Predecessors have several times made, not in the least moved thereto by human interests, but in fulfillment of the sacred duty of their charge to defend the rights and dignity of this Apostolic See; once again demanding and with even greater insistence, now that peace is made among the nations, that "for the Head of the Church, too, an end may be put to that abnormal condition which in so many ways does such serious harm to tranquillity among the peoples."[219]

678. Things being thus restored, the order required by justice and charity re-established and the nations reconciled, it is much to be desired, Venerable Brethren, that all States, putting aside mutual suspicion, should unite in one league, or rather a sort of family of peoples, calculated both to maintain their own independence and safeguard the order of human society. What specially, amongst other reasons, calls for such an association of nations, is the need generally recognized of making every effort to abolish or reduce the enormous burden of the military expenditures which States can no longer bear, in order to prevent these disastrous wars or at least to remove the danger of them as far as possible. So would each nation be assured not only of its independence but also of the integrity of its territory within its just frontiers.

679. The Church will certainly not refuse her zealous aid to States united under the Christian law in any of their undertakings inspired by justice and charity, inasmuch as she is herself the most perfect type of universal society. She possesses in her organization and institutions a wonderful instrument for bringing this brotherhood among men, not only for their eternal salvation but also for

[219] Encyclical *Ad Beatissimi*, November 1, 1914. See *supra* n. 296.

their material well-being in this world; she leads them through temporal well-being to the sure acquisition of eternal blessings. It is the teaching of history that when the Church pervaded with her spirit the ancient and barbarous nations of Europe, little by little the many and varied differences that divided them were diminished and their quarrels extinguished; in time they formed a homogeneous society from which sprang Christian Europe which, under the guidance and auspices of the Church, whilst preserving a diversity of nations, tended to a unity that favored its prosperity and glory. On this point St. Augustine well says: "This celestial city, in its life here on earth, calls to itself citizens of every nation, and forms out of all the peoples one varied society; it is not harassed by differences in customs, laws and institutions, which serve to the attainment or the maintenance of peace on earth; it neither rends nor destroys anything but rather guards all and adapts itself to all; however, these things may vary among the nations, they are all directed to the same end of peace on earth as long as they do not hinder the exercise of religion, which teaches the worship of the true supreme God."[220] And the same holy Doctor thus addresses the Church: "Citizens, peoples, and all men, thou, recalling their common origin, shalt not only unite among themselves, but shalt make them brothers."[221]

680. To come back to what We said at the beginning, We turn affectionately to all Our children and conjure them in the name of Our Lord Jesus Christ to forget mutual differences and offenses and draw together in the bonds of Christian charity, from which none are excluded and within which none are strangers. We fervently exhort all the nations, under the inspiration of Christian benevolence, to establish a true peace among themselves and join together in an alliance which shall be just and, therefore, lasting. And lastly We appeal to all men and all peoples to join in mind and heart with the Catholic Church and through the Church with Christ, the Redeemer of the human race, so that We may address to them in very truth the words of St. Paul to the Ephesians: *But now in Christ Jesus you who sometime were afar off, are made nigh by the Blood of Christ. For He is our peace, Who hath made both one, and breaking down the middle wall 'of partition . . .*

[220] *De Civitate Dei*, bk. XIX, ch. 17, in Migne, *P.L.*, v. 41, c. 646.
[221] *De Moribus Ecclesiae Catholicae*, bk. I, ch. 30, in Migne, *P.L.*, v. 32, c. 1336.

*killing the enmities in Himself. And coming He preached peace
to you that were afar off and peace to them that were nigh.*[222]

681. Nor less appropriate are the words which the same Apostle
addressed to the Colossians: *Lie not one to another: stripping yourselves of the old man with his deeds. And putting on the new,
him who is renewed unto knowledge according to the image of
Him that created him. Where there is neither Gentile nor Jew,
circumcision nor uncircumcision, Barbarian nor Scythian, bond nor
free. But Christ is all and in all.*[223]

682. Meanwhile, trusting in the protection of Mary, the Virgin
Immaculate, who not long ago We directed should be universally
invoked as "Queen of Peace," as also in the intercession of the three
Blessed to whom We have decreed the honor of Saints, We humbly
implore the Holy Ghost, the Paraclete, that He may "graciously
grant to the Church the gifts of unity and peace,"[224] and may renew
the face of the earth by a fresh outpouring of His charity for the
salvation of all. As an earnest of these heavenly gifts and as a pledge
of Our paternal benevolence, We impart with all Our heart to you,
Venerable Brethren, to all your clergy and people, the Apostolic
Benediction.

LETTER *Intelleximus* TO CARDINAL LA FONTAINE, ARCHBISHOP OF
    VENICE, AND TO THE OTHER BISHOPS OF THE TERRITORY OF
    VENICE.[225]

*The application of Christian social principles will bring
internal peace to those lands where there now is strife
between opposing factions.*

June 14, 1920

683. We understand from the letters which you sent Us recently that you are deeply concerned over those popular movements
by which the tranquillity of your territory is disturbed at present.
The reasons for your concern are obvious. The issues in dispute
are most difficult and unpleasant; moreover, the Faith itself is
placed in jeopardy. We deeply share in your concern and for the

---

[222] *Ephesians,* II, 13 *sq.*
[223] *Colossians,* III, 9-11.
[224] *Secret* in the Feast of Corpus Christi.
[225] Original Latin, *A.A.S.,* v. 12, p. 290 (July 1, 1920).

same reasons. It is Our duty principally to bring back a Christian reconciliation among opposing factions, and to safeguard the eternal salvation of all. First of all, you have done well to establish certain proper boards for the benefit of the workingman, which, with the right use of the principles of Christian wisdom, will do away with any disputes between owners and workers. And certainly, as We have written recently to the Bishop of Bergamo, these boards can be of great advantage, as long as they use Christian principles, and as long as those questions or problems which pertain to religion or morals or doctrine are duly referred to the authority of the Church.

684. For the Church alone has the medicine and the remedy for the cure of the sickness which exists in these difficulties — a remedy, by the way, which is conformed to the eternal laws of justice — a remedy which We hear the human race to-day loudly imploring on all sides. But these laws of justice are to be observed indeed in such a way that within their proper fields they may remain both just and firm. Consequently, when We exhort the rich to cultivate generosity and to emphasize fairness much more than their rights, We at the same time earnestly advise the working-men that their very Faith may be endangered if they seek to impose and to make immoderate and unreasonable demands. . . . . . .

MOTU PROPRIO—*Bonum Sane*—ON DEVOTION TO ST. JOSEPH.[226]
Many serious moral evils have arisen as a consequence of the war.

July 25, 1920

685. . . . . . . What is lacking to restore a common and properly ordered peace after so hard a struggle of war, We have recently shown in the Encyclical *On the Christian Restoration of Peace*,[227] in which We paid particular attention to the public relations both of nations and men with one another. Now, however, there is another cause of disturbance which calls for attention, and that a far greater one inasmuch as it attacks the very veins and sinews of human society. The calamity of war came upon the nations precisely at that time when Naturalism, the greatest plague in the

[226] Original Latin, *A.A.S.,* v. 12, pp. 313-315 (August 2, 1920).
[227] Cf. *supra* nn. 662-682.

world, had completely tainted them. As soon as Naturalism takes root, it weakens the desire for heavenly treasures, smothers the flame of love for God, draws man away from the healing and supernaturalizing grace of Christ, and finally robs him of the light of faith, and abandons him, armed only with the weak and corrupt forces of his nature, to the unbridled lusts of his soul. Since too many men, therefore, had their desires turned only to perishable goods, and since the bitterest quarrels and jealousies existed between rich and poor, the greatness and length of the war increased mutual class hatred and rendered it even more bitter, particularly because it brought unbearable want to the masses and a sudden abundance of wealth to a very few.

686. In addition to this list of woes it added these: that the sanctity of marital fidelity and respect for parental authority suffered no slight loss on account of the war, because the remoteness of one of the parties weakened the bond of duty in the other and the absence of a guardian led rash young girls in particular to indulge their passions without restraint. We must, therefore, deplore the fact that morals are much more depraved and corrupt than formerly, and on this account what is called the *social question* is growing so serious from day to day that the worst evils are now to be feared. The fond hope and wish of every renegade is the speedy rise of some universal state, which is based on complete equality of men and common ownership of property as a fundamental principle, in which neither any distinctions of nationality, nor authority of parents over their children, nor of public authority over citizens, nor of God over man living in society is acknowledged. If these principles are put into practice, dreadful horrors must necessarily follow; and at this very moment not a small part of Europe is experiencing and feeling them. We even see that such a state of affairs is being sought for all other nations, and that great upheavals are shortly to ensue everywhere among the masses, stirred up by the madness and audacity of a few.

687. Particularly concerned by this trend of events, We have not neglected when opportunity presented itself, to remind the children of the Church of their duty, as in a letter recently written to the Bishop of Bergamo and also to the bishops of the province of Venice.[228] Now for the same reason, to keep all Our children

228 Cf. *supra* nn. 683-684.

wherever they be, who earn their living by the work of their hands, on the path of duty and to keep them intact from the contagion of Socialism, and there is nothing more opposed to Christian teaching, We especially set before them in all earnestness Saint Joseph, whom they shall follow as their special guide in life and venerate as their patron. . . . . . .

LETTER *Con Vivo Compiacimento* TO CARDINAL POMPILI, VICAR OF ROME.[229]

> *Prayers are ordered for Poland because her national existence is threatened.*

August 5, 1920

688. It is with the greatest pleasure that We have heard that, following Our suggestion, you have ordered that on Sunday next, in the venerable church of the Gesù, solemn prayers shall be raised to the Most High to invoke the mercy of the Lord on unhappy Poland. The gravest considerations lead Us to hope, My Lord Cardinal, that your example will be followed by all the bishops of the Catholic world. In truth, the anxious motherly care with which the Holy See has always followed the vicissitudes of the Polish nation is well known. When all the civil nations were silent in front of the predominance of might over right, the Holy See alone protested against the iniquitous partition of Poland and against the no less iniquitous oppression of the Polish people. But now there is much more. Now not only is the national existence of Poland in danger, but all Europe is threatened by the horrors of fresh wars. So it is not only love for Poland, but love for all Europe that moves Us to hope that all the faithful will join Us in praying the Most High that through the intercession of the Most Blessed Virgin, Protectress of Poland, the people of that country may be spared this last disaster, and at the same time this fresh scourge may be lifted from Europe, already bled almost to death. Praying Almighty God that the hearts of the faithful may respond to the Father's appeal, We impart to you with all Our heart, My Lord Cardinal, the Apostolic Benediction.

[229] Translation from *The Tablet,* v. 137, p. 249 (August 21, 1920). Original Italian, *Civiltà Cattolica,* 1920, v. 3, p. 369 (August 14, 1920).

ALLOCUTION *E Bella* TO THE FIRST GERMAN PILGRIMAGE AFTER
THE WAR.[230]

*Benedict XV will not be content until the armistice is
followed by a complete reconciliation of hearts.*

October 31, 1920

689. . . . . . . Indeed, how lively and great is Our joy now
that We receive the first pilgrims of Germany to come here after
the terrible scourge of the World War! . . . . . . We do not wish to
mention anew what We have recently said, that Our heart will
not be at peace until a complete reconciliation of hearts has followed the armistice. . . .

690. You, Our dear ones, are the first to make the journey to
Rome since those enmities of war have come to an end. Those
hostilities made Our position so perilous, since We well knew that
We had sons in each of the two opposing camps. Not only in the
order of time are you the first to come to Us, but you shall also
lead others to the re-establishment of cordial relations, at least among
all sons of the Catholic Church. . . . We confine Ourself now
to remind you, that the Apostolic See cannot enjoy this peace that
you desire, without the concord of all its sons in the profession of
one and the same teaching and in the practice of one and the
same love. . . .

691. . . . We offer the German Catholics Our blessings and
good wishes, because they are united with Us in the same Faith
by the bond of the love of Christ—*Propter fratres meos et proximos
meos loquebar pacem de te. For the sake of my brethren, and of
my neighbors, I spoke peace of thee.*[231] . . .

692. To Germany, too, We say: May there be peace in your
midst! But, without departing from the language of the Bible,
We wish you, in these words, not only that the horrors of a new
war may forever remain far from your land, but also that fine
customs, domestic peace, progress in industry and commerce, art
and science—in a word, all those goods that are the fruit of peace—
may blossom there.

693. Our yearnings for your well-being, Our dearest sons, are

[230] German text from Lama, *Papst und Kurie*, pp. 202-204. Original text in *Osservatore Romano*, November 1, 1920.
[231] *Psalms*, 121, v. 8.

so strong that it would be folly to expect their fulfillment by merely
natural powers. And, therefore, We expect them first through the
blessing of God, which We now call down on all German Catholics.
May it please the Lord to strengthen by the superabundance of His
grace and blessing the illustrious German episcopate, which We
here and now cordially greet in the person of its worthy representative, the Archbishop of Cologne, here present. May God bless
all the clergy and the whole Catholic population of Germany, and
may this blessing of God draw the clergy and the people more and
more closely around their bishops and through these around the
Holy See. May the Lord bless in a special manner these pilgrims
who have gathered around Us on this memorable day. May their
families and communities, too, share in this blessing. And, why
should We not extend Our wishes and blessings also to those Germans who have not yet returned into the arms of Holy Mother the
Church? Yes, the whole land of St. Boniface be blessed in memory
of the joy that this, the first pilgrimage of several of its sons, has
given Us.

LETTER *Plane Intelligimus* TO CARDINAL PIFFL, ARCHBISHOP OF
VIENNA, AND TO THE OTHER BISHOPS OF AUSTRIA.[232]

The Pope is gravely concerned over the Austrian youth.

November 26, 1920

694. We clearly understand from your common letter the
enormity of fear that is yours, the superabundant cares that are
yours and, for these reasons, you and your flock are constantly before Our eyes and in Our heart. We are gravely concerned about
these troubles, especially the needs of youth and We intend once
again to come to their aid. The subjects, with which, as you announce, your careful planning in your meeting was engaged, confirm again the praise bestowed upon your diligence and merit from
yet another motive Our good wishes for you. Regardless of the
present state of your affairs, regardless of what the future has in
store, you shall not labor in vain. For the rest, Beloved Son and
Venerable Brethren, be of brave heart, trust in God, for He is
faithful and will not leave the just man in uncertainty forever. . . .

[232] Original Latin, *A.A.S.,* v. 13, p. 12 (January 3, 1921).

ENCYCLICAL *Annus Jam Plenus* ON THE CHILDREN, VICTIMS OF THE WAR.[233]

A call to Christians, especially the young, to contribute to the relief of the suffering children of the belligerent nations.

December 1, 1920

695. A whole year has now passed since We (when the war was but a thing of yesterday) called upon all Christians, at the approach of the birthday of Our Lord,[234] to turn their hearts in pity toward the children of Central Europe, who were so severely afflicted by hunger and want that they were wasting away with disease and were face to face with death. And, indeed, a wondrous joy it is to Us that Our appeal has not fallen vainly to the ground— an appeal which was actuated by that charity which enfolds in its kindly embrace all men, without distinction of race or nation, whosoever bear within them the image of God. The happy issue of Our supplication, Venerable Brethren, is especially well known to you who assisted Us zealously in so salutary an enterprise. For, in truth, a generous supply of money has been collected from the peoples of every land. There has been, as it were, a noble competition in liberality, with the result that the Common Father of so many innocent children has been able to look to their necessities and dissipate their sorrows. Nor do We cease to proclaim the kindly Providence of God, Whom it has pleased to use Us as a channel whereby the manifold blessings of Christian charity might flow to His abandoned little ones. In this matter We cannot desist from offering a public tribute of praise to the society, entitled the "Save the Children Fund," which has exerted all possible care and diligence in the collection of money, clothing and food. But, indeed, the general scarcity and the high cost of living, which the war has brought in its train, are of such a complex and varied character that the assistance We have rendered has perhaps neither succeeded in reaching those parts of Europe where necessity pressed hard, nor, where help was given, has it always been adequate to the actual need. To this must be added the fact that in the course of

---

[233] Translation from *The Tablet*, v. 137, p. 872 (December 25, 1920). Original Latin, *A.A.S.*, v. 12, pp. 553-556 (December 1, 1920).
[234] See *supra* nn. 655-660.

the year following the Encyclical Letter which We addressed to you, Venerable Brethren, on this very topic, there has been no appreciable improvement in the lot of most of those areas where it is evident that the people, and especially the young, find life growing yet harder and harder owing to the shortage of the necessaries of life. Nay, in some parts, war has flamed out anew and calamities of every kind, to the serious loss of those very elements that it is necessary to re-establish; in other parts where the civil state has been overthrown and where most frightful and disgraceful massacres have been perpetrated, it has come about that numberless families have been reduced to penury; that wives have been bereft of their husbands, and children of their parents; there are many districts, too, where it is so difficult to make provision for the food supply that as a consequence the population is afflicted by almost the same hardships which pressed upon it in the hideous days of the war.

696. Wherefore once again, inspired by the consciousness of that universal fatherhood which it is Our office to sustain, and with the words of the Divine Master on Our lips—*I have compassion on the multitude . . . for they have nothing to eat*—[235] now, when the anniversary day of the birth of Christ draws nigh, a second time We call loudly upon Christian peoples to give Us the means whereby We may offer some relief to the sick and suffering children, of whatsoever nationality they may be. Yes, We call on all who have hearts of kindness and pity to make a generous offering, but in particular We turn to those young children who dwell in the more prosperous cities of the world, to those who can with comparative ease stretch out a helping hand to their poor little brothers in Christ. Is not the birthday of Christ Jesus in an especial manner the feast of the young? See, then, how the desolate children of those scattered districts strain suppliant hands to those other happier children, and seem to point to the cradle where the Divine Infant cries in helplessness! Yet, is not that Infant the Common Brother of them all, He, Who *being rich became poor,*[236] Who from that manger, as from the throne of heavenly wisdom, silently teaches us not only the value of brotherly love but also how men from their tenderest years onward must detach themselves from the longing for the goods of this world and share them with the poor? . . .

[235] *Matthew,* XV, 32.
[236] II *Corinthians,* VIII, 9.

697. Surely the children of the richer parts of Europe will have it in their power to nourish and clothe those little ones of their own age who languish in want, and especially should this be so at the approaching season of the Nativity of Our Lord, which parents are wont to render still happier for their children by little gifts and presents. And shall We think that these last are endowed with such a spirit as to be unwilling to contribute even a part of their own little savings, whereby they might strengthen the weakness of children who are in want? Oh, what a deep consolation, what joys they will secure for themselves, if haply they become the means whereby those little brothers of theirs, who are deprived of all help and all pleasure, should spend the approaching Christmas time just a little more comfortably, just a little more happily. For even as the Infant Jesus on the night of His birth blessed with a most sweet smile the shepherds who came to Him with gifts to lighten the burden of His poverty, and even as He brightened their souls with the supreme gift of faith, so He will reward with His blessing and heavenly graces those children who, fired with love for Him, shall soften the misery and the sorrow of their little brothers. Nay, there is nothing else more acceptable to the Infant Jesus that they could do or offer at this season. And so We earnestly exhort all Christian parents, to whom the Heavenly Father has committed the grave charge of training their offspring in the practice of charity and the other virtues, to use this happy opportunity of exciting and cultivating in the minds of their children sentiments of humanity and holy compassion. . . .

698. . . . Oh, how Our heart would expand if We were certain that throughout the Christmas festivities there would be no home destitute of consolation and joy, that there would be no child whose sorrow should wring the dear heart of its mother, and that there would be no mother who should look upon her little ones with weeping eyes. And so, Venerable Brethren, We entrust Our project to you, even as We did a year ago, that you may bring it into effect, especially those of you who dwell in districts which enjoy a happier fortune and a more tranquil state of affairs.

699. And inasmuch as those words of Christ Our Lord should take deep possession of your souls, *He that shall receive one such little child in My name, receiveth Me,*[237] We beg that you leave

[237] *Matthew*, XVIII, 5.

no measure untried whereby the liberality and generosity of the faithful over whom you are set may correspond to the urgency of the present need. Accordingly it is Our wish that you forthwith announce throughout the whole of your several dioceses that a collection of alms is to be made on the twenty-eighth day of this month, the feast of the Holy Innocents, or if you prefer, on the Sunday immediately preceding, for the support of the children made needy by the war, and that you particularly recommend this collection to the children in your diocese; further, that with all the diligence in your power you see that the money thus collected is sent either to Us or to the "Save the Children Fund," which We have before mentioned. For Ourself, in order that, after exhorting the faithful by Our words, We may stir their generosity by Our example, We have set apart 100,000 Italian lire for this most sacred work of charity. . . .

ALLOCUTION *Cum Multa Hoc Tempore* TO THE COLLEGE OF CARDINALS.[238]

The provisions of the Versailles Treaty for the Catholic Missions have not been satisfactorily fulfilled.

December 16, 1920

700. . . . . . . Another cause for particular concern to Us comes from the fact that the Catholic Missions are in great peril; in fact, nothing must be nearer Our heart, whose special duty it is to carry on the work of Christ, than the Missions. You remember what We said on this very important topic last year while We were addressing you on the third of July,[239] that decisions of the Versailles Conference which affected the Catholic Missions seemed to Our joy in great measure, if not completely, to be well adapted to their needs, and that We were confident at the same time that the honorable delegates would show the same fairness of mind in carrying out their decisions which they used in making them. However, the matter did not in all cases have that result for which We rightly were hoping. For in many places it continued for some time to be the case that the Apostolic work of Holy Church among the

[238] Original Latin, *A.A.S.*, v. 12, p. 588 (December 17, 1920).
[239] Cf. *supra* n. 635.

unbelievers was hindered and slowed up by numerous difficulties. We indeed, as far as it was in Our power, left nothing undone to remove anything which stood in the way, nor was the effort entirely in vain. Nevertheless, there remain even now, in some places, conditions which are causing delay and hindrance to the Missions with incredible loss of souls. These are, no doubt, the sad consequences of the war by which the world has so long been disturbed. That they may be removed as soon as possible, and that the Church be in no way hindered in spreading Christianity, is the demand not only of religion, but of civilization as well. . . . . . .

ALLOCUTION *Tanto Più Graditi* TO THE COLLEGE OF CARDINALS.[240]

War causes not only material but also moral ruin.

December 24, 1920

701. . . . . . . You, My Lord Cardinal, in presenting to Us the wishes of the Sacred College for the coming Feast of Christmas, have been obliged to bring before Our notice again that, although hostility of arms has ceased in great measure, nevertheless, "there still lies upon the world an immense burden of misgivings and ills, aggravated by the internal strife of peoples and by the struggles of the classes of society." . . . . . .

702. As you have declared, My Lord Cardinal, there still remains a task so serious and difficult as not to have had its counterpart in any other period of history; the duty, before all, of restoring peace to souls, which, if it is evidently necessary where actual warfare is still raging, is no less so where the external war of arms has yielded place to the internal war of souls; and with the task of pacification there remains another, equally important, that of restoring order and custom without which there is no civil life.

703. The war . . . now allayed for two years, but not yet spent in all parts of the globe, if it has sown material ruin which has wasted humanity, and which even at present moves every heart to pity, especially on beholding the wretched plight of children, much more has it sown moral ruin, to which human wisdom, preoccupied only with thoughts of power, boundaries, and material resources, has never given a thought. . . . . . .

[240] Original Italian, *La Civiltà Cattolica*, 1921, v. 1, pp. 113-114 (January 7, 1921).

ENCYCLICAL *Sacra Propediem* ON THE SEVENTH CENTENARY OF THE THIRD ORDER OF ST. FRANCIS.[241]

Mankind needs the peace which Christ brought to the world.

January 6, 1921

704. . . . . . . For above all things Francis wished Tertiaries to be distinguished, as by a special badge, by brotherly love, such as is keenly solicitous of peace and harmony. Knowing this to be the particular precept of Jesus Christ, containing in itself the fulfillment of the Christian law, he was most anxious to conform to it the minds of his followers. By that very fact he succeeded in rendering the Third Order the greatest boon to human society. Burning with a seraphic love of God and man, Francis could not contain his charity within his bosom; he must pour it forth upon all within reach. Hence, though he began by reforming the private and domestic life of the members and adorning it with Christian virtues, as though he intended nothing else, still he had no mind to content himself with that. He employed the reformation of individuals as a means to arouse in the hearts of the people a love of Christian wisdom and to win all unto Jesus Christ. This plan of Francis, to have his Tertiaries act as heralds and messengers of peace amid the far-spread hostilities and civil upheavals of his age, We also entertained when recently almost all the world was aflame with a horror-laden war; and We entertain it still, for the conflagration is not totally extinguished, rather, its embers are smoking everywhere and in some places even flaring. Coupled with this mischief is an ailment in the vitals of our government—brought on by long-standing oblivion and contempt of Christian principles— namely, class struggling so bitterly with class about the distribution of wealth that the world is threatened with ruin.

705. On this immense field of action, to which We, as Vicar of the King of Peace, have devoted special care and thought, We desire to gather the concerted efforts of all children of Christian peace, but especially of the Tertiaries, whose influence in restoring harmony of sentiments will be something wonderful, once their number and their enterprise have generally increased. It is desir-

---

[241] Translation from *Rome Hath Spoken*, pp. 41-43. Original Latin, *A.A.S.*, v. 13, pp. 36-37 (January 24, 1921).

able, therefore, that every town and village and hamlet should have many members of the Order—not indeed slack members, content with the mere name of Tertiaries, but active and eager for their own and their neighbor's salvation. Why should not the numerous and various associations of young people, of workmen, of women, existing everywhere throughout the Catholic world, join the Third Order, and inspired with St. Francis' zeal for peace and charity devote themselves persistently to the glory of Christ and the prosperity of the Church? Mankind needs not the sort of peace that is built up on the laborious deliberations of worldly prudence, but that peace which was brought to us by Christ when He declared, *My peace I give unto you; not as the world gives, do I give unto you.*[242] A man-made treaty, whether of States or of classes among themselves, can neither endure nor have at all the value of real peace, unless it rests upon a peaceful disposition; but the latter can exist only where duty, as it were, puts the bridle on the passions, for it is they that give rise to discord of whatever kind. *From whence,* asks the Apostle, *are wars and contentions among you? Are they not hence, from your concupiscences, which war in your members?*[243] Now, it is Christ Who avails to harmonize all that is in man, making him, not serve, but command his desires, obedient and submissive always to the will of God; and this harmony is the foundation of all peace. In the Order of Franciscan Tertiaries, that power of Christ displays itself to wonderful effect. . . . . . .

LETTER *La Singolare* TO CARDINAL GASPARRI, SECRETARY OF STATE.[244]

> *Conditions in Austria, as constituted by the Versailles Treaty, are absolutely intolerable.*

January 24, 1921

706. The specially unhappy conditions now prevailing in Austria, following on the fortunes of the war and the Treaty of Peace, have now assumed such a serious character that We can no longer remain silent. This noble and illustrious nation, which has acquired

---

[242] *John*, XIV, 27.
[243] *James*, IV, 1.
[244] Translation from *The Tablet*, v. 138, p. 177 (February 5, 1921). Original Italian, *Civiltà Cattolica*, 1921, v. 1, pp. 258-259 (January 29, 1921).

so many merits during the course of centuries for its defense of the Faith and Christian civilization, has lost all its ancient splendor and is reduced to about six million inhabitants, of whom at least a third live in the city of Vienna alone. Previously that capital was the center of a vast and flourishing empire, from which it received an abundance of resources and products of every kind; now it is like a head severed from its body, and is in the throes of misery and desperation. Commerce has ceased, industry is paralyzed, money is enormously depreciated, and it is impossible to see how Austria can find in itself the means to exist as a State and give its people bread and work. The results of such a condition of things are being felt grievously by all classes, especially the poor, the sick and the young, on whose behalf We have appealed repeatedly to the charity of all good people. It is true that various Governments have been moved to pity by the realization of this terrible state of things, and have promised help and subsidies to this afflicted country; but even if this help were given immediately it could not be thoroughly effective, inasmuch as, as We have said, Austria lacks the elements necessary for its own proper existence. In drawing attention to this very unhappy state of things We do not intend to seek where to place responsibility or blame. We simply lament— and public opinion is unanimously with Us—that the actual conditions in Austria are absolutely intolerable, as they take away from an entire nation the possibility of getting the means of existence which the Creator has put at the disposition of all men. In thus speaking, My Lord Cardinal, We are sure that We are voicing the sentiments of humanity and Christian fraternity in the hearts of all good men, and which all civil peoples, without distinction of conquerors, conquered or neutral, have shown clearly when faced with the unhappy lot of Austria. For the rest, it is not for Us to propose a practical solution of the question, the solution of which, as it is of an eminently political character, is the business of the Governments, specially those who signed the Treaty of Peace. We are moved by the love of the Divine Master, which embraces all, particularly those suffering, and We confine Ourself, My Lord Cardinal, to asking you to call the attention of the Diplomatic Corps accredited to the Holy See to this very serious matter, specially those who are in a position to act with most effect, that they may bring Our wish before their respective Governments, and that, inspired by the principles of humanity and justice, they may take the necessary practical steps. . . .

LETTER *Cum Semper* TO CARDINAL MERCIER, ARCHBISHOP OF MALINES, AND TO THE OTHER BISHOPS OF BELGIUM.[245]

The Pope discusses the "Flanders Question" and gives advice on the language problem.

February 10, 1921

707. We have always, as you well know, exercised Our paternal care and affection for the well-being of the Belgian people not only while the horrible struggle was in progress, but also when the Peace of Versailles had been completed; consequently, We thank God, the Giver of all good things, that He has granted Us to see how your country, due to the unhesitating patriotism and ingenuity of all ranks of citizens, is already happily revived and renewed to the point that even the hope of realizing its former prosperity can now be envisioned.

708. Nevertheless, We want you to know, Venerable Brethren, that We are deeply concerned over rumors of dissension and discord, brought about by that long discussed controversy, known as the "Flanders Question." Yes, it is a difficult problem and a complex one, and even those who agree in principle cannot agree on the solution. At this time, therefore, We intend only to touch upon those aspects of the problem which pertain to religion, for Our care, as it always must be, is for the good of souls. Similarly, Our Predecessor, Leo XIII, in writing to the Bishops of Bohemia and Moravia (August 20, 1901)[246] about differences which had arisen between their people because of language, stated that he would not participate in these disputes; but because of his Apostolic Office, he would always be on guard lest the cause of religion suffer because of these quarrels. "We have decided"—so he said—"to abstain from proposing any solution to this affair. A defense of one's native language is not reprehensible, if it is kept within reasonable limits. For the principles which hold for the defense of other private rights can be applied here, so long as the common good does not suffer from their application. It is the duty of those

[245] Original Latin, *A.A.S.*, v. 13, pp. 127-128 (March 11, 1921).
[246] *Cf. supra* nn. 230-233.

who administer the affairs of State to safeguard the rights of individuals in such a way that the common good may be protected. Our duty, however, is clear. It is to watch carefully lest religion, which is the first and chief good of souls, and the origin of all other benefits, be imperiled by these controversies."

709. We are motivated, Venerable Brethren, by the same concern. We are prompted to write to you for the same reason. There is a danger that in these controversies the bonds of charity between fellow citizens may be weakened, or that that harmony by which small projects grow into great projects, and without which the greatest achievements can be destroyed — that harmony may be wiped out. There is a danger, too, and this is the greatest, that the clergy may lose something of its dignity and the efficacy of its ministry, if it takes sides too zealously in these disputes. . . . . . .

710. Therefore, it will be your duty, Venerable Brethren, to watch and to see that the priest fashion the education of the youth upon a supernatural plane (a work, by the way, to which he should be drawn by a consciousness of his office). And, consequently, the priest will be easily identified and acknowledged as the "man of God." If the priest is to gather those abundant fruits of his labor, which he so ardently desires, let him be above all instructed in all those things which "the times" demand, and which will make him useful, pleasing, and acceptable to his flock. Above all, he must understand and correctly use the vernacular, which people of particular sections may have, and with which he must communicate Catholic doctrine; otherwise the exercise of his ministry will be patently a failure. . . . . . .

ALLOCUTION *Gratum Vehementer* TO THE COLLEGE OF CARDINALS.[247]

*Christian regeneration will of itself bring back peace
and tranquillity.*

March 7, 1921

711. It is indeed a pleasure for Us to see your august body assembled round Us once more, that We may speak with you on

[247] Translation from *The Tablet*, v. 138, pp. 373-374 (March 19, 1921). Original Latin, *A.A.S.*, v. 13, pp. 121-123 (March 11, 1921).

the interests of the Church and the good of souls entrusted to Our charge. We wish that We could put a bright picture before you, but the sad state of things prevents it, and indeed the disorder and strife still prevailing in various parts of the world cause Us serious anxiety. In Our unfailing desire to do everything possible to remedy these evils, We have lost no opportunity of helping society toward peace and tranquillity; which tranquillity frequently society gained for itself in centuries past by listening to the Church. That is why We took advantage recently of the celebration of the seventh centenary of the Third Order of St. Francis to invite the whole world to that spirit of self-sacrifice and Christian charity by means of which St. Francis of Assisi, in his desire to bring back souls to God, remedied in such great measure the disorders of his times. And, indeed, never was there such need as there is today of calling to the practice of self-sacrifice and brotherly love this poor humanity, first scourged by war, now thrown into disorder by lust for the things of this earth and by political passions; never was it so necessary as it is today that the reformation of the individual on Christian lines should be raised to check effectively the paganism which is really infiltrating into every manifestation of public and private life. If it is true indeed that the actual state of war has ceased, still a sure and lasting peace has not yet come to bring consolation to the world, much less has there come back into families and all classes, social and national, the tranquillity and order which arise from the spirit of brotherhood and Christian solidarity. We see today the miserable spectacle of fratricidal strife among citizens of the same nation, among peoples born and grown up almost on the same land, and now fighting hand to hand for it, raising a barrier of hatred and enmity between themselves. We see, too, old latent differences between nations breaking out again in a display of violence utterly at variance with the rules of humanity and morality and which We deplore, from whichever side it comes. By now it is evident to all that the rules of peace so laboriously elaborated by even the most experienced politicians are truly written on treaties, but they can never become living things, nor have strength or power, nor penetrate consciences unless in the first place they are based on the principles of justice and equity, and in the second place there arise again in minds and hearts those principles which transformed the world from pagan to Christian and in the day of St. Francis of Assisi healed and restored a society full of disorder and corruption. Only by the control of one's own passion comes the interior order of the individual, base of social order; only by the Christian practice of brotherly love will arise again among social classes and peoples the mutual trust which is the fount of true and lasting peace. This is what We invoke with Our whole heart of the Divine Goodness, this Christian regeneration which of itself will bring back peace and tranquillity on earth, hoping at the same time that the centenary we have been celebrating may spread the spirit of St. Francis. . . . . . .

LETTER *Ubi Primum Cum Arderet* TO CARDINAL LOGUE, ARCH-BISHOP OF ARMAGH.[248]

The Pope exhorts the Irish and the English to submit their difficulties to arbitration.

.April 27, 1921

712.   When in the mysterious designs of God We were raised to this Chair of Peter, Europe was ablaze with war. You are aware that with a full consciousness of Our Apostolic Office We endeavored, to the utmost of Our power, to remedy the numerous and terrible evils begotten of this dreadful conflict, and to reconcile men to peace. We are grieved to say, that though We left nothing undone to restore peace, Our efforts more than once proved ineffectual. But indeed, as We have already frequently said, nations will never enjoy, either at home or abroad, lasting tranquillity unless they return to those Christian principles which they have abandoned, and which the Church hands down by her teaching. Meanwhile We are filled with anguish, when We consider that not a few nations are still oppressed by the weight of woes produced by the war. For although the clash of arms has almost everywhere ceased, yet, on account of the extreme scarcity of the necessaries of life, many of every age and sex, and those the innocent, are being cut off, whilst everywhere, even amongst the nations that have emerged victorious from the conflict, there are apparent signs of solicitude and anxiety which compel all good

[248] Translation from *Irish Ecclesiastical Record,* ser. 5, v. 17, pp. 646-647 (June, 1921). Original Latin, *A.A.S.,* v. 13, pp. 256-258 (June 1, 1921).

men to dread disaster yet to come. It is, however, a matter of some consolation to Us that from the contributions so liberally sent Us from all countries We have been enabled more than once to bring some measure of relief to impoverished peoples.

713. But while We are filled with anxiety in regard to all nations, We are most especially concerned about the condition of Ireland. Unflinching, even unto the shedding of blood, in her devotion to the ancient Faith and in her reverence for the Holy See, she is subjected today to the indignity of devastation and slaughter. There is assuredly no doubt that harsh and cruel occurrences of this kind are in great part attributable to the recent war, for neither has sufficient consideration been given to the desires of nations, nor have the fruits of peace which peoples promised to themselves been reaped. But in the public strife which is taking place in your country it is the deliberate counsel of the Holy See—a counsel consistently acted upon up to the present—in similar circumstances—to take sides with neither of the contending parties. Such neutrality, however, by no means prevents Us from wishing and desiring, nor even from praying and beseeching the contending parties, that the frenzy of the strife may as soon as possible subside, and that a lasting peace and a sincere union of hearts may take the place of this terrible enmity. For, indeed, We do not perceive how this bitter strife can profit either of the parties, when property and homes are being ruthlessly and disgracefully laid waste, when villages and farmsteads are being set aflame, when neither sacred places nor sacred persons are spared, when on both sides a war resulting in the death of unarmed people, even of women and children, is carried on.

714. Mindful, therefore, of the Apostolic Office and moved by that charity which embraces all men, We exhort English as well as Irish to consider calmly whether the time has not arrived to abandon violence and treat of some means of mutual agreement. For this end We think it would be opportune if effect were given to the plan recently suggested by distinguished men as well as skilled politicians: that is to say, that the question at issue should be referred for discussion to some body of men selected by the whole Irish nation, and when this conference has published its findings, let the more influential among both parties meet together and having put forward and discussed the views and conclusions ar-

rived at on both sides, let them determine by common consent
on some means of settling the question in a sincere spirit of peace
and reconciliation. . . . . . .

ALLOCUTION *Causa Nobis Quidem* TO THE COLLEGE OF CAR-
DINALS.[249]

> *If the flame of war has been almost quenched, the
> iniquitous spirit of it remains.*

June 13, 1921

715. . . . . . . If We turn Our eyes from Palestine to Europe,
there, too, is seen an unhappy spectacle. Recent events, as you
know well, Venerable Brethren, have shown all too clearly that
disagreements and competitions between the peoples have not
ceased, and that if indeed the flame of war has been almost
quenched, the iniquitous spirit of it remains, nevertheless. Wherefore, renewing once again Our urgent appeal to all heads of
Governments of good will, We ask that by their counsel and instance they may bring about that the peoples, each and every one,
may put aside enmity one to another, and after discussion in the
spirit of Christian charity may resolve all such differences as still
exist between them, and so may come to troubled Europe the
peace for which all long. . . . . . .

LETTER *Ex Iis Litteris* TO CARDINAL KAKOWSKI, ARCHBISHOP OF
WARSAW, TO CARDINAL DALBOR, ARCHBISHOP OF GNESEN AND
POZNAN, AND TO THE OTHER BISHOPS OF POLAND.[250]

> *Benedict XV insists that Poland must be an inde-
> pendent nation.*

July 16, 1921

716. . . . . . . In the same letter you mention some of those
benefits which We have striven to confer upon the Polish people.
But far greater and far more illustrious examples are at hand from
history as proofs of that special love which this Apostolic See has

---

[249] Translation from *The Tablet*, v. 138, p. 822 (June 25, 1921). Original Latin,
    A.A.S., v. 13, p. 283 (June 18, 1921).
[250] Original Latin, *A.A.S.*, v. 13, pp. 424-425 (September 1, 1921).

always felt toward your nation. . . . When in the recent great war there were some who affirmed that Poland would be sufficiently provided for if there should be granted to her a sort of *autonomy* which was being promised, this Holy See alone affirmed many times and emphatically that full and perfect liberty, that is, what is called *independence,* was necessary for Poland, and that the greatest care should be taken that she might flourish again in her pristine dignity as a moral person.

717. This love and this zeal of Ours toward your nation, Beloved Sons and Venerable Brethren, is fixed by one limit only, namely, that which is indicated by duty and justice. For when peoples contend with one another about their individual designs, it is the duty of the Roman Pontiff, the Common Parent of all men, to favor neither side and to keep himself impartial toward both parties. This procedure the Roman Pontiffs have always followed, and We maintained it while the great war was being waged, and even recently before the plebiscite of Upper Silesia, whatever malevolent men, or certainly men having too little respect for this Holy See, may have said or continue to say. But if, when the greedy desires of men are enkindled, it happens—and experience teaches that it happens not rarely—that the right of another is violated, We are led by the same sanctity of duty to censure and condemn such violation, from whatever source it may have arisen. . . . . . .

PRAYER *O Dio di Bontà* COMPOSED BY BENEDICT XV.[251]

The Pope prays for peace in Italy.

July 25, 1921

718. God of goodness and forgiveness, with lacerated heart we surround Thy altars and implore pity. After the horror of war the most terrible scourge is this fierce hatred which makes men of the same family persecute and kill each other in party strife. The land most famed for Christian piety, cradle of civil kindness, is becoming once again a bloodstained field of civil war. Have pity, O Lord! Thou Who hast revealed the noble law of pardon of offenses and

---

[251] Translation from *The Tablet,* v. 138, pp. 181-182 (August 6, 1921). Original Italian, *A.A.S.,* v. 13, pp. 369-370 (August 1, 1921).

love of enemies, cause those who are not even enemies but are indeed brothers to embrace again, cause that, after the bloody weapons of war have been laid down, all may repeat in the beloved mother tongue the prayer that Thou didst teach: *Our Father Who art in heaven;* and that all who have seen Thy Son open His heart and His arms to those who crucified Him may feel their souls flooded with burning love and may say with humility and trust: *Forgive us our trespasses as we forgive them that trespass against us.* Virgin Immaculate, Queen of Hearts, come down among thy children and make them hear thy Mother's voice. Thou alone by thy intercession canst reconcile them with Almighty God and reconcile them among themselves; thou alone canst give them a taste of the sweetness of the peace that is a prelude of eternal life. Amen.

LETTER *Le Notizie* TO CARDINAL GASPARRI, SECRETARY OF STATE.[252]

In Russia the war is followed by plague and famine which the Holy Father endeavors to relieve.

August 5, 1921

719. The news which has reached Us lately of the conditions of the Russian people is, as you, My Lord Cardinal, well know, terribly serious. As far as can be gathered from the first short and reserved accounts, We are faced with one of the most appalling catastrophes in history. Masses of human beings, at the very last stage of exhaustion, and ravaged by hunger, typhus and cholera, are wandering desperately through a land now barren, and seeking to reach the more populous centres where they hope to find bread, and whence they are being driven back by force of arms. From the Volga basin, faced by the most terrible of deaths, many millions of men are invoking the aid of their human kind. This cry of suffering, My Lord Cardinal, has wounded Us deeply. It is a case of a people already terribly tried by the scourge of war; a people on whom shines the character of Christ and one always firm in its determination to belong to the great Christian family. Separated indeed as they are from Us by the barriers which long centuries

[252] Translation from *The Tablet*, v. 138, p. 245 (August 20, 1921). Original Italian, *A.A.S.*, v. 13, pp. 428-429 (September 1, 1921).

have raised, they are the nearer to Our heart of a father in proportion to the greatness of the trials through which they are passing.
My Lord Cardinal, We feel the duty laid on Us to do all that Our
poverty makes possible to help Our far-off children. But the ruin
is so vast that the peoples must unite to make provision, and no
effort, however great, will be excessive in face of the immensity
of the disaster. Therefore, We ask you, My Lord Cardinal, to use
all the means at your disposal to bring home to the governments of
the different nations the need for prompt and efficacious common
action. Our appeal is directed first of all to the Christian peoples
who know the infinite charity of the Divine Redeemer Who gave
His blood to make all brothers; then it is addressed to all other
civil peoples, because every man worthy of the name must feel the
duty of helping where another man is dying. More than once during the years of suffering through which We are passing the Holy
See has raised its voice among the nations, mindful of the high and
sweet mission which Almighty God has entrusted to it. If Our
word is now heard again, imploring charity before the last echo
of Our recent exhortations and prayers has died away, that is solely
because the new disaster is equal to, perhaps greater than past
troubles. And at the same time may all the faithful of the Church
of Christ scattered throughout the world, while they bring their
offering for their brothers dying of hunger, raise to Almighty God
in all trust their prayers that He may deign to help Us to hasten
the end of so terrible a scourge. . . .

TELEGRAM OF BENEDICT XV TO THE LEAGUE OF NATIONS.[253]

The Holy Father exhorts all nations to help Russia.

September, 1921

720. The reports arriving from Russia become even more
grave, and the misery is so great that only the united effort of all,
the collaboration of both people and government, can bring about a
remedy. Hence, We address, by means of Your Excellency, the
Representatives of the nations reassembled there, and We appeal to
their sense of humanity and fraternity in order that adequate measures may quickly be taken to save the unhappy Russians.

[253] Original Italian, *Civiltà Cattolica*, 1921, v. 4, p. 167 (October 6, 1921).

ALLOCUTION *Generalmente* TO THE DELEGATION OF THE THIRD ORDER OF ST. FRANCIS.[254]

Despite the peace treaties wars continue in the world.

September 19, 1921

721. . . . . . . It is a sorrowful sight to see the troubles which the poisoned germ of discord, nourished by a partisan spirit, has raised in the midst of peoples that were but yesterday calm and peaceful; one's heart aches at seeing brothers tearing and killing each other; certainly it is hardly in conformity with the customs of civilized peoples to perpetuate bellicose attitudes between the subjects of nations which, belligerents yesterday, are to-day joined by peace treaties.

722. What is the source of so much evil? It is because men have lost sight of the order which must prevail in the world; it is because they refuse to recognize in practice the class differences which God has established in society; it is because they make the mistake of believing that everything ends with this earthly existence, without thinking that the goods of the exile must be used only to acquire those of heaven.

723. Now, it is these false ideas rooted in men's minds, these vicious attachments of the heart that are directly combated by the spirit of St. Francis, which has been aptly defined as a "spirit of concord, of charity and of peace." Thus, what a joy it is for Us to learn that it is this spirit which has hovered over the recent Congress. Therefrom We can conclude that the resolutions which were there made will not be long in manifesting themselves as the salt of the earth, the proper remedy for the evils of our time. . . . . . .

TELEGRAM TO PRESIDENT HARDING OF THE UNITED STATES AT THE OPENING OF THE ARMS CONFERENCE IN WASHINGTON.[255]

Benedict XV prays for the success of the Conference.

November 10, 1921

724. On the eve of the opening of the Conference met to resolve the great international questions regarding the Far East and

---

[254] Original Italian, *Civiltà Cattolica*, 1921, v. 4, pp. 72-73 (September 23, 1921).
[255] Translation from *The Tablet*, v. 138, p. 741 (December 3, 1921). Original Italian, *Civiltà Cattolica*, 1921, v. 4, p. 458 (November 26, 1921).

thus to reach disarmament, We pray fervently to God for the happy success of the initiative taken by the Chief Magistrate of the great American Republic for the uplifting of trembling humanity.

ALLOCUTION *In Hac Quidem* TO THE COLLEGE OF CARDINALS.[256]

> *Peace at home and abroad is the one thing now desired by all people.*

November 21, 1921

725. While it is a pleasure to meet you once again, there are at the same time many reasons for anxious consideration, the most important of which is the new organization of relations between the Church and several States. No one can help noting how, since the recent terrible war, new States have arisen and also some previously existing have now largely increased territory. There is much that might be said on this point which for the moment need not be dwelt on, but it is obvious that these States have no right to claim those privileges which the Holy See had granted to others by Concordats or special conventions inasmuch as arrangements made between certain parties must not carry either advantage or detriment to others. We see, too, how, in consequence of serious and radical political changes, some States are now in a condition that they cannot be considered to be the same moral entity with which the Holy See treated before. From that it follows naturally that the agreements and conventions previously concluded between the Holy See and those States have no longer any value. Still, if the heads of such republics or States desire to stipulate new agreements with the Church more consonant with the changed political conditions, they may be assured that, where there is no special obstacle, the Holy See is disposed to treat with them as indeed it is already treating with some nations. But We declare once again to you, Venerable Brethren, that never will We allow that in such agreements anything shall find place that is contrary to the liberty and dignity of the Church, for it is most distinctly necessary in the interests of civil society itself, especially in such times as these, that the liberty and dignity of the Church should be secure and intact. For it is undeniable that harmony between the civil and religious society

---

[256] Translation from *The Tablet*, v. 138, pp. 741-742 (December 3, 1921). Original Latin, *A.A.S.*, v. 13, pp. 521-524 (November 23, 1921).

is most necessary for the tranquillity of public order, the foundation of well-being in every sense. Peace, indeed, at home and abroad is the one thing now desired by the peoples who have suffered so much, and We see with the greatest sorrow and anxiety that the solemn Peace Treaty has not received the seal of peace of minds, and nearly all nations, especially in Europe, are even now being torn by such serious and bitter dissensions that for their settlement more than ever is felt the need of God's intervention. . . .

726. Let us, then, have recourse to His mercy and not only seek it with humble prayers but endeavor to make it propitious to us with holiness of life and charity to those in need. . . .

727. But if We turn specially to Almighty God to seek ready and efficacious remedy for the evils with which human society is overborne, not on that account do We intend that any means and remedies must be neglected that are suggested by reason and experience. Certainly the rulers of the peoples must use such means and remedies in seeking to ensure the common good, but it would be in the highest degree wrong to count on them alone and not on divine aid. So We see with pleasure, Venerable Brethren, that the representatives of several nations have met in Washington for the purpose of coming to an agreement with regard to the reduction of armaments; and not only do We sincerely hope that their labors may reach a happy issue, but also, together with all good men, We pray God to illuminate them with the light of His wisdom, for not only is the object to lift a weight now insupportable from the peoples—which in itself is no small thing—but, what is more important, to remove . . . the danger of future wars. . . . . . .

TELEGRAM OF CARDINAL GASPARRI, SECRETARY OF STATE, TO THE *Congrès Démocratique International.*[257]

The Holy Father blesses all true peace efforts.

December 4, 1921

728. The Holy Father thanks you for the sentiments which you have expressed to him in the name of the delegates to the First International Democratic Congress in Paris, and he prays God to bless the common efforts which you propose to make in the service of true peace for the peoples' welfare.

[257] Original French, *Documentation Catholique,* v. 7, c. 1165 (May 13, 1922).

PART FOUR

PIUS XI

1922-1939

INTRODUCTION

No PRELATE in modern times has come to the Throne of Peter with a background more varied than that of Achilles Cardinal Ratti, who, as Pius XI, succeeded Benedict XV in 1922. Country curate, Oxford lecturer, professor of sacred eloquence, apostle of Milanese chimney-sweeps, prefect of two great libraries, mountain climber, chaplain of a nun's convent, Papal Nuncio to the Republic of Poland, archbishop of a great diocese—these were some of the positions he had filled before his election. A strong character, a devotion to exacting scholarship, a life so rich in experience, all blended to form one of the greatest popes of the past three hundred years.

Desio, in the foothills of Lombardy, was the town in which he was born on May 31, 1857, the fourth son of a silk weaver. His ecclesiastical studies were made at the Seminary of San Carlo in Milan and the Collegio Lombardo in Rome. After ordination in 1879 and two years of graduate work for doctorates in canon law and theology at the Gregorian University and the Sapienza in Rome, he returned to Milan to do parochial work in the village of Barni. Shortly afterward he was selected to teach theology and sacred eloquence in his alma mater at Milan, till, five years later, he received an appointment as associate in the historic Ambrosian library. During the thirty-odd years he labored among the documents of the library, he was a frequent contributor to learned reviews of Italy, concentrating largely on historical and paleographical problems. Ever the priest, he acted as chaplain to the nuns of the Convent of the Cenacle, and gave much of his spare time to apostolic work among the working boys of the city. His holidays were spent in travel and in mountain climbing, and in 1889 he was the first Italian ever to scale the peak of Monte Rosa from the Italian side. Called to Rome in 1911, he was made Pro-Prefect of the Vatican Library, and in 1914 succeeded Father Ehrle as Prefect. Benedict XV sent Monsignor Ratti to Poland in 1918 as Apostolic Visitor to assist in the reorganization of the newly erected Polish Republic. His status was raised to Nuncio in 1919, and he was consecrated titular Archbishop of Lepanto in the Cathedral of Warsaw. Returning to Rome in 1921, he was appointed Cardinal Archbishop of Milan, and was elected pope on February 6, 1922.

"The Peace of Christ in the Reign of Christ" he chose as the ideal of his pontificate. A strong-willed, far-sighted, outspoken character, with a passion for work and the habit of initiative, Pius gave his flock seventeen years of vigorous leadership. Seldom has a pope seemed so conscious of the universal character of the Church. In thirty-seven penetrating encyclicals, he spoke his mind on the problems of his age, taking the entire world into his confidence. Never has a pope done more to encourage the laymen to share in the apostolate of the priesthood.

His accomplishments in the field of diplomacy were impressive. In 1929 he ended the troublesome Roman Question by concluding the Treaty of the Lateran with Italy, creating a tiny but independent state under his sovereignty. He concluded concordats with Latvia, Poland, Bavaria, Rumania, Lithuania, Prussia, Baden, Germany, Austria, Jugoslavia, and working agreements with Portugal and Czechoslovakia. Keenly aware of the dangers of Nationalism, he did not hesitate to condemn instances of exaggerated patriotism or State encroachment on the rights of the Church and the individual. L'Action Française of the French Royalists was condemned in 1925; the governments of Russia, Germany, Spain, Italy and Mexico felt the sting of his criticism when they infringed on the rights of the Church.

His death on February 10, 1939, elicited an outpouring of admiration for his character and achievements from every quarter of the world.

DOCUMENTS

LETTER *Con Vivo Piacere* TO ARCHBISHOP SIGNORI OF GENOA.[1]

The best guarantee of peace is not a forest of bayonets,
but mutual confidence and friendship.

April 7, 1922

729. It is with lively pleasure that We have read the timely letter which you have addressed to your people on the occasion of the international conference which brings together for the first time, in this glorious town, in amicable discussion, the victors and the vanquished, and toward which turn all the general hopes of the peoples. As the representative of the God of peace and love, Who with particular providence has regard to the poor and needy, and Who in an unfathomable decision called Us so suddenly to take up, along with Our succession to the Pontificate, the mission of charity and peace of Our regretted Predecessor, We confidently hope that the representatives of the Powers will, with calm and in a spirit ready for any sacrifice on the altar of the common weal, consider the sad circumstances under which all nations are suffering, this being the first condition for the finding of an efficacious remedy and the first real step toward that universal peace which everyone so ardently desires.

730. If in the very shock of arms, according to the beautiful device of the Red Cross—*Inter arma caritas*—Christian charity ought to reign, that should hold good with all the stronger reason after arms have been laid down and treaties of peace have been signed, the more so since international enmities, which are the sad heritage of war, are prejudicial to the victor nations and the prelude of a difficult future for all.

731. It should not be forgotten that the best guarantee of peace is not a forest of bayonets, but mutual confidence and friendship. If the conference should exclude from its discussions not only existing treaties but also the reparations required, that need not prevent a further exchange of views which might help the conquered to a

[1] Translation from *The Tablet*, v. 139, p. 485 (April 15, 1922). Original Italian, *A.A.S.*, v. 14, pp. 217-218 (April 20, 1922).

speedier fulfillment of their obligations, and would work out to the advantage of the victors.

732. Animated by these sentiments of equal love toward all nations, which is inspired by the charge laid upon Us by the Divine Redeemer, We extend to all the faithful the invitation which you, Venerable Brother, have addressed to your people, and We exhort them to join their prayers with Ours for the success of the conference. May the blessing of Our Lord be upon it, and may the result of its decisions, which We are sure will be taken in a sentiment of good-will, bring to suffering mankind that concord which, whilst bringing people together, may set them again, after eight years of sorrow and ruin, on the shining path of work, progress and civilization, and so realize the ideal of the Church. . . .

LETTER *Il Vivissimo Desiderio* TO CARDINAL GASPARRI, SECRETARY OF STATE.[2]

Peace consists not merely in the cessation of hostilities, but chiefly in the reconciliation of men.

April 29, 1922

733. The strong desire We feel to see established in the world the reign of true peace, which consists not merely in the cessation of hostilities, but chiefly in the reconciliation of men, makes Us follow with the liveliest interest and even with great anxiety, the course of the Conference at Genoa for the blessing of God on which We have already invited the faithful to offer fervent prayers.

734. We cannot conceal from Your Eminence the keen satisfaction with which We learned that, thanks to the good-will of all, the great obstacles which from the beginning seemed to preclude the possibility of any accord had been overcome. No one can doubt that the happy issue of so great a Congress, including as it does representatives of nearly every civilized nation, will mark an historic date for Christian civilization, especially in Europe. The peoples which have suffered so much in the past conflict and its recent unhappy consequences justly desire that the work of the Conference may result in the removal, as far as is possible, of the

[2] Translation from *The Tablet*, v. 139, p. 582 (May 6, 1922). Original Italian, *A.A.S.*, v. 14, pp. 265-267 (May 8, 1922).

danger of fresh wars, and, as soon as may be, in the economic restoration of Europe. With the complete realization of such noble aims, which are indeed interdependent, or with the preparation of the foundations for their future fulfillment, the Genoa Conference will have deserved well of mankind by preparing almost a new era of peace and progress, in which one will be able to say in the words of the Bible: *Justitia et pax osculatæ sunt*[3]—that charity must not be separated from justice.

735. Such a return to the normal state of human society in its essential elements, according to the rules of right reason which is certainly a divine ordinance, will be of the utmost advantage for all, victors and vanquished, but particularly for the poor suffering peoples in Eastern Europe, who, already desolated by war, internal strife and religious persecution, are now decimated by famine and disease, though they possess so many sources of wealth that could be precious elements in social restoration.

736. To reach these people, though separated from Our Communion by a misfortune of ancient times, may Our words, with those of Our lamented Predecessors, be a message of pity and comfort, and at the same time of the ardent prayer of Our fatherly heart that they may enjoy with Us the same gifts of unity and peace in the common participation in the Holy Mysteries.

737. If by a stroke of misfortune the efforts for sincere pacification and lasting accord at this Conference should come to nought, who can think without trembling how greatly would be aggravated the conditions already so miserable and menacing of Europe, with the prospect of still greater sufferings and the danger of a conflagration which would bring down the whole fabric of Christian civilization, since, as St. Thomas says *(De Regimine Principum, I. 10)* and as experience confirms: *desperatio audacter ad quælibet attentanda præcipitat.*

738. Therefore, in the name of the universal mission of charity entrusted to Us by the Divine Redeemer, We again implore all peoples to unite in a Christian spirit and mutual good-will, in the effort to promote the common good which will give to each nation so acting great and lasting benefits.

739. But as this cannot be fully achieved without the grace of that God Who is, and ought to be, recognized as the prime Author

[3] *Psalms,* LXXXIV, 11.

and supreme Sustainer of society—*Rex regum et Dominus Dominantium*[4]—We exhort all Christian people to have recourse to Him, on behalf of civilized society, in the beautiful prayer which in the venerable liturgy of Holy Week We have offered up for the Church: "That our God and Lord would be pleased to give it peace, maintain it in union and preserve it over the earth. . . . And grant us who live in peace and tranquillity grace to glorify God, the Father Almighty." So, verily, may be attained that public prosperity which is the natural aim of all civilized society, as well as of the Church which guides men toward their supernatural end: "That we may so pass through the good things of time that we may not lose those that are eternal."

740. In bringing these feelings and wishes to your knowledge, in order that Our diplomatic representatives may be Our interpreters with their respective Governments and peoples, We impart to Your Eminence with all Our heart Our Apostolic Blessing.

MEMORANDUM SENT BY CARDINAL GASPARRI, SECRETARY OF STATE, TO THE DIPLOMATIC REPRESENTATIVES AT THE GENOA PEACE CONFERENCE.[5]

The Holy See requests that religious rights be safeguarded in any agreement with Russia.

May 15, 1922

741. In the letter which the Holy Father sent on April 29 to the Cardinal Secretary of State, His Eminence was charged to communicate to the Powers with which the Holy See has diplomatic relations His Holiness' wishes for the success of the Genoa Conference, particularly as regards the Russian nation. Inasmuch as conditions do not permit the Holy See approaching each one of the Chancelleries through the ordinary channel of the Pontifical representatives to the different nations, it uses the opportunity of the presence at Genoa of the delegations of the States with which it has diplomatic relations to deliver to them directly the text of that Pontifical document, and to call their attention, and through them

[4] I *Timothy*, VI, 15.
[5] Translation from *The Tablet*, v. 139, pp. 641-642 (May 20, 1922). Original French, *Documentation Catholique*, v. 7, c. 1211 (May 20, 1922).

the attention of the Conference, to certain points of special importance. At the historic moment at which there is question of the
readmission of Russia in the association of the civil nations, the
Holy See desires that the religious interests, which are the basis
of all true civilization, shall be safeguarded in Russia. In consequence, the Holy See asks that in the agreement to be established
between the Powers represented at Genoa there shall be inserted
in some manner, but in a very explicit manner, the three following
clauses: (1) Full liberty of conscience for all citizens, Russian or
foreign, is guaranteed in Russia; (2) private and public exercise of
religion and worship is also guaranteed (this clause is in agreement
with the declarations made at Genoa by the Russian delegate, M.
Tchitcherin); (3) religious immovable property which belonged or
still belongs to any religious confession whatsoever shall be restored
to it and respected.

ALLOCUTION *Très Opportunément* ON THE OPENING OF THE
TWENTY-SIXTH INTERNATIONAL EUCHARISTIC CONGRESS IN
ROME.[6]

*Peace is the first and indispensable condition of all
social reconstruction.*

May 24, 1922

742. . . . . . . And with this Eucharistic Congress, the first of
a new series, must begin, and by the grace of God, by the infinite
goodness and mercy of the Eucharistic Heart of Jesus, will begin
that full pacification which is the first and indispensable condition
of all social reconstruction. That is to say, that there must begin
a real and true regeneration which consists in the return of society
to Jesus Christ and the return of Jesus Christ in human society;
the regeneration which holds in itself the truest, soundest substance
of all reconstruction and reconstitution. The pride and vainglory of
the human mind have driven out Jesus Christ, exiled Him, confined Him in His solitary tabernacles; unbridled lust for worldly
goods has made the minds of men mutually bitter, barbarous and
hostile. Together with the banishment of the Lord peace has left

[6] Translation from *The Tablet*, v. 139, pp. 706-707 (June 3, 1922). Original French,
Actes de Pie XI, v. 1, pp. 65-66.

humanity. The Sacrament of the Eucharist, solemn recognition, solemn adoration of this the most holy among all holy Sacraments, most divine among divine things, that is the remedy. Here it is, where the human mind bows itself before the majesty of God, offering Him the homage of the faith which believes, sees not but adores and acknowledges; it is in this Sacrament that minds become softened and regain gentleness; it is in this Sacrament that all are seated at the same Table and feel themselves truly brothers, great and small, masters and servants, rulers and ruled. Peace, the peace that all are seeking because it has not yet returned to spread its white wings over troubled humanity, the peace that the world cannot give because it can offer nothing more than goods unworthy of the human heart and insufficient for its happiness, this peace Jesus Christ in the Blessed Sacrament alone can give. You have asked Him and He comes to you; breaking the silence of the tabernacle, once more He is seen amongst men and peace smiles on the world. Not the image but the living reality of that peace, which the world cannot give but neither can it take away. You are the true peace, you who have come from all parts of the world, from all the countries harried only yesterday by awful war, come here, forgetting the past, remembering only the bonds of unity joining you in the faith and charity of Jesus Christ. Our dear daughters, the International Union of Catholic Women, have just given an eloquent example of this great thing. Always first, the Christian women—at the Sepulchre, at the Cross—you, Our dear children, have followed them here, in a wonderfully impressive assembly, a magnificently solemn representation of all those who are following you in spirit, a superb flight of souls coming to rest here, in this land sanctified by the blood of martyrs, in this Rome through which Christ is Roman, Rome which, for that very reason, is the country of all Christian souls wherever they may be, from whatever corner of the world their prayers may rise. Welcome, then, in your Father's house, the house of peace, the peace we all desire, of which all feel with more or less urgency the need: all, in the complete light of the Faith, in the impulse which seeks salvation where alone it can be found, all in the one same recognition of the need that human society should turn to God, that God should turn Himself to human society. . . . . . .

LETTER *Pochi Giorni* TO CARDINAL POMPILI, VICAR OF ROME.[7]

May Christ in the Holy Eucharist bring peace to human society!

May 29, 1922

743. . . . . . . May it please the Lord, the Prince of Peace, to extend His Kingdom over every branch of human society, that the minds of all men may be brought together in the brotherhood of faith and love, and over the land but lately drowned in blood and tears the dawn of peace may rise, from the mystic ark of the holy tabernacles the dove with the olive branch may wend its flight through the skies. . . .

LETTER OF CARDINAL GASPARRI, SECRETARY OF STATE, TO M. EUGÈNE DUTHOIT, PRESIDENT OF THE SEMAINE SOCIALE OF STRASBOURG.[8]

Above all else the Holy Father has social peace at heart.

July 10, 1922

744. . . . . . . As a matter of fact, by choosing as your subject for this year, "The State and Economic Life," you intend to advance still further your studies on the economic restoration of society. The Holy See cannot but pray for the happy realization of this plan; in reality, nothing that is able to re-establish or strengthen good order in human relations can be a matter of indifference to the Holy Father. He has at heart, above all else, social peace within nations as well as international peace among them. He is constantly concerned with problems relative to the economic improvement of the working classes; he is always ready to aid in bringing about general prosperity which will spread reasonable well-being among the down-trodden, and which, moreover, will be very useful for the perfection of the religious and moral life. . . . . . .

---

[7] Translation from *The Tablet*, v. 139, pp. 745-746 (June 10, 1922). Original Italian, *A.A.S.*, v. 14, p. 343 (June 8, 1922).
[8] Original French, *Documentation Catholique*, v. 8, c. 281 (August 19, 1922).

LETTER *I Disordini* TO THE BISHOPS OF ITALY.[9]

The Pope exhorts the Bishops of Italy to work for the pacification of their country.

August 6, 1922

745. The disorders which saddened Italy in the past weeks brought to all who love their country with sincere affection a deep sorrow together with a distressing fear for the future. While the sad condition of Italy most urgently demands the unanimous meeting together of all classes of citizens, . . . factional passions drag them into bloody conflict.

746. The sublime mission of peace and of love which the Divine Redeemer wishes to be entrusted to Us in times so sad, and with it also the congenital feeling of love of country, ennobled, and not extinguished, by the universality of Our pastoral care, do not permit Us to remain silent any longer in the face of such a painful spectacle.

747. The cruel tempest which has swept over the earth has left in Italy also, in fact, more in Italy than elsewhere, very sad germs of hatred and violence, while in many hearts it has lulled to sleep the natural horror of shedding blood. Hence, we see factions multiply, their adherents becoming more bitter every day, running often now in one direction, now in another, to perpetrate bloody crimes with an endless train of reprisals which overturn the whole structure of social life. Out of this come immense losses, at home as well as abroad . . . . . . consequences of this fratricidal war, which is most contrary to the elementary principles of Christian society, no less than to the genuine spirit of divine charity, which is the essence of Catholicism.

748. There can be no remedy for all these evils save by returning to God and to the complete observance of His laws, the contempt of which has been the cause of so much misfortune. . . . Let men return, therefore, to Christ, Who desired to make them all brothers at the price of His own Blood. In turning to Him, men will also love one another, because in the love of God and of one's neighbor is contained the whole law of the Gospel. And with the return of all to Christ, the social relations between rulers and subjects, between peoples and governments will be regulated, relations

[9] Original Italian, *A.A.S.*, v. 14, pp. 481-484 (August 31, 1922).

on which every well-ordered society is based, and which are wonderfully directed even in their details by the law of the Gospel. . . .

749. Now, as Leo XIII, in his Encyclical *Immortale Dei* of November 1, 1885, and in his discourse to the Eminent Cardinals of April 11, 1899, teaches with such eloquence and efficacy, the mission of the Church is precisely to reconcile men with God, and thus restore among them Christian peace and brotherhood and, at the same time, social prosperity. . . .

750. We are not ignorant, Venerable Brethren, of your fidelity to this divine mission of the Church; continue, with ever-increasing zeal, especially in these fearful days, your work as peace-makers, which is indeed not the least part of that *ministerium reconciliationis* which the Lord has given us, in keeping with the words of the Apostle: *But all things are of God, Who hath reconciled us to Himself by Christ; and hath given to us the ministry of reconciliation.*[10] Continue it in your instruction and in your enlightened direction of souls; continue it with all the means proper to your exalted pastoral office and, above all else, with public and private prayer, already so highly recommended by Our Predecessor, who wished to give an example of it himself and proposed the touching formula for it. . . .

LETTER *Cum Tertio* TO CARDINAL BOURNE, ARCHBISHOP OF WESTMINSTER, ON THE OCCASION OF THE NATIONAL MISSIONARY CONFERENCE.[11]

> *Christian charity extends to all men without distinction of race.*

September 17, 1922

751. . . . . . . Indeed, We are confident that the clergy and faithful of Great Britain will derive from the Conference an increase of faith, and will imbibe that spirit of brotherly love which should inspire the citizens of the nation whose Empire extends so widely over land and sea. We speak of that brotherly love whereby we are all brethren in Christ Jesus, Whose power is such that when

[10] II *Corinthians*, V, 18.
[11] Translation from *The Tablet*, v. 140, p. 469 (October 7, 1922). Original Latin, *A.A.S.*, v. 14, pp. 547-548 (October 31, 1922).

allowed to take deep root in the heart, all distinctions of nationality are set aside; and in the Catholic missionary, to whatever nation or congregation he belongs, a Catholic recognizes a brave and generous man who is duly exercising the function of the Apostolate to the heathen at the cost of the utmost toil and often of life itself. Moreover, imbued with this spirit, Catholics will contribute generously to the support of the Sacred Missions without distinction, just as Christian charity extends to all men whatsoever without distinction of race from which they have sprung. . . . . . .

LETTER *Ora Sono Pochi Mesi* TO THE BISHOPS OF ITALY.[12]

The Italian people must strive to preserve peace in their own country.

October 28, 1922

752. Only a few months ago, confronted by the evils and the fratricidal struggles which saddened Our beloved country, We sent you an earnest appeal, exhorting you to devote your pastoral care to the task of pacifying the souls and the hearts of men. We fully appreciate the eagerness with which you answered Our paternal invitation, but, unfortunately, the tranquillity so greatly to be desired has not yet returned among the beloved people of Italy, and Our soul is again deeply grieved in beholding the ever-growing calamities that are menacing their material, moral and religious well-being, and all the longer delaying the healing of their deep wounds, the painful aftermath of the long years of war.

753. Faithful, however, to that mission of charity entrusted to Us by the Divine Saviour, We are urgently prompted to address a word of charity and peace to all Italian citizens. In the name of that brotherhood that binds them all in the love of this land so blessed by God, above all in the name of that nobler, because supernatural, brotherhood that in the Religion of Our Lord Jesus Christ binds the sons of Italy into one family, We cry to all in the words of St. Stephen: *Viri, fratres estis; ut quid nocetis alterutrum? Men, you are brethren; why do you injure each other?*[13]

754. And as for you, Venerable Brethren, let your zeal be re-

[12] Original Italian, *A.A.S.*, v. 14, pp. 537-538 (October 31, 1922).
[13] *Acts,* VII, 26.

doubled for this holy enterprise of pacification which you have so earnestly undertaken. Urge all entrusted to your care to moderate their own desires and, if necessary, to sacrifice them for the sake of the common good, taking inspiration from the Christian principles of order, and from those sentiments of charity, meekness and forgiveness which the Divine Teacher has given to His faithful as supreme law.

755. Let them sincerely return to Jesus Christ *qui est pax nostra* —*Who is our peace*[14] because only in loving Him will they love one another and, in brotherly co-operation, they will contribute to the general prosperity from which they all will benefit. May the Apostolic Blessing which We so wholeheartedly bestow upon you, Venerable Brothers, your clergy and all the faithful entrusted to your care be a token and an auspicious omen of this reconciliation so greatly to be desired.

DIPLOMATIC NOTE OF CARDINAL GASPARRI, SECRETARY OF STATE, TO THE CONFERENCE OF LAUSANNE.[15]

The Holy See requests that peace be restored in the Orient.

December 5, 1922

756. Very distressing news daily reaches the Holy See from Constantinople. Christians of Europe are panic-stricken. They flee. Many are not in a position to take flight. Those who want to leave the city must submit a written promise never to return. Their property has been confiscated. All property of Europeans and of religious congregations is in extreme peril. There is reason to fear the arrival of irregular troops which would have disastrous consequences. The Armenians, who have no place of refuge, are exposed to even greater dangers than the others and are literally victims of terror. In bringing these conditions to the attention of the Powers represented at Lausanne to restore peace in the Orient, the Holy See urgently entreats, in the name of humanity, that immediate and effective steps be taken on behalf of the safety of the cruelly persecuted population.

[14] *Ephesians,* II, 14.
[15] Original German, Lama, *Papst und Kurie,* p. 508.

ALLOCUTION *Vehementer Gratum Est* TO THE COLLEGE OF CARDINALS.[16]

Charity must temper justice in international agreements.

December 11, 1922

757. . . . . . . And just as We have striven to provide material help for Our children most in need, so We have made every effort to gain for all the blessings of peace, the peace for which Our Predecessor longed so ardently but which has not yet come to console miserable humanity with its health-giving light. While the representatives of the Powers were meeting at Genoa, We urged them to consider the terrible condition of the peoples and the best remedies to apply to all the disasters. At the same time We invited all the faithful to unite their prayers with Ours to implore of Jesus, Prince of Peace, a successful result of the Conference. And as it seems that there is soon to be another meeting of the delegates of the various Powers at Brussels, where the economic situation of Europe, which has become much worse in these last few months, is to be again considered, We repeat that urgent exhortation. In very truth those meetings, which follow one another almost uninterruptedly, can be of hardly any use at all, become indeed bitter and dangerous delusions, until the Governments decide once for all to temper reasons of justice with those of charity, which in the long run will be to the advantage of conquerors and conquered alike. We have all trust, Venerable Brethren, that this mission of charity and peace of the Church will do much for the pacification and restoration of society, and Our keen desire is that Our work may be as that which Our two immediate Predecessors consecrated to the good of the Catholic world: the one proposing to restore all things in Christ, the other never ceasing to bring Christian peace into the hearts of men. These two programs of the Supreme Pontificate We desire to unite, so that Our motto may be "The Peace of Christ in the Reign of Christ"—*Pax Christi in Regno Christi*. But of this We shall be able to speak better in the Encyclical Letter which We hope to issue, as an offering for Christmas and New Year, to all the bishops of the Catholic world. . . . . . .

[16] Translation from *The Tablet*, v. 140, p. 854 (December 23, 1922). Original Latin, *A.A.S.*, v. 14, pp. 612-613 (December 15, 1922).

Encyclical *Ubi Arcano Dei* on the Peace of Christ in the Kingdom of Christ.[17]

> *The ills of the world are accurately diagnosed and remedies for their cure are proposed.*

December 23, 1922

758. . . . . . . Many reasons have prevented Us up to this time from fulfilling Our wish to write. . . . We were called upon to experience personally and for the first time what St. Paul has called *my daily instance, the solicitude for all the churches.*[18] . . . Then there were to be considered international meetings and treaties which deeply influenced the future of whole peoples and of nations. Faithful to the ministry of peace and reconciliation which has been confided to Our care by God, We strove to make known far and wide the law of justice, tempered always by charity, and to obtain merited consideration for those values and interests which, because they are spiritual, are nonetheless grave and important. As a matter of fact, they are much more serious and important than any merely material thing whatsoever. We were occupied, too, with the almost unbelievable sufferings of those peoples, living in districts far remote from Us, who had been stricken with famine and every kind of calamity. We hastened to send them all the help which Our own straitened circumstances permitted, and did not fail to call upon the whole world to assist Us in this task. Finally, there did not escape Us those uprisings accompanied by acts of violence which had broken out in the very midst of Our own beloved people, here where We were born, here where the Hand of Divine Providence has set down the Chair of St. Peter. For a time these troubles seemed to threaten the very future of Our country, nor could We rest easy until We had done everything within Our power to quiet such serious disorders. . . . . . .

759. These different events, some sad and some joyful, the history of which We wish to record for the edification of posterity, spoke most eloquently to Us, making more and more clear to Our mind those objectives which seem to claim the foremost place in Our Apostolic Ministry and of which it behooves Us to speak now

[17] Translation from Ryan, *The Encyclicals of Pius XI*, pp. 4-46. Original Latin, *A.A.S.*, v. 14, pp. 674-700 (December 27, 1922).
[18] II *Corinthians*, XI, 28.

in as solemn a manner as possible in this, Our very first message
to you.

760. One thing is certain to-day. Since the close of the Great
War individuals, the different classes of society, the nations of the
earth have not as yet found true peace. They do not enjoy, therefore, that active and fruitful tranquillity which is the aspiration
and the need of mankind. This is a sad truth which forces itself
upon us from every side. For anyone who, as We do, desires profoundly to study and successfully to apply the means necessary to
overcome such evils, it is all-important that he recognize both the
fact and the gravity of this state of affairs and attempt beforehand
to discover its causes. This duty is imposed upon Us in commanding fashion by the very consciousness which We have of Our Apostolic Office. We cannot but resolve to fulfill that which is so clearly
Our duty. This We shall do now by this Our first Encyclical, and
afterward with all solicitude in the course of Our Sacred Ministry.

761. Since the selfsame sad conditions continue to exist in the
world to-day which were the object of constant and almost heartbreaking preoccupation on the part of Our respected Predecessor,
Benedict XV, during the whole period of his Pontificate, naturally
We have come to make his thoughts and his solutions of these
problems Our own. May they become, too, the thoughts and ideals
of everyone, as they are Our thoughts, and if this should happen
we would certainly see, with the help of God and the co-operation
of all men of good will, the most wonderful effects come to pass
by a true and lasting reconciliation of men one with another.

762. The inspired words of the Prophets seem to have been
written expressly for our own times: *We looked for peace and no
good came: for a time of healing, and behold fear,*[19] *for the time of
healing, and behold trouble.*[20] *We looked for light, and behold
darkness . . . we have looked for judgment, and there is none: for
salvation, and it is far from us.*[21]

763. The belligerents of yesterday have laid down their arms
but on the heels of this act we encounter new horrors and new
threats of war in the Near East. The conditions in many sections
of these devastated regions have been greatly aggravated by famine,

[19] *Jeremias,* VIII, 15.
[20] *Jeremias,* XIV, 19.
[21] *Isaias,* LIX, 9, 11.

333

epidemics and the laying waste of the land, all of which have not failed to take their toll of victims without number, especially among the aged, women and innocent children. In what has been so justly called the immense theater of the World War, the old rivalries between nations have not ceased to exert their influence, rivalries at times hidden under the manipulations of politics or concealed beneath the fluctuations of finance, but openly appearing in the Press, in reviews and magazines of every type, and even penetrating into institutions devoted to the cultivation of the arts and sciences, spots where otherwise the atmosphere of quiet and peace would reign supreme.

764. Public life is so enveloped, even at the present hour, by the dense fog of mutual hatreds and grievances that it is almost impossible for the common people so much as freely to breathe therein. If the defeated nations continue to suffer most terribly, no less serious are the evils which afflict their conquerors. Small nations complain that they are being oppressed and exploited by great nations. The great Powers, on their side, contend that they are being judged wrongly and circumvented by the smaller. All nations, great and small, suffer acutely from the sad effects of the late war. Neither can those nations which were neutral contend that they have escaped altogether the tremendous sufferings of the war or failed to experience its evil results almost equally with the actual belligerents. These evil results grow in volume from day to day because of the utter impossibility of finding anything like a safe remedy to cure the ills of society, and this in spite of all the efforts of politicians and statesmen whose work has come to naught if it has not unfortunately tended to aggravate the very evils they tried to overcome. Conditions have become increasingly worse because the fears of the people are being constantly played upon by the ever-present menace of new wars, likely to be more frightful and destructive than any which have preceded them. Whence it is that the nations of today live in a state of armed peace which is scarcely better than war itself, a condition which tends to exhaust national finances, to waste the flower of youth, to muddy and poison the very fountainheads of life, physical, intellectual, religious and moral.

765. A much more serious and lamentable evil than these threats of external aggression is the internal discord which menaces

the welfare not only of nations but of human society itself. In the first place, we must take cognizance of the war between the classes, a chronic and mortal disease of present-day society, which like a cancer is eating away the vital forces of the social fabric, labor, industry, the arts, commerce, agriculture—everything, in fact, which contributes to public and private welfare and to national prosperity. This conflict seems to resist every solution and grows worse because those who are never satisfied with the amount of their wealth contend with those who hold on most tenaciously to the riches which they have already acquired, while to both classes there is common the desire to rule the other and to assume control of the other's possessions. From this class war there result frequent interruptions of work, the causes for which most often can be laid to mutual provocations. There result, too, revolutions, riots and forcible repression of one side or other by the government, all of which cannot but end in general discontent and in grave damage to the common welfare.

766. To these evils we must add the contests between political parties, many of which struggles do not originate in a real difference of opinion concerning the public good or in a laudable and disinterested search for what would best promote the common welfare, but in the desire for power and for the protection of some private interest which inevitably result in injury to the citizens as a whole. From this course there often arise robberies of what belongs rightly to the people, and even conspiracies against and attacks on the supreme authority of the State, as well as on its representatives. These political struggles also beget threats of popular action and, at times, eventuate in open rebellion and other disorders which are all the more deplorable and harmful since they come from a public to whom it has been given, in our modern democratic States, to participate in very large measure in public life and in the affairs of government. Now, these different forms of government are not of themselves contrary to the principles of the Catholic Faith, which can easily be reconciled with any reasonable and just system of government. Such governments, however, are the most exposed to the danger of being overthrown by one faction or another.

767. It is most sad to see how this revolutionary spirit has penetrated into that sanctuary of peace and love, the family, the original nucleus of human society. In the family these evil seeds of dissen-

335

sion, which were sown long ago, have recently been spread about more and more by the fact of the absence of fathers and sons from the family fireside during the war and by the greatly increased freedom in matters of morality which followed on it as one of its effects. Frequently we behold sons alienated from their fathers, brothers quarreling with brothers, masters with servants, servants with masters. Too often likewise have we seen both the sanctity of the marriage tie and the duties to God and to humankind, which this tie imposes upon men, forgotten.

768. Just as the smallest part of the body feels the effect of an illness which is ravaging the whole body or one of its vital organs, so the evils now besetting society and the family afflict even individuals. In particular, We cannot but lament the morbid restlessness which has spread among people of every age and condition in life, the general spirit of insubordination and the refusal to live up to one's obligations which has become so widespread as almost to appear the customary mode of living. We lament, too, the destruction of purity among women and young girls as is evidenced by the increasing immodesty of their dress and conversation and by their participation in shameful dances, which sins are made the more heinous by the vaunting in the faces of people less fortunate than themselves their luxurious mode of life. Finally, We cannot but grieve over the great increase in the number of what might be called social misfits who almost inevitably end by joining the ranks of those malcontents who continually agitate against all order, be it public or private.

769. Is it surprising, then, that we should no longer possess that security of life in which we can place our trust and that there remains only the most terrible uncertainty, and from hour to hour added fears for the future? Instead of regular daily work there is idleness and unemployment. That blessed tranquillity which is the effect of an orderly existence and in which the essence of peace is to be found no longer exists, and, in its place, the restless spirit of revolt reigns. As a consequence industry suffers, commerce is crippled, the cultivation of literature and the arts becomes more and more difficult, and, what is worse than all, Christian civilization itself is irreparably damaged thereby. In the face of our much praised progress, we behold with sorrow society lapsing back slowly but surely into a state of barbarism.

770. We wish to record, in addition to the evils already mentioned, other evils which beset society and which occupy a place of prime importance but whose very existence escapes the ordinary observer, the sensual man—he who, as the Apostle says, does not perceive *the things that are of the Spirit of God*,[22] yet which cannot but be judged the greatest and most destructive scourges of the social order of today. We refer specifically to those evils which transcend the material or natural sphere and lie within the supernatural and religious order properly so-called; in other words, those evils which affect the spiritual life of souls. These evils are all the more to be deplored since they injure souls whose value is infinitely greater than that of any merely material object.

771. Over and above the laxity in the performance of Christian duties which is so widespread, We cannot but sorrow with you, Venerable Brothers, over the fact that very many churches, which during the war had been turned to profane uses, have not yet been restored to their original purpose as temples of prayer and of divine worship; moreover, that many seminaries whose existence is vital for the preparation and formation of worthy leaders and teachers of the religious life have not yet been reopened; that the ranks of the clergy in almost every country have been decimated, either because so many priests have died on the battlefield in the exercise of their Sacred Ministry or have been lost to the Church because they proved faithless to their holy vocation, due to the unfavorable conditions under which they were compelled to live for so long; and, finally, that in many places even the preaching of the Word of God, so necessary and so fruitful for *the edifying of the body of Christ*[23] has been silenced.

772. The evil results of the Great War, as they affect the spiritual life, have been felt all over the world, even in out-of-the-way and lonely sections of far-off continents. Missionaries have been forced to abandon the field of their Apostolic labors, and many have been unable to return to their work, thus causing interruptions to and even abandonment of those glorious conquests of the Faith which have done so much to raise the level of civilization, moral, material and religious. It is quite true that there have been some worth-while compensations for these great spiritual misfortunes.

[22] I *Corinthians*, II, 14.
[23] *Ephesians*, IV, 12.

Among these compensations is one which stands out in bold relief and gives the lie to many ancient calumnies, namely, that a pure love of country and a generous devotion to duty burn brightly in the souls of those consecrated to God, and that through their Sacred Ministry the consolations of religion were brought to thousands dying on the fields of battle wet with human blood. Thus, many, in spite of their prejudices, were led to honor again the priesthood and the Church by reason of the wonderful examples of sacrifice of self, with which they had become acquainted. For these happy results we are indebted solely to the infinite goodness and wisdom of God, Who draws good from evil.

773. Our letter so far has been devoted to a recital of the evils which afflict present-day society. We must now search out, with all possible care, the causes of these disorders, some of which have already been referred to. At this point, Venerable Brothers, there seems to come to Us the voice of the Divine Consoler and Physician Who, speaking of these human infirmities, says: *All these evil things come from within*.[24]

774. Peace indeed was signed in solemn conclave between the belligerents of the late war. This peace, however, was only written into treaties. It was not received into the hearts of men, who still cherish the desire to fight one another and to continue to menace in a most serious manner the quiet and stability of civil society. Unfortunately, the law of violence held sway so long that it has weakened and almost obliterated all traces of those natural feelings of love and mercy which the law of Christian charity has done so much to encourage. Nor has this illusory peace, written only on paper, served as yet to reawaken similar noble sentiments in the souls of men. On the contrary, there has been born a spirit of violence and of hatred which, because it has been indulged in for so long, has become almost second nature in many men. There has followed the blind rule of the inferior parts of the soul over the superior, that rule of the lower elements *fighting against the law of the mind,* which St. Paul grieved over.[25]

775. Men today do not act as Christians, as brothers, but as strangers, and even enemies. The sense of man's personal dignity and of the value of human life has been lost in the brutal domina-

[24] *Mark,* VII, 23.
[25] *Romans,* VII, 23.

338

tion begotten of might and mere superiority in numbers. Many are intent on exploiting their neighbors solely for the purpose of enjoying more fully and on a larger scale the goods of this world. But they err grievously who have turned to the acquisition of material and temporal possessions and are forgetful of eternal and spiritual things, to the possession of which Jesus, Our Redeemer, by means of the Church, His living interpreter, calls mankind.

776. It is in the very nature of material objects that an inordinate desire for them becomes the root of every evil, of every discord, and, in particular, of a lowering of the moral sense. On the one hand, things which are naturally base and vile can never give rise to noble aspirations in the human heart which was created by and for God alone and is restless until it finds repose in Him. On the other hand, material goods (and in this they differ greatly from those of the spirit which the more of them we possess the more remain to be acquired) the more they are divided among men the less each one has and, by consequence, what one man has another cannot possibly possess unless it be forcibly taken away from the first. Such being the case, worldly possessions can never satisfy all in equal manner nor give rise to a spirit of universal contentment, but must become perforce a source of division among men and of vexation of spirit, as even the Wise Man, Solomon, experienced: *Vanity of vanities, and vexation of spirit.*[26]

777. The same effects which result from these evils among individuals may likewise be expected among nations. *From whence are wars and contentions among you?* asks the Apostle St. James. *Are they not hence, from your concupiscences, which war in your members?*[27] The inordinate desire for pleasure, *concupiscence of the flesh,* sows the fatal seeds of division not only among families but likewise among States; the inordinate desire for possessions, *concupiscence of the eyes,* inevitably turns into class warfare and into social egotism; the inordinate desire to rule or to domineer over others, *pride of life,* soon becomes mere party or factional rivalries, manifesting itself in constant displays of conflicting ambitions and ending in open rebellion, in the crime of *lèse majesté,* and even in national parricide.

778. These unsuppressed desires, this inordinate love of the

---

[26] *Ecclesiastes,* I, 2, 14.
[27] *James,* IV, 1.

things of the world, are precisely the source of all international misunderstandings and rivalries, despite the fact that oftentimes men dare to maintain that acts prompted by such motives are excusable and even justifiable because, forsooth, they were performed for reasons of State or of the public good, or out of love for country. Patriotism—the stimulus of so many virtues and of so many noble acts of heroism when kept within the bounds of the law of Christ —becomes merely an occasion, an added incentive to grave injustice when true love of country is debased to the condition of an extreme nationalism, when we forget that all men are our brothers and members of the same great human family, that other nations have an equal right with us both to life and to prosperity, that it is never lawful nor even wise, to dissociate morality from the affairs of practical life, that, in the last analysis, it is *justice which exalteth a nation: but sin maketh nations miserable.*[28]

779. Perhaps the advantages to one's family, city or nation obtained in some such way as this may well appear to be a wonderful and great victory (this thought has been already expressed by St. Augustine), but in the end it turns out to be a very shallow thing, something rather to inspire us with the most fearful apprehensions of approaching ruin. *It is a happiness which appears beautiful but is brittle as glass. We must ever be on guard lest with horror we see it broken into a thousand pieces at the first touch.*[29]

780. There is, over and above the absence of peace and the evils attendant on this absence, another deeper and more profound cause for present-day conditions. This cause was even beginning to show its head before the war and the terrible calamities consequent on that cataclysm should have proven a remedy for them if mankind had only taken the trouble to understand the real meaning of those terrible events. In the Holy Scriptures we read: *They that have forsaken the Lord shall be consumed.*[30] No less well-known are the words of the Divine Teacher, Jesus Christ, Who said: *Without Me you can do nothing*[31] and again, *He that gathereth not with Me, scattereth.*[32]

781. These words of the Holy Bible have been fulfilled and are

[28] *Proverbs*, XIV, 34.
[29] St. Augustine, *De Civitate Dei*, bk. IV, ch. 3.
[30] *Isaias*, I, 28.
[31] *John*, XV, 5.
[32] *Luke*, XI, 23.

now at this very moment being fulfilled before our very eyes. Because men have forsaken God and Jesus Christ, they have sunk to the depths of evil. They waste their energies and consume their time and efforts in vain sterile attempts to find a remedy for these ills, but without even being successful in saving what little remains from the existing ruins. It was a quite general desire that both our laws and our governments should exist *without recognizing God* or Jesus Christ, on the theory that all authority comes from men, not from God. Because of such an assumption, these theorists fell very short of being able to bestow upon law not only those sanctions which it must possess but also that secure basis for the supreme criterion of justice which even a pagan philosopher like Cicero saw clearly could not be derived except from the divine law. Authority itself lost its hold upon mankind, for it had lost that sound and unquestionable justification for its right to command on the one hand and to be obeyed on the other. Society, quite logically and inevitably, was shaken to its very depths and even threatened with destruction, since there was left to it no longer a stable foundation, everything having been reduced to a series of conflicts, to the domination of the majority, or to the supremacy of special interests.

782. Again, legislation was passed which did not recognize that either God or Jesus Christ had any rights over marriage—an erroneous view which debased matrimony to the level of a mere civil contract, despite the fact that Jesus Himself had called it a *great Sacrament*[33] and had made it the holy and sanctifying symbol of that indissoluble union which binds Him to His Church. The high ideals and pure sentiments with which the Church has always surrounded the idea of the family, the germ of all social life, these were lowered, were unappreciated, or became confused in the minds of many. As a consequence, the correct ideals of family government, and with them those of family peace, were destroyed; the stability and unity of the family itself were menaced and undermined, and, worst of all, the very sanctuary of the home was more and more frequently profaned by acts of sinful lust and soul-destroying egotism—all of which could not but result in poisoning and drying up the very sources of domestic and social life.

783. Added to all this, God and Jesus Christ, as well as His doctrines, were banished from the school. As a sad but inevitable

[33] *Ephesians,* V, 32.

341

consequence, the school became not only secular and non-religious but openly atheistical and anti-religious. In such circumstances it was easy to persuade poor ignorant children that neither God nor religion are of any importance as far as their daily lives are concerned. God's name, moreover, was scarcely ever mentioned in such schools unless it were perchance to blaspheme Him or to ridicule His Church. Thus, the school forcibly deprived of the right to teach anything about God or His law could not but fail in its efforts really to educate, that is, to lead children to the practice of virtue, for the school lacked the fundamental principles which underlie the possession of a knowledge of God and the means necessary to strengthen the will in its efforts toward good and in its avoidance of sin. Gone, too, was all possibility of ever laying a solid groundwork for peace, order and prosperity, either in the family or in social relations. Thus the principles based on the spiritualistic philosophy of Christianity having been obscured or destroyed in the minds of many, a triumphant materialism served to prepare mankind for the propaganda of anarchy and of social hatred which was let loose on such a great scale.

784. Is it to be wondered at, then, that with the widespread refusal to accept the principles of true Christian wisdom, the seeds of discord sown everywhere should find a kindly soil in which to grow and should come to fruit in that most tremendous struggle, the Great War, which unfortunately did not serve to lessen but increased, by its acts of violence and of bloodshed, the international and social animosities which already existed?

785. Up to this We have analyzed briefly the causes of the ills which afflict present-day society, the recital of which, however, Venerable Brothers, should not cause us to lose hope of finding their appropriate remedy, since the evils themselves seem to suggest a way out of these difficulties.

786. First, and most important of all, for mankind is the need of spiritual peace. We do not need a peace that will consist merely in acts of external or formal courtesy, but a peace which will penetrate the souls of men and which will unite, heal and reopen their hearts to that mutual affection which is born of brotherly love. The Peace of Christ is the only peace answering this description: *Let the Peace of Christ rejoice in your hearts.*[34] Nor is there any other peace

---

[34] *Colossians,* III, 15.

possible than that which Christ gave to His disciples[35] for since He is God, He *beholdeth the heart*[36] and in our hearts His kingdom is set up. Again, Jesus Christ is perfectly justified when He calls this peace of soul His own, for He was the first Who said to men, *All you are brethren.*[37] He gave likewise to us, sealing it with His own life's Blood, the law of brotherly love, of mutual forbearance—*This is My commandment, that you love one another, as I have loved you.*[38] *Bear ye one another's burdens; and so you shall fulfill the law of Christ.*[39]

787. From this it follows, as an immediate consequence, that the Peace of Christ can only be a peace of justice according to the words of the prophet, *the work of justice shall be peace,*[40] for He is God *Who judgest justice.*[41] But peace does not consist merely in a hard, inflexible justice. It must be made acceptable and easy by being compounded almost equally of charity and a sincere desire for reconciliation. Such peace was acquired for us and the whole world by Jesus Christ, a peace which the Apostle, in a most expressive manner, incarnates in the very Person of Christ Himself when he addresses Him, *He is our Peace,* for it was He Who satisfied completely divine justice by His death on the Cross, destroying thus in His own flesh all enmities toward others and making peace and reconciliation with God possible for mankind.[42] Therefore, the Apostle beholds in the work of Redemption, which is a work of justice at one and the same time, a divine work of reconciliation and of love. *God indeed was in Christ, reconciling the world to Himself.*[43] *God so loved the world, as to give His only begotten Son.*[44]

788. Thomas Aquinas, the Angel of the Schools, also discovered in this fact the very formula and essence of our belief, for he writes that a true and lasting peace is more a matter of love than of justice. The reason for his statement is that it is the function of justice merely to do away with obstacles to peace, as for example, the in-

[35] *John*, XIV, 27.
[36] I *Kings*, XVI, 7.
[37] *Matthew*, XXIII, 8.
[38] *John*, XV, 12.
[39] *Galatians*, VI, 2.
[40] *Isaias*, XXXII, 17.
[41] *Psalms*, IX, 5.
[42] *Ephesians*, II, 14 *sq.*
[43] II *Corinthians*, V, 19.
[44] *John*, III, 16.

jury done or the damage caused. Peace itself, however, is an act and results only from love.[45]

789. Of this Peace of Christ, which dwells in our hearts and is, in effect, the love of God, We can repeat what the Apostle has said of the Kingdom of God which also rules by love—*the Kingdom of Christ is not meat and drink.*[46] In other words, the Peace of Christ is not nourished on the things of earth, but on those of heaven. Nor could it well be otherwise, since it is Jesus Christ Who has revealed to the world the existence of spiritual values and has obtained for them their due appreciation. He has said, *For what doth it profit a man, if he gain the whole world, and suffer the loss of his own soul?*[47] He also taught us a divine lesson of courage and constancy when He said, *Fear ye not them that kill the body, and are not able to kill the soul: but rather fear him that can destroy both soul and body in hell.*[48]

790. This does not mean that the Peace of Christ, which is the only true peace, exacts of us that we give up all worldly possessions. On the contrary, every earthly good is promised in so many words by Christ to those who seek His peace: *Seek ye first the kingdom of God, and His justice, and all these things shall be added unto you.*[49]

791. This Peace of Christ, however, surpasses all human understanding—*the Peace of God which surpasseth all understanding*[50] and for this very reason dominates our sinful passions and renders such evils as division, strife and discord, which result solely from the unrestrained desire for earthly possessions, impossible. If the desire for worldly possessions were kept within bounds and the place of honor in our affections given to the things of the spirit, which place undoubtedly they deserve, the Peace of Christ would follow immediately, to which would be joined in a natural and happy union, as it were, a higher regard for the value and dignity of human life. Human personality, too, would be raised to a higher level, for man has been ennobled by the Blood of Christ and made kin to God Himself by means of holiness and the bond of brotherly

[45] *Summa Theologica,* 2a 2ae, q.29, a.3, ad 3um.
[46] *Romans,* XIV, 17.
[47] *Matthew,* XVI, 26.
[48] *Matthew,* X, 28.
[49] *Matthew,* VI, 33; *Luke,* XII, 31.
[50] *Philippians,* IV, 7.

love which unites us closely with Christ, by prayer and by the reception of the Sacraments, means infallibly certain to produce this elevation to and participation in the life of God, by the desire to attain everlasting possession of the glory and happiness of heaven which is held out to all by God as our goal and final reward.

792. We have already seen and come to the conclusion that the principal cause of the confusion, restlessness, and dangers which are so prominent a characteristic of false peace, is the weakening of the binding force of law and lack of respect for authority, effects which logically follow upon denial of the truth that authority comes from God, the Creator and Universal Law-giver.

793. The only remedy for such state of affairs is the Peace of Christ since the Peace of Christ is the Peace of God, which could not exist if it did not enjoin respect for law, order and the rights of authority. In the Holy Scriptures We read: *My children, keep discipline in peace.*[51] *Much peace have they that love thy law, O Lord.*[52] *He that feareth the commandment, shall dwell in peace.*[53] Jesus Christ very expressly states: *Render to Cæsar the things that are Cæsar's.*[54] He even recognized that Pilate possessed authority from on High[55] as He acknowledged that the scribes and Pharisees, who, though unworthy, sat in the chair of Moses,[56] were not without a like authority. In Joseph and Mary, Jesus respected the natural authority of parents and was subject to them for the greater part of His life.[57] He also taught, by the voice of His Apostle, the same important doctrine: *Let every soul be subject to higher powers: for there is no power but from God.*[58]

794. If we stop to reflect for a moment that these ideals and doctrines of Jesus Christ, for example, His teachings on the necessity and value of the spiritual life, on the dignity and sanctity of human life, on the duty of obedience, on the divine basis of human government, on the sacramental character of matrimony and by consequence the sanctity of family life—if we stop to reflect, let Us repeat, that these ideals and doctrines of Christ (which are in fact

---

[51] *Ecclesiasticus*, XLI, 17.
[52] *Psalms*, CXVIII, 165.
[53] *Proverbs*, XIII, 13.
[54] *Matthew*, XXII, 21.
[55] *John*, XIX, 11.
[56] *Matthew*, XXIII, 2.
[57] *Luke*, II, 51.
[58] *Romans*, XIII, 1; *cf.* also I *Peter*, II, 13, 18.

but a portion of the treasury of truth which He left to mankind) were confided by Him to His Church and to her alone for safe-keeping, and that He has promised that His aid will never fail her at any time, for she is the infallible teacher of His doctrines in every century and before all nations, there is no one who cannot clearly see what a singularly important role the Catholic Church is able to play, and is even called upon to assume, in providing a remedy for the ills which afflict the world today and in leading mankind toward a universal peace.

795. Because the Church is by divine institution the sole de-pository and interpreter of the ideals and teachings of Christ, she alone possesses in any complete and true sense the power effectively to combat that materialistic philosophy which has already done and still threatens such tremendous harm to the home and to the State. The Church alone can introduce into society and maintain therein the prestige of a true, sound spiritualism, the spiritualism of Christianity which, both from the point of view of truth and of its practical value, is quite superior to any exclusively philosophical theory. The Church is the teacher and an example of world good-will, for she is able to inculcate and develop in mankind the "true spirit of brotherly love,"[59] and, by raising the public estimation of the value and dignity of the individual's soul, help thereby to lift us even unto God.

796. Finally, the Church is able to set both public and private life on the road to righteousness by demanding that everything and all men become obedient to God "Who beholdeth the heart," to His commands, to His laws, to His sanctions. If the teachings of the Church could only penetrate, in some such manner as We have described, the inner recesses of the consciences of mankind, be they rulers or be they subjects, all eventually would be so apprised of their personal and civic duties and their mutual responsibilities that in a short time *Christ would be all, and in all.*[60]

797. Since the Church is the safe and sure guide to conscience, for to her safe-keeping alone there has been confided the doctrines and the promise of the assistance of Christ, she is able not only to bring about at the present hour a peace that is truly the peace of Christ, but can, better than any other agency which We know of,

[59] St. Augustine, *De Moribus Ecclesiae Catholicae*, I, 30, in Migne, *P.L.*, v. 32, c. 1336.
[60] *Colossians*, III, 11.

contribute greatly to the securing of the same peace for the future, to the making impossible of war in the future. For the Church teaches (she alone has been given by God the mandate and the right to teach with authority) that not only our acts as individuals but also as groups and as nations must conform to the eternal law of God. In fact, it is much more important that the acts of a nation follow God's law, since on the nation rests a much greater responsibility for the consequences of its acts than on the individual.

798. When, therefore, governments and nations follow in all their activities, whether they be national or international, the dictates of conscience grounded in the teachings, precepts and example of Jesus Christ, and which are binding on each and every individual, then only can we have faith in one another's word and trust in the peaceful solution of the difficulties and controversies which may grow out of differences in point of view or from clash of interests. An attempt in this direction has already and is now being made; its results, however, are almost negligible and, especially so, as far as they can be said to affect those major questions which divide seriously and serve to arouse nations one against the other. No merely human institution of to-day can be as successful in devising a set of international laws which will be in harmony with world conditions as the Middle Ages were in the possession of that true League of Nations, Christianity. It cannot be denied that in the Middle Ages this law was often violated; still it always existed as an ideal, according to which one might judge the acts of nations, and a beacon light calling those who had lost their way back to the safe road.

799. There exists an institution able to safeguard the sanctity of the law of nations. This institution is a part of every nation; at the same time it is above all nations. She enjoys, too, the highest authority, the fullness of the teaching power of the Apostles. Such an institution is the Church of Christ. She alone is adapted to do this great work, for she is not only divinely commissioned to lead mankind, but moreover, because of her very make-up and the constitution which she possesses, by reason of her age-old traditions and her great prestige, which has not been lessened but has been greatly increased since the close of the war, cannot but succeed in such a venture where others assuredly will fail.

800. It is apparent from these considerations that true peace, the

Peace of Christ, is impossible unless we are willing and ready to accept the fundamental principles of Christianity, unless we are willing to observe the teachings and obey the law of Christ, both in public and private life. If this were done, then society being placed at last on a sound foundation, the Church would be able, in the exercise of its divinely given ministry and by means of the teaching authority which results therefrom, to protect all the rights of God over men and nations.

801. It is possible to sum up all We have said in one word, "the Kingdom of Christ." For Jesus Christ reigns over the *minds of individuals* by His teachings, in their hearts by His love, in each one's life by the living according to His law and the imitating of His example. Jesus reigns over the *family* when it, modeled after the holy ideals of the Sacrament of matrimony instituted by Christ, maintains unspotted its true character of sanctuary. In such a sanctuary of love, parental authority is fashioned after the authority of God, the Father, from Whom, as a matter of fact, it originates and after which even it is named.[61]

802. The obedience of the children imitates that of the Divine Child of Nazareth, and the whole family life is inspired by the sacred ideals of the Holy Family. Finally, Jesus Christ reigns over *society* when men recognize and reverence the sovereignty of Christ, when they accept the divine origin and control over all social forces, a recognition which is the basis of the right to command for those in authority and of the duty to obey for those who are subjects, a duty which cannot but ennoble all who live up to its demands. Christ reigns where the position in society which He Himself has assigned to His Church is recognized, for He bestowed on the Church the status and the constitution of a society which, by reason of the perfect ends which it is called upon to attain, must be held to be supreme in its own sphere; He also made her the depository and interpreter of His divine teachings, and, by consequence, the teacher and guide of every other society whatsoever, not, of course, in the sense that she should abstract in the least from their authority, each in its own sphere supreme, but that she should really perfect their authority, just as divine grace perfects human nature, and should give to them the assistance necessary for men to attain their true final end, eternal happiness, and by that very fact make

[61] *Cf. Ephesians*, III, 15.

them the more deserving and certain promoters of their happiness here below.

803. It is, therefore, a fact which cannot be questioned that the true Peace of Christ can only exist in the Kingdom of Christ—"the Peace of Christ in the Kingdom of Christ." It is no less unquestionable that, in doing all we can to bring about the re-establishment of Christ's Kingdom, we will be working most effectively toward a lasting world peace.

804. Pius X, in taking as his motto, "To restore all things in Christ," was inspired from on High to lay the foundations of that "work of peace" which became the program and principal task of Benedict XV. These two programs of Our Predecessors We desire to unite in one—the re-establishment of the Kingdom of Christ by peace in Christ—"the Peace of Christ in the Kingdom of Christ." With might and main We shall ever strive to bring about this peace, putting Our trust in God, Who, when He called Us to the Chair of Peter, promised that the divine assistance would never fail Us. We ask that all assist and co-operate with Us in this Our mission. Particularly We ask you to aid Us, Venerable Brothers, you, His sheep, whom Our leader and Lord, Jesus Christ, has called to feed and to watch over as the most precious portion of His flock, which comprises all mankind. . . .

805. Of your praiseworthy industry, We have had a quite recent proof on the occasion of the International Eucharistic Congress held in Rome and of the celebration of the Centenary of the Sacred Congregation of the Propagation of the Faith, when several hundred bishops from all sections of the globe were reunited with Us before the tomb of the Holy Apostles. That brotherly reunion, so solemn, because of the great number and high dignity of the bishops who were present, carried Our thoughts to the possibility of another similar meeting of the whole episcopate here in the center of Catholic unity, and of the many effective results which might follow such a meeting toward the re-establishment of the social order after the terrible disorders through which we have just passed. The very proximity of the Holy Year fills Us with the solemn hope that this Our desire may be fully realized. . . . . . .

806. From the reports received from you by Us and by public fame, which is amply confirmed in the Press and in many other ways, We know only too well what thanks We should, in union

349

with you, render to the Good God for the great work which, as the occasion permitted, He has done through you and through your predecessors, both for your clergy and for your faithful people, a work which has come to maturity in our own times and which We see being multiplied on all sides in a most fruitful manner. . . . . . .

807. The fruits of such piety are manifest, the widespread diffusion and great activity of the apostolate which, by prayer, word of mouth, by the religious Press, by personal example, by works of charity seeks in every way possible to lead souls to the Sacred Heart of Jesus and to restore to the same Sacred Heart His sovereign rule over the family and over society. We refer also to the *holy battle* waged on so many fronts to vindicate for the family and the Church the natural and divinely given rights which they possess over education and the school. Finally, We include among these fruits of piety that whole group of movements, organizations and works so dear to Our fatherly heart which passes under the name of "Catholic Action," and in which We have been so intensely interested.

808. All these organizations and movements ought not only to continue in existence, but ought to be developed more and more, always, of course, as the conditions of time and place seem to demand. There can be no question of the fact that these conditions are at times very difficult and exact of both pastors and the faithful a great and increasing amount of sacrifice and labor. But since such work is vitally necessary, it is without question an essential part of our Christian life and of the Sacred Ministry and is, therefore, indissolubly bound up with the restoration of the Kingdom of Christ and the re-establishment of that true peace which can be found only in His Kingdom—"the Peace of Christ in the Kingdom of Christ." . . . . . .

809. Tell your faithful children of the laity that when, united with their pastors and their bishops, they participate in the works of the apostolate, both individual and social, the end purpose of which is to make Jesus Christ better known and better loved, then they are more than ever *a chosen generation, a kingly priesthood, a holy nation, a purchased people,* of whom St. Peter spoke in such laudatory terms.[62] Then, too, they are more than ever united with Us and with Christ, and become great factors in bringing about world peace because they work for the restoration and spread of

---

[62] I *Peter*, II, 9.

the Kingdom of Christ. Only in this Kingdom of Christ can we find that true human equality by which all men are ennobled and made great by the selfsame nobility and greatness, for each is ennobled by the precious Blood of Christ. As for those who are in authority, they are, according to the example of Our Lord Jesus Christ, but ministers of the good, servants of the servants of God, particularly of the sick and of those in need.

810. However, these very social changes, which have created and increased the need of co-operation between the clergy and laity to which We have just referred, have themselves brought along in their wake new and most serious problems and dangers. As an after-effect of the upheaval caused by the Great War and of its political and social consequences, false ideas and unhealthy sentiments have, like a contagious disease, so taken possession of the popular mind that We have grave fears that even some among the best of our laity and of the clergy, seduced by the false appearance of truth which some of these doctrines possess, have not been altogether immune from error.

811. Many believe in or claim that they believe in and hold fast to Catholic doctrine on such questions as social authority, the right of owning private property, on the relations between capital and labor, on the rights of the laboring man, on the relations between Church and State, religion and country, on the relations between the different social classes, on international relations, on the rights of the Holy See and the prerogatives of the Roman Pontiff and the episcopate, on the social rights of Jesus Christ, Who is the Creator, Redeemer, and Lord not only of individuals but of nations. In spite of these protestations, they speak, write, and what is more, act as if it were not necessary any longer to follow, or that they did not remain still in full force, the teachings and solemn pronouncements which may be found in so many documents of the Holy See, and particularly in those written by Leo XIII, Pius X and Benedict XV.

812. There is a species of moral, legal and social modernism which We condemn, no less decidedly than We condemn theological modernism. . . . . . .

813. From this Apostolic Center of the Church of Christ, We turn Our eyes toward those who, unfortunately in great numbers, are either ignorant of Christ and His Redemption or do not follow

in their entirety His teachings, or who are separated from the unity of His Church and thus are without His Fold, although they, too, have been called by Christ to membership in His Church. The Vicar of the Good Shepherd, seeing so many of his sheep gone astray, cannot but recall and make his own the simple but expressive words of Christ, words which are permeated through and through by the longings born of divine desire: *And other sheep I have, that are not of this fold: them also I must bring.*[63] He cannot but rejoice in that wonderful prophecy which filled even the Sacred Heart of Jesus with joy. *And they shall hear My voice, and there shall be one Fold and one Shepherd.*[64] May God, and We join with you and with all the faithful in this prayer, shortly bring to fulfillment His prophecy by transforming this consoling vision of the future into a present reality.

814. One of the outstanding manifestations of this religious unity, and a happy augury for the future, is that altogether unexpected, but well-known fact of which you have knowledge, Venerable Brothers, a fact not pleasing to some perhaps, but certainly very consoling both to Us and to you, namely, that recently the representatives and rulers of practically every nation, motivated by a common and instinctive desire for union and peace, have turned to this Apostolic See in order to bind themselves closer to Us or to renew in some cases the bonds of amity and friendship which had joined us together previously. We rejoice at this fact, not merely because it increases the prestige of Holy Church, but because it is becoming increasingly evident on all sides, and especially from actual experience, what great possibilities for peace and happiness, even here below, such a union with Us possesses for human society. Although the Church is committed by God, first of all, to the attainment of spiritual and imperishable purposes, however, because of the very intimate and necessary connection of things one with another, such a mission serves likewise to advance the temporal prosperity of nations and individuals, even more so than if she were instituted primarily to promote such ends.

815. The Church does not desire, neither ought she to desire, to mix up without a just cause in the direction of purely civil affairs. On the other hand, she cannot permit or tolerate that the State use

[63] *John*, X, 16.
[64] *Ibidem.*

the pretext of certain laws or unjust regulations to do injury to the rights of an order superior to that of the State, to interfere with the constitution given the Church by Christ, or to violate the rights of God Himself over civil society.

816. We make Our very own, Venerable Brothers, the words which Benedict XV, of happy memory, used in the last allocution which he pronounced at the Consistory of November twenty-first of last year, when he spoke of the treaties asked for or proposed to Us by various States: "We cannot possibly permit that anything harmful to the dignity or liberty of the Church creep into these treaties, for it is all-important that the safety and freedom of the Church be guarded at all times, and especially in our own days, and this in the lasting interests of human society itself."[65]

817. It is scarcely necessary to say here how painful it is to Us to note that from this galaxy of friendly powers which surround Us, one is missing, Italy, Our own dear native land, the country where the Hand of God, Who guides the course of history, has set down the Chair of His Vicar on earth, in this city of Rome which, from being the capital of the wonderful Roman Empire, was made by Him the capital of the whole world, because He made it the seat of a sovereignty which, since it extends beyond the confines of nations and States, embraces within itself all the peoples of the whole world. The very origin and divine nature of this sovereignty demand, the inviolable rights of conscience of millions of the faithful of the whole world demand that this sacred sovereignty must not be, neither must it ever appear to be, subject to any human authority or law whatsoever, even though that law be one which proclaims certain guaranties for the liberty of the Roman Pontiff.

818. The true guaranties of liberty, in no way injurious, but on the contrary of incalculable benefit to Italy, which Divine Providence, the Ruler and Arbiter of mankind, has conferred upon the sovereignty of the Vicar of Christ here below, these guaranties which for centuries have fitted in so marvelously with the divine designs in order to protect the liberty of the Roman Pontiff, neither Divine Providence itself has manifested nor human ingenuity has as yet discovered any substitute which would compensate for the loss of these rights; these guaranties We declare have been and are

[65] See *supra* n. 725.

still being violated. Whence it is that there has been created a certain abnormal condition of affairs which has grievously troubled and, up to the present hour, continues to trouble the consciences of the Catholics of Italy and of the entire world.

819.   We, therefore, who are now the heirs and depositories of the ideals and sacred duties of Our Venerated Predecessors, and like them alone invested with competent authority in such a weighty matter and responsible to no one but God for Our decisions, We protest, as they have protested before Us, against such a condition of affairs in defense of the rights and of the dignity of the Apostolic See, not because We are moved by any vain earthly ambition of which We should be ashamed, but out of a sense of Our duty to the dictates of conscience itself, mindful always of the fact that We, too, must one day die and of the awful account which We must render to the Divine Judge of the ministry which He has confided to Our care.

820.   At all events, Italy has not nor will she have in the future anything to fear from the Holy See. The Pope, no matter who he shall be, will always repeat the words: *I think thoughts of peace, not of affliction,*[66] thoughts of a true peace which is founded on justice and which permit him truthfully to say: *Justice and Peace have kissed.*[67]

821.   It is God's task to bring about this happy hour and to make it known to all; men of wisdom and of good-will surely will not permit it to strike in vain. When it does arrive, it will turn out to be a solemn hour, one big with consequences not only for the restoration of the Kingdom of Christ, but for the pacification of Italy and the world as well.

822.   We pray most fervently, and ask others likewise to pray, for this much-desired pacification of society, especially at this moment when, after twenty centuries, the day and hour approach when all over the world men will celebrate the humble and meek coming among us of the sweet Prince of Peace, at whose birth the heavenly hosts sang: *Glory be to God in the highest; and on earth peace to men of good-will.*[68]

823.   As an augury of this peace for mankind, may the Apostolic

---

[66] *Jeremias,* XXIX, 11.
[67] *Psalms,* LXXXIV, 11.
[68] *Luke,* II, 14.

Blessing, which We invoke upon you and your flock, on your clergy, your people, on their families and homes bring happiness to the living, peace and eternal rest to the dead. From the depths of Our heart as a sign of Our fatherly love, We impart to you, to your clergy, and to your people, the Apostolic Blessing.

LETTER *Quando alla Vigilia* TO CARDINAL POMPILI, VICAR OF ROME.[69]

The Pope asks prayers that humanity may be saved from new scourges of war.

January 31, 1923

824. When, on the eve of Christmas, as an echo, so to speak, of the Angels' message of peace promised to men of good will, We sent out to the whole society of mankind the paternal entreaty, the affectionate augury of "The Peace of Christ in the Kingdom of Christ," We could not but express at the same time the feeling of sadness and anxiety caused by sorrow for existing evils and fear of more to come, both the one and the other a miserable heritage of the war. But We were far from foreseeing such an immediate unhappy confirmation of Our words. You, My Lord Cardinal, surely feel, in unison with Us, all the misery, all the gravity of the present situation. Far from Us is the thought of entering into the merits of the many questions disturbing the peoples; but We cannot help a feeling of anguish at the terrible spectre of new conflagrations with all their effects of loss and sorrow for individuals, families, cities and provinces. And if this causes anxiety in all minds, most of all must it do so with Us, who feel Ourself equally Father of all in the spiritual paternity belonging to Our Apostolic Ministry. That is why, as We lack human means of preventing all these troubles, We repeat the invocation of supplication: *O our God, as we know not what to do we can only turn our eyes to Thee;*[70] and We ask you, My Lord Cardinal, to invite the faithful of Our city of Rome to join Us in prayer to obtain that the Lord, *Author and Lover of peace,* may save suffering humanity from

---

[69] Translation from *The Tablet,* v. 141, p. 191 (February 10, 1923). Original Italian, *A.A.S.,* v. 15, pp. 97-98 (March 5, 1923).
[70] II *Paralipomenon,* XX, 12.

new scourges and may bring back peoples and governments to those feelings of fraternity and love, justice and equity, which may inspire friendly agreements among them. . . .

ALLOCUTION *Non È Piccolo* TO THE FRANCISCAN TERTIARIES OF ARA COELI, ROME.[71]

The Franciscan Tertiaries have an apostolate of peace and reconciliation.

February 26, 1923

825. . . . . . . We have already signified with what sentiments We give you the Apostolic Blessing, which, with sentiments of filial piety, you have come to ask at the house of your Father. . . . May it effect, by the divine assistance, the realization of the pious aspirations just expressed and expounded in your name. May it effect that they may lead you on to ever higher perfection, rendering ever more effective the apostolate of your Christian life, and especially the apostolate of peace and reconciliation which shall eventually carry the world to the triumph of "the Peace of Christ in the Kingdom of Christ."

ALLOCUTION *Gratum Nobis* TO THE COLLEGE OF CARDINALS.[72]

The Church proves her sincere desire for peace by fulfilling the offices of Christian charity toward her persecutors.

May 23, 1923

826. . . . . . . In the Near East, in Europe and Asia, where Christianity has so many and such vital records and interests, the horizon is still covered by dark and threatening clouds. Conditions are still those of unspeakable tribulation for entire peoples and countries, with incalculable harm not only to our holy Religion but also to the most elementary interests of humanity and civilization. It is almost superfluous to add that, just as We have always

---

[71] Translation from *Rome Hath Spoken*, pp. 50-51. Original Italian, *Acta Ordinis Fratrum Minorum*, v. 42, p. 121 (April, 1923).
[72] Translation from *The Tablet*, v. 141, pp. 731-732 (June 2, 1923). Original Latin, *A.A.S.*, v. 15, pp. 249-252 (June 1, 1923).

defended, and will always defend to the utmost of Our power, the rights of Catholics, as inalienable as they are evident and above all preponderant, over the Holy Places, so also We will continue to give all the comfort and help in Our power to relieve the many miseries to which We have alluded. We can only wish that it had been given Us to rescue all the homeless and find a refuge for all the orphans, as We have been able to do for some—very few indeed in comparison with the need—by the aid of the wide charitable generosity for which We take the opportunity of this solemn moment and meeting to express Our thanks.

827. Europe itself, too, suffers from many serious ills. On the Continent and in the great islands, peoples of old and magistral civilization are contending and wearing themselves out in fratricidal and exhausting strife, with actual enormous mutual damage of every sort and kind, with danger of immensely greater damage for all Europe, indeed for all human society . . . a spectacle unspeakably sad and grievous for Us, Father of all the contending parties. They are divided and agitated by a different conception of, or a different desire for, political liberty and independence; or the reciprocally disastrous point of divergence is a different interpretation of treaties or a different valuation of the rights and duties emerging from them. But whether they have remained always at home or have left their homes either recently or long ago, they are always, every one of them, children of the Father who delights in sitting at the common table with his children who have remained, and desires and hopes always to see the return of those who have gone away. They are all, every one of them, sheep and lambs of the same Fold to which the one Divine Shepherd is ever lovingly calling them.

828. Among the host of those thus striving, We see children endeared to Us under many different titles: children of the Isle of Saints and of the Isle of Angels, of the Eldest Daughter and of Catholic Germany, which put in the balance against the great falling away of four centuries ago such noble fervor and sound, fruitful organization of Catholic life, even through the terrible war and the present troubles. Nor can We help seeing amid the damage of every kind the immense sufferings of all the religious institutions and works of those Our children who, by their very sufferings, are rendered ever more dear to Us. Is there need to say with what sorrow We see all these things happening, the long continuance

357

of such miserable conditions? God knows We have done and attempted everything that was possible, materially and morally, to bring them to an end or at least alleviate them; as long as some hope shines forth, We shall not cease to do this. We shall speak peace, at least by preaching and inculcating peace to Our children fighting one another. This peace We now invoke from the bottom of Our heart. And it is and will always be possible for Us to pray the God of Peace that He bring back and establish His Peace in all hearts, inspiring in them justice and charity, leading them to friendly understandings, and this prayer We offer and will offer with all the ardor of Our soul.

829. Even more terrible happenings We have seen in Russia. There is no need here to recall in detail what all know so well, as the story has been told fully in the public Press. But one thing We must note. Messengers and ministers of the Head of the Catholic Religion were pouring out, on the suffering and starving children of great Russia, with devotion and self-sacrifice which deserved and indeed received the praise and admiration of all, the benefits which were made possible by the help We implored and which was given so generously and unfailingly by the Catholics of the whole world. While that was happening, authorized representatives of the Catholic Religion were tried and condemned to suffer in prison, and one of them even was killed. . . . . . .

830. It is needless to add that all that has happened will not stop the charitable work, undertaken and continued now for many months, to alleviate the terrible suffering. We shall go on with it as long as We see need and as long as We are able, remembering the Apostle's words: *Be not overcome by evil; but overcome evil by good.*[73] And this, too, will be a means of showing how We long for peace with all, preserving all rights due in justice to the feeble, the poor and the suffering, especially those who suffer for justice and truth; safeguarding, above all things and before all things, in the supreme interests also of civil society, the rights of the Catholic Church, established by divine disposition as the one and only mistress and upholder of justice and truth, because the one and only guardian of the incorruptible teaching and the Blood of the Divine Redeemer. The inviolability of these rights will always be for Us a line over which it is not possible to pass,

[73] *Romans*, XII, 21.

desirous as We ever are to be in peace with all and to co-operate in the universal pacification; willing as We are, where it is possible, to make concessions and even sacrifices which may be necessary to attain less troubled conditions of life for the Church, and pacification of minds, in the different countries. . . . . . .

LETTER *Quando nel Principio* TO CARDINAL GASPARRI, SECRETARY OF STATE.[74]

Principles on reparations and military occupation are proposed.

June 24, 1923.

831. When, at the beginning of Our Pontificate, with a heart full of anguish on account of present ills and fear of ills to come, at a moment which seemed decisive for the tranquillity of Europe and the salvation of society, We gave you the charge of putting before the representatives of the peoples assembled in Council Our greetings and Our wishes as a father, We asked all to consider how very much worse would be the condition of Europe, already so miserable and threatening, if the attempts to reach sincere pacification and a lasting agreement should fail once again.

832. Little more than a year has gone by and it is needless to point out how justified Our fear was; in the short time that has intervened, international relations have not only not improved, as there was every right to hope would result from the Genoa Conference, rather have they become worse, so as to justify anxiety and no small fear for the future. You, My Lord Cardinal, daily witness of and sharer in Our cares, know well what sorrow this causes Us. Common Father and Head of the whole Christian family, We cannot remain indifferent to the troubles of Our children and the dangers threatening them. We are taught by the example of St. Paul, who said: *Who is weak and I am not weak; who is scandalized and I am not on fire.*[75]

833. Therefore, while We endeavor with all Our power and all the means which Our children entrust to Us to this end to alleviate the sufferings, so serious and so general, of the present time, it is

[74] Translation from *The Tablet,* v. 142, pp. 24-25 (July 7, 1923). Original Italian, *A.A.S.,* v. 15, pp. 353-355 (July 5, 1923).
[75] II *Corinthians,* XI, 29.

Our duty to take advantage of every occasion that offers to co-operate as best We may in the pressing work of pacification and restoration in Christ, longed for by peoples and individuals.

834. Now that among the governments of the Powers most closely concerned in the war, new diplomatic conversations are in view, based on new proposals, in order to reach a friendly solution of the questions which are troubling Central Europe and inevitably recoiling on all the nations, We believe it to be Our duty to raise again Our voice, disinterested, impartial and of good-will toward all, as the voice of the Common Father must be. Considering the grave responsibility lying at the moment on Us, and on those who hold in their hands the destinies of the peoples, We conjure them once again to examine the different questions, and particularly the question of reparations, in that Christian spirit which does not set a dividing line between reasons of justice and the reasons of social charity on which the perfection of civil society is based. If and when the debtor, with the intention of paying reparation for the very serious damage suffered by populations and places once so prosperous and flourishing, gives proof of his serious will to reach a fair and definite agreement, invoking an impartial judgment on the limits of his own capacity to pay and undertaking to hand over to the judges every means of true and exact control, then justice and social charity, as well as the very interests of the creditors and of all the nations, wearied of strife and longing for peace, seem to require that no demand shall be made from the debtor that he cannot meet without entirely exhausting his resources and his capacity for production, with irreparable damage to himself and to his creditors, with danger of social disturbances which would be the ruin of Europe, and with resentment which would be a perpetual menace of new and worse conflagrations. In equal measure it is just that the creditors should have guarantees in proportion to their dues, to ensure the payments on which depend interests vital for them, too; We leave it, however, to them to consider whether for that purpose it is necessary to maintain in every case territorial occupations which impose heavy sacrifices on occupied and occupiers, or whether it would not be better to substitute for these, possibly by degrees, other guarantees equally effective and certainly less painful.

835. If these pacific bases be agreed to by both sides and, in

consequence, the bitterness caused by the territorial occupation is eliminated and by degrees the occupation itself is reduced until it comes to an end entirely, it will be possible to reach that true pacification of the peoples which is also a necessary condition for the economic restoration which all keenly desire. Such pacification and restoration are of such great benefit for all the nations, conquerors and conquered, that no sacrifice seen to be necessary ought to seem too great in order to obtain them.

836. But just because these benefits are so great there is no other way to obtain them except by special favor of Almighty God from Whom come *every best gift and every perfect gift*.[76] Therefore, to Almighty God *in Whose Hands are the hearts of rulers,* We raise Our prayers and We call on all Christian people together, to pray with increasing fervor and union, that the Lord may inspire in all *thoughts of peace and not of affliction,* and together with the thoughts of peace, the noble purpose to actuate them and power to carry them out. Thus we shall see happily brought about, to the comfort of all, what Mother Church invokes on the whole world in the prayer which she puts on the lips of her ministers in the liturgy: *Da quæsumus Domine, ut et mundi cursus pacifice nobis tuo ordine dirigatur et Ecclesia tua tranquilla devotione laetetur. . . .*

OFFICIAL INTERPRETATION BY CARDINAL GASPARRI, SECRETARY OF STATE, OF THE LETTER, *Quando nel Principio.*[77]

Further explanation of the Pope's ideas on reparations and the occupation of the Ruhr.

June 29, 1923

837. . . . . . . His spiritual fatherhood, which embraces all peoples, does not permit the Sovereign Pontiff to remain indifferent to the present evils and to the threat of even greater evils which the future holds; it urges him to profit by every occasion which offers itself in order to collaborate in some way in the necessary task of pacifying and restoring in Christ, nations and individuals, in accord with their desires.

838. Reflecting on the heavy responsibility which weighs upon him at the present hour, upon him as well as upon those who hold

[76] *James,* I, 17.
[77] Original French, *Documentation Catholique,* v. 10, cc. 70-71 (July 21, 1923).

the destiny of nations in their hands, the Holy Father implores them once again to examine the various questions, and in particular the problem of reparations, in that Christian spirit which does not separate the demands of justice from those of social charity. With a view to dissipating any future misunderstandings, let us see what the demands of justice and social charity are according to the papal document; let us give a brief commentary on the text itself, but let us scrupulously respect the sense of the text.

839. In pursuance of the rule laid down in the letter of the Pope, Germany, the debtor nation—by asking for an impartial judgment on the limits of its own ability to pay, engaging itself the while implicitly to put the judges honestly in possession of the facts and furnishing them with every means of exercising a genuine and exact check—admits its obligation to make reparation to the extent that this is possible for the damages caused to populations and regions once prosperous and flourishing.

840. At the same time, on their side, the creditors—the Powers of the Entente, above all France and Belgium, who are more specially interested—certainly have the right to demand of the debtor, reparation for the damages suffered but not beyond the limits of its ability to pay. In other words, they cannot demand of Germany what it would not be able to give without exhausting its own resources and its own capacity for production; such a demand would be contrary to justice and to social charity, as also to the interests not only of the debtor but even of the creditors themselves, and would entail the danger of grave social upheavals and of bitterness which would constitute a continual menace of new and more disastrous conflagrations.

841. As a matter of fact, the creditors do not present such demands, but they deny the sincerity of Germany's new proposals and are of the opinion that the reparations now demanded, after the successive reductions already made, do not exceed the solvency of Germany, without there being any need of proving their contention by making the estimate and the check-up which the Germans demand. These are questions which must be the subject of diplomatic conversations in the near future. The Holy See neither can nor wishes to interfere here; it is sufficient for her to have recalled the principles of justice and charity which God Himself has charged her with conserving and teaching to the world.

842. There is reason to hope that in a friendly way or by means of an expert appraisement and of the check-up demanded by Germany, the Powers will arrive at the fixation of the amount which Germany can and must pay as reparations; and they will succeed in this if they are animated by *thoughts of peace and not of affliction,* to use the Biblical expression quoted in the Pope's letter.

843. This point made, there is also another, equally important, which the pontifical document touches upon, and it is that of guarantees. The Holy Father recognizes the right of the creditors to obtain guarantees proportioned to the amount of their credit and assuring its payment, on which payment depend interests that are equally vital for them. Actually territorial occupations are the gage or guarantee; but the Holy Father leaves to the creditors themselves the duty of deciding whether, in order to secure the payments, it is necessary to maintain territorial occupations which impose heavy sacrifices on the populations of the occupied territories and upon the occupying Powers themselves, and if it would not be preferable to substitute, even if it were only by degrees, other guarantees equally efficacious but less odious to the people.

844. If the Powers would adopt the suggestions of the Holy Father, the occupations would gradually lose some of their rigor, they would be more easily borne by the people and would be progressively reduced until they would be totally taken away. And then, but only then, one could arrive at last at the sincere peace among nations which is also a necessary condition of that economic restoration so ardently desired by all. . . . . . .

ENCYCLICAL *Studiorum Ducem* ON ST. THOMAS AQUINAS.[78]

The Summa Theologica contains the doctrinal basis for a real "League of Nations."

June 29, 1923

845. . . . . . . Hence, in the second part of the *Summa Theologica,* those teachings are famous which regard the paternal or domestic rule, the legal rule of State or nation, the law of peoples, peace, war, justice and dominion, laws and their observance, the

---

[78] Translation from *The Catholic Mind,* v. 21, pp. 311-312 (August 22, 1923). Original Latin, *A.A.S.,* v. 15, p. 319 (July 5, 1923).

duty of providing for private necessity as for public prosperity, and all this as well in the natural as in the supernatural order. Because, if privately and publicly and in the mutual relations of nation with nation, these precepts are preserved holily and inviolately, nothing else is required for that conciliating "Peace of Christ in the Reign of Christ" which the whole world so much desires.

846. It is, therefore, to be hoped that the doctrines of Aquinas, concerning the ruling of peoples and the laws which establish their relations with one another, may be better known, since they contain the true foundations of that which is termed the "League of Nations." . . . . . .

TELEGRAM OF CARDINAL GASPARRI, SECRETARY OF STATE, TO ARCHBISHOP PACELLI, APOSTOLIC NUNCIO IN MUNICH.[79]

Pius XI condemns acts of sabotage under the color of passive resistance.

July 1, 1923

847. The Holy Father, in his letter, is endeavoring to bring the Powers to a friendly understanding and asks for the suspension of everything that might hinder it. He has been bitterly grieved to hear that in the occupied territories acts of sabotage and of wrong-doing in other ways are being committed under color of passive resistance. His Holiness charges Your Excellency to act energetically to the end that the Government may once and for all condemn such criminal resistance, as the Holy Father himself condemns it.

LETTER *In Litteris* TO CARDINAL LA FONTAINE, PATRIARCH OF VENICE.[80]

The nations are still kept apart by quarrels.

July 15, 1923

848. . . . But assuredly nothing would give Us greater joy than that the quarrels which still keep nations apart should be settled

---

[79] Translation from *The Tablet*, v. 142, p. 49 (July 14, 1923). Original Italian, *L'Osservatore Romano* (July 2, 1923).
[80] Original Latin, *A.A.S.,* v. 15, p. 498 (October 1, 1923).

in the mutual kiss of justice and peace. But to come to the point which more immediately furnished the reason for writing, We were glad to hear that you had assembled at Venice to discuss and prepare the decrees of the Provincial Council which you will soon hold. The enactment of these laws will be of greatest advantage to each one of your dioceses, We predict, on account of the love for souls and skill in administration in which you excel. Both these qualities assuredly will have the result that the laws will be precisely thought out and most fittingly put into practice. Nevertheless, since you yourself sought the efficacy of Our blessing as a support for the task you have undertaken, We both praise your sentiments of filial devotion, and call down the Divine Blessing upon the Council of this Ecclesiastical Province which is soon to be convened. And We wish and desire that the clergy and laity of the Province of Venice, who have ever been known for their purity of faith and devotion to religion, will gladly respond to the attention and care of their bishops by submission and obedience. . . .

LETTER OF CARDINAL GASPARRI, SECRETARY OF STATE, TO MR. JOHN EPPSTEIN, AN OFFICER OF THE LEAGUE OF NATIONS UNION.[81]

*The Vatican's attitude toward participation in the •
League of Nations.*

August 11, 1923

849. . . . . . . The project[82] could be accepted only in the sense that the Holy See would be at the disposal of the League for matters coming within its competence; that is to say, for the elucidation of questions of principle in regard to morality and public international law, and also to give help to the League's relief work, where its [the Holy See's] intervention would be of value to suffering peoples. On this occasion I feel that I must tell you how much the Holy Father appreciates the zeal with which, as an officer of the League of Nations Union, you uphold Catholic principles in all circumstances. . . .

[81] Original English, Eppstein, *The Catholic Tradition of the Law of Nations,* p. 320.
[82] Mr. Eppstein had suggested that diplomatic relations might be established, to the mutual advantage of both, between the Council of the League and the Holy See.

BRIEF *Post Immanes* GRANTING INDULGENCES TO "THE EUCHA-
RISTIC UNION FOR THE PEACE OF CHRIST THROUGH THE
RESTORATION OF THE KINGDOM OF CHRIST."[83]

*Even though the war has ended, mutual enmities and
internal disputes remain.*

August 25, 1923

850. Now after the vast ruins of that terrible war, in which all
of Europe was enkindled, while internal disputes are still in evidence, and also the mutual enmities of nations remain, even though
the sound of cannons has been stilled, in Our opinion there is
nothing more efficacious for the salvation of Christian peoples than
the restoration on earth of the true peace of Christ. Consequently,
it was with much joy that We discovered in the city of Rome, in
the Patriarchal Basilica of St. Mary Major, that a pious society of
the faithful had been canonically organized under the title: "Peace
of Christ in the Kingdom of Christ" or "The Eucharistic Union
for the Peace of Christ through the Restoration of the Kingdom of
Christ." The aim of this movement is to labor spiritually for the
peace of the world, in keeping with the spirit of the Gospels and
the admonitions of the Roman Pontiffs, especially by a fervent devotion to the Holy Eucharist, the Sacrament of Divine Love. . . .

LETTER *Prope Adsunt* TO CARDINAL POMPILI, VICAR OF ROME.[84]

*Catholics must pray for all victims of the war without
distinction of nationality, class or party.*

October 21, 1923

851. . . . While none of those who have passed to the other
life can be forgotten by Our charity as the Common Father of all,
yet at this All Souls' Day Our thoughts turn at once to those
innumerable multitudes who, during the last few years, were killed
during the war or who died from wounds or illness which it caused,
or who fell during the civil wars that have followed upon the death-
struggle in Europe. Let Us add, too, that Our thoughts turn especially to those who, as We have reason to think, now find them-

---

[83] Original Latin, *Il Monitore Ecclesiastico*, v. 36, p. 33 (February, 1924).
[84] Original Latin, *Actes de Pie XI*, v. 1, pp. 288-290.

selves deprived of tributes of affection and help from prayer, because those whom they held most dear neglect them. . . .

852. Those who have died in the embrace of the Lord have already lost all resentment and hatred. United forever in the grace and the love of Christ, they wait only to be raised to that glory which is reserved for the children of God from every people, tribe and nation. We want Catholics to pray for all those who have died because of the war or the dissensions which followed it, without distinction of nationality, class or party. This universal communion of prayers must be brought about in order that the blessed vision of peace may be quickened for these, Our beloved children, and in order that charity, which is the bond of perfection, having been planted more deeply in the souls of men on earth, "The Peace of Christ in the Kingdom of Christ" may dawn and hasten to appear. . . .

ALLOCUTION *Il Benvenuto a Voi* TO THE KING OF SPAIN.[85]

Peace and unity, prosperity and glory are the fruit of "The Peace of Christ in the Kingdom of Christ."

November 19, 1923

853. . . . . . . Tell your people that in that Divine Heart in which you have placed them We find them again, and every day shall find them in Our daily approach to our Sacramental Lord; and tell them, too, that of that Heart, Breath and Life of the universe, We pray and shall pray, as We do for the King and the Royal Family, for every grace and every gift of peace and unity, prosperity and glory. And if there be any among you, Our poor but ever dear children, who do not wish to approach the Divine Heart, tell them that for that very reason We turn toward them with a more ardent sentiment of paternal love Our thoughts and affection, such as the Divine Shepherd turned to the sheep far off, praying for the unity of the Fold. Peace and unity, prosperity and glory, these gifts will come all together, as a cortège of the heavenly Queen, when there comes "The Peace of Christ in the Kingdom of Christ." Peace and unity, prosperity and glory—no one of these gifts, Our heart

[85] Translation from *The Tablet*, v. 142, p. 678 (December 1, 1923). Original Italian, *Civiltà Cattolica*, 1923, v. 4, pp. 465-466 (November 24, 1923).

assures Us, will be lacking to your people if, under your guidance and following your example, they remain and ever go forward on the roads which their fathers marked out and sowed with such splendor of examples to be imitated; if, with the perpetual regrowth in the children of their fathers' Faith and piety, Our holy Catholic Religion, the uniquely complete expression of Christianity and all its life-giving energies, can continue to carry, in the laws and in the school and by these roads—the only true ones which can lead to the end—in society, in the family, in public and private life, its salutary influx of holiness and real civilization, of science and art, of concord in minds and hearts. . . . . . .

ALLOCUTION *Ex Quo Proximum* TO THE COLLEGE OF CARDINALS.[86]

The Pope appeals for aid in helping the post-war suffering of Europe.

December 20, 1923

854. . . . . . . And first, as regards the conditions of the peoples, in foreign and home affairs, as far as concerns peace, on which Our anxiety has been shown so often, you see in very truth no great improvement. The Letter, known to you, which under the impulse of paternal love We sent to Our beloved son, Pietro Gasparri, Cardinal Secretary of State, in the endeavor to remedy in some sort the terrible ills afflicting Central Europe, although not entirely fruitless—for, indeed, something has been done in the sense We indicated—did not have the result for which We had the right to hope. We did indeed see some result from Our insistent prayer for kindness and humanity, but there still remains bitter enmity in men's minds; there remain, and indeed increase, poverty and need of every sort by which populations afflicted by the war are harrowed, to relieve which, now especially that winter approaches bringing hunger in its train, that same Cardinal has appealed in Our name, through the Nuncios and Legates of the Apostolic See, to the nations best provided with foodstuffs, asking them to alleviate the suffering to the best of their ability.

[86] Translation from *The Tablet*, v. 142, p. 841 (December 29, 1923). Original Latin, *A.A.S.*, v. 15, pp. 605-606 (December 31, 1923).

855. That Our plea for pity will have satisfactory result for those in need, We feel assured, and not without reason; for having, more than once before now, called for the help of others on behalf of the peoples who have fallen into the worst suffering through the war, Our appeal was never made in vain; indeed, the measure of generous assistance that came in response was marvelous. Through this generosity, for which here once more We express all the gratitude that it deserves, We have been enabled to snatch almost from the jaws of death numbers who, in Central Europe and even more in the Near East and the Far East, too, were dying through famine and terrible calamities. We wish it were given to Us in the same way to comfort with opportune help, as We would like to do, those brave men who are suffering scandalous ill-treatment on account of their steadfast attachment to the Catholic Faith. . . .

ALLOCUTION *Amplissimum Consessum Vestrum* TO THE COL-LEGE OF CARDINALS.[87]

Religion suffers much from war and national unrest.

March 24, 1924

856. . . . . . . Although in the uncertainty and suspense prevailing in Europe, there still remains a considerable amount of trouble and difficulty, it seems, nevertheless, that both in the several States and in international relations, a somewhat happier condition of affairs is maturing; and from this We trust that some advantage will accrue to religion which has suffered so much from the past unrest in national affairs and in the minds of men. . . . . . .

857. Rightly, therefore, Venerable Brethren, we may all be lifted up with the hope that the course of this year of expiation[88] may do so much to carry forward the Kingdom of God and to promote peace among men that "The Peace of Christ in the Kingdom of Christ," which We have most ardently desired and sought with prayers and sighs, may shine forth sooner than We had anticipated. . . . . . .

[87] Translation from *The Tablet*, v. 143, p. 460 (April 5, 1924). Original Latin, *A.A.S.*, v. 16, pp. 127-129 (April 1, 1924).
[88] The approaching Holy Year of 1925.

Bull *Infinita Dei Misericordia* PROCLAIMING THE JUBILEE OF 1925.[89]

> *In this Jubilee the pilgrims are asked to pray for peace among nations.*

May 29, 1924

858. . . . . . . True it is that Catholicism has made no small progress in the most recent times, and that the multitudes—who have learned from long experience that without God it is vain to hope for better things and peace of soul — are showing a more burning thirst for religion; but it is still necessary that the appetites of the peoples and the immoderate and unjust desires of the nations be curbed according to the precepts of the Gospel, and that men re-unite themselves in divine charity. Never can this habit of brotherly love among the peoples be restored, never can there be lasting peace, unless that charity—too long extinguished, indeed entirely forgotten, as a result of the last war—be once more taken to heart by the peoples and taken as inspiration by Governments. There is no one who will not realize how the Holy Year can help toward this pacification of individuals and peoples and how opportune the moment is. What could bring individuals and peoples together better than that a great multitude of pilgrims should come together from every part of the world in Rome, this second country of the Catholic nations, should gather round the Common Father, approach in holy freedom of association that Cement of Union, the Most Blessed Eucharist, and there reach up to and increase that spirit of charity which the sacred monuments of Rome record and so wonderfully put into the hearts of all as a characteristic note of all Christians? . . . . . .

859. You know, beloved children, what are, in general, the intentions of the Roman Pontiff; this Jubilee, however, gives Us occasion to ask of Almighty God something in particular which you, too, will ask together with Us. We mean peace, not so much the peace written in treaties as that impressed on souls, that which must be restored among the peoples. It may not indeed be so far off as it was in past times; nevertheless, it is farther off than Our

[89] Translation from *The Tablet*, v. 143, pp. 769-770 (June 7, 1924). Original Latin, *A.A.S.*, v. 16, pp. 211-213 (June 2, 1924).

hopes and the hopes of all would desire. If, then, you who live in Rome and you who come here, with your souls purified of sin and lit up by charity, pray at the tombs of the Apostles for such a precious blessing, shall it not be that we may hope that Christ, the Prince of Peace, Who once calmed with a gesture the waves of the Sea of Galilee, moved at last with pity for His people, may ordain that the storms, by which Europe has been overcome now for so long, may be checked and calmed? . . . . . .

ALLOCUTION *Nostis Qua Praecipue* TO THE COLLEGE OF CARDINALS.[90]

His Holiness sends alms to Russia for relief of the starving masses, although he completely condemns Communism.

December 18, 1924

860. . . . . . . On Our part We have decided, as far as it is possible to do so, to continue, as We have in the past, to help the Russians, both those who are living in Russia and those who are exiles and who are afflicted with a heavier cross. To more than one, We may seem in some way, by this charity toward the Russian people which We have mentioned,[91] to have helped a form of government which is so far from meriting Our approval that in spite of the fact that We have striven, with might and main, for so long a time to alleviate the many and great evils which exist among these same Russians, We consider it part of the duty of Universal Fatherhood committed to Us by God, to admonish and earnestly to beseech all in the Lord, but especially the rulers of nations, that as lovers of prosperity and peace and as promoters of the sanctity of the family and of human dignity, they make a united and serious effort to protect themselves and their people from the very grave and certain dangers and losses arising from Socialism and Communism, as they are called, using, however, at the same time, the necessary means and care to better the lot of workingmen and, in general, of all men in humble condition. For this We pray unceasingly to

[90] Original Latin, *A.A.S.*, v. 16, pp. 494-495 (December 31, 1924).
[91] Pius XI sent several million dollars to Russia for the sick and starving peasants. Cf. Hughes, *Pope Pius the Eleventh*, p. 164.

Almighty God, the Lord of nations and the Saviour of peoples, and We earnestly ask that all the faithful in the whole world pray with Us during the Holy Jubilee Year. . . . . . .

LETTER OF CARDINAL GASPARRI, SECRETARY OF STATE, TO EUGÈNE DUTHOIT, PRESIDENT OF THE SEMAINE SOCIALE OF LYONS.[92]

Society has denied the concept of lawful authority and, therefore, struggles between the disorder of license and a desperate recourse to violence.

July 16, 1925

861. . . . . . . The program has authority as its subject, and this is, without a doubt, from the viewpoint of social science, one of the most vital and comprehensive questions; it is also one of the most opportune questions of our day when we see human society, because it has denied or falsified the concept of authority, struggling between the contrary consequences of the error, between the disorder of license and of anarchy, and the desperate recourse to violence, the last expedient for maintaining some kind of order, when moral force has ceased to exercise its beneficent rule. Catholic doctrine keeps its steady balance between these two extremes; it does not cease to recognize and support authority, properly understood, which is, by that very fact, always reconcilable with sane liberty and public prosperity. . . . . . .

ENCYCLICAL *Quas Primas* ON THE KINGSHIP OF CHRIST.[93]

If all men recognize Christ as King there will be peace among individuals and among nations.

December 11, 1925

862. In the first Encyclical Letter[94] which We addressed at the beginning of Our Pontificate to the bishops of the Universal Church, We referred to the chief causes of the difficulties under which mankind was laboring. And We remember saying that these manifold

---

[92] Original French, *Documentation Catholique*, v. 14, c. 413 (September 26, 1925).
[93] Translation from *The Kingship of Christ* (C.T.S. Pamphlet), pp. 3-18. Original Latin, *A.A.S.*, v. 17, pp. 593-605 (December 28, 1925).
[94] *Ubi Arcano Dei*, December 23, 1922; see *supra* nn. 758-823.

evils in the world were due to the fact that the majority of men had thrust Jesus Christ and His holy law out of their lives; that these had no place either in private affairs or in politics: and We said further that, as long as individuals and States refused to submit to the rule of our Saviour, there would be no really hopeful prospect of a lasting peace among nations. Men must look for "The Peace of Christ in the Kingdom of Christ"; and this We promised to do as far as lay in Our power. In the Kingdom of Christ, that is, it seemed to Us that peace could not be more effectually restored nor fixed upon a firmer basis than through the restoration of the Empire of our Lord. . . . . . .

863. When once men recognize, both in private and in public life, that Christ is King, society will at last receive the great blessings of real liberty, well-ordered discipline, peace and harmony. Our Lord's regal office invests the human authority of princes and rulers with a religious significance; it ennobles the citizen's duty of obedience. It is for this reason that St. Paul, while bidding wives revere Christ in their husbands, and slaves respect Christ in their masters, warns them to give obedience to them not as to men, but as to the vicegerents of Christ; for it is not meet that men redeemed by Christ should serve their fellow men. *You are bought with a price; be not made the bond-slaves of men.*[95] If princes and magistrates duly elected are filled with the persuasion that they rule, not by their own right, but by the mandate and in the place of the Divine King, they will exercise their authority piously and wisely; they will make laws and administer them, having in view the common good and also the human dignity of their subjects. The result will be order, peace and tranquillity, for there will be no longer any cause of discontent. Men will see in their king or in their rulers men like themselves, perhaps unworthy or open to criticism, but they will not on that account refuse obedience if they see reflected in them the authority of Christ, God and Man. Peace and harmony, too, will result; for with the spread and the universal extension of the Kingdom of Christ men will become more and more conscious of the link that binds them together, and thus many conflicts will be either prevented entirely or at least their bitterness will be diminished.

864. If the Kingdom of Christ, then, receives, as it should, all

[95] I *Corinthians,* VII, 23.

nations under its sway, there seems no reason why We should despair of seeing that peace which the King of Peace came to bring on earth—He Who came to reconcile all things, Who came not to be ministered unto but to minister, Who, though Lord of all, gave Himself to us as a model of humility, and with His principal law united the precept of charity; Who said also: *My yoke is sweet and my burden light.*[96] Oh, what happiness would be Ours if all men, individuals, families and nations, would but let themselves be governed by Christ. "Then at length," to use the words addressed by Our Predecessor, Pope Leo XIII, twenty-five years ago, to the bishops of the Universal Church,[97] "will many ills be cured; then will the law regain its former authority, peace with all its blessings be restored. Men will sheathe their swords and lay down their arms when all freely acknowledge and obey the authority of Christ, and every tongue confesses that the Lord Jesus Christ is in the glory of God, the Father." That these blessings may be abundant and lasting in Christian society, it is necessary that the Kingship of our Saviour should be as widely as possible recognized and understood, and to this end nothing would serve better than the institution of a special feast in honor of the Kingship of Christ. . . . . . .

865. If We ordain that the whole Catholic world shall revere Christ as King, We shall minister to the need of the present day, and at the same time provide an excellent remedy for the plague which now infects society. We refer to the plague of secularism, its errors and impious activities. This evil spirit, as you are well aware, Venerable Brethren, has not come into being in one day; it has long lurked beneath the surface. The Empire of Christ over all nations was rejected. The right which the Church has from Christ Himself, to teach mankind, to make laws, to govern peoples in all that pertains to their eternal salvation, that right was denied. Then gradually the Religion of Christ came to be likened to false religions and to be placed ignominiously on the same level with them. It was then put under the power of the State and tolerated more or less at the whim of princes and rulers. Some men went further, and wished to set up in the place of God's Religion a natural religion consisting in some instinctive affection of the heart. There were even some nations who thought they could dispense

---

[96] *Matthew*, XI, 30.
[97] Encyclical *Annum Sacrum*, May 25, 1899; see *supra* nn. 214-216.

with God, and that their religion should consist in impiety and the neglect of God. The rebellion of individuals and of nations against the authority of Christ has produced deplorable effects. We lamented these in the Encyclical *Ubi Arcano;* We lament them to-day: the seeds of discord sown far and wide; those bitter enmities and rivalries between nations, which still hinder so much the cause of peace; that insatiable greed which is so often hidden under a pretense of public spirit and patriotism, and gives rise to so many private quarrels; a blind and immoderate selfishness, making men seek nothing but their own comfort and advantage, and measure everything by these; no peace in the home, because men have forgotten, or neglect their duty; the unity and stability of the family undermined; society, in a word, shaken to its foundations and on the way to ruin. We firmly hope, however, that the Feast of the Kingship of Christ, which in future will be yearly observed, may hasten the return of society to our loving Saviour. . . . . . .

ALLOCUTION *Jam Annus* TO THE COLLEGE OF CARDINALS.[98]

> *Reconciliation with God is the best preparation for peace among peoples.*

December 14, 1925

866. . . . . . . From which happy story[99] derives the hope, confident because well founded . . . of much precious aid for true peace among the peoples and between the peoples, one of Our intentions given to the people for their prayers in this Holy Year. This We add because nothing could be more clearly true than that the best preparation for peace among the peoples is their reconciliation with Almighty God. . . .

867. No less evident is it that a wonderful harmony governs events from on High when, on the one hand, the Holy Year brings the peoples together as brothers in the charity of Christ and of the Church and sets all the world praying for "The Peace of Christ in the Kingdom of Christ," and, on the other, such notable advance is made and solemn agreements concluded in the peaceful directions

---

[98] Translation from *The Tablet,* v. 146, p. 879 (December 26, 1925). Original Latin, *A.A.S.,* v. 17, pp. 639-642 (December 28, 1925).

[99] The story of the Holy Year which the Pope had just related.

so often indicated and recommended by the Vicar of Christ as Father of all. . . . . . .

868. You see, then, Venerable Brothers, that We had reason for saying that Our joy in this Holy Year was tinged with sadness. And not from one cause only. While appreciating in fullest measure everything which tends to prevent or even only attenuate class warfare and to co-ordinate the work of all citizens for the common good, We regret that, while in these days laws are being framed in what are called economic and social matters, it has not been thought possible to take full and due account of Catholic teaching and of the Catholic action which is charged to develop that teaching and put it in practice, above all in the very field in which both teaching and action are specially necessary and salutary; for there are laws of liberty which the Church, by reason of its office, is bound to safeguard and vindicate. The Church, by its teaching and in its institution, is as far removed from that license and anarchy to which Liberalism and Socialism, which the Church condemns, inevitably lead society, as from every political conception which makes society or the State an end in itself, from which naturally, fatally indeed, it finishes in absorbing or destroying private rights, with results clearly no less calamitous. . . . . . .

APOSTOLIC CONSTITUTION *Servatoris Jesu Christi* EXTENDING THE JUBILEE TO THE WHOLE WORLD.[100]

The Pope requests the bishops to instruct the people to pray for peace.

December 25, 1925

869. . . . . . . Moreover, the same bishops shall instruct the faithful entrusted to them that they must pray for those intentions which We announced in proclaiming the Jubilee for the city of Rome, namely: for the spread of the Catholic Faith, for peace and harmony among nations, for a solution of the problems besetting the Holy Places in Palestine, which will respect the rights of the Catholic Church. . . . . . .

---

[100] Original Latin, *A.A.S.*, v. 17, p. 612 (December 28, 1925).

LETTER *Ab Ipsis Pontificatus Primordiis* TO THE VICARS APOSTOLIC OF CHINA.[101]

The Church is not hostile to national aspirations.

June 15, 1926

870. ... . The most holy work of the missions would be still more fruitful, if one could destroy a prejudice, from day to day more tenacious and wider spread, notably amongst young people badly informed in whose mind it takes root: We refer to the prejudice which attributes to the action of the Catholic Church and her missionaries, not the service of religion, but that of the interests and the politics of foreign nations. Whence one concludes that the Church is hostile to the independence of the peoples whom she evangelizes, as well as to the free exercise of their national aspirations. . . . . .

LETTER OF CARDINAL GASPARRI, SECRETARY OF STATE, TO M. EUGÈNE DUTHOIT, PRESIDENT OF THE SEMAINE SOCIALE OF HAVRE.[102]

The peace that exists is more nominal than real.

June 29, 1926

871. . . . . . . The Holy Father, justly concerned over the state of affairs created by the recent world-wide conflict and conscious of the grave obligations incumbent upon him by reason of his Universal Fatherhood, has already set forth at different times the means best suited to improve the condition of international relationships and to effect in the greatest measure possible the best understanding between the different peoples.

872. It is, therefore, with peculiar satisfaction that His Holiness congratulates you upon the selection of the program for the forthcoming deliberations of the Social Week, for the selection made proves how deeply you are penetrated with the importance of these problems which are so intimately bound up with the prosperity of the nations.

[101] Translation from Schaefer, *A Papal Peace Mosaic*, p. 42. Original Latin, *A.A.S.*, v. 18, p. 304 (August 2, 1926).
[102] Original French, *Documentation Catholique*, v. 16, c. 220 (August 14, 1926).

873. Even while aware of the many difficulties which this program imposes upon you, the Holy Father never doubts but that the noble intellects who have consecrated themselves to the task will, by their conscientious studies and their practical solutions for each problem, bring it about that society takes a big step forward toward that social peace which is still the object of so many desires and the universal aspiration of the nations.

874. Though nations are divided by their respective boundaries, this does not mean that they must divest themselves of interest in one another's progress and in their mutual well-being. Because this truth has been lost sight of, the most disastrous consequences have resulted; and it is not hard to see that even the peace recently concluded has been more nominal than real, since it has not done away with the serious difficulties that face us at this moment. Being the outcome of this painful problem, the program of the 18th Social Week of France is also more than a promise of a better future. As the principal aim of these "Weeks" has been to study this problem in the light of the direction of the Holy See, the Holy Father does not doubt of their success, since they will conform rigorously to the teachings of the Vicar of Christ, who alone is able to bring about for nations the desire of Christ expressed to His apostles in the Cenacle: *Pax Vobis*. . . . . . .

ENCYCLICAL *Mortalium Animos* ON TRUE RELIGIOUS UNITY.[103]

There is a widespread desire for peace and unity among nations.

January 6, 1928

875. The will to strengthen and to diffuse for the common good of human society that brotherhood in which we are all closely united by the bonds of a common nature and origin has never perhaps so taken hold of men's minds as in our times. When nations do not fully enjoy the blessings of peace, and old and new discords break forth into mutiny and conflict; when, indeed, it is impossible to settle the numerous controversies that strike at the peace and prosperity of peoples without the harmonious action of those who govern States and rule and promote their interests, it is easy to

[103] Translation from *The Promotion of True Religious Unity* (N.C.W.C. pamphlet), pp. 1-2. Original Latin, *A.A.S.,* v. 20, p. 5 (January 10, 1928).

understand, and all the more so now that all accept the unity of mankind, how it is that, impelled by the desire for universal brother-hood, many should be anxious that the various nations stand ever more closely together. . . . . . .

LETTER OF CARDINAL GASPARRI, SECRETARY OF STATE, TO M. EUGÈNE DUTHOIT, PRESIDENT OF THE SEMAINE SOCIALE OF PARIS.[104]

Justice, united to charity, is the mother of peace.

July 7, 1928

876. . . . . . . In hearts in which the Divine Goodness is mir-rored, justice is steeped in charity; it does not, therefore, instigate against one another groups of men who are still enemies; on the contrary, it reconciles them, for it basically and effectively solves their conflicts. Wherefore, it is to this justice thus animated by charity that His Holiness, Pius XI, in his Encyclical *Ubi Arcano*,[105] has declared that the words of the prophet are applicable: *Opus justitiae pax*.[106] It is justice, inseparably united to charity, which is the mother of peace—a sincere peace which penetrates hearts and tranquilizes them once more, which disposes them mutually to the most fraternal good-will, an enduring peace which corresponds to the wish expressed by Leo XIII, concerning the welfare of society, a fruitful peace wherein the most magnificent progress becomes possible for Christian civilization. . . . . . .

TELEGRAM FROM CARDINAL GASPARRI, SECRETARY OF STATE, TO ARCHBISHOP COSTANTINI, APOSTOLIC DELEGATE TO CHINA.[107]

The Pope rejoices in the establishment of peace which he hopes is founded on charity and justice.

August 1, 1928

877. The Holy Father, who has followed and follows with very great interest the course of events in China, and who has been

---

[104] Original French, *Documentation Catholique*, v. 20, c. 228 (August 18, 1928).
[105] *Cf. supra* nn. 758-823.
[106] *Isaias*, XXXII, 17.
[107] Translation from *The Tablet*, v. 152, pp. 213-214 (August 18, 1928). Original Italian, *A.A.S.*, v. 20, pp. 245-246 (August 1, 1928).

the first to treat China not only on terms of perfect equality, but by an act of sincere and very special sympathy, has consecrated by his own hands at Rome in St. Peter's the first Chinese bishops, gives fervent thanks to God for the conclusion of the civil war, and hopes that the peace thus restored may be enduring and fruitful, within and without, based upon the principles of justice and charity.

878. Through the attainment of this peace, His Holiness trusts that the legitimate rights and aspirations of a people, the most numerous in the world, a people of ancient culture, who have known periods of greatness and splendor in the past, may be fully recognized, and that the Chinese people, persevering in the paths of justice and order, may have a great future opened out before them.

879. The Holy Father desires the Catholic missions to bring their contributions to the peace, well-being and progress of China, and in accordance with his letter of June 15, 1926, *Ab Ipsis Pontificatus Primordiis,* directed to the Chinese Ordinaries, he again repeats that the Catholic Church professes, teaches and preaches respect and obedience to lawfully constituted authority, and demands for her missionaries and faithful the security and liberty of the common rights.

880. To the same Ordinaries His Holiness recommends, as the crown of their evangelical work, the organization and development of Catholic Action amongst the faithful of both sexes, more especially amongst the young, that by prayer, good words and works they may bring their due contribution to the peace, well-being and social greatness of their country, by making better known the salutary principles of the Gospel and assisting the bishops and priests in the spread of the Christian ideal, and of individual and social Christian charity. Finally, His Holiness reiterates his augury for the peace and prosperity of China, and, imploring Almighty God to grant his prayer in abundant measure, imparts to all his fatherly and Apostolic Benediction.

LETTER *Quae Nobis* TO CARDINAL BERTRAM, ARCHBISHOP OF BRESLAU.[108]

Catholic Action contributes to the peace and security of human society.

November 13, 1928

881. . . . . . . Therefore, it cannot be said that Catholic Action neglects the true welfare of the State, since this welfare pertains, just as the promotion of every kind of public prosperity, to the scope of Christian charity. Is not that welfare wherein is contained the immediate end of civil society furthered by Catholic Action when it requires that its members respect legitimate authority and obey the laws, and that they guard and defend those things in which the well-being and happiness of the people consist, such as the integrity of moral life, the protection of the home, and agreement between all classes, in short, everything that contributes to the peace and security of human society? . . . . . .

ADDRESS *Ella Ha Avuto* ON THE OCCASION WHEN THE STATUE OF BENEDICT XV WAS UNVEILED IN ST. PETER'S.[109]

Benedict XV relied greatly on prayer to bring peace to Europe.

November 22, 1928

882. . . . . . . Truly this monument recalls before all else that vast and devastating event which occupied all, it can well be said, of the Pontificate of Benedict XV; that event in which it appeared that the fierce fury which took hold of the world wanted to drag it all to a terrible suicide. There returns to Our memory that day when we were still not far from the beginning of his Pontificate, yet already some months advanced into the terrible World War— and We almost see and hear it again—when to the Sacred College, to the prelates come to comfort him with their homage and festive wishes, and especially to the Dean of the Sacred College, who, acting as interpreter of the whole gathering, nay of the entire world, begged him not to stop crying out his word of peace, the

---

[108] Translation from Loeffler, *Directives for Catholic Action*, p. 16. Original Latin, *A.A.S.*, v. 20, pp. 386-387 (December 3, 1928).

[109] Original Italian, *Il Monitore Ecclesiastico*, v. 41, pp. 61-62 (February, 1929).

afflicted Pontiff responded: "No, Lord Cardinal,"—We seem to hear him again because We, too, were present—"We will not speak more to men: men do not listen to Us: We will speak to God in prayer— and let all pray with Us." And from that day more than ever he sank—that is exactly the word—in prayer, seeking in it not so much his own comfort but that help which he saw clearly could not come from men but only from God; and he prayed and prayed; they knew it well who lived more intimately with him; all know it and particularly those who, like Ourself, saw him come here to this very basilica to pray, and exactly as he is portrayed in this monument, having laid aside all the ornamentation of the solemn liturgical vestments, as if in the garment of penance, in the act of prayer and supplication. And it is well thus; the solemn vestments would not have ornamented so much as crushed the slender and frail figure. Thus all see the dear and beloved fatherly figure, and it seems as though the internal force of prayer diffuses itself and appears through the slender form of his body. And in the background which the artist has so aptly placed, there one seems to see the great sorrow of the images and thoughts which anguished the grieved spirit of the Pope in prayer, because certainly while he prayed he saw in his soul the ravished countries and the cities in ashes and the clash of opposing ranks and the mountains of thousands of dead piled one on top of another, and from afar, as the poet would express it, "the misery of the burning city" of Europe and of so great a part of the world. . . . . . .

LETTER *Le Notizie Che* TO THE PRESIDENTS OF BOLIVIA AND PARA-GUAY.[110]

The Pope appeals to both countries to seek a peaceful settlement of their dispute.

December 18, 1928

883. The news that has reached Us concerning the two Republics of Bolivia and Paraguay has deeply grieved Us, as We have reason to fear that the solution of the conflict will be sought by force of arms. Representative upon earth of Him Whose advent brought peace to men of good-will, and as the spiritual Father of

[110] Translation from *The Tablet*, v. 152, p. 895 (December 29, 1928). Original Italian, *L'Osservatore Romano* (December 20, 1928).

both peoples, both alike very dear to Us, We appeal to the Christian sentiments of Your Excellency, of your Government, and of your people that with all your strength you endeavor to spare your country and humanity from the scourge of a war, of which it is always difficult to see the consequences. In this sense We pray to the Most High, and with this augury We send to you, the President, and all your people, Our Paternal Benediction.

ALLOCUTION TO THE COLLEGE OF CARDINALS.[111]
Pius XI rejoices over the return of peaceful relations between Bolivia and Paraguay.

December 24, 1928

884. . . . . . . We have again trembled and prayed before the peril of yet another war, when the memory of the last is still fresh in Our mind—a war between two peoples and two Republics both equally dear to Us. And again behold the Divine Goodness and Mercy gives Us an assurance of returning concord between Our far-distant children. . . . . . .

THE LATERAN TREATY BETWEEN THE HOLY SEE AND THE ITALIAN GOVERNMENT.[112]
The Holy See declares its policy in the field of international relations.

February 11, 1929

885. . . . . . . With regard to the sovereignty pertaining to it in the field of international relations, the Holy See declares that it wishes to remain, and will remain, extraneous to all temporal disputes between nations, and to international congresses convoked for the settlement of such disputes, unless the contending parties make a joint appeal to its mission of peace; nevertheless, it reserves the right in every case to exercise its moral and spiritual power. In consequence of this declaration, the State of the Vatican will always and in every case be considered neutral and inviolable territory. . . . . . .

[111] Translation from *The Tablet*, v. 153, p. 20 (January 5, 1929). Original Italian, *Civiltà Cattolica*, 1929, v. 1, p. 14 (December 28, 1928).
[112] Translation from *Treaty and Concordat between the Holy See and Italy* (N.C.W.C. pamphlet), pp. 10-11. Original Italian, *A.A.S.*, v. 21, p. 220 (June 7, 1929).

ADDRESS *Il Nostro* TO THE LENTEN PREACHERS OF ROME.[113]

Tranquillity is a necessary condition for stable peace and general prosperity.

February 11, 1929

886. . . . . . . Before everything else, We have always wished to be a father dealing with his children, for Our desire is not to make things difficult and complicated, but as easy and simple as possible. Also, We would calm and banish all causes of alarm. We would make wholly unjust and utterly unreasonable all reproaches raised, or to be raised, on the grounds of—We were going to say—superstitious regard for the territorial integrity of the country. It seems to Us that We have followed a course that will benefit all, both now and in the future, by producing greater tranquillity—the first and most indispensable condition for stable peace and general prosperity. . . . . . .

ADDRESS *Vogliamo Anzitutto* TO THE PROFESSORS AND STUDENTS OF THE CATHOLIC UNIVERSITY OF MILAN.[114]

The Lateran Treaty is an important contribution to world peace.

February 13, 1929

887. . . . . . . This is the moment which Divine Providence has chosen to summon Us to accomplish acts and inaugurate events that certainly—as far as human, and not only human but super-natural, foresight can perceive—are destined, We firmly hope and trust, as We have long been convinced, to produce precious fruits for the glory of God and Christ the King, for the honor of Holy Mother Church, for the good of souls, for the good of Italy and of so many dear souls—the dearer to Us as they are the nearer—for the good of the whole world. We cannot but make the obvious reflection that these events are calculated to evoke the sympathy of the entire world, of all upright souls, of all hearts that cherish

[113] Translation from *How the Roman Question Was Settled* (C.T.S. pamphlet), pp. 12-13. Original Italian, *A.A.S.*, v. 21, p. 108 (March 6, 1929).

[114] Translation from *How the Roman Question Was Settled* (C.T.S. pamphlet), pp. 18-19. Original Italian, *A.A.S.*, v. 21, pp. 111-112 (March 6, 1929).

lofty feelings and aspirations because of the great contribution these same events bring to the work of pacification, to that peace which the Divine Jesus has called *His Peace*—"The Peace of Christ in the Kingdom of Christ." . . . . . .

DISCOURSE *Voilà une Magnifique Audience* TO THE DIPLOMATIC CORPS.[115]

> *To establish peace on a firm foundation, there must be not only juridical but also moral guarantees.*

March 9, 1929

888. This is a magnificent audience, an audience, We do not hesitate to say, which surpasses in size and in importance all others. This is not merely a compliment, gentlemen, for from a certain point of view, a real and positive point of view, your joint visit is truly the greatest and most important that could be made to Us, and it is you who suggest this point of view. For it is not only your esteemed and amiable persons that We see. Behind each one of you We cannot help perceiving your respective rulers—kings, presidents, regents—whatever title they may hold, and with them your governments, your peoples, your entire countries, altogether—a vision of a greatness truly apocalyptic, of a world-wide immensity, a *visionem magnam,* a great vision!

889. And you come to thank Us for something which, owing to you, has become rather a new reason for Our gratitude toward you. Indeed it is owing to you, to your good offices, that the communication, which, by the instrumentality of Our Cardinal Secretary of State, We have wished to make to you concerning the events which were about to be accomplished, it is owing to your intelligent and kind transmission and interpretation, that this communication has brought Us the most consoling and also the most desirable proofs of sympathy and fidelity from your States and your peoples. Fidelity and sympathy which have never been belied and have sometimes even been accentuated since the year 1870, but which at the present time, at a point (We can truly say at a turning point) so important in the history of the Holy See, have been expressed in demonstrations so solemn, so grandiose, that they have replaced

[115] Original French, *The Tablet*, v. 153, p. 351 (March 16, 1929).

and surpassed without measure all the guarantees that We could have desired.

890. We say the guarantees that We could have desired, because there are some guarantees that We could in no way desire or accept. This is a distinction which has been forgotten by the numerous dilettantes and amateurs (as your eloquent interpreter has called them) of international law. This distinction goes back to that which arises between juridical and moral guarantees. The juridical guarantee is that which the ancient and solemn language of law translates by defense, protection: *defensio, tutela. Defensio:* defense against the enemy or against the insolvent. Against the enemy? But We are no one's enemy, and We do not believe that We have any other enemies than the enemies of truth and goodness. Defense against the insolvent? But We have believed, and We still believe, in the loyalty and the persevering good-will of those who have shown themselves ready and desirous of negotiating. If not defense, protection? But even less could We accept this: it is the Apostle, St. Paul, who says that even the rich heir *nihil differt a servo . . . . . quamdiu sub tutoribus est.*[116] And whether defense or protection, how could We impose on others such cares and such responsibilities?

891. But if We can speak of juridical guarantees, We can also speak of moral guarantees. Such is, magnificent in its kind, the guarantee (it can also be called a diplomatic guarantee) which you, gentlemen, represent, which you form, and which your eloquent interpreter has so opportunely recalled, so luminously set forth in all the extent and force of its meaning.

892. There is another guarantee which, since the eleventh of February, has continued to fill the country and the entire world. It is this great, incomparable (and perhaps up to the present, never before realized) plebiscite, not only of Italy, but of all parts of the world. There is no exaggeration in these words. We have just received letters and dispatches, not only from all the cities and villages of Italy, not only from all the cities and many villages of all the countries of Europe, but also from the two Americas, the Indies, China, Japan, Australia, New Zealand, from the north, the center, and the south of Africa, from Alaska, from the Mac-Kenzie, from the Hudson, as if there were question of a local

[116] *Galatians,* IV, 1-2.

event. A truly impressive fact, and one that authorizes Us to say that not only the people, all the people of Italy, but the people of the whole world are with Us: a true plebiscite, not only national but world-wide. This is the most imposing guarantee that one can think of or imagine. In this vast and immense plebiscite We cannot fail to recognize and call attention to some voices which have moved Us profoundly. There is first of all the voice of the small number of survivors in your different countries among the brave men who for years, in the spirit of Catholic faith, have put their lives at the disposition and the defense of the Holy See. You will tell these brave men that the Holy Father has prayed and offered Masses for all their dead, who are also Our dead—unforgettable.

893. Another touching voice is that of those who, especially in Italy, have said to Us, "Now we will again fulfill our Easter duty." It is a whole trend, an entire region which is revealed: the region of consciences, the trend of religious pacification; it is the most elevated point of view, infinitely more worthy of consideration than civil and political pacification of a country, although the latter may itself be a great and inestimable treasure. This thought brings Us back once again to the beautiful and dear mountains of Our youth. One must rise to reach the highest points of view; one must reach the tops, the summits: from up there, one no longer sees the pretty valleys, the picturesque houses, the pensive belfries, but the vision becomes infinitely wider and more sublime.

894. We also, at the point at which We have arrived, when We think of the pacification of so many souls, of so many consciences, not only of Italy but of the whole world, cannot but feel the duty of thanking with all Our heart the good God and all men who have given Us the assistance of their good-will in making their contribution—and a contribution which certainly is not indifferent nor of little value—to this great work of pacification. It seems to Us also that We have the right to rejoice at this and to invite everybody to rejoice with Us.

895. There only remains to Us, gentlemen, to give you (as St. Peter, the first Pope, used to say) *what We have*[117] — Our Benediction. We give it with all Our heart to your families, to your countries, to the peoples and Governments that you represent, and to all that each one of you bears in his mind and in his heart.

[117] *Acts,* III, 6.

DISCOURSE *Ecco Una* TO THE STUDENTS OF THE COLLEGE OF MONDRAGONE.[118]

The State must not train its youth to be warriors.

May 14, 1929

896. . . . . . . We shall not say that for the work in the field of education to be accomplished it is necessary, convenient or fitting for the State to rear conquerors brought up to conquer. What is done in one State could also be done throughout the world; and if all the States were to rear conquerors, what would then happen? In this manner one would contribute not to universal peace but to universal war. Unless it were meant (and maybe just this was meant) that one must rear conquerors of truth and virtue, in which case We would most heartily agree. . . . . . .

ENCYCLICAL *Rappresentanti in Terra* ON THE CHRISTIAN EDUCATION OF YOUTH.[119]

Without true Christian education, order, peace and prosperity, whether in the family or in society, will be impossible.

December 31, 1929

897. . . . . . . It is the inalienable right as well as the indispensable duty of the Church, to watch over the entire education of her children, in all institutions, public or private, not merely in regard to the religious instruction there given, but in regard to every other branch of learning and every regulation insofar as religion and morality are concerned.

898. Nor should the exercise of this right be considered undue interference, but rather maternal care on the part of the Church in protecting her children from the grave danger of all kinds of doctrinal and moral evil. Moreover, this watchfulness of the Church not only can create no real inconvenience, but must, on the contrary, confer valuable assistance in the right ordering and well-

[118] Original Italian, *Civiltà Cattolica*, 1929, v. 2, p. 466 (May 25, 1929).
[119] Translation from *The Catholic Mind*, v. 28, pp. 66-85 (February 22, 1930). Original Italian, *A.A.S.*, v. 21, pp. 730-753 (December 31, 1929). The Latin text known as *Divini Illius Magistri* is a translation from the Italian.

being of families and of civil society; for it keeps far away from youth the moral poison which at that inexperienced and changeable age more easily penetrates the mind and more rapidly spreads its baneful effects. For it is true, as Leo XIII has wisely pointed out, that without proper religious and moral instruction "every form of intellectual culture will be injurious; for young people not accustomed to respect God, will be unable to bear the restraint of a virtuous life, and never having learned to deny themselves anything, they will easily be incited to disturb the public order."[120] . . . . . .

899. The family, therefore, holds directly from the Creator the mission and, hence, the right to educate the offspring, a right inalienable because inseparably joined to the strict obligation, a right anterior to any right whatever of civil society and of the State, and therefore, inviolable on the part of any power on earth. . . . . . .

900. It must be borne in mind also that the obligation of the family to bring up children, includes not only religious and moral education, but physical and civic education as well, principally insofar as it touches upon religion and morality. This incontestable right of the family has at various times been recognized by nations anxious to respect the natural law in their civil enactments. Thus, to give one recent example, the Supreme Court of the United States of North America, in a decision on an important controversy, declared that it is not in the competence of the State to fix any uniform standard of education by forcing children to receive instruction exclusively in public schools, and it bases its decision on the natural law: the child is not the mere creature of the State; those who nurture him and direct his destiny have the right, coupled with the high duty, to educate him and prepare him for the fulfillment of his obligations.[121] . . . . . .

901. These rights have been conferred upon civil society by the Author of nature Himself, not by title of fatherhood, as in the case of the Church and of the family, but in virtue of the authority which it possesses to promote the common temporal welfare, which

[120] Encyclical *Nobilissima Gallorum Gens,* February 8, 1884.
[121] "The fundamental theory of liberty upon which all governments in this Union repose excludes any general power of the State to standardize its children by forcing them to accept instruction from public teachers only. The child is not the mere creature of the State; those who nurture him and direct his destiny have the right coupled with the high duty, to recognize and prepare him for additional duties."— U. S. Supreme Court Decision in the Oregon School Case, June 1, 1925.

is precisely the purpose of its existence. Consequently, education cannot pertain to civil society in the same way in which it pertains to the Church and to the family, but in a different way corresponding to its own particular end and object.

902. Now this end and object, the common welfare in the temporal order, consists in that peace and security in which families and individual citizens have the free exercise of their rights, and at the same time enjoy the greatest spiritual and temporal prosperity possible in this life, by the mutual union and co-ordination of the work of all. The function, therefore, of the civil authority residing in the State is twofold, to protect and to foster, but by no means to absorb the family and the individual, or to substitute itself for them. . . . . .

903. In general, then, it is the right and duty of the State to protect, according to the rules of right reason and faith, the moral and religious education of youth, by removing public impediments that stand in the way. In the first place, it pertains to the State, in view of the common good, to promote in various ways the education and instruction of youth. It should begin by encouraging and assisting, of its own accord, the initiative and activity of the Church and the family, whose successes in this field have been clearly demonstrated by history and experience. It should, moreover, supplement their work whenever this falls short of what is necessary, even by means of its own schools and institutions. For the State, more than any other society, is provided with the means put at its disposal for the needs of all, and it is only right that it use these means to the advantage of those who have contributed them.[122]

904. Over and above this, the State can exact, and take measures to secure that all its citizens have the necessary knowledge of their civic and political duties, and a certain degree of physical, intellectual and moral culture, which, considering the conditions of our times, is really necessary for the common good.

905. However, it is clear that in all these ways of promoting education and instruction, both public and private, the State should respect the inherent rights of the Church and of the family concerning Christian education, and, moreover, have regard for distributive justice. Accordingly, unjust and unlawful is any monopoly, educational or scholastic, which, physically or morally, forces fami-

[122] *Cf.* Discourse *Ecco Una* to the students of the College of Mondragone, May 14, 1929.

lies to make use of government schools, contrary to the dictates of their Christian conscience, or contrary even to their legitimate preferences.

906. This does not prevent the State from making due provision for the right administration of public affairs and for the protection of its peace, within or without the realm. These are things which directly concern the public good and call for special aptitudes and special preparation. The State may, therefore, reserve to itself the establishment and direction of schools intended to prepare for certain civic duties and especially for military service, provided it be careful not to injure the rights of the Church or of the family in what pertains to them. It is well to repeat this warning here; for in these days there is spreading a spirit of nationalism which is false and exaggerated, as well as dangerous to true peace and prosperity. Under its influence various excesses are committed in giving a military turn to the so-called physical training of boys (sometimes even of girls, contrary to the very instincts of human nature); or again in usurping unreasonably, on Sunday, the time which should be devoted to religious duties and to family life at home. It is not Our intention, however, to condemn what is good in the spirit of discipline and legitimate bravery promoted by these methods; We condemn only what is excessive, as, for example, violence, which must not be confounded with courage nor with the noble sentiment of military valor in defense of country and public order; or again exaltation of athleticism which even in classic pagan times marked the decline and downfall of genuine physical training. . . . . . .

907. While treating of education, it is not out of place to show here how an ecclesiastical writer, who flourished in more recent times, during the Renaissance, the holy and learned Cardinal Silvio Antoniano, to whom the cause of Christian education is greatly indebted, has set forth most clearly this well-established point of Catholic doctrine. He had been a disciple of that wonderful educator of youth, St. Philip Neri; he was teacher and Latin secretary to St. Charles Borromeo, and it was at the latter's suggestion and under his inspiration that he wrote his splendid treatise on *The Christian Education of Youth*. In it he argues as follows: "The more closely the temporal power of a nation aligns itself with the spiritual, and the more it fosters and promotes the latter, by so

much the more it contributes to the conservation of the common-wealth. For it is the aim of the ecclesiastical authority, by the use of spiritual means, to form good Christians in accordance with its own particular end and object; and in doing this it helps at the same time to form good citizens, and prepares them to meet their obligations as members of a civil society. This follows of necessity because in the City of God, the Holy Roman Catholic Church, a good citizen and an upright man are absolutely one and the same thing. How grave, therefore, is the error of those who separate things so closely united, and who think that they can produce good citizens by ways and methods other than those which make for the formation of good Christians. For, let human prudence say what it likes and reason as it pleases, it is impossible to produce true temporal peace and tranquillity by things repugnant or opposed to the peace and happiness of eternity."[123] . . . . . .

908. Parents, therefore, and all who take their place in the work of education, should be careful to make right use of the authority given them by God, Whose vicars, in a true sense, they are. This authority is not given for their own advantage, but for the proper up-bringing of their children in a holy and filial "fear of God, the beginning of wisdom," on which foundation alone all respect for authority can rest securely; and without which, order, tranquillity and prosperity, whether in the family or in society, will be im-possible. . . . . . .

909. And let no one say that in a nation where there are differ-ent religious beliefs, it is impossible to provide for public instruc-tion otherwise than by neutral or mixed schools. In such a case it becomes the duty of the State; indeed, it is the easier and more reasonable method of procedure, to leave free scope to the initiative of the Church and the family, while giving them such assistance as justice demands. That this can be done to the full satisfaction of families and to the advantage of education and of public peace and tranquillity, is clear from the actual experience of some countries comprising different religious denominations. There the school legislation respects the rights of the family and Catholics are free to follow their own system of teaching in schools that are entirely Catholic. Nor is distributive justice lost sight of, as is evidenced by the financial aid granted by the State to these schools. . . . . . .

[123] *Dell' Educazione Cristiana*, bk. I, c. 43.

LETTER *Ci Commuovono Profondamente* TO CARDINAL POMPILI, VICAR OF ROME.[124]

The Holy Father protests against the persecution in Russia.

February 2, 1930

910. We are profoundly moved by the horrible and criminal sacrileges which are repeated and increased every day against God and the souls of the innumerable population of Russia, all dear to Our heart on account of their great sufferings, and especially the many devout and generous sons of this Holy, Catholic, Apostolic, Roman Church found amongst them, devout and generous even unto heroism and martyrdom.

911. From the beginning of Our Pontificate, following the example of Our Predecessor, We have multiplied Our efforts to arrest this terrible persecution and to avert the grave evils which threaten these peoples. We have also hastened to ask the representatives of the Governments assembled at Geneva to come to a common agreement and declaration, which would have saved Russia and the world from many woes, proclaiming, as a previous condition to any recognition of the Soviet Government, respect for conscience, liberty of worship and the property of the Church.

912. Alas! these three points, useful above all to those ecclesiastical hierarchies separated from Catholic unity, were abandoned in favor of temporal interests, which would have been better safeguarded had the different Governments had regard also for all the rights of God, His kingdom and His justice. Our intervention was rejected which sought to save sacred vessels and icons from destruction and preserve them for their traditional use, things which formed a treasure of sacred art and piety dear to the hearts of all Russians; nevertheless, We had the happiness to secure the withdrawal of a capital process and succor the head of that hierarchy long withdrawn from Catholic unity, the Patriarch Tikhon, while the generous offerings of the Catholic world saved from starvation and a horrible death 150,000 children nourished daily by those sent by Us, until they were compelled to abandon this work of charity by those who preferred to see innocent children die rather than that they should be succored by Christian charity. . . . . . .

[124] Translation from *The Tablet*, v. 155, p. 209 (February 15, 1930). Original Italian, *A.A.S.*, v. 22, pp. 89-90 (February 22, 1930).

ALLOCUTION *Benedetto il Natale* TO THE COLLEGE OF CARDINALS.[125]

> *It is impossible for peace to rule among men so long as*
> *they turn avidly in search of material things.*

December 24, 1930

913. . . . . . . And now, Venerable Brothers and most Beloved Sons, Our wish to you, inspired in Our heart and placed on Our tongue by the solemn and dear feast which We are once again preparing to celebrate: "Peace on earth."—It is a wish come from heaven and first sung by the angels over the cradle of the new-born Eternal King, Who came on earth to bring peace between men and God, between men and men, sacrificing Himself for all, calling back everyone to the Universal Divine Fatherhood and the Universal Human Brotherhood, to the idea and practice of fraternal charity, to a just valuation of and detachment from earthly things, to the search, first and foremost, for spiritual things.

914. What wish could be more timely or more attuned to the universal call for peace, peace? And for this very reason, Our wish is addressed not only to you but to all the world. To all the world because Christ came to save all, but especially to all the beloved sons of the great Catholic family of the Church which Christ came to found. It is the peace brought by Christ, the Peace of Christ; and one is not with Christ and of Christ, save by being in the Catholic Church and with the Catholic Church: *Ubi Ecclesia ibi Christus.*

915. Thereby Catholics are called not only to a wider and more perfect enjoyment of the Peace of Christ but to the strengthening and widening of the Kingdom of Christ, and, therefore, to the strengthening and widening of His peace through the manifold apostolate of word, deed and prayer, so easy to all and so powerful, yes, all powerful with God. The glory and the duty of this apostolate of peace belong principally to Us and to all called to be ministers of the God of Peace. But here is a vast and glorious field for all the Catholic laity, too, whom We unceasingly call upon and ask to share in the hierarchical apostolate. To Catholics of all the world and particularly those who study, labor and pray in Catholic Action,

---

[125] Translation from *Appeals for Peace of Pope Benedict XV and Pope Pius XI* (C.A.I.P. pamphlet), pp. 8-11. Original Italian, *A.A.S.,* v. 22, pp. 533-536 (December 31, 1930).

We turn to-day with this warm invitation and plea. May they all unite in the Peace of Christ and for the Peace of Christ in a full concord of thoughts and emotions, of desires and prayers, of deeds and words—the spoken word, the written word, the printed word— and then an atmosphere of genuine peace, warming and beneficent, will envelop all the world.

916. But We wish you the "Peace of Christ," not a sentimental, confused, unwise pacifism, because that only is true peace that comes from God and that bears the essential and indispensable marks and priceless fruits of true peace. The Church, incomparable teacher, called this to mind a few days ago in enclosing within the sacredness of the Divine Sacrifice those beautiful and profound words of the Apostle of the Gentiles: *And the Peace of God, which surpasseth all understanding, keep your hearts and minds in Jesus Christ.*[126]

917. The Peace of Christ, the true peace, transcends, therefore, the senses. It is a grave error to believe that true and lasting peace can rule among men and among peoples so long as they turn first and foremost and avidly in search of sensible, material, earthly things. These being limited, can with difficulty satisfy all, even if no one (which is hard to imagine) should wish to take the lion's share. They are necessarily unsatisfying because the greater the number of sharers, the smaller the share of each. Whence they are, almost inevitably, sources of discord and opposition as they are of greed and envy. The contrary is true of spiritual treasures—truth, goodness, virtue—which the more widely they are shared, the more they abound and give fruit to the advantage of each and of all.

918. Another error, against which the apostolic word, divinely inspired, wishes to fortify us, is that of supposing that true external peace can reign between men and peoples where there is not internal peace, where, that is to say, the spirit of peace does not possess the intelligence and hearts, or better, the souls of men—the intelligence so as to recognize and respect the claims of justice, the hearts so that charity may be joined to and even prevail over justice. For if peace, according to the prophet, must be the work and fruit of justice,[127] it belongs, as St. Thomas luminously teaches,[128] and this

---

[126] *Philippians*, IV, 7.
[127] *Isaias*, XXXII, 17.
[128] *Summa Theologica*, 2a, 2ae, q. 29, a.3 *ad 3um*.

is true, by the very nature of things, more to charity than to justice.

919. It is, however, difficult for the internal peace of minds and hearts to rule lastingly among citizens and social classes if a strong sense of contrast arises and is maintained among them by an unequal distribution and proportion of benefits and burdens, of rights and duties, of the contribution made by capital, management and labor and of the participation in those fruits which can be produced only by their friendly collaboration.

920. Even more difficult—not to say impossible—is it for peace to last between peoples and States if, in the place of true and genuine love of country, there rules and abounds a hard and selfish nationalism, which is the same as saying hatred and envy, in place of mutual desire for the good, distrust and suspicion in place of the confidence of brothers, competition and struggle in place of willing co-operation, ambition for hegemony and mastery in place of respect and care for the rights of all, even those of the weak and the small.

921. It is totally impossible for peoples to possess and enjoy that tranquillity in order and freedom, which is the essence of peace, so long as they are beset at home and abroad by threats and dangers which are not balanced by sufficient measures and provisions for defense. And certainly threats and dangers are inseparable from anti-social and anti-religious propaganda; yet not with material defenses alone can they be scattered and conquered.

922. As for threats of new wars, while the peoples of the world are still feeling so deeply the scourge of the last merciless war, We cannot believe they are real, because We are unable to believe any civilized State exists which would become so monstrously murderous and almost certainly suicidal. If We should even only suspect the existence of such a State, We should turn to God with the inspired prayer of the Prophet-King, who indeed knew both war and victory: *Scatter Thou the nations that delight in wars,*[129] and the daily and universal prayer of the Church: "Give us peace!" . . . . . .

---

[129] *Psalms,* LXVII, 31.

LETTER *Con Suma Satisfacción* TO THE ARCHBISHOP OF BUENOS AIRES AND THE BISHOPS OF ARGENTINA.[130]

The purpose of Catholic Action is "The Peace of Christ in the Kingdom of Christ."

February 4, 1931

923. . . . . . . Because on various occasions We have treated about the nature, the end and the necessity of Catholic Action, especially in recent times, it does not seem necessary to insist more on this matter because We know that it is fully known. Permit Us, nevertheless, to recall that Catholic Action is nothing more than the help which the laity gives to the ecclesiastical hierarchy in the exercise of its apostolate and that Catholic Action was born together with the Church and has recently assumed new directions and new forms in order to satisfy more fully the necessities of the present times. And precisely because it is an apostolate, it does not procure only self-sanctification, though that is its necessary basis, but it also tends toward the greater sanctification of others by means of the organized action of Catholics, who, following in all things the directions imposed by the hierarchy, valiantly help to spread the Kingdom of Christ among the nations. The end of Catholic Action is, therefore, very noble because it coincides with the very end of the Church: "The Peace of Christ in the Kingdom of Christ; *Pax Christi in regno Christi."* . . . . . .

ENCYCLICAL *Quadragesimo Anno* ON RECONSTRUCTING THE SOCIAL ORDER.[131]

Pius XI lays bare the root of the existing social confusion and points the only way to sound restoration: namely, the Christian reform of morals.

May 15, 1931

924. Forty years have passed since Leo XIII's peerless Encyclical, *On the Condition of Workers,* first saw the light, and the whole Catholic world, filled with grateful recollection, is undertaking to

[130] Original Spanish, *Colección de Encíclicas y Otras Cartas,* pp. 691-692.
[131] Translation from *Two Basic Social Encyclicals.* Original Latin, *A.A.S.,* v. 23, pp. 177-228 (June 1, 1931).

commemorate it with befitting solemnity. Other Encyclicals of Our Predecessor had in a way prepared the path for that outstanding document and proof of pastoral care: namely, those on the family and the holy Sacrament of matrimony as the source of human society,[132] on the origin of civil authority[133] and its proper relations with the Church,[134] on the chief duties of Christian citizens,[135] against the tenets of Socialism,[136] against false teachings on human liberty,[137] and others of the same nature fully expressing the mind of Leo XIII. Yet the Encyclical, *On the Condition of Workers,* compared with the rest, had this special distinction that at a time when it was most opportune and actually necessary to do so, it laid down for all mankind the surest rules to solve aright that difficult problem of human relations, called "the social question."

925. For, toward the close of the nineteenth century, the new kind of economic life that had arisen and the new developments of industry had gone to the point in most countries that human society was clearly becoming divided more and more into two classes. One class, very small in number, was enjoying almost all the advantages which modern inventions so abundantly provided; the other, embracing the huge multitude of working people, oppressed by wretched poverty, was vainly seeking escape from the straits wherein it stood.

926. Quite agreeable, of course, was this state of things to those who thought it, in their abundant riches, the result of inevitable economic laws and, accordingly, as if it were for charity to veil the violation of justice which lawmakers not only tolerated but at times sanctioned, wanted the whole care of supporting the poor committed to charity alone. The workers, on the other hand, crushed by their hard lot, were barely enduring it and were refusing longer to bend their necks beneath so galling a yoke; and some of them, carried away by the heat of evil counsel, were seeking the overturn of everything, while others, whom Christian training restrained from such evil designs, stood firm in the judgment that much in this had to be wholly and speedily changed. The same feeling those

---

[132] Encyclical *Arcanum,* February 10, 1880.
[133] Encyclical *Diuturnum,* June 29, 1881; cf. *supra* nn. 23-26.
[134] Encyclical *Immortale Dei,* November 1, 1885; cf. *supra* nn. 52-67.
[135] Encyclical *Sapientiae Christianae,* January 10, 1890; cf. *supra* nn. 109-116.
[136] Encyclical *Quod Apostolici Muneris,* December 28, 1878; cf. *supra* nn. 17-18.
[137] Encyclical *Libertas Praestantissimum,* June 20, 1888; cf. *supra* nn. 89-99.

many Catholics, both priests and laymen, shared, whom a truly wonderful charity had long spurred on to relieve the unmerited poverty of the non-owning workers, and who could in no way convince themselves that so enormous and unjust an inequality in the distribution of this world's goods truly conforms to the designs of the all-wise Creator.

927. Those men were, without question, sincerely seeking an immediate remedy for this lamentable disorganization of States and a secure safeguard against worse dangers. Yet such is the weakness of even the best of human minds that, now rejected as dangerous innovators, now hindered in the good work by their very associates, advocating other courses of action, and uncertain in the face of various opinions, they were at a loss which way to turn.

928. In such a sharp conflict of minds, therefore, while the question at issue was being argued this way and that, nor always with calmness, all eyes, as often before, turned to the Chair of Peter, to that sacred depository of all truth whence words of salvation pour forth to all the world. And to the feet of Christ's Vicar on earth were flocking, in unaccustomed numbers, men well versed in social questions, employers, and workers themselves, begging him with one voice to point out, finally, the safe road to them.

929. The wise Pontiff long weighed all this in his mind before God; he summoned the most experienced and learned to counsel; he weighed the issues carefully and from every angle. At last, admonished "by the consciousness of His Apostolic Office"[138] lest silence on his part might be regarded as failure in his duty,[139] he decided, in virtue of the Divine Teaching Office entrusted to him, to address not only the whole Church of Christ but all mankind. Therefore, on the fifteenth day of May, 1891, that long-awaited voice thundered forth; neither daunted by the arduousness of the problem nor weakened by age but with vigorous energy, it taught the whole human family to strike out in the social question upon new paths.

930. You know, Venerable Brethren and Beloved Children, and understand full well the wonderful teaching which has made the Encyclical, *On the Condition of Workers,* illustrious forever.

[138] Encyclical *On the Condition of Workers,* May 15, 1891, n. 119 in this book.
[139] *Ibid., cf.* n. 132 in this book.

The Supreme Pastor in this Letter, grieving that so large a portion of mankind should "live undeservedly in miserable and wretched conditions,"[140] took it upon himself with great courage to defend "the cause of the workers whom the present age had handed over, each alone and defenseless, to the inhumanity of employers and the unbridled greed of competitors."[141] He sought no help from either Liberalism or Socialism, for the one had proved that it was utterly unable to solve the social problem aright, and the other, proposing a remedy far worse than the evil itself, would have plunged human society into greater dangers.

931. Since a problem was being treated "for which no satisfactory solution" is found "unless religion and the Church have been called upon to aid,"[142] the Pope, clearly exercising his right and correctly holding that the guardianship of religion and the stewardship over those things that are closely bound up with it had been entrusted especially to him and relying solely upon the unchangeable principles drawn from the treasury of right reason and Divine Revelation, confidently and *as one having authority*,[143] declared and proclaimed "the rights and duties within which the rich and the proletariat—those who furnish material things and those who furnish work—ought to be restricted in relation to each other,"[144] and what the Church, heads of States and the people themselves directly concerned ought to do.

932. The Apostolic voice did not thunder forth in vain. On the contrary, not only did the obedient children of the Church hearken to it with marveling admiration and hail it with the greatest applause, but many also who were wandering far from the truth, from the unity of the Faith, and nearly all who since then, either in private study or in enacting legislation, have concerned themselves with the social and economic question. Feeling themselves vindicated and defended by the Supreme Authority on earth, Christian workers received this Encyclical with special joy. So, too, did all those noble-hearted men who, long solicitous for the improvement of the condition of the workers, had up to that time encountered almost nothing but indifference from many, and even rankling

---

[140] Encyclical *On the Condition of Workers*, n. 121 in this book.
[141] *Ibid.*, n. 121 in this book.
[142] *Ibid.*, n. 132 in this book.
[143] *Matthew*, VII, 29.
[144] Encyclical *On the Condition of Workers*, n. 120 in this book.

suspicion, if not open hostility from some. Rightly, therefore, have all these groups constantly held the Apostolic Encyclical from that time in such high honor that to signify their gratitude they are wont, in various places and in various ways, to commemorate it every year.

933. However, in spite of such great agreement, there were some who were no little disturbed; and so it happened that the teaching of Leo XIII, so noble and lofty and so utterly new to worldly ears, was held suspect by some, even among Catholics, and to certain ones it even gave offense. For it boldly attacked and over-turned the idols of Liberalism, ignored long-standing prejudices, and was in advance of its time beyond all expectation, so that the slow of heart disdained to study this new social philosophy and the timid feared to scale so lofty a height. There were some also who stood, indeed, in awe at its splendor, but regarded it as a kind of imaginary ideal of perfection more desirable than attainable.

934. Venerable Brethren and Beloved Children, as all everywhere, and especially Catholic workers who are pouring from all sides into this Holy City, are celebrating with such enthusiasm the solemn commemoration of the fortieth anniversary of the Encyclical *On the Condition of Workers,* We deem it fitting on this occasion to recall the great benefits this Encyclical has brought to the Catholic Church and to all human society; to defend the illustrious master's doctrine on the social and economic question against certain doubts and to develop it more fully as to some points; and lastly, summoning to court the contemporary economic regime and passing judgment on Socialism, to lay bare the root of the existing social confusion and at the same time point the only way to sound restoration: namely, the Christian reform of morals. All these matters which We undertake to treat will fall under three main headings, and this entire Encyclical will be devoted to their development.

935. To begin with the topic which We have proposed first to discuss, We cannot refrain, following the counsel of St. Ambrose,[145] who says that "no duty is more important than that of returning thanks," from offering Our fullest gratitude to Almighty God for the immense benefits that have come through Leo's Encyclical to

[145] St. Ambrose, *De Excessu Fratris Sui Satyri,* I, 44.

the Church and to human society. If indeed We should wish to review these benefits even cursorily, almost the whole history of the social question during the last forty years would have to be recalled to mind. These benefits can be reduced conveniently, however, to three main points, corresponding to the three kinds of help which Our Predecessor ardently desired for the accomplishment of his great work of restoration.

936. In the first place, Leo himself clearly stated what ought to be expected from the Church:[146] "Manifestly it is the Church which draws from the Gospel the teachings through which the struggle can be composed entirely, or, after its bitterness is removed, can certainly become more tempered. It is the Church, again, that strives not only to instruct the mind, but to regulate by her precepts the life and morals of individuals, and that ameliorates the condition of the workers through her numerous and beneficent institutions."

937. The Church did not let these rich fountains lie quiescent in her bosom, but from them drew copiously for the common good of the longed-for peace. Leo himself and his Successors, showing paternal charity and pastoral constancy always, in defense especially of the poor and the weak,[147] proclaimed and urged without ceasing again and again by voice and pen the teaching on the social and economic question which *On the Condition of Workers* presented, and adapted it fittingly to the needs of time and of circumstance. And many bishops have done the same, who in their continual and able interpretation of this same teaching have illustrated it with commentaries and, in accordance with the mind and instructions of the Holy See, provided for its application to the conditions and institutions of diverse regions.[148] It is not surprising, therefore, that many scholars, both priests and laymen, led especially by the desire that the unchanged and unchangeable teaching of the Church should meet new demands and needs more effectively, have zeal-

---

[146] Encyclical *On the Condition of Workers*, n. 133 in this book.

[147] Let it be sufficient to mention some of these only: Leo XIII's Apostolic Letter *Praeclara Gratulationis*, June 20, 1894, *cf. supra* nn. 191-193; and his Encyclical *Graves de Communi*, January 18, 1901; Pius X's Motu Proprio *De Actione Populari Christiana*, December 8, 1903; Benedict XV's Encyclical *Ad Beatissimi*, November 1, 1914, *cf. supra* 280-297; Pius XI's Encyclical *Ubi Arcano Dei*, December 23, 1922, *cf. supra* 758-823; and his Encyclical *Rite Expiatis*, April 30, 1926.

[148] *Cf. La Hiérarchie Catholique et le Problème Social Depuis l'Encyclique "Rerum Novarum,"* 1891-1931, pp. xvi-335: ed. "Union internationale d'Etudes Sociales fondée à Malines, en 1920, sous la présidence du Card. Mercier." Paris, Édition Spes, 1931.

ously undertaken to develop, with the Church as their guide and teacher, a social and economic science in accord with the conditions of our time.

938. And so, with Leo's Encyclical pointing the way and furnishing the light, a true Catholic social science has arisen, which is daily fostered and enriched by the tireless efforts of those chosen men whom We have termed auxiliaries of the Church. They do not, indeed, allow their science to lie hidden behind learned walls. As the useful and well-attended courses instituted in Catholic universities, colleges and seminaries, the social congresses and "Weeks" that are held at frequent intervals with most successful results, the study groups that are promoted, and finally the timely and sound publications that are disseminated everywhere and in every possible way, clearly show, these men bring their science out into the full light and stress of life.

939. Nor is the benefit that has poured forth from Leo's Encyclical confined within these bounds; for the teaching which *On the Condition of Workers* contains has gradually and imperceptibly worked its way into the minds of those outside Catholic unity who do not recognize the authority of the Church. Catholic principles on the social question have, as a result, passed little by little into the patrimony of all human society, and We rejoice that the eternal truths which Our Predecessor of glorious memory proclaimed so impressively have been frequently invoked and defended not only in non-Catholic books and journals but in legislative halls also and courts of justice.

940. Furthermore, after the terrible war, when the statesmen of the leading nations were attempting to restore peace on the basis of a thorough reform of social conditions, did not they, among the norms agreed upon to regulate in accordance with justice and equity the labor of the workers, give sanction to many points that so remarkably coincide with Leo's principles and instructions as to seem consciously taken therefrom? The Encyclical *On the Condition of Workers,* without question, has become a memorable document and rightly to it may be applied the words of Isaias: *He shall set up a standard to the nations.*[149]

941. Meanwhile, as Leo's teachings were being widely diffused in the minds of men, with learned investigations leading the way,

[149] *Isaias,* XI, 12.

they have come to be put into practice. In the first place, zealous
efforts have been made, with active good-will, to lift up that class
which, on account of the modern expansion of industry, had increased to enormous numbers but not yet had obtained its rightful
place or rank in human society and was, for that reason, all but
neglected and despised—the workers, We mean—to whose improvement, to the great advantage of souls, the diocesan and regular
clergy, though burdened with other pastoral duties, have, under
the leadership of the bishops, devoted themselves. This constant
work, undertaken to fill the workers' souls with the Christian
spirit, helped much also to make them conscious of their true dignity and render them capable, by placing clearly before them the
rights and duties of their class, of legitimately and happily advanc-
ing and even of becoming leaders of their fellows.

942. From that time on, fuller means of livelihood have been
more securely obtained; for not only did works of beneficence and
charity begin to multiply at the urging of the Pontiff, but there
have also been established everywhere new and continuously ex-
panding organizations in which workers, craftsmen, farmers and
employees of every kind, with the counsel of the Church and frequently under the leadership of her priests, give and receive mutual
help and support.

943. With regard to civil authority, Leo XIII, boldly breaking
through the confines imposed by Liberalism, fearlessly taught that
government must not be thought a mere guardian of law and of
good order, but rather must put forth every effort so that "through
the entire scheme of laws and institutions . . . both public and
individual well-being may develop spontaneously out of the very
structure and administration of the State."[150] Just freedom of action
must, of course, be left both to individual citizens and to families,
yet only on condition that the common good be preserved and
wrong to any individual be abolished. The function of the rulers
of the State, moreover, is to watch over the community and its
parts; but in protecting private individuals in their rights, chief
consideration ought to be given to the weak and the poor. "For the
nation, as it were, of the rich is guarded by its own defenses and
is in less need of governmental protection, whereas the suffering
multitude, without the means to protect itself, relies especially on

[150] Encyclical *On the Condition of Workers,* n. 145 in this book.

the protection of the State. Wherefore, since wage-workers are numbered among the great mass of the needy, the State must include them under its special care and foresight."[151]

944. We, of course, do not deny that even before the Encyclical of Leo, some rulers of peoples had provided for certain of the more urgent needs of the workers and curbed more flagrant acts of injustice inflicted upon them. But after the Apostolic voice had sounded from the Chair of Peter throughout the world, rulers of nations, more fully alive at last to their duty, devoted their minds and attention to the task of promoting a more comprehensive and fruitful social policy.

945. And while the principles of Liberalism were tottering, which had long prevented effective action by those governing the State, the Encyclical *On the Condition of Workers* in truth impelled peoples themselves to promote a social policy on truer grounds and with greater intensity, and so strongly encouraged good Catholics to furnish valuable help to heads of States in this field that they often stood forth as illustrious champions of this new policy even in legislatures. Sacred ministers of the Church, thoroughly imbued with Leo's teaching, have, in fact, often proposed to the votes of the peoples' representatives the very social legislation that has been enacted in recent years and resolutely demanded and promoted its enforcement.

946. A new branch of law, wholly unknown to the earlier time, has arisen from this continuous and unwearied labor to protect vigorously the sacred rights of the workers that flow from their dignity as men and as Christians. These laws undertake the protection of life, health, strength, family, homes, workshops, wages and labor hazards, in fine, everything which pertains to the condition of wage workers, with special concern for women and children. Even though these laws do not conform exactly, everywhere and in all respects, to Leo's recommendations, still it is undeniable that much in them savors of the Encyclical *On the Condition of Workers* to which great credit must be given for whatever improvement has been achieved in the workers' condition.

947. Finally, the wise Pontiff showed that "employers and workers themselves can accomplish much in this matter, manifestly through those institutions by the help of which the poor are oppor-

[151] Encyclical *On the Condition of Workers,* n. 150 in this book.

tunely assisted and the two classes of society are brought closer to each other."[152] First place among these institutions, he declares, must be assigned to associations that embrace either workers alone or workers and employers together. He goes into considerable detail in explaining and commending these associations and expounds with a truly wonderful wisdom their nature, purpose, timeliness, rights, duties and regulations.

948. These teachings were issued indeed most opportunely. For at that time, in many nations, those at the helm of State, plainly imbued with Liberalism, were showing little favor to workers' associations of this type; nay, they rather openly opposed them, and while going out of their way to recognize similar organizations of other classes and show favor to them, they were, with criminal injustice, denying the natural right to form associations to those who needed them most to defend themselves from ill treatment at the hands of the powerful. There were even some Catholics who looked askance at the efforts of workers to form associations of this type as if they smacked of a socialistic or revolutionary spirit.

949. The rules, therefore, which Leo XIII issued in virtue of his authority, deserve the greatest praise in that they have been able to break down this hostility and dispel these suspicions; but they have even a higher claim to distinction in that they encouraged Christian workers to found mutual associations according to their various occupations, taught them how to do so, and resolutely confirmed in the path of duty a goodly number of those whom Socialist organizations strongly attracted by claiming to be the sole defenders and champions of the lowly and oppressed.

950. With respect to the founding of these societies, the Encyclical *On the Condition of Workers* most fittingly declared that "workers' associations ought to be so constituted and so governed as to furnish the most suitable and most convenient means to attain the object proposed, which consists in this, that the individual members of the association secure, so far as is possible, an increase in the goods of the body, of the soul and of property."[153] Yet it is clear that "the improvement of religion and morals ought to be regarded as their principal concern, as it were, and that their social organization as such ought to be, above all, directed completely by this concern."

[152] Encyclical *On the Condition of Workers*, n. 162 in this book.
[153] Encyclical *On the Condition of Workers*, n. 170 in this book.

For "when the regulations of associations are founded upon religion, the way is easy toward establishing the mutual relations of the members, so that peaceful living together and prosperity will result."[154]

951. To the founding of these associations the clergy and many of the laity devoted themselves everywhere with truly praiseworthy zeal, eager to bring Leo's program to full realization. Thus associations of this kind have molded truly Christian workers who, in combining harmoniously the diligent practice of their occupation with the salutary precepts of religion, protect effectively and resolutely their own temporal interests and rights, keeping a due respect for justice and a genuine desire to work together with other classes of society for the Christian renewal of all social life.

952. These counsels and instructions of Leo XIII were put into effect differently in different places according to varied local conditions. In some places one and the same association undertook to attain all the ends laid down by the Pontiff; in others, because circumstances suggested or required it, a division of work developed and separate associations were formed. Of these, some devoted themselves to the defense of the rights and legitimate interests of their members in the labor market; others took over the work of providing mutual economic aid; finally, still others gave all their attention to the fulfillment of religious and moral duties and other obligations of like nature.

953. This second method has especially been adopted where either the laws of a country, or certain special economic institutions, or that deplorable dissension of minds and hearts, so widespread in contemporary society, and an urgent necessity of combating with united purpose and strength the massed ranks of revolutionarists, have prevented Catholics from founding purely Catholic labor unions. Under these conditions, Catholics seem almost forced to join secular labor unions. These unions, however, should always profess justice and equity and give Catholic members full freedom to care for their own conscience and obey the laws of the Church. It is clearly the office of bishops, when they know that these associations are, on account of circumstances, necessary and are not dangerous to religion, to approve of Catholic workers joining them, keeping before their eyes, however, the principles and precautions

[154] Encyclical *On the Condition of Workers*, n. 171 in this book.

407

laid down by Our Predecessor, Pius X of holy memory.[155] Among these precautions the first and chief is this: side by side with these unions there should always be associations zealously engaged in imbuing and forming their members in the teaching of religion and morality so that they in turn may be able to permeate the unions with that good spirit which should direct them in all their activity. As a result, the religious associations will bear good fruit even beyond the circle of their own membership.

954. To the Encyclical of Leo, therefore, must be given this credit, that these associations of workers have so flourished everywhere that while, alas, still surpassed in numbers by Socialist and Communist organizations, they already embrace a vast multitude of workers and are able, within the confines of each nation, as well as in wider assemblies, to maintain vigorously the rights and legitimate demands of Catholic workers and insist also on the salutary Christian principles of society.

955. Leo's learned treatment and vigorous defense of the natural right to form associations began, furthermore, to find ready application to other associations also and not alone to those of the workers. Hence, no small part of the credit must, it seems, be given to this same Encyclical of Leo for the fact that among farmers and others of the middle class most useful associations of this kind are seen flourishing to a notable degree and increasing day by day, and other institutions of a similar nature in which spiritual development and economic benefit are happily combined.

956. But if this cannot be said of organizations which Our same Predecessor intensely desired established among employers and managers of industry—and We certainly regret that they are so few—the condition is not wholly due to the will of men but to far graver difficulties that hinder associations of this kind which We know well and estimate at their full value. There is, however, strong hope that these obstacles also will be removed soon, and even now We greet with the deepest joy of Our soul, certain by no means insignificant attempts in this direction, the rich fruits of which promise a still richer harvest in the future.[156]

957. All these benefits of Leo's Encyclical, Venerable Brethren

[155] Pius X, Encyclical *Singulari Quadam*, September 24, 1912.
[156] *Cf.* Letter of the Sacred Congregation of the Council to the Bishop of Lille, June 5, 1929.

and Beloved Children, which We have outlined rather than fully described, are so numerous and of such import as to show plainly that this immortal document does not exhibit a merely fanciful, even if beautiful, ideal of human society. Rather did Our Predecessor draw from the Gospel and, therefore, from an ever-living and life-giving fountain, teachings capable of greatly mitigating, if not immediately terminating that deadly internal struggle which is rending the family of mankind. The rich fruits which the Church of Christ and the whole human race have, by God's favor, reaped therefrom unto salvation, prove that some of this good seed, so lavishly sown forty years ago, fell on good ground. On the basis of the long period of experience, it cannot be rash to say that Leo's Encyclical has proved itself the *Magna Charta* upon which all Christian activity in the social field ought to be based, as on a foundation. And those who would seem to hold in little esteem this Papal Encyclical and its commemoration, either blaspheme what they know not, or understand nothing of what they are only superficially acquainted with, or, if they do understand, convict themselves formally of injustice and ingratitude.

958. Yet since, in the course of these same years, certain doubts have arisen concerning either the correct meaning of some parts of Leo's Encyclical or conclusions to be deduced therefrom, which doubts in turn have even among Catholics given rise to controversies that are not always peaceful; and since, furthermore, new needs and changed conditions of our age have made necessary a more precise application of Leo's teaching or even certain additions thereto, We most gladly seize this fitting occasion, in accord with Our Apostolic Office, through which We are debtors to all,[157] to answer, so far as in Us lies, these doubts and these demands of the present day.

959. Yet before proceeding to explain these matters, that principle which Leo XIII so clearly established must be laid down at the outset here, namely, that there resides in Us the right and duty to pronounce with supreme authority upon social and economic matters.[158] Certainly the Church was not given the commission to guide men to an only fleeting and perishable happiness but to that which is eternal. Indeed "the Church holds that it is unlawful for

---

[157] *Cf. Romans*, I, 14.
[158] *Cf.* Encyclical *On the Condition of Workers*, nn. 124 and 125 in this book.

her to mix without cause in these temporal concerns;"[159] however, she can in no wise renounce the duty God entrusted to her to interpose her authority, not, of course, in matters of technique for which she is neither suitably equipped nor endowed by office, but in all things that are connected with the moral law. For as to these, the deposit of truth that God committed to Us and the grave duty of disseminating and interpreting the whole moral law, and of urging it in season and out of season, bring under and subject to Our supreme jurisdiction not only social order but economic activities themselves.

960. Even though economics and moral science employs each its own principles in its own sphere, it is, nevertheless, an error to say that the economic and moral orders are so distinct from and alien to each other that the former depends in no way on the latter. Certainly the laws of economics, as they are termed, being based on the very nature of material things and on the capacities of the human body and mind, determine the limits which productive human effort cannot, and which it can attain in the economic field and by what means. Yet it is reason itself that clearly shows, on the basis of the individual and social nature of things and of men, the purpose which God ordained for all economic life.

961. But it is only the moral law which, just as it commands us to seek our supreme and last end in the whole scheme of our activity, so likewise commands us to seek directly in each kind of activity those purposes which we know that nature, or rather God, the Author of nature, established for that kind of action, and in orderly relationship subordinate such immediate purposes to our supreme and last end. If we faithfully observe this law, then it will follow that the particular purposes, both individual and social, that are sought in the economic field will fall in their proper place in the universal order of purposes, and we, in ascending through them, as it were, by steps, shall attain the final end of all things, that is, God, to Himself and to us, the Supreme and Inexhaustible Good.

962. But to come down to particular points, We shall begin with ownership or the right of property. Venerable Brethren and Beloved Children, you know that Our Predecessor of happy memory strongly defended the right of property against the tenets of

[159] Pius XI, Encyclical *Ubi Arcano Dei*, December 23, 1922; *cf. supra* n. 815.

the Socialists of his time by showing that its abolition would result, not to the advantage of the working class, but to their extreme harm. Yet since there are some who calumniate the Supreme Pontiff and the Church herself, as if she had taken and were still taking the part of the rich against the non-owning workers—certainly no accusation is more unjust than that—and since Catholics are at variance with one another concerning the true and exact mind of Leo, it has seemed best to vindicate this, that is, the Catholic teaching on this matter, from calumnies and safeguard it from false interpretations.

963. First, then, let it be considered as certain and established that neither Leo nor those theologians who have taught under the guidance and authority of the Church have ever denied or questioned the twofold character of ownership, called usually individual or social according as it regards either separate persons or the common good. For they have always unanimously maintained that nature, rather the Creator Himself, has given man the right of private ownership not only that individuals may be able to provide for themselves and their families but also that the goods which the Creator destined for the entire family of mankind may, through this institution, truly serve this purpose. All this can be achieved in no wise except through the maintenance of a certain and definite order.

964. Accordingly, twin rocks of shipwreck must be carefully avoided. For, as one is wrecked upon, or comes close to, what is known as "individualism" by denying or minimizing the social and public character of the right of property, so by rejecting or minimizing the private and individual character of this same right, one inevitably runs into "collectivism" or at least closely approaches its tenets. Unless this is kept in mind, one is swept from his course upon the shoals of that moral, juridical and social modernism which We denounced in the Encyclical issued at the beginning of Our Pontificate.[160] And, in particular, let those realize this who, in their desire for innovation, do not scruple to reproach the Church with infamous calumnies, as if she had allowed to creep into the teachings of her theologians, a pagan concept of ownership which must be completely replaced by another that they, with amazing ignorance, call "Christian."

[160] Pius XI, Encyclical *Ubi Arcano Dei*, December 23, 1922; *cf. supra* nn. 758-823.

965. In order to place definite limits on the controversies that have arisen over ownership and its inherent duties, there must be first laid down as a foundation a principle established by Leo XIII: the right of property is distinct from its use.[161] That justice called commutative commands sacred respect for the division of possessions and forbids invasion of others' rights through the exceeding of the limits of one's own property; but the duty of owners to use their property only in a right way does not come under this type of justice, but under other virtues, obligations of which "cannot be enforced by legal action."[162] Therefore, they are in error who assert that ownership and its right use are limited by the same boundaries; and it is much farther still from the truth to hold that a right to property is destroyed or lost by reason of abuse or non-use.

966. Those, therefore, are doing a work that is truly salutary and worthy of all praise who, while preserving harmony among themselves and the integrity of the traditional teaching of the Church, seek to define the inner nature of these duties and their limits whereby either the right of property itself or its use, that is, the exercise of ownership, is circumscribed by the necessities of social living. On the other hand, those who seek to restrict the individual character of ownership to such a degree that, in fact, they destroy it, are mistaken and in error.

967. It follows from what We have termed the individual and at the same time social character of ownership, that men must consider in this matter not only their own advantage but also the common good. To define these duties in detail, when necessity requires and the natural law has not done so, is the function of those in charge of the State. Therefore, public authority, under the guiding light always of the natural and divine law, can determine more accurately upon consideration of the true requirements of the common good, what is permitted and what is not permitted to owners in the use of their property. Moreover, Leo XIII wisely taught "that God has left the limits of private possessions to be fixed by the industry of men and institutions of peoples."[163] That history proves ownership, like other elements of social life, to be not absolutely unchanging, We once declared as follows: "What

---

[161] Encyclical *On the Condition of Workers*, n. 137 in this book.
[162] Encyclical *On the Condition of Workers*, n. 137 in this book.
[163] Encyclical *On the Condition of Workers*; this part is not included in this book.

diverse forms has property had, from that primitive form among rude and savage peoples, which may be observed in some places even in our time, to the form of possession in the patriarchal age; and so further to the various forms under tyranny (We are using the word tyranny in its classical sense); and then through the feudal and monarchic forms down to the various types which are to be found in more recent times!"[164] That the State is not permitted to discharge its duty arbitrarily is, however, clear. The natural right itself both of owning goods privately and of passing them on by inheritance ought always to remain intact and inviolate, since this indeed is a right that the State cannot take away: "For man is older than the State,"[165] and also "domestic living together is prior both in thought and in fact to uniting into a polity."[166] Wherefore the wise Pontiff declared that it is grossly unjust for a State to exhaust private wealth through the weight of imposts and taxes. "For since the right of possessing goods privately has been conferred not by man's law, but by nature, public authority cannot abolish it, but can only control its exercise and bring it into conformity with the common weal."[167] Yet when the State brings private ownership into harmony with the needs of the common good, it does not commit a hostile act against private owners but rather does them a friendly service; for it thereby effectively prevents the private possession of goods, which the Author of nature, in His most wise providence, ordained for the support of human life, from causing intolerable evils and thus rushing to its own destruction; it does not destroy private possessions, but safeguards them; and it does not weaken private property rights, but strengthens them.

968. Furthermore, a person's superfluous income, that is, income which he does not need to sustain life fittingly and with dignity, is not left wholly to his own free determination. Rather, the Sacred Scriptures and the Fathers of the Church constantly declare in the most explicit language that the rich are bound by a very grave precept to practice almsgiving, beneficence and munificence. Expending larger incomes so that opportunity for gainful work may be abundant, provided, however, that this work is ap-

[164] Allocution to the Convention of Italian Catholic Action, May 16, 1926.
[165] Encyclical *On the Condition of Workers;* this part is not included in this book.
[166] Encyclical *On the Condition of Workers,* n. 128 in this book.
[167] Encyclical *On the Condition of Workers,* n. 161 in this book.

plied to producing really useful goods, ought to be considered, as We deduce from the principles of the Angelic Doctor,[168] an outstanding exemplification of the virtue of munificence and one particularly suited to the needs of the times.

969. That ownership is originally acquired both by occupancy of a thing not owned by any one and by labor, or, as is said, by specification, the tradition of all ages as well as the teaching of Our Predecessor, Leo, clearly testify. For, whatever some idly say to the contrary, no injury is done to any person when a thing is occupied that is available to all but belongs to no one; however, only that labor which a man performs in his own name and by virtue of which a new form or increase has been given to a thing grants him title to these fruits.

970. Far different is the nature of work that is hired out to others and expended on the property of others. To this indeed especially applies what Leo XIII says is "incontestible," namely, that "the wealth of nations originates from no other source than from the labor of workers."[169] For is it not plain that the enormous volume of goods that makes up human wealth is produced by and issues from the hands of the workers that either toil unaided or have their efficiency marvelously increased by being equipped with tools or machines? Everyone knows, too, that no nation has ever risen out of want and poverty to a better and nobler condition save by the enormous and combined toil of all the people, both those who manage work and those who carry out directions. But it is no less evident that, had not God, the Creator of all things, in keeping with His goodness, first generously bestowed natural riches and resources—the wealth and forces of nature—such supreme efforts would have been idle and vain, indeed could never even have been begun. For what else is work but to use or exercise the energies of mind and body on or through these very things? And in the application of natural resources to human use the law of nature, or rather God's Will promulgated by it, demands that right order be observed. This order consists in this: that each thing have its proper owner. Hence, it follows that unless a man is expending labor on his own property, the labor of one person and the property of another must be associated, for neither can produce anything

[168] *Summa Theologica,* 2a 2ae, Q.cxxxiv.
[169] Encyclical *On the Condition of Workers,* n. 147 in this book.

without the other. Leo XIII certainly had this in mind when he wrote: "Neither capital can do without labor, nor labor without capital."[170] Wherefore, it is wholly false to ascribe to property alone or to labor alone whatever has been obtained through the combined effort of both, and it is wholly unjust for either, denying the efficacy of the other, to arrogate to itself whatever has been produced.

971. Property, that is, "capital," has undoubtedly long been able to appropriate too much to itself. Whatever was produced, whatever returns accrued, capital claimed for itself, hardly leaving to the worker enough to restore and renew his strength. For the doctrine was preached that all accumulation of capital falls by an absolutely insuperable economic law to the rich, and that by the same law the workers are given over and bound to perpetual want, to the scantiest of livelihoods. It is true, indeed, that things have not always and everywhere corresponded with this sort of teaching of the so-called Manchesterian Liberals; yet it cannot be denied that economic-social institutions have moved steadily in that direction. That these false ideas, these erroneous suppositions, have been vigorously assailed, and not by those alone who through them were being deprived of their innate right to obtain better conditions, will surprise no one.

972. And, therefore, to the harassed workers there have come "intellectuals," as they are called, setting up in opposition to a fictitious law the equally fictitious moral principle, that all products and profits, save only enough to repair and renew capital, belong by very right to the workers. This error, much more specious than that of certain of the Socialists, who hold that whatever serves to produce goods ought to be transferred to the State, or, as they say, "socialized," is consequently all the more dangerous and the more apt to deceive the unwary. It is an alluring poison which many have eagerly drunk whom open Socialism had not been able to deceive.

973. Unquestionably, so as not to close against themselves the road to justice and peace through these false tenets, both parties ought to have been forewarned by the wise words of Our Predecessor: "However the earth may be apportioned among private owners, it does not cease to serve the common interest of all."[171] This

---

[170] Encyclical *On the Condition of Workers,* n. 135 in this book.
[171] Encyclical *On the Condition of Workers;* this part is not included in this book.

same doctrine We Ourself also taught above in declaring that the division of goods which results from private ownership was established by nature itself in order that created things may serve the needs of mankind in fixed and stable order. Lest one wander from the straight path of truth, this is something that must be continually kept in mind.

974. But not every distribution among human beings of property and wealth is of a character to attain, either completely or to a satisfactory degree of perfection, the end which God intends. Therefore, the riches that economic-social developments constantly increase ought to be so distributed among individual persons and classes that the common advantage of all, which Leo XIII had praised, will be safeguarded; in other words, that the common good of all society will be kept inviolate. By this law of social justice, one class is forbidden to exclude the other from sharing in the benefits. Hence, the class of the wealthy violates this law no less, when, as if free from care on account of its wealth, it thinks it the right order of things for it to get everything and the worker nothing, than does the non-owning working class when, angered deeply at outraged justice and too ready to assert wrongly the one right it is conscious of, it demands for itself everything as if produced by its own hands, and attacks and seeks to abolish, therefore, all property and returns or incomes, of whatever kind they are or whatever the function they perform in human society, that have not been obtained by labor, and for no other reason save that they are of such a nature. And in this connection We must not pass over the unwarranted and unmerited appeal made by some to the Apostle when he said: *If any man will not work neither let him eat.*[172] For the Apostle is passing judgment on those who are unwilling to work, although they can and ought to, and he admonishes us that we ought diligently to use our time and energies of body and mind and not be a burden to others when we can provide for ourselves. But the Apostle in no wise teaches that labor is the sole title to a living or an income.[173]

975. To each, therefore, must be given his own share of goods, and the distribution of created goods, which, as every discerning person knows, is laboring today under the gravest evils due to the

[172] II *Thessalonians*, III, 10.
[173] *Cf.* II *Thessalonians*, III, 8-10.

huge disparity between the few exceedingly rich and the unnumbered propertyless, must be effectively called back to and brought into conformity with the norms of the common good, that is, social justice.

976. The redemption of the non-owning workers—this is the goal that Our Predecessor declared must necessarily be sought. And the point is the more emphatically to be asserted and more insistently repeated because the commands of the Pontiff, salutary as they are, have not infrequently been consigned to oblivion either because they were deliberately suppressed by silence or thought impracticable, although they both can and ought to be put into effect. And these commands have not lost their force and wisdom for our time because that "pauperism" which Leo XIII beheld in all its horror is less widespread. Certainly the condition of the workers has been improved and made more equitable, especially in the more civilized and wealthy countries where the workers can no longer be considered universally overwhelmed with misery and lacking the necessities of life. But since manufacturing and industry have so rapidly pervaded and occupied countless regions, not only in the countries called new, but also in the realms of the Far East that have been civilized from antiquity, the number of the non-owning working poor has increased enormously and their groans cry to God from the earth. Added to them is the huge army of rural wage workers, pushed to the lowest level of existence and deprived of all hope of ever acquiring "some property in land,"[174] and, therefore, permanently bound to the status of non-owning worker unless suitable and effective remedies are applied.

977. Yet while it is true that the status of non-owning workers is to be carefully distinguished from pauperism, nevertheless, the immense multitude of the non-owning workers on the one hand and the enormous riches of certain very wealthy men on the other establish an unanswerable argument that the riches which are so abundantly produced in our age of "industrialism," as it is called, are not rightly distributed and equitably made available to the various classes of the people.

978. Therefore, with all our strength and effort we must strive that at least in the future the abundant fruits of production will accrue equitably to those who are rich and will be distributed in

[174] Encyclical *On the Condition of Workers*, n. 161 in this book.

ample sufficiency among the workers—not that these may become remiss in work, for man is born to labor as the bird to fly—but that they may increase their property by thrift; that they may bear, by wise management of this increase in property, the burdens of family life with greater ease and security and, emerging from that insecure lot in life in whose uncertainties non-owning workers are cast, they may be able not only to endure the vicissitudes of earthly existence but have also assurance that when their lives are ended they will provide, in some measure, for those they leave after them.

979. All these things which Our Predecessor has not only suggested but clearly and openly proclaimed, We emphasize with renewed insistence in Our present Encyclical; and unless utmost efforts are made without delay to put them into effect, let no one persuade himself that public order, peace and the tranquillity of human society can be effectively defended against agitators of revolution.

980. As We have already indicated, following in the footsteps of Our Predecessor, it will be impossible to put these principles into practice unless the non-owning workers, through industry and thrift, advance to the state of possessing some little property. But except from pay for work, from what source can a man, who has nothing else but work from which to obtain food and the necessaries of life, set anything aside for himself through practicing frugality? Let us, therefore, explaining and developing wherever necessary Leo XIII's teachings and precepts, take up this question of wages and salaries which he called one "of very great importance." [175]

981. First of all, those who declare that a contract of hiring and being hired is unjust of its own nature, and, hence, a partnership-contract must take its place, are certainly in error and gravely misrepresent Our Predecessor whose Encyclical not only accepts working for wages or salaries but deals at some length with its regulation in accordance with the rules of justice. We consider it more advisable, however, in the present condition of human society that, so far as is possible, the work-contract be somewhat modified by a partnership-contract, as is already being done in various ways and with no small advantage to workers and owners. Workers and other employees thus become sharers in ownership or management or participate in some fashion in the profits received.

[175] Encyclical *On the Condition of Workers*, n. 156 in this book.

982. The just amount of pay, however, must be calculated not on a single basis but on several, as Leo XIII already wisely declared in these words: "To establish a rule of pay in accord with justice, many factors must be taken into account."[176] By this statement he plainly condemned the shallowness of those who think that this most difficult matter is easily solved by the application of a single rule or measure—and one quite false. For they are greatly in error who do not hesitate to spread the principle that labor is worth and must be paid as much as its products are worth, and that consequently the one who hires out his labor has the right to demand all that is produced through his labor. How far this is from the truth is evident from what We have already explained in treating of property and labor.

983. It is obvious that, as in the case of ownership, so in the case of work, especially work hired out to others, there is a social aspect also to be considered in addition to the personal or individual aspect. For man's productive effort cannot yield its fruits unless a truly social and organic body exists, unless a social and juridical order watches over the exercise of work, unless the various occupations, being interdependent, co-operate with and mutually complete one another, and, what is still more important, unless mind, material things and work combine and form, as it were, a single whole. Therefore, where the social and individual nature of work is neglected, it will be impossible to evaluate work justly and pay it according to justice. Conclusions of the greatest importance follow from this two-fold character which nature has impressed on human work, and it is in accordance with these that wages ought to be regulated and established.

984. In the first place, the worker must be paid a wage sufficient to support him and his family.[177] That the rest of the family should also contribute to the common support, according to the capacity of each, is certainly right, as can be observed especially in the families of farmers, but also in the families of many craftsmen and small shopkeepers. But to abuse the years of childhood and the limited strength of women is grossly wrong. Mothers, concentrating on household duties, should work primarily in the home or in its immediate vicinity. It is an intolerable abuse, and to be

---

[176] Encyclical *On the Condition of Workers*, n. 135 in this book.
[177] Encyclical *Casti Connubii*, December 31, 1930.

abolished at all cost, for mothers, on account of the father's low wage, to be forced to engage in gainful occupations outside the home to the neglect of their proper cares and duties, especially the training of children. Every effort must, therefore, be made that fathers of families receive a wage large enough to meet ordinary family needs adequately. But if this cannot always be done under existing circumstances, social justice demands that changes be introduced as soon as possible whereby such a wage will be assured to every adult workingman. It will not be out of place here to render merited praise to all, who with a wise and useful purpose, have tried and tested various ways of adjusting the pay for work to family burdens in such a way that, as these increase, the former may be raised and indeed, if the contingency arises, there may be enough to meet extraordinary needs.

985. In determining the amount of the wage, the condition of a business and of the one carrying it on must also be taken into account; for it would be unjust to demand excessive wages which a business cannot stand without its ruin and consequent calamity to the workers. If, however, a business makes too little money, because of lack of energy or lack of initiative or because of indifference to technical and economic progress, that must not be regarded a just reason for reducing the compensation of the workers. But if the business in question is not making enough money to pay the workers an equitable wage because it is being crushed by unjust burdens or forced to sell its product at less than a just price, those who are thus the cause of the injury are guilty of grave wrong, for they deprive workers of their just wage and force them, under the pinch of necessity, to accept a wage less than fair.

986. Let, then, both workers and employers strive with united strength and counsel to overcome the difficulties and obstacles and let a wise provision on the part of public authority aid them in so salutary a work. If, however, matters come to an extreme crisis, it must be finally considered whether the business can continue or the workers are to be cared for in some other way. In such a situation, certainly most serious, a feeling of close relationship and a Christian concord of minds ought to prevail and function effectively among employers and workers.

987. Lastly, the amount of the pay must be adjusted to the public economic good. We have shown above how much it helps

the common good for workers and other employees, by setting aside some part of their income which remains after necessary expenditures, to attain gradually to the possession of a moderate amount of wealth. But another point, scarcely less important, and especially vital in our times, must not be overlooked: namely, that the opportunity to work be provided to those who are able and willing to work. This opportunity depends largely on the wage and salary rate, which can help as long as it is kept within proper limits, but which can be, on the other hand, an obstacle if it exceeds these limits. For everyone knows that an excessive lowering of wages, or their increase beyond due measure, causes unemployment. This evil, indeed, especially as We see it prolonged and injuring so many during the years of Our Pontificate, has plunged workers into misery and temptation, ruined the prosperity of nations, and put in jeopardy the public order, peace and tranquillity of the whole world. Hence, it is contrary to social justice when, for the sake of personal gain and without regard for the common good, wages and salaries are excessively lowered or raised; and this same social justice demands that wages and salaries be so managed, through agreement of plans and wills, insofar as can be done, as to offer to the greatest possible number the opportunity of getting work and obtaining suitable means of livelihood.

988. A right proportion among wages and salaries also contributes directly to the same result; and with this is closely connected a right proportion in the prices at which the goods are sold that are produced by the various occupations, such as agriculture, manufacturing and others. If all these relations are properly maintained, the various occupations will combine and coalesce into, as it were, a single body, and like members of the body mutually aid and complete one another. For then only will the social economy be rightly established and attain its purposes when all and each are supplied with all the goods that the wealth and resources of nature, technical achievement, and the social organization of economic life can furnish. And these goods ought indeed to be enough both to meet the demands of necessity and decent comfort and to advance people to that fuller condition of life which, when it is wisely cared for, is not only no hindrance to virtue but helps it greatly.[178]

---

[178] Cf. St. Thomas, *De Regimine Principum,* I, 15; Encyclical *On the Condition of Workers,* nn. 156-147 in this book.

989. What We have thus far stated regarding an equitable distribution of property and just wages concerns individual persons and only indirectly touches social order, to the restoration of which according to the principles of sound philosophy and to its perfection according to the sublime precepts of the law of the Gospel, Our Predecessor, Leo XIII, devoted all his thought and care. Still, in order that what he so happily initiated may be solidly established, what remains to be done may be accomplished, and that even more copious and richer benefits may accrue to the family of mankind, two things are especially necessary: reform of institutions and correction of morals.

990. When We speak of the reform of institutions, the State comes chiefly to mind, not as if universal well-being were to be expected from its activity, but because things have come to such a pass through the evil of what We have termed "individualism," that, following upon the overthrow and near extinction of that rich social life which was once highly developed through associations of various kinds, there remain virtually only individuals and the State. This is to the great harm of the State itself; for, with a structure of social governance lost, and with its taking over all the burdens which the wrecked associations once bore, it has been overwhelmed and crushed by almost infinite tasks and duties.

991. As history abundantly proves, it is true that on account of changed conditions many things which were done by small associations in former times cannot be done now save by large associations. Still, that most weighty principle, which cannot be set aside or changed, remains fixed and unshaken in social philosophy: Just as it is gravely wrong to take from individuals what they can accomplish by their own initiative and industry and give it to the community, so also it is an injustice and at the same time a grave evil and disturbance of right order to assign to a greater and higher association what lesser and subordinate organizations can do. For every social activity ought of its very nature to furnish help to the members of the body social, and never destroy and absorb them.

992. The supreme authority of the State ought, therefore, to let subordinate groups handle matters and concerns of lesser importance, which would otherwise dissipate its efforts greatly. Thereby it will more freely, powerfully and effectively do all those things

that belong to it alone because it alone can do them: directing, watching, urging, restraining, as occasion requires and necessity demands. Therefore, those in power should be sure that the more perfectly a graduated order is kept among the various associations, in observance of the principle of "subsidiary function," the stronger social authority and effectiveness will be and the happier and more prosperous the condition of the State.

993. First and foremost, the State and every good citizen ought to look to and strive toward this end: that the conflict between the hostile classes be abolished and an harmonious co-operation of the industries and professions be encouraged and promoted. The social policy of the State, therefore, must devote itself to the re-establishment of the industries and professions. In actual fact, human society now, for the reason that it is founded on classes with divergent aims, and, hence, opposed to one another and, therefore, inclined to enmity and strife, continues to be in a violent condition and is unstable and uncertain.

994. Labor, as Our Predecessor explained well in his En-cyclical,[179] is not a mere commodity. On the contrary, the worker's human dignity in it must be recognized. It, therefore, cannot be bought and sold like a commodity. Nevertheless, as the situation now stands, hiring and offering for hire in the so-called labor market separate men into two divisions, as into battle lines, and the contest between these divisions turns the labor market itself almost into a battlefield where face to face the opposing lines struggle bitterly. Everyone understands that this grave evil which is plunging all human society to destruction must be remedied as soon as possible. But complete cure will not come until this opposition has been abolished and well-ordered members of the social body — industries and professions — are constituted in which men may have their place, not according to the position each has in the labor market but according to the respective social functions which each performs. For under nature's guidance it comes to pass that just as those who are joined together by nearness of habitation establish towns, so those who follow the same industry or profession—whether in the economic or other field—form guilds or associations, so that many are wont to consider these self-governing organizations, if not essential, at least natural to civil society.

[179] Encyclical *On the Condition of Workers*, n. 135 in this book.

423

995. Because order, as St. Thomas well explains,[180] is unity arising from the harmonious arrangement of many objects, a true, genuine social order demands that the various members of a society be united together by some strong bond. This unifying force is present not only in the producing of goods or the rendering of services—in which the employers and employees of an identical industry or profession collaborate jointly—but also in that common good to achieve which all industries and professions together ought, each to the best of its ability, to co-operate amicably. And this unity will be the stronger and more effective, the more faithfully individuals and the industries and professions themselves strive to do their work and excel in it.

996. It is easily deduced from what has been said, that the interests common to the whole industry or profession should hold first place in these guilds. The most important among these interests is to promote the co-operation in the highest degree of each industry and profession for the sake of the common good of the country. Concerning matters, however, in which particular points, involving advantage or detriment to employers or workers, may require special care and protection, the two parties, when these cases arise, can deliberate separately or, as the situation requires, reach a decision separately.

997. The teaching of Leo XIII on the form of political government, namely, that men are free to choose whatever form they please, provided that proper regard is had for the requirements of justice and of the common good, is equally applicable in due proportion, it is hardly necessary to say, to the guilds of the various industries and professions.[181] Moreover, just as inhabitants of a town are wont to found associations with the widest diversity of purposes, which each is quite free to join or not, so those engaged in the same industry or profession will combine with one another into associations equally free for purposes connected in some manner with the pursuit of the calling itself. Since these free associations are clearly and lucidly explained by Our Predecessor of illustrious memory, We consider it enough to emphasize this one point: People are quite free not only to found such associations, which are a matter of private order and private right, but also in respect to

---

[180] St. Thomas, *Contra Gentiles,* III, 71; *cf. Summa Theologica,* I, Q.lxv, art. 2.
[181] *Cf.* Leo XIII, Encyclical *Immortale Dei,* November 1, 1885; *supra* n. 53.

them "freely to adopt the organization and the rules which they judge most appropriate to achieve their purpose."[182] The same freedom must be asserted for founding associations that go beyond the boundaries of individual callings. And may these free organizations, now flourishing and rejoicing in their salutary fruits, set before themselves the task of preparing the way, in conformity with the mind of Christian social teaching, for those larger and more important guilds, industries and professions, which We mentioned before, and make every possible effort to bring them to realization.

998. Attention must be given also to another matter that is closely connected with the foregoing. Just as the unity of human society cannot be founded on an opposition of classes, so also the right ordering of economic life cannot be left to a free competition of forces. For from this source, as from a poisoned spring, have originated and spread all the errors of individualist economic teaching. Destroying through forgetfulness or ignorance the social and moral character of economic life, it held that economic life must be considered and treated as altogether free from and independent of public authority, because in the market, that is, in the free struggle of competitors, it would have a principle of self-direction which governs it much more perfectly than through the intervention of any created intellect. But free competition, while justified and certainly useful, provided it is kept within certain limits, clearly cannot direct economic life—a truth which the outcome of the application in practice of the tenets of this evil individualistic spirit has more than sufficiently demonstrated. Therefore, it is most necessary that economic life be again subjected to and governed by a true and effective directing principle. This function is one that the economic dictatorship which has recently displaced free competition can still less perform, since it is a headstrong power and a violent energy that, to benefit people, needs to be strongly curbed and wisely ruled. But it cannot curb and rule itself. Loftier and nobler principles—social justice and social charity—must, therefore, be sought whereby this dictatorship may be governed firmly and fully. Hence, the institutions themselves of peoples, and particularly those of all social life, ought to be penetrated with this justice, and it is most necessary that it be truly effective, that is, establish a juridical and social order which will, as it were, give form and shape to all

[182] Encyclical *On the Condition of Workers*, n. 170 in this book.

economic life. Social charity, moreover, ought to be as the soul of this order, an order which public authority ought to be ever ready effectively to protect and defend. It will be able to do this the more easily as it rids itself of those burdens which, as We have stated above, are not properly its own.

999. Furthermore, since the various nations largely depend on one another in economic matters and need one another's help, they should strive with a united purpose and effort to promote, by wisely conceived pacts and institutions, a prosperous and happy international co-operation in economic life. If the members of the body social are, as was said, reconstituted, and if the directing principle of economic-social life is restored, it will be possible to say, in a certain sense, even of this body what the Apostle says of the Mystical Body of Christ: *The whole body (being closely joined and knit together through every joint of the system according to the functioning in due measure of each single part) derives its increase to the building up of itself in love.*[183] Recently, as all know, there has been inaugurated a special system of syndicates and corporations of the various callings which, in view of the theme of this Encyclical, it would seem necessary to describe here briefly and comment upon appropriately.

1000. The civil authority itself constitutes the syndicate as a juridical personality in such a manner as to confer on it simultaneously a certain monopoly-privilege, since only such a syndicate, when thus approved, can maintain the rights (according to the type of syndicate) of workers or employers, and since it alone can arrange for the placement of labor and conclude the so-termed labor agreements. Anyone is free to join a syndicate or not, and only within these limits can this kind of syndicate be called free; for syndical dues and special assessments are exacted of absolutely all members of every specified calling or profession, whether they are workers or employers; likewise all are bound by the labor agreements made by the legally recognized syndicate. Nevertheless, it has been officially stated that this legally recognized syndicate does not prevent the existence, without legal status, however, of other associations made up of persons following the same calling.

1001. The associations, or corporations, are composed of delegates from the two syndicates (that is, of workers and employers)

[183] *Ephesians,* IV, 16.

respectively of the same industry or profession and, as true and proper organs and institutions of the State, they direct the syndicates and co-ordinate their activities in matters of common interest toward one and the same end. Strikes and lock-outs are forbidden; if the parties cannot settle their dispute, public authority intervenes.

1002. Anyone who gives even slight attention to the matter, will easily see what are the obvious advantages in the system We have thus summarily described: The various classes work together peacefully, Socialist organizations and their activities are repressed, and a special magistracy exercises a governing authority. Yet, lest We neglect anything in a matter of such great importance, and that all points treated may be properly connected with the more general principles which We mentioned above and with those which We intend shortly to add, We are compelled to say that to Our certain knowledge there are not wanting some who fear that the State, instead of confining itself, as it ought, to the furnishing of necessary and adequate assistance, is substituting itself for free activity; that the new syndical and corporative order savors too much of an involved and political system of administration; and that (in spite of those more general advantages mentioned above, which are, of course, fully admitted) it rather serves particular political ends than leads to the reconstruction and promotion of a better social order.

1003. To achieve this latter lofty aim, and in particular to promote the common good truly and permanently, We hold it is, first and above everything, wholly necessary that God bless it and, secondly, that all men of good-will work with united effort toward that end. We are further convinced, as a necessary consequence, that this end will be attained the more certainly the larger the number of those ready to contribute toward it their technical, occupational and social knowledge and experience; and also, what is more important, the greater the contribution made thereto of Catholic principles and their application, not indeed by Catholic Action (which excludes strictly syndical or political activities from its scope) but by those sons of Ours whom Catholic Action imbues with Catholic principles and trains for carrying on an apostolate under the leadership and teaching guidance of the Church—of that Church which in this field, as in every other field where moral questions are involved and discussed, can never forget or neglect through indifference its divinely-imposed mandate to be vigilant and to teach.

427

1004. What We have taught about the reconstruction and perfection of social order can surely in no wise be brought to realization without reform of morality, the very record of history clearly shows. For there was a social order once which, although indeed not perfect or in all respects ideal, nevertheless, met in a certain measure the requirements of right reason, considering the conditions and needs of the time. If that order has long since perished, that surely did not happen because the order could not have accommodated itself to changed conditions and needs by development and by a certain expansion, but rather because men, hardened by too much love of self, refused to open the order to the increasing masses as they should have done, or because, deceived by allurements of a false freedom and other errors, they became impatient of every authority and sought to reject every form of control.

1005. There remains to Us, after again calling to judgment the economic system now in force and its most bitter accuser, Socialism, and passing explicit and just sentence upon them, to search out more thoroughly the root of these many evils and to point out that the first and most necessary remedy is a reform of morals. Important indeed have the changes been which both the economic system and Socialism have undergone since Leo XIII's time.

1006. That, in the first place, the whole aspect of economic life is vastly altered, is plain to all. You know, Venerable Brethren and Beloved Children, that the Encyclical of Our Predecessor of happy memory had in view chiefly that economic system wherein, generally, some provide capital while others provide labor for a joint economic activity. And in a happy phrase he described it thus: "Neither capital can do without labor, nor labor without capital." [184] With all his energy Leo XIII sought to adjust this economic system according to the norms of right order; hence, it is evident that this system is not to be condemned in itself. And surely it is not of its own nature vicious. But it does violate right order when capital hires workers, that is, the non-owning working class, with a view to and under such terms that it directs business and even the whole economic system according to its own will and advantage, scorning the human dignity of the work-

[184] Encyclical *On the Condition of Workers*, n. 135 in this book.

ers, the social character of economic activity and social justice itself, and the common good.

1007. Even to-day this is not, it is true, the only economic system in force everywhere; for there is another system also, which still embraces a huge mass of humanity, significant in numbers and importance, as for example, agriculture, wherein the greater portion of mankind honorably and honestly procures its livelihood. This group, too, is being crushed with hardships and with difficulties, to which Our Predecessor devotes attention in several places in his Encyclical. . . .

1008. But, with the diffusion of modern industry throughout the whole world, the "capitalist" economic regime has spread everywhere to such a degree, particularly since the publication of Leo XIII's Encyclical, that it has invaded and pervaded the economic and social life of even those outside its orbit and is unquestionably impressing on it its advantages, disadvantages and vices, and, in a sense, is giving it its own shape and form.

1009. Accordingly, when directing Our special attention to the changes which the capitalist economic system has undergone since Leo's time, We have in mind the good not only of those who dwell in regions given over to "capital" and industry, but of all mankind. In the first place, it is obvious that not only is wealth concentrated in our times but an immense power and despotic economic dictatorship is consolidated in the hands of a few, who often are not owners but only the trustees and managing directors of invested funds which they administer according to their own arbitrary will and pleasure.

1010. This dictatorship is being most forcibly exercised by those who, since they hold the money and completely control it, control credit also and rule the lending of money. Hence, they regulate the flow, so to speak, of the life-blood whereby the entire economic system lives, and have so firmly in their grasp the soul, as it were, of economic life that no one can breathe against their will.

1011. This concentration of power and might, the characteristic mark, as it were, of contemporary economic life, is the fruit that the unlimited freedom of struggle among competitors has of its own nature produced, and which lets only the strongest survive, which is often the same as saying, those who fight the most violently, those who give least heed to their conscience.

1012. This accumulation of might and of power generates in turn three kinds of conflict. First, there is the struggle for economic supremacy itself; then there is the bitter fight to gain supremacy over the State in order to use in economic struggles its resources and authority; finally, there is conflict between States themselves, not only because countries employ their power and shape their policies to promote every economic advantage of their citizens, but also because they seek to decide political controversies that arise among nations through the use of their economic supremacy and strength.

1013. The ultimate consequences of the individualist spirit in economic life are those which you yourselves, Venerable Brethren and Beloved Children, see and deplore: free competition has destroyed itself; economic dictatorship has supplanted the free market; unbridled ambition for power has likewise succeeded greed for gain; all economic life has become tragically hard, inexorable and cruel. To these are to be added the grave evils that have resulted from an intermingling and shameful confusion of the functions and duties of public authority with those of the economic sphere —such as, one of the worst, the virtual degradation of the majesty of the State, which, although it ought to sit on high like a queen and supreme arbitress, free from all partiality and intent upon the one common good and justice, is become a slave, surrendered and delivered to the passions and greed of men. And as to international relations, two different streams have issued from the one fountain-head: On the one hand, economic nationalism or even economic imperialism; on the other, a no less deadly and accursed internationalism of finance or international imperialism whose country is where profit is.

1014. In the second part of this Encyclical where We have presented Our teaching, We have described the remedies for these great evils so explicitly that We consider it sufficient at this point to recall them briefly. Since the present system of economy is founded chiefly upon ownership and labor, the principles of right reason, that is, of Christian social philosophy, must be kept in mind in theory regarding ownership and labor and their association together, and must be put into actual practice. First, so as to avoid the reefs of individualism and collectivism, the two-fold character, that is, individual and social, both of capital or ownership and of work or labor must be given due and rightful weight. Relations of one to the other must be made to conform to the laws of strictest justice — commutative justice, as it is called — with the support, however, of Christian charity. Free competition, kept within definite and due limits, and still more economic dictatorship, must be effectively brought under public authority in these matters which pertain to the latter's function. The public institutions themselves of peoples, moreover, ought to make all human society conform to the needs of the common good, that is, to the norm of social justice. If this is done, that most important division of social life, namely, economic activity, cannot fail likewise to return to right and sound order.

1015. Socialism, against which Our Predecessor, Leo XIII, had especially to inveigh, has since his time changed no less profoundly than the form of economic life. For Socialism, which could then be termed almost a single system, and which maintained definite teachings reduced into one body of doctrine, has since then split chiefly into two sections, often opposing one another and even bitterly hostile, without either one, however, abandoning a position fundamentally contrary to Christian truth that was characteristic of Socialism.

1016. One section of Socialism has undergone almost the same change that the capitalistic economic system, as We have explained above, has undergone. It has sunk into Communism. Communism teaches and seeks two objectives: Unrelenting class warfare and absolute extermination of private ownership. Not secretly or by hidden methods does it do this, but publicly, openly, and by employing every and all means, even the most violent. To achieve these objectives there is nothing which it does not dare, nothing for which it has respect or reverence; and when it has come to power, it is incredible and portent-like in its cruelty and inhumanity. The horrible slaughter and destruction through which it has laid waste vast regions of eastern Europe and Asia are the evidence; how much an enemy and how openly hostile it is to Holy Church and to God Himself is, alas, too well proved by facts and fully known to all. Although We, therefore, deem it superfluous to warn upright and faithful children of the Church regarding the impious and iniquitous character of Communism, yet We cannot without deep sorrow contemplate the heedless-ness of those who apparently make light of these impending dangers, and with sluggish inertia allow the wide-spread propagation of doctrine which seeks by violence and slaughter to destroy society altogether. All the more gravely to be condemned is the folly of those who neglect to remove or change the conditions that inflame the minds of peoples. . . .

1017. The other section, which has kept the name Socialism, is surely more moderate. It not only professes the rejection of violence, but modifies and tempers to some degree, if it does not reject entirely, the class struggle and the abolition of private ownership. One might say that, terrified by its own principles and by the conclusions drawn therefrom by Communism, Socialism inclines toward, and in a certain measure approaches, the truths which Christian tradition has always held sacred; for it cannot be denied that its demands at times come very near those that Christian reformers of society justly insist upon.

1018. For if the class struggle abstains from enmities and mutual hatred, it gradually changes into an honest discussion of differences founded on a desire for justice, and if this is not that blessed social peace which we all seek, it can and ought to be the point of departure from which to move forward to the mutual co-operation of the industries and professions. So also the war declared on private ownership, more and more abated, is being so restricted that now, finally, not the possession itself of the means of production is attacked but rather a kind of sovereignty over society which ownership, contrary to all right, has seized and usurped. For such sovereignty belongs in reality not to owners but to the public authority. If the foregoing happens, it can come even to that point that imperceptibly these ideas of the more moderate Socialism will no longer differ from the desires and demands of those who are striving to remold human society on the basis of Christian principles. For certain kinds of property, it is rightly contended, ought to be reserved to the State since they carry with them a dominating power so great that it cannot, without danger to the general welfare, be entrusted to private individuals. Such just demands and desires have nothing in them now which is inconsistent with Christian truth, and much less are they special to Socialism. Those who work solely toward such ends have, therefore, no reason to become Socialists.

1019. Yet let no one think that all the Socialist groups or factions that are not Communist have, without exception, recovered their senses to this extent either in fact or in name. For the most part they do not reject the class struggle or the abolition of ownership, but only in some degree modify them. Now if these false principles are modified and to some extent erased from the program, the question arises, or rather is raised without warrant by some, whether the principles of Christian truth cannot perhaps be also modified to some degree and be tempered so as to meet Socialism half-way and, as it were, by a middle course, come to agreement with it. There are some allured by the foolish hope that Socialists in this way will be drawn to us. A vain hope. Those who want to be apostles among Socialists ought to profess Christian truth whole and entire, openly and sincerely, and not connive at error in any way. If they truly wish to be heralds of the Gospel, let them above all strive to show to Socialists that Socialist claims, so far as they are just, are far more strongly supported by the principles of Christian faith and much more effectively promoted through the power of Christian charity.

1020. But what if Socialism has really been so tempered and modified as to the class struggle and private ownership that there is in it no longer anything to be censured on these points? Has it thereby renounced its nature contradictory to the Christian religion? This is the question that holds many minds in suspense. And numerous are the Catholics who, although they clearly understand that Christian principles can never be abandoned or diminished, seem to turn their eyes to the Holy See and earnestly beseech Us to decide whether this form of Socialism has so far recovered from false doctrines that it can be accepted without the sacrifice of any Christian principle and, in a certain sense, be baptized. That We, in keeping with Our fatherly solicitude, may answer their petitions, We make this pronouncement: whether considered as a doctrine, or an historical fact, or a movement, Socialism, if it remains truly Socialism, even after it has yielded to truth and justice on the points which We have mentioned, cannot be reconciled with the teachings of the Catholic Church because its concept of society itself is utterly foreign to Christian truth.

1021. For, according to Christian teaching, man, endowed with a social nature, is placed on this earth so that, by leading a life in society and under an authority ordained of God,[185] he may fully cultivate and develop all his faculties unto the praise and glory of his Creator; and that by faithfully fulfilling the duties of his craft or other calling he may obtain for himself temporal and at the same time eternal happiness. Socialism, on the other hand, wholly ignoring and indifferent to this sublime end of both man and society, affirms that human association has been instituted for the sake of material advantage alone.

1022. Because of the fact that goods are produced more efficiently by a suitable division of labor than by the scattered efforts of individuals, Socialists infer that economic activity, only the material ends of which enter into their thinking, ought of necessity to be carried on socially. Because of this necessity, they hold that men are obliged, with respect to the producing of goods, to surrender and subject themselves entirely to society. Indeed, possession of the greatest possible supply of things that serve the advantages of this life is considered of such great importance that the higher goods of man, liberty not excepted, must take a secondary place and even be sacrificed to the demands of the most efficient production of goods. This damage to human dignity, undergone in the "socialized" process of production, will be easily offset, they say, by the abundance of socially produced goods which will pour out in profusion to individuals to be used freely at their pleasure for comforts and cultural development. Society, therefore, as Socialism conceives it, can on the one hand neither exist nor be thought of without an obviously excessive use of force; on the other hand, it fosters a liberty no less false since there is no place in it for social authority, which rests not on temporal and material advantages but descends from God alone, the Creator and last end of all things.[186]

1023. If Socialism, like all errors, contains some truth (which, moreover, the Supreme Pontiffs have never denied), it is based nevertheless on a theory of human society peculiar to itself and irreconcilable with true Christianity. Religious Socialism, Christian Socialism, are contradictory terms; no one can be at the same time a good Catholic and a true Socialist.

1024. All these admonitions which have been renewed and

[185] Cf. Romans, XIII, 1.
[186] Cf. Leo XIII, Encyclical Diuturnum Illud, June 29, 1881.

confirmed by Our solemn authority must likewise be applied to a certain new kind of Socialist activity, hitherto little known but now carried on among many Socialist groups. It devotes itself above all to the training of the mind and character. Under the guise of affection it tries in particular to attract children of tender age and win them to itself, although it also embraces the whole population in its scope in order finally to produce true Socialists who would shape human society to the tenets of Socialism.

1025. Since in Our Encyclical, *The Christian Education of Youth*,[187] We have fully taught the principles that Christian education insists on and the ends it pursues, the contradiction between these principles and ends and the activities and aims of this Socialism that is pervading morality and culture is so clear and evident that no demonstration is required here. But they seem to ignore or underestimate the grave dangers that it carries with it who think it of no importance courageously and zealously to resist them according to the gravity of the situation. It belongs to Our Pastoral Office to warn these persons of the grave and imminent evil: let all remember that Liberalism is the father of this Socialism that is pervading morality and culture and that Bolshevism will be its heir.

1026. Accordingly, Venerable Brethren, you can well understand with what great sorrow We observe that not a few of Our sons, in certain regions especially, although We cannot be convinced that they have given up the true Faith and right will, have deserted the camp of the Church and gone over to the ranks of Socialism, some to glory openly in the name of Socialist and to profess Socialist doctrines, others through thoughtlessness or even almost against their wills to join associations which are Socialist by profession or in fact.

1027. In the anxiety of Our paternal solicitude, We give Ourself to reflection and try to discover how it could happen that they should go so far astray and We seem to hear what many of them answer and plead in excuse: the Church and those proclaiming attachment to the Church favor the rich, neglect the workers and have no concern for them; therefore, to look after themselves they had to join the ranks of Socialism.

1028. It is certainly most lamentable, Venerable Brethren, that

[187] Encyclical *Divini Illius Magistri,* December 31, 1929; *cf. supra* nn. 897-909.

there have been, nay, that even now there are men who, although professing to be Catholics, are almost completely unmindful of that sublime law of justice and charity that binds us not only to render to everyone what is his but to succor brothers in need as Christ, the Lord Himself,[188] and, what is worse, out of greed for gain do not scruple to exploit the workers. Even more, there are men who abuse religion itself, and under its name try to hide their unjust exactions in order to protect themselves from the manifestly just demands of the workers. The conduct of such We shall never cease to censure gravely. For they are the reason why the Church could, even though undeservedly, have the appearance of and be charged with taking the part of the rich and with being quite unmoved by the necessities and hardships of those who have been deprived, as it were, of their natural inheritance. The whole history of the Church plainly demonstrates that such appearances are unfounded and such charges unjust. The Encyclical itself, whose anniversary we are celebrating, is clearest proof that it is the height of injustice to hurl these calumnies and reproaches at the Church and her teaching.

1029. Although pained by the injustice and downcast in fatherly sorrow, it is so far from Our thought to repulse or to disown children who have been miserably deceived and have strayed so far from the truth and salvation that We cannot but invite them with all possible solicitude to return to the maternal bosom of the Church. May they lend ready ears to Our voice; may they return whence they have left, to the home that is truly their Father's, and may they stand firm there where their own place is, in the ranks of those who, zealously following the admonitions which Leo promulgated and We have solemnly repeated, are striving to restore society according to the mind of the Church on the firmly established basis of social justice and social charity. And let them be convinced that nowhere, even on earth, can they find full happiness save with Him Who, being rich, became poor for our sakes that through His poverty we might become rich,[189] Who was poor and in labors from His youth, Who invited to Himself all that labor and are heavily burdened that He might refresh them fully in the love of His heart,[190] and Who, lastly, without any respect

---

[188] *Cf.* James, II.
[189] *Cf.* II *Corinthians*, VIII, 9.
[190] *Cf. Matthew*, XI, 28.

for persons, will require more of them to whom more has been given[191] and *will render to everyone according to his conduct.*[192]

1030. Yet, if we look into the matter more carefully and more thoroughly, we shall clearly perceive that, preceding this ardently desired social restoration, there must be a renewal of the Christian spirit, from which so many immersed in economic life have, far and wide, unhappily fallen away, lest all our efforts be wasted and our house be built not on a rock but on shifting sand.[193] And so, Venerable Brethren and Beloved Sons, having surveyed the present economic system, We have found it laboring under the gravest of evils. We have also summoned Communism and Socialism again to judgment and have found all their forms, even the most modified, to wander far from the precepts of the Gospel.

1031. "Wherefore," to use the words of Our Predecessor, "if human society is to be healed, only a return to Christian life and institutions will heal it."[194] For this alone can provide effective remedy for that excessive care for passing things that is the origin of all vices; and this alone can draw away men's eyes, fascinated by and wholly fixed on the changing things of the world, and raise them toward heaven. Who would deny that human society is in most urgent need of this cure now? Minds of all, it is true, are affected almost solely by temporal upheavals, disasters and calamities. But if we examine things critically with Christian eyes, as we should, what are all these compared with the loss of souls? Yet it is not rash by any means to say that the whole scheme of social and economic life is now such as to put in the way of vast numbers of mankind most serious obstacles which prevent them from caring for the one thing necessary — namely, their eternal salvation.

1032. We, made Shepherd and Protector by the Prince of Shepherds, Who redeemed them by His Blood, of a truly innumerable flock, cannot hold back Our tears when contemplating this greatest of their dangers. Nay rather, fully mindful of Our Pastoral Office and with paternal solicitude, We are continually meditating on how We can help them; and We have summoned to Our aid the untiring zeal also of others who are concerned on grounds of

[191] *Cf. Luke,* XII, 48.
[192] *Matthew,* XVI, 27.
[193] *Cf. Matthew,* VII, 24 *sq.*
[194] Encyclical *On the Condition of Workers,* n. 140 in this book.

justice or charity. For what will it profit men to become expert in more wisely using their wealth, even to gaining the whole world, if thereby they suffer the loss of their souls?[195] What will it profit to teach them sound principles of economic life if in unbridled and sordid greed they let themselves be swept away by their passion for property so that, *hearing the commandments of the Lord they do all things contrary?*[196]

1033.   The root and font of this defection from the Christian law, in economic and social life, and of the consequent apostasy of great numbers of workers from the Catholic Faith, are the disordered passions of the soul, the sad result of original sin which has so destroyed the wonderful harmony of man's faculties that, easily led astray by his evil desires, he is strongly incited to prefer the passing goods of this world to the lasting goods of heaven. Hence arises that unquenchable thirst for riches and temporal goods, which has at all times impelled men to break God's laws and trample upon the rights of their neighbors, but which, on account of the present system of economic life, is laying far more numerous snares for human frailty. Since the instability of economic life, and especially of its structure, exacts of those engaged in it most intense and unceasing effort, some have become so hardened to the stings of conscience as to hold that they are allowed, in any manner whatsoever, to increase their profits and use means, fair or foul, to protect their hard-won wealth against sudden changes of fortune. The easy gains, that a market unrestricted by any law opens to everybody, attract large numbers to buying and selling goods, and they, their one aim being to make quick profits with the least expenditure of work, raise or lower prices by their uncontrolled business dealings so rapidly, according to their own caprice and greed, that they nullify the wisest forecasts of producers. The laws passed to promote corporate business, while dividing and limiting the risk of business, have given occasion to the most sordid license. For We observe that consciences are little affected by this reduced obligation of accountability; that furthermore, by hiding under the shelter of a joint name, the worst of injustices and frauds are perpetrated; and that, too, directors of business companies, forgetful of their trust, betray the rights of those whose savings they have undertaken

[195] *Cf. Matthew*, XVI, 26.
[196] *Judges*, II, 17.

438

to administer. Lastly, We must not omit to mention those crafty men who, wholly unconcerned about any honest usefulness of their work, do not scruple to stimulate the baser human desires and, when they are aroused, use them for their own profit.

1034. Strict and watchful moral restraint enforced vigorously by governmental authority could have banished these enormous evils and even forestalled them; this restraint, however, has too often been sadly lacking. For since the seeds of a new form of economy were bursting forth just when the principles of rationalism had been implanted and rooted in many minds, there quickly developed a body of economic teaching far removed from the true moral law, and, as a result, completely free rein was given to human passions.

1035. Thus it came to pass that many, much more than ever before, were solely concerned with increasing their wealth by any means whatsoever, and that in seeking their own selfish interests before everything else, they had no conscience about committing even the gravest of crimes against others. Those first entering upon this broad way that leads to destruction[197] easily found numerous imitators of their iniquity by the example of their manifest success, by their insolent display of wealth, by their ridiculing the conscience of others, who, as they said, were troubled by silly scruples, or lastly by crushing the more conscientious competitors.

1036. With the rulers of economic life abandoning the right road, it was easy for the rank and file of workers everywhere to rush headlong also into the same chasm; and, all the more so, because very many managements treated their workers like mere tools, with no concern at all for their souls, without indeed even the least thought of spiritual things. Truly the mind shudders at the thought of the grave dangers to which the morals of workers (particularly younger workers) and the modesty of girls and women are exposed in modern factories; when we recall how often the present economic scheme, and particularly the shameful housing conditions, create obstacles to the family bond and normal family life; when we remember how many obstacles are put in the way of the proper observance of Sundays and Holy Days; and when we reflect upon the universal weakening of that truly Christian sense through which even rude and unlettered men were wont

[197] Cf. Matthew, VII, 13.

to value higher things, and upon its substitution by the single pre-occupation of getting in any way whatsoever one's daily bread. And thus bodily labor, which Divine Providence decreed to be performed after original sin for the good at once of man's body and soul, is being everywhere changed into an instrument of perversion; for dead matter comes forth from the factory ennobled, while men there are corrupted and degraded.

1037. No genuine cure can be furnished for this lamentable ruin of souls, which, so long as it continues, will frustrate all efforts to regenerate society, unless men return openly and sincerely to the teaching of the Gospel, to the precepts of Him Who alone has the words of everlasting life,[198] words which will never pass away, even if heaven and earth will pass away.[199] All experts in social problems are seeking eagerly a structure so fashioned in accordance with the norms of reason that it can lead economic life back to sound and right order. But this order, which We Ourself ardently long for and with all Our efforts promote, will be wholly defective and incomplete unless all the activities of men harmoniously unite to imitate and attain, insofar as it lies within human strength, the marvelous unity of the Divine plan. We mean that perfect order which the Church with great force and power preaches and which right human reason itself demands, that all things be directed to God as the first and supreme end of all created activity, and that all created good under God be considered as mere instruments to be used only insofar as they conduce to the attainment of the supreme end. Nor is it to be thought that gainful occupations are thereby belittled or judged less consonant with human dignity; on the contrary, we are taught to recognize in them with reverence the manifest Will of the Divine Creator Who placed man upon the earth to work it and use it in a multitude of ways for his needs. Those who are engaged in producing goods, therefore, are not forbidden to increase their fortune in a just and lawful manner; for it is only fair that he who renders service to the community and makes it richer should also, through the increased wealth of the community, be made richer himself according to his position, provided that all these things be sought with due respect for the laws of God and without impairing the rights of others and that

[198] Cf. John, VI, 70.
[199] Cf. Matthew, XXIV, 35.

they be employed in accordance with faith and right reason. If these principles are observed by everyone, everywhere and always, not only the production and acquisition of goods but also the use of wealth, which now is seen to be so often contrary to right order, will be brought back soon within the bounds of equity and just distribution. The sordid love of wealth, which is the shame and great sin of our age, will be opposed in actual fact by the gentle yet effective law of Christian moderation which commands man to seek first the Kingdom of God and His justice, with the assurance that, by virtue of God's kindness and unfailing promise, temporal goods also, insofar as he has need of them, shall be given him besides.[200]

1038. But in effecting all this, the law of charity, *which is the bond of perfection,*[201] must always take a leading role. How completely deceived, therefore, are those rash reformers who concern themselves with the enforcement of justice alone—and this, commutative justice—and in their pride reject the assistance of charity! Admittedly, no vicarious charity can substitute for justice which is due as an obligation and is wrongfully denied. Yet even supposing that everyone should finally receive all that is due him, the widest field for charity will always remain open. For justice alone can, if faithfully observed, remove the causes of social conflict but can never bring about union of minds and hearts. Indeed, all the institutions for the establishment of peace and the promotion of mutual help among men, however perfect these may seem, have the principal foundation of their stability in the mutual bond of minds and hearts whereby the members are united with one another. If this bond is lacking, the best of regulations come to naught, as we have learned by too frequent experience. And so, then only will true co-operation be possible for a single common good when the constituent parts of society deeply feel themselves members of one great family and children of the same Heavenly Father; nay, that they are one body in Christ, *but severally members one of another,*[202] so that *if one member suffers anything, all the members suffer with it.*[203] For then the rich and others in positions of power will change their former indifference toward their poorer brothers into

[200] *Cf. Matthew,* VI, 33.
[201] *Colossians,* III, 14.
[202] *Romans,* XII, 5.
[203] I *Corinthians,* XII, 26.

a solicitous and active love, listen with kindliness to their just demands, and freely forgive their possible mistakes and faults. And the workers, sincerely putting aside every feeling of hatred or envy which the promoters of social conflict so cunningly exploit, will not only accept without rancor the place in human society assigned them by Divine Providence, but rather will hold it in esteem, knowing well that everyone, according to his function and duty, is toiling usefully and honorably for the common good and is following closely in the footsteps of Him Who, being in the form of God, willed to be a carpenter among men and be known as the Son of a carpenter.

1039.   Therefore, out of this new diffusion throughout the world of the spirit of the Gospel, which is the spirit of Christian moderation and universal charity, We are confident there will come that longed-for and full restoration of human society in Christ, and that "Peace of Christ in the Kingdom of Christ," to accomplish which, from the very beginning of Our Pontificate, We firmly determined and resolved within Our heart to devote all Our care and all Our pastoral solicitude;[204] and toward this same highly important and most necessary end now, you also, Venerable Brethren, who with Us rule the Church of God under the mandate of the Holy Ghost,[205] are earnestly toiling with wholly praiseworthy zeal in all parts of the world, even in the regions of the holy missions to the infidels. Let well-merited acclamations of praise be bestowed upon you and at the same time upon all those, both clergy and laity, whom We rejoice to see daily participating and valiantly helping in this same great work, Our beloved sons engaged in Catholic Action, who with a singular zeal are undertaking with Us the solution of the social problem insofar as by virtue of her divine institution this is proper to and devolves upon the Church. All these We urge in the Lord, again and again, to spare no labors and let no difficulties conquer them, but rather to become day by day more courageous and more valiant.[206] Arduous indeed is the task which We propose to them, for We know well that on both sides, both among the upper and the lower classes of society, there are many obstacles and barriers to be overcome. Let them not, however, lose heart;

---

[204] Encyclical *Ubi Arcano*, December 23, 1922; *cf. supra* n. 804.
[205] *Cf. Acts*, XX, 28.
[206] *Cf. Deuteronomy*, XXXI, 7.

to face bitter combats is a mark of Christians, and to endure grave labors to the end is a mark of them who, as good soldiers of Christ,[207] follow Him closely.

1040. Relying, therefore, solely on the all-powerful aid of Him *Who wishes all men to be saved*,[208] let us strive with all our strength to help those unhappy souls who have turned from God and, drawing them away from the temporal cares in which they are too deeply immersed, let us teach them to aspire with confidence to the things that are eternal. Sometimes this will be achieved much more easily than seems possible at first sight to expect. For if wonderful spiritual forces lie hidden, like sparks beneath ashes, within the secret recesses of even the most abandoned man—certain proof that his soul is naturally Christian—how much the more in the hearts of those many upon many who have been led into error rather through ignorance or environment?

1041. Moreover, the ranks of the workers themselves are already giving happy and promising signs of a social reconstruction. To Our soul's great joy, We see in these ranks also the massed companies of young workers, who are receiving the counsel of Divine Grace with willing ears and striving with marvelous zeal to gain their comrades for Christ. No less praise must be accorded to the leaders of workers' organizations who, disregarding their own personal advantage and concerned solely about the good of their fellow members, are striving prudently to harmonize the just demands of their members with the prosperity of their whole occupation and also to promote these demands, and who do not let themselves be deterred from so noble a service by any obstacle or suspicion. Also, as anyone may see, many young men, who, by reason of their talent or wealth, will soon occupy high places among the leaders of society, are studying social problems with deeper interest, and they arouse the joyful hope that they will dedicate themselves wholly to the restoration of society.

1042. The present state of affairs, Venerable Brethren, clearly indicates the way in which we ought to proceed. For we are now confronted, as more than once before in the history of the Church, with a world that in large part has almost fallen back into paganism. That these whole classes of men may be brought back to

[207] *Cf.* II *Timothy*, II, 3.
[208] I *Timothy*, II, 4.

Christ Whom they have denied, we must recruit and train from among them, themselves, auxiliary soldiers of the Church who know them well and their minds and wishes, and can reach their hearts with a tender brotherly love. The first and immediate apostles to the workers ought to be workers; the apostles to those who follow industry and trade ought to be from among them themselves.

1043. It is chiefly your duty, Venerable Brethren, and that of your clergy, to search diligently for these lay apostles both of workers and of employers, to select them with prudence, and to train and instruct them properly. A difficult task, certainly, is thus imposed on priests, and, to meet it, all who are growing up as the hope of the Church must be duly prepared by an intensive study of the social question. Especially is it necessary that those whom you intend to assign in particular to this work should demonstrate that they are men possessed of the keenest sense of justice, who will resist with true manly courage the dishonest demands or the unjust act of anyone, who will excel in the prudence and judgment which avoids every extreme, and, above all, who will be deeply permeated by the charity of Christ, which alone has the power to subdue firmly but gently the hearts and wills of men to the laws of justice and equity. Upon this road so often tried by happy experience, there is no reason why we should hesitate to move forward with all speed.

1044. These, Our Beloved Sons, who are chosen for so great a work, We earnestly exhort in the Lord to give themselves wholly to the training of the men committed to their care, and in the discharge of this eminently priestly and Apostolic duty to make proper use of the resources of Christian education by teaching youth, forming Christian organizations, and founding study groups guided by principles in harmony with the Faith. But above all, let them hold in high esteem and assiduously employ for the good of their disciples that most valuable means of both personal and social restoration which, as We taught in Our Encyclical, *Mens Nostra,*[209] is to be found in the spiritual exercises. In that Letter We expressly mentioned and warmly recommended not only the spiritual exercises for all the laity, but also the highly beneficial workers' retreats. For in that school of the spirit, not only are the best of Christians developed but true apostles also are trained for every condition of

[209] Encyclical *Mens Nostra,* December 20, 1929.

life and are enkindled with the fire of the Heart of Christ. From this school they will go forth as did the Apostles from the Upper Room of Jerusalem, strong in faith, endowed with an invincible steadfastness in persecution, burning with zeal, interested solely in spreading everywhere the Kingdom of Christ.

1045. Certainly there is the greatest need now of such valiant soldiers of Christ who will work with all their strength to keep the human family safe from the dire ruin into which it would be plunged were the teachings of the Gospel to be flouted, and that order of things permitted to prevail which tramples underfoot no less the laws of nature than those of God. The Church of Christ, built upon an unshakable rock, has nothing to fear for herself, as she knows for a certainty that the gates of hell shall never prevail against her.[210] Rather, she knows full well, through the experience of many centuries, that she is wont to come forth from the most violent storms stronger than ever and adorned with new triumphs. Yet her maternal heart cannot but be moved by the countless evils with which so many thousands would be afflicted during storms of this kind, and above all by the consequent enormous injury to spiritual life which would work eternal ruin to so many souls redeemed by the Blood of Jesus Christ. To ward off such great evils from human society nothing, therefore, is to be left untried; to this end may all our labors turn, to this all our energies, to this our fervent and unremitting prayers to God! For with the assistance of Divine Grace the fate of the human family rests in our hands.

1046. Venerable Brethren and Beloved Sons, let us not permit the children of this world to appear wiser in their generation than we who, by the Divine Goodness, are the children of the light.[211] We find them, indeed, selecting and training with the greatest shrewdness alert and resolute devotees who spread their errors ever wider day by day through all classes of men and in every part of the world. And whenever they undertake to attack the Church of Christ more violently, We see them put aside their internal quarrels, assembling in full harmony in a single battle line with a completely united effort, and work to achieve their common purpose.

1047. Surely there is not one that does not know how many and how great are the works that the tireless zeal of Catholics is

[210] *Cf. Matthew*, XVI, 18.
[211] *Cf. Luke*, XVI, 8.

striving everywhere to carry out, both for social and economic welfare as well as in the fields of education and religion. But this admirable and unremitting activity not infrequently shows less effectiveness because of the dispersion of its energies in too many different directions. Therefore, let all men of good-will stand united, all who under the Shepherds of the Church wish to fight this good and peaceful battle of Christ; and, under the leadership and teaching guidance of the Church, let all strive according to the talent, powers and position of each to contribute something to the Christian reconstruction of human society which Leo XIII inaugurated through his immortal Encyclical, *On the Condition of Workers,* seeking not themselves and their own interests, but those of Jesus Christ;[212] not trying to press at all costs their own counsels, but ready to sacrifice them, however excellent, if the greater common good should seem to require it, so that in all and above all Christ may reign, Christ may command, to Whom be *honor and glory and dominion forever and ever.*[213]

1048. That this may happily come to pass, to all of you, Venerable Brethren and Beloved Children, who are members of the vast Catholic family entrusted to Us, but with the especial affection of Our heart to workers and to all others engaged in manual occupations, committed to Us more urgently by Divine Providence, and to Christian employers and managements, with paternal love We impart the Apostolic Benediction.

ENCYCLICAL *Non Abbiamo Bisogno* ON CATHOLIC ACTION.[214]

The Pope condemns the proposal to monopolize completely the young for the exclusive advantage of a party or a regime.

June 29, 1931

1049. ......The interior peace—that peace which comes to anyone with full and clear knowledge that one is arrayed on the side of Truth and Justice and that one is striving and suffering

---

[212] *Cf. Philippians,* II, 21.
[213] *Apocalypse,* V, 13.
[214] Translation from *Catholic Action* (N.C.W.C. pamphlet), pp. 4-31. Original Italian, *A.A.S.,* v. 23, pp. 286-312 (July 6, 1931).

for these virtues—that peace which only God can give and which the world, in the same way that it cannot give, neither can it take away—that blessed and consoling peace has never left Us, thanks to Divine Goodness and Mercy; and We have fullest confidence that, come what may, it will never leave Us. But the possession of this peace—and this was verified in the Heart of Our suffering Saviour and is also verified in the hearts of His faithful followers—does not prevent the torment of bitterness, as well you know, Venerable Brethren, and We also have experienced the truth of those mysterious words: *Behold in peace is my bitterness most bitter.*[215] . . . . . .

1050. We and the bishops and the clergy and all the faithful—in fact, all citizens desirous of peace and order—have worried and suffered and are worrying and suffering in the presence of a systematic campaign all too quickly begun against the most reasonable and precious liberties of religion and of consciences, such as were the attacks on Catholic Action and its different associations, especially those of the young. . . . . . . We know of impious parodies of sacred processions, all of which were permitted to take place to the profound sorrow of the faithful and the great amazement of all citizens who desire peace and order, who were obliged to witness peace and order undefended, and even worse than undefended, by those very persons who have both the solemn duty and vital interest to defend them. . . . . . .

1051. We are, as We stated above, happy and proud to wage the good fight for the liberty of consciences, not indeed (as someone, perhaps inadvertently, has quoted Us as saying) for the liberty of conscience which is an equivocal expression too often distorted to mean the absolute independence of conscience, which is absurd in a soul created and redeemed by God. . . . . . .

1052. And here We find Ourself in the presence of authentic affirmations on the one hand and not less authentic facts on the other hand, which reveal, without the slightest possibility of doubt, the proposal, already in great part actually put into effect, to monopolize completely the young, from the tenderest years up to manhood and womanhood, and all for the exclusive advantage of a party, of a regime based on an ideology which clearly resolves itself into a true and real pagan worship of the State, which is no less

---

[215] *Isaias,* XXXVIII, 17.

in contrast with the natural rights of the family than it is in contradiction to the supernatural rights of the Church. To propose and promote such a monopoly, to persecute for this reason Catholic Action, as has been done for some time more or less openly or under cover, to reach this end by striking Catholic Action in the way that has recently occurred, is truly and actually to prevent children from going to Jesus Christ, since it prevents them from going to His Church. . . . . . .

1053. A conception of the State, which makes the young generations belong entirely to it without any exception from the tenderest years up to adult life, cannot be reconciled by a Catholic with the Catholic doctrine; nor can it be reconciled with the natural right of the family. It is not possible for a Catholic to reconcile with Catholic doctrine the pretense that the Church and the Pope must limit themselves to the external practices of religion, such as Mass and the Sacraments, and then to say that the rest of education belongs to the State. . . . . . .

1054. Everything is definitely promised in answer to prayer: if the answer will not be the re-establishment of serene and tranquil relations, it will have its answer at any rate in Christian patience, in holy courage, in the infallible joy of suffering something with Jesus and for Jesus, with the youth and for the youth so dear to Him, until the hour hidden in the mystery of the Divine Heart which will infallibly be the most opportune for the cause of truth and of good.

1055. And since from so many prayers We must hope for everything, and since everything is possible to that God Who has promised everything in answer to prayer, We have confident hope that He will illumine minds to truth and turn wills to good, so that the Church of God, which wishes nothing from the State that belongs to the competence of the State, will cease to be asked for that which is the Church's competence—the education and the Christian formation of youth—and this not through human favor, but by divine mandate, and that which, therefore, she always asks and will always ask with an insistence and an intransigeance which cannot cease or waver because it does not come from human desire or design, or from human ideas, changeable in different times and places and circumstances, but from the divine and inviolable disposition. . . . . . .

ENCYCLICAL *Nova Impendet* ON THE ECONOMIC CRISIS.[216]

Excessive competition in armaments causes in no small way the rivalry among nations and the enormous squandering of public moneys.

October 2, 1931

1056. . . . . . . To this crusade of compassion We exhort all as to a sacred duty, a duty rooted in that commandment so distinctly peculiar to the evangelical law and proclaimed by Christ our Lord as the first and greatest commandment, the summary and compendium of all the rest, the commandment, namely, of charity. It was the commandment which Our immediate beloved Predecessor urged so frequently and so insistently at a time when war and bitter enmity raged well-nigh throughout the world, and which he made the distinctive note, as it were, of his pontificate. To this sweet precept We, too, now appeal. . . . . . .

1057. The acute crisis which We lament is at one and the same time the effect of the rivalry among nations, and the cause of enormous squandering of public moneys, and these two evils are to no small extent due to the excessive and ever-increasing competition in the output of military stores and implements of war. Hence, We cannot refrain from renewing on this occasion Our timely warnings,[217] as well as that of Our Predecessor,[218] a warning which We regret has not so far been successfully put into practice. At the same time We exhort you, Venerable Brethren, to strive by every means in your power, in the pulpit and in the Press, to enlighten men's minds and to shape their hearts in conformity with the saner dictates of right reason and Christian law. . . . . . .

1058. The solemn feast draws near of Christ the King Whose reign and Whose peace from the beginning of Our Pontificate We have desired and implored; it seems to Us in every way opportune at this time to celebrate a triduum of supplication in all churches, to beg assistance from the Lord of Mercies, and the blessings of peace. . . .

---

[216] Translation from *On the Economic Crisis* (C.T.S. pamphlet), pp. 6-10. Original Latin, *A.A.S.*, v. 23, pp. 395-397 (October 3, 1931).

[217] Allocution *Benedetto il Natale,* December 24, 1930, *cf. supra* nn. 913-922; and Letter *Con Vivo Piacere,* April 7, 1922, *cf. supra* nn. 729-732.

[218] Exhortation *Dès le Début,* August 1, 1917, *cf. supra* nn. 519-534.

ALLOCUTION *E Questo È Veramente* TO THE COLLEGE OF
CARDINALS.[219]

The Holy Father condemns isolation, reciprocal exclusiveness, distrust and intimidation.

December 24, 1931

1059. . . . . . . Many will surely say: But the Holy Father has not said a word, not even one word, about peace, disarmament, the cessation or suspension of armaments, about which the atmosphere of the whole world is full and palpitating with arguments. Verily, no. He does not intend to pronounce that word. He has not spoken it, first of all, because he has already spoken many times, as have also his Predecessors; and also because it has been said already by the angels who have come from heaven for the Divine Nativity. It has already been repeated and proclaimed to the world with the return to the cradle of the unarmed King of Peace, the unarmed Omnipotence.

1060. This word has been uttered literally in the expectation of the coming of Jesus, in the expectation of the birth of the Divine Infant. The prophet had already said and seen it when he saw the sword transformed into a ploughshare and the lion and the lamb lying down together. It was a word full of peace: peace of heart, peace of soul, peace between creatures capable of feeling the desire, the benefit and the necessity of it. Then that other peace, external peace, and finally the means of peace which are evidently not arms, but the instruments of good and well-being.

1061. We have not uttered that word for another reason: because it is manifest that this word is liable to much abuse, so that We know by experience that We cannot speak upon this matter without Our words being subjected to the most absurd and contradictory interpretations. And then? Why, then Our words of peace and concord become new occasions of discord and division among men.

1062. Our final observation shall be this: instead of speaking to men of peace, tranquillity, mutual benevolence and mutual beneficence, We shall speak only to God, since men do not and are not disposed to listen to Us. In the midst of all this disquiet, what is

[219] Translation from *The Tablet*, v. 159, pp. 18-19 (January 2, 1932). Original Italian, *Civiltà Cattolica*, 1932, v. 1, pp. 176-177 (January 9, 1932).

there that is really solid? There is only the solidarity of disquiet, pain and suffering. And besides all this, there is a competition of isolation, of reciprocal exclusiveness, distrust, and, We may almost add, of intimidation. On the one side there is universal suffering; on the other armaments which lead nowhere, while in the extreme East war has broken out between two great peoples. When the earth presents such ill prospects, so unpromising, and more, so menacing, it is clear that to call upon heaven with a strong cry is the duty incumbent upon all; instead, they have neither heeded nor felt the need of it.

1063. Who is there who does not see that it is the Hand of God which enters into human things; who does not see that this universal suffering depends not upon human hands? Human events, then, do not obey the human will. See all on their feet, all engaged in profound studies, all absorbed in a competition of research to discover the cause of this universal disquiet, this general evil, in order to find remedies. And it all results in nothing. The remedies are not found; and, what is still more sad, none see what is so evident, the Hand of God in it. There is no thought of God. True, in far-away America, there was such a remembrance, especially in thanksgiving for the great benefits which Divine Providence had bestowed upon that immense country; nor was the accent of gratitude wanting that the present evil was not so grave there as elsewhere. But what is this in such a universal suffering?

1064. In all this going and coming, meeting, discussing and research on the part of so many eminent personages, so many learned men, there is no mention of God, and it increases the fear of what We see in part already: the fear that God, after having made us feel the weight of His justice—perhaps after making us feel it yet more heavily—will have nothing else to do save to leave us to act by ourselves, leave us poor men to ourselves, leave us to act without Him.

1065. What can we do, what can so many men do, what can the whole world do, without God, forgetful of Him and not turning to Him? Here comes in the formidable evidence of the Divine Word, the infallible, incontrovertible truth: *Nisi Dominus ædificaverit domum, in vanum laboraverunt qui ædificant eam.*[220] The city, the house, cannot be built and protected except by God. From

[220] *Psalms*, CXXVI, 1.

this it necessarily follows that we must turn in heart, thought, and with our whole soul, to Him. It is to God that We intend to speak, it is to God that We shall upraise Our prayer. . . . . . .

ENCYCLICAL *Lux Veritatis* ON THE FIFTEENTH CENTENARY OF THE COUNCIL OF EPHESUS.[221]

Public welfare and peace are founded on Christian principles and precepts.

December 25, 1931

1066. . . . . . . If the Church falls on difficult times, if faith wanes and charity grows cold, if morals, private and public, grow worse, if any danger threatens the Catholic cause or civil society, let us have recourse to her (Mary), begging help from heaven; in the supreme trial of death, when all hope, all help, is gone, let us lift up our eyes in tears and trembling, imploring through her, pardon from her Son and eternal joy in heaven.

1067. With more ardent effort, therefore, in the present needs under which we labor, let all go to her, and with supplication beg earnestly "that, by interceding with her Son, the erring nations may return to Christian principles and precepts, on which the foundation of public welfare rests, and through which desirable peace and true happiness flourish in abundance. From her also let them more earnestly pray for what all should have most at heart, that Mother Church may have liberty and the fruit of it in tranquillity, a liberty which it will use for the sole purpose of procuring the highest interests of mankind, and from which harm has never come to individuals or States, but always many very great benefits."[222] . . . . .

1068. If all these things should result as We counsel, if domestic society—the principle and foundation of all human intercourse—should revert to the most exalted standard of this holiness, we could in time provide a remedy for our dangerous evil conditions. May it so happen that *the Peace of God which surpasseth all understanding*[223] keep the minds and hearts of all and, with all our minds and forces united, may Christ's Kingdom be established! . . .

[221] Translation from *The Light of Truth* (N.C.W.C. pamphlet), pp. 22-25. Original Latin, *A.A.S.*, v. 23, pp. 514-516 (December 26, 1931).
[222] Encyclical *Octobri Mense*, September 22, 1891.
[223] *Philippians*, IV, 7.

ADDRESS TO THE LENTEN PREACHERS OF ROME.[224]

In vain do statesmen assemble to consider the difficult problems of peace if they forget God, the Author of all true peace.

February 8, 1932

1069. . . . . . . We also find ourselves assembled between two international conferences of which the world has expected so much, because it perceives how grievously it is oppressed and tormented. Of these two conferences one has been put off *sine die;*[225] and the other,[226] what will it effect? As yet no one can say, but one thing is very evident: the absence of any rosy hopes and the presence of an ever-growing pessimism. All the same, we must go on hoping that Divine Providence will come to our help in these human affairs, that the Hand of God may accomplish what the hands of men cannot. It is manifest that this sorrowful state of affairs demonstrates in the clearest manner the insufficiency and incapacity of man to guide the affairs of the world, and it is also evident enough that the things of the world both great and small depend not upon men, but upon the Hand of God.

1070. We are living at a time of extreme anxiety, not only on account of this sense of fear, not only on account of international political difficulties, but on account of a state of restriction which affects each and all, which, indeed, in the proper sense of the word has entered every house and affected every family. It is necessary, then, that We advert to these things, so vast and so important, and also that We suggest some thoughts and reflections which will not be without use to the preachers. Such thoughts and reflections make us meditate upon the true cause of all these evils, a cause of which we must never lose sight: sin. We especially urge the preachers, therefore, to kindle in the hearts of their hearers this truth and enlighten their consciences with certain salutary ideas.

---

[224] Translation from *The Tablet,* v. 159, pp. 245-246 (February 20, 1932). Original Italian, *L'Osservatore Romano,* February 10, 1932. We have been unable to obtain the original text but we have consulted the French version in *Documentation Catholique,* v. 31, cc. 777-780. It is necessary to note here that this is one of the many later papal discourses that were not reported entirely verbatim. Parts of this speech were reported in the third person and this is true of the introduction. Hence, it is impossible to designate this address in the usual manner by citing the opening words.

[225] The Conference at Lausanne.

[226] The Conference on the Young Plan at Basle.

1071. As to ourselves, we are all in the Hands of God, and, therefore, in good Hands. But too often this truth is forgotten, even there where it ought to be most remembered, there where they consider the destiny of peoples, there where they strive to find a remedy for so many evils! This is the sad spectacle which so impresses Us. Men of State, of politics, of industry, of finance, of war, of peace, all assembled to reason, discuss and treat of this grave crisis, and yet not once in all their discussions and efforts do they turn a glance toward heaven, or direct a thought toward the God of Heaven and Earth, or give a thought to the fact that all things in the world do not obey the hands of men, but those of God. All these men are on their feet, all are in movement, and yet not one of them can point out the way to a solution. Before such forgetfulness We must recall the thought of God and Divine Providence. We give too little thought to it, and when this deplorable example of forgetfulness is manifested in high places, it necessarily becomes widely imitated amongst the masses. And the danger which results from all this is exceedingly grave, and even terrifying. For God can only say, "Do they wish to act without Me? Very well, then, act without Me"; and so doing they can only come to utter ruin. . . . . . .

1072. But yet another thought presents itself as We look at this world-wide misery and universal distress. We are reminded of those severe words *per quae quis peccat, per haec et torquetur.*[227] Yes, this torment comes from sin. We see how all have rushed madly along the paths of the new paganism, a paganism which materializes the whole life. Many thought, and continue to think, that money is all-sufficient, the rapid gaining of it for the enjoyment, power, and dominion it brings is the sole end. It is a paganism which enters both public and private life; it enters the family, bringing with it an abandonment of those principles of moderation, self-control, self-denial, self-respect, and respect for others, and of all those things which must and ought to be respected. Humanity is stricken just where it has sinned, and where the sin yet remains. They have forsaken supernatural good for earthly good, and now there only remain to them, as is too evident, desolation, disquiet and fear. . . We merely wish to accentuate this great fact. For it is enough merely to raise our eyes and look around to see it. . . . . . .

[227] *Wisdom*, XI, 17.

454

ALLOCUTION *È Piaciuto* ON THE TENTH ANNIVERSARY OF THE
POPE'S CORONATION.[228]

*The Pope invites all in a spirit of penitence to pray
for peace.*

February 12, 1932

1073. It has pleased the Divine Goodness and Mercy to bring
Us once more, after ten years of Our Pontificate, to this anniversary,
which your gathering together with such devotion has made most
solemn and consoling, bringing Us a sweet and precious relief
amidst the enormous burden of responsibility, which on the completion of these ten years makes Us debtors toward God and man.
And the Divine Providence has thus disposed things, that this
should happen at a moment of universal distress, one of the gravest
suffering for the great mass of people, of grave preoccupation for
their rulers, and of anxious search after peace and the means of
securing it. We are aware that in these circumstances many of
Our children belonging to the great Catholic family—indeed, the
whole human family, although far distant—desire to hear by means
of the radio, as you do who stand beside Us, the voice of the Father,
and to receive from the Vicar of Christ a word of light and comfort. The Immaculate Virgin, whose beneficent apparition at
Lourdes We celebrated yesterday, has inspired Us to satisfy this
devout desire. We, therefore, invite all, far and near, to raise a
prayer to God, Creator, Lord and Supreme Ruler of the world
and its peoples, to call to mind and deplore in a spirit of penitence
sins which arm the Divine Justice against us, presenting our
tribulations to His Infinite Mercy, imploring of Him and His inspirations that peace and the means for attaining it which seem
to escape the research of men. We invite you to do this in the very
words of the sacred liturgy of Holy Church, incomparable Mistress
of Prayer, which she puts upon our lips and hearts and commends
to our meditation. Let us pray, then, in a perfect unity of hearts and
minds—for this peace, the first and most necessary for us. . . . . . .

---

[228] Translation from *The Tablet,* v. 159, pp. 246-247 (February 20, 1932). Original
Italian, *A.A.S.,* v. 24, pp. 65-66 (March 5, 1932).

ENCYCLICAL *Caritate Christi Compulsi* ON PRAYER AND EX-
PIATION.[229]

> *To create the atmosphere of lasting peace, neither peace*
> *treaties, nor solemn pacts, nor international conferences,*
> *not even the noblest efforts of any statesman will be*
> *enough, unless the sacred rights of natural and divine*
> *law are recognized.*

May 3, 1932

1074. Urged by the charity of Christ, We have invited with
the Apostolic Letter *Nova Impendet* of October 2, 1931,[230] all members of the Catholic Church, indeed all men of good-will, to unite
in a holy crusade of love and succor, in order to alleviate in some
measure the terrible consequences of the economic crisis under
which the human race is struggling. And truly wonderful was the
unanimous enthusiasm with which the generosity and activity of
all answered Our appeal. But distress has increased, the number
of the unemployed has grown in practically all parts, and subversive
elements are making use of the fact for their propaganda; hence,
public order is threatened more and more, and the peril of terrorism
and anarchy hangs over society ever more ominously. Such being
the case, the same charity of Christ moves Us to turn once again to
you, Venerable Brethren, to the faithful in your charge, to the
whole world, and to exhort all to unite, and to resist with all their
might the evils that are crushing humanity, and the still graver evils
that are threatening.

1075. If We pass in review the long and sorrowful sequence
of woes, that, as a sad heritage of sin, mark the stages of fallen
man's earthly pilgrimage, from the flood on, it would be hard to
find spiritual and material distress so deep, so universal, as that
which we are now experiencing; even the greatest scourges that left
indelible traces in the lives and memories of peoples, struck only
one nation at a time. Now, on the contrary, the whole of humanity
is held bound by the financial and economic crisis so fast, that the
more it struggles the harder appears the task of loosening its bonds;
there is no people, there is no State, no society or family which

---

[229] Translation from *The Sacred Heart and World Distress* (N.C.W.C. pamphlet),
pp. 3-21. Original Latin, *A.A.S.*, v. 24, pp. 177-192 (June 1, 1932).
[230] *Cf. supra* nn. 1056-1058.

in one way or another, directly or indirectly, to a greater or less extent, does not feel the repercussion. Even those, very few in number, who appear to have in their hands, together with enormous wealth, the destinies of the world, even those very few who with their speculations were and are in great part the cause of so much woe, are themselves quite often the first and most notorious victims, dragging down with themselves into the abyss the fortunes of countless others; thus verifying in a terrible manner and before the whole world what the Holy Ghost had already proclaimed for every sinner in particular: *By what things a man sinneth, by the same also he is tormented.*[231]

1076. This deplorable state of things, Venerable Brethren, makes Our paternal heart groan; and makes Us feel more and more deeply the need of adopting, in the measure of Our insufficiency, the sublime sentiment of the Sacred Heart of Jesus: *I have compassion on the multitude.*[232] But still more deplorable is the root from which springs this condition of affairs: for, if what the Holy Ghost affirms through the mouth of St. Paul is ever true, much more is it true at present: *The desire of money is the root of all evils.*[233] Is it not that lust of earthly goods, that the pagan poet called, with righteous scorn, "the accursed hunger for gold"; is it not that sordid egoism which too often regulates the mutual relations of individuals and society; is it not, in fine, greed, whatever be its species and form, that has brought the world to a pass we all see and deplore? From greed arises mutual distrust, that casts a blight on all human dealings; from greed arises hateful envy which makes a man consider the advantages of another as losses to himself; from greed arises narrow individualism which orders and subordinates everything to its own advantage without taking account of others—on the contrary, cruelly trampling under foot all rights of others. Hence the disorder and inequality from which arises the accumulation of the wealth of nations in the hands of a small group of individuals who manipulate the market of the world at their own caprice, to the immense harm of the masses, as We showed last year in Our Encyclical Letter *Quadragesimo Anno.*[234]

1077. Right order of Christian charity does not disapprove of

---

[231] *Wisdom*, XI, 17.
[232] *Mark*, VIII, 2.
[233] I *Timothy*, VI, 10.
[234] *Cf. supra* nn. 924-1048.

lawful love of country and a sentiment of justifiable nationalism; on the contrary, it controls, sanctifies and enlivens them. If, however, egoism, abusing this love of country and exaggerating this sentiment of nationalism, insinuates itself into the relations between people and people, there is no excess that will not seem justified; and that which between individuals would be judged blameworthy by all, is now considered lawful and praiseworthy if it is done in the name of this exaggerated nationalism. Instead of the great law of love and human brotherhood, which embraces and holds in a single family all nations and peoples with one Father Who is in heaven, there enters hatred, driving all to destruction. In public life sacred principles, the guide of all social intercourse, are trampled upon; the solid foundations of right and honesty, on which the State should rest, are undermined; polluted and closed are the sources of those ancient traditions which, based on faith in God and fidelity to His law, secured the true progress of nations.

1078. Profiting by so much economic distress and so much moral disorder, the enemies of all social order, be they called Communists, or any other name, boldly set about breaking through every restraint. This is the most dreadful evil of our times, for they destroy every bond of law, human or divine; they engage openly and in secret in a relentless struggle against religion and against God Himself; they carry out the diabolical program of wresting from the hearts of all, even of children, all religious sentiment; for well they know that when once belief in God has been taken from the heart of mankind they will be entirely free to work out their will. Thus we see to-day, what was never before seen in history, the satanical banners of war against God and against religion brazenly unfurled to the winds in the midst of all peoples and in all parts of the earth.

1079. There were never lacking impious men, nor men who denied God; but they were relatively few, isolated and individual, and they did not care or did not think it opportune to reveal too openly their impious mind, as the inspired Psalmist appears to suggest, when he exclaims: *The fool hath said in his heart: there is no God.*[235] The impious, the atheist, lost in the crowd, denied God, his Creator, only in the secret of his heart. To-day, on the contrary, atheism has already spread through large masses of the

[235] *Psalms,* XIII, 1 and LII, 1.

people: well-organized, it works its way even into the common schools; it appears in theaters; in order to spread, it makes use of its own cinema films, of the gramophone and the radio; with its own printing presses it prints booklets in every language; it promotes special exhibitions and public parades; it has formed its own political parties and its own economic and military systems. This organized and militant atheism works untiringly by means of its agitators, with conferences and projections, with every means of propaganda, secret and open, among all classes, in every street, in every hall; it secures for this nefarious activity the moral support of its own universities, and holds fast the unwary with the mighty bonds of its organizing power. At the sight of so much activity placed at the service of so wicked a cause, there comes spontaneously to Our mind and to Our lips the mournful lament of Christ: *The children of this world are wiser in their generation than the children of light.*[236]

1080. The leaders of this campaign of atheism, turning to account the present economic crisis, inquire with diabolic reasoning into the cause of this universal misery. The Holy Cross of Our Lord, symbol of humility and poverty, is joined together with the symbols of modern imperialism, as though religion were allied with those dark powers which produce such evils among men. Thus they strive, and not without effect, to combine war against God with men's struggle for their daily bread, with their desire to have land of their own, suitable wages and decent dwellings — in fine, a condition of life befitting human beings. The most legitimate and necessary desires, just as the most brutal instincts, everything serves their anti-religious program, as if the order established by God stood in contradiction with the welfare of mankind, and were not on the contrary its only sure safeguard; as if human forces by means of modern mechanical power could combat the divine forces and introduce a new and better ordering of things.

1081. Now it is a lamentable fact that millions of men, under the impression that they are struggling for existence, grasp at such theories to the utter subversion of truth, and cry out against God and religion. Nor are these assaults directed only against the Catholic Religion, but against all who still recognize God as Creator of heaven and earth and as absolute Lord of all things. And the

[236] *Luke,* XVI, 8.

459

secret societies, always ready to support war against God and the Church no matter who wages it, do not fail to inflame ever more this insane hatred which can give neither peace nor happiness to any class of society, but will certainly bring all nations to disaster.

1082. Thus, this new form of atheism, whilst unchaining man's most violent instincts, with cynical impudence proclaims that there will be neither peace nor welfare on earth until the last remnant of religion has been torn up and until its last representative has been crushed out of existence; as if in this way could be silenced the marvelous concert in which creation chants the glory of its Creator. . . . . . .

1083. Confronted with so much impiety, such destruction of all the holiest traditions, such slaughter of immortal souls, such offenses against the Divine Majesty, We cannot, Venerable Brethren, refrain from pouring out the bitter grief of Our soul, We cannot refrain from raising Our voice, and, with all the energy of Our Apostolic heart taking the defense of the downtrodden rights of God, and of the most sacred sentiments of the human heart that has an absolute need of God; and this, all the more, since these hostile forces, impelled by the spirit of evil, do not content themselves with mere clamor, but unite all their strength in order to carry out at the first opportunity their nefarious designs. Woe to mankind, if God, thus spurned by His creatures, allows in His justice free course to this devastating flood and uses it as a scourge to chastise the world. It is necessary, therefore, Venerable Brethren, that without faltering we *set up a wall for the house of Israel,*[237] that we likewise unite all our forces in one solid, compact line against the battalions of evil, enemies of God no less than of the human race. For in this conflict there is really question of the fundamental problem of the universe and of the most important decision proposed to man's free will. For God or against God, this once more is the alternative that shall decide the destinies of all mankind in politics, in finance, in morals, in the sciences and arts, in the State, in civil and domestic society. In the East and in the West, everywhere this question confronts us as the deciding factor because of the consequences that flow from it. Thus even the advocates of an altogether materialistic conception of the world, always see rising before them the question of the existence of God,

[237] *Ezechiel,* XIII, 5.

that they thought had been ruled out once and for all, are ever constrained to take up again its discussion.

1084. In the name of the Lord, therefore, We conjure individuals and nations, in the face of such problems and in the throes of a conflict of such vital interest for mankind, to put aside that narrow individualism and base egoism that blinds even the most clear-sighted, that withers up all noble initiative as soon as it is no longer confined to a limited circle of paltry and particular interests. Let them all unite together even at the cost of heavy sacrifices, to save themselves and mankind. In such a union of minds and forces, they naturally ought to be the first, who are proud of the Christian name, mindful of the glorious tradition of Apostolic time, when *the multitude of believers had but one heart and one soul.*[238] But let all those also loyally and heartily concur, who still believe in God and adore Him, in order to ward off from mankind the great danger that threatens all alike. For in truth, belief in God is the unshaken foundation of all social order and of all responsible action on earth; and, therefore, all those who do not want anarchy and terrorism, ought to take energetic steps in order that the enemies of religion may not attain the goal they have so loudly proclaimed to the world.

1085. We are aware, Venerable Brethren, that in this battle for the defense of religion We must make use of all lawful means at Our disposal. Therefore, following in the wise path of Our Predecessor, Leo XIII of saintly memory, in Our Encyclical *Quadragesimo Anno*[239] We advocated so energetically a more equitable distribution of the goods of the earth and indicated the most efficacious means of restoring health and strength to the ailing social body, and tranquillity and peace to its suffering members. For the unquenchable aspiration to reach a suitable state of happiness even on earth is planted in the heart of man by the Creator of all things, and Christianity has always recognized and ardently promoted every just effort of true culture and sound progress for the perfecting and developing of mankind. . . .

1086. When Our Lord, coming down from the splendors of Thabor, had healed the boy tormented by the devil, whom the disciples had not been able to cure, to their humble question, *Why*

---

[238] *Acts*, IV, 32.
[239] *Cf. supra* nn. 924-1048.

could not we cast him out, He made reply in the memorable words, *This kind is not cast out but by praying and fasting.*[240] It appears to Us, Venerable Brethren, that these divine words find a peculiar application in the evils of our times, that can be averted only by means of prayer and penance.

1087. Mindful, then, of our condition, that we are essentially limited and absolutely dependent on the Supreme Being, before everything else let us have recourse to prayer. We know through faith how great is the power of humble, trustful, persevering prayer; and to no other pious work have ever been attached such ample, such universal, such solemn promises as to prayer! *Ask and it shall be given you, seek and you shall find, knock and it shall be opened to you. For everyone that asketh, receiveth, and he that seeketh, findeth; and to him that knocketh it shall be opened.*[241] *Amen, amen, I say to you if you ask the Father anything in My name He will give it to you.*[242] . . . . . .

1088. In addition, prayer will remove the fundamental cause of present-day difficulties which We have mentioned above, that is, the insatiable greed for earthly goods. The man who prays looks above to the goods of heaven whereon he meditates and which he desires; his whole being is plunged into the contemplation of the marvelous order established by God, which knows not the frenzy of success and does not lose itself in futile competitions of ever-increasing speed; and thus automatically, as it were, will be re-established that equilibrium between work and rest, whose entire absence from society to-day is responsible for grave dangers to life—physical, economic and moral. If, therefore, those who, through the excessive production of manufactured articles, have fallen into unemployment and poverty made up their minds to give the proper time to prayer, there is no doubt that work and production would soon return to reasonable limits and that the conflict which now divides humanity into two great camps struggling for transient interests would be changed into a noble and peaceful contest for goods heavenly and eternal.

1089. In like manner will the way be opened to the peace we long for, as St. Paul beautifully remarks in the passage where he

---

[240] *Matthew,* XVII, 18, 20.
[241] *Matthew,* VII, 7-8.
[242] *John,* XVI, 23.

joins the precept of prayer to holy desires for the peace and salvation of all men: *I desire, therefore, first of all, that supplications, prayers, intercessions and thanksgivings be made for all men; for kings and all that are in high station, that we may lead a quiet and peaceful life in all piety and chastity. For this is good and acceptable in the sight of God, Our Saviour, Who will have all men to be saved, and to come to the knowledge of truth.*[243] Let peace be implored for all men, but especially for those who, in human society, have the grave responsibilities of government; for how could they give peace to their peoples if they have it not themselves? And it is prayer precisely that, according to the Apostle, will bring the gift of peace; prayer that is addressed to the Heavenly Father Who is the Father of all men; prayer that is the common expression of family feelings, of that great family which extends beyond the boundaries of any country and continent.

1090. Men who in every nation pray to the same God for peace on earth cannot be at the same time bearers of discord among peoples; men who turn in prayer to the Divine Majesty cannot foment that nationalistic imperialism which of each people makes its own god; men who look to the *God of Peace and of Love,*[244] who turn to Him through the mediation of Christ, Who is *Our Peace,*[245] will know no rest until finally that peace which the world cannot give, comes down from the Giver of every good gift, on *men of good-will.*[246] *'Peace be to you,*[247] was the Easter greeting of Our Lord to His Apostles and first disciples; and this blessed greeting from those first times until our day has never been absent from the sacred liturgy of the Church, and to-day, more than ever, it should comfort and refresh aching and oppressed human hearts. . . . . . .

1091. In place of moral laws which disappear, together with the loss of faith in God, brute force is imposed, trampling on every right. Old-time fidelity and honesty of conduct and mutual intercourse extolled so much even by the orators and poets of paganism, now give place to speculations in one's own affairs as in those of others without reference to conscience. In fact, how can any contract be maintained and what value can any treaty have, in which

[243] I *Timothy,* II, 1-4.
[244] II *Corinthians,* XIII, 11.
[245] *Ephesians,* II, 14.
[246] *Luke,* II, 14.
[247] *John,* XX, 26.

every guarantee of conscience is lacking? And how can there be talk of guarantees of conscience when all faith in God and all fear of God has vanished? Take away this basis, and with it all moral law falls, and there is no remedy left to stop the gradual but inevitable destruction of peoples, families, the State, civilization itself.

1092. Penance, then, is as it were a salutary weapon placed in the hands of the valiant soldiers of Christ who wish to fight for the defense and restoration of the moral order in the universe. It is a weapon that strikes at the root of all evil, that is, at the dust of material wealth and the wanton pleasures of life. By means of voluntary sacrifices, by means of practical and even painful acts of self-denial, by means of various works of penance, the noble-hearted Christian subdues the base passions that tend to make him violate the moral order. But if zeal for divine law and brotherly love are as great in him as they should be, then not only does he practice penance for himself and his own sins, but he takes upon himself the expiation of the sins of whole generations, imitating even the Divine Redeemer, Who became the Lamb of God, *Who taketh away the sins of the world*.[248]

1093. Is there not perchance, Venerable Brethren, in this spirit of penance also a sweet mystery of peace? *There is no peace to the wicked*,[249] says the Holy Spirit, because they live in continuous struggle and conflict with the order established by nature and by its Creator. Only when this order is restored, when all peoples faithfully and spontaneously recognize and profess it, when the internal conditions of peoples and their outward relations with other nations are founded on this basis, then only will stable peace be possible on earth. But to create this atmosphere of lasting peace, neither peace treaties, nor the most solemn pacts, nor international meetings or conferences, not even the noblest and most disinterested efforts of any statesman will be enough unless in the first place are recognized the sacred rights of natural and divine law. No leader in public economy, no power of organization will even be able to bring social conditions to a peaceful solution, unless first in the very field of economics there triumphs moral law based on God and conscience. This is the underlying value of every value in the political life as well as in the economic life of nations; this is the soundest

248 *John*, I, 29.
249 *Isaias*, XLVIII, 22.

"rate of exchange." If it is kept steady all the rest will be stable, being guaranteed by the immutable and eternal law of God.

1094. And even for men individually, penance is the foundation and bearer of true peace, detaching them from earthly and perishable goods, lifting them up to goods that are eternal, giving them, even in the midst of privations and adversity, a peace that the world with all its wealth and pleasures cannot give. . . .

1095. Prayer, then, and penance are the two potent inspirations sent to Us at this time by God, that We may lead back to Him mankind that has gone astray and wanders about without a guide; they are the inspirations that will dispel and remedy the first and principal cause of every revolt and every revolution, the revolt of man against God. But the peoples themselves are called upon to make up their minds to a definite choice; either they entrust themselves to these benevolent and beneficent inspirations and are converted, humble and repentant, to the Lord and the Father of Mercies, or they abandon themselves and what little remains of happiness on earth to the mercy of the enemy of God, to the spirit of vengeance and destruction.

1096. Nothing remains for Us, therefore, save to invite this poor world that has shed so much blood, has dug so many graves, has destroyed so many works, has deprived so many men of bread and labor, nothing else remains for Us, We say, but to invite it in the loving words of the sacred liturgy: "Be thou converted to the Lord thy God." . . . . . .

LETTER OF CARDINAL PACELLI, SECRETARY OF STATE, TO M. EUGÈNE DUTHOIT, PRESIDENT OF THE SEMAINE SOCIALE AT LILLE.[250]

All States have the obligation to promote the international common good.

June 28, 1932

1097. . . . . . . It will be a good thing that the lessons of this Social Week are to be proclaimed in an environment so well adapted to give them a wide publicity, because they will be animated—your program assures this—by a marshaling of capital truths which must constitute the spiritual bulwark of a sound international economy.

[250] Original French, *Documentation Catholique.* v. 28, c. 173 (July 30, 1932).

1098. Such is, first of all, the fundamental unity of the great human family which has been taught by Christ that it has one Father in heaven; from this it follows that it is a bounden duty for the members of the different nations to cause to overflow generously upon other peoples the love which they must first entertain for their own country; and it is likewise a duty for each people to take into account the legitimate interests of other peoples. Hence, too, there arises for all nations the obligation of mutual justice and charity; above all, the various political entities taken together have the duty to promote and to serve the common international welfare, just as the citizens and the governing class of each individual State are bound to promote and to serve a common good that touches them more closely and is narrower in extent. And by the same token, it is necessary for all peoples to keep in view their interdependence, and to work into the various types of their national solidarity corresponding forms of collaboration with those of other nationalities. Granted that it be necessary for them in a general way to build up their national economy, this must not then be done by systematically isolating themselves behind economic barriers that grow ever more impassable; rather must it be brought about by a renewed honorable practice of the austere virtues recommended by His Holiness, Pius XI, in his last Encyclical. This Encyclical *Caritate Christi Compulsi*[251] and that other *Quadragesimo Anno*[252] have furnished you. . . with precious lights by which to discern the ways of the reconstruction that must be effected. You will be faithful to this letter and their spirit, if, for an undertaking assuredly difficult, you implore extraordinary assistance from God. . . . . . .

ENCYCLICAL *Acerba Animi* ON THE PERSECUTION OF THE CHURCH IN MEXICO.[253]

Papal conciliatory efforts in Mexico were met with new persecutions.

September 29, 1932

1099. . . . . . . Seeing, therefore, some hope of remedying greater evils, and judging that the principal motives that had induced

---

[251] May 3, 1932; cf. *supra* nn. 1074-1096.
[252] May 15, 1931; cf. *supra* nn. 924-1048.
[253] Translation from *The Mexican Persecution* (C.T.S. pamphlet), pp. 6-9. Original Latin, *A.A.S.*, v. 24, pp. 324-327 (October 1, 1932).

the episcopate to suspend public worship no longer existed, We asked Ourself whether it were not advisable to order its resumption. In this there was certainly no intention of accepting the Mexican regulations of worship, nor of withdrawing Our protests against these regulations, much less of ceasing to combat them. It was merely a question of abandoning, in view of the Government's new declarations, one of the methods of resistance, before it could bring harm to the faithful, and of having recourse instead to others deemed more opportune. Unfortunately, as all know, Our wishes and desires were not followed by the peace and favorable settlement for which We had hoped. On the contrary, bishops, priests and faithful Catholics continued to be penalized and imprisoned, contrary to the spirit in which the *modus vivendi* had been established. . . . . . . We wished briefly to rehearse the salient points in the grievous condition of the Church in Mexico, so that all lovers of order and peace among nations, on seeing that such an unheard-of persecution differs but little, especially in certain States, from the one raging within the unhappy borders of Russia, may from this iniquitous similarity of purpose conceive fresh ardor to stem the torrent which is subverting all social order. . . . . . .

Allocution *Abbiamo Nominato* to the College of Cardinals.[254]

> *The mutual distrust and conflicts between peoples and States sadden the Holy Father.*

December 24, 1932

1100. . . . . . . We have referred to Our sorrows, and We can do no less than bring into relief both the gravity and duration of the sorrowful events due to the iniquitous acts against the hierarchy, the faithful and our holy religion in Spain, Mexico and Russia. Not less profound is the grief which We experience at the continual difficulties, the mutual distrust, the divisions and conflicts between peoples and States, from which are not excluded the horrors of war and civil war. Besides all these, there are the consequences of the universal financial and economic crisis, a crisis without precedent in history, which not only continues but becomes daily

---

[254] Translation from *The Tablet*, v. 161, pp. 17-18 (January 7, 1933). Original Italian, *Civiltà Cattolica*, 1933, v. 1, pp. 7-10 (December 28, 1932).

more aggravated, inflicting most painful sufferings upon the poor and laboring classes, those whose need is greatest and who are deserving of all the help that social justice and Christian charity can give them. We have also referred to the many and great consolations which God has granted Us, and for which no words of Ours can adequately express Our gratitude toward the Divine Goodness and toward all who have been His generous and faithful instruments in those things. . . .

1101. We must not omit the consolation which has been afforded Us at this last hour, and the hopes of a permanent and durable peace engendered by it, in consequence of the Christmas armistice, although brief, arranged between two beloved Christian nations engaged in war.[255] . . . It is a due and beneficent celebration[256] which is desired by many. It will be no light benefit if, for a while, the world ceases to be wholly concerned with conflicts and disagreements, distrust and diffidence, armaments and disarmaments, injuries and reparations, debts and payments, delay and insolvency, economic and financial interests, individual and social miseries; if, for a while, it ceases to fix itself only on these things, and turns to those of high spirituality: to the interests and life of the soul, to the dignity and value of this Blood and Grace of Christ, the brotherhood of all men, all equally sealed by the Divine Blood, the saving mission of the Church for humanity, and to all the other high and holy thoughts which spring naturally from the divine facts of such a celebration. . . . . .

BULL *Quod Nuper* ANNOUNCING THE JUBILEE YEAR OF 1933.[257]

The Pope exhorts all to pray that the Holy Year may bring true peace to souls and to peoples.

January 6, 1933

1102. . . . . . . Moved, therefore, by this most happy centenary, men should turn their thoughts, at least in part, from earthly and passing things in which to-day they are struggling so unhappily, to

---

255 These two nations were Bolivia and Paraguay engaged in the Chaco War.
256 This celebration was the Holy Year in honor of the Nineteenth Centenary of our
    Redemption.
257 Translation from the *American Ecclesiastical Review,* v. 88, pp. 302-303 (March,
    1933). Original Latin, *A.A.S.,* v. 25, pp. 5-7 (January 30, 1933).

celestial and eternal things. Let them lift their minds from the fearful and sad conditions of these days to the hope of that happiness to which our Lord Jesus Christ called us when He poured out His Blood and conferred immense benefits of every kind. Let them withdraw themselves from the din of daily life, and reflect in their hearts with themselves, especially during this Centenary Year. Inasmuch as our Saviour loved us and with such ardent zeal liberated us from the slavery of sin, so undoubtedly they will feel themselves seized with greater charity and will be almost necessarily impelled to love again this most loving Lord. . . . . . . Let us stimulate ourselves to prayer, to penitence for the sins committed by us, having in mind in our prayers and acts of expiation not only our eternal salvation, but also that of all mankind led astray by so many errors, torn by so many discords and hostilities, laboring under so many miseries, and fearful of so many dangers. Oh! may the most merciful Lord bring it about that the Holy Year which We shall shortly inaugurate will bring peace to souls, to the Church that liberty everywhere due her, to all peoples concord and true prosperity. . . . . . .

DISCOURSE *Ecco la Bolla* ON THE OCCASION OF PUBLISHING THE JUBILEE BULL.[258]

Christ came to bring peace upon the earth.

January 15, 1933

1103. . . . . . . To the one who has had the happy and truly enviable fortune to announce solemnly and officially the good news, the Vicar of Jesus Christ feels able to address those words mentioned by the Apostle: *How beautiful are the feet of them that preach the Gospel of peace, of them that bring glad tidings of good things!*[259] It is indeed a word of peace, of great, of most sublime peace, which the reader of the Bull would tell the world: peace in the highest and broadest sense that one can imagine. And if every peace is a means and a condition of good (because sometimes above peace there is order, and order by itself is a good higher than any other), if almost every peace is a messenger of good and is a requisite condition for good; then this should be said first of all

[258] Original Italian, *Il Monitore Ecclesiastico*, v. 45, p. 37 (February, 1933).
[259] *Romans*, X, 15.

of that great peace which does not pertain merely to pacification
between man and man, between people and people. These external
peaces are small, however great they may seem to be and may be
in reality, when compared with the internal peace even of one soul
alone with God. Moreover, they are still small when one thinks
of the great peace of the whole world to which all human kind is
called. This is the peace which Christ the Redeemer has come to
bring upon the earth, fastening to His Cross the decree of death
and transforming it into a sentence of salvation. And this is the
peace which the Supreme Pontiff wishes to be proclaimed during
the impending extraordinary Holy Year, along with that motto
which he has already announced: "We adore Thee, O Christ, and
We bless Thee because by Thy cross Thou hast redeemed the
world." . . . . . .

LETTER *Tra i Sacrosanti* TO CARDINAL MARCHETTI SELVAG-GIANI, VICAR OF ROME, DECREEING A HOLY HOUR ON HOLY THURSDAY.[260]

*Pius XI hopes that the Holy Year will bring the much
desired peace among all nations.*

March 2, 1933

1104. . . . . . . We do not doubt, Lord Cardinal, that the clergy
and people of Our city will respond with holy fervor to Our
fatherly invitation; and We trust that all the Venerable Brethren
of the Catholic episcopate who can possibly do so will follow Our
example and exhort their faithful to unite with Our beloved children
of Rome, with all the centers of the pious Association of the Holy
Hour, and with Ourself, in this loving and dutiful remembrance
of the bitter pain the Heart of Jesus deigned to endure for our
salvation. Thus the Holy Year will open with the upraising of
expiatory prayer toward heaven in every part of the world, a prayer
which shall unite in the Divine Heart all the hearts of men, of
every race, tongue and nation, and obtain, as We trustfully expect,
from the Divine Majesty the conversion of sinners, the perseverance
and ever greater sanctification of the just, the relief of such great

[260] Translation from *The Tablet,* v. 161, pp. 306-307 (March 11, 1933). Original
Italian, *A.A.S.,* v. 25, pp. 74-75 (March 4, 1933).

miseries which, owing to the present crisis, afflict the whole earth, and finally the longed-for peace among all nations. Moreover, desiring that this Holy Hour be verily holy, We wish all the faithful to unite with Us according to Our intentions, especially for those countries where our most loving Redeemer is most outraged. . . . . . .

ALLOCUTION *Iterum Vos* TO THE COLLEGE OF CARDINALS.[261]

The Pope has not ceased to preach peace among nations.

March 13, 1933

1105. . . . . . . The critical international situation continues as heretofore, a situation rendered uncertain, uneasy and disquieting by reciprocal mistrust, by conflicting interests, by inadequate and frequently contradictory measures proposed and attempted by exaggerated and unjust nationalism, than which nothing is more contrary to that brotherhood of men and peoples which can find its vital roots healthy and can find satisfying nourishment only in the dictates, inspirations and practice of Christian charity. In the name of this charity and solely under its impulse, We have not ceased to preach peace among nations. And We obtained some slight benefit, or rather a brief respite from strife at Christmas and in the name of the new-born Redeemer of the world. But alas, in the Old World as in the New, again one hears the clash of fraternal arms, and from the stained and devastated soil there rises to heaven the voice of brothers' blood.

1106. The economic crisis still continues throughout the world, and it is the weakest who suffer most: innocent children, first and delicate blossoms of life; the infirm, already afflicted and now in greater need; aged folk, already worn out and often broken by their long journey. There is the material and moral suffering of thousands and millions of workingmen and artisans, who are deprived not merely of wages earned in justice and with dignity, but also and especially of work, and are reduced to unemployment with all its perils and temptations, to say nothing of the cost of the difficulties and anxieties that fall upon society in general and upon those in whose hands rests responsibility for public order and security.

[261] Translation from *The Catholic Mind,* v. 31, pp. 126-129 (April 8, 1933). Original Latin, *A.A.S.,* v. 25, pp. 112-118 (March 16, 1933).

1107. There is, however, one class of men who derive advantage, sad advantage, from general hardship and misery, the enemies of all political, social and religious order. War on human society, on religion, on God Himself—that is their well-known program. No less well-known are their subversive, murderous principles. Occurrences of recent, very recent date show how capable, how determined they are to translate these principles into acts. What has been happening this long time and is still happening throughout the huge expanse of unhappy Russia, in Mexico, in Spain, and lately in small and large countries in Central Europe, shows only too clearly what may and must be feared wherever their nefarious propaganda and influence penetrate.

1108. And where do they not penetrate? And yet, until quite recently, Our voice had remained single and solitary, pointing out the serious danger that threatens Christian civilization in each and every country in the world which enjoys its inestimable benefits that cannot be replaced. Our voice was alone in indicating and urging a radical cure and remedy, namely, the sound and solid principles of charity and justice and the fundamental, indestructible truths and teachings on the value of souls and the dignity of the human individual, on man's origin and destiny and his essential relations with God, his Creator, Redeemer, Lord and Judge, and with his fellow men and the rest of creation. . . . . . .

1109. Those who would overthrow all order turn their most violent, unwearying, relentless assaults against God and against all religion, principally against the Catholic Religion and the Catholic Church. Does not this mean, and do not the facts show, that they, too, see in God and in the Catholic Religion the surest support and strongest bulwark of all that they combat and would destroy? . . . But when the Spirit of God sees the impious arise in a host of many peoples, He sees at the same time their efforts frustrated, God mocking and smiting them, arming all creation to wreak Divine Vengeance and the whole earth doing battle with Him against the insensate. Is not this a call for all to reflect and consider whether and to what extent the present war on God, more impious and provocative than ever before, is responsible for the world-wide catastrophes of war and economic crisis from which all are still suffering so terribly on every hand? . . . . . .

1110. Since this great Jubilee and Holy Year of the Redemption of mankind, recently promulgated by Us, is meant to be and with God's grace will be, a year of greater expiation and remission of sins, of seeking and practicing justice in every department of Christian life, for this reason We cherish full and certain confidence that it will be especially, above all, a year of spiritual exaltation for the whole Christian world and for all mankind; and, secondly, a relief, which, God grant, may be an entire cessation, from the hardships and miseries with which the world is still sorely afflicted.

1111. The first result, a spiritual raising up of hearts and minds, will be brought about by grateful remembrance and meditation on the Redemption of man, consummated in the death and blood of a God Who came down among men and was the Teacher and Model of every virtue. The second, the beneficent relief, will be obtained from Divine Mercy by the universal concert of prayers and good works, were it only by drawing down the necessary light and still more necessary concord upon conferences and conversations that will take place precisely during this Holy Year for world economic readjustment, for disarmament — may it be effective materially and morally — and for war debts. For all these intentions We propose to pray every day and We invite everyone to do so with Us. . . . . . .

ENCYCLICAL *Dilectissima Nobis* ON SPAIN.[262]

The Church knows how to reconcile legitimate liberty with authority, the exigencies of justice with peace.

June 3, 1933

1112. . . . . . . Nor can it be believed that Our words are inspired by sentiments of aversion to the new form of government or other purely political changes which recently have transpired in Spain. Universally known is the fact that the Catholic Church is never bound to one form of government more than to another, provided the divine rights of God and of Christian consciences are safe. She does not find any difficulty in adapting herself to various civil institutions, be they monarchic or republican, aristocratic or democratic. Speaking only of recent facts, evident proof of this lies in

---

[262] Translation from *Encyclical on Spain* (America Press pamphlet), pp. 2-3. Original Latin, *A.A.S.*, v. 25, pp. 262-264 (June 5, 1933).

the numerous Concordats and agreements concluded in late years, and in the diplomatic relations the Holy See has established with different States in which, following the Great War, monarchic governments were succeeded by republican forms. Nor have these new republics ever had to suffer in their institutions and just aspirations toward national grandeur and welfare through their friendly relations with the Holy See, or through their disposition, in a spirit of reciprocal confidence, to conclude conventions on subjects relating to Church and State, in conformity with changed conditions and times. Nay, We can with certainty affirm that from these trustful understandings with the Church, the States themselves have derived remarkable advantages, since it is known no more effective dyke can be opposed to an inundation of social disorders than the Church, which is the greatest educator of the people and always knows how to unite, in fecund agreement, the principle of legitimate liberty with that of authority, the exigencies of justice with welfare and peace.

1113. The government of the new Republic could not be ignorant of all this. Nay, it knew well Our good disposition and that of the Spanish episcopate to concur in maintaining order and social tranquillity. In harmony with Us was the immense multitude not only of the clergy both secular and regular, but likewise of the Catholic laity, or, rather, the great majority of the Spanish people, who, notwithstanding their personal opinions and provocations and vexations by adversaries of the Church, kept themselves aloof from acts of violence and reprisals, in tranquil subjection to the constituted power, without having resort to disorder and much less to civil war.

1114. Certainly to no other causes than to this discipline and subjection inspired by Catholic teachings and spirit have we the right to attribute the possibility of maintaining some peace and public tranquillity while the turbulence of parties and the passions of revolutionaries work to propel the nation toward the abyss of anarchy. It has, therefore, caused Us great amazement and profound anguish to learn that some, as if it were to justify the iniquitous proceedings against the Church, publicly alleged a necessity of defending the new Republic. From the foregoing, it appears so evident that the alleged motive was non-existent, that we can only conclude the struggle against the Church in Spain is not so much due to a misunderstanding of the Catholic Faith and its beneficial institutions, as to a hatred against the Lord and His Christ nourished by groups subversive to any religious and social order, as, alas, we have seen in Mexico and Russia. . . . . . .

ADDRESS *L'Auguste Pontife* TO A PILGRIMAGE FROM SPAIN.[263]

The prayers for peace during the Holy Year have received an answer in the Four-Power Pact.

June 9, 1933

1115. . . . . . . The world is still in quest of peace, union of minds. In the House of Peter thousands upon thousands of men who were divided and quarreling in their respective countries have listened in agreement to the paternal words of the Holy Father and have knelt together to receive the Apostolic Benediction. And most recently, what is known to the world as the Four-Power Pact,[264] which had for some time, in the midst of contradictions, remained in doubt and uncertainty, has been concluded. This pact of the great European nations assures—what a precious assurance— the entire world of at least a ten-year period of peace, of better mutual understanding, of improved and easier harmony of mutual interests, although there are some interests which are quite contradictory and difficult to reconcile. Now this result We have the right and duty to attribute to the prayers which, more than ever in these recent times and above all during this Holy Year, We have asked from all peoples in all places for the peace and the relief of the world. . . . . . .

ALLOCUTION TO THE COLLEGE OF CARDINALS.[265]

We must never cease to pray for peace.

December 23, 1933

1116. . . . . . . Now We have a word also which We would repeat not three, but many times to all who inquire of Us . . . what they

---

[263] French translation from *Documentation Catholique*, v. 30, c. 139 (July 29, 1933). The original Italian, which we have not been able to consult, is in *L'Osservatore Romano*, June 11, 1933.
[264] Pact signed in Rome, June 7, 1933, between France, Great Britain, Italy and Germany.
[265] Translation from *The Tablet*, v. 163, p. 17 (January 6, 1934). Original Italian, *Civiltà Cattolica*, 1934, v. 1, p. 101 (January 3, 1934).

should do, who wish for peace, general concord and the well-being of the whole human race. . . . Our reply is: "Pray! and in the second place, pray! and in the third place, pray!" We repeat the words of the Divine Redeemer: *Oportet orare semper et numquam deficere.*[266] . . . . . .

DISCOURSE TO THE LENTEN PREACHERS OF ROME.[267]

Peace made chiefly by arguments and discussions produces only new conflicts.

February 13, 1934

1117. . . . . . . On other occasions, at other times and in other circumstances, We have made many recommendations; but on this occasion, at the beginning of Our thirteenth year, We would go back to the words, source of all good, *Pax Christi in regno Christi:* "The Peace of Christ in the Kingdom of Christ." Not a peace made by words, by arguments and discussions which produce only new conflicts and fresh divisions; but the peace of souls in Christ, the peace won by the truth, in tranquillity of conscience, in the possession of truth, in understanding and virtue. This peace ought to exist in the Kingdom of Christ. . . . . . .

APOSTOLIC CONSTITUTION *Quod Superiore Anno* EXTENDING THE JUBILEE TO THE WHOLE WORLD.[268]

Again the Pope asks the world to pray for the return of peace, concord and prosperity.

April 2, 1934

1118. The extraordinary jubilee proclaimed by Us last year to commemorate the nineteenth centenary of the Redemption, has already come to a happy conclusion. . . . Almost innumerable hosts of Our children have been coming in pilgrimages, small and great,

---

[266] *Luke*, XVIII, 1.
[267] Translation from *The Tablet*, v. 163, p. 241 (February 24, 1934). Original Italian, *Civiltà Cattolica*, 1934, v. 1, pp. 541-542 (February 26, 1934).
[268] Translation from *The Australasian Catholic Record*, v. 11, pp. 169-170 (July, 1934). Original Latin, *A.A.S.*, v. 26, pp. 137-139 (April 3, 1934).

to this Mother City, where We have received them and consoled them with words of paternal affection. They represented every social class. The working classes, who earn their daily bread by manual labor, flocked hither and found themselves side by side with members of the aristocracy and men who direct the destinies of States. The example given by such statesmen is certainly worthy of all praise, for, amidst the difficulties of the times, they wished to obtain divine help not only for themselves but for their colleagues and countries. . . . . . . Besides the things mentioned in the Apostolic Letter *Quod Nuper,*[269] namely, the restoration of due liberty to the Church in all countries and the return of all peoples to peace, concord and true prosperity, We desire, moreover, that the prayers of the faithful be directed to obtaining the blessing of continued and fruitful success for the strenuous labors of the Church's missionaries and also to obtaining the eagerly desired re-entrance of separated Christians into the one sheepfold of Jesus Christ. . . . . . .

RADIO ADDRESS *Christus Rex* TO THE XXXII INTERNATIONAL EUCHARISTIC CONGRESS IN BUENOS AIRES.[270]

Only Christianity can maintain true international peace.

October 14, 1934

1119. . . . . . . Christ, the Eucharistic King, triumphs! Would, indeed, that together with victory, regal sway and empire—all belonging to Him by necessary title—the peaceful triumph of our meek and loving King at long last might extend from the noble shores of the Argentine to all parts of the earth and even to all minds and wills. Thus this poor world, only recently stricken by the affliction of witnessing scenes of fraternal and regal bloodshed,[271] shall find lasting peace and be liberated from its many evils. This peace shall be found only where it flourishes and is given, for We mean "The Peace of Christ in the Kingdom of Christ." . . . . . .

[269] *Cf. supra* n. 1102.
[270] Translation from *The Australasian Catholic Record,* v. 12, p. 94 (April, 1935). Original Latin, *A.A.S.,* v. 26, p. 577 (November 3, 1934).
[271] Pius XI is probably referring here to the Hitler "Blood Purge" of June, 1934, and the assassination of King Alexander of Jugoslavia in October, 1934.

ALLOCUTION *Felicemente Tutto* TO THE COLLEGE OF CAR-
DINALS.[272]

The Pope laments the preparations being made for war.

December 24, 1934

1120. . . . . . . Another happy memory is that of the International Juridical Congress, which after seven centuries has celebrated together the Justinian Code and the Gregorian Decretals,
as if to unite in a living unity the Civil and the Canon Law. In
this way the whole world has been reminded of the benefits derived
from the Catholic Church through the gift of Christian Law, the
Law of Christianity, a real superhuman creation in which assuredly
the Hand of God operated in His Church, by means of His Church.
This reminder is all the more opportune at a time when everyone
is concerned about law and justice. In the turbid atmosphere of
to-day We hear expressions which speak of the Law of Race, the
Law of Nationality, as if law and justice could be sustained or
founded on these particular types. It is justice which judges all
things. This is so true and sure that the pagan mind of Cicero
understood it and good sense alone is sufficient to suggest it. It is
not law which makes justice, but justice which makes law; it is
justice which makes just laws. . . . . . .

1121. The world is still troubled by that universal crisis which
not only continues but daily becomes more menacing. Not only
so, but to all the miseries and wretchedness, all the evils of public
and private life, we have to-day the added evil of confused but
widely diffused rumors of war, or at least of preparations for war.
That is something which disorientates, and before which the spirit
stands arrested. We are just on the eve of the day on which, in
heaven and on an earth which is overclouded, there resounds once
more, as at the Nativity, the inaugural canticle: *Glory be to God
on high, and on earth peace to men of good-will.*[273] This canticle
must with good reason become our prayer, our ceaseless supplication, just as to-morrow it will be on the lips of all in every land.
This is properly the prayer alike of the Church and of her visible
Head, their dominant thought, their most profound desire. Men

---

[272] Translation from *The Tablet*, v. 165, pp. 17-18 (January 5, 1935). Original Italian,
Civiltà Cattolica, 1935, v. 1, pp. 85-86 (December 31, 1934).
[273] *Luke*, II, 14.

say: *Si vis pacem, para bellum,* as if in all these armaments we should only see precautions and the guarantee of peace. We wish to believe that it is so; We wish to believe and to hope—for too terrible would be a reality contrary to this desire. We do indeed wish for peace. We invoke peace, We bless peace, We want peace. But if peradventure it happen—by an impossible supposition, so to say, through a new phenomenon of homicidal and suicidal madness of the nations—that they prefer war to peace, then We have another prayer, which it will become Our duty to raise to God: *Dissipa gentes quae bella volunt.*[274] But We wish instead to have ever in Our heart and on Our lips that other prayer, and with it We would reciprocate your auguries and filial desires: Glory to God in heaven, and peace upon earth. Peace, peace, peace!

LETTER *Quod Tam Alacri* TO BISHOP GERLIER OF LOURDES.[275]

If men seek to establish peace and prosperity only by human measures, then these blessings will ever elude their grasp.

January 10, 1935

1122. . . . . . . To-day, if ever, we need to pray for the divine assistance; the whole world needs it, and the whole community of nations. The evils which are even now impending are so great as to leave little prospect of relief, while the future fills every mind with anxiety and suspense. But it is especially for the stubborn pride of man that humanity must pay the penalty. To Our paternal solicitude and grief, We perceive that the remedy, which is necessary to cure so many ills, cannot be applied because God is denied, His law is spurned, His help is neglected. If it is only by human measures and by human prudence that men seek to establish peace and prosperity, then these blessings will ever elude their grasp. Let all, therefore, who glory in the name of Christians, let all who live by divine faith ask from God, Who alone can grant it, the health which ailing humanity needs. And during the forthcoming triduum of prayers at Lourdes and at the numerous Eucharistic sacrifices which will be offered, let us pray most earnestly for those

[274] *Psalms*, LXVII, 31.
[275] Translation from *The Tablet*, v. 165, pp. 141-142 (February 2, 1935). Original Latin, *A.A.S.*, v. 27, pp. 6-7 (January 24, 1935).

intentions which We named in extending the Jubilee to the whole of the Catholic world.[276] Let us pray especially that men may happily compose their quarrels and settle their differences so that all nations may receive the blessing of true peace: the peace which Christ brought at His birth, as the angels sang; the peace which after rising from the dead He gave to His disciples, and which, as He was about to ascend to His Father, He left as a sacred pledge to all.

1123. And We most earnestly pray that the Immaculate Virgin Mary, who by God's gift has granted and still grants so many miraculous favors at the grotto of Massabielle, may graciously hear the voice of her supplicants. May she at last propitiate her Son and obtain from Him happier times for our sorely afflicted humanity; so that minds which are blinded—especially the minds of those who openly and arrogantly proclaim rebellion against God—may be enlightened by truth and virtue; that those who have gone astray may be brought back to the path of rectitude; that the Church may enjoy throughout the world the freedom which is her due; and that all nations may be granted peace and true prosperity. . . . . . . Then will the world, distracted as it is by earthly anxieties and divided by so many conflicts, see the whole family of Christians united in one intention, in one faith, and in one prayer, imploring pardon for sinners, peace for the fearful, comfort for the afflicted, bread for the hungry, the light of truth and the harbor of salvation for all those who have gone astray. . . . . . .

ALLOCUTION *Pergratus Nobis* TO THE COLLEGE OF CARDINALS.[277]

A new war would be an enormous crime, a manifestation of mad folly.

April 1, 1935

1124. . . . . . . While the evils produced by the last European War have not yet been repaired, behold a dense cloud obscures the horizon once more, from which fresh lightnings proceed, so that men hold themselves in fear and trembling in a way that recalls

---

[276] *Cf.* Bull *Quod Nuper,* January 6, 1933, *supra* n. 1102. *Cf.* Apostolic Constitution *Quod Superiore Anno,* April 2, 1934, *supra* n. 1118.
[277] Translation from *The Tablet,* v. 165, pp. 473-474 (April 13, 1935). Original Latin, *A.A.S.,* v. 27, pp. 131-133 (April 5, 1935).

the words of Jesus Christ: *You shall hear of wars and rumors of wars and sedition . . . there shall be pestilence and famine, terrors from heaven. Men's hearts failing them for fear of those things which are coming to pass in the whole world.*[278] We do not marvel, then, if the peoples, in such consternation and pressure of nations, from every side, turn their eyes to the Common Father, asking from him light, solace and hope.

1125. As We desire to respond as far as possible to this filial expectation, We would open to you Our mind, which, although in trepidation, rests with secure confidence on the help of the merciful God. If at all times men have need of the Christian virtue of hope, it is specially necessary that they seek it with greater intensity in these calamitous times, holding fast the assurance that all things are governed by the command of God. If we rest the anxiety of our souls on this virtue, which we transform into ardent prayer to the Father of Infinite Mercy, finally happier times will dawn for the human race. As the Apostles, agitated and almost overwhelmed by the waves, turned suppliantly to Christ, so also do we, that finally He may make a great calm; and we repeat their prayer: *Lord, save us or we perish.*[279]

1126. Since the universal rumors of war are diffused abroad and cause the greatest fear and agitation amongst all, We consider it opportune, by virtue of the Apostolic Office entrusted to Us, to speak Our mind. That the peoples should once more take to arms against each other, that brethren should again shed each other's blood, that from earth, sea and sky should come ruin and destruction, this is a crime so enormous, a manifestation of such mad folly that We hold it to be absolutely impossible, according to the judicial saying: *Quae contra jus fiunt nec fieri posse credenda sunt.*

1127. We cannot be persuaded that those who should have at heart the prosperity and well-being of the peoples are ready for the ruin and extermination not only of their own nation but of a great part of humanity. But if anyone thinks to commit this infamous crime—may God put far off such a sorrowful presage, which on Our part We believe unthinkable—then We can only again direct to God with anguished soul the prayer, *Dissipa gentes quae bella volunt.*[280] A new war, impossible morally, appears to

[278] *Luke, XXI, 9-26.*
[279] *Matthew, VIII, 25.*
[280] *Psalms, LXVII, 31.*

Us, as to others, manifestly impossible also both physically and materially, in the present most grave circumstances—in these times of agonizing sorrows, which leave Us to fear a future still more sorrowful unless God All-merciful renews, with His heavenly lights, the minds of those who govern the lot of peoples. As you know full well, last January We ordered a public triduum of prayers at Lourdes. . . . We trust that to the abundant fruits of salvation gathered during the Holy Year there may be added others yet more copious, and that through the intercession of the Immaculate Virgin there may come to this troubled world the longed-for vision of peace.

PAPAL BLESSING *Fratres et Filii Dilectissimi* TRANSMITTED TO LOURDES AT THE CLOSE OF THE TRIDUUM.[281]

Pius XI prays that all peoples may enjoy the gift of peace.

April 28, 1935

1128. Dear Brethren and Children, let us all pray to our Common Mother:

Immaculate Queen of peace, have pity on us.
Immaculate Queen of peace, pray for us.
Immaculate Queen of peace, intercede for us.

O Mother of Compassion and Mercy, who assisted thy sweet Son, while on the Altar of the Cross He fulfilled the Redemption of Mankind, being a co-redeemer and participator in His suffering; and who here from your holy grotto have deigned to bless so many bishops and priests of all the Catholic world, renewing, during this most holy triduum, the Sacrifice of the Cross; let this be a commemoration with grateful soul, of thy benign and beneficent apparitions; let this be the offering of acts of grace to God in happy fulfillment of the Holy Year of the Redemption. Preserve in us and increase each day, we beg of you, the precious fruits of the Redemption and of thy passion. Thou who art mother of all, grant that in purity of customs and dignity of life, in unity of minds and harmony of souls, the peace of peoples remaining safe, we may finally enjoy untroubled the gifts of peace. Amen. . . .

[281] Translation from Schaefer, *A Papal Peace Mosaic*, p. 49. Original Latin, *Documentation Catholique*, v. 33, cc. 1159-1160 (May 11, 1935).

DISCOURSE *Il Venerabile Servo* ON THE OCCASION OF HONORING THE VENERABLE GIUSTINO DE JACOBIS.[282]

> The Pope trusts that the difficulties between Italy and
> Abyssinia may be solved without war.

July 28, 1935

1129. . . . . . . There is a second coincidence, grave, solemn, historical, which may well give Us pause to think, and also to hope. We find Ourself celebrating the glory of this great Italian, Giustino de Jacobis, who was still more a great servant of God, of God the Redeemer, and who became the Apostle of Abyssinia, the apostle and the benefactor and father of all Abyssinia, remembered even to-day as if his life were a fresh event. We find Ourself honoring this great Italian, this great Abyssinian by adoption when there are between Italy and Abyssinia clouds which cross the sky, clouds of which the presence, the significance, or rather the mystery, because such it is still, can escape the observation of no one.

1130. Most dear sons, in a moment so solemn, so historically solemn and important, We wish to add only a very few words: some, to say to all, to invite all to the imitation of this high example of virtue and heroism in the performance of all duties; others, to say that We hope, We still hope, We shall always hope, for "The Peace of Christ in the Kingdom of Christ"; and that We nourish every confidence that nothing will come to pass which is not in accordance with truth, with justice, with charity. . . . . . .

DISCOURSE *Voilà un Coup d'Oeil* TO THE INTERNATIONAL CONGRESS OF CATHOLIC NURSES.[283]

> Expansion is a need of which account must be taken,
> but the right of defense has limits and restrictions
> which cannot be ignored without culpability.

August 27, 1935

1131. . . . . . . We thought to finish here, but We have not finished. You have said something else, something actual, which

---

[282] Original Italian, *L'Osservatore Romano*, July 29, 1935.
[283] Translation partly from *The Tablet*, v. 166, p. 274 (August 31, 1935), pp. 308-309 (September 7, 1935). Original French, *Documentation Catholique*, v. 34, cc. 325-327 (September 14, 1935).

We would not pass over. By the voice of your interpreter you have assured Us that you would pray for Us, particularly for Our intention of "The Peace of Christ in the Kingdom of Christ." We would wish all to have the great joy of seeing peace established in the world. We thank you very particularly for that filial promise; so doing, you will accomplish much. Nurses know well what war means; they have seen it, and if any of you have seen the last war, you will not forget it. We have seen it. We crossed Europe in the midst of the war, and We saw the ravages it had caused when traversing Central Europe to follow the appeal of Divine Providence which called Us to Poland. We came to Poland just after the Russian evacuation, when the traces of devastation were yet burning; and We saw there the reality of war. We want you to pray particularly on this subject, that war may be kept far away, and that we may be spared from it. . . .

1132. The joy and Peace of Christ—that is Our great desire, the object of Our continual prayers, of Our daily petitions to God, the God of Peace, that in the heart and on the lips there may be peace: *Pax vobis. Pax vobis.* Above all when He appeared He announced peace. *Pax vobis.* I give you My Peace, that Peace which in a particular way belongs to Me, that Peace which the world cannot give, but which happily it knows. *Pax Vobis.*

1133. Just as peace is the will of God, it is also a necessary condition for obtaining all the benefits of social and individual life. It is a necessary condition also for the good of souls. Recall only what the missions have suffered as a result of the war. Just the thought of the good of souls, even outside the missions, ought to make us pray for peace. Even in non-missionary countries, what spiritual havoc has there been as a result of the war, what ravages and devastations among souls! Nurses know this better than others. Indeed We hope for peace; indeed We pray the good God to spare Us from war.

1134. The thought of war alone, without adding anything to it—if it were possible to add anything to it—makes Us tremble. Yet, outside Italy, there is talk about a war of conquest, a war of aggression. On such a supposition We find it hard to fix Our thought, so greatly does it disconcert Us. A war of sheer conquest and nothing else would certainly be an unjust war. It ought, therefore, to be unimaginable—a thing sad and horrible beyond expression.

An unjust war is unthinkable. We cannot admit its possibility, and We deliberately reject it. We neither believe nor are willing to believe it.

1135. In Italy, on the other hand, the talk is about a possible war which would be just, inasmuch as it would be a war of defense, to assure the frontiers against continual and incessant dangers, as well as a war necessitated by the expansion of a population growing larger every day, and, therefore, a war justified by the defensive and material needs of a country.

1136. Dear daughters, if it be true that the need for expansion and the need for frontier defense do, indeed, exist, then We cannot forbid Ourself from hoping that the need will be met by means other than war. If any ask, "How?" it is evidently not easy to answer; but nonetheless We cannot believe that an answer is impossible. The possibility must be studied. One thing, however, seems clear to Us. Allowing that expansion is a need of which account must be taken, the right of defense has limits and restrictions which cannot be ignored without culpability.

1137. In any event, We implore Almighty God to prosper the efforts of those clear-eyed men who understand the claims of the common good of peoples and of social justice, of those men who are doing all in their power for peace, not by threats which can only make things worse and aggravate the situation by exciting others, thus making things more difficult and more menacing every day—of those men also who do their utmost, not by delays which are only a loss of valuable time but with a really humane and good intention—of those men, too, who do all in their power for the work of pacification and peace with a sincere intention of preventing war. We pray Almighty God to bless these efforts, this industry, and We enlist you to pray to Him with Us. . . . . . .

ADDRESS *Cari Combattenti* TO A PILGRIMAGE OF WAR VETERANS.[284]

Peace is the essential condition of all prosperity.

September 7, 1935

1138. . . . . . . We have prayed for peace, interpreting the common wish of the ex-combatants, not only for the peace of the dead,

---

[284] Translation from *The Tablet*, v. 166, p. 338 (September 14, 1935). Original Italian, *L'Osservatore Romano*, September 8, 1935.

but also of the living, of the whole world; because the whole world sighs for, desires and pleads for peace; the whole world, mindful of the war, of the memories of the World War, desires peace. We have prayed for peace, because all the ex-combatants desire peace. As Vicar of Jesus Christ, Who is called Prince of Peace, foretold by the prophets as Prince of Peace, Whóse entry into the world was announced by the angelic song: *Peace to men of good-will*[285]— as Vicar of this Divine Lord, and Common Father of all, since all are embraced in the Redemption wrought by the Son of God, We pray for peace. That is Our particular duty, without which We could not be thought of as Pope.

1139. We wish with peace that the hopes, the necessities of a great and good people, Our people, may be recognized and satisfied, that their rights may be assured and recognized, but with justice and peace. With justice, because without justice there is sin, and sin brings misery to the people. With justice and peace, because peace alone can drive away the evils of war, which afflict all people. Peace is the essential condition of all prosperity; the foundation of all good in this world comes from peace and order.

1140. Wherefore We pray always for peace, and it is an inexpressible joy for Us to see, verily at this moment, the appearance of a rainbow on the horizon which We hope is the augury and preservative of peace. We thank the Lord, and pray more insistently that this beneficent rainbow may spread its sympathetic colors from one extreme of the horizon to the other. May God will it and give this peace to the world—a peace of justice, of truth, of charity, made with honor and dignity, made with right and with respect for all rights, and one which, wherever it comes, brings felicity for all. . . .

RADIO ADDRESS *Ecce Os Nostrum* TO THE NATIONAL EUCHARISTIC CONGRESS AT CLEVELAND.[286]

The Pope deprecates the unspeakable havoc of wars.

September 26, 1935

1141. . . . With earnestness We have desired to share with you in the spiritual sweetness of this rich Feast and to join Our prayers

---

[285] *Luke*, II, 14.
[286] Translation from *Catholic Action*, v. 17, October, 1935, p. 11. Original Latin, *L'Osservatore Romano*, September 28, 1935.

and intercession with yours, to obtain an ever-renewed, an ever-greater increase of faith and Catholic life and action in the battle for moral uprightness and for modesty and decency; to deprecate the unspeakable material and moral havoc of wars and their dire aftermath of tears and sorrow — an action which We can never sufficiently commend; to implore that peace so much desired by all—peace to those who are near and peace to those who are far; and to supplicate at least a less intolerable burden of life for a world worn to exhaustion by the ravages of the great depression. . . .

RADIO ADDRESS *Ci Rallegriamo Intensamente* TO THE FIRST NATIONAL EUCHARISTIC CONGRESS OF PERU.[287]

The Catholic faith of Peru led this country very recently to make peace with its adversary.[288]

October 27, 1935

1142. . . . . . . Now, together with the news of your Eucharistic Congress, your faith is proclaimed to all the world. Now, all the world sees with what spirit you, a few years ago and very recently, have been led to the inestimable benefits of peace. May God grant that this Christian spirit, the sole source of true peace, be diffused over all the earth and quickly come and move and reconcile the hearts in those parts, above all of Europe and Africa, where peace, alas, is already too disturbed and gives fear of worse misfortune. For this peace, never separated from justice, truth and charity, pray with Us to the peaceful, Eucharistic King. . . .

LETTER *Quamvis Nostra* TO THE BRAZILIAN HIERARCHY ON CATHOLIC ACTION.[289]

Catholic Action promotes justice, peace and love.

October 27, 1935

1143. . . . . . . Catholic Action, therefore, when rightly and wisely organized, augmented in forces and enriched by strong

[287] Translation from Schaefer, *A Papal Peace Mosaic*, p. 52. Original Italian, *L'Osservatore Romano*, October 28, 1935.

[288] This refers to the agreement between Colombia and Peru concerning the province of Leticia.

[289] Translation from Loeffler, *Directives for Catholic Action*, p. 43. Original Latin, *A.A.S.*, v. 28, pp. 163-164 (April 30, 1936).

auxiliaries, will truly become that pacific army which will undertake the glorious warfare to spread and defend the Kingdom of Christ, a kingdom of justice, of peace and of love. Consequently, Catholic Action, while of its very nature avoiding partisan political aims and methods, does truly and effectively look to the good of the whole State. . . . . . .

ALLOCUTION *Graves Equidem* TO THE COLLEGE OF CARDINALS.[290]

Pius XI ardently strives to procure that peace which is conjoined with truth, justice and charity.

December 16, 1935

1144. . . . . . . Reasons for sadness are not wanting, sufficient to fill with profound grief Our fatherly heart; for example, the happenings in Russia and Mexico and, in part, in Germany. But We do not wish to continue the enumeration of sorrowful facts; especially We do not wish to accentuate those conflicts which preoccupy not only Europe and Africa, but, so to say, the whole world, because in such uncertainty of men and happenings there is danger that Our words, whatever they are, might be not well understood or even openly distorted. For the rest, that which might be justly and legitimately looked for from Us in favor of truth, justice and charity, We have manifested many times already. We know that the words spoken by Us under diverse circumstances, which have been largely divulged by means of the Press, cannot fail to come to the knowledge of those who not only desire the truth but ask it of Us with sincerity and real interest. This may serve as a warning, particularly to those who yet seem to marvel or be scandalized at Us as if We had not fulfilled Our divine mission of Teacher of the faithful. But as We have not failed to affirm in the past and shall not in the future, so now—before We end this Our Allocution—We solemnly repeat that We ardently desire and strive to procure that peace which is conjoined with justice, with truth and charity, fervently praying to God for all *men of good will*[291] to whatever land they belong. . . . . . .

[290] Translation from *The Tablet*, v. 166, p. 853 (December 28, 1935). Original Latin, *A.A.S.*, v. 27, pp. 458-459 (December 31, 1935).
[291] *Luke*, II, 14.

ENCYCLICAL *Ad Catholici Sacerdotii* ON THE CATHOLIC PRIEST-HOOD.[292]

The priest brings peace to hearts embittered by moral and economic hardship.

December 20, 1935

1145. . . . . . . The priest contributes most effectively to the solution, or at least the mitigation of social conflicts, since he preaches Christian brotherhood, declares to all their mutual obligations of justice and charity, brings peace to hearts embittered by moral and economic hardship, and, alike to rich and poor, points out the only true riches to which all men both can and should aspire. . . . . . .

1146. Amidst all the aberrations of human thought, infatuated by a false emancipation from every law and curb; and amidst the awful corruptions of human malice, the Church rises up like a bright lighthouse warning, by the clearness of its beam, every deviation to right or left from the way of truth, and pointing out to one and all the right course that they should follow. Woe if ever this beacon should be—We do not say extinguished, for that is impossible owing to the unfailing promises on which it is founded—but if it should be hindered from shedding far and wide its beneficent light! We see already with Our own eyes whither the world has been brought by its arrogant rejection of divine Revelation and its pursuit of false philosophical and moral theories that bear the specious name of "science." That it has not fallen still lower down the slope of error and vice is due to the guidance of the light of Christian truth that always shines in the world. Now, the Church exercises her "ministry of the word" through her priests of every grade of the hierarchy, in which each has his wisely allotted place. These she sends everywhere as unwearied heralds of the good tidings which alone can save and advance true civilization and culture, or help them to rise again. The word of the priest enters the soul and brings light and power; the voice of the priest rises calmly above the storms of passion, fearlessly to proclaim the truth and exhort to the good; that truth which elucidates and solves

[292] Translation from *The Catholic Priesthood* (America Press pamphlet), pp. 3-10. Original Latin, *A.A.S.*, v. 28, pp. 7-17 (January 2, 1936).

the gravest problems of human life; that good which no misfortune can take from us, which death but secures and renders immortal.

1147.   Consider the truths themselves which the priest, if faithful to his ministry, must frequently inculcate. Ponder them one by one and dwell upon their inner power; for they make plain the influence of the priest and how strong and beneficent it can be for the moral education, social concord and peaceful development of peoples. He brings home to young and old the fleeting nature of the present life; the perishableness of earthly goods; the value of spiritual goods and of the immortal soul; the severity of divine judgment; the spotless holiness of the Divine Gaze that reads the hearts of all; the justice of God which *will render to every man according to his works.*[293] These and similar lessons the priest teaches: a teaching fitted indeed to moderate the feverish search for pleasure and the uncontrolled greed for worldly goods, that debase so much of modern life and spur on the different classes of society to fight one another like enemies, instead of helping one another like friends. In this clash of selfish interest, unleashed hate, and dark plans of revenge, nothing could be better or more powerful to heal, than loudly to proclaim the *new commandment*[294] of Christ. That commandment enjoins a love which extends to all, knows no barriers nor national boundaries, excludes no race, excepts not even its own enemies. . . . . . .

ALLOCUTION *Il Santo Padre* TO THE COLLEGE OF CARDINALS.[295]

> *The faithful must keep Christian hope even in the darkest hours.*

December 24, 1935

1148. . . . . . . Your eminent interpreter has shown Us how we have arrived at these feasts, and clearly pointed out by what ways we have come to them. Various ways, various paths, through moments illumined by the very light of heaven, of supernatural almost divine

[293] *Matthew*, XVI, 27.
[294] *Cf. John*, XIII, 34.
[295] Translation from *The Tablet*, v. 167, p. 18 (January 4, 1936). Original Italian, *L'Osservatore Romano*, December 25, 1935. It is not clear whether the first section of this address contains the direct words of Pius XI; but in our title the first words given in the official report are cited.

light; through moments shadowed by threatening clouds, already tinged by human blood. It is verily along these ways that we have come to Christmas; in these last days especially the way has become more rugged, so difficult, so unpromising of good, and so menacing —to adopt a term used on the mountain heights—of bad weather. We Ourself have traversed this path amidst the most grievous preoccupations, extremely sorrowful and grievous, down to this last preoccupation which threatens peace and menaces war. May God disperse the vision which is presented to Us! . . . . . .

1149. Finally, there come these last preoccupations, so grave that they hold the whole world in suspense—agonizing suspense. We have *pro modulo suo,* as far as We have been able and according to Our limited possibilities, endeavored and willed to give Our beneficent contribution to heal this sorrowful complication of affairs. We had hoped until these last hours, at this sacred moment, to be able to give some word of serenity. That hope, unhappily, has not been realized. We do not say We have lost all hope; indeed We cannot lose it, for this is Our happy situation, to keep this hope even in the worst of hypotheses. This is not merely Our need but Our Christian duty. At the very foundation of Christian life is the virtue of hope, supernatural hope above all, but also natural, for the supernatural does not destroy nature, but upraises it. . . . . . .

ALLOCUTION *La Vostra Presenza* TO THE SPANISH REFUGEES.[296]

The Spanish Civil War proclaims to the whole world that the very foundations of all order, of all culture, of all civilization are being menaced.

September 14, 1936

1150. . . . . . . Louder than all this confusion and this clash of unrestrained violence, passing through these burnings and massacres, a voice is heard proclaiming to the world the truly horrifying news: "Brothers have murdered brothers." Civil war, war between the sons of a common country, of a common people, of a common fatherland! God knows that war, even in the least tragic of circumstances, is always something so fearful and so inhuman: men seek-

[296] Translation from *The Pope on the Spanish Terror* (C.T.S. pamphlet), pp. 7-20. Original Italian, *A.A.S.,* v. 28, pp. 375-381 (September 15, 1936).

ing other men to kill them, to kill as many as possible, to destroy persons and property and with means increasingly and fatally effective. But what is to be said when war is fratricidal? It has been well said that "the blood of a single man shed by the hand of his brother is more than enough for all time and for the whole earth";[297] what is to be said when we are confronted with the fratricidal strife whose tale is not yet ended?

1151. Above the bond of humanity and fatherland there is a brotherhood which is infinitely more sacred and more precious, the brotherhood which makes us one in Christ Our Redeemer, our sonship in the Catholic Church, which is the Mystical Body of Christ Himself, the full treasury of all the benefits that our Redemption has brought us. And it is precisely this sublime brotherhood (which made Spain Christian) which in the present calamity has had to suffer and which has to suffer yet more.

1152. One would say that a satanic preparation has rekindled, and more fiercely in our neighbor, Spain, that flame of hatred and savage persecution which has been professedly reserved for the Catholic Church and the Catholic Religion, as for the one real obstacle in the way of those forces which have already given proof and estimate of their quality in the attempts to subvert established order of every kind, from Russia to China, from Mexico to South America.

1153. These attempts and preparations have been preceded and unfailingly accompanied by a universal, persistent and most astute propaganda, intent on subjecting the whole world to those absurd and disastrous ideologies which, once they have seduced and stirred up the masses, aim at nothing less than arming them and throwing them madly against every institution, human and divine. And how can this awful consummation fail to be inevitable, and that in the most aggravated conditions and proportions, if, through deluded scheming and self-interest and because of disastrous rivalry and egoistic pursuit of personal supremacy, those who should, do not hasten to repair the breach — if indeed it is not already too late?

1154. We, who share in that universal, divine Fatherhood, which embraces all souls created by One God and by the Blood of that same God redeemed, and all destined for God, We, who share this Fatherhood which strengthens human solidarity by such new

[297] Manzoni, *Osservazioni sulla Morale Cattolica*, ch. VII.

and sublime bonds and duties, We cannot but give expression once more to all the anguish of a father's heart, particularly in this gathering which your presence here, beloved sons, has rendered so solemn and so momentous by reason of the sacredness of your sufferings. We must bewail not merely evils and disasters in general, but more in particular the widespread fratricidal carnage, the many offenses to Christian life and dignity, the rack and ruin of the most sacred and precious heritage of a great and noble people, and of a people so singularly dear to Us.

1155. But, beloved sons, the doings which your presence brings so vividly to mind, are something more than a mere succession, however impressive, of devastations and disasters; they are likewise a school in which the most serious lessons are being taught to Europe and the whole world—to a world now at last wholly steeped in, ensnared and threatened by subversive propaganda, and more especially to a Europe battered and shaken to its very foundations. These tragic happenings in Spain speak to Europe and the whole world and proclaim, once more, to what extent the very foundations of all order, of all culture, of all civilization are being menaced.

1156. This menace, it must be added, is all the more serious, and is kept more lively and active, the more profound the ignorance and refusal to see the truth, along with truly satanic hatred against God and against humanity redeemed by Him, and against all that concerns religion and the Catholic Church. This point has been so often admitted and, as We just observed, openly confessed, that it is superfluous for Us to insist on the matter further, and now less than ever, when the events of Spain have spoken with such frightening eloquence.

1157. It is not superfluous, but rather is it opportune and a sad necessity, a duty incumbent upon Us, to warn all against the insidiousness with which the heralds of the forces of subversion are seeking to find some common ground for a possible *rapprochement* and for collaboration on the part of Catholics, and this on the basis of a distinction between ideology and application, between ideas and action, between the economic and moral orders. This insidiousness is dangerous in the extreme, its origin and end being simply to delude and to render defenseless Europe and the whole world, to the entire advantage of those same designs of hatred, subversion and destruction, by which they are being threatened.

493

1158. Another truth is this, that with this renewed revelation and open confession of that inveterate hate for religion and the Catholic Church, through these melancholy happenings in Spain, a further lesson is being offered to Europe and the world, a lesson precious and highly salutary for all who do not care to close their eyes and grope in the dark. It is, then, at last certain and clear as day, from the very confession of these forces of subversion which are threatening everything and everybody, that the one real obstacle in their way is Christian teaching and the consistent practice of Christian living, as these are taught and enjoined by the Catholic Religion and the Catholic Church. This is to say, it is certain and evident that wherever war is being made on religion and the Catholic Church and her beneficent influence on the individual, on the family, on the mass of the people, such war is waged in alliance with the forces of subversion, by these same forces and for the same disastrous purpose. . . . . . .

1159. To all this good and faithful people, to this dear and noble Spain which has suffered so much, We direct Our Benediction, and We desire that it may reach them; and to them, no less, Our daily prayer goes out and will continue to go out until the happiness of peace fully and finally returns. . . . . . . And what of the others? What is to be said of all those others who also are, and never cease to be, Our sons, in spite of their deeds and methods of persecution, so odious and so cruel, against persons and things to Us so dear and sacred? What of those who, as far as distance permitted, have not even spared Our person, and who with expressions and gestures so highly offensive have treated Us not as sons with a Father, but as foes with an enemy who is particularly detested?

1160. We have, beloved sons, divine precepts and examples which may seem too difficult for poor and unaided human nature to obey and imitate, but which are in reality, with divine grace, so beautiful and attractive to the Christian soul—to your souls, beloved sons—that We cannot, and could not for one moment, doubt as to what is left for Us to do: to love them, and to love them with a special love born of mercy and compassion, to love them, and since We can do nothing else, to pray for them; to pray that the serene vision of truth will return to their minds and will reopen their hearts to the desire and quest in brotherly love for the real common good; to pray that they may return to the Father who awaits them with such longing, and will make a joyous festival of their return; to pray that they may be one with Us, when shortly—of this We have full confidence in Almighty God and in the glorious encouragement of this present feast of the Exaltation of the Holy Cross, *per Crucem ad lucem* — the rainbow of peace will shine forth in the clear sky of Spain, bearing the news of peace to the whole of your great and splendid country—a peace glad and abiding, the comforter of all sorrows, the healer of all wounds, the fulfillment of all just and kindly aspirations that run not counter to the common good, the harbinger of a future of ordered tranquillity and of honorable prosperity. . . . . . .

RADIO ADDRESS *Se Nelle* TO THE UNIVERSAL CHURCH.[298]

Pius XI offers his personal sufferings for the peace of the whole Church.

December 24, 1936

1161. . . . . . . Thus on each anniversary of these most holy days . . . We have purposely added to Our message of spiritual joy an expression of the bitter sorrow which oppresses Our paternal heart at this time when so many calamities are afflicting mankind, civil society and the Church: warning all against the deadly dangers which are at hand, exhorting all to be on active guard and to unite all their good works against the propaganda and the constantly recurring attacks of the enemy on the most precious possessions of society, of the family and of the individual; above all recalling them to those unfailing remedies: truth, justice and brotherly charity, of which the Church is the sole depository and divinely appointed teacher.

1162. The sorrowful note which mixes this year with Christmas joys is deeper and more afflicting, while civil war continues to rage with all its horrors of hate, massacre and destruction in Spain, where it appears that that propaganda, that those hostile activities of which We were speaking, have decided to make a supreme test of the forces of destruction which are at their service, and which are now spread through every country: a new warning, graver and

[298] Translation from *The Tablet*, v. 169, pp. 5-6 (January 2, 1937). Original Italian, *A.A.S.*, v. 29, pp. 6-9 (January 20, 1937).

more threatening, perhaps, than ever for the whole world, but principally for Europe and her Christian civilization. The revelation of a threat terrifying in its reality of what is being prepared for Europe and the world unless immediate and effective steps for defense and help are taken.

1163. Among those, moreover, who claim to be the defenders of order against the forces of ruin, of civilization against the ravages of Communism, and who even claim a pre-eminence on this ground, We see with grief a great number, who, in the choice of their means and in the opinion of their adversaries, let themselves be dominated and guided by false and disastrous notions. False and disastrous indeed are the ideas which seek to lessen or to extinguish in the hearts of men, and especially in youth, faith in Christ and in the divine representation which the Church of Christ stands for as depository of the divine promises, and by her divine mission, teacher of the peoples. Whoever treats her as the declared enemy of prosperity and progress of the nation is no builder of a happy future for mankind and for his own country, but destroys the most effective and decisive means of defense against formidable evil, and collaborates unwittingly with those whom he flatters himself he is fighting against. . . . . . .

1164. This year, dear children, the Divine Goodness allows Us to contribute to the prayers, works and sacrifices of all, by personal experience of suffering, from which We had hitherto been wonderfully spared. The same Divine Goodness has been pleased, moreover, to console Us immediately and abundantly by the impressive and moving collective concert of prayer, which from all parts of the Church has been raised in these last days, and continues ever more fervently for the relief of the Common Father. It is with a full heart that We seize an occasion so fitting to thank each and every one for this proof so tender and intense of filial piety, and although what We have to suffer is small indeed in comparison with what is suffered in so large a part of the world, or in comparison with what He, the Chief, the Founder, the King of this divine Church suffered for us in body and soul, We pray Him nevertheless to accept this offering which We make to Him, which We wish to be now and always in full conformity with His most holy will. May it be accepted for His glory, attacked more satanically than ever today, for the conversion of all those separated from

Him, for the peace and for the good of the whole Church, and in a special fashion for sorely-tried Spain, which, by reason of her trials, is particularly dear to Us. . . . . . .

1165. Paul, the tireless preacher of the Peace of Christ, who wrote to the Corinthians that profound sentence, *For God is a God of peace, not of disorder,*[299] and Sylvester, who, after a long night of persecutions, could salute the dawn of liberty and peace, invite Us this year to address to the governments and peoples of the earth a new, more urgent, and more heartening exhortation to peace: to its maintenance where it still reigns, to its re-establishment where it is no more than a memory and the victim of tragic destruction and baffled hope. And with this appeal to the world We join more fervently today than ever Our prayer to God for that *tranquillitas ordinis* in which alone peace can reside, and for the realization of that justice, individual and collective, without which no order is possible. We lay this prayer for peace humbly before the crib of the Prince of Peace. . . . . . .

RADIO ADDRESS *Quamquam Vobis* TO THE THIRTY-THIRD INTERNATIONAL EUCHARISTIC CONGRESS AT MANILA.[300]

The Holy Father prays for the general restoration of public tranquillity.

February 7, 1937

1166. . . . . . . While, therefore, in this our age, all too many men, blinded by false teaching, beguiled by lust of gain or by seduction of vice, or contending fiercely among themselves in mutual envy and rivalry, are drawn away from Jesus Christ, the Way, the Truth and the Light, and make a miserable end, may you, Venerable Brethren and Beloved Children, come closer into ever more intimate union with Him, and even as you offer to Him in reparation the honor which is His due, let all your energies be bent to this goal: that your wandering brothers and all those *who sit in darkness and in the shadow of death*[301] may as soon as possible attain through Him to light, truth and life. Him, may all men

---

[299] I *Corinthians,* XIV, 33.
[300] Translation from *Catholic Action,* v. 19, March, 1937, p. 11. Original Latin, *A.A.S.,* v. 29, p. 18 (February 20, 1937).
[301] *Luke,* I, 79.

acknowledge, adore and follow, for He alone *hath the words of eternal life*[302] so that with the general restoration of public tranquillity and the reconciliation of souls in justice and charity, the Peace of Christ may finally shine upon the wearied race of men. . . .

ENCYCLICAL *Mit Brennender Sorge* ON THE CONDITION OF THE CHURCH IN GERMANY.[303]

> *Pius XI ardently desires the restoration of a true peace between Church and State in Germany; but he will not and cannot compromise with the religious errors propagated by the Nazi Government.*

March 14, 1937

1167. . . . . . . In the summer of 1933, Venerable Brethren, We accepted the offer made by the Government of the Reich to institute negotiations for a Concordat in connection with a proposal of the previous year, and, to the satisfaction of you all, brought them to a conclusion with a solemn agreement. In this We were guided by the solicitude incumbent on Us to safeguard the freedom of the Church in the exercise of her Apostolic Ministry in Germany and the salvation of the souls entrusted to her, and at the same time by the sincere wish of rendering an essential service to the progress and prosperity of the German people. In spite of many serious misgivings at the time, We forced Ourself to decide that We should not withhold Our consent. We wished to spare Our faithful sons and daughters in Germany, so far as was humanly possible, the anxiety and suffering which, in the given circumstances, We would certainly have otherwise had to expect. Through Our act We wished to prove to all, that, seeking only Christ and the things of Christ, We do not refuse the hand of peace of Mother Church to anyone who does not himself reject it.

1168. If the tree of peace which We planted with pure intention in German soil has not borne the fruit We desired in the interests of your people, no one in the wide world who has eyes to see and ears to hear can say to-day that the fault lies with the

---

[302] *John,* VI, 69.
[303] Translation from *The Church in Germany* (N.C.W.C. pamphlet), pp. 2-35. Original German, *A.A.S.,* v. 29, pp. 146-167 (April 10, 1937).

Church and her Head. The lessons of the past years make it clear where the responsibility lies. They disclose machinations that from the beginning had no other aim than a war of extermination. In the furrows where We labored to plant the seeds of sincere peace, others were sowing—like the enemy in Holy Scripture[304]—the tares of distrust, of discord, hatred, calumny, of secret and open enmity against Christ and His Church, an enmity in principle, fed from a thousand springs and working with every means at its disposal. With them and only with them, as well as with their open and silent supporters, lies the responsibility that now, instead of the rainbow of peace, the storm-clouds of destructive religious conflicts are visible on the German horizon.

1169. We have not tired, Venerable Brethren, of portraying to the responsible guides of the destinies of your country the consequences that necessarily follow if such trends are left unhindered and much more if they are viewed with favor. We have done everything to defend the sanctity of a word solemnly pledged, to protect the inviolability of obligations freely undertaken, against theories and practices which, if officially approved, must destroy all confidence and render valueless any word that might also be pledged in the future. When once the time shall have come to place before the eyes of the world these Our endeavors, all right-minded persons will know where they have to look for those who kept the peace, and where for those who broke it. Everyone in whose mind there is left the least perception of the truth, in whose heart there is a trace of feeling for justice, will then have to admit that in these grievous and eventful years after the signing of the Concordat, in every word and in every action of Ours We have stood faithful to the terms of the agreement. But with amazement and deep aversion he will be obliged to admit that to change the meaning of the agreement, to evade the agreement, to empty the agreement of all its significance, and finally more or less openly to violate the agreement, has been made the unwritten law of conduct by the other party.

1170. The moderation We have shown in spite of everything was neither dictated by considerations of human expediency nor motivated by unseemly weakness, but simply by the desire that We might not perchance tear up valuable wheat with the tares; by the

[304] Cf. Matthew, XIII, 25.

intention not to pronounce judgment openly until minds were made ready for the inevitability of this judgment; by the determination not to deny definitely the good faith of others before the hard language of facts had torn away the coverings under which a systematic camouflage has been able and is able to disguise the attack on the Church. Even to-day, when the open campaign waged against the denominational school guaranteed by the Concordat, when the nullification of the freedom of the vote for Catholics who should have the right to decide in the matter of education, shows the dreadful seriousness of the situation in a most important field of the Church's life and the unparalleled torment of conscience of believing Christians, Our pastoral care for the salvation of souls counsels Us not to leave unheeded even the slight prospects of return to a loyal adherence to a responsible agreement. In compliance with the prayers of the most reverend episcopate, We shall not weary in the future also of pleading the cause of outraged right with the rulers of your people. Unconcerned with the success or failure of the day and obeying only Our conscience and in accordance with Our pastoral mission, We shall oppose an attitude of mind that seeks to stifle chartered right with open or covered violence.

1171. The purpose of the present letter, however, Venerable Brethren, is a different one. As you kindly visited Us as We lay on Our bed of sickness, so to-day We turn to you and through you to the Catholic faithful of Germany, who, like all suffering and oppressed children, are particularly close to the heart of the Common Father. In this hour, when their faith is being tried like pure gold in the fire of tribulation and concealed and open persecution, when they are surrounded by a thousand forms of organized bondage in matters of religion, when the lack of true information and absence of the customary means of defense weigh heavy on them, they have a double right to words of truth and spiritual comfort from him, to whose first Predecessor the significant words of the Saviour were spoken: *But I have prayed for thee, that thy faith fail not; and thou being once converted, confirm thy brethren.*[305]

1172. Take care, Venerable Brethren, that first of all, belief in God, the primary and irreplaceable foundation of all religion, be preserved true and unadulterated in German lands. He is not a believer

[305] *Luke*, XXII, 32.

in God who uses the word of God rhetorically but he who associates with the sacred word the true and worthy idea of God. . . . . . . He who takes the race, or the people, or the State, or the form of Government, the bearers of the power of the State or other fundamental elements of human society—which in the temporal order of things have an essential and honorable place—out of the system of their earthly valuation, and makes them the ultimate norm of all, even of religious values, and deifies them with an idolatrous worship, perverts and falsifies the order of things created and commanded by God. Such a one is far from true belief in God and a conception of life corresponding to true belief. . . . . . .

1173. This God has given His commandments in His capacity as Sovereign. They apply regardless of time and space, country or race. As God's sun shines on all that bear human countenance, so does His law know no privileges or exceptions. The rulers and the ruled, crowned and uncrowned, high and low, rich and poor, all alike are subject to His law. From the sum total of His rights as Creator flows connaturally the sum total of His claims to obedience on the part of the individual and every kind of society. This claim to obedience comprehends every walk of life, in which moral questions demand a settlement in harmony with God's law, and consequently the adjustment of transitory human legislation to the structure of the immutable law of God. Only superficial minds can lapse into the heresy of speaking of a national God, of a national religion; only such can make the mad attempt of trying to confine within the boundaries of a single people, within the narrow blood stream of a single race, God, the Creator of the world, the King and Lawgiver of all peoples before Whose greatness all peoples are as small as a drop in a bucket.[306]

1174. The bishops of the Church of Christ set up *for the things that appertain to God*[307] must be watchful that such pernicious errors, which are usually followed by more pernicious practices, find no foothold among the faithful. It is the holy duty of your office, as far as in you lies, to do everything to bring it about that the commandments of God shall be regarded and obeyed as the obligatory basis of morally ordered private and public life, that the sovereign rights of God, the name and the word of God, be not

[306] *Cf. Isaias*, XL., 15.
[307] *Hebrews*, V, 1.

blasphemed;[308] that the blasphemies—in word, writing and picture, at times countless as the sands by the sea—be made to cease; that over against the defying Promethean spirit of deniers, scorners and haters of God the propitiatory prayer of the faithful never falters but that, like incense, it may rise hour after hour to the Most High and stay His Hand raised to punish.

1175. We thank you, Venerable Brethren, your priests and all the faithful, who have done and continue to do their duty in defending the sovereign rights of God against the aggressive neopaganism that unfortunately in many instances is favored in influential quarters. Our thanks are doubly sincere and coupled with admiration and approval of those who in the exercise of their duty were found worthy of making earthly sacrifices for God's sake and of enduring earthly suffering. . . . . . .

1176. The climax of revelation reached in the Gospel of Jesus Christ is definite, is obligatory forever. This revelation knows no addition from the hand of man, above all, knows no substitution and no replacement by arbitrary "revelations" that certain speakers of the present day wish to derive from the myth of blood and race. Since Christ, the Anointed, accomplished the work of redemption, broke the dominion of sin, and merited for us the grace of becoming children of God — since then no other name has been given under heaven to men, through which they can be saved, but the name of Jesus.[309] No man, though all knowledge, all power, all outward might on earth should be embodied in him, can lay any other foundation than that which is already laid in Christ[310]. He, who, sacrilegiously disregarding the yawning abyss of essential distinction between God and creature, between the God-Man and the children of men, dares to place any mortal, were he the greatest of all times, beside Christ, or worse, above Him and against Him, must be told that he is a false prophet, in whom the words of Scripture find terrible application: *He that dwelleth in heaven, shall laugh at them.*[311]

1177. The Church founded by the Redeemer is one—for all peoples and nations. Beneath her vault, which like God's firmament arches over the whole earth, there is a place and home for all peo-

---

[308] *Cf. Titus*, II, 5.
[309] *Cf. Acts*, IV, 12.
[310] *Cf.* I *Corinthians*, III, 11.
[311] *Psalms*, II, 4.

ples and tongues; there is room for the development of all the particular qualities, points of excellence, missions and callings, that God has assigned to individuals and peoples. The heart of Mother Church is wide and big enough to see in the development, according to God's purpose, of such special qualities and gifts rather the richness of variety than the danger of separation. She rejoices in the intellectual advancement of individuals and peoples. With the joy and pride of a mother she sees in their genuine achievements the fruits of education and progress, that she blesses and furthers whenever she can in conscience do so. But she knows, too, that limits are set to this freedom by the majesty of God's law that has willed and founded this Church one and indivisible in all essentials. He who touches this unity and indivisibility, takes from the Bride of Christ one of the diadems with which God Himself has crowned her. He subjects her divine structure that rests on eternal foundations to the re-examination and remodeling of architects, to whom the Heavenly Father has granted no plenipotentiary powers to build. . . . . . .

1178. . . . A Christianity that enters into itself in all its members, that strips off all mere outward show and worldliness, that takes the commandments of God seriously, and proves itself in love of God and active love of one's neighbor, can and must be the pattern and leader to a world sick to its very heart and seeking for support and guidance if unspeakable misfortune and a cataclysm far beyond all imagination are not to burst over it. In the final analysis every true and lasting reform has proceeded from the sanctuary; from men who were inflamed and driven by love of God and their neighbor. From their magnanimity and readiness to hearken to every call of God and to realize that call first of all in themselves, they grew in humility and in the conviction of their calling to be luminaries and renewers of their times. When zeal for reform did not spring from the pure source of personal singleness of heart, but was the expression and outbreak of passionate frenzy, it caused confusion instead of bringing light, tore down instead of building up; and not seldom was the point of departure for errors more disastrous than were the evils that it was the intention or the pretended intention to correct. . . .

1179. In your districts, Venerable Brethren, voices are raised in ever louder chorus, urging men on to leave the Church. Among the spokesmen there are many, who, by reason of their official position, seek to create the impression that leaving the Church, and the disloyalty to Christ the King which it entails, is a particularly convincing and meritorious form of profession of loyalty to the present State. With cloaked and with manifest methods of coercion, by intimidation, by holding out the prospect of economic, professional, civic and other advantages, the loyalty of Catholics and especially of certain classes of Catholic officials to their Faith is put under a pressure that is as unlawful as it is unworthy of human beings. All Our fatherly sympathy and deepest condolence We offer to those who pay so high a price for their fidelity to Christ and the Church. But here We reach the point of supreme importance, where it is question of safety or destruction, and where, consequently, for the believer, the way of heroic fortitude is the only way of salvation. . . .

1180. . . . When people who do not even agree on their faith in Christ hold before you as a thing to be desired or allure you with the picture of a German national church, know this: it is nothing but the denial of the Church of Christ, a manifest apostasy from the command to evangelize the whole world, to whose fulfillment only a universal church can be commensurate. The history of other national churches, their spiritual torpor, their attachment to or enslavement by earthly powers, shows the hopeless sterility that comes over every branch that separates itself from the living vine of the Church. To be on the alert right from the very start and to oppose an unflinching "No" to such sophistries, render a service not only to the purity of one's faith in Christ, but also to the well-being and vital forces of one's people.

1181. You must be especially alert, Venerable Brethren, when fundamental religious conceptions are robbed of their intrinsic content and made to mean something else in a profane sense. Revelation, in the Christian sense, is the word of God to man. To use the same word for the "whispered inspirations" of blood and race, for the manifestations of the history of a people, is confusing in any case. Such false coinage does not deserve to be received into the vocabulary of a believing Christian. . . . . . .

1182. The moral conduct of mankind is grounded on faith in God kept true and pure. Every attempt to dislodge moral teaching and moral conduct from the rock of faith, and to build them on the unstable sands of human norms, sooner or later leads the individual and the community to moral destruction. The fool, who hath said in his heart, there is no God, will walk the ways of corruption.[312] The number of such fools, who to-day attempt to separate morality and religion, has become legion. They do not or will not see that by expelling confessional, that is, clear and definite, Christianity from instruction and education, from the formation of social and public life, they are treading the ways of spiritual impoverishment and decline. No coercive power of the State, no mere earthly ideals, though they be high and noble in themselves, will be able in the long run to replace the final and decisive motives that come from belief in God and Christ. Take the moral support of the eternal and divine, of comforting and consoling belief in the Rewarder of all good and the Punisher of all evil, from those who are called on to make the greatest sacrifices, to surrender their petty selves to the common weal, the result will be, in countless instances, not the acceptance, but the shirking, of duty. The conscientious observance of the Ten Commandments of God and the Commandments of the Church—the latter are only the practical applications of the principles of the Gospel—is for every individual an incomparable schooling of systematic self-discipline, moral training and character formation—a schooling that demands much, but not too much. The God of kindness, Who as Lawgiver says: "Thou shalt," gives in His grace also the power to do. To disregard such profound and efficacious factors in moral training, or knowingly to bar their way to the field of popular education, is inexcusable co-operation in the religious undernourishment of the community. To hand over moral teaching to subjective human opinions that change with the trend of the time, instead of anchoring it to the holy Will of the Eternal God and to His Commandments, is to open wide the door to the forces of destruction. Thus to have ushered in the betrayal of the eternal principles of an objective morality for the schooling of conscience, for the ennoblement of every sphere and branch of life, is a sin against the future of the people, whose bitter fruits the coming generations will taste.

1183. It is part of the trend of the day to sever more and more not only morality but also the foundation of law and jurisprudence, from true belief in God and from His revealed commandments. Here We have in mind particularly the so-called natural law that

---

[312] Cf. Psalms, XIII, 1.

is written by the Finger of the Creator Himself in the tables of the hearts of men[313] and which can be read on these tables by sound reason not darkened by sin and passion. Every positive law, from whatever lawgiver it may come, can be examined as to its moral implications, and consequently as to its moral authority to bind in conscience, in the light of the commandments of the natural law. The laws of man that are in direct contradiction with the natural law bear an initial defect that no violent means, no outward display of power can remedy. By this standard must we judge the principle: "What helps the people is right." A right meaning may be given to this sentence if understood as expressing that what is morally illicit can never serve the true interests of the people. But even ancient paganism recognized that the sentence, to be perfectly accurate, should be inverted and read: "Never is anything useful, if it is not at the same time morally good. And not because it is useful, is it morally good, but because it is morally good, it is also useful." [314] Cut loose from this rule of morality, that principle would mean, in an international life, a perpetual state of war between the different nations. In political life within the State, since it confuses considerations of utility with those of right, it mistakes the basic fact that man as a person possesses God-given rights, which must be preserved from all attacks aimed at denying, suppressing or disregarding them. To pay no heed to this truth is to overlook the fact that the true public good is finally determined and recognized by the nature of man, with his harmonious co-ordination of personal rights and social obligations, as well as by the purpose of the community which in turn is conditioned by the same human nature. The community is willed by the Creator as the means to the full development of individual and social attainments, which the individual, in give and take, has to employ to his own good and that of others. Also those higher and more comprehensive values, that cannot be realized by the individual but only by the community, in the final analysis are intended by the Creator for the sake of the individual, for his natural and supernatural development and perfection. A deviation from this order loosens the supports on which the community is placed, and thereby imperils the tranquillity, security and even the existence of the community itself.

[313] Cf. *Romans*, II, 15.
[314] Cicero, *De Officiis*, III, 30.

1184. The believer has an inalienable right to profess his faith and put it into practice in the manner suited to him. Laws that suppress or make this profession and practice difficult contradict the natural law.

1185. Conscientious parents, aware of their duty in the matter of education, have a primary and original right to determine the education of the children given to them by God in the spirit of the true Faith and in agreement with its principles and ordinances. Laws or other regulations concerning schools that disregard the rights of parents guaranteed to them by the natural law, or by threat and violence nullify those rights, contradict the natural law and are utterly and essentially immoral.

1186. The Church, the guardian and exponent of the divine natural law, cannot do otherwise than declare that the registrations which have just taken place in circumstances of notorious coercion are the result of violence and void of all legality.

1187. As the vicegerent of Him Who said to the young man of the Gospel: *If thou wilt enter into life, keep the commandments*,[315] do We especially address fatherly words to youth. By a thousand tongues to-day a gospel is preached in your ears that is not revealed by your Heavenly Father. A thousand pens write in the service of a sham Christianity that is not the Christianity of Christ. Day by day the Press and the radio overwhelm you with productions hostile to your Faith and Church and, with no consideration or reverence, attack what must be to you sacred and holy.

1188. We know that many, very many of you, for the sake of loyalty to your Religion and Church, for the sake of belonging to Church associations guaranteed by the Concordat, have borne and still endure bitter days of misunderstanding, of suspicion, of contempt, of denial of your patriotism, of manifold injury in your professional and social life. We are aware that many an unknown soldier of Christ stands in your ranks, who with heavy heart but head erect bears his lot and finds comfort solely in the thought of suffering reproach for the Name of Jesus.[316]

1189. To-day, when new perils and conflicts threaten, We say to this youth: *If anyone preach to you a gospel, besides that which you have received* at the knees of a pious mother, from the lips

[315] *Matthew*, XIX, 17.
[316] *Cf. Acts*, V, 41.

of a Catholic father, from the education of a teacher true to his God and his Church, *let him be anathema*.[317] If the State founds a State-Youth to which all are obliged to belong, then it is—without prejudice to the rights of Church associations—an obvious, an inalienable right of the young men themselves, and of their parents responsible for them before God, to demand that this obligatory organization should be cleansed of all manifestations of a spirit hostile to Christianity and the Church, which, up to the recent past and even at the present moment, place Catholic parents in hopeless conflicts of conscience, since they cannot give to the State what is demanded in the name of the State without robbing God of what belongs to God.

1190. No one has any intention of obstructing the youth of Germany on the road that is meant to bring them to the realization of true popular union, to the fostering of the love of freedom, to steadfast loyalty to the fatherland. What We object to, and what We must object to, is the intentional and systematically fomented opposition which is set up between these educational purposes and those of religion. Therefore, We call out to youth: sing your songs of freedom, but do not forget the freedom of the sons of God while singing them. Do not allow this noble freedom, for which there is no substitute, to pine away in the slave chains of sin and sensuality. He who sings the song of loyalty to his earthly country must not, in disloyalty to God, to his Church, to his eternal country, become a deserter and a traitor. . . .

1191. . . . The trials and sorrows through which your people have passed since the war have left their mark on its soul. They have left behind conflicts and bitterness that can be healed only slowly, that can be overcome only in the spirit of unselfish and active charity. This charity, which is the indispensable armor of the Apostle, especially in the world of the present day stirred up and distorted with hate, We pray and beg the Lord to bestow on you in superabundant measure. This Apostolic love will make you, if not forget, at least forgive the many undeserved offenses that more plentifully than ever before are strewn in the path of your priestly ministration. This comprehending and merciful charity toward the erring, and even toward the contemptuous, does not mean and cannot mean, that you renounce in any way the proclaim-

[317] *Galatians*, I, 9.

ing of, the insisting on, and the courageous defense of the truth and its free and unhindered application to the realities about you. The first and obvious duty the priest owes to the world about him is service to the truth, the whole truth, the unmasking and refutation of error in whatever form or disguise it conceals itself. . . . . . .

1192. We address a particularly heartfelt greeting to Catholic parents. Their God-given rights and duties in education are this present moment at the very center of a struggle which could not conceivably be fraught with graver consequences for the future. The Church of Christ cannot wait until her altars have been overthrown, until sacrilegious hands have set the houses of God on fire, before she begins to mourn and lament. When the attempt is made to desecrate the tabernacle of a child's soul sanctified in baptism by an education that is hostile to Christ; when from this living temple of God the eternal lamp of belief in Christ is cast out and in its place is brought the false light of a substitute faith that has nothing in common with the faith of the Cross, then the time of spiritual profanation of the temple is at hand, then it is the duty of every professing Christian to separate clearly his responsibility from that of the other side, to keep his conscience clear of any culpable co-operation in such dreadful work and corruption. The more the opponents are at pains to deny and gloss over their dark intentions, all the more is vigilant distrust called for, and distrustful vigilance that has been aroused by bitter experience. The formal maintaining of religious instruction, especially when controlled and shackled by those who are not competent, in the framework of a school that in other departments systematically and invidiously works against the same religion, can never be a justification for a believing Christian to give his free approval to such a school that aims at destroying religion. . . . . . .

1193. Every word of this letter has been weighed in the scales of truth and of charity. We did not desire to share any accountability, by reason of untimely silence, for a want of enlightenment, nor, by needless severity, for the hardening of heart of any one of those who are placed under Our pastoral responsibility and are no less included in Our pastoral charity because at the moment they are walking estranged in the ways of error. Though many of those who adapt themselves to the ways of their new environment, who have for their deserted Father's house and for the Father

tion, far superior even to that which up to this time had been laboriously achieved by certain more privileged nations.

1196. Nevertheless, the struggle between good and evil remained in the world as a sad legacy of the original fall. Nor has the ancient tempter ever ceased to deceive mankind with false promises. It is on this account that one convulsion following upon another has marked the passage of the centuries, down to the revolution of our own days. This modern revolution, it may be said, has actually broken out or threatens everywhere, and it exceeds in amplitude and violence anything yet experienced in the preceding persecutions launched against the Church. Entire peoples find themselves in danger of falling back into a barbarism worse than that which oppressed the greater part of the world at the coming of the Redeemer.

1197. This all too imminent danger, Venerable Brethren, as you have already surmised, is Bolshevistic and atheistic Communism, which aims at upsetting the social order and at undermining the very foundations of Christian civilization.

1198. In the face of such a threat, the Catholic Church could not and does not remain silent. This Apostolic See, above all, has not refrained from raising its voice, for it knows that its proper and social mission is to defend truth, justice and all those eternal values which Communism ignores or attacks. Ever since the days when groups of "intellectuals" were formed, in an arrogant attempt to free civilization from the bonds of morality and religion, Our Predecessors overtly and explicitly drew the attention of the world to the consequences of the de-Christianization of human society. With reference to Communism, Our Venerable Predecessor, Pius IX, of holy memory, as early as 1846 pronounced a solemn condemnation, which he confirmed in the words of the Syllabus directed against "that infamous doctrine of so-called Communism which is absolutely contrary to the natural law itself, and if once adopted would utterly destroy the rights, property and possessions of all men, and even society itself."[321] Later on, another of Our Predecessors, the immortal Leo XIII, in his Encyclical *Quod Apostolici Muneris,* defined Communism as "the fatal plague which insinuates itself into the very marrow of human society only to

---

[321] Encyclical *Qui Pluribus,* November 9, 1846 (*Acta Pii IX,* v. 1, p. 13). *Cf. Syllabus,* IV (*A.S.S.,* v. 3, p. 170).

bring about its ruin."[322] With clear intuition he pointed out that the atheistic movements existing among the masses of the Machine Age had their origin in that school of philosophy which for centuries had sought to divorce science from the life of the Faith and of the Church.

1199. During Our Pontificate We, too, have frequently and with urgent insistence denounced the current trend to atheism which is alarmingly on the increase. In 1924 when Our relief-mission returned from the Soviet Union We condemned Communism in a special Allocution[323] which We addressed to the whole world. In our Encyclicals *Miserentissimus Redemptor*,[324] *Quadragesimo Anno*,[325] *Caritate Christi*,[326] *Acerba Animi*,[327] *Dilectissima Nobis*,[328] We raised a solemn protest against the persecutions unleashed in Russia, in Mexico and now in Spain. Our two Allocutions of last year, the first on the occasion of the opening of the International Catholic Press Exposition, and the second during Our audience to the Spanish refugees, along with Our message of last Christmas, have evoked a world-wide echo which is not yet spent. In fact, the most persistent enemies of the Church, who from Moscow are directing the struggle against Christian civilization, themselves bear witness, by their unceasing attacks in word and act, that even to this hour the Papacy has continued faithfully to protect the sanctuary of the Christian religion, and that it has called public attention to the perils of Communism more frequently and more effectively than any other public authority on earth.

1200. To Our great satisfaction, Venerable Brethren, you have, by means of individual and even joint pastoral letters, accurately transmitted and explained to the faithful these admonitions. Yet, despite Our frequent and paternal warning, the peril only grows greater from day to day because of the pressure exerted by clever agitators. Therefore, We believe it to be Our duty to raise Our voice once more, in a still more solemn missive, in accord with the tradition of this Apostolic See, the Teacher of Truth, and in accord

---

[322] Encyclical *Quod Apostolici Muneris*, December 28, 1878 (*Acta Leonis XIII*, v. 1, p. 170).
[323] Allocution *Nostis Qua Praecipue*, December 18, 1924; see *supra* n. 860.
[324] May 8, 1928 (*A.A.S.*, v. 20, pp. 165-178).
[325] See *supra* nn. 924-1048.
[326] See *supra* nn. 1074-1096.
[327] See *supra* n. 1099.
[328] See *supra* nn. 1112-1114.

with the desire of the whole Catholic world, which makes the appearance of such a document but natural. We trust that the echo of Our voice will reach every mind free from prejudice and every heart sincerely desirous of the good of mankind. We wish this the more because Our words are now receiving sorry confirmation from the spectacle of the bitter fruits of subversive ideas, which We foresaw and foretold, and which are, in fact, multiplying fearfully in the countries already stricken, or threatening every other country of the world.

1201. Hence, We wish to expose once more in a brief synthesis the principles of atheistic Communism as they are manifested chiefly in Bolshevism. We wish also to indicate its method of action and to contrast with its false principles the clear doctrine of the Church, in order to inculcate anew and with greater insistence the means by which the Christian civilization, the true *civitas humana,* can be saved from the satanic scourge, and not merely saved, but better developed for the well-being of human society.

1202. The Communism of to-day, more emphatically than similar movements in the past, conceals in itself a false messianic idea. A pseudo-ideal of justice, of equality and fraternity in labor impregnates all its doctrine and activity with a deceptive mysticism, which communicates a zealous and contagious enthusiasm to the multitudes entrapped by delusive promises. This is especially true in an age like ours, when unusual misery has resulted from the unequal distribution of the goods of this world. This pseudo-ideal is even boastfully advanced as if it were responsible for a certain economic progress. As a matter of fact, when such progress is at all real, its true causes are quite different, as, for instance, the intensification of industrialism in countries which were formerly almost without it, the exploitation of immense natural resources, and the use of the most brutal methods to insure the achievement of gigantic projects with a minimum of expense.

1203. The doctrine of modern Communism, which is often concealed under the most seductive trappings, is in substance based on the principles of dialectical and historical materialism previously advocated by Marx, of which the theorists of Bolshevism claim to possess the only genuine interpretation. According to this doctrine there is in the world only one reality, matter, the blind forces of which evolve into plant, animal and man. It teaches that even human society is nothing but a kind or a form of matter which evolves in the same way and which moves by a law of inevitable necessity and by a perpetual conflict of forces to its final synthesis, namely, a classless society. In such a doctrine, as is evident, there is no room for the idea of God; there is no difference between matter and spirit, between soul and body; there is neither survival of the soul after death nor any hope in a future life. Insisting on the dialectical aspect of their materialism, the Communists claim that the conflict which carries the world toward its final synthesis can be accelerated by man. Hence, they endeavor to sharpen the antagonisms which arise between the various classes of society. Thus the class-struggle with its consequent violent hate and destruction takes on the aspects of a crusade for the progress of humanity, and all other forces whatever, as long as they resist such systematic violence, must be annihilated as hostile to the human race.

1204. Communism, moreover, strips man of his liberty, robs human personality of all its dignity, and removes all the moral restraints that check the eruptions of blind impulse. There is no recognition of any right of the individual in his relations to the collectivity; no natural right is accorded to human personality, which is a mere cog-wheel in the Communist system. In man's relations with other individuals, besides, Communists hold the principle of absolute equality, rejecting all hierarchy and divinely-constituted authority, including the authority of parents. What men call authority and subordination, they assert, is derived from the community as its first and only font. Nor is the individual (according to them) granted any property rights over material goods or the means of production, for inasmuch as these are the source of further wealth, they claim their possession would give one man power over another. Precisely on this score, Communists insist that all forms of private property must be eradicated, for they are at the origin of all economic enslavement.

1205. Refusing to human life any sacred or spiritual character, such a doctrine logically makes of marriage and the family a purely artificial and civil institution, the outcome of a specific economic system, and insists that there exists no matrimonial bond of a juridico-moral nature that is not subject to the whim of the individual or of the collectivity. Naturally, therefore, the notion of an indissoluble marriage-tie is scouted. Communism is particularly characterized by the rejection of any link that binds woman to the family and the home, and her emancipation is proclaimed as a basic principle. She is withdrawn from the family and the care of her children, to be thrust instead into public life and collective production under the same conditions as man. The care of home and children then devolves upon the State. Finally, the right of education is denied to parents, for it is conceived as the exclusive prerogative of the community, in whose name and by whose mandate alone parents may exercise this right.

1206. What would be the condition of a human society based on such materialistic tenets? It would be a State with no other hierarchy than that of the economic system. It would have only one mission: the production of material things by means of collective labor, so that the goods of this world might be enjoyed in a paradise where each would "give according to his powers" and would "receive according to his needs." Communism recognizes in the State the right, or rather, unlimited discretion, to draft individuals for the labor of the State with no regard for their personal welfare; so that even violence could be legitimately exercised to dragoon the recalcitrant against their wills. In the Communistic commonwealth morality and law would be nothing but a derivation of the existing economic order, purely earthly in origin and unstable in character. In a word, the Communists claim to inaugurate a new era and a new civilization which is the result of blind evolutionary forces culminating in a humanity without God.

1207. When all men have finally acquired the collectivist mentality in this Utopia of a really classless society, the political State, which is now conceived by Communists merely as the instrument by which the proletariat is oppressed by the capitalists, will have lost all reason for its existence and will "wither away." However, until that happy consummation is realized, the State and the powers of the State furnish Communism with the most efficacious and most extensive means for the achievement of its goal.

1208. Such, Venerable Brethren, is the new gospel which Bolshevistic and atheistic Communism offers the world as the glad tidings of deliverance and salvation! It is a system full of errors and sophisms. It is in opposition both to reason and to Divine Revelation. It subverts the social order, because it means the destruction of its foundations; because it ignores the true origin and purpose of the State; because it denies the rights, dignity and liberty of human personality.

1209. How is it possible that such a system, long since rejected scientifically and now proved erroneous by experience, how is it, We ask, that such a system could spread so rapidly in all parts of the world? The explanation lies in the fact that too few have been able to grasp the nature of Communism. The majority instead succumb to its deception, skillfully concealed by the most extravagant promises. By pretending to desire only the betterment of the condition of the working classes, by urging the removal of the very real abuses chargeable to the liberalistic economic order, and by demanding a more equitable distribution of this world's goods (objectives entirely and undoubtedly legitimate), the Communist takes advantage of the present world-wide economic crisis to draw into the sphere of his influence even those sections of the populace which on principle reject all forms of materialism and terrorism. And as every error contains its element of truth, the partial truths to which We have referred are astutely presented according to the needs of time and place, to conceal, when convenient, the repulsive crudity and inhumanity of Communistic principles and tactics. Thus the Communist ideal wins over many of the better-minded members of the community. These in turn become the apostles of the movement among the younger intelligentsia who are still too immature to recognize the intrinsic errors of the system. The preachers of Communism are also proficient in exploiting racial antagonisms and political divisions and oppositions. They take advantage of the lack of orientation characteristic of modern agnostic science in order to burrow into the universities, where they bolster up the principles of their doctrine with pseudo-scientific arguments.

1210. If we would explain the blind acceptance of Communism by so many thousands of workmen, we must remember that the way had been already prepared for it by the religious and moral destitution in which wage-earners had been left by liberal economics. . . . It can surprise no one that the Communistic fallacy should be spreading in a world already to a large extent de-Christianized.

1211. There is another explanation for the rapid diffusion of the Communistic ideas now seeping into every nation, great and small, advanced and backward, so that no corner of the earth is free from them. This explanation is to be found in a propaganda so truly diabolical that the world has perhaps never witnessed its like before. It is directed from one common center. It is shrewdly adapted to the varying conditions of diverse peoples. It has at its disposal great financial resources, gigantic organizations, international congresses, and countless trained workers. It makes use of pamphlets and reviews, of cinema, theater and radio, of schools and even universities. Little by little it penetrates into all classes of the people and even reaches the better-minded groups of the community, with the result that few are aware of the poison which increasingly pervades their minds and hearts.

1212. A third powerful factor in the diffusion of Communism is the conspiracy of silence on the part of a large section of the non-Catholic Press of the world. We say conspiracy, because it is impossible otherwise to explain how a Press usually so eager to exploit even the little daily incidents of life has been able to remain silent for so long about the horrors perpetrated in Russia, in Mexico and even in a great part of Spain; and that it should have relatively so little to say concerning a world organization as vast as Russian Communism. This silence is due in part to short-sighted political policy, and is favored by various occult forces which for a long time have been working for the overthrow of the Christian Social Order.

1213. Meanwhile the sorry effects of this propaganda are before our eyes. Where Communism has been able to assert its power— and here We are thinking with special affection of the people of Russia and Mexico—it has striven by every possible means, as its champions openly boast, to destroy Christian civilization and the Christian religion by banishing every remembrance of them from the hearts of men, especially of the young. Bishops and priests were exiled, condemned to forced labor, shot and done to death in inhuman fashion; laymen suspected of defending their religion were vexed, persecuted, dragged off to trial and thrown into prison.

1214. Even where the scourge of Communism has not yet had time enough to exercise to the full its logical effect, as witness Our beloved Spain, it has, alas, found compensation in the fiercer violence of its attack. Not only this or that church or isolated monastery was sacked, but as far as possible every church and every monastery was destroyed. Every vestige of the Christian religion was eradicated, even though intimately linked with the rarest monuments of art and science. The fury of Communism has not confined itself to the indiscriminate slaughter of bishops, of thousands of priests and religious of both sexes; it searches out, above all, those who have been devoting their lives to the welfare of the working classes and the poor. But the majority of its victims have been laymen of all conditions and classes. Even up to the present moment, masses of them are slain almost daily for no other offense than the fact that they are good Christians or at least opposed to atheistic Communism. And this fearful destruction has been carried out with a hatred and a savage barbarity one would not have believed possible in our age. No man of good sense, nor any statesman conscious of his responsibility, can fail to shudder at the thought that what is happening today in Spain may perhaps be repeated tomorrow in other civilized countries.

1215. Nor can it be said that these atrocities are a transitory phenomenon, the usual accompaniment of all great revolutions, the isolated excesses common to every war. No, they are the natural fruit of a system which lacks all inner restraint. Some restraint is necessary for man considered either as an individual or in society. Even the barbaric peoples had this inner check in the natural law written by God in the heart of every man. And where this natural law was held in higher esteem, ancient nations rose to a grandeur that still fascinates—more than it should—certain superficial students of human history. But tear the very idea of God from the hearts of men, and they are necessarily urged by their passions to the most atrocious barbarity.

1216. This, unfortunately, is what we now behold. For the first time in history we are witnessing a struggle, cold-blooded in purpose and mapped out to the least detail, between man and *all that is called God*.[329] Communism is by its nature anti-religious. It considers religion as "the opiate of the people" because the principles of religion which speak of a life beyond the grave dissuade the proletariat from the dream of a Soviet paradise which is of this world.

1217. But the law of nature and its Author cannot be flouted

[329] II *Thessalonians,* II, 4.

with impunity. Communism has not been able, and will not be able, to achieve its objectives even in the merely economic sphere. It is true that in Russia it has been a contributing factor in rousing men and materials from the inertia of centuries, and in obtaining by all manner of means, often without scruple, some measure of material success. Nevertheless, We know from reliable and even very recent testimony that not even there, in spite of slavery imposed on millions of men, has Communism reached its promised goal. After all, even the sphere of economics needs some morality, some moral sense of responsibility, which can find no place in a system so thoroughly materialistic as Communism. Terrorism is the only possible substitute, and it is terrorism that reigns to-day in Russia, where former comrades in revolution are exterminating each other. Terrorism, having failed despite all to stem the tide of moral corruption, cannot even prevent the dissolution of society itself.

1218. In making these observations it is no part of Our intention to condemn *en masse* the peoples of the Soviet Union. For them We cherish the warmest paternal affection. We are well aware that not a few of them groan beneath the yoke imposed on them by men who in very large part are strangers to the real interests of the country. We recognize that many others were deceived by fallacious hopes. We blame only the system, with its authors and abettors who considered Russia the best-prepared field for experimenting with a plan elaborated decades ago, and who from there continue to spread it from one end of the world to the other.

1219. We have exposed the errors and the violent, deceptive tactics of Bolshevistic and atheistic Communism. It is now time, Venerable Brethren, to contrast with it the true notion, already familiar to you, of the *civitas humana* or human society, as taught by reason and Revelation through the mouth of the Church, *Magistra Gentium.*

1220. Above all other reality there exists one supreme Being: God, the omnipotent Creator of all things, the all-wise and just Judge of all men. This Supreme Reality, God, is the absolute condemnation of the impudent falsehoods of Communism. In truth, it is not because men believe in God that He exists; rather because He exists do all men whose eyes are not deliberately closed to the truth believe in Him and pray to Him.

1221. In the Encyclical on Christian Education[330] We explained the fundamental doctrine concerning man as it may be gathered from reason and faith. Man has a spiritual and immortal soul. He is a person, marvelously endowed by his Creator with gifts of body and mind. He is a true "microcosm," as the ancients said, a world in miniature, with a value far surpassing that of the vast inanimate cosmos. God alone is his last end, in this life and the next. By sanctifying grace he is raised to the dignity of a son of God, and incorporated into the Kingdom of God in the Mystical Body of Christ. In consequence he has been endowed by God with many and varied prerogatives: the right to life, to bodily integrity, to the necessary means of existence; the right to tend toward his ultimate goal in the path marked out for him by God; the right of association and the right to possess and use property. . . . . . .

1222. But God has likewise destined man for civil society according to the dictates of his very nature. In the plan of the Creator, society is a natural means which man can and must use to reach his destined end. Society is for man and not vice versa. This must not be understood in the sense of liberalistic individualism, which subordinates society to the selfish use of the individual; but only in the sense that by means of an organic union with society and by mutual collaboration the attainment of earthly happiness is placed within the reach of all. In a further sense, it is society which affords the opportunities for the development of all the individual and social gifts bestowed on human nature. These natural gifts have a value surpassing the immediate interests of the moment, for in society they reflect the divine perfection, which would not be true were man to live alone. But on final analysis, even in this latter function, society is made for man, that he may recognize this reflection of God's perfection, and refer it in praise and adoration to the Creator. Only man, the human person, and not society in any form, is endowed with reason and a morally free will.

1223. Man cannot be exempted from his divinely-imposed obligations toward civil society, and the representatives of authority have the right to coerce him when he refuses without reason to do his duty. Society, on the other hand, cannot defraud man of

[330] See *supra* nn. 897-909.

his God-granted rights, the most important of which We have indicated above. Nor can society systematically void these rights by making their use impossible. It is, therefore, according to the dictates of reason that ultimately all material things should be ordained to man as a person, that through his mediation they may find their way to the Creator. In this wise we can apply to man, the human person, the words of the Apostle of the Gentiles, who writes to the Corinthians on the Christian economy of salvation: *All things are yours, and you are Christ's, and Christ is God's.*[331] While Communism impoverishes human personality by inverting the terms of the relation of man to society, to what lofty heights is man not elevated by reason and Revelation!

1224. The directive principles concerning the social-economic order have been expounded in the social Encyclical of Leo XIII on the question of labor.[332] Our own Encyclical on the Reconstruction of the Social Order[333] adapted these principles to present needs. Then, insisting anew on the age-old doctrine of the Church concerning the individual and social character of private property, We explained clearly the rights and dignity of labor, the relations of mutual aid and collaboration which should exist between those who possess capital and those who work, the salary due in strict justice to the worker for himself and for his family.

1225. In this same Encyclical of Ours We have shown that the means of saving the world of today from the lamentable ruin into which amoral liberalism has plunged us, are neither the class-struggle nor terror, nor yet the autocratic abuse of State power, but rather the infusion of social justice and the sentiment of Christian love into the social-economic order. We have indicated how a sound prosperity is to be restored according to the true principles of a sane corporative system which respects the proper hierarchic structure of society; and how all the occupational groups should be fused into an harmonious unity inspired by the principle of the common good. And the genuine and chief function of public and civil authority consists precisely in the efficacious furthering of this harmony and co-ordination of all social forces.

1226. In view of this organized common effort toward peace-

[331] I *Corinthians,* III, 22-23.
[332] See *supra* nn. 118-175.
[333] See *supra* nn. 924-1048.

ful living, Catholic doctrine vindicates to the State the dignity
and authority of a vigilant and provident defender of those divine
and human rights on which the Sacred Scriptures and the Fathers
of the Church insist so often. It is not true that all have equal
rights in civil society. It is not true that there exists no lawful social
hierarchy. Let it suffice to refer to the Encyclicals of Leo XIII
already cited, especially to that on State powers,[334] and to the other
on the Christian Constitution of States.[335] In these documents the
Catholic will find the principles of reason and the Faith clearly
explained, and these principles will enable him to defend himself
against the errors and perils of a Communistic conception of the
State. The enslavement of man despoiled of his rights, the denial
of the transcendental origin of the State and its authority, the
horrible abuse of public power in the service of a collectivistic terrorism, are the very contrary of all that corresponds with natural
ethics and the Will of the Creator. Both man and civil society
derive their origin from the Creator, Who has mutually ordained
them one to the other. Hence, neither can be exempted from their
correlative obligations, nor deny or diminish each other's rights.
The Creator Himself has regulated this mutual relationship in its
fundamental lines, and it is by an unjust usurpation that Communism arrogates to itself the right to enforce, in place of the
divine law based on the immutable principles of truth and charity,
a partisan political program which derives from the arbitrary human
will and is replete with hate.

1227. In teaching this enlightening doctrine the Church has
no other intention than to realize the glad tidings sung by the
Angels above the cave of Bethlehem at the Redeemer's birth:
Glory to God . . . and . . . peace to men . . . ,[336] true peace and
true happiness, even here below as far as is possible, in preparation
for the happiness of heaven—but to men of good-will. This doctrine
is equally removed from all extremes of error and all exaggerations
of parties or systems which stem from error. It maintains a constant equilibrium of truth and justice, which it vindicates in theory
and applies and promotes in practice, bringing into harmony the
rights and duties of all parties. Thus authority is reconciled with

[334] Encyclical *Diuturnum Illud,* June 29, 1881. See *supra* nn. 23-26.
[335] Encyclical *Immortale Dei,* November 1, 1885. See *supra* nn. 52-67.
[336] *Luke,* II, 14.

liberty, the dignity of the individual with that of the State, the human personality of the subject with the divine delegation of the superior; and in this way a balance is struck between the due dependence and well-ordered love of a man for himself, his family and country, and his love of other families and other peoples, founded on the love of God, the Father of all, their first principle and last end. The Church does not separate a proper regard for temporal welfare from solicitude for the eternal. If she subordinates the former to the latter, according to the words of her divine Founder, *Seek ye first the Kingdom of God and His justice, and all these things shall be added unto you,*[337] she is, nevertheless, so far from being unconcerned with human affairs, so far from hindering civil progress and material advancement, that she actually fosters and promotes them in the most sensible and efficacious manner. Thus even in the sphere of social-economics, although the Church has never proposed a definite technical system, since this is not her field, she has, nevertheless, clearly outlined the guiding principles which, while susceptible of varied concrete applications according to the diversified conditions of times and places and peoples, indicate the safe way of securing the happy progress of society.

1228. The wisdom and supreme utility of this doctrine are admitted by all who really understand it. With good reason outstanding statesmen have asserted that, after a study of various social systems, they have found nothing sounder than the principles expounded in the Encyclicals *Rerum Novarum* and *Quadragesimo Anno*. In non-Catholic, even in non-Christian countries, men recognize the great value to society of the social doctrine of the Church. Thus, scarcely a month ago, an eminent political figure of the Far East, a non-Christian, did not hesitate to affirm publicly that the Church, with her doctrine of peace and Christian brotherhood, is rendering a signal contribution to the difficult task of establishing and maintaining peace among the nations. Finally, We know from reliable information that flows into this Center of Christendom from all parts of the world, that the Communists themselves, where they are not utterly depraved, recognize the superiority of the social doctrine of the Church, when once explained to them, over the doctrines of their leaders and their teachers. Only those blinded

---

[337] *Matthew*, VI, 33.

by passion and hatred close their eyes to the light of truth and obstinately struggle against it.

1229. But the enemies of the Church, though forced to acknowledge the wisdom of her doctrine, accuse her of having failed to act in conformity with her principles, and from this conclude to the necessity of seeking other solutions. The utter falseness and injustice of this accusation is shown by the whole history of Christianity. To refer only to a single typical trait, it was Christianity that first affirmed the real and universal brotherhood of all men of whatever race and condition. This doctrine she proclaimed by a method, and with an amplitude and conviction, unknown to preceding centuries; and with it she potently contributed to the abolition of slavery. Not bloody revolution, but the inner force of her teaching made the proud Roman matron see in her slave a sister in Christ. It is Christianity that adores the Son of God made Man for love of man, and become not only the *Son of a Carpenter* but Himself a *Carpenter.*[338] It was Christianity that raised manual labor to its true dignity, whereas it had hitherto been so despised that even the moderate Cicero did not hesitate to sum up the general opinion of his time in words of which any modern sociologist would be ashamed: "All artisans are engaged in sordid trades, for there can be nothing ennobling about a workshop."[339]

1230. Faithful to these principles, the Church has given new life to human society. Under her influence arose prodigious charitable organizations, great guilds of artisans and workingmen of every type. These guilds, ridiculed as "medieval" by the Liberalism of the last century, are today claiming the admiration of our contemporaries in many countries, who are endeavoring to revive them in some modern form. And when other systems hindered her work and raised obstacles to the salutary influence of the Church, she was never done warning them of their error. We need but recall with what constant firmness and energy Our Predecessor, Leo XIII, vindicated for the workingman the right to organize, which the dominant Liberalism of the more powerful States relentlessly denied him. Even to-day the authority of this Church doctrine is greater than it seems; for the influence of ideas in the realm of facts, though invisible and not easily measured, is predominantly important.

[338] *Matthew,* XIII, 55; *Mark,* VI, 3.
[339] *De Officiis,* bk. I, c. 42.

1231. It may be said in all truth that the Church, like Christ, goes through the centuries doing good to all. There would be to-day neither Socialism nor Communism if the rulers of the nations had not scorned the teachings and maternal warnings of the Church. On the bases of Liberalism and Laicism they wished to build other social edifices which, powerful and imposing as they seemed at first, all too soon revealed the weakness of their foundations, and to-day are crumbling one after another before our eyes, as everything must crumble that is not grounded on the one Cornerstone which is Christ Jesus.

1232. This, Venerable Brethren, is the doctrine of the Church, which alone in the social as in all other fields can offer real light and assure salvation in the face of Communistic ideology. But this doctrine must be consistently reduced to practice in every-day life, according to the admonition of St. James, the Apostle: *Be ye doers of the word and not hearers only, deceiving your own selves.*[340] The most urgent need of the present day is, therefore, the energetic and timely application of remedies which will effectively ward off the catastrophe that daily grows more threatening. We cherish the firm hope that the fanaticism with which the sons of darkness work day and night at their materialistic and atheistic propaganda will at least serve the holy purpose of stimulating the sons of light to a like and even greater zeal for the honor of the Divine Majesty.

1233. What, then, must be done, what remedies must be employed to defend Christ and Christian civilization from this pernicious enemy? As a father in the midst of his family, We should like to speak quite intimately of those duties which the great struggle of our day imposes on all the children of the Church; and We would address Our paternal admonition even to those sons who have strayed far from her.

1234. As in all the stormy periods of the history of the Church, the fundamental remedy to-day lies in a sincere renewal of private and public life according to the principles of the Gospel by all those who belong to the Fold of Christ, that they may be in truth the salt of the earth to preserve human society from total corruption. . . . . . . The Catholic who does not live really and sincerely according to the Faith he professes will not long be master of himself in these days when the winds of strife and persecution blow

[340] *James*, I, 22.

so fiercely, but will be swept away defenseless in this new deluge which threatens the world. And thus, while he is preparing his own ruin, he is exposing to ridicule the very name of Christian.

1235. And here We wish, Venerable Brethren, to insist more particularly on two teachings of Our Lord which have a special bearing on the present condition of the human race: detachment from earthly goods and the precept of charity. *Blessed are the poor in spirit* were the first words that fell from the lips of the Divine Master in His Sermon on the Mount.[341] This lesson is more than ever necessary in these days of materialism athirst for the goods and pleasures of this earth. All Christians, rich or poor, must keep their eye fixed on heaven, remembering that *we have not here a lasting city, but we seek one that is to come.*[342] . . . . . .

1236. Still more important as a remedy for the evil We are considering, or certainly more directly calculated to cure it, is the precept of charity. We have in mind that Christian charity, *patient and kind,*[343] which avoids all semblance of demeaning paternalism, and all ostentation; that charity which from the very beginning of Christianity won to Christ the poorest of the poor, the slaves. . . . But when on the one hand We see thousands of the needy, victims of real misery for various reasons beyond their control, and on the other so many round about them who spend huge sums of money on useless things and frivolous amusement, We cannot fail to remark with sorrow not only that justice is poorly observed, but that the precept of charity also is not sufficiently appreciated, is not a vital thing in daily life. . . .

1237. To be sure of eternal life, therefore, and to be able to help the poor effectively, it is imperative to return to a more moderate way of life, to renounce the joys, often sinful, which the world to-day holds out in such abundance; to forget self for love of the neighbor. There is a divine regenerating force in this *new precept* (as Christ called it) of Christian charity.[344] Its faithful observance will pour into the heart an inner peace which the world knows not, and will finally cure the ills which oppress humanity.

1238. But charity will never be true charity unless it takes justice into constant account. . . . From this it follows that a

[341] *Matthew*, V, 3.
[342] *Hebrews*, XIII, 14.
[343] I *Corinthians*, XIII, 4.
[344] *John*, XIII, 34.

"charity" which deprives the workingman of the salary to which he has a strict title in justice, is not charity at all, but only its empty name and hollow semblance. The wage-earner is not to receive as alms what is his due in justice. And let no one attempt with trifling charitable donations to exempt himself from the great duties imposed by justice. Both justice and charity often dictate obligations touching on the same subject-matter, but under different aspects; and the very dignity of the workingman makes him justly and acutely sensitive to the duties of others in his regard.

1239.   Therefore, We turn again in a special way to you, Christian employers and industrialists, whose problem is often so difficult for the reason that you are saddled with the heavy heritage of an unjust economic regime whose ruinous influence has been felt through many generations. We bid you be mindful of your responsibility. It is unfortunately true that the manner of acting in certain Catholic circles has done much to shake the faith of the working-classes in the Religion of Jesus Christ. These groups have refused to understand that Christian charity demands the recognition of certain rights due to the workingman, which the Church has explicitly acknowledged. What is to be thought of the action of those Catholic employers who in one place succeeded in preventing the reading of Our Encyclical, *Quadragesimo Anno,* in their local churches? Or of those Catholic industrialists who even to this day have shown themselves hostile to a labor movement that We Ourselves recommended? Is it not deplorable that the right of private property defended by the Church should so often have been used as a weapon to defraud the workingman of his just salary and his social rights?

1240.   In reality, besides commutative justice, there is also social justice with its own set obligations, from which neither employers nor workingmen can escape. Now it is of the very essence of social justice to demand from each individual all that is necessary for the common good. But just as in the living organism it is impossible to provide for the good of the whole unless each single part and each individual member is given what it needs for the exercise of its proper functions, so it is impossible to care for the social organism and the good of society as a unit unless each single part and each individual member—that is to say, each individual man in the dignity of his human personality—is supplied with all that is necessary for the exercise of his social functions. If social justice be satisfied, the result will be an intense activity in economic life as a whole, pursued in tranquillity and order. This activity will be proof of the health of the social body, just as the health of the human body is recognized in the undisturbed regularity and perfect efficiency of the whole organism.

1241. But social justice cannot be said to have been satisfied as long as workingmen are denied a salary that will enable them to secure proper sustenance for themselves and for their families; as long as they are denied the opportunity of acquiring a modest fortune and forestalling the plague of universal pauperism; as long as they cannot make suitable provision through public or private insurance for old age, for periods of illness and unemployment. . . .

1242. It happens all too frequently, however, under the salary system, that individual employers are helpless to ensure justice unless, with a view to its practice, they organize institutions the object of which is to prevent competition incompatible with fair treatment for the workers. Where this is true, it is the duty of contractors and employers to support and promote such necessary organizations as normal instruments enabling them to fulfill their obligations of justice. But the laborers, too, must be mindful of their duty to love and deal fairly with their employers, and persuade themselves that there is no better means of safeguarding their own interests.

1243. If, therefore, We consider the whole structure of economic life, as We have already pointed out in Our Encyclical, *Quadragesimo Anno,* the reign of mutual collaboration between justice and charity in social-economic relations can only be achieved by a body of professional and interprofessional organizations, built on solidly Christian foundations, working together to effect, under forms adapted to different places and circumstances, what has been called the Corporation.

1244. To give to this social activity a greater efficacy, it is necessary to promote a wider study of social problems in the light of the doctrine of the Church and under the aegis of her constituted authority. If the manner of acting of some Catholics in the social-economic field has left much to be desired, this has often come about because they have not known and pondered sufficiently the teachings of the Sovereign Pontiffs on these questions. Therefore, it is of the utmost importance to foster in all classes of society an intensive program of social education adapted to the varying degrees of intellectual culture. It is necessary with all care and diligence to procure the widest possible diffusion of the teachings of the Church, even among the working-classes. . . .

1245. In this renewal the Catholic Press can play a prominent part. Its foremost duty is to foster in various attractive ways an ever better understanding of social doctrine. It should, too, supply accurate and complete information on the activity of the enemy and the means of resistance which have been found most effective in various quarters. It should offer useful suggestions and warn against the insidious deceits with which Communists endeavor, all too successfully, to attract even men of good faith.

1246. . . . In the beginning Communism showed itself for what it was in all its perversity; but very soon it realized that it was thus alienating the people. It has, therefore, changed its tactics, and strives to entice the multitudes by trickery of various forms, hiding its real designs behind ideas that in themselves are good and attractive. Thus, aware of the universal desire for peace, the leaders of Communism pretend to be the most zealous promoters and propagandists in the movement for world amity. Yet at the same time they stir up a class-warfare which causes rivers of blood to flow, and, realizing that their system offers no internal guarantee of peace, they have recourse to unlimited armaments. Under various names which do not suggest Communism, they establish organizations and periodicals with the sole purpose of carrying their ideas into quarters otherwise inaccessible. They try perfidiously to worm their way even into professedly Catholic and religious organizations. Again, without receding an inch from their subversive principles, they invite Catholics to collaborate with them in the realm of so-called humanitarianism and charity; and at times even make proposals that are in perfect harmony with the Christian spirit and the doctrine of the Church. Elsewhere they carry their hypocrisy so far as to encourage the belief that Communism, in countries where faith and culture are more strongly entrenched, will assume another and much milder form. It will not interfere with the practice of religion. It will respect liberty of conscience. There are some even who refer to certain changes recently introduced into Soviet legislation as a proof that Communism is about to abandon its program of war against God.

1247. See to it, Venerable Brethren, that the faithful do not allow themselves to be deceived! Communism is intrinsically wrong, and no one who would save Christian civilization may collaborate with it in any undertaking whatsoever. Those who permit themselves to be deceived into lending their aid toward the triumph of Communism in their own country, will be the first to fall victims of their error. And the greater the antiquity and grandeur of the Christian civilization in the regions where Communism successfully penetrates, so much more devastating will be the hatred displayed by the godless.

1248. But *unless the Lord keep the city, he watcheth in vain that keepeth it.*[345] And so, as a final and most efficacious remedy, We recommend, Venerable Brethren, that in your dioceses you use the most practical means to foster and intensify the spirit of prayer joined with Christian penance. When the Apostles asked the Saviour why they had been unable to drive the evil spirit from a demoniac, Our Lord answered: *This kind is not cast out but by prayer and fasting.*[346] So, too, the evil which to-day torments humanity can be conquered only by a world-wide holy crusade of prayer and penance. . . . . . .

1249. To priests in a special way We recommend anew the oft-repeated counsel of Our Predecessor, Leo XIII, to go to the workingman. We make this advice Our own, and faithful to the teachings of Jesus Christ and His Church, We thus complete it: "Go to the workingman, especially where he is poor; and in general, go to the poor." The poor are obviously more exposed than others to the wiles of agitators who, taking advantage of their extreme need, kindle their hearts to envy of the rich and urge them to seize by force what fortune seems to have denied them unjustly. If the priest will not go to the workingman and to the poor, to warn them or to disabuse them of prejudice and false theory, they will become an easy prey for the apostles of Communism.

1250. Indisputably much has been done in this direction, especially after the publication of the Encyclicals, *Rerum Novarum* and *Quadragesimo Anno.* We are happy to voice Our paternal approval of the zealous pastoral activity manifested by so many bishops and priests who have, with due prudence and caution, been planning

[345] *Psalms,* CXXVI, 1.
[346] *Matthew,* XVII, 20.

and applying new methods of apostolate more adapted to modern needs. But for the solution of our present problem, all this effort is still inadequate. When our country is in danger, everything not strictly necessary, everything not bearing directly on the urgent matter of unified defense, takes second place. So we must act in to-day's crisis. Every other enterprise, however attractive and helpful, must yield before the vital needs of protecting the very foundation of the Faith and of Christian civilization. Let our parish priests, therefore, while providing, of course, for the normal needs of the faithful, dedicate the better part of their endeavors and their zeal to winning back the laboring masses to Christ and to His Church. Let them work to infuse the Christian spirit into quarters where it is least at home. The willing response of the masses, and results far exceeding their expectations, will not fail to reward them for their strenuous pioneer labor. . . . . . .

1251. After this appeal to the clergy, We extend Our paternal invitation to Our beloved sons among the laity who are doing battle in the ranks of Catholic Action. On another occasion[347] We have called this movement so dear to Our heart "a particularly providential assistance" in the work of the Church during these troublous times. Catholic Action is in effect a *social* apostolate also, inasmuch as its object is to spread the Kingdom of Jesus Christ not only among individuals, but also in families and in society. . . .

1252. The militant leaders of Catholic Action, thus properly prepared and armed, will be the first and immediate apostles of their fellow workmen. . . . . . . Ranged with Catholic Action are the groups which We have been happy to call its auxiliary forces. With paternal affection We exhort these valuable organizations also to dedicate themselves to the great mission of which We have been treating, a cause which to-day transcends all others in vital importance.

1253. We are thinking likewise of those associations of workmen, farmers, technicians, doctors, employers, students and others of like character, groups of men and women who live in the same cultural atmosphere and share the same way of life. Precisely these groups and organizations are destined to introduce into society that order which We have envisaged in Our Encyclical, *Quadragesimo*

[347] Address *Siamo Ancora* at the inauguration of the Catholic Press Exposition, May 12, 1936, in *Civiltà Cattolica*, 1936, v. 2, p. 420 (June 1, 1936).

Anno, and thus to spread in the vast and various fields of culture and labor the recognition of the Kingdom of Christ. . . . . .

1254. Here We should like to address a particularly affectionate word to Our Catholic workingmen, young and old. They have been given, perhaps as a reward for their often heroic fidelity in these trying days, a noble and an arduous mission. Under the guidance of their bishops and priests, they are to bring back to the Church and to God those immense multitudes of their brother-workmen who, because they were not understood or treated with the respect to which they were entitled, in bitterness have strayed far from God. Let Catholic workingmen show these their wandering brethren by word and example that the Church is a tender Mother to all those who labor and suffer, and that she has never failed, and never will fail, in her sacred maternal duty of protecting her children. If this mission, which must be fulfilled in mines, in factories, in shops, wherever they may be laboring, should at times require great sacrifices, Our workmen will remember that the Saviour of the world has given them an example not only of toil but of self-immolation.

1255. To all Our children, finally, of every social rank and every nation, to every religious and lay organization in the Church, We make another and more urgent appeal for union. Many times Our paternal heart has been saddened by the divergencies—often idle in their causes, always tragic in their consequences—which array in opposing camps the sons of the same Mother Church. Thus it is that the radicals, who are not so very numerous, profiting by this discord, are able to make it more acute, and end by pitting Catholics one against the other. In view of the events of the past few months, Our warning must seem superfluous. We repeat it nevertheless once more, for those who have not understood, or perhaps do not desire to understand. Those who make a practice of spreading dissension among Catholics assume a terrible responsibility before God and the Church.

1256. But in this battle, joined by the powers of darkness against the very idea of Divinity, it is Our fond hope that, besides the host which glories in the name of Christ, all those—and they comprise the overwhelming majority of mankind—who still believe in God and pay Him homage may take a decisive part. We, therefore, renew the invitation extended to them five years ago in Our Encyclical, *Caritate Christi,* invoking their loyal and hearty collaboration "in order to ward off from mankind the great danger that threatens all alike." Since, as We then said, "belief in God is the unshakable foundation of all social order and of all responsibility on earth, it follows that all those who do not want anarchy and terrorism ought to take energetic steps to prevent the enemies of religion from attaining the goal they have so brazenly proclaimed to the world." [348]

1257. Such is the positive task, embracing at once theory and practice, which the Church undertakes in virtue of the mission, confided to her by Christ, of constructing a Christian society, and, in our own times, of resisting unto victory the attacks of Communism. It is the duty of the Christian State to concur actively in this spiritual enterprise of the Church, aiding her with the means at its command, which, although they be external devices, have nonetheless for their prime object the good of souls.

1258. This means that all diligence should be exercised by States to prevent within their territories the ravages of an anti-God campaign which shakes society to its very foundations. For there can be no authority on earth unless the authority of the Divine Majesty be recognized; no oath will bind which is not sworn in the Name of the Living God. We repeat what We have said with frequent insistence in the past, especially in Our Encyclical, *Caritate Christi:* "How can any contract be maintained, and what value can any treaty have, in which every guarantee of conscience is lacking? And how can there be talk of guarantees of conscience when all faith in God and all fear of God have vanished? Take away this basis, and with it all moral law falls, and there is no remedy left to stop the gradual but inevitable destruction of peoples, families, the State, civilization itself." [349]

1259. It must likewise be the special care of the State to create those material conditions of life without which an orderly society cannot exist. The State must take every measure necessary to supply employment, particularly for the heads of families and for the young. To achieve this end demanded by the pressing needs of the common welfare, the wealthy classes must be induced to assume those burdens without which human society cannot be saved nor they themselves remain secure. However, measures taken by the

[348] See *supra* n. 1084.
[349] See *supra* n. 1091.

State with this end in view ought to be of such a nature that they will really affect those who actually possess more than their share of capital resources, and who continue to accumulate them to the grievous detriment of others.

1260. The State itself, mindful of its responsibility before God and society, should be a model of prudence and sobriety in the administration of the commonwealth. To-day more than ever the acute world crisis demands that those who dispose of immense funds, built up on the sweat and toil of millions, keep constantly and singly in mind the common good. Public officials and State employees are obliged in conscience to perform their duties faithfully and unselfishly, imitating the brilliant example of distinguished men of the past and of our own day, who with unremitting labor sacrificed their all for the good of their country. In international trade-relations let all means be sedulously employed for the removal of those artificial barriers to economic life which are the effects of distrust and hatred. All must remember that the peoples of the earth form but one family in God.

1261. At the same time the State must allow the Church full liberty to fulfill her divine and spiritual mission, and this in itself will be an effectual contribution to the rescue of nations from the dread torment of the present hour. Everywhere to-day there is an anxious appeal to moral and spiritual forces; and rightly so, for the evil we must combat is at its origin primarily an evil of the spiritual order. From this polluted source the monstrous emanations of the Communistic system flow with satanic logic. Now, the Catholic Church is undoubtedly preeminent among the moral and religious forces of to-day. Therefore, the very good of humanity demands that her work be allowed to proceed unhindered.

1262. Those who act otherwise, and at the same time fondly pretend to attain their objective with purely political or economic means, are in the grip of a dangerous error. When religion is banished from the school, from education and from public life, when the representatives of Christianity and its sacred rites are held up to ridicule, are we not really fostering the materialism which is the fertile soil of Communism? Neither force, however well organized it be, nor earthly ideals, however lofty or noble, can control a movement whose roots lie in the excessive esteem for the goods of this world.

1263. We trust that those rulers of nations, who are at all aware of the extreme danger threatening every people to-day, may be more and more convinced of their supreme duty not to hinder the Church in the fulfillment of her mission. . . .

1264. We cannot conclude this Encyclical Letter without addressing some words to those of Our children who are more or less tainted with the Communist plague. We earnestly exhort them to hear the voice of their loving Father. We pray the Lord to enlighten them that they may abandon the slippery path which will precipitate one and all to ruin and catastrophe, and that they recognize that Jesus Christ, Our Lord, is their only Saviour: *For there is no other name under heaven given to man, whereby we must be saved.*[350]

1265. To hasten the advent of that "Peace of Christ in the Kingdom of Christ,"[351] so ardently desired by all, We place the vast campaign of the Church against world Communism under the standard of St. Joseph, her mighty Protector. He belongs to the working-class, and he bore the burdens of poverty for himself and the Holy Family, whose tender and vigilant head he was. . . . With eyes lifted on high, our Faith sees the new heavens and the new earth described by Our first Predecessor, St. Peter.[352] While the promises of the false prophets of this earth melt away in blood and tears, the great apocalyptic prophecy of the Redeemer shines forth in heavenly splendor: *Behold, I make all things new.* . . .[353]

ENCYCLICAL *Firmissimam Constantiam* ON THE RELIGIOUS SITUATION IN MEXICO.[354]

The Church promotes peace and order even at the cost of great sacrifices to herself.

March 28, 1937

1266. . . . . . . In answer to the accusations that are frequently made against the Church, of neglecting social problems or of being

---

[350] *Acts,* IV, 12.
[351] See *supra* n. 804.
[352] *Cf.* II *Peter,* III, 13; *Isaias,* LXV, 17 and LXVI, 22; *Apocalypse,* XXI, 1.
[353] *Apocalypse,* XXI, 5.
[354] Translation from *Catholicism in Mexico* (C.T.S. pamphlet), pp. 9-19. Original Latin, *A.A.S.,* v. 29, pp. 193-199 (April 10, 1937). This Encyclical is occasionally cited under the title of the Spanish translation *Nos Es Muy Conocida.* This may be found in *A.A.S.,* v. 29, pp. 200-211 (April 10, 1937).

unable to solve them, do not cease to proclaim that only the teaching and work of the Church, through the presence of her Divine Founder, can offer the remedy for the very grave evils which afflict humanity. It is for you, therefore, to apply these principles (as you are already striving to do) in order to solve the grave social problems which trouble your country, as, for example, the agrarian problem, the reduction of the large estates, the betterment of the living conditions of the workers and their families.

1267. You will remember that, without detriment to the essence of primary and fundamental rights such as that of property, the common good sometimes requires that these rights be limited and that recourse be had more frequently than in times past to the dictates of social justice. In some cases, the defense of the dignity of the human person will necessitate the frank denunciation of unjust and unworthy living conditions; but at the same time great care must be taken lest violence be approved on the pretext of remedying the sufferings of the masses, and lest encouragement be given to sudden and turbulent changes in the age-old structure of society without regard to equity and moderation and with results more disastrous than the very evils they set out to remedy. . . . . . .

1268. It is only natural that when even the most elementary religious and civil liberties are attacked Catholic citizens should not passively resign themselves to forego them. However, the opportunity of vindicating these rights and liberties, and how vigorously this should be done, will vary according to circumstances.

1269. You have more than once reminded your flock that the Church promotes peace and order even at the cost of great sacrifices to herself, and that she condemns every unjust rebellion or act of violence against properly constituted civil power. On the other hand, you have also affirmed that if the case arose where the civil power should so trample on justice and truth as to destroy even the very foundations of authority, there would appear no reason to condemn citizens for uniting to defend the nation and themselves by lawful and appropriate means against those who make use of the power of the State to drag the nation to ruin.

1270. Although it is true that the practical solution depends on concrete circumstances, it is nevertheless Our duty to remind you of some general principles which must always be kept in mind, namely:

(1) That the methods used for vindicating these rights are

means to an end, or constitute a relative end, not a final and absolute end;

(2) That, as means to an end, they must be lawful and not intrinsically evil acts;

(3) That since they should be means proportionate to the end,
they must be used only insofar as they serve to attain that end, in
whole or in part, and in such a way that they do not bring greater
harm to the community than the harm they were to remedy;

(4) That the use of such means and the exercise of civic and
political rights in all their fullness, involving matters of a purely
temporal and technical kind or of recourse to force in self-defense,
do not fall directly within the province of Catholic Action as such,
although, on the other hand, it is part of the function of Catholic
Action to prepare Catholics for the proper use of their rights and
for the defense of those rights by all just means, as required by the
common good;

(5) Since the clergy and Catholic Action are, by reason of their
mission of peace and love, consecrated to the purpose of uniting
all men *in the bond of peace,*[355] they ought to contribute greatly to
the prosperity of the nation, by promoting the union of citizens
and of social classes, and by collaborating in all those social measures that are not contrary to Christian doctrine and morality. . . . . . .

1271. We once more ardently exhort Our beloved sons of Mexico, who during Our Pontificate have been the special object of Our
solicitude, to unity, charity and peace in the apostolic work of
Catholic Action which has been called to restore Christ to Mexico
and to bring you peace and even temporal prosperity.

ENCYLICAL *Ingravescentibus Malis* ON THE HOLY ROSARY OF
THE BLESSED VIRGIN MARY.[356]

> *Catholics must pray to the Blessed Virgin Mary that
> real peace may return to this world.*

September 29, 1937

1272. . . . . . . Thus the faithful of every age, both in public
misfortune and in private need, turn in supplication to Mary, the

---

[355] *Ephesians,* IV, 3.
[356] Translation from *On the Recitation of the Rosary* (N.C.W.C. pamphlet), pp. 2-8.
Original Latin, *A.A.S.,* v. 29, pp. 374-378 (October 7, 1937).

benignant, so that she may come to their aid and grant help and remedy against sorrows of body and soul. And never was her most powerful aid hoped for in vain by those who besought it with pious and trustful prayer.

1273. But also in our day, dangers no less grave than in the past beset civil and religious society. In fact, because the supreme and eternal authority of God, which commands and forbids, is despised and completely repudiated by men, the result is that the consciousness of Christian duty is weakened, and that faith becomes tepid in souls or entirely lost, and this afterward affects and ruins the very basis of human society.

1274. Thus on the one hand are seen citizens intent on an atrocious struggle among themselves because some are provided with abundant riches and others must gain bread for themselves and their dear ones by the sweat of their brows. Indeed, as we all know, in some regions the evil has reached such a pitch that it seeks to destroy all private right of property, so that everything might be shared in common.

1275. On the other hand, there are not lacking men who declare that they honor and exalt, above all, the power of the State. They say they must use every means to assure civil order and enforce authority, and pretend that only thus are they able totally to repulse the execrable theories of the Communists. However, they despise the light of evangelic wisdom and endeavor to revive the errors of the pagans and their way of life.

1276. To this is added the clever and lamentable sect of those who, denying and hating God, declare themselves the enemies of the Eternal, and who insinuate themselves everywhere. They discredit and uproot all religious belief from souls. Finally, they trample on every human and divine right. And while they cast scorn on the hope of heavenly reward, they incite men to seek, even by illicit means, false earthly happiness, and, therefore, drive them with brazen temerity to the dissolution of the social order, causing disorder, cruel rebellions and even the conflagration of civil war. . . . . . .

1277. Nevertheless, if men in our century, with its derisive pride, refuse the Holy Rosary, there is an innumerable multitude of holy men of every age and every condition who have always held it dear. They have recited it with great devotion, and in every moment they have used it as a powerful weapon to put the demons to flight, to preserve the integrity of life, to acquire virtue more easily, and, in a word, to attain real peace among men. . . . . . . And as in the times of the Crusades in all Europe there was raised one voice of the people, one supplication, so it is to-day: in all the world, the cities and even the smallest villages, united with courage and strength, with filial and constant insistence, the people seek to obtain from the great Mother of God that the enemies of Christian and human civilization be defeated, and thus that real peace may shine again over tired and straying men. If, then, all will do this with due disposition, with great faith and with fervent piety, it is right to hope that as in the past, so in our day, the Blessed Virgin will obtain from her divine Son that the waves of the present tempests be calmed and that a brilliant victory crown this rivalry of Christians in prayer. . . . . . .

ALLOCUTION *Il Santo Padre Ha Incominciato* TO THE COLLEGE OF CARDINALS.[357]

In Germany there is a real religious persecution.

December 24, 1937

1278. . . . . . . It shall not be said of Us, in the words of an ancient historian, that We have forgotten the real names of things. No, by the grace of God, We have not forgotten the true names; We shall call things by their real names. In Germany there is indeed a real religious persecution. It is said, and it has been said for some time past, that this is not true. We know, on the contrary, that there is a terrible persecution; only a few times previously has there been a persecution so terrible, so fearful, so grievous and so lamentable in its far-reaching consequences. This is a persecution in which neither brutality, nor violence, nor the deceits of cunning and falsehood have been lacking. . . . . . .

1279. It is said that the Catholic Religion is no longer what it was but that it is political; this pretext, this qualification is offered to justify the persecution, as though there were no persecution but only, so to speak, a defense movement. Our beloved sons have

---

[357] Original Italian, *A.A.S.,* v. 30, pp. 21-23 (January 31, 1938). The opening part of this allocution was not reported in the direct words of the Pope.

furnished and are furnishing their Father with proof that here it is a case of the same accusation made against Our Lord when He was dragged before Pilate, when all accused Him of engaging in politics, of being a usurper, a conspirator against the government, an enemy of Caesar. . . .

1280. If We concerned Ourself with politics, which is charged against Us, which is attributed to Us, then in these discussions of re-arming and of war, perhaps there would be a place, however narrow and small, also for Us. No, the Supreme Pontiff has no need of that: *My kingdom is not of this world.*[358] The Pope does not engage in politics, he does not live, he does not work to engage in politics but to render testimony to the truth, to teach the truth: that truth which the world so little appreciates and cares for so little while it cares for everything else, just as Pilate did not wait for an answer to his question: *What is truth?* [359]

1281. The Supreme Pontiff wishes to state and to repeat, to protest proudly in the face of the entire world: We do not engage in politics; on the contrary, to return to the words of Our Lord Jesus Christ, if it were so, Our people—and throughout the whole world are found Our people: dear sons, devoted faithful, believers, worshipers of God—would come to Our help. None of these sons of Ours, scattered as they are over the entire world, believes that We are engaged in politics; but they can all see and testify again and again that it is religion with which We are concerned, and nothing else. . . . . . .

Address of Cardinal Pacelli, Secretary of State, to the Thirty-Fourth International Eucharistic Congress at Budapest.[360]

The race in armaments has become the predominant occupation of mankind in the twentieth century.

May 25, 1938

1282. . . . . . . Face to face with us is drawn up the lugubrious array of the militant godless, shaking the clenched fist of the Antichrist against everything that we hold most sacred. Face to face

[358] *John,* XVIII, 36.
[359] *John,* XVIII, 38.
[360] Translation from *The Catholic Mind,* v. 36, pp. 256-259 (July 8, 1938). Original French, Pacelli, *Discorsi e Panegirici,* pp. 715-730.

with us spreads the army of those who would like to make all the peoples of the earth and each individual human being believe that they can find prosperity only by receding from the Gospel of Christ, and that the happiness and greatness of society, as of individuals, can but grow dim in the shadow of the Cross. Face to face with us lags the amorphous mass of those who, without being personally hostile to Jesus Christ, allowed themselves to be tossed by the muddy waves of indifference and frivolity or, carried away by the currents of fashion, to become at the end the unconscious accomplices of incredulity and the fight against Christ. Also face to face with us are the often sanguinary stations which the Church of Christ in these days of disorder suffers with Him on the Way of the Cross.

1283. And while our souls contemplate this gigantic drama and our hearts beat faster at the spectacle of this duel where the *mysterium gratiae* and the *mysterium iniquitatis* meet each other, the irresistible force of our faith and our love, fanned by the breath of divine grace, forces the *Credo* from our lips, no longer as the calm psalmody of days of quiet but as the virile hymn of days of battle. . . . . . . He who has once crossed, under the guidance of grace, the threshold which leads to the central mystery of our faith . . . is mightily armed against enterprises of faithlessness, of the hatred of God and denial of Christ, against the pretensions of pride and human prejudices which surround him, trying to draw him into the nets of their errors and their mistakes. . . . . . .

1284. The philosophers of godlessness, in breaking the bonds which bound man to his Creator, have at the same time without knowing it, and perhaps without even wishing it, disrupted those spiritual forces which gave to the human community its dignity, its cohesion, its very existence, and which drew their strength and their efficiency exclusively from the faith in the Father Who is in heaven. The deniers of the Christian revelation who reject all His mysteries, including that of the Blessed Eucharist, have defiled man in his private and social life; they have robbed the relations of man with man of their high nobility, of their sacred character, they have destroyed them in depriving them of the only sanction which really counts and which the earth expects from heaven.

1285. A slow but long-continued work of disintegration has insensibly separated intellectual and moral life from the faith in God and in Christ, unshakable Rock on which it was originally

541

founded; blind presumption has little by little relaxed and finally broken the link between the duty of man and the eternal principles without having been able to substitute anything else but transcendental morals without foundation or blessing; drunk with the pride of a purely extraneous progress, they have detached education from the foundation which God had given it, and we now contemplate with horror the term of this evolution, the fruit of this progress and of this education: instead of the proud humanity, conscious and free, which has been promised us, we see nothing but a world in disequilibrium, without joy and peace, sorry product of secular errors and mistakes.

1286. Has the world ever known such exasperated hatred, divisions and deep discords as those among which it is hopelessly involved to-day? The value of a given word, has it ever been lower than it is to-day, since utilitarian materialism has been openly and officially substituted for the eternal moral principles? Are we surprised, in a world in which the idea of the fear of God is lost and the teachings of Christ are not applied to the practice of real life, to see suspicion rule between class and class, between man and man, between nation and nation, between people and people, suspicion which has arrived at such a degree that its brutal force threatens every moment to cause a catastrophe, and that in any case it covers with dark clouds the horizon of to-day and the near future? Is not this race in armaments an object of pitiless horror and aversion for every thinking human being, this race which under the nightmare of this universal suspicion has become the predominant occupation of mankind in the twentieth century, equipped for new conflicts of which the destructive fury would surpass in savagery everything which the past has known?

1287. In face of the violent upheaval which the pioneers of atheistic Communism are trying to spread through the world, it is the right, it is the duty of the threatened nations to oppose it for their own sake, and not to allow the destroyers of Christian society to carry into other nations' their incendiary torches of revolution and class war. On the other hand, no illusion could be more pitiful, nor in the long run more dangerous than to try in this reaction to do without the spiritual strength which faith in God and Christ gives the individual and society. Nothing can be more deplorable than just at the moment when this monster is trying to spread its tentacles over Europe and the rest of the world, to weaken the forces of resistance of the Christian front by forcibly taking away from the Church its mission of educating the young in that spirit of heroic fidelity to Christ which alone can give the victory over such a desperate enemy. . . . . . .

1288. We cannot praise too highly the superhuman efforts of those statesmen who, trying to reduce through education or compulsion the bad instincts tending to destroy social peace, put in practice different means according to the temperament of the various peoples and the character of their institutions which seem most apt to bring to an end the open or latent war in which humanity is being used up. It is only just to render homage to their good-will, to the straightness and the nobility of their intentions, to the energy with which they pursue their hard task. Nevertheless, it is the conviction of every observer who looks attentively into things that neither the mightiest organization, nor the strictest education imposed by the temporal authorities will ever alone effect a change of heart. Yet without this change of heart the most perfect institutions of social peace will never be anything but a machine without a soul, and, therefore, devoid of life and fruitfulness.

1289. Until those who are on both sides of the line have their hearts penetrated by the spirit of Bethlehem, by the example of Nazareth, by the doctrine of the Sermon on the Mount, by the *Misereor super turbam*,[361] all the official statutes, all human arbitration will remain doomed to impotence at the great risk of arriving one day at the full bankruptcy of their promises. . . . . . .

Radio Address *Dum Datur Nobis* to the Thirty-Fourth International Eucharistic Congress at Budapest.[362]

> *Pius XI prays that the dark clouds threatening the peace may be dispersed.*

May 29, 1938

1290. . . . . . . First of all, We address Ourself to you, beloved people of Hungary. Together with those divine gifts that support the supernatural life, for you We presage from God not only that

---

[361] *Mark*, VIII, 2: *I have compassion on the crowd.*
[362] Original Latin, *A.A.S.*, v. 30, p. 182 (June 10, 1938).

tranquillity of peace without which there can be no real peace but also that dignity of peace which the Hungarian nation deserves.

1291. Finally We bless from Our paternal heart each and all of you from all nations, who are celebrating the Eucharistic Congress at Budapest. While our Redeemer, hidden beneath the Eucharistic veils but visible as it were to the eyes of faith, achieves this great triumph, We earnestly pray, together with you, that He may foster, increase, and strengthen the present consolations and the hope which We see for a better future. Thus, when those clouds which seem to portend new storms have been driven from the sky, may He enlighten and calm, with the rays of His divine light and the gifts of His grace, the darkness and unrest of souls, whose plight presses upon Us. . . . . . .

RADIO ADDRESS *Hac Sollemni Hora* TO THE CANADIAN NATIONAL EUCHARISTIC CONGRESS IN QUEBEC.[363]

The pilgrims are asked to pray for peace.

June 26, 1938

1292. . . . . . . You know well, Venerable Brethren and Beloved Sons, whence they[364] drew that power and strength, by which, moved and fortified, they entered upon the way of sanctity with a determined and vigorous spirit. It was, of course, from the August Sacrament of the altar, which truly is *the corn of the elect and wine springing forth virgins.*[365] Let all of us, therefore, approach this Heavenly Banquet, this Mystery of Divine Love with the utmost holiness and with burning love; and having been refreshed and strengthened there by Christ, our Lord, Who "causes joy in heaven and preserves the whole world," [366] let us ask for truth, peace and charity not only for ourselves and for all Christian peoples, but also for those men who have strayed from the path of virtue, too frequently blinded by worldly lust, or falsely inflamed by hate. And in a special way We implore the gifts of peace, unity and love, which have their source in the Eucharist for the Canadian nation in which men from so many nations and races are settling; so that there may be indeed "one faith of mind and piety of action." . . .

[363] Original Latin, *A.A.S.*, v. 30, pp. 224-225 (July 15, 1938).
[364] The Canadian Martyrs.
[365] *Zacharias*, IX, 17.
[366] *Imitation of Christ*, bk. 4, c. I, 11.

Address *Le Missioni e il Nazionalismo* to the students of the Collegio de Propaganda Fide in Rome.[367]

Exaggerated nationalism is a veritable curse.

August 21, 1938

1293. . . . . . . Beware of the grave danger of exaggerated nationalism. For there is nationalism and nationalism, which amounts to saying that there is nation and nation, personality and personality. Nations as well as nationalism are existing realities, for nations were made by God. There is, therefore, room for a fair and moderate nationalism, which is the breeding ground of many virtues, but beware of exaggerated nationalism as of a veritable curse. Unfortunately, it seems to Us that the facts justify Our terms—a veritable curse—for it breeds constant division and the threat of war. It is no less a curse of sterility where missions are concerned, for it is not along this path that the fertility of grace will be revealed, or that apostleship will flourish. . . . . . .

Address *Egli, Che all'Inizio* to four hundred teachers enrolled in Catholic Action.[368]

The primary aim of a true colonial policy is to civilize the less gifted races.

September 6, 1938

1294. . . . . . . It has been said that Italian racialism refuses to start a polemic on what only concerns religion and philosophy. Neither does the Pope wish to embark upon polemics any more than the Apostles themselves did, but he owes it to himself to state nothing but the truth, just as they did. But no reader who is the least familiar with Christian doctrine can remain indifferent to words of that kind. Why, indeed, should relations between the races not interest philosophy and religion? There do exist races more or less gifted, just as there are families similarly endowed. But when a

---

[367] Translation from *The Tablet*, v. 172, p. 266 (August 27, 1938). Original Italian, *Civiltà Cattolica*, 1938, v. 3, pp. 464-465 (August 27, 1938).

[368] Translation from *The Tablet*, v. 172, p. 363 (September 17, 1938). Original Italian, *Civiltà Cattolica*, 1938, v. 4, p. 79 (September 23, 1938). It is not clear whether these are the Pope's direct words or not. Although they are partially in the third person, both *The Tablet* and the *Civiltà Cattolica* report the entire passage as a direct quotation.

race more abundantly gifted by Divine Providence enters into contact with another race that is less favored, or when a country seeks to possess colonies, it is evident that the colonizing country's first aim must be to civilize, that is, to allow its colonies to participate in the benefits of civilization. What else are colonies for, if they are not meant to educate races less civilized? . . . We are not particularly referring to the Italian colonies; We are speaking generally; if nations do not colonize in order to spread civilization, then they are open to the accusation that they found colonies only to exploit them. . . . And whoever does civilizing work, cannot disregard religion and philosophy. . . . If We are so insistent on this point, it is because We cannot let an opinion spread as erroneous as that which holds that education can ever do without religion and philosophy. . . . . . .

ADDRESS *Voilà une Audience* TO A PILGRIMAGE OF THE FRENCH CHRISTIAN WORKERS' SYNDICATES.[369]

Pius XI condemns the Totalitarian State.

September 18, 1938

1295. . . . . . . In the first place, We treat an important doctrine. You have included among your guiding principles—We have seen it, and it couldn't be otherwise with Christian workers—a denial of the doctrine, so frequently heard to-day, that the State is all and the individual nothing. You have done well, for the Church does not speak that way; such is not the doctrine of the Church. One might sum up this doctrine with brutal simplicity: all for the State, nothing for the individual. No, the Church does not teach such a doctrine. But neither does it teach the contrary doctrine: all for the individual, nothing for the State. No, this is its privilege: to walk, as it were, among the peoples and the continents, among all the nations of the earth—We do not say races—and to safeguard in all and everywhere that middle path in which virtue always lies, *in medio stat virtus*. Real virtue is always in the middle path.

1296. The Church professes and teaches a doctrine which clearly marks out the relations between the State and the individual. Certainly (there is clear evidence), because of the necessities of life, the

<hr>

369 Original French, *L'Osservatore Romano*, September 19, 1938.

individual, from birth until death, needs the State for his life and his own development. But it is not true that the State is a person, an independent person speaking in its own name. . . . Thus when one speaks of the soul of the State, it is a way of speaking that has its foundation in reality, but which is really an abstraction. And the State can exercise no personal function except through the individuals who compose it. That is the evidence, but in our day it is no longer recognized in many places. It is said almost everywhere in one way or another—everyone is used to hearing it— that everything belongs to the State, nothing to the individual. Oh! dear sons, what an error lies in this expression! In the first place, it is against the facts, for if the individual is really dependent upon society in some way, society without the individuals would be nothing but a pure abstraction. But there is something very grave behind this; those who say that all belongs to the State also say that the State is something divine. Then the individual is divinized, but in a new way; it is a species of social pantheism. Listen, dear sons, to the lesson which the elementary catechism taught us: it is the enemy of man who says *you will be like gods, eritis sicut dii.*[370] You all know what this phrase means and how it has become the tragedy of all ages for poor, sinful humanity.

1297. Almost everywhere it is said that everything belongs to the State; that is, the totalitarian State, as it is called; nothing without the State, everything for the State. There is an error here so evident that it is astonishing that men, otherwise serious and talented, say it and teach it to the masses. . . . . . .

RADIO ADDRESS *Mentre Milioni di Uomini* TO THE WHOLE WORLD.[371]

Pius XI offers his life for the peace of the world.

September 29, 1938

1298. Whilst millions of people are living in anxiety, fear of war and the threat of massacre and ruin, We gather to Our fatherly heart the troubles of so many of Our sons, and invite bishops, clergy, religious and faithful to unite in confident prayer for the preserva-

---

[370] *Genesis*, III, 5.
[371] Translation from *The Tablet*, v. 172, p. 459 (October 8, 1938). Original Italian, *A.A.S.*, v. 30, p. 309 (October 14, 1938).

tion of peace in justice and in charity. Let the faithful have recourse
once more to the unarmed but invincible power of prayer, so that
God, Who holds in His Hands the fate of the world, may sustain
in rulers, especially at this moment, a confidence in the peaceful
methods of sincere negotiations and lasting agreements, and that
He may inspire all with sentiments and acts true to their repeated
peaceful words and calculated to foster peace and to place it on the
secure foundations of right and evangelical teaching.

1299. We are grateful beyond expression for the prayers which
the faithful of the world have said and are saying on Our behalf;
but We willingly offer the life which, on the strength of those
prayers, the Lord has restored and renewed for the salvation and
the peace of the world, whether the Master of life and death wishes
to cut short the wonderful gift of so long a life, or lengthen the
working day of a tired and sorrowful worker. . . . . . .

ADDRESS TO THE MEMBERS OF THE SACRED ROMAN ROTA.[372]

*Men must be grateful to Divine Providence for preserv-
ing the peace.*

October 1, 1938

1300. . . . . . . It looks as though men, up to the last moment,
had not made ready any avenues to peace; it looks as though they
did not want peace. But Divine Providence has thought of us—
and in ways which have not occurred to men. Therefore, we must
be infinitely grateful to the Lord for having heard the prayers of
His Church. . . . . . .

ADDRESS *Anzitutto Egli* TO THE FOURTH INTERNATIONAL CONGRESS OF CHRISTIAN ARCHEOLOGY.[373]

*In these sad times the Christian must look forward
with hope to the future.*

October 20, 1938

1301. . . . . . . These persecutions in Germany and Austria are
carried out with strange audacity, as witnessed by the evidence that

---

[372] Original Italian, *Civiltà Cattolica,* 1938, v. 4, p. 183 (October 8, 1938).
[373] Translation from *The Tablet,* v. 172, p. 555 (October 29, 1938). Original Italian,
   L'Osservatore Romano, October 22, 1938.

lies under Our eyes. This persecution not only saddens the Pope as a Father of the faithful, but simply as a man, seeing human dignity betrayed as it was under Julian the Apostate: for this persecution spares no one. . . . What to do? Do as the Pope does, who remains an optimist; though his optimism bears rather on the future. The present is what it is, as God permits it to be, and as He allows men to make it. The future, chiefly the future of great things, is in the Hands of God, and it is in excellent Hands. . . . . . .

ALLOCUTION *Con Grande* TO THE COLLEGE OF CARDINALS.[374]

The Holy Father is deeply grieved by the violation of the Concordat on the part of the Italian Government.

December 24, 1938

1302. . . . . . . We might give without further addition that paternal Apostolic Blessing which you, as the good sons that you are, so fully desire and have so amply deserved. However, We are now almost on the eve, not only of Christmas, but also of another anniversary to which We are asked to devote a thought and an allusion which seem necessary, that is, the eve of the tenth anniversary of the conciliation; moreover, We have before Us an audience which could not be more opportune, that is, more intelligent, more enlightened and answering better in a word to a subject so important in itself and rendered even more important, though assuredly not the easier to handle, through present circumstances.

1303. We hasten to say and to proclaim in this place that Our celebration of this tenth anniversary must be a hymn of the liveliest thanksgiving, Our *Magnificat,* Our *Nunc Dimittis,* Our and your *Te Deum,* to that Divine Goodness which, from the time of Our first Encyclical, recalled to Our memory and Our pen those beautiful words: *Ego cogito cogitationes pacis et non afflictionis;*[375] this made Us anticipate in Our heart that hour which Divine Providence was soon to cause to strike and about which it was Our duty to see that it would not be struck in vain.

1304. It is hardly necessary to say, and yet We say it aloud, that, after God, Our recognition and Our thanks are due to those

---

[374] Translation from *The Catholic Mind,* v. 37, pp. 549-553 (February 22, 1939).
  Original Italian, *Civiltà Cattolica,* 1939, v. 1, pp. 83-86 (December 29, 1938).
[375] *Jeremias,* XXIX, 11.

very eminent persons—We mean Our noble Sovereign and his incomparable Minister—to whom is due the fact that this so important and beneficial work has been crowned with a happy end and a great success. We must mention also those eminent persons— Cardinal Gasparri and the Marquis Francesco Pacelli—who helped Us with an heroic assiduity in their work, a fact which may have hastened their death, and it is for this reason that We recall with gratitude their honor and their names.

1305.   But the duty of acknowledging Our recognition toward God and toward men having been accomplished, and having given Our cordial congratulations to the whole of that Italy which is so particularly dear to Us among the many other dear parts of Our great Catholic family, We are obliged unhappily to state because of Our Apostolic duty and on behalf of sincere truth, as well as because of the reverence paid to Us because of Our age—that this long expected anniversary cannot bring Us that serene joy for which alone We wished to make place, but rather grave and veritable preoccupations and bitter sorrows.

1306.   Bitter sorrows, indeed, when it is a question of genuine and manifold vexations—We do not say that they are general—but certainly they are very numerous and taking place in many localities against that Catholic Action which, as is well known, is the apple of Our eye, and—it must also be recognized and admitted—by the violation of various offices of Catholic Action and of its archives. Catholic Action has no concern with politics and is not a matter for rivalry—a thing for which We have no desire—but solely purposes to make good Christians, living their Christianity, and by that very token, elements of the first importance for the public good, especially in a Catholic country like Italy, as the facts have shown. When We observe the fervor in this regard of the less important circles, it appears only too clearly that even though Catholic Action was definitely mentioned in Our Pact of Conciliation, gestures of laxity and of encouragement have amply (though secretly) come from high quarters, for the vexations, indeed, continue in different places from one end to the other of the Peninsula, and these are not only unimportant places. . . . . . .

1307.   The offense, the wound struck at Our Concordat and precisely in that which concerns Holy Matrimony—and for every Catholic it is enough to say that—has not only caused the heart of the old Father bitter griefs because of the evil treatment meted out toward his so well-beloved Catholic Action, but veritable and grave preoccupations to the head of Catholicism and the guardian of morality and truth. We have no need to add further words to underline how the wound has gone straight and most painfully to Our heart. We know that it has been asserted that the Concordat has not been broken, but rather that it has remained intact. We are far from wishing to enter into a discussion of this kind. We believe, on the contrary, that if, in the case of the observation or non-observation of every bilateral pact, its interpretation cannot be usurped by one of the parties alone, this is even truer in the case of an interpretation which frees one so resolutely from all engagements to it.

1308. We have another observation to make: it is a reminder of the great and glorious memory of Leo XIII. When thinking again of the recent apotheosis prepared in Rome itself for a cross which is the enemy of the Cross of Christ, of that blow struck at the Concordat and of all the other things of which We have spoken to you, it did not seem to Us excessive to hope for some regard for Our white hairs; instead, We met further rudeness.[376] This reminder We make both to honor the truly honorable memory of that great Pontiff and to remind Ourself of that spirit of magnificent pardon and to imitate as We do with all Our heart, that most noble example, while praying God that He will deign to illuminate intellects and move hearts in the senses of truth and justice which are the only true and solid bases of the well-being of persons and peoples, as is written in Holy Writ: *Miseros facit populos peccatum.*[377]

1309. We have offered Our life, now an old one, for the peace and prosperity of peoples: We offer it again in order that inner peace, the peace of souls and consciences, may remain intact, as well as that the flourishing prosperity of Italy, which amidst all peoples is so dear to Us just as His own country was so dear to Jesus Who gave Himself to His passion and death for the human race. That is Our Christmas vow and wish and it is with Him that We bless you again, both you and all whom you have in your hearts.

[376] *Cf. Leonis XIII Pontificis Maximi Acta*, v. 15, p. 369. In this letter to Cardinal Rampolla Leo XIII laments the fact that the Italian revolutionaries not only had no respect for his white hairs, but even intensified their persecution in the later years of his Pontificate.
[377] *Proverbs*, XIV, 34.

PART FIVE

PIUS XII

1939–

INTRODUCTION

T HE DRAMATIC swiftness with which the College of Cardinals elevated Eugenio Cardinal Pacelli, Secretary of State, to the papacy on March 2, 1939, proclaimed how heartily they endorsed the forceful policy of Pius XI, how deeply they admired the saintly prelate who had been most intimately associated with him. The conclave of 1939 was the shortest since 1623, and marked the first election of a Secretary of State since 1775. A priest of outstanding piety, a diplomat of forty years' experience and first-hand knowledge of continental Europe, England, North and South America, the *Alter Ego* of Pius XI seemed pre-eminently fitted for the strenuous tasks of the papacy in a world poised on the brink of another devastating war.

He was born on March 2, 1876, the second son of Filippo Pacelli, aristocratic dean of the Vatican law corps. Of delicate health yet extraordinary piety even as a boy, Eugenio entered the Capranica College in Rome, and, after an unusually brilliant course, was ordained in 1899. Shortly afterward, at the invitation of Monsignor Gasparri, Father Pacelli relinquished a professorship of law at the Roman seminary and entered the papal secretariate of state, a department he was to leave only when elected pope. In 1914, when

Benedict XV made Cardinal Gasparri Secretary of State, Monsignor Pacelli was promoted to Secretary of the Sacred Congregation for Extraordinary Ecclesiastical Affairs, charged with supervising the work of exchanging prisoners, of moving the wounded to hospitals, of relaying information to relatives of missing soldiers during the World War.

In May, 1917, he was consecrated titular Archbishop of Sardes by Benedict XV himself, and sent as Papal Nuncio to Bavaria to sound out the Central Powers on the possibilities of a negotiated peace. Throughout the revolutionary outbreaks he stayed on in Munich, although repeatedly his life was threatened. In 1925, after concluding a concordat with Bavaria, Archbishop Pacelli was sent to Berlin, where, as dean of the diplomatic corps, he was highly respected by statesmen and citizens alike. Recalled to Rome in 1929, he was created cardinal and succeeded Cardinal Gasparri as Secretary of State.

In spite of the ever-increasing diplomatic work of the secretariate and the modernization of Vatican City after the Lateran Treaty, Cardinal Pacelli, at the command of the Pope, saw more of the Church Universal than any Vatican prelate in history. His travels in England and Germany, made during the earlier years of his diplomatic career, were supplemented by extensive journeys in South America, whither he went as Legate to the Eucharistic Congress in Buenos Aires in 1934; in North America, where he traveled eight thousand miles by plane in 1936; in France for the dedication of the Cathedral of Lisieux in 1937; in Hungary in 1938 for the Eucharistic Congress at Budapest.

Having been appointed Camerlengo in 1935, Cardinal Pacelli presided during the interregnum after the death of Pius XI. He was elected pope on the first day of the conclave. Extraordinarily gifted in languages, as this book bears witness, the reigning Supreme Pontiff speaks fluently seven languages—Italian, French, German, Spanish, Portuguese, English and Latin and is thus enabled to speak to great numbers of his flock in their own tongues. Many of his addresses have been delivered over the radio and in this way a living contact, more intimate than ever before, has been established between the Holy Father and his children.

DOCUMENTS

RADIO BROADCAST *Dum Gravissimum* TO THE ENTIRE WORLD.[1]

At the beginning of his Pontificate Pius XII prays for peace, the fairest of all God's gifts.

March 3, 1939

1310. . . . . . . To this Our fatherly message We desire to add an invitation to, and indeed an augury of peace. We speak of that peace which Our Predecessor of beloved memory so earnestly besought from God, offering indeed his own life for the harmonious reconciliation of men; peace, the fairest of all God's gifts, that passes all understanding, the peace that all men of feeling cannot but strive for; the peace, in fine, which arises from justice and charity. This is the peace to which We exhort all, the peace which brings new warmth to those already joined in friendship with God, which moderates and tempers private interests with the sacred love of Jesus Christ, the peace which joins nations and peoples through mutual brotherly love, so that each race, by a feeling common to all, by friendly helping alliances, strives with God's inspiration and aid for the greater happiness of the whole human family.

1311. Moreover, in such anxious times as these, while so many difficulties, such grave difficulties seem to prevent that true peace which all so earnestly desire, and to keep it at a distance, We humbly pray to God for all who are placed in authority over States, upon whom falls the heavy burden and the high distinction of leading their peoples to prosperity and to civic progress. Such, Eminent Fathers, Venerable Brethren and most dear children, is the first desire with which God has inspired Our father's heart.

1312. The very serious ills that afflict men everywhere do not escape Our gaze, those ills which, though We be resourceless save in the aid of the Most High, in which indeed We place all Our trust, it is Our office to heal. Borrowing the words of St. Paul, We urge all, *Receive Us.*[2] We take courage in Our trust that you,

---

[1] Translation from *The Tablet*, v. 173, p. 309 (March 11, 1939). Original Latin, *A.A.S.*, v. 31, pp. 86-87 (March 3, 1939).
[2] II *Corinthians*, VII, 2.

Brethren and most dear children, will be the last to fall short in all that belongs to the work of furthering this desire of Our heart, the peaceful reconciliation of mankind. After the help of God it is in your prompt and eager good-will that Our confidence chiefly lies. . . . . . .

ALLOCUTION *Quae Venerandus* TO THE COLLEGE OF CARDINALS.[3]

It is the duty of the Holy See to serve truth and to promote peace.

March 12, 1939

1313. . . . . . . Turning Our eyes toward Him Who is the Father of light and the God of all consolation, and under the protection of the Virgin of Good Counsel who was the patron of the Conclave, We assume the government of the Bark of Peter to direct it amid so many waves and tempests toward the port of peace. Through the centuries the duty of the Sovereign Pontificate has had no other purpose than the service of truth; We speak of the truth which should be complete and undefiled, which no cloud veils, which is subject to no weakening, which is never separated from the charity of Jesus Christ. In fact, under every pontificate and especially under Ours, which is called to fulfill its mission in favor of the human community afflicted by so many discords and conflicts, these words of the Apostle, St. Paul, stand out as a sacred mandate: *Doing the truth in charity.*[4]

1314. We ask, then, Venerable Brothers and Dear Sons, your help and your zeal so that with this aid We may conform entirely to this special precept of the Apostle of the Gentiles, to the exercise of this immense responsibility solemnly inaugurated to-day, and to spread over the whole human race those celestial gifts which in a certain manner are contained in the responsibility of the pontificate. Recognizing fully the grandeur and the gravity of Our office and not ignoring the confidence and the hope placed in the Holy See not only by those who are intimately united with Us by faith and charity but also by numerous brothers separated from Us, and by almost the whole human family which sighs for the peace of

---

[3] Translation from *Pius XII and Peace*, pp. 2-3. Original Latin, *Discorsi e Radiomessaggi*, v. 1, pp. 9-10.

[4] *Ephesians*, IV, 15.

reconciliation; in this moment, when the majesty and the might of the tiara are placed on Our brow, We conjure you, Our Senate, and We exhort you, Our intimate counsellors, in the words of St. John Chrysostom: "You who know our labor, aid us by prayer, by solicitude, by zeal, by fellowship, so that we may be your glory and you may be ours."[5] . . .

EASTER HOMILY *Quoniam Paschalia Sollemnia* IN ST. PETER'S BASILICA.[6]

> *If charity be not joined with strict and rigid justice, in a kind of brotherly bond, then the world will not know the blessings of peace.*

April 9, 1939

1315. . . . We say to you that there is no more fitting way in which to introduce what We propose for your consideration than to repeat those most beautiful words which our Divine Master, raised up from the dead, spoke on this day to His disciples: *Peace be to you.*[7] Behold a greeting of peace, behold an omen of peace indeed! It was indeed as *the Prince of Peace*[8] that the Redeemer of mankind was foretold to the world that awaited His coming. It was with the angelic choirs singing, *Glory to God in the highest: and on earth peace to men of good-will*[9] that He was born into the world. Our Redeemer stood forth, the Herald and Ambassador of peace, and, in the words of St. Paul, *He preached the gospel of peace.*[10] Nor has this peace been made void by the disputes and the struggles. For Christ our Lord, when "death and life engaged in marvelous fight,"[11] fought unto death itself, bought this peace at the price, as it were, of His blood, won it as the pacifying fruit of the victory He gained, *by the blood of His cross, whether the things in earth, or the things that are in heaven.*[12]

---

[5] *Homilia XXIX in Epistolam ad Romanos*, n. 5, in Migne, *P.G.*, v. 60, c. 660.
[6] Translation from *The Tablet*, v. 173, pp. 483-484 (April 15, 1939). Original Latin, *A.A.S.*, v. 31, pp. 146-151 (April 24, 1939).
[7] *John* XX, 19.
[8] *Isaias*, IX, 6.
[9] *Luke*, II, 14.
[10] *Ephesians*, II, 17.
[11] The Paschal Sequence.
[12] *Colossians*, I, 20.

1316. With good reason, therefore, does the Apostle, St. Paul,
not only repeat, time and again, his invocation, abounding in comfort, *God of Peace, Lord of Peace*,[13] but, taking up yet once again,
as it were, the word of the prophets of old,[14] declares Jesus Christ
to be Himself our Peace.[15] Such are the thoughts which, at this
moment, We think it profitable for all to note and to reflect upon,
that their spirits may be raised up and refreshed—at this moment
when all mankind is so earnestly crying out for peace, is so desirous
of peace, so concerned to invoke peace. "For such is the great goodness of peace that . . . nothing is to man more welcome hearing,
of all desirable things there is none he more longs for. There is
nothing his invention can devise that can better it."[16]

1317. But to-day, more perhaps than at any other time, it is the
words of Jeremias that best describe the situation, who portrays for
us men crying, *Peace, peace: and there was no peace*.[17] On all sides,
indeed, wherever we turn our gaze, it is a sad spectacle that meets
us. For in every part of the world we can descry great numbers
of men greatly disturbed, anxious as to their fate, tormented with
fearful misgivings, that seem to hint at still more frightful things
about to come. A fearsome anxiety possesses the souls of men, as
though worse dangers yet were hanging over them in direful
menace. How far removed is this unhappy state of things from
that serene, secure "tranquillity of order"[18] which is bound up with
peace really worthy of its name!

1318. And yet, how can there be real and solid peace while even
men with a common nationality, heedless of their common stock
or their common fatherland, are torn apart and kept asunder by
intrigues and dissensions and the interests of factions? How can
there be peace, We repeat, while hundreds of thousands of men,
millions even, lack work? For work is not only, for every man, a
means of decent livelihood, but it is the means through which all
those manifold powers and faculties with which nature, training
and art have endowed the dignity of the human personality, find
their necessary expression, and this with a certain natural comeliness.

---

[13] *Romans*, XV, 33; XVI, 20; I *Corinthians*, XIV, 33; *Philippians*, IV, 9; I *Thessalonians*, V, 23; II *Thessalonians*, III, 16; *Hebrews*, XIII, 20.
[14] *Cf. Micheas*, V, 5.
[15] *Cf. Ephesians*, II, 14.
[16] St. Augustine, *De Civitate Dei*, XIX, 11.
[17] *Jeremias*, VI, 14; VIII, 11; *Ezechiel*, XIII, 10.
[18] St. Augustine, *De Civitate Dei*, XIX, 13.

Who is there, then, who cannot see how, in such crises of unemployment as those our own time experiences, huge multitudes are created, through this very lack of work, of men utterly wretched, whose unhappy condition is increased by the bitter contrast it presents with the pleasures and luxurious living of others altogether unconcerned about these armies of the needy? Who does not see how these poor men fall an easy prey to others whose minds are deceived by a specious semblance of truth, and who spread their corrupting teaching with ensnaring attractions?

1319. Moreover, how can there be peace, if there be lacking between the different States that common, equitable judgment of reason and consent of minds, which have been the power guiding the nations of the world along the shining road of civil progress? When, on the contrary, solemnly sanctioned treaties and pledged faith are stripped of that force and security which plighted faithfulness implies and by which it is strengthened, when this force and security are taken away, it becomes every day more difficult to lessen the increase of armaments and to pacify the minds of men, twin desires to-day of all men everywhere.

1320. We, therefore, exhort all, as this fearful storm approaches, to make their way back to the King of Peace, the Conqueror of Death, from Whom we have heard the comforting words, "Peace be to you." May He bountifully grant to us that peace He promised, His own peace, which the world cannot give, that peace which alone can calm and allay the fears and the confusion of men's minds. *My peace I give you; not as the world giveth do I give to you. Let not your heart be troubled, nor fear.*[19]

1321. Now with men it is so ordered that their outward tranquillity must be the reflection of something within. Whence the first care must be to bring about peace in men's souls. If peace be lacking to any man's soul, let him have a care, as soon as may be, to seek it. If he already possesses peace of soul, let him diligently foster it, guard it and keep it unharmed. For on this very day, when He first gave Himself, risen from the dead, to the sight of the Apostles, Christ our Lord, not without a most weighty deliberation, willed to add to His greeting of peace that most precious gift of peace, the Sacrament of Penance. He so willed it that on this solemn day of His Resurrection, there should arise that

[19] *John*, XIV, 27.

institution which restores and renews in souls the life which is divine, and which is the victory of life over death—that is, over sin. To this inexhaustible fount of pardon and of peace, our loving Mother, the Church, most earnestly, in this sacred paschal time, calls all her children. And if all and each of them would hearken to her voice, zealously, willingly, what a rich and flourishing life in Christ would be theirs! And, moreover, what serene enjoyment would be theirs, of that peace, through which, lovingly and perfectly obedient to the Divine Redeemer, they would be able to conquer the enticements of pleasurable desires. "Would your spirit see itself fitted to conquer your lusts?" we ask with St. Augustine. "Let it subject itself to the Higher Power and it shall triumph over the lower: and you shall be filled with peace, true, certain peace in most orderly guise. What is the scheme of this peace? God ruling the mind: the mind ruling the body: there is not any more perfect scheme of things."[20]

1322. You see, therefore, Venerable Brethren and most dear children, how peace, in the true sense, is built upon a single and most firm foundation. That is to say, it is built upon the Eternal God, to acknowledge Whom, to honor and to worship Whom, to obey Whose commandments, is a duty laid upon every living creature. To diminish the obedience due to the Divine Creator, to regulate it out of existence, is thus nothing else than to throw into confusion and to break up entirely the tranquillity of the individual citizen's life, of the life of the family, of the separate nations and, ultimately, of the whole human race. For it is God alone Who *will speak peace unto His people: and unto His saints: and unto them that are converted to the heart.*[21] At His bidding alone, Who is the Supreme Defender of Justice, the Supreme Dispenser of Peace, *have Peace and Justice kissed.*[22] And this is to be expected seeing that, as Isaias sings, *The work of justice shall be peace, and the service of justice quietness and security forevermore.*[23]

1323. This is but natural, for just as without order in human affairs there can be no peace, so, likewise, if justice be done away with, there can be no such thing as order. Now justice requires

[20] St. Augustine, *Sermones post Maurinos reperti*, in *Miscellanea Agostiniana*, v. 1, p. 633, n. 15-18.
[21] *Psalms*, LXXXIV, 9.
[22] *Psalms*, LXXXIV, 11.
[23] *Isaias*, XXXII, 17.

that to lawfully constituted authority there be given that respect and obedience which is its due; that the laws which are made shall be in wise conformity with the common good; and that, as a matter of conscience, all men shall render obedience to these laws. Justice requires that all men acknowledge and defend the sacrosanct rights of human freedom and human dignity, and that the infinite wealth and resources with which God has endowed the whole of the earth, shall be distributed, in conformity with right reason, for the use of all His children. Justice, finally, requires this, too: that the activities of the saving Catholic Church, the unerring mistress of the truth, the inexhaustible fountain of the life of the spirit, the special nurse of civil society, shall not suffer any disparagement, still less any prohibiting impediment. But if the noble reign of justice is usurped by the arms of violence, will anyone then marvel if the new age now dawning shows forth not the much-desired brightness of peace, but the dark and bloody furies of war? It is also part of the office of justice to determine and to maintain the norm of that order in human affairs which is the primary and the principal foundation of lasting peace. But justice only, and alone, cannot overcome the difficulties and obstacles which very frequently lie in the way of establishing a tranquillity that will endure. If charity be not joined with strict and rigid justice, in a kind of brotherly bond, the eye of the mind is very easily clouded and thereby hindered, so that it does not discern the rights of another; the ears become deaf, so that they do not hear the voice of that equity which has the power, by explanation to the wise man willing to listen, to make clear in reasonable and orderly fashion whatever may be matter of dispute, even the bitterest and the rudest of differences.

1324. We must, of course, be understood, when We speak here of charity, to mean that effective and generous charity which led the Divine Redeemer to die for each of us: *Who loves me and delivered Himself for me;*[24] that charity which *urgeth us*[25] and which brings it about that, *they also who live, may not now live to themselves, but to Him Who died for them and rose again;*[26] that charity, in fine, moved by which Christ Our Lord took *the form of a servant,*[27] that we all might be made brethren in Him Who

[24] *Galatians,* II, 20.
[25] II *Corinthians,* V, 14.
[26] II *Corinthians,* V, 15.
[27] *Philippians,* II, 7.

is *the first-born*,[28] children of that same God, heirs of that same Kingdom, called to the joys of that same eternal happiness. If the minds of mortal men would somewhat drink in the kindliness of this love, and in it repose themselves, then, beyond all doubting, the light of peace would begin to shine upon the laboring human race. Then, to provocative anger would succeed the tranquillity of a reasoning mind; to exaggerated and unbridled demands, the benevolent co-operation of helping effort, so that trustful repose and serenity would take the place of all that dreadful unrest of mind.

1325. Let men seek once more that road by which they may journey back to friendly alliances in which the convenience and the profit of each are carefully considered in a just and kindly system; in which individual sacrifices for the higher good of the human family are not shirked; in which, finally, faith publicly given shall flourish as an example to all men of good-will. To the end that these effects may follow, and that these Our most cherished desires may be brought to a happy fulfillment, We cannot refrain from repeating to all the peoples of the world and to their rulers, that fervent invitation, exhortation even, to a peace bred of justice and charity, which We addressed to them in the very moment almost of Our elevation to the Supreme Pontificate. . . . . . .

ADDRESS *C'Est avec un Vif Sentiment* TO THE INTERNATIONAL UNION OF CATHOLIC WOMEN'S LEAGUES.[29]

The cause of the world unrest is materialistic egoism amongst individuals and peoples.

April 14, 1939

1326. . . . . . . Our human society threatens soon to be no longer one, to such an extent are its constituent elements disintegrating under our very eyes under the influence of materialistic egoism—or are aligning themselves against each other. Whatever remains of true social life tends to be governed only by the play of individual interests and the competition of collective desires. It is true that efforts are not wanting to restore some unity in this

[28] *Romans*, VIII, 29.
[29] Original French, *Discorsi e Radiomessaggi*, v. 1, pp. 46-47.

disintegration of human personalities. But the plans proposed will always be basically at fault if they stem from the same principle as the evil they are meant to remedy. The wound will not be healed nor will the deep rent in our individualistic and materialistic humanity be mended by any system whatever that itself remains materialistic in its principles and mechanistic in its application.

1327. There is only one efficacious balm with which to dress this wound: the return of the human mind and heart to the knowledge and love of God, the Common Father, and of Him Whom He has sent to save the world, Jesus Christ. . . . . . Then only will be realized that unity in order, *"Unitas ordinis,"* of which St. Thomas speaks, and which must be the ideal of your souls, the supreme goal of your efforts. But then, too, by working for the universal good, each of you will work for the good of your country and for the welfare of your family, precisely because order is one: it can reign in souls, in nations, in the whole of humanity, only if everything is in its proper place; and, therefore, only if God everywhere occupies the only place which is proper to Him: the first. And thus finally, in the stability of order, there will descend upon the earth that peace, which is so much sought after in the agonized desires of the people and, saddest above all, in the hopeless sobbing of mothers.

1328. There is your mission; it requires spirit and perseverance; it will often necessitate heroism. But victory is assured, because mind always ends by conquering over matter, and right by triumphing over the ruins accumulated by violence. History demonstrates this and God has promised it to us; the measure of our victory is that of our faith. *Haec est victoria, quae vincit mundum, fides nostra — This is the victory that overcometh the world, our faith.*[30] . . . . .

---

[30] I *John*, V, 4.

RADIO ADDRESS *Con Inmenso Gozo* TO THE CATHOLICS OF SPAIN.[31]

The Holy Father rejoices because peace has returned to Spain.

April 16, 1939

1329. With immense joy We approach you, most beloved sons of Catholic Spain, to express Our fatherly congratulations for the gift of peace and victory with which God has deigned to crown the Christian heroism of your faith and charity, proved through such great and generous sufferings. With mingled anxiety and confidence Our Predecessor of blessed memory looked to this providential peace, the fruit, no doubt, of that blessing which, from the first days of the conflict he gave to those who had taken on themselves "the difficult and dangerous task of defending and restoring the rights and the honor of God and religion,"[32] and We do not doubt that the peace will be such as he hoped for, "the harbinger of a future of tranquillity in order and honor in prosperity."[33]

1330. The designs of Providence, most beloved children, have been manifested once again over heroic Spain. The nation chosen by God as the principal instrument for the evangelization of the New World, and as the impregnable bulwark of the Catholic Faith, has given the loftiest proof to the champions of the materialistic atheism of our age, that above everything stand the eternal values of religion and the spirit. The tenacious propaganda and abundant strength of the enemies of Jesus Christ suggest that they wanted to give in Spain a supreme proof of the disintegrating power at their command, spread throughout the world, and, thanks to God, they have not been allowed to succeed; but they were, nevertheless, permitted to realize a measure of their terrible consequences, so that the whole world could see how religious persecution, threatening the fixed bases of justice and charity, which are the love of God and respect for His holy law, can drag a modern society to unsuspected depths of passionate discord and evil destruction. Persuaded of this truth, the healthy people of Spain, with that generosity and

---

[31] Translation from *The Tablet*, v. 173, p. 514 (April 22, 1939). Original Spanish, *A.A.S.*, v. 31, pp. 151-154 (April 24, 1939).
[32] Allocution of Pius XI to the Spanish refugees, *A.A.S.*, v. 28, p. 380.
[33] *Ibidem*, p. 381.

openness which are two characteristics of its most noble spirit, rose at once in defense of the ideals of the Faith and Christian civilization, deeply implanted in the fertile soil of Spain, and helped by God, Who does not abandon those who trust in Him, knew how to resist the attack of those who, inflamed by what they thought a humanitarian ideal for the elevation of the lowly, were in reality fighting on behalf of atheism. This, the chief meaning of your victory, encourages Us to indulge the greatest hopes that in His mercy God will deign to lead Spain along the secure road of her traditional and Catholic greatness, which ought to be for all Spaniards who are lovers of their religion and their country, the starting point for the vigorous effort to reorganize the life of the nation in perfect conformity with its most noble history of faith, piety and Catholic civilization.

1331. We especially exhort the rulers and pastors of Catholic Spain to illumine the minds of those led astray, showing to them, in all love, the roots of materialism and laicism from which their errors and wrongdoing sprung, and whence they might again spring up, putting before them the principles of individual and social justice contained in the Holy Gospel and in the doctrine of the Church, without which the peace and prosperity of nations, however powerful, cannot endure. We do not doubt that this will be done, and that for this, Our firm hope, there stand as warranty the most noble Christian sentiments of which the head of the State and his many loyal collaborators have given proof, together with the legal protection granted to the supreme interests of religion and society in conformity with the doctrines of the Holy See. . . . . . . And now, beloved children, that the rainbow of peace has reappeared shining in the Spanish sky, let us all heartily unite in a fervent hymn of thanksgiving to the God of peace and in a prayer of pardon and mercy for all those who have died; and in order that this peace may be fruitful and lasting, We exhort you with all the fervor of Our heart *to   preserve the unity of the Spirit in the bond of peace*.[34] . . . . . .

---

[34] *Ephesians*, IV, 3.

LETTER *Quandoquidem in Gubernanda* TO CARDINAL MAGLIONE, SECRETARY OF STATE.[35]

Pius XII invites the faithful to join a crusade of prayer for peace during the month of May.

April 20, 1939

1332. You who so closely assist Us in the government of the Catholic Church know very well how ardently We desire and invoke God that ultimately minds may change to sentiments of justice and charity so that the so greatly longed-for Christian peace among all nations and peoples, now so agitated and preoccupied, may be consolidated profoundly and permanently. When We were elevated to the Supreme Pontificate it was precisely concerning this peace—the sublime gift of God—that We, with the heart of a father, exhorted not only Our individual sons in Christ scattered everywhere throughout the world, but all nations and their governments.

1333. And on the solemn day of Easter in the Basilica of St. Peter, where among a numberless multitude of people We offered pontifically the Divine Sacrifice, We repeated the same invitation and same exhortation, begging concord and tranquillity for all of Jesus Christ, Conqueror of Death and Giver of Celestial Peace. Now, then, as the month of May approaches, when the faithful are accustomed to raise special prayers to the Holy Virgin, it is close to Our heart to express the very earnest desire that in this very period public prayers in the cause herein indicated be offered in various dioceses and parishes.

1334. But in this crusade of prayer We like to incite especially those whom We, following the example of the Divine Redeemer of Whom We are Vicar on earth, love with especially tender affection: We mean children who in the first flower of life radiate innocence, gentleness and grace. May fathers and mothers, with pious custom, accompany their children, even to the littlest ones, every day to the Altar of the Virgin, presenting them to her along with flowers from their gardens and fields and together with their prayers and those of their children. And how could the Heavenly Mother fail to heed so many supplicant voices, imploring peace for citizens, for peoples, for nations? How could she fail to heed them if with the prayers of the angels of heaven there should be inter-

[35] Translation from *Pius XII and Peace*, pp. 8-9. Original Latin, *A.A.S.*, v. 31, pp. 154-156 (April 24, 1939).

twined those of children whom one may call angels of this earth? Certainly the Virgin Mother of God, invoked by such prayers, will offer her aid and her intercession in this moment of universal trepidation and by inviting the favor of her Divine Son, offended by so many sins, will obtain from Him liberation from present anxieties, the peace of hearts and fraternal concord among peoples.

1335. And will the same blessed Jesus Who, during His mortal life, loved the age of innocence with particular affection and Who, with the words, *Suffer the little children to come unto Me and forbid them not, for of such is the Kingdom of God,*[36] rebuked the Apostles because they desired to remove children from His embrace; will the same blessed Jesus, We say, hear any other prayers more readily than those of children who raise to Him and to His Celestial Mother their white supplicant hands? . . . Since, therefore, everywhere, in cities, in towns and even in the most remote villages illuminated by the light of the Gospel, children will troop to the churches during the coming month of May to offer up their supplications, it may be hoped that once mutual rancors are appeased, minds pacified and dissension among peoples controlled, better times may arrive for humanity under the auspices of the Virgin. . . .

DISCOURSE *Wir Begrüssen* TO A GROUP OF GERMAN PILGRIMS.[37]

Pius XII exhorts the German Catholics to remain firm in their Faith and to pray for peace.

April 23, 1939 .

1336. . . . . . . Remain true to the Catholic Faith and do everything in your power to preserve it for your children. Profess this holy Faith with so pure an intention and in so lofty a manner that it will be clear to everyone that Catholics are contending only for the rights of God and of the Church of Jesus Christ. Let no one say that We do not long for a happy, prosperous Germany. It is precisely because We desire this that We insist on religious values. Only upon these can be built lasting greatness, prosperity and happiness. Let us pray ardently—especially now in the month of May— to the Mother of God for peace, for the Catholic Church in Germany, and for the German youth. . . .

[36] *Mark,* X, 14.
[37] Original German, *Discorsi e Radiomessaggi,* v. I, p. 65.

RESPONSE *Las Palabras Pronunciadas* TO THE HOMAGE OF THE NEW AMBASSADOR OF ARGENTINA, ENRICO GUIÑAZÚ.[38]

International relations must be founded on justice and charity.

May 4, 1939

1337. . . . . . . When the Church and the State inform their mutual relations with the spirit that is manifested in your words, Mr. Ambassador, there is created between both powers an atmosphere of reciprocal cordiality and loyal support. This atmosphere is in accordance with the intimate aspirations of the most faithful Argentine people and from which the same people have received so many benefits in the past. It also constitutes a most secure foundation for their further development in the ways of prosperity and peace.

1338. In the midst of the grave problems which in the present hour agitate and weigh heavily on the peoples, the noble adherence of Your Excellency to the idea of an international understanding which seeks a solution of the fortuitously existing differences between the principles of justice and the spirit of fraternity, constitutes an omen whose symbolic importance, especially at the present time, We come to appreciate adequately. . . . Therefore, with all Our heart We pray to the Lord that the spirit of conscientious and generous understanding may find each day more numerous and more devoted defenders and collaborators among the nations and peoples, and that it may also make easier the way for the readjustment and perfecting of the internal peace founded in justice and fraternal charity. . . . . . .

RADIO ADDRESS *Pour la Douzième Fois* TO THE FRENCH NATIONAL EUCHARISTIC CONGRESS IN ALGIERS.[39]

Christ is the Author of the peace which society needs.

May 7, 1939

1339. . . . . . . We are, in fact, really present in two ways: visibly in the person whom We have chosen as Our Legate, so that

[38] Original Spanish, *Discorsi e Radiomessaggi,* v. 1, pp. 95-96.
[39] Translation from *Pius XII and Peace,* p. 10. Original French, *A.A.S.,* v. 31, p. 222 (June 9, 1939).

he should preside over the Eucharistic days in Our name, that is to say, Our Beloved Son, the Cardinal Archbishop of Paris; invisibly, but really, with Our prayers joined to those of your holy and enthusiastic throng. Neither the waves of the sea nor the roar, as it were of armaments, of surf raging on the shore could withstand your mystic impetus. Notre Dame de la Garde [the great sentinel statue of Our Lady, overlooking the harbor of Marseilles] has sent you to the Madonna of Africa, and in this Holy Host there irradiates from both these hills the faith shown to you by the Prince of Peace—Who is also Author of that peace which is to-day so ardently supplicated by a human society now so troubled.

1340. This is what has brought you here and encouraged you. This is what unites Us intimately to you in this month of May, which We wish to be entirely dedicated to prayer (and particularly the prayer of children, who are the beloved of the Saviour) to draw down from heaven upon the earth, through the hands of the Immaculate Virgin, that peace promised to men of good-will; peace to souls troubled by the call and seduction of false doctrines; peace between nations trembling in constant anxiety. . . . . . .

ADDRESS *Magnam Tibi Gratiam Habemus* ON THE OCCASION
. OF THE POPE'S VISIT TO THE LATERAN BASILICA.[40]

*Abiding by the wishes of his Predecessor, Pius XII
prays for peace in the Lateran Basilica.*

May 18, 1939

1341. . . . . . . Lovingly recalling the memory of Pius XI, Our glorious Predecessor, who, under happy auspices, after the signing of the Lateran Treaty, entered this Basilica, and gladly abiding by his wishes, We pray for peace for all men, and ardently desire peace for this house of God. "Everlasting peace to this house from the Eternal One. May Eternal Peace, the Word of the Father, be peace to this house. May the loving Consoler grant peace to this house."[41] May the peace of the Gospel, the grace of the Holy Spirit, the peace of unshaken hope, pure love, boundless mercy, ever be with you in

[40] Original Latin, *Discorsi e Radiomessaggi*, v. 1, p. 136.
[41] *Pontificale Romanum*, Dedication of a Church.

rich measure who stand around Us, and as a pledge of this We
bless you with all Our heart.

ALLOCUTION *In Questo Giorno* TO THE COLLEGE OF CARDINALS
ON THE POPE'S NAME-DAY, THE FEAST OF ST. EUGENE.[42]

> *The Church offers her services to stay the imminent
> irruption of force.*

June 2, 1939

1342. . . . . . . At this very moment in so many places the
world is seething with activities, with the birth and culmination of
happenings, whereof not even the most far-sighted human wisdom
could say whether the final result of their course will end in construction or in ruin. The Church is not the child of this world.
But she is in the world, she exists in its midst, and from it she
receives her children. She has her part in the alternations of joy
and of sorrow. And it is in the midst of the world that she suffers,
strives, prays. As in her primal times, she prays with the great
Apostle, Paul, making *supplications, prayers, and thanksgivings for
all men: for kings, and for all that are in high station: that we
may lead a quiet and a peaceable life in all piety and chastity. For
this is good and acceptable in the sight of God, our Saviour, Who
will have all men to be saved, and to come to the knowledge of
the truth.*[43] And what is that if it is not a prayer for peace between
nations, which since the dawn of Christianity the Church has sent
up before that God Who would have all men to be saved, and to
come to the knowledge of the truth?

1343. But throughout the course of history, facing those things
that fall across that course, the forward march of the Church has
become more difficult and arduous than in times past. She finds
herself engulfed in a world of oppositions and contrary purposes,
of conflicting feelings and interests, of immoderate ideas and un-
curbed ambitions, of fear and of insolence. She is surrounded by
humanity that seems neither to know how to decide which side
to take: whether to admit the decision of the sword or the noble
sovereignty of right as the first principle of action and supreme

---

[42] Translation from *The Catholic Mind*, v. 37, pp. 790-794 (August 22, 1939). Original
Italian, *Discorsi e Radiomessaggi*, v. 1, pp. 152-155.
[43] I *Timothy*, II, 1-4.

arbiter of their proper destinies; whether to confide in the empire of reason or trust to that of force. Hence, the Spouse of Christ encounters obstacles in her efforts to secure for her principles and admonitions, which are dictated by her religious mission and in their development tend to the welfare of each nation and of the whole human community, that welcome which she expects, that readiness in acceptance, without which her word is no more than a voice crying in the wilderness.

1344. But for all that, the bounden duty of Our Apostolic Ministry cannot permit these external obstacles, whether fear of being misinterpreted or of Our intentions and aims being misunderstood even when their object is good, to hinder Us in the salutary work of pacification which is proper to the Church. The Church does not permit herself to be turned aside or restrained by any private interests. Unless invited thereunto, she dreams not of busying herself in the territorial disputes of States, nor of allowing herself to be entangled in the complexity of conflicts which easily spring therefrom. For all that, she may not, in these hours when peace suffers the greatest dangers and the most violent of passions enter into discussions, forbear to speak maternally and, should conditions permit, offer maternally her services to stay the imminent irruption of force, with its incalculable material, spiritual and moral consequences.

1345. In this spirit of justice and peace which, as the Father of all, We feel in the depth of Our heart, We considered it to be opportune, after mature deliberation at a time particularly grave in the life of the peoples, at the beginning of last May, to make known to certain statesmen of the great European nations the anxieties that preoccupied Us regarding the situation, and Our fear lest international dissensions should become exasperated, and we should drift into conflict and bloodshed. That step—We can refer to it thankfully—has in the main met with the sympathy of the Governments, and being made public (without which We could have done nothing) called forth the gratitude of the nations. We received assurances of good-will and a desire to preserve peace as the peoples hoped.

1346. Who could be more satisfied than We in perceiving the beginning of a relaxation of tension in souls? Who could want and hope for with more zeal, the strengthening of every good point

gained? Nor do We pretend to conceal the fact that other information was brought Us regarding the intentions and sentiments of
influential statesmen. We are very grateful to them, for in a distinct
measure they have raised Our hopes; the consideration of noble
humanity, the consciousness of the unavoidable responsibility they
have incurred before God and before history, as well as a proper
idea of the true interests of their peoples, have sufficient force and
weight to induce the governments to safeguard both a stable peace
and the liberty and honor of the nations, to overcome the material
and moral obstacles which prevent a firm and sincere understanding. That itself has opened the way for new offers and appeals
on Our part.

1347. But the destiny and welfare of the peoples are in the
hands of "the Emperor Who reigns in Heaven,"[44] of the Father of
Light, the Source of every perfect good that is in the world. With
the destinies and happiness of the peoples He holds also in His
Hands the hearts of men. And as He wills, so does He incline
them, enlarge them, restrain, check or direct their wills without
changing the nature of them. In man's work everything is weak,
as is man himself. His thoughts are timid, his foresight uncertain, his limbs stiff, and his steps feeble: he marches toward an
end that is forever obscure. But in the handiwork of God all is
powerful, like unto Himself. His designs have no uncertainty; His
dominion extends throughout the governing of the world. His
delight is with the children of men, but nothing may withstand
Him. In His Hands the very obstacles themselves are become the
means whereby ends are shaped, and human spirit and free will
are directed toward the sublimities of His mercy and justice—twin
stars of His universal sway. In Him rests our strongest hope.

1348. In order to implore the divine illumination and blessing
on the actions of to-day as well as the decisions to which they lead,
last May We had already called the Catholic world around the altar
of Mary, to a crusade of prayer, and placed the white legions of the
children in the vanguard—children, the flowering lilies at the feet
of the Most Blessed Virgin, protected by the Holy Angels, called
by Jesus to Himself, by Him embraced, blessed and proffered as a
pattern to every heir to the Kingdom of Heaven. Innocence praying
and supplicating is a manifestation and an example. And on this

[44] Dante, *Inferno,* canto I, 124.

occasion We are gladdened in testifying to the gracious joy that is disclosed in Our heart at the recollection of that praiseworthy and pious striving, that burning fervor, that holy and heartfelt emulation which has sprung forth among the faithful of the whole world in response to that appeal.

1349. And now, entering upon the delightful month of June, dedicated to the Sacred Heart of Jesus, We direct Ourself with increased ardor, with a greater and more insistent hope toward Him Who is the King and focal point of all hearts, *Rex et centrum omnium cordium;* the Refuge and Sustainer of all the agonizing and fearful. May He, to Whom is given all power in heaven and on earth, vouchsafe to allay the surge of a troubled and stricken world, and bring to pass among men and nations the breathing of a new spirit. May Our appeals for peace, through Him, find echo in the hearts of both rulers and peoples. And in the actions and decisions of those that are responsible may there be those practical realizations, for which the yearnings and prayers of all men of good-will are breathed forth. . . .

RESPONSE *Las Palabras Pronunciadas por Vuestra Excelencia* TO THE HOMAGE OF THE NEW AMBASSADOR OF BOLIVIA, GABRIELE GOSÁLVEZ.[45]

Christians make sacrifices willingly for the common good.

June 16, 1939

1350. . . . . . . The present hour, with its entangled multitude of new and serious obligations, imposes on the energy, courage and decisions of those to whom the destinies of people are entrusted, tasks almost unknown in more normal times. Those people who do not wish to see themselves condemned to remain behind in the material and cultural field cannot refrain from the necessity of seeking and finding a reply to and a solution of the urgent problems of the new times, with their economic, political and social repercussions. For the realization of these ends, the power of the State often is obliged to ask all classes of people to make heavy sacrifices for the common good.

[45] Translation from the *N.C.W.C. News Service,* June 19, 1939. Original Spanish, *Discorsi e Radiomessaggi,* v. 1, pp. 189-190.

1351. However, where the doctrine of Christ informs intelligences and hearts and directs men's activities, the concept of sacrifice, the subordination of one's own interests to the necessities and obligations of the community, form a part of those laws and fundamental rules from which no Christian conscience can withdraw—as long as the public authorities themselves respect the sacred and inviolable limits of divine law. And happy are the people whose rulers are penetrated with the benefit which comes from religion through her efforts for prosperity and pacific projects, and who, in recognition of this fact, endeavor to open the way for the activities of the Church of Christ, to establish and implant Christian sentiment in public and private life.

1352. Therefore, the lofty words of Your Excellency have given Us very great satisfaction upon learning how profound is the consciousness in the Government and in the Bolivian people of the indispensable and irreplaceable function of education in the Church and what a deep impression the solicitude and vigilance of the Common Father in favor of peace has created in your country. May Our Lord increase in all the people and in all statesmen sentiments of sincere and efficacious love of peace, which may inspire in them wise and salutary resolutions. . . .

RESPONSE *En Este Momento* TO THE HOMAGE OF THE NEW AMBASSADOR OF URUGUAY, GIOACCHINO SECCO ILLA.[46]

Desires for peace will find their triumph in the doctrine of Christ.

June 20, 1939

1353. . . . . . . In a time when the life and peace of nations are beset with so many responsibilities and formidable problems, Your Excellency must be assured that the fulfillment of the noble aims of your mission will find in Us a full and hearty approval. Confidently We invoke the protection of the Almighty upon the Uruguayan people, so beloved by Us, upon the head of the State, his Government, and, above all, upon Your Excellency, while We make fervent wishes that the unity of spiritual powers that flows from the doctrine and law of Christ may bring triumph to the holy

[46] Original Spanish, *Discorsi e Radiomessaggi,* v. 1, p. 200.

desires for peace, which in this hour constitute the fervent wish of all the world.

ADDRESS *Sempre Gradite* TO A LARGE AUDIENCE, INCLUDING A GROUP OF FRANCISCAN PARISH PRIESTS.[47]

For the peace of the world, nothing is more urgent and imperative than prayer.

July 5, 1939

1354. . . . . . . In this same audience We are given the opportunity of addressing a special invitation to the numerous Franciscan parish priests of Italy who are with Us today to carry this message with them and to intensify devotion and prayer among Christian people. Since they, the Franciscans, are direct heirs of the spirit of peace of the beatific Poverello, their spiritual activity among the souls entrusted to their care should be particularly full of such spirit; and prayer, of which they are the accredited ministers because of the end of their pastoral office, should all the more fervently be employed by them in serving the cause of peace, inasmuch as nothing at this moment is more urgent and nothing is more imperative upon the charity of all the sons of the Church. Under the sign of peace, let them take back to their parishes the blessing that We here give with all Our heart to each shepherd and his fold, and, interpreting both your deep feeling and Our own, may they employ their endeavors in such a way that a similar prayer full of hope and perseverance may arise from all classes of mankind. . . . . . .

LETTER OF CARDINAL MAGLIONE, SECRETARY OF STATE, TO LA SEMAINE SOCIALE DE FRANCE MEETING IN BORDEAUX.[48]

The Vatican discusses the problem of the social classes.

July 11, 1939

1355. It is with interest altogether paternal that His Holiness turns his attention to the program of the Semaine Sociale of Bordeaux: *The problem of the classes in the national community and*

[47] Original Italian, *Discorsi e Radiomessaggi*, v. 1, p. 238.
[48] Original French, *Documentation Catholique*, v. 40, cc. 982-984 (August 5, 1939).

in the human order. Such a subject is very opportune. It is clear that in our times there is such confusion of minds and of morals that everything that can help to give society a more wholesome and reasonable frame of mind ought to be retained as an essential factor of peace, as the pontifical teachings have very pertinently indicated. Now, from this point of view no one will gainsay that the problem of the classes appears as one of the most important.

1356. As a matter of fact, that society is made up of diverse classes is something which no impartial observer would deny, no more than he would deny the diversity of the members of a single body. However, these social classes have certain constituent elements which must be clearly distinguished. They are not, in point of fact, a kind of voluntary association; they are not an hermetically sealed caste, a clan, a party, in which prejudices of birth, or of custom or of politics, play a predominant role; neither are they, properly speaking, an order, a state, a profession, implying a well-defined juridical organization.

1357. Class is something more natural, more extensive and more profound: it results from a similarity of conditions of life and of labor, from a community of moral and material interests which are the cause that men and families spontaneously group together and seek solidarity, because they are subject to the identical necessities of existence, share in the same culture, the same needs, the same aspirations: which process, by the way, verifies a fundamental law of nature that can be discovered in all the degrees of creation. Thus we have the working class, the employer class, the middle classes, to cite only these few.

1358. The variety of classes composing the social body has been the object of deep study, especially during the course of the last century, at a time when the doctrines of Liberalism and the development of "machinism" were bound to give a very characteristic impress to the world of labor, but an impress so little human, so little Christian. Historians and economists, often of materialist inspiration, have analyzed the fact of the social classes, its contents and results. However, their works, devoid of any spirituality, necessarily ended in dangerous conclusions. The Marxist school in particular, having no other aim than the overturning of the existing order by means of revolution, and considering, in the variety of the members of the social body, nothing but their oppositions and antagonisms, set up as a dogma the warfare of the classes. The great Encyclical of Pius XI on *Atheistic Communism* informs us only too well of the deadly fruits which result from such experiments!

1359. On the contrary, the very title itself of the approaching Semaine Sociale of Bordeaux makes sufficiently clear how and where the problem of the classes must be placed. They have meaning and life only as a function of the national community and of human order. For, as a matter of fact, if the classes appear to us to be different, it is that they may find themselves in the position of the members in relation to the body, or of parts in relation to the whole. Since order results, as St. Thomas and the Encyclical *Divini Redemptoris* explain, from the unity of diverse objects harmoniously disposed, the social body will be truly ordered only if a true unity solidly binds all of its constituent members together. And let it be well noted that on this unity depends their welfare, for, as the Angelic Doctor has said, "as the part and the whole are in a certain manner one and the same thing, so what belongs to the whole belongs in a certain way to each part."

1360. In other words, the health of the body is nothing else than the health of the members which compose it. This rule is essentially verified in what concerns the classes in relation to the body of the nation. Each of them has, undoubtedly, its particular law, its character, its proper functions, its specific aspirations, which are natural to it, and, therefore, are instilled by the Creator. There can be no question for Catholic sociology of mistaking them, and even less of being in opposition to them or of suppressing them, but rather it has the duty to preserve and guide them along the way of fruitful and intelligent collaborations, avoiding thus the deviations ever-possible, and alas! even frequent, in the state of humanity wounded by original sin. Thus it is by integrating the classes, with all the respect that they deserve, into the general plan of society, that the greatest material and spiritual progress will be realized for the one and the other.

1361. And not only are the classes constituted for the purpose of collaborating among themselves within the limits of the national community, but they go even further, as the second part of your program justly states, in order to take in the whole of the human order. In fact, as history teaches us, the very instinct of the classes could not but early make them leap the bounds of particular countries to join and unite on the plane of the human community. And are not the national communities the members of this human community just as families are the constituent elements of the nation? Thus, the classes as essential parts of the national community must, in the last analysis, take the human order as their starting point, and they must bring about a collaboration on a world-wide scale. At a time when countries have a tendency to withdraw within themselves, to the very great misfortune of all of them, it is fitting to emphasize the advantages of a universal solidarity of the classes whose movements, if wisely ordered—far from stopping at the political boundaries of a State—will want, by their very vocation, to extend to the entire human family.

1362. In this matter, we likewise receive a supreme and decisive lesson from the Holy Scriptures themselves, where one sees this social economy elevated to the supernatural order, the sublime model from which the other institutions, for their happiness and their welfare, must draw their inspiration. Since the grace of the Incarnation and of the Redemption has formed the Mystical Body of Christ and since the Eucharist, made from the multiplicity of grains of wheat, has achieved in the Transubstantiated Bread the mystery of a transcendant unity, one can truly say with St. Paul: *For we, being many, are one bread, one body, all that partake of one Bread.*[49] Far from seeing their legitimate particularities destroyed, the classes find themselves reunited by the bonds of divine charity. It is in his First Epistle to the Corinthians that the Apostle gives a detailed exposition of this ravishing doctrine: You are the Body of Christ and His members in particular. . . . For, while you are many, you are only one body. . . . And, by grace, let the members be filled with solicitude for one another.[50] Thus, is it not true that this is the sovereign model of the collaboration of the classes in the national community as well as in the human order? . . . . . .

1363. This is the ardent appeal which His Holiness addresses to you, echoing the last words of the Saviour, Whose August Vicar he is here below: *That they all may be one, as Thou, Father, in Me, and I in Thee; that they also may be one in Us . . . that they may be one, as We also are one.*[51] It is, therefore, in this spirit that the

[49] I *Corinthians*, X, 17.
[50] *Cf.* I *Corinthians*, XII, 27, 12, 25.
[51] *John*, XVII, 21-22.

Semaine Sociale will approach the difficult problem of class collaboration and it will contribute effectively toward the mutual harmony between the classes and toward their mutual understanding in justice and charity. . . . . . .

ADDRESS *L'Augurio* TO A GROUP OF THREE HUNDRED NEWLY-WEDS.[52]

Peace is the source of true happiness for the Christian family.

July 19, 1939

1364. The wish usually addressed to newly-weds is always and everywhere for happiness. It seeks to be the full and complete expression of the sentiments and desires of the fathers and mothers, of relatives, of friends and of all those who share their joy. Such is also the prayer with which the Church finishes the Mass for Bride and Bridegroom: "Almighty God, keep in abiding peace those whom Thou has joined together in lawful bond." And that is likewise the paternal good wish that We are accustomed to offer to the newly-weds who come to Rome to ask the Apostolic Benediction: a Benediction which is a pledge of heavenly favors, a true pledge of peace and happiness for you, most dear sons. In addressing it to you to-day, We desire to call your attention to the high meaning of this profoundly Christian wish, precious heritage that the Divine Master has left us: *Pax vobis.*[53]

1365. Peace, source of true happiness, can come only from God, can be found only in God: "Oh! Thou hast made us for Thyself, and our heart is restless until it rests in Thee." [54] That is why absolute peace, complete and perfect happiness exists only in heaven, in the Beatific Vision. But, even in earthly life, the fundamental condition of true peace and sane joy is in a loving and filial dependence upon the Will of God. Everything which weakens, everything which breaks or stops this conformity and union of wills is opposed to peace: sin above all. Sin is rupture and disunion, dis-

---

[52] Translation from *Pius XII and Peace*, pp. 12-14. Original Italian, *Discorsi e Radiomessaggi*, v. 1, pp. 259-261.
[53] *Luke*, XXIV, 36.
[54] St. Augustine, *Confessiones*, bk. 1, c. 1.

order and trouble, remorse and fear, and those who resist the Will of God have not, cannot have peace. *Who hath resisted Him and hath had peace?* [55] Then peace is the happy lot of those who observe the law of God. *Much peace have they that love Thy law.*[56]

1366. On this solidly established foundation, Christian spouses, Christian parents find the generative principle of happiness and the support of peace in the family. The Christian family, in fact, enemy of egoism and of the pursuit of personal satisfactions, is entirely impregnated with love and charity; and when the passing charms of the senses are dissipated, when the flowers of youthful beauty fall, one after another, when the illusory phantoms of the imagination have vanished, the bond of the hearts remains unbreakable between husband and wife, between children and their parents, and equally immovable, love, the great principle of domestic life, and with it happiness and peace.

1367. On the contrary, he who considers the sacred rite of Christian marriage as a simple, external ceremony, necessary by custom, he who presents himself thereto with a soul deprived of God's grace, he profanes the Sacrament of Christ, corrupts the source of supernatural graces which in the admirable designs of Providence are destined to fructify the garden of the family, and to make grow there the flowers of the virtues and the fruits of true peace and pure joy. Families which are born in sin, during the first storm will strike upon the rocks or, like ships abandoned to the mercy of the waves, they will wander off their course with doctrines, which, while proclaiming liberty or license, prepare the way for the most cruel bondage. Those who profane the family will not have peace; only the Christian family respectful of the law of the Creator and of the Redeemer, aided by grace, has the guarantee of peace. Such is the fervent and sincere wish which goes out for you from Our paternal heart: peace with God, in conformity to His will, peace with men in love of the truth, peace with yourselves in victory over passions: threefold peace which constitutes the only true happiness which is possible here below. May the paternal Benediction which We bestow upon you from the depths of Our heart be an augury of this peace. . . . . . .

[55] *Job*, IX, 4.
[56] *Psalms*, CXVIII, 165.

RESPONSE *Les Paroles Prononcées* TO THE HOMAGE OF THE NEW
AMBASSADOR OF POLAND, CASIMIR PAPÉE.[57]

*The Church is opposed to materialism which teaches
the supremacy of might over right.*

July 24, 1939

1368. That Our message to the world in favor of a true and
substantial peace, based on justice, honor and the liberty of the
nations, has corresponded to the intimate convictions and the ardent
desires of the Polish people and has been perfectly understood by
them—such a testimony gathered from the lips of one who speaks
with such authority is very precious to Us and constitutes so important an adherence to the great idea of peace among the nations,
that We do not hesitate to express here Our grateful acknowledgment.

1369. The allusion made on this occasion by Your Excellency to
the preponderant and decisive role which religion and morality
play in the great problems at this time of such concern to the life
of the peoples, is to-day of capital importance. When the Polish
nation, looking back over the vicissitudes of its history, remembers
with gratitude what it has received from the Religion of Christ and
from western civilization developed in the very shadow thereof, it
makes an avowal which is valuable for the present and also for the
future. The more the materialistic spirit, which is so far from the
religious ideals of old Christian Europe, gains ground, the more
does the harsh struggle to live and to retain gainful employment
expose individuals and groups to the temptation of attributing to
the factors of physical force an unmerited and destructive primacy
over the sacred idea of right—the more indispensable, too, to the
present generation are the educative wisdom and the maternal love
of the Church, which, in the midst of strifes and tensions, inevitable
on this earth, never tires of preaching and propagating to all, without distinction of nation or language, the Gospel and spirit of Him
Whose doctrine and life contain for all time the moral foundations
of all prosperity and all true peace. . . .

---

[57] Original French, *Discorsi e Radiomessaggi*, v. 1, pp. 283-284.

LETTER OF CARDINAL MAGLIONE, SECRETARY OF STATE, TO REV.
J. P. ARCHAMBAULT, S.J., PRESIDENT OF THE CANADIAN SOCIAL
WEEK.[58]

*Neither co-operation among classes nor corporative
organizations nor sound nationalism will ever realize
social or national peace in justice, as long as self-renunciation is excluded in favor of strict justice.*

July 26, 1939

1370. The topic selected by the *Ecole Sociale Populaire* for discussion at the forthcoming Seventeenth Social Study Week for
French-Canadian Catholics, that is, "Peace," could not be more
timely. No subject preoccupies the minds so much and none causes
such deep anxiety as peace, the object of every national as well as
individual desire. Conscious of the fact that the general crisis arises
from passions that obliterate all right views on truth and justice, the
Ecole Sociale Populaire intends to study the problem of peace from
its social, as well as from its national and international angle in the
light of Christian principles, which supply the key for its solution
and, above all, in the light of the great reality called love and, better
still, love for our neighbor, without which justice is but a blind
and a snare. By thus retracing the sources of peace as preserved and
regulated by justice, one truth, among others, will be set in a new
light: the urgent necessity for realizing the great benefits of peace
and justice by way of self-renunciation that makes one give rather
than take. Neither syndicalism, co-operation among classes, corporative organizations, nor sound nationalism and perfect national
training will ever realize social or national peace in justice, as long
as self-renunciation is excluded in favor of strict justice.

1371. But, however much peace among nations stands in the
foreground of all present events, it is no less true that all exterior
peace springs from the interior peace of conscience, and that all
collective peace is rooted in individual peace, the fruit of Christian
justice. It is, therefore, matter of exceptional satisfaction to the Holy
Father that your Social Study Week has given such prominence to
individual and domestic peace. It is there, indeed, that the nations'
peace strikes its roots. Nothing contributes so much to the happi-

[58] Translation from *The Tablet*, v. 174, p. 239 (August 19, 1939). Original French,
L'Osservatore Romano, August 9, 1939.

ness of nations as the training of Christian personality by the exercise of personal virtue and the deepening of the religious sense according to the principles of the Gospel. It is by insisting on this point that your Social Study Week will work on safe ground, where man's fundamental happiness will not be forgotten: *Seek ye first the Kingdom of God and His justice.*[59] It is oblivion of this principle that has brought disaster on society, when faith in it would have brought men and nations the peace in order, which alone can save the children of God from ruin. On this assumption, the Social Study Week could not be more timely, for it will revive a doctrine whose urgency none can escape. The thoughts that will be expressed in those days reflect those of the Holy See in circumstances that so deeply interest both the Church and the world. Whatever be the practical results of the meetings, ideas will, at any rate, be released that will further the teachings of Jesus Christ and of His representative at a most critical time. Meanwhile the Holy Father prays God to shed His light on the preachers of His Word and to give fertility to their good will. . . .

DISCOURSE *Un Grande Pensiero* TO A PILGRIMAGE FROM VENICE.[60]

Pius XII gives the first place in his ministry to the work for peace.

August 20, 1939

1372. . . . . . . In the present circumstances, We desire of this blessing that, above all things, it should bring Us peace—peace for Italy, peace for Europe, peace for the world. The intimate agony caused by the outbreak of the war broke the heart of the admirable Pontiff whose holy and dear memory We have recalled with you to-day, broke it almost as if he had foreseen and felt in advance all the horrors and ruin of the world conflict. His successor, Benedict XV of happy memory, sighed, spoke and prayed for peace—called for that moderation in soul which is forgetfulness of struggle in the concord of nations. For peace, Our immediate Predecessor, Pius XI, whose venerable figure is living before the eyes of Our spirit at this

---

[59] *Matthew,* VI, 33.
[60] Translation from *Pius XII and Peace,* pp. 16-17. Original Italian, *Discorsi e Radiomessaggi,* v. I, pp. 300-301.

moment, together with that of Pius X, offered his life to God, nearly a year ago, in a paternal act that moved the whole world.

1373. In the present hour, which renews the acute anxiety and trepidation of Our heart, We, Ourself, since the first day of Our Pontificate, have attempted and done everything in Our power to remove the danger of war and to co-operate in the attainment of a firm peace founded on justice, which would safeguard the liberty and honor of peoples. We have even, within the limits of what is possible and as much as Our Apostolic Ministry permitted, laid aside other tasks and other preoccupations which weighed on Our soul. We have imposed on Ourself a prudent reserve, in order not to render in any way more difficult or impossible for Us the work for peace—conscious of all that We owe to the sons of the Catholic Church and to the whole of humanity. We do not desire, nor have We the heart even now, to give up hope that a sense of moderation and objectivity will prevail in avoiding a conflict which, according to all previsions, would even surpass the past in material destruction and spiritual ruin.

1374. We do not think that the rulers of peoples, in the decisive hours, will take upon themselves the indescribable responsibility of a call to arms. But, above all, human hope is placed in Divine Goodness and Our eyes lift themselves to the All Powerful, to the Father of Mercies, to the God of All Comfort, Who has rendered nations liable to be cured. From Him, in Whose Hands are the hearts, as well as the minds, of the heads of States, We (united in this memorable day with you, Venerable Brothers and Beloved Sons, with all the Catholics of the world, and having also in Our prayers so many souls of good-will who, though living outside the Church, also aspire to peace) desire to implore Him that, in His infinite goodness and mercy toward the human race, He put an end to war where it is now raging and benevolently preserve all from the scourge of new and more inhuman conflicts. Let God show, and let there shine over this world—anxious and troubled as a sea in a storm—a rainbow of calm, of peace, and of fruitful concord among peoples and nations. Let us not cease to pray, but with redoubled fervor let us raise to God the ardent supplication: "Give us peace, O Lord, in our days."

RADIO PLEA *Un'Ora Grave* TO THOSE IN POWER AND TO THEIR
PEOPLES.[61]

Nothing is lost with peace; all may be lost with war.

August 24, 1939

1375. Once again a critical hour strikes for the great human
family—an hour of tremendous deliberations, toward which Our
heart cannot be indifferent and from which Our spiritual authority,
coming to Us from God to lead souls in the ways of justice and
peace, must not hold itself aloof. Behold Us, then, with all of you
who this moment are carrying the burden of so great a responsibility, in order that through Our voice you may hear the voice of
that Christ from Whom the world received the most exalted example of living, and in Whom millions and millions of souls repose
their trust—in a crisis in which His word alone is capable of master-
ing all the tumultuous disturbances of the earth. Behold Us with
you leaders of peoples, men of State and men of arms, writers,
orators of the radio and of the public rostrum, and all those others
who have the power to influence the thought and action of their
fellow men for whose destiny they are responsible.

1376. We, armed only with the word of truth, and standing
above all public disputes and passions, speak to you in the Name
of God, from Whom all paternity in heaven and earth is named;
in the Name of Jesus Christ Our Lord, Who desired that all men
be brothers; in the Name of the Holy Ghost, the Gift of God Most
High, the inexhaustible Source of love in the hearts of men. To-day,
notwithstanding Our repeated exhortations and Our very particular
interest, the fear of bloody international conflict becomes more excruciating. To-day when the tension of minds seems to have arrived
at such a pass as to make an outbreak of the awful scourge of war
appear imminent, We direct, with paternal feeling, a new and more
heartfelt appeal to those in power and to their peoples — to the
former that, laying aside accusations, threats and causes of mutual
distrust, they may attempt to resolve their present differences with
the sole means suitable thereto, namely by reciprocal and trusting
agreements; to the latter that, in calm tranquillity, without disor-

[61] Translation from *Pius XII and Peace,* pp. 17-19. Original Italian, *A.A.S.,* v. 31,
pp. 333-335 (September 11, 1939).

dered agitation, they may encourage the peaceful efforts of those who govern them.

1377. It is by force of reason, and not by force of arms, that justice makes progress, and empires which are not founded on justice are not blessed by God. Statesmanship emancipated from morality betrays those very ones who would have it so. The danger is imminent, but there is yet time. Nothing is lost with peace; all may be lost with war. Let men return to mutual understanding! Let them begin negotiations anew, conferring with good-will and with respect for reciprocal rights. Then will they find that to sincere and conscientious negotiations an honorable solution is never precluded. They will feel a sense of greatness in the true sense of the word if, by silencing the voices of passion—be it collective or private —and by leaving to reason its rightful rule, they will have spared the blood of their fellow men and saved their countries from ruin.

1378. May the Almighty grant that the voice of this Father of the Christian family, of this Servant of Servants, who bears amongst men, unworthily indeed but nevertheless really, the person, the voice and the authority of Jesus Christ, find in the minds and hearts of men a ready and willing reception. May the strong hear Us that they may not become weak through injustice. May the powerful hear Us if they desire that their power be not destruction, but rather protection for their peoples and a safeguard to tranquillity in public order and in their labor. We beseech them by the Blood of Christ, Whose conquering force in the world was His mildness in life and in death. And beseeching them, We know and feel that We have with Us all those who are upright of heart, all those who hunger and thirst after justice, all those who already suffer every sorrow through the evils of life. We have with Us the hearts of mothers, which beat as one with Ours; of fathers, who would be obliged to abandon their families; of the lowly, who labor and do not understand; of the innocent, upon whom weighs heavily the awful threat; of the young men, generous knights of purest and noblest ideals. And with Us also is the soul of this ancient Europe, which was the product of Faith and Christian genius.

1379. With Us, all humanity seeks justice, bread and freedom; not steel, which kills and destroys. With Us is that Christ Who has made His solemn commandment, love of one's brother, the very substance of His Religion and the promise of salvation for

individuals and for nations. Recalling finally that human efforts
are of no avail without Divine assistance, We invite all to raise
their eyes to heaven and to beseech the Lord with fervent prayers
that His divine grace descend in abundance upon this world in its
upheaval, that it placate dissensions, reconcile hearts and evoke the
resplendent dawn of a more serene future. To this end, and with
this hope, We impart to all, from Our heart, Our Paternal Benediction.

MESSAGE *Le Souverain Pontife* TO THE HEADS OF THE EUROPEAN
GOVERNMENTS.[62]

The Holy Father pleads at the last moment for peace.

August 31, 1939

1380. The Holy Father cannot abandon hope that conversations now being held may bring about a just and peaceful solution
such as the whole world has not ceased to implore. Therefore, His
Holiness beseeches, in the Name of God, the Governments of Germany and Poland to do everything possible to avoid any incident
whatsoever, and to abstain from taking any measure capable of
aggravating the present tension. He asks the Governments of
England, France and Italy to support this, his request.

TELEGRAM FROM CARDINAL MAGLIONE, SECRETARY OF STATE, TO
THE PAX ROMANA CONGRESS IN WASHINGTON, D. C.[63]

*Pius XII praises the Pax Romana crusade of prayer for
peace.*

September 1, 1939

1381. Paternal heart Common Father deeply touched announcement inauguration new crusade of prayer for peace by Pax Romana.
Prays at this moment of anxiety and sorrow, petitions this international gathering may be efficacious bringing peace so earnestly
desired to troubled world. Token loving gratitude pledge plenteous

---

[62] Translation from *Pius XII and Peace*, p. 20. Original French, *A.A.S.*, v. 31, pp.
335-336 (September 11, 1939).
[63] Original English, *N.C.W.C. News Service*, September 4, 1939.

heavenly favor Holy Father bestows from heart to officers, members Pax Romana paternal Apostolic Benediction.

RESPONSE *C'Est une Vive Satisfaction* TO THE HOMAGE OF THE NEW BELGIAN AMBASSADOR, ADRIAN NIEUWENHUYS.[64]

> *Recourse to armed might is the inevitable consequence of abandoning the principle of negotiation.*

September 14, 1939

1382. . . . . . . The beginnings of this mission coincide with an hour of tragic tension, which fills Our heart with a profound sadness. That which, since the last world war, was the anguish and the terror of peoples, is again a reality, the reality of an immeasurable catastrophe! For of this new war, which already shakes the soil of Europe, and particularly that of a Catholic nation, no human prevision can calculate the frightful potential of carnage which it bears within itself, nor what its extension and its successive complications will be. Your Excellency recalls, with good reason, the efforts made by your Sovereign, up until the very last minute, to preserve the peace that was menaced and to safeguard the peoples of Europe from even greater calamities. And who would be more ardently disposed to lend help to these generous plans and proposals than the Common Father of Christianity? Placed, by the duties of Our Apostolic Ministry, above particular conflicts—and anxious in Our paternal solicitude for the true good of all peoples—We, with aching heart, beheld drawing nearer day by day the cataclysm that would follow as an inevitable consequence upon the abandonment of the principle of negotiation and the recourse to armed might.

1383. We Ourself need not repeat how the prevision of such great misfortune has incessantly been with Us, since the very first day of Our Pontificate; how, even up to the final moment which preceded the outbreak of hostilities, We attempted everything within Our power, whether by prayers and public exhortations, or by confidential approaches repeated and precise, to enlighten minds on the gravity of the peril, and to lead them to loyal and peaceful negotiations, on the bases, the only solid and durable ones possible, of justice and charity; justice rendered to

[64] Original French, *A.A.S.*, v. 31, pp. 367-369 (September 25, 1939).

the weakest as well as to the strongest; charity which steers safe of the errors of egoism so that the safeguarding of the rights of the individual does not degenerate into forgetfulness, or negation, or positive violation of the rights of others. . . . . . .

1384. Since We are, despite Our unworthiness, the Vicar of Him Who came down to earth as the *Princeps Pacis,*[65] feeling Ourself sustained besides by the prayers of the faithful and comforted by the intimate certitude of having innumerable souls of good-will with Us, We shall not cease to be attentively on the alert, in order to help them with all Our power, on any occasion that may offer itself; above all, to lead anew the peoples to-day stirred up and divided, toward the conclusion of a peace honorable for all, in conformity with the human and Christian conscience, a peace which protects the vital rights of each and safeguards the security and tranquillity of the nations; and then, as long as the former course is impossible, at least to alleviate the wounds already inflicted, or those which will be in the future. With a view to this, it pleases Us to recall certain declarations, by which the belligerents at the beginning of the conflict publicly affirmed their will to observe, in the conduct of the war, the laws of humanity and to act in accordance with the stipulations of international agreements. Therefore, We cling in a special manner to the hope, that civilian populations will be preserved from all direct military operations; that, in the occupied territories, the life, property, honor and religious sentiments of the inhabitants will be respected; that the prisoners of war will be treated humanely and that they will be able, without any hindrance, to receive the comforts of religion; that the use of asphyxiating and poison gases will be excluded. . . .

DISCOURSE *Seid Uns Herzlich Willkommen* TO A GROUP OF GERMAN PILGRIMS.[66]

War is a scourge from God.

September 26, 1939

1385. . . . . . . You have come to Us in a very grave hour. It is so grave and the future so dark that at present We can see and

[65] *Isaias,* IX, 6.
[66] Original German, *Discorsi e Radiomessaggi,* v. 1, p. 321.

say only this: the war which has just broken out is, for all peoples who will be drawn into it, a terrible scourge of God. The priest must now, more than ever before, be above all political and national feelings. He must console, comfort, help, exhort to prayer and penance, and must himself pray and do penance. Pray that God may shorten the misery of war and restore peace, peace in honor, in justice, in reconciliation and agreement for all participants, a peace that will again grant the Catholic Church in your beloved fatherland happier days and greater freedom. . . .

DISCOURSE *Vous Êtes Venus* TO CARDINAL HLOND, ARCHBISHOP OF GNESEN AND POSNAN, AND A GROUP OF POLISH PILGRIMS.[67]

Despite unjust persecution, the Polish Catholics must persevere in prayer and in the practice of good works.

September 30, 1939

1386. . . . . . . You have come neither to formulate vindication nor to express loud laments, but to ask from Our heart and lips words of consolation in your sufferings. To give them is Our duty as a father, and no one, certainly, has a right to wonder that We do so. A father's love interests itself in all things that affect his children and is moved by that which wounds them. To each We would repeat the words of St. Paul: *Who is weak, and I am not weak? Quis infirmatur et ego non infirmor?*[68] There are already thousands, hundreds of thousands of poor human beings who are suffering; victims struck in their flesh and souls by this war, from which all of Our efforts have sought so obstinately, so ardently, but so uselessly, alas, to preserve Europe and the world.

1387. Before Our eyes pass as a vision frightened crowds and, in black desperation, a multitude of refugees and wanderers—all those who no longer have a country or a home. There rise toward Us the agonized sobs of mothers and wives, who weep for dear ones fallen on the field of battle. We hear the desolate lament of so many of the old and infirm, who too often are left deprived of every assistance; the cries of children who have lost their parents;

[67] Translation from *Pius XII and Peace*, pp. 24-25. Original French, *Discorsi e Radio-messaggi*, v. 1, pp. 325-328.
[68] II *Corinthians*, XI, 29.

the cries of the wounded in battle who are dying—not all of whom were soldiers. All of their sufferings, miseries and mourning We make Ours.

1388. The Pope's love for his children, like that of God, knows no limit, just as it knows no frontiers. All the children of the Church are at home when they are near their Common Father; all have a place in his heart. But this paternal tenderness, which reserves its special affection for the afflicted and would linger with each of them, is not the only good that remains for you. There endure before God, His Vicar and all men of good faith other treasures which are not laid by in safes of iron but in the hearts and souls of men. . . . . . .

1389. We hope, moreover, that God, in His mercy, will not permit the free exercise of religion in your country to become shackled; We even hope, in spite of reasons to the contrary, inspired by the all too well-known designs of the enemies of God, that Catholic life will be able to continue profound and fruitful among you; that you will be able to renew the ceremonies of worship, the manifestations of piety toward the Eucharist and of homage to the Kingship of Christ, of which your cities and the countryside gave such a magnificent display recently; that the Catholic Press, the charitable institutions, social works, religious teaching will enjoy the liberty which is their due. That is why We especially exhort your spiritual pastors to continue, even to increase, their initiative in the fields which, with God's help, still will remain open to their zeal. Whatever may be the new circumstances in which this zeal must be employed, the first duty of all, pastors and sheep, is to persevere not only in prayer but also courageously in good works with steadfast confidence. . . .

1390. As the flowers of your country, often covered with winter's snow, await the warm breath of spring, you will know that you, too, may expect the hour of heavenly consolation, praying with trust. Your sufferings, thus tempered with hope, will not then be mixed with rancor, much less with hatred. Your striving for justice will be in the same spirit, for so it must be to accord with the divine law of charity. In fact, it is through justice and charity (and through them alone, as We have never ceased to reiterate) that at length may be restored to a world so upset that peace for which, amid the din of arms, men plead so anxiously and for which from one end of the world to the other millions of sincere souls, even among those who do not profess the Catholic Faith, raise their prayers to God, the Sovereign Ruler of men and things. . . . . . .

RESPONSE *Heureux Est pour Nous* TO THE HOMAGE OF THE NEW LITHUANIAN MINISTER, STANISLAUS GIRDVAINIS.[69]

Christian justice, fraternity and charity will furnish the solution for many otherwise insoluble problems.

October 18, 1939

1391. . . . . . . Aware of the duties proper to Our office as Supreme Pastor, We will not permit—unless We are requested—that Our activity, ever directed toward the salvation of souls, become involved in purely temporal controversy and territorial competitions between States. But the very duty of this office does not permit Us to close Our eyes when, precisely for the salvation of souls, new and incommensurable dangers arise; when, over the face of Europe, Christian in all its fundamental features, a sinister shadow of the thought and the work of the enemies of God is cast more threateningly each day. In these circumstances, more than in any period in history, the preservation, care and defense of the Christian heritage acquire a decisive importance for the future destinies of Europe and the prosperity of each of its peoples, large or small.

1392. The State which, with noble loftiness of views, recognizes the liberty suitable to the expansion and practice of Christian doctrine, stores up for itself resources of spiritual forces on which it may count with full security when troubled and difficult hours arise. Wherever full freedom is left to evangelical doctrine, Christian sentiment will penetrate not only the souls of the citizens but the manifold and diverse activities of public life. The more Christian justice, fraternity and charity animate and guide individuals and groups, so much the more is established among nations a spiritual atmosphere, making possible, indeed easy, the solution of many problems which to-day appear, or really are, insolvable. If in the midst of present events Christian nations are particularly entitled

[69] Translation from *Pius XII and Peace*, pp. 25-26. Original French, *A.A.S.*, v. 31, p. 612 (November 10, 1939).

to Our solicitude and Our pastoral vigilance, Our sons and daughters of Lithuania can understand how close We are to them. We are united with them also by Our unshakable assurance of their fidelity to and confidence in God, Whose all-powerful aid can open new roads toward progress and prosperity in a pacified Europe, returned to a sense of justice, fraternity and its Christian vocation. . . .

ENCYCLICAL *Summi Pontificatus* ON THE FUNCTION OF THE STATE IN THE MODERN WORLD.[70]

The disorders of the modern world are keenly diagnosed and suitable remedies for their cure are prescribed.

October 20, 1939

1393. . . . . . . As Vicar of Him Who in a decisive hour pronounced before the highest earthly authority of that day the great words: *For this was I born, and for this came I into the world; that I should give testimony to the truth. Every one that is of the truth, heareth My voice,*[71] We feel We owe no greater debt to Our office and to Our time than to testify to the truth with Apostolic firmness: "to give testimony to the truth." This duty necessarily entails the exposition and confutation of errors and human faults; for these must be made known before it is possible to tend and to heal them, *you shall know the truth, and the truth shall make you free.*[72] In the fulfillment of this, Our duty, We shall not let Ourselves be influenced by earthly considerations nor be held back by mistrust or opposition, by rebuffs or lack of appreciation of Our words, nor yet by fear of misconceptions and misinterpretations. We shall fulfill Our duty, animated ever with that paternal charity which, while it suffers from the evils which afflict Our children, at the same time points out to them the remedy; We shall strive to imitate the Divine Model of shepherds, Jesus, the Good Shepherd, Who is Light as well as Love: *doing the truth in charity.*[73]

1394. At the head of the road which leads to the spiritual and

[70] Official English translation, *A.A.S.*, v. 31, pp. 543-564 (October 28, 1939). Original Latin, *A.A.S.*, v. 31, pp. 420-453 (October 28, 1939).
[71] *John*, XVIII, 37.
[72] *John*, VIII, 32.
[73] *Ephesians*, IV, 15.

moral bankruptcy of the present day stand the nefarious efforts of not a few to dethrone Christ; the abandonment of the law of truth which He proclaimed and of the law of love which is the life breath of His Kingdom. In the recognition of the loyal prerogatives of Christ and in the return of individuals and of society to the law of His truth and of His love lies the only way to salvation.

1395. Venerable Brethren, as We write these lines the terrible news comes to Us that the dread tempest of war is already raging despite all Our efforts to avert it. When We think of the wave of suffering that has come on countless people who, but yesterday, enjoyed in the environment of their homes some little degree of well-being, We are tempted to lay down Our pen. Our paternal heart is torn by anguish as We look ahead to all that will yet come forth from the baneful seed of violence and of hatred for which the sword to-day ploughs the blood-drenched furrow. But precisely because of this apocalyptic foresight of disaster, imminent and remote, We feel We have a duty to raise with still greater insistence the eyes and hearts of those in whom there yet remains good-will to the One from Whom alone comes the salvation of the world—to the One Whose almighty and merciful Hand can alone calm this tempest—to the One Whose truth and Whose love can enlighten the intellects and inflame the hearts of so great a section of mankind plunged in error, selfishness, strife and struggle, so as to give it a new orientation in the spirit of the Kingship of Christ.

1396. Perhaps—God grant it—one may hope that this hour of direst need may bring a change of outlook and sentiment to those many who, till now, have walked with blind faith along the path of popular modern errors, unconscious of the treacherous and insecure ground on which they trod. Perhaps the many who have not grasped the importance of the educational and pastoral mission of the Church will now understand better her warnings, scouted in the false security of the past. No defense of Christianity could be more effective than the present straits. From the immense vortex of error and anti-Christian movements there has come forth a crop of such poignant disasters as to constitute a condemnation surpassing in its conclusiveness any merely theoretical refutation.

1397. Hours of painful disillusionment are often hours of grace —*a passage of the Lord*,[74] when doors which in other circumstances

[74] *Exodus*, XII, 11.

would have remained shut, open at Our Saviour's words: *Behold, I stand at the gate, and knock.*[75] God knows that Our heart goes out in affectionate sympathy and spiritual joy to those who, as a result of such painful trials, feel within them an effective and salutary thirst for the truth, justice and peace of Christ. But for those also for whom as yet the hour of light from on high has not come, Our heart knows only love, Our lips move only in prayer to the Father of Light that He may cause to shine in their hearts, indifferent as yet or hostile to Christ, a ray of that Light which once transformed Saul into Paul; of that Light which has shown its mysterious power strongest in the times of greatest difficulty for the Church. . . . . . .

1398. The present age, Venerable Brethren, by adding new errors to the doctrinal aberrations of the past, has pushed these to extremes which lead inevitably to a drift toward chaos. Before all else, it is certain that the radical and ultimate cause of the evils which We deplore in modern society is the denial and rejection of a universal norm of morality as well for individual and social life as for international relations; We mean the disregard, so common nowadays, and the forgetfulness of the natural law itself, which has its foundation in God, Almighty Creator and Father of all, Supreme and Absolute Lawgiver, All-wise and Just Judge of human actions. When God is denied, every basis of morality is undermined; the voice of conscience is stilled or, at any rate, grows very faint, that voice which teaches even to the illiterate and to uncivilized tribes what is good and what is bad, what lawful, what forbidden, and makes men feel themselves responsible for their actions to a Supreme Judge.

1399. The denial of the fundamentals of morality had its origin, in Europe, in the abandonment of that Christian teaching of which the Chair of Peter is the depository and exponent. That teaching had once given spiritual cohesion to a Europe which, educated, ennobled and civilized by the Cross, had reached such a degree of civil progress as to become the teacher of other peoples, of other continents. But, cut off from the infallible teaching authority of the Church, not a few separated brethren have gone so far as to overthrow the central dogma of Christianity, the Divinity of the Saviour, and have hastened thereby the progress of spiritual decay.

[75] *Apocalypse*, III, 20.

1400. The Holy Gospel narrates that when Jesus was crucified *there was darkness over the whole earth*[76]; a terrifying symbol of what happened and what still happens spiritually wherever incredulity, blind and proud of itself, has succeeded in excluding Christ from modern life, especially from public life, and has undermined faith in God as well as faith in Christ. The consequence is that the moral values by which, in other times, public and private conduct was gauged have fallen into disuse; and the much-vaunted laicization of society, which has made ever more rapid progress, withdrawing man, the family and the State from the beneficent and regenerating effects of the idea of God and the teaching of the Church, has caused to reappear, in regions in which for many centuries shone the splendors of Christian civilization, in a manner ever clearer, ever more distinct, ever more distressing, the signs of a corrupt paganism: *There was darkness when they crucified Jesus.*[77]

1401. Many perhaps, while abandoning the teaching of Christ, were not fully conscious of being led astray by a mirage of glittering phrases, which proclaimed such estrangement as an escape from the slavery in which they were before held; nor did they then foresee the bitter consequences of bartering the truth that sets free, for error which enslaves. They did not realize that, in renouncing the infinitely wise and paternal laws of God, and the unifying and elevating doctrine of Christ's love, they were resigning themselves to the whim of a poor, fickle human wisdom; they spoke of progress, when they were going back; of being raised, when they groveled; of arriving at man's estate, when they stooped to servility. They did not perceive the inability of all human effort to replace the law of Christ by anything equal to it; *they . . . became vain in their thoughts.*[78]

1402. With the weakening of faith in God and in Jesus Christ, and the darkening in men's minds of the light of moral principles, there disappeared the indispensable foundation of the stability and quiet of that internal and external, private and public order which alone can support and safeguard the prosperity of States. It is true that even when Europe had a cohesion of brotherhood through identical ideals gathered from Christian preaching, she was not free from dissensions, convulsions and wars which laid her waste;

[76] *Matthew*, XXVII, 45.
[77] *Roman Breviary, 5th responsory of Good Friday.*
[78] *Romans*, I, 21.

595

but perhaps they never felt the intense pessimism of to-day as to the possibility of settling them, for they had then an effective moral sense of the just and of the unjust, of the lawful and of the un-lawful, which, by restraining outbreaks of passion, left the way open to an honorable settlement. In our days, on the contrary, dissensions come not only from the surge of rebellious passion, but also from a deep spiritual crisis which has overthrown the sound principles of private and public morality.

1403. Among the many errors which flow from the poisoned source of religious and moral agnosticism, We would draw your attention, Venerable Brethren, to two in particular, as being those which more than others render almost impossible, or at least precarious and uncertain, the peaceful intercourse of peoples.

1404. The first of these pernicious errors, widespread to-day, is the forgetfulness of that law of human solidarity and charity which is dictated and imposed by our common origin and by the equality of rational nature in all men, no matter to what people they belong, and by the redeeming Sacrifice offered by Jesus Christ on the Altar of the Cross to His Heavenly Father on behalf of sinful mankind.

1405. In fact, the first page of the Scripture, with magnificent simplicity, tells us how God, as a culmination to His creative work, made man to His own image and likeness[79]; and the same Scripture tells us that He enriched man with supernatural gifts and privileges, and destined him to an eternal and ineffable happiness. It shows us besides how other men took their origin from the first couple, and then goes on, in unsurpassed vividness of language, to recount their division into different groups and their dispersion to various parts of the world. Even when they abandoned their Creator, God did not cease to regard them as His children, who, according to His merciful plan, should one day be reunited once more in His friendship.[80] The Apostle of the Gentiles later on makes himself the herald of this truth which associates men as brothers in one great family, when he proclaims to the Greek world that God *hath made of one, all mankind, to dwell upon the whole face of the earth, determining appointed times, and the limits of their habitation, that they should seek God.*[81]

[79] Cf. *Genesis*, I, 26-27.
[80] Cf. *Genesis*, XII, 3.
[81] *Acts*, XVII, 26-27.

1406. It is a marvelous vision, which makes us see the human race in the unity of one common origin in God, *One God and Father of all, Who is above all, and through all, and in us all;*[82] in the unity of nature which in every man is composed of material body and spiritual, immortal soul; in the unity of the immediate end and mission in the world; in the unity of dwelling place, the earth of whose resources all men can, by natural right, avail themselves to sustain and develop life; in the unity of the supernatural end, God Himself, to Whom all should tend; in the unity of means to secure that end.

1407. It is the same Apostle who portrays for us mankind in the unity of its relations with the Son of God, Image of the invisible God, in Whom all things have been created: *in Him were all things created*[83]; in the unity of its ransom, effected for all by Christ, Who, through His holy and most bitter Passion, restored the original friendship with God which had been broken, making Himself the Mediator between God and men: *For there is one God, and one Mediator of God and men—the Man, Christ Jesus.*[84] And to render such friendship between God and mankind more intimate, this same divine and universal Mediator of salvation and of peace, in the sacred silence of the Supper Room, before He consummated the Supreme Sacrifice, let fall from His divine Lips the words which reverberate mightily down the centuries, inspiring heroic charity in a world devoid of love and torn by hate: *This is My commandment, that you love one another, as I have loved you.*[85]

1408. These are supernatural truths which form a solid basis and the strongest possible bond of a union, that is reinforced by the love of God and of our Divine Redeemer, from Whom all receive salvation *for the edifying of the Body of Christ: Until we all meet into the unity of faith, and of the knowledge of the Son of God, unto a perfect man, unto the measure of the age of the fullness of Christ.*[86] In the light of this unity of all mankind, which exists in law and in fact, individuals do not feel themselves isolated units, like grains of sand, but feel united by the very force of their nature and by their internal destiny, into an organic, harmonious mutual

[82] *Ephesians,* IV, 6.
[83] *Colossians,* I, 16.
[84] I *Timothy,* II, 5.
[85] *John,* XV, 12.
[86] *Ephesians,* IV, 12-13.

relationship which varies with the changing of times. And the nations, despite a difference of development due to diverse conditions of life and of culture, are not destined to break the unity of the human race, but rather to enrich and embellish it by the sharing of their own peculiar gifts and by that reciprocal interchange of goods which can be possible and efficacious only when a mutual love and a lively sense of charity unite all the sons of the same Father and all those redeemed by the same divine Blood.

1409. The Church of Christ, the faithful depository of the teaching of divine wisdom, cannot and does not think of depreciating or disdaining the particular characteristics which each people, with jealous and intelligible pride, cherishes and retains as a precious heritage. Her aim is a supernatural union in all-embracing love, deeply felt and practiced, and not the unity which is exclusively external and superficial and, by that very fact, weak. The Church hails with joy and follows with her maternal blessing every method of guidance and care which aims at a wise and orderly evolution of particular forces and tendencies having their origin in the individual character of each race, provided that they are not opposed to the duties incumbent on men from their unity of origin and common destiny. She has repeatedly shown in her missionary enterprises that such a principle of action is the guiding star of her universal apostolate. Pioneer research and investigation, involving sacrifice, devotedness and love on the part of her missionaries of every age, have been undertaken in order to facilitate the deeper appreciative insight into the most varied civilizations and to put their spiritual values to account for a living and vital preaching of the Gospel of Christ. All that in such usages and customs is not inseparably bound up with religious errors will always be subject to kindly consideration and, when it is found possible, will be sponsored and developed.

1410. Our immediate Predecessor, of holy and venerated memory, applying such norms to a particularly delicate question, made some generous decisions which are a monument to his insight and to the intensity of his Apostolic spirit. Nor need We tell you, Venerable Brethren, that We intend to proceed without hesitation along this way. Those who enter the Church, whatever be their origin or their speech, must know that they have equal rights as children in the Lord's House, where the law and peace of Christ prevail.

1411. In accordance with these principles of equality, the Church devotes her care to the forming of a cultured native clergy and to the gradual increasing of the number of native bishops. And in order to give external expression to these, Our intentions, We have chosen the forthcoming Feast of Christ the King to raise to the episcopal dignity at the Tomb of the Apostles twelve representatives of widely different peoples and races. In the midst of the disruptive contrasts which divide the human family, may this solemn act proclaim to all Our sons, scattered over the world, that the spirit, the teaching and the work of the Church can never be other than that which the Apostle of the Gentiles preached: *putting on the new [man], him who is renewed unto knowledge, according to the image of Him that created him. Where there is neither Gentile nor Jew, circumcision nor uncircumcision, Barbarian nor Scythian, bond nor free. But Christ is all, and in all.*[87]

1412. Nor is there any fear lest the consciousness of universal brotherhood, aroused by the teaching of Christianity and the spirit which it inspires, be in contrast with love of traditions or the glories of one's fatherland, or impede the progress of prosperity or legitimate interests. For that same Christianity teaches that in the exercise of charity we must follow a God-given order, yielding the place of honor in our affections and good works to those who are bound to us by special ties. Nay, the Divine Master Himself gave an example of this preference for His own country and fatherland, as He wept over the coming destruction of the Holy City. But legitimate and well-ordered love of our native country should not make us close our eyes to the all-embracing nature of Christian charity, which calls for consideration of others and of their interests in the pacifying light of love.

1413. Such is the marvelous doctrine of love and peace which has been such an ennobling factor in the civil and religious progress of mankind. And the heralds who proclaimed it, moved by supernatural charity, not only tilled the land and cared for the sick, but, above all, they reclaimed, moulded and raised life to divine heights, directing it toward the summit of sanctity in which everything is seen in the light of God. They have raised mansions and temples which show to what lofty and kindly heights the Christian ideal urges man; but, above all, they have made of men, wise or ignorant,

[87] *Colossians*, III, 10-11.

strong or weak, living temples of God and branches of the very Vine which is Christ. They have handed on to future generations the treasures of ancient art and wisdom and have secured for them that inestimable gift of eternal wisdom which links men as brothers by the common recognition of a supernatural ownership. Venerable Brethren, forgetfulness of the law of universal charity — of that charity which alone can consolidate peace by extinguishing hatred and softening envies and dissensions—is the source of very grave evils for peaceful relations between nations.

1414. But there is yet another error no less pernicious to the well-being of the nations and to the prosperity of that great human society which gathers together and embraces within its confines all races. It is the error contained in those ideas which do not hesitate to divorce civil authority from every kind of dependence upon the Supreme Being—First Cause and Absolute Master of man and of society—and from every restraint of a Higher Law derived from God as from its First Source. Thus, they accord the civil authority an unrestricted field of action that is at the mercy of the changeful tide of human will, or of the dictates of casual historical claims and of the interests of a few.

1415. Once the authority of God and the sway of His law are denied in this way, the civil authority as an inevitable result tends to attribute to itself that absolute autonomy which belongs exclusively to the Supreme Maker. It puts itself in the place of the Almighty and elevates the State or group into the last end of life, the supreme criterion of the moral and juridical order, and, therefore, forbids every appeal to the principles of natural reason and of the Christian conscience. We do not, of course, fail to recognize that, fortunately, false principles do not always exercise their full influence, especially when age-old Christian traditions, on which the peoples have been nurtured, remain still deeply, even if unconsciously, rooted in their hearts.

1416. Nonetheless, one must not forget that the essential insufficiency and weakness of every principle of social life, which rests upon a purely human foundation, is inspired by merely earthly motives, and relies for its force on the sanction of a purely external authority. Where the dependence of human right upon the divine is denied, where appeal is made only to some insecure idea of a merely human authority, and where an autonomy is claimed which rests only upon a utilitarian morality, there human law itself justly forfeits in its more weighty application the moral force which is the essential condition for its acknowledgment and also for its demand of sacrifices.

1417. It is quite true that power, based on such weak and unsteady foundations, can attain at times, under chance circumstances, material successes apt to arouse wonder in superficial observers. But the moment comes when the inevitable law triumphs, which strikes down all that has been constructed upon a hidden or open disproportion between the greatness of the material and outward success, and the weakness of the inward value and of its moral foundation. Such disproportion exists whenever public authority disregards or denies the dominion of the Supreme Lawgiver, Who, as He has given rulers power, has also set and marked its bounds.

1418. Indeed, as Our great Predecessor, Leo XIII, wisely taught in the Encyclical *Immortale Dei,* it was the Creator's will that civil sovereignty should regulate social life after the dictates of an order changeless in its universal principles; should facilitate the attainment in the temporal order, by individuals, of physical, intellectual and moral perfection; and should aid them to reach their supernatural end.

1419. Hence, it is the noble prerogative and function of the State to control, aid and direct the private and individual activities of national life that they converge harmoniously toward the common good. That good can neither be defined according to arbitrary ideas nor can it accept for its standard primarily the material prosperity of society, but rather it should be defined according to the harmonious development and the natural perfection of man. It is for this perfection that society is designed by the Creator as a means.

1420. To consider the State as something ultimate to which everything else should be subordinated and directed, cannot fail to harm the true and lasting prosperity of nations. This can happen either when unrestricted dominion comes to be conferred on the State as having a mandate from the nation, people, or even a social class, or when the State arrogates such dominion to itself as absolute master, despotically, without any mandate whatsoever. If, in fact, the State lays claim to and directs private enterprises, these, ruled as they are by delicate and complicated internal principles which guarantee and assure the realization of their special aims, may be damaged to the detriment of the public good, by being wrenched from their natural surroundings, that is, from responsible private action.

1421. Further, there would be danger lest the primary and essential cell of society, the family, with its well-being and its growth, should come to be considered from the narrow standpoint of national power, and lest it be forgotten that man and the family are by nature anterior to the State, and that the Creator has given to both of them powers and rights and has assigned them a mission and a charge that correspond to undeniable natural requirements.

1422. The education of the new generation in that case would not aim at the balanced and harmonious development of the physical powers and of all the intellectual and moral qualities, but at a one-sided formation of those civic virtues that are considered necessary for attaining political success, while the virtues which give society the fragrance of nobility, humanity and reverence would be inculcated less, for fear they should detract from the pride of the citizen.

1423. Before Us stand out with painful clarity the dangers We fear will accrue to this and the coming generation from the neglect or non-recognition, the minimizing and the gradual abolition of the rights peculiar to the family. Therefore, We stand up as determined defenders of those rights in the full consciousness of the duty imposed on Us by Our Apostolic Office. The stress of our times, as well external as internal, material and spiritual alike, and the manifold errors with their countless repercussions are tasted by none so bitterly as by that noble little cell, the family.

1424. True courage and a heroism worthy in its degree of admiration and respect, are often necessary to support the hardships of life, the daily weight of misery, growing want and restrictions on a scale never before experienced, whose reason and necessity are not always apparent. Whoever has the care of souls and can search hearts knows the hidden tears of mothers, the resigned sorrow of so many fathers, the countless bitternesses of which no statistics tell or can tell. He sees with sad eyes the mass of sufferings ever on the increase; he knows how the powers of disorder and destruction stand on the alert, ready to make use of all these things for their dark designs. No one of good-will and vision will think of refusing the State, in the exceptional conditions of the world of to-day, correspondingly wider and exceptional rights to meet the public needs. But even in such emergencies, the moral law, established by God, demands that the lawfulness of each such measure and its real necessity be scrutinized with the greatest rigor according to the standards of the common good.

1425. In any case, the more burdensome the material sacrifices demanded of the individual and the family by the State, the more must the rights of conscience be to it sacred and inviolable. Goods, blood it can demand; but the soul redeemed by God, never. The charge laid by God on parents to provide for the material and spiritual good of their offspring and to procure for them a suitable training saturated with the true spirit of religion, cannot be wrested from them without grave violation of their rights.

1426. Undoubtedly, that formation should aim as well at the preparation of youth to fulfill with intelligent understanding and pride those offices of a noble patriotism which give to one's earthly fatherland all due measure of love, self-devotion and service. But, on the other hand, a formation which forgot or, worse still, deliberately neglected to direct the eyes and hearts of youth to the heavenly country would be an injustice to youth, an injustice against the inalienable duties and rights of the Christian family and an excess to which a check must be opposed, in the interests even of the people and of the State itself.

1427. Such an education might seem perhaps to the rulers responsible for it, a source of increased strength and vigor; it would be, in fact, the opposite, as sad experience would prove. The crime of high treason against the *King of Kings and Lord of Lords*,[88] perpetrated by an education that is either indifferent or opposed to Christianity, the reversal of *Suffer the little children . . . to come to Me*,[89] would bear most bitter fruits. On the contrary, the State which lifts anxiety from the bleeding and torn hearts of fathers and mothers and restores their rights, only promotes its own internal peace and lays foundations of a happy future for the country. The souls of children given to their parents by God and consecrated in Baptism with the royal character of Christ, are a sacred charge over which watches the jealous love of God. The same Christ Who pronounced the words, *Suffer little children to come to*

[88] I *Timothy*, VI, 15; cf. *Apocalypse*, XIX, 6.
[89] *Matthew*, XIX, 14.

Me, has threatened, for all His mercy and goodness, with fearful evils, those who give scandal to those so dear to His Heart.

1428. Now what scandal is more permanently harmful to generation after generation than a formation of youth which is misdirected toward a goal that alienates from Christ, *the Way and the Truth and the Life,* and leads to open or hidden apostasy from Christ? That Christ from Whom they want to alienate the youthful generations of the present day and of the future is the same Christ Who has received from His Eternal Father all power in heaven and on earth. He holds in His omnipotent Hand the destiny of States, of peoples and of nations. His it is to shorten or prolong life; His to grant increase, prosperity and greatness. Of all that exists on the face of the earth, the soul alone has deathless life. A system of education that should not respect the sacred precincts of the Christian family, protected by God's holy law, that should attack its foundations, bar to the young the way to Christ, to the Saviour's fountains of life and joy,[90] that should consider apostasy from Christ and the Church as a proof of fidelity to the people or a particular class, would pronounce its own condemnation and experience in its day the inevitable truth of the prophet's words: *they that depart from thee, shall be written in the earth.*[91]

1429. The idea which credits the State with unlimited authority is not simply an error harmful to the internal life of nations, to their prosperity, and to the larger and well-ordered increase in their well-being, but likewise it injures the relations between peoples, for it breaks the unity of supra-national society, robs the law of nations of its foundation and vigor, leads to violation of others' rights and impedes agreement and peaceful intercourse. A disposition, in fact, of the divinely-sanctioned natural order divides the human race into social groups, nations or States, which are mutually independent in organization and in the direction of their internal life. But for all that, the human race is bound together by reciprocal ties, moral and juridical, into a great commonwealth directed to the good of all nations and ruled by special laws which protect its unity and promote its prosperity. Now no one can fail to see how the claim to absolute autonomy for the State stands in open opposition to this natural law that is inherent in man—nay, denies it utterly—

[90] *Cf. Isaias,* XII, 3.
[91] *Jeremias,* XVII, 13.

and, therefore, leaves the stability of international relations at the mercy of the will of rulers, while it destroys the possibility of true union and fruitful collaboration directed to the general good.

1430.   So, Venerable Brethren, it is indispensable for the existence of harmonious and lasting contacts and of fruitful relations, that the peoples recognize and observe these principles of international natural law which regulate their normal development and activity. Such principles demand respect for corresponding rights to independence, to life and to the possibility of continuous development in the paths of civilization; they demand, further, fidelity to compacts agreed upon and sanctioned in conformity with the principles of the law of nations.

1431.   The indispensable presupposition, without doubt, of all peaceful intercourse between nations, and the very soul of the juridical relations in force among them, is mutual trust: the expectation and conviction that each party will respect its plighted word; the certainty that both sides are convinced that *Better is wisdom, than weapons of war*,[92] and are ready to enter into discussion and to avoid recourse to force or to threats of force in case of delays, hindrances, changes or disputes, because all these things can be the result not of bad-will, but of changed circumstances and of genuine interests in conflict. But, on the other hand, to tear the law of nations from its anchor in divine law, to base it on the autonomous will of States, is to dethrone that very law and deprive it of its noblest and strongest qualities. Thus it would stand abandoned to the fatal drive of private interest and collective selfishness exclusively intent on the assertion of its own rights and ignoring those of others.

1432.   Now, it is true that with the passage of time and the substantial change of circumstances, which were not and perhaps could not have been foreseen in the making of a treaty, such a treaty or some of its clauses can in fact become, or at least seem to become, unjust, impracticable or too burdensome for one of the parties. It is obvious that should such be the case, recourse should be had in good time to a frank discussion with a view to modifying the treaty or making another in its stead. But to consider treaties on principle as ephemeral and tacitly to assume the authority of rescinding them unilaterally when they are no longer to one's ad-

[92] *Ecclesiastes*, IX, 18.

vantage, would be to abolish all mutual trust among States. In this way, natural order would be destroyed and there would be seen dug between different peoples and nations trenches of division impossible to refill.

1433. To-day, Venerable Brethren, all men are looking with terror into the abyss to which they have been brought by the errors and principles which We have mentioned, and by their practical consequences. Gone are the proud illusions of limitless progress. Should any still fail to grasp this fact, the tragic situation of to-day would rouse them with the prophet's cry: *Hear, ye deaf, and, ye blind, behold.*[93] What used to appear on the outside as order, was nothing but an invasion of disorder: confusion in the principles of moral life. These principles, once divorced from the majesty of the divine law, have tainted every field of human activity.

1434. But let us leave the past and turn our eyes toward that future which, according to the promises of the powerful ones of this world, is to consist, once the bloody conflicts of to-day have ceased, in a new order founded on justice and on prosperity. Will that future be really different; above all, will it be better? Will treaties of peace, will the new international order at the end of this war be animated by justice and by equity toward all, by that spirit which frees and pacifies? Or will there be a lamentable repetition of ancient and of recent errors?

1435. To hope for a decisive change exclusively from the shock of war and its final issue is idle, as experience shows. The hour of victory is an hour of external triumph for the party to whom victory falls, but it is in equal measure the hour of temptation. In this hour the angel of justice strives with the demon of violence; the heart of the victor all too easily is hardened; moderation and far-seeing wisdom appear to him weakness; the excited passions of the people, often inflamed by the sacrifices and sufferings they have borne, obscure the vision even of responsible persons and make them inattentive to the warning voice of humanity and equity, which is overwhelmed or drowned in the inhuman cry, *"Vae victis, Woe to the conquered."* There is danger lest settlements and decisions born in such conditions be nothing else than injustice under the cloak of justice. No, Venerable Brethren, safety does not come to peoples from external means, from the sword, which can impose

___
[93] *Isaias,* XLII, 18.

conditions of peace but does not create peace. Forces that are to renew the face of the earth should proceed from within, from the spirit.

1436. Once the bitterness and the cruel strifes of the present have ceased, the new order of the world, of national and international life, must rest no longer on the quicksands of changeable and ephemeral standards that depend only on the selfish interests of groups and individuals. No, it must rest on the unshakable foundation, on the solid rock of natural law and of Divine Revelation. There the human legislator must attain to that balance, that keen sense of moral responsibility, without which it is easy to mistake the boundary between the legitimate use and the abuse of power. Thus only will his decisions have internal consistency, noble dignity and religious sanction, and be immune from selfishness and passion.

1437. For true though it is that the evils from which mankind suffers to-day come in part from economic instability and from the struggle of interests regarding a more equal distribution of the goods which God has given man as a means of sustenance and progress, it is not less true that their root is deeper and more intrinsic, belonging to the sphere of religious belief and moral convictions which have been perverted by the progressive alienation of the peoples from that unity of doctrine, faith, customs and morals which once was promoted by the tireless and beneficent work of the Church. If it is to have any effect, the re-education of mankind must be, above all things, spiritual and religious. Hence, it must proceed from Christ as from its indispensable foundation; must be actuated by justice and crowned by charity.

1438. The accomplishment of this task of regeneration, by adapting her means to the altered conditions of the times and to the new needs of the human race, is an essential and maternal office of the Church. Committed to her by her Divine Founder, the preaching of the Gospel, by which are inculcated to men truth, justice and charity, and the endeavor to implant its precepts solidly in mind and conscience, are the most noble and most fruitful works for peace. That mission would seem as if it ought to discourage by its very grandeur the hearts of those who make up the Church Militant. But that co-operation in the spread of the Kingdom of God which in every century is effected in different ways, with varying instruments, with manifold hard struggles, is a duty incumbent on everyone who has been snatched by Divine Grace from the slavery of Satan and called in Baptism to citizenship of the Kingdom of God.

1439. And if belonging to it, living according to its spirit, laboring for its increase and placing its benefits at the disposition of that portion of mankind also which as yet has no part in them, mean in our days having to face obstacles and oppositions as vast and deep and minutely organized as never before, that fact does not dispense a man from the frank, bold profession of our Faith. Rather, it spurs one to stand fast in the conflict even at the price of the greatest sacrifices. Whoever lives by the spirit of Christ refuses to let himself be beaten down by the difficulties which oppose him, but on the contrary feels himself impelled to work with all his strength and with the fullest confidence in God. He does not draw back before the straits and the necessities of the moment but faces their severity ready to give aid with that love which flies no sacrifice, is stronger than death, and will not be quenched by the rushing waters of tribulation.

1440. It gives Us, Venerable Brethren, an inward strength, a heavenly joy, for which We daily render to God Our deep and humble thanks, to see in every region of the Catholic world evident signs of a spirit which boldly faces the gigantic tasks of our age, which with generous decision is intent on uniting in fruitful harmony the first and essential duty of individual sanctification, with Apostolic activity for the spread of the Kingdom of God. From the movement of the Eucharistic Congresses furthered with loving care by Our Predecessors and from the collaboration of the laity formed in Catholic Action toward a deep realization of their noble mission, flow forth fountains of grace and reserves of strength, which could hardly be sufficiently prized in the present time, when threats are more numerous, needs multiply and the conflict between Christianity and anti-Christianism grows intense.

1441. At a moment when one is forced to note with sorrow the disproportion between the number of priests and the calls upon them, when one sees that even to-day the words of Our Saviour apply: *The harvest indeed is great, but the laborers are few*,[94] the collaboration of the laity in the apostolate of the hierarchy, a col-

---

[94] *Matthew*, IX, 37; *Luke*, X, 2.

laboration indeed given by many and animated with ardent zeal and generous self-devotion, stands out as a precious aid to the work of priests and shows possibilities of development which justify the brightest hopes. The prayer of the Church to the Lord of the Harvest that He send workers into His vineyard[95] has been granted to a degree proportionate to the present needs, and in a manner which supplements and completes the powers, often obstructed and inadequate, of the priestly apostolate. Numbers of fervent men and women, of youth obedient to the voice of the Supreme Pastor and to the directions of their bishops, consecrate themselves with the full ardor of their souls to the works of the apostolate in order to bring back to Christ the masses of peoples who have been separated from Him. To them in this moment so critical for the Church and for mankind go out Our paternal greeting, Our deepfelt gratitude, Our confident hope. These have truly placed their lives and their work beneath the standard of Christ the King; and they can say with the Psalmist: *I speak my works to the King.*[96] *Thy Kingdom come* is not simply the burning desire of their prayers; it is, besides, the guide of their activity.

1442. This collaboration of the laity with the priesthood in all classes, categories and groups reveals precious industry, and to the laity is entrusted a mission than which noble and loyal hearts could desire none higher nor more consoling. This Apostolic work, carried out according to the mind of the Church, consecrates the layman as a kind of "Minister to Christ" in the sense which St. Augustine explains as follows: "When, brethren, you hear Our Lord saying: *Where I am, there, too, will My servant be,* do not think solely of good bishops and clerics. You, too, in your way minister to Christ by a good life, by almsgiving, by preaching His Name and teaching whom you can. Thus every father should recognize that it is under this title that he owes paternal affection to his family. Let it be for the sake of Christ and for life everlasting, that he admonishes all his household, teaches, exhorts, reproves, shows kindness, corrects; and thus in his own home he will fulfill an ecclesiastical and, in a way, an episcopal office, ministering to Christ, that he may be forever with Him." [97]

[95] Cf. *Matthew*, IX, 37; *Luke*, X, 2.
[96] *Psalms*, XLIV, 2.
[97] *On the Gospel according to St. John,* tract 51, n. 13, in Migne, *P.L.,* v. 35, c. 1768.

1443. In promoting this participation by the laity in the apostolate, which is so important in our times, the family has a special mission, for it is the spirit of the family that exercises the most powerful influence on that of the rising generation. As long as the sacred flame of the Faith burns on the domestic hearth, and the parents forge and fashion the lives of their children in accordance with this Faith, youth will be ever ready to acknowledge the royal prerogatives of the Redeemer, and to oppose those who wish to exclude Him from society or wrongly to usurp His rights. When churches are closed, when the Image of the Crucified is taken from the schools, the family remains the providential and, in a certain sense, impregnable refuge of Christian life. And We give thanks to God as We see that numberless families accomplish this, their mission, with a fidelity undismayed by combat or by sacrifice. A great host of young men and women, even in those regions where faith in Christ means suffering and persecution, remain firm around the Throne of the Redeemer with a quiet, steady determination that recalls the most glorious days of the Church's struggles.

1444. What torrents of benefits would be showered on the world; what light, what order, what peace would accrue to social life; what unique and precious energies would contribute toward the betterment of mankind, if men would everywhere concede to the Church, teacher of justice and love, that liberty of action to which, in virtue of the divine mandate, she has a sacred and indisputable right! What calamities could be averted, what happiness and tranquillity assured, if the social and international forces working to establish peace would let themselves be permeated by the deep lessons of the Gospel of Love in their struggle against individual or collective egoism! There is no opposition between the laws that govern the life of faithful Christians and the postulates of a genuine brotherly humanitarianism, but rather unity and mutual support. In the interests of suffering mankind, shaken to the depth both materially and spiritually, We have no more ardent desire than this: that the present difficulties may open the eyes of many to see Our Lord Jesus Christ and the mission of His Church on this earth in their true light, and that all those who are in power may decide to allow the Church a free course to work for the formation of the rising generation according to the principles of justice and peace.

1445. This work of pacification presupposes that obstacles are not put to the exercise of the mission which God has entrusted to His Church; that the field of this activity is not restricted, and that the masses, and especially youth, are not withdrawn from her beneficent influence. Accordingly, We, as representative on earth of Him Who was proclaimed by the Prophet, *Prince of Peace*,[98] appeal to the rulers of the peoples, and to those who can in any way influence public life, to let the Church have full liberty to fulfill her role as educator by teaching men truth, by inculcating justice, and by inflaming hearts with the Divine Love of Christ.

1446. While the Church cannot renounce the exercise of this, her mission, which has for its final end to realize here below the divine plan and to *re-establish all things in Christ, that are in heaven and on earth*,[99] her aid, nonetheless, is shown to be indispensable as never before, now that sad experience teaches that external means and human provisions and political expedients of themselves bring no efficacious healing to the ills which afflict mankind. Taught precisely by the sad failure of human expedients to avert the tempests that threaten to sweep civilization away, many turn their gaze with renewed hope to the Church, the rock of truth and of charity, to that Chair of Peter from which, they feel, can be restored to mankind that unity of religious teaching and of the moral code which of old gave consistency to pacific international relations. Unity, toward which so many, answerable for the destiny of nations, look with regretful yearning as they experience from day to day the vanity of the very means in which once they had placed their trust! Unity, the desire of those many legions of Our sons who daily call upon *the God of peace and of love!*[100] Unity, the hope of so many noble minds separated from Us, who yet in their hunger and thirst for justice and peace turn their eyes to the See of Peter and from it await guidance and counsel!

1447. These last are recognizing in the Catholic Church principles of belief and life that have stood the test of two thousand years and the strong cohesion of the ecclesiastical hierarchy, which in union with the Successor of Peter spends itself in enlightening minds with the teaching of the Gospel, in guiding and sanctifying men, and which is generous in its maternal condescension toward

[98] *Isaias*, IX, 6.
[99] *Ephesians*, I, 10.
[100] II *Corinthians*, XIII, 11.

all, but firm when, even at the cost of torments or martyrdom, it
has to say: *"Non licet;* It is not allowed!"

1448.   And yet, Venerable Brethren, the teaching of Christ, which
alone can furnish man with such solid bases of belief as will greatly
enlarge his vision, divinely dilate his heart and apply an efficacious remedy to the very grave difficulties of to-day—this and the
activity of the Church in teaching and spreading that doctrine, and
in forming and modeling men's minds by its precepts, are at times
an object of suspicion, as if they shook the foundations of civil authority or usurped its rights. Against such suspicions We solemnly
declare with Apostolic sincerity that—without prejudice to the
declarations, regarding the power of Christ and of His Church,
made by Our Predecessor, Pius XI, of venerable memory, in his
Encyclical *Quas Primas* of December 11, 1925[101]—any such aims are
entirely alien to that same Church, which spreads its maternal arms
toward this world not to dominate but to serve. She does not claim
to take the place of other legitimate authorities in their proper
spheres, but offers them her help after the example and in the spirit
of her Divine Founder Who *went about doing good.*[102]

1449.   The Church preaches and inculcates obedience and respect for earthly authority which derives from God its whole origin
and holds to the teaching of her Divine Master Who said: *Render,
therefore, to Caesar the things that are Caesar's*[103]; she has no desire
to usurp, and sings in the liturgy: "He takes away no earthly realms
who gives us the celestial." [104] She does not suppress human energies
but lifts them up to all that is noble and generous and forms characters which do not compromise with conscience. Nor has she who
civilizes the nations ever retarded the civil progress of mankind, at
which on the contrary she is pleased and glad with a mother's pride.
The end of her activity was admirably expressed by the Angels over
the cradle of the Word Incarnate, when they sang of glory to God
and announced peace to men of good-will: *Glory to God in the
highest; and on earth peace to men of good-will.*[105] This peace,
which the world cannot give, has been left as a heritage to His
disciples by the Divine Redeemer Himself: *Peace I leave with you,*

[101] *Cf. supra* nn. 862-865.
[102] *Acts,* X, 38.
[103] *Matthew,* XXII, 21.
[104] Hymn for the Feast of Epiphany.
[105] *Luke,* II, 14.

My peace I give unto you[106]; and thus following the sublime teaching of Christ, summed up by Him in the two-fold precept of love of God and of the neighbor, millions of souls have reached, are reaching, and will reach peace.

1450. History, wisely called by a great Roman, "The Teacher of Life," has proved for close on two thousand years how true is the word of Scripture that he will not have peace who resists God.[107] For Christ alone is the *cornerstone*[108] on which man and society can find stability and salvation. On this Cornerstone the Church is built, and, hence, against her the adversaries can never prevail: *the gates of hell shall not prevail,*[109] nor can they ever weaken her; nay, rather, internal and external struggles tend to augment the force and multiply the laurels of her glorious victories. On the other hand, any other building which has not been founded solidly on the teaching of Christ rests on shifting sands and is destined to perish miserably.[110]

1451. Venerable Brethren, the hour when this, Our first Encyclical, reaches you is in many respects a real *hour of darkness,*[111] in which the spirit of violence and of discord brings indescribable suffering on mankind. Do We need to give assurance that Our paternal heart is close to all Our children in compassionate love, and especially to the afflicted, the oppressed, the persecuted? The nations swept into the tragic whirlpool of war are perhaps as yet only at the *beginnings of sorrows,*[112] but even now there reign in thousands of families death and desolation, lamentation and misery. The blood of countless human beings, even non-combatants, raises a piteous dirge over a nation such as Our dear Poland, which, for its fidelity to the Church, for its services in the defense of Christian civilization, written in indelible characters in the annals of history, has a right to the generous and brotherly sympathy of the whole world, while it awaits, relying on the powerful intercession of Mary, Help of Christians, the hour of a resurrection in harmony with the principles of justice and true peace.

1452. What has already happened and is still happening was

[106] *John,* XIV, 27.
[107] *Cf. Job,* IX, 4.
[108] *Ephesians,* II, 20.
[109] *Matthew,* XVI, 18.
[110] *Cf. Matthew,* VII, 26-27.
[111] *Cf. Luke,* XXII, 53.
[112] *Matthew,* XXIV, 8.

presented, as it were, in a vision before Our eyes, when, while still some hope was left, We left nothing undone in the form suggested to Us by Our Apostolic Office and by the means at Our disposal, to prevent recourse to arms and to keep open the way to an understanding honorable to both parties. Convinced that the use of force on one side would be answered by recourse to arms on the other, We considered it a duty inseparable from Our Apostolic Office and one of Christian charity to try every means to spare mankind and Christianity the horrors of a world conflagration, even at the risk of having Our intentions and Our aims misunderstood. Our advice, if heard with respect, was not, however, followed, and while Our pastoral heart looks on with sorrow and foreboding, the image of the Good Shepherd comes up before Our gaze, and it seems as though We ought to repeat to the world in His name: *If thou . . . hadst known . . . the things that are to thy peace; but now they are hidden from thy eyes.*[113]

1453. In the midst of this world which to-day presents such a sharp contrast to "The Peace of Christ in the Reign of Christ," the Church and her faithful are in times and in years of trial such as have rarely been known in her history of struggle and suffering. But in such times, especially, he who remains firm in his faith and strong at heart knows that Christ the King is never so near as in the hour of trial, which is the hour for fidelity. With a heart torn by the sufferings and afflictions of so many of her sons, but with the courage and the stability that come from the promises of Our Lord, the Spouse of Christ goes to meet the gathering storms. This she knows, that the truth which she preaches, the charity which she teaches and practices, will be the indispensable counsellors and aids to men of good-will in the reconstruction of a new world based on justice and love, when mankind, weary from its course along the way of error, has tasted the bitter fruits of hate and violence.

1454. In the meantime, however, Venerable Brethren, the world and all those who are stricken by the calamity of the war must know that the obligation of Christian love, the very foundation of the Kingdom of Christ, is not an empty word, but a living reality. A vast field opens up for Christian Charity in all its forms. We have full confidence that all Our sons, especially those who are not being tried by the scourge of war, will be mindful in imitation of

[113] *Luke,* XIX, 42.

the Divine Samaritan, of all those, who, as victims of the war, have a right to compassion and help.

1455. The "Catholic Church, the City of God, whose King is Truth, whose law love and whose measure eternity," [114] preaching fearlessly the whole truth of Christ and toiling as the love of Christ demands with the zeal of a mother, stands as a blessed vision of peace above the storm of error and passion awaiting the moment when the all-powerful Hand of Christ the King shall quiet the tempest and banish the spirits of discord which have provoked it.

1456. Whatever We can do to hasten the day when the dove of peace may find on this earth, submerged in a deluge of discord, somewhere to alight, We shall not omit to do, trusting in those statesmen who, before the outbreak of war, nobly toiled to avert such a scourge from the peoples; trusting in the millions of souls of all countries and of every sphere, who call not for justice alone but for love and mercy; above all, trusting in God Almighty to Whom We daily address the prayer: *in the shadow of Thy wings will I hope, until iniquity pass away.* [115]

1457. God can do all things. As well as the happiness and the fortunes of nations, He holds in His Hands human counsels and sweetly turns them in whatever direction He wills: even the obstacles are for His Omnipotence means to mould affairs and events and to direct minds and free wills to His all-high purposes.

1458. Pray, then, Venerable Brethren, pray without ceasing; pray especially when you offer the Divine Sacrifice of Love. Do you, too, pray, you whose courageous profession of the faith entails to-day hard, painful and, not rarely, heroic sacrifices; pray, you suffering and agonizing members of the Church, when Jesus comes to console and to heal your pains, and do not forget with the aid of a true spirit of mortification and worthy practice of penance to make your prayers more acceptable in the eyes of Him Who *lifteth up all that fall: and setteth up all that are cast down,* [116] that He in His mercy may shorten the days of trial and that thus the words of the Psalmist may be verified: *Then they cried to the Lord in their affliction: and He delivered them out of their distresses.* [117] . . . . . .

---

[114] St. Augustine, *Ep.* CXXXVIII, *ad Marcellinum,* c. 3, n. 17, in Migne, *P.L.,* v. 33, c. 533.
[115] *Psalms,* LVI, 2.
[116] *Psalms,* CXLIV, 14.
[117] *Psalms,* CVI, 13.

ADDRESS *La Devota Accoglienza* TO A GROUP FROM CASTEL GANDOLFO.[118]

> *The world needs that peace which is ordered harmony among men.*

October 22, 1939

1459. . . . . . . Here is peace; the countryside is peaceful, the sky of Italy is peaceful, and peaceful is the lake which We view nearby. But far away We see the restless waves of the sea reflect the rays of the sun, waves which are images of the tribulation of human passions let loose in Europe and the world. The world is without peace. The world has need of peace, not of that peace which is not peace—*peace, peace and there was no peace*[119]—but of that peace of which St. Augustine says, "peace which is ordered harmony among men"[120]—that peace which the new-born Redeemer brought to men of good-will, subduers and dominators of themselves living together. In the present hour of storm and tempest among nations, the dawn of peace which the Church of Christ invokes from God in the Litany of the Saints is "that Thou mayest give peace and true concord to Christian kings and princes; that Thou mayest give peace and unity to the entire Christian people." . . . . . .

HOMILY *Audistis, Venerabiles Fratres* AT THE CONSECRATION OF TWELVE MISSIONARY BISHOPS.[121]

> *Peace and prosperity are the rewards of nations which establish laws inspired by the doctrine of the Gospel.*

October 29, 1939

1460. . . . . . . Blessed the families over whom the most just scepter of Christ the King rules! In fact, these are cemented by a reciprocal love, are reinforced by an admirable order, enjoy peace and prosperity, and are gladdened with numerous progeny on

---

[118] Translation from *Pius XII and Peace*, p. 30. Original Italian, *Discorsi e Radiomessaggi*, v. 1, p. 346.
[119] *Jeremias*, VI, 14.
[120] *De Civitate Dei*, bk. XIX, c. 13.
[121] Translation from *Pius XII and Peace*, pp. 31-33. Original Latin, *A.A.S.*, v. 31, pp. 596-598 (November 10, 1939).

whom repose the best hopes of the country, and in whom again
live the examples of the virtue of the fathers, in constant imitation.
Most happy, then, are those States that establish laws inspired by the
doctrine of the Gospel, and do not refuse to render public homage
to the majesty of Christ, the King. In these nations, in fact, the
interests and mutual relations of the citizens are harmonized according to the rules of morals and of justice; in them tyranny is
not known, nor is respect lacking toward the authorities; nor is
that just liberty lacking which is due to the dignity of the human
person. In these States, finally, in virtue of concord, their power
grows and they accomplish great undertakings and every good thing
receives an ever greater development.

1461. If, therefore, recognizing the regal dignity of Christ, and
willingly actuating the precepts either in public or in private life,
bring many and such great benefits to each citizen, it is absolutely
necessary, Venerable Brothers and Beloved Sons, that all those who
glory in the name of Christian strive according to their own possibilities to bring their contribution to this most important purpose.
And that especially in our days, when men, too often absorbed in
the covetous search for earthly things, are distracted from the
heavenly good; so that "the kingdom of truth and of life, the kingdom of holiness and of grace, the kingdom of justice, of love and
of peace" [122] is either neglected and forgotten or quite unhappily
repulsed. If with paternal soul We exhort all present to actuate
these holy resolutions, We especially exhort you, whom to-day, here
in the majesty of the Vatican Basilica, at the Tomb of the Prince of
the Apostles, We have raised to the episcopal dignity. As one day,
the Divine Redeemer sent forth a small band of Apostles without
any human means to conquer the whole world, not with the force
of arms, but with the power of truth and charity, so We, to-day—
as We are on earth in His stead—send forth you, the twelve heralds
of the Divine Word. Upheld not by your own force or that of
others, but trusting solely in that divine grace that transforms souls,
you must, at the cost of whatever sacrifice, render so many nations
—far removed in space but so near Our heart—participants of the
evangelic doctrine and of Christian civilization.

1462. The magnificent spectacle of the happy event of to-day
rises up before Our mind and strongly moves Our soul and raises

[122] Preface from the Mass of Christ the King.

the hope of abundant future fruits. Whilst in fact, with the passing of years and with the alternate vicissitudes of events, innumerable things rise, grow and fall, and then, changed and renewed again, emerge or, quite consumed, precipitate and perish, the Catholic Church instead is not shaken by the waves of time, is not overcome by difficulties, is not changed by pressing vicissitudes. Instead, the Church advances with firm and sure step, and still to-day, through her vocation and divine mission, accomplishes for the good of mankind what she already accomplished twenty centuries ago. And while the desires for earthly things, the internal hatreds and jealousies too often split and divide the souls of men, the Church of God, beloved mother of all peoples, embraces with immense charity the whole human family, without distinction of race or rank, and provides, either with prayer or with external works, for the salvation and the true felicity of all. . . . . . .

ENCYCLICAL *Sertum Laetitiae* TO THE BISHOPS OF THE UNITED STATES ON THE ONE HUNDRED AND FIFTIETH ANNIVERSARY OF THE ESTABLISHMENT OF THE HIERARCHY.[123]

Contempt for the commandments of God is the basis of modern evils.

November 1, 1939

1463. . . . . . . Not with the conquest of material space does one approach to God, separation from Whom is death, conversion to Whom is life, to be established in Whom is glory; but under the guidance of Christ, with the fullness of sincere faith, with unsullied conscience and upright will, with holy works, with the achievement and the employment of that genuine liberty whose sacred rules are found proclaimed in the Gospel. If, instead, the commandments of God are spurned, not only is it impossible to attain that happiness which has place beyond the brief span of time which is allotted to earthly existence, but the very basis upon which rests true civilization is shaken, and naught is to be expected but ruins over which belated tears must be shed; for the same means which lead to the attainment of the Eternal assure also to tem-

---

[123] Official English translation, *A.A.S.*, v. 31, pp. 649-655 (November 25, 1939). Original Latin, *A.A.S.*, v. 31, pp. 639-644 (November 25, 1939).

poral goods their stability and safe keeping. How in fact can the public weal and the glory of civilized life have any guarantee of stability when right is subverted and virtue despised and derided? Is not God the source and the giver of law? Is He not the inspiration and the reward of virtue, with none like unto Him among lawgivers? [124] This according to the admission of all reasonable men is everywhere the bitter and prolific root of evils: the refusal to recognize the divine Majesty, the neglect of the moral law whose origin is from heaven, or that regrettable inconstancy which makes its victims waver between the lawful and the forbidden, between justice and iniquity. Thence arise immoderate and blind egoism, the thirst for pleasure, the vice of drunkenness, immodest and costly styles in dress, the prevalence of crime even among minors, the lust for power, neglect of the poor, base craving for ill-gotten wealth, the flight from the land, levity in entering into marriage, divorce, the break-up of the family, the cooling of mutual affection between parents and children, birth control, the enfeeblement of the race, the weakening of respect for authority, or obsequiousness, or rebellion, neglect of duty towards one's country and towards mankind. We raise Our voice in strong albeit paternal complaint, that in so many schools of your land Christ is often despised or ignored, the explanation of the universe and mankind is forced within the narrow limits of materialism or of rationalism, and new educational systems are sought after which cannot but produce a sorrowful harvest in the intellectual and moral life of the nation. . . . . . .

1464. We desire to touch upon another question of weighty importance, the social question, which, remaining unsolved, has been agitating States for a long time and sowing among the classes the seeds of hatred and mutual hostility. You know full well what aspect it assumes in America, what acrimonies, what disorders it produces. It is not necessary, therefore, that we dwell on these points. The fundamental point of the social question is this, that the goods created by God for all men should in the same way reach all, justice guiding and charity helping. The history of every age teaches that there were always rich and poor; that it will always be so, we may gather from the unchanging tenor of human destinies. Worthy of honor are the poor who fear God because theirs is the kingdom of Heaven and because they readily abound in spir-

[124] Cf. Job, XXXVI, 22.

itual graces. But the rich, if they are upright and honest, are God's dispensers and providers of this world's goods. As ministers of Divine Providence they assist the indigent, through whom they often receive gifts for the soul and whose hand—so they may hope —will lead them into the eternal tabernacles. God, Who provides for all with counsels of supreme bounty, has ordained that for the exercise of virtue and for the testing of one's worth there be in the world rich and poor; but He does not wish that some have exaggerated riches while others are in such straits that they lack the bare necessities of life. But a kindly mother of virtue is honest poverty which gains its living by daily labor in accordance with the scriptural saying: *Give me not (O God) mendicancy or opulence, but provide me only with what is necessary for my sustenance.*[125]

1465. Now if the rich and the prosperous are obliged, out of ordinary motives of pity to act generously toward the poor, their obligation is all the greater to do them justice. The salaries of the workers, as is just, are to be such that they are sufficient to maintain them and their families. Solemn are the words of Our Predecessor, Pius XI, on this question: "Every effort must, therefore, be made that fathers of families receive a wage sufficient to meet adequately normal domestic needs. If under present circumstances this is not always feasible, social justice demands that reforms be introduced without delay which will guarantee such a wage to every adult workingman. In this connection We praise those who have most prudently and usefully attempted various methods by which an increased wage is paid in view of increased family burdens and special provision made for special needs."[126]

1466. May it also be brought about that each and every able-bodied man may receive an equal opportunity for work in order to earn the daily bread for himself and his own. We deeply lament the lot of those—and their number in the United States is large indeed—who, though robust, capable and willing, cannot have the work for which they are anxiously searching. May the wisdom of the governing powers, a far-seeing generosity on the part of the employers, together with the speedy re-establishment of more favorable conditions, effect the realization of these reasonable hopes to the advantage of all.

[125] *Proverbs*, XXX, 8.
[126] *Quadragesimo Anno*, May 15, 1931; cf. *supra* n. 984.

1467. Because sociability is one of man's natural requirements and since it is legitimate to promote by common effort, decent livelihood, it is not possible without injustice to deny or to limit either to the producers or to the laboring and farming classes, the free faculty of uniting in associations by means of which they may defend their proper rights and secure the betterment of the goods of soul and of body, as well as the honest comforts of life. But to unions of this kind, which in past centuries have procured immortal glory for Christianity, and for the professions an untarnishable splendor, one cannot everywhere impose an identical discipline and structure which, therefore, can be varied to meet the different temperaments of the people and the diverse circumstances of time. But let the unions in question draw their vital force from principles of wholesome liberty. Let them take their form from the lofty rules of justice and of honesty; and, conforming themselves to those norms, let them act in such a manner that in their care for the interests of their class they violate no one's rights; let them continue to strive for harmony and respect the commonweal of civil society.

1468. It is a source of joy to Us to know that the above-cited Encyclical, *Quadragesimo Anno,* as well as that of the Sovereign Pontiff, Leo XIII, *Rerum Novarum,*[127] in which is indicated the solution of the social question in accordance with the postulates of the Gospel and of the eternal philosophy, are the object, in the United States, of careful and prolonged consideration on the part of some men of keener intellect whose generous wish pushes them on toward social restoration and the restrengthening of the bonds of love amongst men, and that some employers themselves have desired to settle the ever-recurring controversies with the workingman in accordance with the norms of these encyclicals, respecting always the common good and the dignity of the human person. What a proud vaunt it will be for the American people, by nature inclined to grandiose undertakings and to liberality, if they untie the knotty and difficult social question by following the sure paths illuminated by the light of the Gospel, and thus lay the basis of a happier age. . . . . . .

---

[127] May 15, 1891; *cf. supra* nn. 118-175.

Response *D'une Nation Lointaine* to the homage of the
new Minister of Haiti, Nicolas Léger.[128]

*To have peace men must renounce the cult of might
employed against right.*

November 10, 1939

1469. . . . . . . The joy We feel in welcoming you is a sad contrast to happenings outside, a universal source of worry, the economic consequences of which are felt beyond continents and seas.
The unity of the great human family, above all of the faithful in
Christ, imposes on those peoples happily preserved from war the
obligation to interest themselves in those who suffer and to multiply
their appeals to the mercy of God, so that His omnipotent Hand
may restore order and peace to the world.

1470. But as We have often said, the world will enjoy peace
and order, which is its indispensable condition, only if men responsible for the government of peoples and their reciprocal relations
renounce the cult of might employed against right; if, recognizing
that morality with a purely human basis is insufficient, they accept
the supreme authority of the Creator as the basis of all individual
and collective morality, and if they render to the Father in heaven
the homage wished by Him of fraternal concord among His children of all countries and languages. Then only will they succeed in
effectuating and perfecting a stable, fruitful international organization such as is desired by men of good-will, an organization which,
respecting the rights of God, will be able to assure the reciprocal
independence of nations big and small, to impose fidelity to agreements loyally agreed upon, and to safeguard the sound liberty and
dignity of the human person in each one's efforts toward the
prosperity of all. . . . . . .

---

[128] Translation from *Pius XII and Peace*, pp. 33-34. Original French, *A.A.S.*, v. 31,
p. 675 (November 25, 1939).

RADIO ADDRESS *It Is from a Heart* TO THE CATHOLICS OF THE
UNITED STATES ON THE FIFTIETH ANNIVERSARY OF THE CATH-
OLIC UNIVERSITY OF AMERICA.[129]

Naturalism and materialism are plunging nations into war.

November 13, 1939

1471. . . . . . . The Christian education of youth was never of
more decisive or vital importance than it is to-day, when We are
faced with the bewildering errors of a naturalism and a materialism
which are plunging the world into war—evidence in themselves of
the hollowness of a philosophy built on purely human standards.
As We see these calamities multiply and intensify, We might
well lose heart, were We not sustained by trust in the loving Providence of God which gives strength and solace more abundantly as
worldly confidence fails.

1472. But Our chief hope, after God, rests in the schools of
Christian culture, old and new, among which stands your Catholic
University as a typical example, assigning in its zeal for truth the
correct place in its programs to natural science and metaphysics,
mind and heart, past and present, reason and Revelation. Thus, in
the austere retirement of your halls, alternating reflection and study
with prayer, you will continue to train the young men of tomorrow
to face false teaching and evil consequences as intrepid champions
of those fundamentals of civilization which, enshrined in the Gospel
of Christ and taught by the Church, are spirit and life. . . . . . .

MESSAGE TO KING LEOPOLD OF BELGIUM.[130]

*The attempt to restore peace made by King Leopold of
Belgium and Queen Wilhelmina of Holland is praised.*

November 14, 1939

1473. . . . Highly appreciate noble sentiments that inspired message of Your Majesty and of Queen of Low Countries and We shall
pray to the Lord, Who holds hearts in His Hands and directs human events, so that in His Mercy He may open ways to real, durable peace. . . .

[129] Original English, *A.A.S.*, v. 31, p. 677 (November 25, 1939).
[130] English translation, *Pius XII and Peace*, p. 34. We have been unable to locate the
original text.

Address *Plusquam Decem Saecula* to the National Croat
Pilgrimage.[131]

*Friendly relations between Church and State contribute
to public peace and prosperity.*

November 15, 1939

1474. . . . . . . The Christian faith and loyalty to the Vicar of
Christ are the foundation and the source of life, of social action and
charity, of every form of sanctity. Make the most of your ecclesiastical institutions and organizations, chiefly of Catholic Action, to let
the Christian Faith radiate to every corner of public life, encouraged
by the thought that in your country friendly relations between
Church and State can only contribute to public peace and prosperity. On these assumptions, We beg of you first to cultivate holiness in private life. Daily prayer, family devotions before the cruci-
fix, open the heart to God's law and Christian perfection; simplicity
of life *in all piety and purity,*[132] a closer union with the Divine
Redeemer in the Blessed Sacrament, and a deep devotion to Our
Lady, will attune your words and actions to your faith. Bring up
and educate your youth in godliness and modesty, and preserve the
Catholic spirit in their readings and their amusements. Domestic
peace and public happiness are possible only on these conditions. . . . . . .

Letter *Comme Vous* to Cardinal Suhard, Archbishop of
Rheims.[133]

*Only a return to Christian morality is capable of stop-
ping the world in its descent toward an abyss of
calamities.*

November 21, 1939

1475. . . . Because We were afflicted and frightened at seeing
spread more widely each day among nations, doctrines and manners
contrary to the sovereign rights of God and to the great law of

---

131 Translation from *The Tablet,* v. 174, p. 607 (November 25, 1939). Original Latin,
    Discorsi e Radiomessaggi, v. 1, pp. 386-387.
132 I *Timothy,* II, 2.
133 Translation from *Pius XII and Peace,* p. 48. Original French, *Documentation
    Catholique,* v. 41, c. 121 (February 5, 1940).

Christian charity, We wished to bring into the light, so that they might be restored to honor, the simple but sublime lessons of the Decalogue and the Gospels. For We believe, in accordance with the teaching of the Church and the testimony of history, that only a return to a fundamentally Christian morality is still capable of stopping the world in its descent toward an abyss of calamities. . . .

1476. It is especially agreeable to Us to find in the faithful people, with a total and filial adherence of spirit, a generous disposition of hearts to walk resolutely in the ways that We have traced. Furthermore, We have the satisfaction of learning that multitudes of just souls, even those foreign to the Catholic Faith, spontaneously render homage to the loyalty of Our intentions and the sincerity of Our efforts with a view to universal appeasement. . . . . . . We think that the French have good reason to rejoice at seeing affirmed in the Encyclical certain principles that are legitimately dear to them; and at seeing reproved certain ideas that they reprove, and blamed, certain procedures which they condemn as the principal source of the present evils. . . . . . .

RESPONSE *La Solenne Presentazione* TO THE HOMAGE OF THE NEW ITALIAN AMBASSADOR, DINO ALFIERI.[134]

Pius XII hopes that his efforts for peace may find a sympathetic welcome in the hearts of the Italian people.

December 7, 1939

1477. . . . . . . In these times, as your honorable mission is beginning, the Holy See's work in favor of peace and international concord, which We look upon as a duty, seems to be as thorny as it is difficult. It is so difficult, because the fundamental conceptions of justice and love, which make for individual happiness and the nobility of common social life, have in many respects fallen into oblivion or contempt by a false process of thought and action which humanizes what is divine and divinizes what is human. This oblivion and contempt reveal themselves in some cases to an alarming extent. This faulty development, nay, this inversion of the principles of justice and moral duties, was intended to substitute for the

---

[134] Translation from *The Tablet*, v. 174, p. 724 (December 23, 1939). Original Italian, *A.A.S.*, v. 31, pp. 705-706 (December 22, 1939).

Christian conception of life of the community and the State, doctrines and practices of a disruptive and destructive character that find civic and human progress in the severance of natural law from the divine Revelation and its radiance over the world from the sacred city of Rome. Each of these errors, like all errors, has its own stages of development: a stage of growth and decadence, its peak and its hurried twilight, when the intoxicating poison of seductive doctrines drugs and subdues the masses, under the very eyes of men more balanced and thoughtful, who now are terrified by the false expectations and promises that allured them into error. How many eyes, blinded so far, are beginning to see the light!

1478. But in a special manner the praise manifested by Your Excellency with such high sentiments for the fundamental thoughts in Our recent Encyclical,[135] on the tranquil and fraternal union of souls and on peace based on justice, gives rise to the joyful hope that the efforts of the Holy See in favor of peace may find a sympathetic echo in the brave, strong and active Italian people. The wisdom of its rulers and its own instinctive inclination have fortunately saved it so far from war and placed it in the most favorable position to contribute to the creation and the restoration of a genuine peace founded on the noble principles of justice and humanity. . . . . . .

EXHORTATION *Asperis Commoti Anxietatibus* TO PRIESTS AND CLERICS WHO HAVE JOINED THE ARMED FORCES.[136]

The chaplain must preach Christianity to the army by his example.

December 8, 1939

1479. Among the poignant anxieties that weigh upon Our mind owing to the raging of a war which We tried by every means, though in vain, to avert, there is one that affects Us especially— that painful situation, which has forcibly and suddenly removed

---

[135] *Summi Pontificatus,* October 20, 1939; *cf. supra* nn. 1393-1458.
[136] Translation from *The Catholic Mind,* v. 38, pp. 9-17 (January 8, 1940). Original Latin, *A.A.S.,* v. 31, pp. 696-701 (December 22, 1939). Reading this document one must bear in mind that in some European countries, notably France, priests and clerics were called into the regular army to serve not as chaplains but as ordinary soldiers.

you, beloved priests and clerics, far from your field of work for souls or from the quiet of your studies and set you down in a new world of camp and battles. Not accustomed to the life that you now lead, you are suddenly put to serve in barracks, in hospitals, in first-aid stations and even in the firing-line itself,—some of you as chaplains, others (and these the majority) to perform tasks far different from those to which your vocation has called you.

1480. The Military Vicars or Chief Chaplains follow you in your present life with vigilance and care; and We are reassured of their immediate and paternal assistance because of a splendid organization untiring, energetic, alert and prudent. Their efforts are precious in every way and not least in the sacrifices they involve; and inspired as they are with a very deep sense of duty, are crowned in every country with the greatest success. It is Our wish, while We bring their work to your notice and assure you of the confidence We place in it, to recommend it at the same time to your gratitude and to that spirit of willing docility on your part, that is a necessary condition for it to be effective. Moreover, that you may not be without those spiritual helps that you have need of, both for yourselves and for your work for souls, it is Our intention to grant to all the Military Vicars or Chief Chaplains of those nations or districts where the state of war or mobilization now exists or shall come to exist — without prejudice to the ordinary powers already granted — new and extraordinary powers that will be an indication to you of the loving care with which We, in Our paternal solicitude, follow you in your difficulties and trials. But the task of active assistance confided by Us to the Military Vicars or Chief Chaplains does not dispense Us from approaching you directly to open to you Our mind and to exhort you, in the extraordinary circumstances in which you are placed, to give attentive consideration to the duties imposed on you by your new conditions of life, that you may fulfill them without reserve in the spirit of your vocation.

1481. However you may have changed your dress, the spirit that is in you should not be changed. This should go with you in the midst of arms no less than in the exercise of your priesthood. He Who to-day permits that you be far from your accustomed habits of study and work, is the same Heavenly Father Who called you to the altar. . . . . . . Know how to make the best of an opportunity that will pass. Do not judge the circumstances, from which the present bitter situation has arisen, from a limited and merely human standpoint. But recognize in them the ever-loving Will of the Heavenly Father, Who can bring good out of evil, and Who from the occasion of your being called to arms wishes, even in the midst of so much ruin, to draw souls to salvation, leading them back by means of you to the paths of faith and good Christian life. There is nothing that cannot prove useful to you in this new apostolate; and the more priestly zeal one has, the more readily will one find at every turn suitable means and opportunities for good.

1482. But first and foremost, it is you yourselves, your own persons We mean, who in the midst of arms should be the living apostles of Christ. And that you will be, even without the use of words, if you do honor to your vocation above all by an exemplary fidelity to your new duties and by a thoroughly blameless conduct. The words that Saint Paul addressed to the Philippians, exhorting them to honor their Faith in the pagan environment in which they lived, We, therefore, repeat to you: *Let your conversation be worthy of the Gospel of Christ;*[137] and with him We add: *And do ye all things without murmurings and hesitations, that you may be blameless and sincere children of God, without reproof, in the midst of a crooked and perverse generation, among whom you shine as lights in the world.*[138] Let there be seen in you at all times the minister of God. This character of yours ought to make of you men of duty, models of obedience to authority without prejudice to the law of God and of readiness for sacrifice; but it ought not, nay it cannot, in any way or for any reason whatsoever, let you yield to any of the frivolous, corrupt or blameworthy influences that may be found in your environment.

1483. In the field of morals your conduct should be especially strict, without compromise, concession or weakness, that it may be at once an exhortation and an example. The strictness, which is the fitting accompaniment of that meekness of heart by which you should make yourselves all things to all men to win all to Christ, and which besides is entirely in accordance with the strict discipline of the soldier, is the real source of courage; and of courage you should be masters, asserting with a calm freedom and inde-

---

[137] *Philippians,* I, 27.
[138] *Philippians,* II, 14-15.

pendence, no matter what the circumstances, the priestly character of your vocation to the priesthood. . . . . . . Thus you will be conscious of not having betrayed your mission and of having borne good witness to Jesus Christ, your Divine Master, in the midst of the most varied society that it is possible to conceive in this world. By means of you every social class, every profession liberal or industrial, men of every sort or culture, of every type of mentality, will have heard yet once more through the roar of cannon the Gospel message of redemption; and to your account there will not be laid the sin of making your companions in arms think that, in the lives of Christ's followers and their leaders, practice does not square with preaching. You will have won for the Church respect and sympathy, and the personal friendships that you form in the worthy exercise of your military duties will be easily turned into conquests of souls, or at least will open the way to such conquests.

1484. But do not lose sight of the warning given by the Apostle to the faithful in those glorious days when the Church was on its way, the way indeed of suffering, to its triumph: *Be not overcome by evil, but overcome evil by good.*[139] You see, most dear sons, what a vast field for good Divine Providence opens up to your zeal by that very act which seems to withdraw you from your holy ministry or from the immediate preparation for it. It is a mission that ought to fill every sincere heart of priest or levite with joy, and at least diminish, if not altogether take away, the pain of the sacrifices that the exceptional conditions of to-day impose on them. Besides, is it not by sacrifice that our actions as well as our teaching become fruitful? And is it not by suffering, yes even more than by labor, that we bear witness to the Truth?

1485. Think, too, of your own personal profit, your spiritual profit, We mean. What experience helpful to your own improvement you will gain from contact with men and events in the course of the varied and painful vicissitudes of your military service! It will be precisely that kind of experience which will give maturity to your virtues and hence also to your apostolate. There will be no loss of time for you as priests, because of what seems to be nothing else than an isolated and harmful episode in your lives; no loss, indeed, if you will be wise and will walk under the eyes of God, not losing hold of His blessed Hand, which, though it lead you by

---

[139] *Romans,* XII, 21.

rugged paths, would guide you to the good and to the heights. . . .
That this is possible even in the midst of arms, you can deduce,
even apart from further proof, from a consideration of the examples
of evangelical piety that the world of arms itself has given in the
persons of so many noble Christians and saints. In circumstances
not unlike yours, they managed to live in God and by God, dominated, as they were, by this central idea rooted in their hearts: the
accomplishment in all their tasks of the will of God. To see the
will of God always, in everything and everywhere and, in spite of
the repugnances of nature, to accept it—that is what you must
strive for daily, the short road, easy and safe, to that piety which
in the midst of the present dangers is as much the bulwark of your
priestly vocation, as throughout the whole course of your life
it ought to be the unfailing fount of strength and power of all your
enterprises. . . . . . .

1486. Renew your strength, then, most dear sons, as much as
you possibly can, from this piety. If this accompanies you in the
arduous trial to which Our Lord calls you, you will pass through
it with advantage to your own souls and with abundant fruit for
the souls of your brethren, to whom there is nothing that the
minister of the Gospel should not, by his toil and suffering, be ready
to give. You will, in the eyes of the world which to-day looks on
you with a particular interest, have done honor to the Catholic
priesthood and to the Church whose responsibility in large measure
you bear. You will have deserved well of your native land itself,
for, in this hour which is so fraught with perils for its fortunes,
by your example you will have strengthened its sons and, by your
efficacious efforts to bring tranquillity to their souls, you will have
upheld their courage and increased their effectiveness. Wives and
mothers will rival each other in blessing you, because your charity
will, in a thousand ways, have consoled them in the persons of their
dear ones. You will, too, be rewarded by the approval of your own
consciences, which will bear you witness that even under present
conditions your priesthood suffered no loss but rather gained in the
deepening of its spirit, its promptness in action and its readiness
for sacrifice. . . . In the firm hope that all this may be verified in
you, We are with you, most dear sons, in Our paternal prayers for
your bodily safety, your escape from danger, your spiritual progress.
And while We beseech the Lord that He shorten for you, and for

all others, the day of trial and, with peace restored to the world, that He restore you to your peaceful abodes of pastoral work or of the training that leads to it, as a pledge of Our paternal good-will and a source of strength, We send you from Our heart Our Apostolic Benediction.

ADDRESS *Magnas Tibi Agimus Gratias* ON THE OCCASION OF THE POPE'S VISIT TO THE BASILICA OF ST. MARY MAJOR.[140]

Through the intercession of the Blessed Virgin Pius XII prays for peace.

December 8, 1939

1487. . . . . . . Torn away from the joy of this occasion, Our heart goes out to those places where in Christian lands a cruel war is slaughtering so many young men and causing ruin and tears. We are stricken with so much grief and afflicted with great and exceeding sorrow. The annals of Christian history narrate that whenever evils weighed heavily upon her children, they were often removed by a most tender and compassionate Mother. While, therefore, she looks upon us with eyes of mercy, let the bitterness of strife cease, and, with hatred put aside and harmony established, let real peace be restored again, a peace which will bind men together in mutual and lasting bonds and make them submissive to God, a peace based on the faithful observance of God's commandments. O, Star of the Sea, calm the sea! During the Solemn Pontifical Mass We will suppliantly pour forth Our prayers to God that, through the intercession of the most Blessed Virgin, the dark clouds may be scattered and the joy of a new era smile upon Us. That is Our ardent desire for all; but you who now stand around Us, a joyous festive gathering, We bless with overflowing love and implore the kindness and favor of the Immaculate Virgin that you may have justice, confidence and joy in greater measure. "May the soul of Mary be in each of you to magnify the Lord; may the spirit of Mary be in each of you to rejoice in the Lord." [141]

---

[140] Original Latin, *A.A.S.*, v. 31, p. 708 (December 22, 1939).
[141] St. Ambrose, *Expositio in Lucam*, II, 26, in Migne, *P.L.*, v. 15, c. 1561.

ADDRESS *La Solenne Visita* ON RECEIVING KING VICTOR EMMANUEL III AND QUEEN ELENA IN THE VATICAN.[142]

The Pope prays that Italy may remain at peace.

December 21, 1939

1488. . . . This visit occurs at a time when other peoples are overthrown or threatened by war and when tranquillity and peace have fled from a great number of hearts. Italy, on the contrary, thanks to the always vigilant, strong and wise hand of the august King and Emperor, and through the far-seeing guidance of her rulers, rests peaceful in civil life, in concord of spirits, in the cult of letters, science and the arts, in works of the fields and industries, in the paths of the sky and of the seas, in the solemn rites of the Catholic Religion. It has been attested before Us to-day how intensely the Faith, which for centuries has animated the illustrious House of Savoy and has raised it to the altars, lives in the royal and imperial dynasty whose glory is exalted in the emblem of the white cross. As the Christmas holidays draw nigh, We invoke upon Your Majesties, upon the beloved Royal Family, upon the Head and the members of the Government, upon all persons here present the most abundant heavenly blessings. May the omnipotent Hand of God guide the destiny of the Italian people, so close and so dear to Us, may it guide the decisions of her rulers in a way that she may be able to contribute with vigilant foresight and conciliating wisdom, not only to internal and external peace, but also to the re-establishment of an honorable and lasting peace between peoples.

ALLOCUTION *In Questo Giorno di Santa* TO THE COLLEGE OF CARDINALS.[143]

Pius XII outlines the requisites for a just and honorable peace.

December 24, 1939

1489. On this holy and happy day, Venerable Brethren and Beloved Sons, when Our anxious expectation of the Divine Coming

---

[142] Original Italian, *A.A.S.*, v. 31, pp. 708-709 (December 22, 1939).
[143] Translation from *The Pope's Five Peace-Points* (C.T.S. pamphlet), pp. 3-19. Original Italian, *A.A.S.*, v. 32, pp. 5-13 (January 22, 1940).

is just about to find fulfillment in the contemplation of the mystery of our Saviour's birth, it is like a foretaste of Christmas joy to see around Us the members of the Sacred College and the Roman prelates and to hear from the beloved and revered Cardinal Dean so eloquent an expression of your affectionate good wishes—wishes which, supernaturalized by the prayers to the heavenly Child that accompany them, are offered to Us by so many faithful and devoted hearts on this joyous feast, the first festival of the liturgical year, and the first Christmas of Our Pontificate.

1490. With you We raise Our heart above this earth to the world of the spirit which the light of faith illumines with its splendor. With you We rejoice, with you We dwell upon the sacred memory of the mystery which, hidden from all ages, was manifested in the cave of Bethlehem. Herein We contemplate the cradle of Universal Redemption; the revelation of peace between heaven and earth, of God's glory in the highest and of peace on earth to men of good-will; the beginning of a new era in history in which men will adore this Divine Mystery, the great Gift of God which brings joy to the whole world. . . . Our Christmas joy is spiritual and supernatural; it takes wing and soars to God. In the words of the liturgy, "amidst the vicissitudes of earthly change, our hearts cleave to the source of all true happiness."[144] Amidst the clash and tumult of earthly events true joy is found only in the repose of the spirit. Here is a fortress which no earthly storm can assail, where the heart rests in God with confidence and unites itself with Christ, the Source and Cause of every joy and every grace. . . .

1491. The heavenly light of this joy and consolation is the source of Christian confidence, and no affliction or labor, no worry or anxiety concerning earthly things can dim that light or trouble its serenity. . . . Where others are at a loss, where the faint-hearted are submerged in the bitter waters of affliction and despair, the souls in which Christ lives are full of strength; they rise above the storms and disorders of this world to sing the praises of God's just judg-ments and decrees. Tempests may rage, but these souls have no fear, not only because they are immortal but also, and chiefly, be-cause they are uplifted to God by their prayer and union with Him. *Sursum corda; Habemus ad Dominum.*[145] . . . . .

[144] Oration for the Fourth Sunday after Easter.
[145] Preface of the Mass.

1492. But while the Vigil of Christmas brings Us the consoling joy of your presence, yet the hour is not without its sorrowful recollections. Before your minds as before Ours rises the figure of Our glorious Predecessor of holy memory, who only a year ago spoke to us words which we shall never forget, words solemn and grave, issuing from the depths of his fatherly heart, words which you heard and understood as We heard and understood them: the *Nunc Dimittis* of another saintly Simeon. They echoed in this very hall in which We now address you. Heavy with foreboding, they were prophetic of the misfortunes that were to come, and the tone of their appeal and admonition, the heroic self-sacrifice which marked that utterance, are still present to our ears and to our hearts.

1493. The unspeakable calamity of war, which Pius XI foresaw with deep misgiving, and which with all the energy of his noble spirit he strove to avert from the comity of nations, is now upon Us as a tragic reality. Our soul is flooded with bitter affliction when We think that this holy festival of Christ, the Prince of Peace, must to-day be celebrated amidst the deadly roll of cannon, under the menace of warlike missiles and the attacks of armed vessels of war. Moreover, since the world seems to have forgotten the peaceful message of Christ, the voice of reason and Christian brotherhood, We have been forced to witness a series of acts irreconcilable alike with the precepts of positive international law and those of the law of nature, as well as with the elementary sentiments of humanity; acts which show in what a vicious circle the juridical sense becomes involved when it is led simply by considerations of expediency. Among such crimes We must include a calculated act of aggression against a small, industrious and peaceful nation, on the pretext of a threat which was neither real nor intended, nor even possible; atrocities (by whichever side committed) and the unlawful use of destructive weapons against non-combatants and refugees, against old men and women and children; a disregard for the dignity, liberty and life of man, showing itself in actions which cry to heaven for vengeance: *The voice of thy brother's blood crieth to Me from the earth;*[146] and finally an ever-growing and increasingly methodical anti-Christian and atheistic propaganda, especially among the young.

1494. It is Our duty, as well as Our sacred desire and purpose, to preserve the Church and its mission from all contact with this

[146] *Genesis*, IV, 10.

anti-Christian spirit, and, therefore, We warmly and insistently urge especially the ministers of the altar and *the dispensers of the mysteries of God*[147] to be ever more assiduous and exemplary in the teaching and the practice of charity, bearing always in mind that in the Kingdom of Christ there is no precept more inviolable or more fundamental than the service of truth and the strengthening of the bond of love.

1495. With deep distress We contemplate the manifest and growing damage to souls caused by the spread of ideas which, more or less purposely and openly, are distorting and obscuring the truth in the minds of individuals and nations, whether belligerent or not; and We are overwhelmed with the thought of the immense labor which will be necessary, when the world has tired of war and turns to thoughts of peace, in order to break down the gigantic walls of hatred and hostility which have been built up in the heat of conflict. Aware of the excesses to which the way is opened and an impulse is given by a policy which takes no account of God's law, We used every endeavor, when war threatened, to avert the supreme catastrophe and to persuade those in power, upon whose shoulders rested the heavy responsibility of decision, to withdraw from an armed conflict and to spare the world a tragedy beyond all foreseeing. But Our efforts, as well as those of other parties enjoying influence and respect, failed to produce the desired effect, chiefly because it appeared impossible to remove the deep feeling of distrust which during recent years had been steadily growing and had placed insurmountable spiritual barriers between one nation and another. The international problems involved were by no means insoluble, but that lack of confidence, due to a series of particular circumstances, presented an almost insuperable obstacle to faith in the efficacy of any promises or in the lasting character of possible agreements. The recollection of the short and troubled duration of similar pacts and agreements in the past finally paralyzed all efforts to promote a peaceful solution.

1496. It remained for Us, Venerable Brethren and Beloved Sons, only to repeat the words of the Prophet: *We have looked for peace and there is no good; and for the time of healing and behold trouble*[148] and to use every possible endeavor meanwhile to alleviate the misfortunes arising out of the war, endeavors which are not a little

---

[147] I *Corinthians*, IV, 1.
[148] *Jeremias*, XIV, 19.

obstructed by the impossibility, not yet overcome, of bringing the aid of Christian charity to those regions where the need of it is most urgently felt. For four months now, and with anguish beyond words, We have gazed upon the ruins which this war, begun under such unusual circumstances, has been piling up. And even though hitherto, if We except the blood-stained soil of Poland and Finland, the number of victims may be considered to be smaller than had been expected, nevertheless the sum-total of calamities and sacrifices has already reached proportions which cannot but cause grave anxiety for the economic, social and spiritual future of Europe, and not of Europe alone. As the war-monster progressively acquires, swallows and demands more and more of the materials available, all of which are inexorably put at the disposal of its ever-increasing requirements, the greater becomes the danger that the nations directly or indirectly affected by the conflict will become victims of a sort of pernicious anemia—and the inevitable question arises: how will an exhausted or attenuated economy contrive to find the means necessary for economic and social reconstruction at a time when difficulties of every kind will be multiplied, difficulties of which the disruptive and revolutionary forces now holding themselves in readiness will not fail to take advantage, in the hope of striking a decisive blow at Christian Europe? Even the fever of conflict should not prevent nations and their rulers from giving due weight to considerations such as these, which ought to cause them to examine the likely consequences and reflect upon the aims and justifiable purposes of the war.

1497. Those who keep a watchful eye upon these future consequences and calmly consider the symptoms in many parts of the world already pointing to such a development of events, will, We think, in spite of the war and its hard necessities, keep their minds open to the prospect of defining clearly, at an opportune moment and so far as it lies with them to do so, the fundamental points of a just and honorable peace; nor will they categorically refuse negotiations for such a peace in the event of a suitable occasion, with the needful guarantees and safeguards, presenting itself.

(1). A fundamental postulate of any just and honorable peace is an assurance for all nations, great or small, powerful or weak, of their right to life and independence. The will of one nation to live must never mean the sentence of death passed upon another. When this equality of rights has been destroyed, attacked, or threatened, order demands that reparation shall be made, and the measure and extent of that reparation is determined, not by the sword nor by arbitrary decision of self-interest, but by the rules of justice and reciprocal equity.

(2). The order thus established, if it is to continue undisturbed and ensure true peace, requires that the nations be delivered from the slavery imposed upon them by the race for armaments, and from the danger that material force, instead of serving to protect right, may become an overbearing and tyrannical master. Any peaceful settlement which fails to give fundamental importance to a mutually agreed, organic and progressive disarmament, spiritual as well as material, or which neglects to ensure the effective and loyal implementing of such an agreement, will sooner or later show itself to be lacking in coherence and vitality.

(3). The maxims of human wisdom require that in any reorganization of international life all parties should learn a lesson from the failures and deficiencies of the past. Hence, in creating or reconstructing international institutions which have so high a mission and such difficult and grave responsibilities, it is important to bear in mind the experience gained from the ineffectiveness or imperfections of previous institutions of the kind. Human frailty renders it difficult, not to say impossible, to foresee every contingency and guard against every danger at the moment in which treaties are signed; passion and bitter feeling are apt to be still rife. Hence, in order that a peace may be honorably accepted and in order to avoid arbitrary breaches and unilateral interpretations of treaties, it is of the first importance to erect some juridical institution which shall guarantee the loyal and faithful fulfillment of the conditions agreed upon, and which shall, in case of recognized need, revise and correct them.

(4). If a better European settlement is to be reached, there is one point in particular which should receive special attention: it is the real needs and the just demands of nations and populations, and of racial minorities. It may be that, in consequence of existing treaties incompatible with them, these demands are unable to establish a strictly legal right. Even so, they deserve to be examined in a friendly spirit with a view to meeting them by peaceful methods, and even, where it appears necessary, by means of an equitable and covenanted revision of the treaties themselves. If the balance between nations is thus adjusted and the foundation of mutual confidence thus laid, many incentives to violent action will be removed.

(5). But even the best and most detailed regulations will be imperfect and foredoomed to failure unless the peoples and those who govern them submit willingly to the influence of that spirit which alone can give life, authority and binding force to the dead letter of international agreements. They must develop that sense of deep and keen responsibility which measures and weighs human statutes according to the sacred and inviolable standards of the law of God; they must cultivate that hunger and thirst after justice which is proclaimed as a beatitude in the Sermon on the Mount and which supposes as its natural foundation the moral virtue of justice; they must be guided by that universal love which is the compendium and most general expression of the Christian ideal, and which, therefore, may serve as a common ground also for those who have not the blessing of sharing the same faith with us.

1498. We are not insensible of the grave difficulties which lie in the way of the achievement of these ends which We have described as needful for establishing and preserving a just peace between nations. But if ever there was an objective deserving the collaboration of all noble and generous minds, if there was ever a spiritual crusade which might assume with a new truth as its motto, "God wills it," then it is this high purpose, it is this crusade enlisting all unselfish and great-hearted men in an endeavor to lead the nations back from the broken cisterns of material and selfish interests to the living fountain of divine justice, which alone is able to provide that morality, nobility and stability of which the need has been so long experienced, to the great detriment of nations and of humanity. To these ideals, which are at the same time the real objectives of a true peace established in justice and love, We hope and trust that all those united with Us in the bond of faith will keep open their minds and hearts; so that when the storm of war shows signs of abating there may arise in every nation men of foresight and good-will, inspired with the courage which can suppress the base instinct of revenge and set up in its stead the grave and noble majesty of justice, sister of love and consort of true wisdom.

1499. Of this justice, which alone can create and preserve peace, We and with Us all those who hear Our voice, know where to find the supreme model, the inner principle, and the sure promise.

Transeamus usque Bethlehem, et videamus: Let us go over to Bethlehem.[149] There we shall find lying in the cradle Him Who is born "the Sun of Justice, Christ our God," and at His side the Virgin Mother who is the "Mirror of Justice" and "Queen of Peace," with the holy Protector Saint Joseph, "the just man." Jesus is the Expected of Nations. The prophets announced His coming and foretold His future triumphs: *His name shall be called Wonderful, Counsellor, God the Mighty, the Father of the World to Come, the Prince of Peace.*[150]

1500. When this heavenly Child was born another prince of peace reigned on the banks of the Tiber; and he with solemn ceremony had dedicated an "Altar of Augustan Peace" whose relics, for long ages hidden beneath the ruins of Rome, have come to light in our own time. On that altar Augustus sacrificed to gods who have no power to save. But we may well believe that the true God and eternal Prince of Peace, Who a few years later came down to dwell amongst men, was not deaf to the sighs for peace which were uttered in that age, and that the Augustan Peace was a symbol of the supernatural peace which He alone can give and in which any true earthly peace is perforce included; We mean the peace which is won, not by the sword but by the wood of the crib of this Infant Lord of Peace, and by the wood of the cross on which He was to die, a wood bedewed with His own Blood, not the blood of rancor and hatred, but the Blood of pardon and love.

1501. Let us, then, go to Bethlehem; let us go to the grotto of the King of Peace—that peace which the choirs of angels sang. Prostrate before Him on behalf of this torn and divided humanity and on behalf of those numberless souls, to whatever people they may belong, who are bleeding and dying, who are mourning and weeping, who have lost their fatherland, let us address to Him our prayers for peace and concord, for help and salvation, using the words which the Church puts upon the lips of her children during this holy season: "O Emmanuel, our King and Lawgiver, the Expected of Nations and their Saviour, come and save us, our Lord and our God."[151] While in this prayer We express Our yearning for a peace in the spirit of Christ, the Mediator of Peace between heaven and

---

[149] *Luke,* II, 15.
[150] *Isaias,* IX, 6.
[151] *The Roman Breviary.*

earth Who with His goodness and kindness has appeared amongst us; while We exhort all Christians to unite their sacrifices and prayers with Our intentions, We impart to you, Venerable Brethren and Beloved Sons, and to all those whom you have in your thoughts, to all men of good-will on earth, especially to the suffering, the distressed and the persecuted, to captives and to the oppressed of every nation, as a pledge of grace, consolation, and heavenly comfort, Our Apostolic Benediction.

1502. At the end of this discourse of Ours We do not wish to deprive you of the joy of announcing to you, Venerable Brethren and Beloved Sons, that there has arrived this morning from the Apostolic Delegation in Washington a telegram, the introductory and essential part of which We are now to read: "The President, having called Monsignor Spellman, Archbishop of New York, this morning after a conversation with him has sent him to me together with Mr. Berle, Assistant Secretary of State, bearing a letter for His Holiness which I here transcribe literally according to the desire of the President himself. In it the President declares that he is nominating a representative of the President with the rank of Extraordinary Ambassador, but without formal title, to the Holy See. This representative will be the Honorable Myron Taylor, who will leave for Rome in about a month. The news will be made officially public tomorrow." . . .

1503. This is a Christmas Message which could not have been more welcome to Us since it represents on the part of the eminent head of a great and powerful nation, a strong and promising contribution to Our desire for the attainment of a just and honorable peace and for a more effective and wider effort to alleviate the sufferings of the victims of war. Therefore, We are bound to express here Our felicitations and Our gratitude for this noble and generous act of President Roosevelt.

ALLOCUTION *In Questo Giorno Auspicato* ON THE OCCASION OF THE VISIT TO KING VICTOR EMMANUEL III IN THE QUIRINAL.[152]

Pius XII praises the peace that has been established between the Vatican and the Quirinal.

December 28, 1939

1504. On this auspicious day . . . We renew the expression of Our lively satisfaction at the solemn visit which Their Majesties paid to Us at the Apostolic Palace of the Vatican, with that sentiment of devotion to the See of Peter which exalts in Our eyes and in those of Rome and of the world the ancient Catholic spirit of the dynasty of Savoy. . . . In this palace, after ten years, a fresh seal is placed upon the happy reconciliation between the Church and the State which makes glorious the names of Our venerated Predecessor, Pius XI, and His Majesty, Victor Emmanuel III. The Vatican and the Quirinal, divided by the Tiber, are united by the bonds of peace and the memories of the religion of our ancestors. The waters of the river have swept away and buried in the depths of the Tyrrhenian Sea the sad recollections of the past, and have caused olive branches to blossom upon their banks.

1505. To-day, for the first time for so many years, the hand of the Roman Pontiff is raised in benediction in this splendid hall as a sign of peace, and Italy beholds it and rejoices. . . . We, therefore, beseech God and His Blessed Mother to extend their protection to the august Sovereigns, to the Princes and Princesses of the Royal Family, to the illustrious Head and to the members of the Government, and to all those here present, in order that that peace which, safeguarded by the wisdom of the rulers, makes Italy a great nation, strong and respected before the world, may serve as a spur and an incentive to future agreement between the peoples who, like brothers become enemies, are fighting each other to-day on land, on the sea and in the air; to that agreement which, in its substance and in its spirit, shall be a sure promise of a new order, calm and lasting, such as would be vain to seek outside the royal ways of justice and Christian charity.

---

[152] Translation from *The Tablet*, v. 175, p. 9 (January 6, 1940). Original Italian, *A.A.S.*, v. 32, pp. 21-22 (January 22, 1940).

REPLY *Los Lazos de Afecto* TO THE HOMAGE OF L. CRUZ-OCAMPO, AMBASSADOR OF CHILE.[153]

Church works for "redemption of the proletariat."

December 30, 1939

1506. . . . . . . The Church, whose maternal hand with anxious watchfulness takes the feverish pulse of the men of our day; the Church, whose discerning eye discovers the necessities, griefs and aspirations that are hidden to others; the Church, whose ear hears in the confidences of the heart the abysses of bitterness in which are sunken the souls of those who believe themselves to be the victims of intentional or unintentional injustices; the Church, We say, sees with all clarity and supports with untiring zeal the imperative obligation of that "redemption of the proletariat" which had its beginning in the cave at Bethlehem and concerning which Our great Predecessor spoke with such enlightening wisdom.

1507. Nothing would be more pleasing to Us, Mr. Ambassador, than to procure in ever increasing degrees for the people of Chile, so dear to Us . . . those precious and irreplaceable helps for the way of true prosperity which come from the doctrine and law of Jesus Christ and from the individual and social formation that is in full correspondence with them. Your Excellency's words have made Us confident that the Church in the exercise of her mission of truth and love will enjoy in Chile that freedom which belongs to her as a perfect society and which is deeply rooted in the conscience of the Catholic people of your country. . . .

LETTER *The Memorable Message* TO PRESIDENT ROOSEVELT OF THE UNITED STATES.[154]

In establishing a just and lasting peace only he will help who unites with high political power a clear understanding of the voice of humanity along with a sincere reverence for the Gospel of Christ.

January 7, 1940

1508. The memorable message that Your Excellency was pleased to have forwarded to Us on the eve of the Holy Feast of Christmas

[153] Original Spanish, *Discorsi e Radiomessaggi*, v. 1, pp. 459-460.
[154] Original English, *A.A.S.*, v. 32, pp. 43-45 (February 20, 1940).

has brightened with a ray of consolation, of hope and confidence, the suffering, the heart-rending fear and the bitterness of the peoples caught up in the vortex of war. For this all right-minded men have paid you the spontaneous tribute of their sincere gratitude. We have been deeply moved by the noble thought contained in your note, in which the spirit of Christmas and the desire to see it applied to the great human problems have found such eloquent expression; and, fully persuaded of its extraordinary importance, We lost no time in communicating it to the distinguished gathering present that very morning in the Consistorial Hall of this Apostolic Vatican Palace, solemnly expressing before the world, Catholic and non-Catholic alike, Our appreciation of this courageous document, inspired by a far-seeing statesmanship and a profound human sympathy.

1509. We have been particularly impressed by one characteristic feature of Your Excellency's message: the vital, spiritual contact with the thoughts and feelings, the hopes and the aspirations of the masses of the people, of those classes, namely, on whom more than others, and in a measure never felt before, weighs the burden of sorrow and sacrifice imposed by the present restless and tempestuous hour. Also for this reason, none perhaps better than We can understand the meaning, the revealing power and the warmth of feeling manifest in this act of Your Excellency. In fact, Our own daily experience tells Us of the deep-seated yearning for peace that fills the hearts of the common people. In the measure that the war with its direct and indirect repercussions spreads; and the more economic, social and family life is forcibly wrenched from its normal bases by the continuation of the war, and is forced along the way of sacrifice and every kind of privation, the bitter need of which is not always plain to all; so much the more intense is the longing for peace that pervades the hearts of men and their determination to find and to apply the means that lead to peace.

1510. When that day dawns—and We would like to hope that it is not too far distant—on which the roar of battle will lapse into silence and there will arise the possibility of establishing a true and sound peace dictated by the principles of justice and equity, only he will be able to discern the path that should be followed who unites with high political power a clear understanding of the voice of humanity along with a sincere reverence for the divine precepts of life as found in the Gospel of Christ. Only men of such moral stature will be able to create the peace that will compensate for the incalculable sacrifices of this war and clear the way for a comity of nations, fair to all, efficacious and sustained by mutual confidence.

1511. We are fully aware of how stubborn the obstacles are that stand in the way of attaining this goal, and how they become daily more difficult to surmount. And if the friends of peace do not wish their labors to be in vain, they should visualize distinctly the seriousness of these obstacles, and the consequently slight probability of immediate success so long as the present state of the opposing forces remains essentially unchanged. As Vicar on earth of the Prince of Peace, from the first days of Our Pontificate We have dedicated Our efforts and Our solicitude to the purpose of maintaining peace, and afterward of re-establishing it. Heedless of momentary lack of success and of the difficulties involved, We are continuing to follow along the path marked out for Us by Our Apostolic Mission. As We walk this path, often rough and thorny, the echo which reaches Us from countless souls, both within and outside the Church, together with the consciousness of duty done, is for Us abundant and consoling reward.

1512. And now that in this hour of world-wide pain and misgiving, the Chief Magistrate of the great North American Federation, under the spell of the Holy Night of Christmas, should have taken such a prominent place in the vanguard of those who would promote peace and generously succor the victims of the war, bespeaks a providential help, which We acknowledge with grateful joy and increased confidence. It is an exemplary act of fraternal and hearty solidarity between the New and the Old World in defense against the chilling breath of aggressive and deadly godless and anti-Christian tendencies, that threaten to dry up the fountainhead, whence civilization has come and drawn its strength. In such circumstances We shall find a special satisfaction, as We have already informed Your Excellency, in receiving with all the honor due to his well-known qualifications and to the dignity of his important mission, the representative who is to be sent to Us as the faithful interpreter of your mind regarding the procuring of peace and the alleviation of sufferings consequent upon the war. Recalling with keen joy the pleasant memories left Us after Our unforgettable visit to your great nation, and living over again the sincere pleasure that personal acquaintance with Your Excellency brought Us, We express in turn

Our hearty good wishes, with a most fervent prayer for the prosperity of Your Excellency and of all the people of the United States.

ADDRESS *Un Duplice Dono* TO THE ROMAN NOBILITY IN RESPONSE TO THEIR NEW YEAR WISHES.[155]

War rages to-day because the law of evangelical charity has been ignored.

January 8, 1940

1513. . . . . . . Because the law of evangelical love has been ignored, denied and outraged, to-day war—from which Divine Mercy so far has preserved Italy—rages in some parts of the world, where whole cities are seen transformed into heaps of smoking ruins and plains, abundant in harvests, have been transformed into cities of tortured dead. Peace wanders timid and alone through deserted ways in the shadow of gloomy hope. On its tracks and in its steps, in the Old and New World, men who are friends of peace go seeking it, preoccupied with the desire of bringing it back into the midst of men on bases that are just, solid and lasting, and of preparing, in a brotherly effort, the arduous task of necessary reconstruction. . . . . . .

ADDRESS *I Sentimenti* TO THE KNIGHTS OF THE ORDER OF MALTA.[156]

The Knights must lavish their charity upon the unfortunate war victims.

January 15, 1940

1514. . . . . . . Long before civilized nations had established international law, a long time before they had given reality to the dream—not yet effectuated—of common force in defense of right and human liberty, of the independence of peoples, of peaceful equity in their reciprocal relations, the Order of St. John, now the Order of Malta, had gathered, in religious fraternity and military discipline, men of eight different tongues consecrated to the defense

---

[155] Translation from *Pius XII and Peace*, p. 47. Original Italian, *Discorsi e Radiomessaggi*, v. I, p. 473.

[156] Original Italian, *Discorsi e Radiomessaggi*, v. I, pp. 483-485.

of the spiritual values which constitute the common endowment of Christianity, namely, faith, justice, social order and peace. . . . . .

1515. It seems to Us that to-day, too, humanity lies prostrate and exhausted on the road of time. While it was foolishly going down from Jerusalem to Jericho, from the city of prayer to that of pleasures, from the regions of the ideal to those of gain, it fell into the hands of robbers whose names are pride, unbelief, ambition, violence, disloyalty, hatred. They robbed it of its riches, of the highest moral values which make man worthy and holily proud: faith in God, brotherhood, mutual trust; they violently snatched away from it a precious treasure: peace. You, then, Beloved Sons and Illustrious Knights, of Jerusalem by origin, good Samaritans by vocation, hospitalers by profession, charitable through your whole tradition and by personal devotion, you ancient founders of hostels for the pilgrims and the travelers in danger, give a generous and compassionate refuge in your prayers, in your alms, in your solicitude to the millions of beings tried by poverty, by misfortunes, by the scourge of war. Like the innkeeper in the parable of the Gospel, you may be sure that Divine Mercy will repay you, not exactly but a hundred fold, for the moneys that you have advanced, that is, all that you have generously offered in prayers, in sacrifices, in wealth, in influence, in your efforts for the relief of suffering humanity. . . .

ADDRESS *Or È Più* TO THE DAUGHTERS OF MARY FROM THE ROMAN PARISH OF ST. MARY IN AQUIRO.[157]

The road to peace can be found in a sincere return to the Gospel.

January 31, 1940

1516. . . . . . . Instructed and educated to virtue under the assiduous preaching and guidance of zealous prelates so near Us, continue, O beloved daughters, to walk in the paths of the garden of the Immaculate Mary. Cultivate in it the most delicate and fragrant flowers: the lilies of purity, the violets of humility, the roses of a generous and active charity, protected by the thorns of an ever-vigilant modesty and of a frank renunciation of worldly frivolities, and strengthened by the vivifying warmth of a strong and valiant

[157] Original Italian, *Discorsi e Radiomessaggi*, v. 1, pp. 506-507.

faith, on account of which adherence to the divine teachings is more valuable than any worldly success and pleasure. And as your dedication to Mary gives you a special title to her benevolence, implore her that, in these turbulent days, men whose souls have all been redeemed by the precious Blood of the Divine Son may recognize the duties of Christian love and brotherhood and discover anew, in a sincere return to the Gospel, the royal road to tranquillity and order, in an unbounded desire for peace.

RADIO MESSAGE *In This Hour* TO THE NEW ZEALAND EUCHARISTIC CONGRESS IN WELLINGTON.[158]

If Christ rules the whole life of a nation, His peace will descend upon it.

February 1, 1940

1517. . . . . . . We rejoice that you are celebrating the first century of the Catholic Church in New Zealand with a Eucharistic Congress. In so doing, you announce your longing and your hope that Christ may rule over the whole life of your nation, over the life of each one as over social life: that His Spirit, His Will, His Word, may fill those who guide your destiny and make your laws: that His Love may smooth out difficulties among you, and heal the wounds of the past: that His peace may descend upon your common life, and mercifully protect you from the horrors of the war. . . . . . .

MESSAGE *Partecipando alla Vivissima Esultanza* TO EMPEROR HIROHITO OF JAPAN.[159]

The Pope hopes that hostilities abroad may cease.

February 10, 1940

1518. We are participating with great rejoicing in the celebration commemorating the twenty-sixth centenary of the founding of your powerful empire and We extend to Your Majesty and to your august house congratulations for the glory of your ancient kingdom, while We reaffirm Our gratitude for the kindliness of your govern-

[158] Original English, *A.A.S.*, v. 32, p. 48 (February 20, 1940).
[159] Translation from *Pius XII and Peace*, p. 50. Original Italian, *Civiltà Cattolica*, 1940, v. 1, pp. 401-402 (February 20, 1940).

ment toward Our Catholic sons. We are praying God that once the hostilities abroad have ceased, the distinguished Japanese people may shine with new grandeur of real greatness and its sovereigns, through Supreme aid, may perpetually enjoy years of happiness.

ADDRESS *Se l'Inizio* TO PILGRIMS FROM MILAN.[160]

Pius XII praises the peace efforts of his Predecessor.

February 11, 1940

1519. . . . . . . In the history of the Church the name of Pius XI will mark the center of a new age, the end and seal of a past as glorious as it was tempestuous, the sign and good omen of a future that from the past derives its strength and its impetus toward greater triumphs of the faith. *Pax Christi in regno Christi* was the motto that inspired all his thoughts and his actions.

1520. Born with an intrepid heart, with a mind open to the widest horizons, with a sagacity penetrating the labyrinths of causes and effects, with the alert imperturbability sustained by eyes fixed on heaven, Pius XI, seated on the Throne of Peter as on the highest peak of the Alps which he used to climb, surveyed the world thrown into confusion by the peoples in conflict with one another because they had forgotten God and His Christ, the Peacemaker, and he invoked "The Peace of Christ in the Kingdom of Christ" as the polar star of his pontifical reign. By the light of this star he guided the Bark of Peter, hoping that the unsearchable Divine Will, which in its justice is never unmindful of mercy, being moved to pity, would forgive the iniquities of mankind and would suspend and remove the scourge that was threatening to fall upon turbulent and discordant humanity. To "The Peace of Christ in the Kingdom of Christ" he dedicated his life and his death; from the first day when he appeared dressed in white, he was seen blessing Italy and the world from the lofty balcony of the Vatican Basilica, embracing all in his new and immense fatherly heart.

1521. To the Peace of Christ he directed his thought; that Apostolic thought which, with the ardor of Paul of Tarsus, leaps over every barrier to exalt and to announce to the whole world the faith

[160] Original Italian, *Discorsi e Radiomessaggi*, v. 1, pp. 529-536.

of Rome,[161] and to gather together in peace all nations, far and near, united or estranged; that thought which, according to the great Bishop of Hippo, is the thought of the heavenly city and of the Kingdom of Christ, because: "this heavenly city, while it is a pilgrim on earth, draws to itself citizens of every nation, and gathers together the members of the pilgrimage of every language, overlooking the differences in their customs, in their laws and in their statutes, by which fact this earthly peace is secured or preserved; neither wasting nor destroying anything, but rather upholding and supporting . . . . . . and that same earthly peace determines the heavenly one, which is so truly a peace that it should be considered the only peace of rational creatures, because it is the highly ordered and harmonious society of mankind, having the fullness of power to enjoy God and one another in God." [162] Thus the genius of Augustine anticipated the thought of Pius XI—with the Peace of Christ on earth in the Kingdom of Christ, the Conqueror of the peoples—in making the earthly peace a prelude and good omen of the heavenly peace, the ultimate goal of humanity, which has been redeemed by God but still sojourns on the face of the earth.

1522. If Pius XI lifted his mind to such lofty thoughts in the contemplation of his Apostolic Office, he afterward came down to the practical application of them, employing as his ministers, will and action, well realizing, as did Paul, his debt to the Greeks and to the barbarians, to the wise and to the unwise: *Graecis ac Barbaris, sapientibus et insipientibus debitor sum.*[163] He sought to establish among souls the Peace of Christ, the peace bequeathed to us by Christ; he sought to establish it among the learned and the unlearned, between science and faith, between capital and labor, between abundance and need, between wealth and poverty, between politics and ethics, between the powerful and the weak, between the persecutors and the oppressed, between the East and the West. If he found obstacles in his path he did not despair; he waited, as in the dim twilight of his Alpine climbings, for the appearance of a dawn favorable to him and his followers.

1523. He was great in action. Intrepid herald and pioneer of peace in the midst of the flames and horrors of war as in the storms

[161]*Romans*, I, 8.
[162] *De Civitate Dei,* bk. XIX, ch. 17.
[163] *Romans*, I, 14.

of the Alps, he also became a messenger of peace to Italy, his beloved native land, giving her "The Peace of Christ in the Kingdom of Christ" by putting an end to a long and painful estrangement that had separated the one from the other "of those whom the same wall and the same moat contain."[164]

1524. Supreme Priest, he experienced the paternal love of mediator of peace between the people and the Church, and found a way of accord with all who responded to his far-sighted and magnanimous pastoral solicitude. . . . And We, embracing all in the universal charity of Christ and in the solicitude of Peter for all the Churches, greatly enjoy seeing you with Us; and We are very pleased to see that you strive to honor ever more nobly your very learned and oldest teacher and most famous Bishop and Patron[165] who, in days not less troublous than ours, was champion of peace and good-will among emperors and rivals of emperors, and who at the beginning of his civil administration, appearing as peacemaker among the citizens of Milan quarreling over the election of a bishop, revealed himself as such a wise mediator of peace, that peace identified itself with him and changed the insignia of the *consularis* to the holier and worthier insignia of Archbishop of the Vicariate of Italy. Therefore, We reverence and venerate him as a great protector of the peace of the Church and of the world, and We exhort you not only to honor him but also to pray to him fervently: *for all men, for kings, and for all in high positions, that we may lead a quiet and peaceful life in all piety and worthy behavior. This is good and agreeable in the sight of God our Saviour, Who wishes all men to be saved and to come to the knowledge of the truth.*[166]

ADDRESS *Os Damos* TO THE ARGENTINIAN MILITARY MISSION.[167]

Forgetfulness of God is the fundamental cause of the ills that are distressing humanity.

February 15, 1940

1525. . . . . . . You Argentinians, and in particular those who see the throes of anguish through which other peoples pass, have

---

[164] Dante, *Purgatorio*, VI, 84.
[165] St. Ambrose.
[166] I *Timothy*, II, 1-4.
[167] Original Spanish *Discorsi e Radiomessaggi*, v. 1, pp. 539-540.

abundant reason for thanking the Provident God for the paternal love with which He watches over you. The statue of Christ on the summit of the Andes, which recalls and blesses your pact of friendship with neighboring peoples, is the symbol of real peace. May God will that we see it soon appear on the highest summits of Europe. . . . Forgetfulness of God is the fundamental cause of the ills that are distressing humanity. Wherever it takes root, it is as a fire which devours everything. It not only dries up souls and deprives them of their eternal happiness, but it also succeeds in destroying the security, the tranquillity and the social order of the State. . . . . . .

HOMILY *Grandi, Diletti Figli* DURING THE CEREMONIES COMMEMORATING THE FIRST ANNIVERSARY OF HIS ELECTION.[168]

A victory over passion is necessary to restore in justice and love the honor and conscience of nations.

March 3, 1940

1526. . . . . . . When the empires of the world in upheaval dash against one another like ocean waves, when the earth trembles under the cannon's roar, when the seas open and swallow up men and riches, when in the skies, storms more deadly than hurricanes strike terror into the hearts of the people; what remains to us, beloved sons, if we do not turn to the God of our Tabernacles, the Conqueror of the World, the King of Ages, Who curbs the wings of the lightning and the roar of the whirlwind, Who holds in His Hand the hearts of kings and rulers, directing them whither He will?

1527. O Jesus, King of Kings and Lord of Lords, before Whom at the tomb of Thy first Vicar, rock of foundation of Thy Church established for the salvation of men, We prostrate Ourself in prayer for all Thy people all over the face of the globe: may the reign of Thy love, O Jesus, triumph in souls! . . . Come down from the mountain as in the night after the multiplication of bread; walk on the waters, hold back the winds, calm the tempest, reassure Thy disciples in their battered ship, drive away the darkness and lead us

[168] Translation from *The Sword of the Spirit,* bulletin 39, p. 2 (February 5, 1942). Original Italian, *Discorsi e Radiomessaggi,* v. 2, pp. 9-11.

to the port of peace. Make men feel that Thou art the Light of the World and that they must turn to Thee. May they lay their arms at Thy Feet! May it be that on the altar of this Christian peace, unknown to Cæsar's pagan legions, the conflicting minds and wills of those who are arbiters of the destiny of nations—with mutual trust and noble sincerity—may offer to Thee, O God, Author and Lover of Peace, that magnanimous victory over passion, that greatly desired sacrifice which, forgetting all offense, will restore in justice and love the honor and conscience of the nations! Amen.

ADDRESS *Dal Fondo* TO A DELEGATION OF THE BYZANTINE RUMANIAN CLERGY.[169]

The Pope prays that Rumania may be spared from the scourge of war.

March 4, 1940

1528. . . . . . When your magnificent Danube issues from the Nera forests and reaches, tired of its thousand-mile course, rich plains, pouring wealth on fields, industrial cities and oil fields, it presents to heaven and earth an unrivaled vision of peace. Peace! This word is the summary of the best wishes We can offer you; but present circumstances, in a world torn by the horrors of war, give it particular significance. We are thinking of a threefold aspect of peace. We wish you the peace of heart which will never fail you, if you keep in close and personal union with Christ. We wish your nation internal peace, remembering that the Catholic social doctrine, the Catholic sense of the family, the Catholic law of brotherly and universal charity, will ever be the most powerful instrument for placating civil discords, for breaking down class hostility between rich and poor, workers and employers and the various races that happen to live in the territories of a State. Lastly, We wish you external peace, praying the Lord that He may save your country from the scourge of war and enable it to carry on its charitable work among those who have been stricken by the present conflict. . . .

---

[169] Translation from *The Tablet*, v. 175, p. 255 (March 16, 1940). Original Italian, *Discorsi e Radiomessaggi*, v. 2, pp. 17-18.

ALLOCUTION *Vive Sempre* TO THE COLLEGE OF CARDINALS ON THE ANNIVERSARY OF HIS CORONATION.[170]

In this war all purely human methods of obtaining peace are revealing their intrinsic deficiency and, hence, Pius XII calls for prayers.

March 12, 1940

1529. . . . . . . A year has gone by which has been filled with so many material and spiritual events and changes; . . . a year in the course of which the interior and exterior aspects of Europe have been transformed. Political, economic and spiritual upheavals have begun, the repercussions and the consequences of which no human mind can foresee, but the gravity of which must be considered with attention and solicitude by those who are called to proclaim the truth and the reign of Christ in the midst of a humanity disturbed and shaken to its foundations by error and by passion.

1530. At this time, when all human forecasts seem false, when all purely human methods are revealing their intrinsic deficiency, the eyes of the faithful turn toward the eternal hills whence only can come salvation. In this world in the grip of the evil desires of men, in which We see men wandering as in a desert among hallucinations and mirages which are but darkness, dashing themselves against each other and falling down, the Church marches surely, holding on high the torch of Christ: the Way, the Truth and the Life; for, without a way one arrives at no end; without truth one enlightens no minds; without life one animates no will and no work. It is truth which enlightens the way and the life, this truth which is the pedestal of justice, this justice which is the foundation of peace.

1531. Yes; it is peace which is founded on the knowledge of God and of Our Lord Jesus Christ—*the Way, the Truth, and the Life*[171]—which is the most profound wish and aspiration of Our soul. It is peace which prompts Us in Our love for men, for all men, which We carry in Our heart, for both those who are near to Us and those who are far away, those who are faithful to Us and those who are separated from Us, those who are at peace and those

---

[170] Translation from *The Tablet*, v. 175, pp. 277-278 (March 23, 1940). Original Italian, *Discorsi e Radiomessaggi*, v. 2, pp. 25-26.
[171] *John*, XIV, 6.

who are at war, for it is to all that We owe the services of truth
and of the charity of Christ. From this hill We contemplate the
troubled world. If peace reigns about Us, by the grace of God, yet
beyond the Alps, beyond the seas and the oceans, there are only
winds and storms, and both religion and humanity call out for peace.
Our hopes and Our confidence repose in God, Who holds in His
Hands the hearts of men and the storms of the land, of the sky, and
of the sea. You, Venerable Brethren and Dear Sons, who are Our
Senate and Our counsellors, assist Our hope with your prayers and
your solicitudes, so that having participated in Our sorrow and
shared Our thorns, you may share Our roses and Our joys, for your
consolation and your glory. . . .

ADDRESS *Più di Una Volta* TO THE ROMAN LADIES OF CHARITY
OF ST. VINCENT DE PAUL.[172]

*It is for disowning charity that the world has lost true
peace.*

March 13, 1940

1532. . . . . . . True charity does not limit itself to giving: it
gives itself, and your mission is not merely to send alms, but to
carry them yourselves. Now to visit the poor, you need to leave
your own homes and your own comforts, to renounce even the spirit
of the world. . . . And to go to the poor does not mean walking on
soft carpets in luxurious apartments: for they live in dismal huts;
they are sometimes roofless, like those poor nomads whose children
are found in this very Rome sleeping on the bare ground under
carts. . . . You must give cheerfully. The poor, who have souls as
well as the rich, have also, like them, hearts; and sometimes how
little it takes to bring serenity to their affliction and to soften the
bitterness of their revolt! . . . . . .

1533. Dear daughters, it is for disowning charity that the world
has lost true peace; and it will never recover it until it finds its way
back to the throne of charity. Threatened by a new upheaval, mankind is anxiously waiting for the return of the dove, the forerunner
of the rainbow of peace. But this winged messenger will not bring

[172] Translation from *The Tablet*, v. 175, p. 305 (March 30, 1940). Original Italian,
Discorsi e Radiomessaggi, v. 2, pp. 30-34.

universal peace to men and nations, unless it can again pluck from
the earth the green olive branch, the emblem of softening unction,
which demands for its growth and fruitfulness the warmth of
charity. . . .

HOMILY *Exsultet Jam Angelica* DELIVERED IN ST. PETER'S
BASILICA ON EASTER SUNDAY.[173]

> *Christ alone can bid the nations settle their disputes,*
> *freely and successfully, not by violence but by the law*
> *of truth, of justice and of charity.*

March 24, 1940

1534. . . . . . . True it is that at this moment almost all the peoples of the world are the prey of panic-stricken anxiety. Some are
rocked by the raging tide of war; others are appalled by the future,
with its outlook of peril. And yet the solemnities of Easter call
men's minds back to the thought of heavenly joys; those Christian
virtues we need so urgently, of faith, hope and charity, spring up
and flourish again under their influence. Ah, Venerable Brethren
and Beloved Sons, Our heart and yours are overflowing with a
heavenly gladness, which these virtues nourish in them; if only that
were true all over the world! If only mankind would listen to
the holy invitation which this day offers, would experience that
holy joy, which alone can soothe grief, wipe away tears and calm
anxieties! We cannot think without profound sadness of those
whose minds have no ray of divine truth to enlighten them; tortured by unhappiness, they cannot derive from the thought of heaven
that hope which can never fail us, that comfort which alone deserves
the name. It is Our prayer that He Who overcame death will make
His heavenly light shine upon them; will so renew them and refashion them that they, too, may attain paschal joy, which is nothing
less than the earnest of everlasting happiness. We celebrate to-day
the feast of Christ's rising again; may it be a principle of spiritual
renewal in individual lives, as history affords clear proof that it
actually gave birth to a new world-order.

1535. It is plain truth that when Our Lord Christ, "overcoming

---

[173] Translation from *Foundations for Peace* (C.T.S. pamphlet), pp. 12-18. Original
Latin, *A.A.S.*, v. 32, pp. 146-150 (April 19, 1940).

the sting of death,"[174] opened the kingdom of heaven to all who believe in Him, a new and a happier age dawned upon the whole human race. As the sun, showing above the high mountain-tops at early morning, scatters the darkness and the mists, bringing back light, heat and life with it; so Jesus Christ, when He rises living from the tomb, "chases away our crimes, washes away our faults . . . restores innocence to the fallen, joy to the sad at heart, sends our quarrels flying, and brings us peace." [175] Three days earlier, the Apostles had abandoned their Master in hasty flight; when they witnessed His amazing victory over the powers of darkness, their wavering faith found new strength, the dying embers of divine love in their hearts were kindled into flame. They had strength from above to rely on, grace from above to aid them; and they prepared to communicate to others the spiritual life which they had drunk in from Jesus Christ, to subdue the whole world, not by arms stained with blood, but by the power of truth and of charity. So it was that *their cry went out into all lands, their words to the ends of the world.*[176] Villages, towns, populous cities were awakened at this new dawning of light, were quickened by this new influence of love, and felt the need of a renewal. . . .

1536. If, then, as We have said (and the annals of the Church are proof of it), the triumph of Jesus Christ over death brought with it an amazing restoration and renewal of the whole world, it should be the same with us now. If we really mean to walk in the steps of our Divine Redeemer, how eagerly, how painstakingly we ought to reproduce in our own lives the image of that spiritual restoration! But this, as we all know by experience, is no easy task. The renewal can only be brought about by Christian strength of character; and such strength, with our human weakness to retard it, means effort, claims effort, if it is to be the ruling principle of our lives.

1537. And yet, Venerable Brethren and Beloved Sons, our Lord Christ has not rested content with giving us commandments, has not rested content, even, with ratifying those commandments by the astonishing example of His life; He has promised us help from above, and if we ask for it, humbly and earnestly, His great mercy

---

[174] Ambrosian hymn, *Te Deum.*
[175] Roman Missal for Holy Saturday.
[176] *Psalms*, XVIII, 5; *Romans*, X, 18.

bestows that help on us without fail, so that nothing can be difficult to the followers of Jesus Christ, if their wills are set on it; nay, as we know by experience, the fiercer our struggle against the *powers of darkness*[177] the more delightful, the more consoling is our victory. We must strive, then, with all our force and all our energy, *to walk in newness of life, just as Christ has risen from the dead through the glory of His Father,*[178] *to live soberly, justly and devoutly in this world, renouncing impiety and all worldly desires.*[179] Our aim must be to *strip off our old nature, with the actions which belong to it, and clothe ourselves with the new nature, which is renewed continually into a fuller knowledge and according to the likeness of Him Who created it.*[180] So we may actually attain the result we long for, *that those who live may no longer live to themselves but to Him Who died and rose again for them.*[181]

1538.   We have seen, then, the course of action which is so clearly defined for us, so earnestly recommended to us, by the Apostle of the Gentiles. If we regulate our lives by it, the holy festival of Easter will bring a gift to each of us—that of reflecting in ourselves, in our characters, the living image of Jesus Christ, undeterred by the labor which it involves. And if we do this, the winds and storms which rock the terrified world of to-day, the multitudinous anxieties which burden men's lives so heavily in our time, will pass us by; we shall enjoy the peace which comes from above, we shall be sustained by the hope of blessings which can never die, we shall have our fill of heavenly comfort. After all, *if we have died with Him, we shall also live with Him; if we wait for Him patiently, we shall also reign with Him;*[182] *if we suffer with Him, we shall also be glorified with Him.*[183]

1539.   But there is also another reason, Venerable Brethren and Beloved Sons, for urging so strongly upon you and upon all men this duty of spiritual renewal and restoration through Christ. It is not only the private lives of individual citizens and their private welfare that depend on this course of action; it is the highest interest of the whole confederacy of mankind. And not least in these times,

---

[177] *Luke*, XXII, 53; *Ephesians*, VI, 12.
[178] *Romans*, VI, 4.
[179] *Titus*, II, 12.
[180] *Colossians*, III, 9-10.
[181] II *Corinthians*, V, 15.
[182] II *Timothy*, II, 11-12.
[183] *Cf. Romans*, VIII, 17.

when all eyes are fixed upon events so lamentable, all hearts are daunted by the fear of worse to come. You can see for yourselves what an age it is we have been born into. Peace between nations lies hopelessly shattered; pacts solemnly confirmed by agreement on both sides are continually being revised, or violated outright, at the discretion of one party, without any attempt at discussion and clear adjustment of mutual relations; the voice of brotherly love and brotherly good-will is silenced. All the fruits of research and experiment, all men's energies, all their wealth and property, are now being devoted to the conduct of war, or to the ever-increasing production of armaments. What was designed to promote the prosperity of nations and the growth of civilization, is now, by a preposterous change of direction, being used for its downfall and ruin. The commerce of peace-time, held up by every possible device, is at a standstill; and this means a want of supply which falls most heavily upon the poorer classes. More than this, and worse than this, in many parts of the world, where men's hearts are blinded by hatred and ill-will, the earth, the seas, and even the sky, noble image of our heavenly country, are being polluted with fratricidal massacre. More than once, to Our great distress, the laws which bind civilized peoples together have been violated; most lamentably, undefended cities, country towns and villages have been terrorized by bombing, destroyed by fire and thrown down in ruins; unarmed citizens, even the sick, helpless old people and innocent children have been turned out of their homes, and often visited with death.

1540.   As these evils crowd in upon us, what hope of remedy is left to us, except that which comes from Christ, from His inspirations, and from His teaching, a healing stream flowing through every vein of our society? Only Christ's law, only Christ's grace, can renew and restore private and public life, redressing the true balance of rights and duties, checking unbridled self-interest, controlling passion, implementing and perfecting the course of strict justice with His overflowing charity. He Who could once give His commands to wind and storm, Who could allay the waves of an angry sea and reduce them to calm, He it is Who alone can turn men's hearts to peace and brotherly love: He alone can bid the nations settle their disputes, freely and successfully, not by violence but by the law of truth, of justice and of charity: He alone can strike the swords from their hands and join those hands at last in a treaty of friendship. We, therefore, whose fatherly love for all makes Us share in the bitter grief and affliction of Our sons, on this day of solemn rejoicing offer Our heart-felt prayers to the Divine Redeemer, that it may please Him "to grant to kings and princes" and to all the Christian people "peace and true concord." [184] Amen.

ADDRESS *In Questa Settimana* TO THE RELIGIOUS OF THE CENACLE, TO MEMBERS ATTENDING A CONVENTION OF THE APOSTLESHIP OF PRAYER AND TO NEWLY-WEDS.[185]

Many nations have lost peace because their prophets and leaders have departed from God.

March 27, 1940

1541. . . . . . . Among others, there are two dangers actually threatening the world to-day. On the one hand, there is pride, rebelling against God and His rights; reason, breaking away from divine authority; and force, being extolled above justice and equity. But Christ has said, *Learn of Me, because I am meek and humble of Heart: and you shall find rest to your souls.*[186] Thus, to spread devotion to His Sacred Heart is really to teach meekness and humility and to work for the peace of the world.

1542. The other danger, which is almost the opposite of the first, is the moral depression and the lack of trust which exist, the results of the decline of faith, hope and charity. These theological virtues, which are like rays of light and love between God and man, acquire a new ardor from the flames emanating from the Sacred Heart of Jesus. In the contemplation of this Heart and of Its open wound, men understand that God is not only their Lord to be served and to be feared, but also their Father, full of pity, Who loves them and is to be loved by them. Then the most downcast spirit raises itself anew, and the most troubled mind becomes calm again. To spread the devotion of the Sacred Heart is, therefore, to spread peace among souls. *Pax vobis!* . . . . . .

1543. Beloved Sons! When Jesus in the silence of the Cenacle uttered the words *Pax vobis* — Peace be to you! — the Apostles

[184] Litany of the Saints.
[185] Original Italian, *Discorsi e Radiomessaggi,* v. 2, pp. 47-50.
[186] *Matthew,* XI, 29.

trembled with dismay, even though they were behind firmly closed doors: *quum . . . fores essent clausæ . . . propter metum Judæorum.*[187] The peace which they had not been able to enjoy in their refuge, but of which they were to be messengers *usque ad ultimum terræ,* to the farthermost corners of the earth, was to accompany them on their journeys and through their sufferings and martyrdom. For them it was not to be the silver-winged dove[188] sweetly cooing in the fragrant foliage, but the sea-gull, which does not make for its nest during the storm but, flying from the crest of the waves to the top of the ship's mast, appears to the dismayed sailor as an example of the vanity of all efforts and the futility of all struggles of man when left to his own devices, and of the power and joyful serenity of the frail creature which abandons itself to its Creator.

1544. Will mankind understand this lesson and strive to find again in a confident return to God that peace, the thought of which fills all minds and all hearts like the haunting remembrance of a vanished happiness? Not a few to-day have lost peace because their prophets and their leaders have departed from God and His Christ. Some, proclaimers of an irreligious culture and government, enclosing themselves within the pride of human reason: *Quum . . . fores essent clausæ!,* have barred the door to the very idea of the divine and the supernatural, banishing from creation the Creator, removing from schools and courts the image of the Divine Crucified Master, and eliminating from institutions, national, social and family, every reference to the Gospel, without, however, succeeding in effacing its deep influence. Others have fled far from Christ and His peace, rejecting centuries of enlightened, beneficent and fraternal civilization to sink in the darkness of ancient paganism or of modern idolatry. May they recognize their error, and understand that Christ the Saviour, notwithstanding their desertions, their denials and their outrage, will remain forever near them, with outstretched Hands and with an open Heart, ready to say to them: *Pax vobis,* if they, in a sincere and confident transport, will fling themselves at His Feet with that cry of faith and love: *Dominus meus et Deus meus! My Lord and My God!*[189]

---

[187] *John,* XX, 19.
[188] See *Psalms,* LXVII, 14.
[189] *John,* XX, 28.

ADDRESS *Vi Siamo Ben Grati* TO THE MEMBERS OF THE ROYAL ACADEMY OF ST. CECILIA IN ROME.[190]

The Pope wishes that international relations could be as harmonious as the music played by the Royal Academy.

April 6, 1940

1545. . . . . . . Music, a gift bestowed by the generosity of God upon men, (*Dei largitate,* as St. Augustine so aptly says,) should, in its turn, lead men to God and help them to walk in His presence by the observance of His Commandments. Indeed, the essential law for Christians—after the adoration and love for God, their Creator and Father—is fraternal harmony among all His children. St. Augustine, meditating upon the example of King David, who was both an inspired poet and an immortal singer, and, at the same time, a wise and glorious king, observed that the true and well-regulated accord of different musical sounds is like a well-governed city where order reigns, due to the organic union of its different elements.[191] Unity in variety; diversity, but in accord, this is the exact meaning of the two words which you have selected as your motto, *Concordia discors,* and which were already found in the ancient poets, Ovid and Horace, *Quid velit et possit rerum concordia discors.*[192]

1546. What your *Concordia discors* intended to express by means of this delightful 'concert has been achieved; however, the gloom that your art has dispelled for a few moments still remains at the bottom of our hearts: distress, because in many parts of the world, instead of hearing nature's divine and serene melodies, we hear the roar of guns; anguish, because we perceive the awful dissonance of all those different elements whose consonance alone can insure order and peace to cities and nations and all mankind: *Concordi varietate compactam bene ordinatæ civitatis . . . unitatem.*

1547. The program of your concert included composers who were of different nationalities but who were brought together in a region above earthly fatherlands in the universal temple of glory and art. May the resonance of this concert spread and linger in the world as a prelude symbolic of the desired harmony of nations!

---

[190] Original Italian, *Discorsi e Radiomessaggi,* v. 2, pp. 60-61.
[191] *De Civitate Dei,* bk. XVII, ch. 14.
[192] Horace, *Epist.* I, 12, 19.

May the present tragic discord of men and nations soon turn into the perfect and lasting accord of an equitable peace inspired by the divine teachings of Christ! Then will nations rise joyously to sing a majestic choral hymn whose power will shake the earth and the sky: *O Praise the Lord, all ye nations . . . for His mercy is confirmed upon us!*[193] Then humanity, tranquil again, will join in that "wonderful song of all creatures," of which St. Augustine speaks, the immortal echoes of which the ecstatic Poverello of Assisi, patron of Italy, gave to the world.

LETTER *Superiore Anno* TO CARDINAL MAGLIONE, SECRETARY OF STATE.[194]

Pius XII calls again upon all Catholics to pray during the month of May to the Blessed Virgin for the restoration of peace.

April 15, 1940

1548. Last year, when dark clouds obscured the horizon, and the talk of armed strife, forerunner of war, held all in trepidation, We who share in Our paternal heart the sufferings and straits of Our children, addressed a Letter[195] to you; through you We bade the whole Catholic world to offer in the month of May, then close at hand, prayers and fervent aspirations to the great Mother of God that she might conciliate her Son, offended by our many sins, and that the just settlement of opposing interests and the restoration of confidence to men's minds might effect the return of peace among nations. Now that the situation is worse, and that this terrible war has broken out, bringing with it already untold harm and suffering, We cannot but call again on Our children, scattered through the world, to gather around the altar of the Virgin Mother of God daily during the next month consecrated to her, to offer her suppliant prayer.

1549. All know now that, from the beginning of the war, We have left nothing undone, but have championed by every means at Our disposal—in Our public utterances written and oral, and in

---

[193] *Psalms,* CXVI, 1-2.
[194] Translation from *The Tablet,* v. 175, p. 399 (April 27, 1940). Original Latin, *A.A.S.,* v. 32, pp. 144-146 (April 19, 1940).
[195] Letter *Quandoquidem in Gubernanda,* April 20, 1939; *cf. supra* nn. 1332-1335.

conversations and interviews — the restoration of that peace and concord which must be based on justice and reach its perfection in mutual fraternal charity. You, Beloved Son, who stand so close by Us in the government of the Universal Church, and have such intimate contact with Us, know well that We are deeply afflicted by the travail and sorrows of the warring nations; that We can repeat and apply to Ourself in this connection, the words of the Apostle, St. Paul, *Who is weak, and I am not weak?*[196] Our heart is full of sorrow, not only for the terrible calamities that overwhelm the countries at war, but also for the evils, every day more menacing, that threaten other nations. But if, as We have said, We have left nothing undone that human power could do and human counsels could suggest, to avert this accumulation of evils, We nonetheless place all Our hope in Him Who alone is all-powerful, Who holds the world in the palm of His Hand, Who guides the destinies of peoples, the thoughts and sentiments of those who rule nations. We desire, therefore, that all should interweave their prayers with Ours, that the Merciful God by His powerful command may hasten the end of this calamitous storm.

1550. And since, as St. Bernard says, "It is the will of God that we should obtain all through Mary," [197] all should have recourse to her, and should lay at the foot of her altar their supplications, their tears, their sorrows, and from her seek solace and comfort. May that which, as history tells us, was for our forebears a constant and effective practice in times of crisis and trial, become for us who follow their footsteps faithfully, a persevering exercise during these trying times. . . . She is in truth the most powerful Mother of God, and is, too—a consoling thought for us—our most loving Mother; accordingly let us be happy to place ourselves under her protection and help, and to entrust ourselves entirely to her motherly goodness.

1551. But above all We desire, Beloved Son, that during next month white hosts of children may flock to the shrines of Our Lady, and through her intercession and peaceful mediation may obtain from God for all peoples and nations the desired tranquillity. Let them be assembled every day before the altar of our heavenly Mother, and on bended knees and with hands joined, let them offer together with their prayers their flowers, they who are them-

---

[196] II *Corinthians*, XI, 29.
[197] *Sermon on the Nativity of Our Lady.*

selves flowers from the mystical garden of the Church. We place great faith in the prayers of those whose *angels in heaven always see the face of My Father*,[198] whose expression radiates innocence and whose glistening eyes seem to reflect the splendors of the heavens. We know that our Divine Redeemer loves them with a special love, and that His most holy Mother has for them a special tenderness; We know that the prayers of the innocent pierce the heavens, disarm Divine Justice, and obtain heavenly graces for themselves and for others. Joined then in a holy rivalry of prayer, may they not fail to hasten the fulfillment of the wish common to all; let them remember Our Lord's promise: *Ask, and it shall be given you; seek, and you shall find; knock, and it shall be opened to you.*[199] May God in His kindness, moved by so many voices praying together, and especially by the voices of children, re-establish men's minds in peace, bind them together again in fraternal union, and restore the order of tranquillity and justice; may the rainbow of peace appear once again, and a happier era open for human society. . . . . . .

ADDRESS *Questa Viva Corona* TO A PILGRIMAGE FROM GENOA.[200]

The Pope implores Mary, Our Lady of Victory, to bring peace to the entire world.

April 21, 1940

1552. . . . . . . Our Beloved Sons, with you We raise Our prayer and praise to Mary, in this hour in which joy is mixed with sadness and fear. It is the hour of the mercy, of the power, and of the protection of Mary, of her who, though beautiful, sweet and resplendent, can be as terrible as an army ready for battle,[201] and who bears, among other titles, that of Lady of Victories, a title well known at Lepanto and Vienna. In her is Our hope, in her is Our peace. Over the world a fog is spreading, dark-hued with wrath and death. In the scales of His Justice, God is weighing potentates and nations, but the protection and the pious intercession of the Queen of Peace and Mercy can have such power over the Heart of

---

[198] *Matthew*, XVIII, 10.
[199] *Matthew*, VII, 7; *Luke*, XI, 9.
[200] Original Italian, *Discorsi e Radiomessaggi*, v. 2, pp. 86-87.
[201] *Cf. Canticle of Canticles*, VI, 3.

God as to change the progress of lightning, to rend clouds asunder, to free us from our sorrows by changing the hearts of men, dispelling hatred and anger, and bringing forth the dawn of peace.

1553. . . . May she, through your prayers and those of your little children who will kneel with you at her feet, and through Our prayers to which yours and those of millions of souls will be joined, obtain that God, Who rules the storms and winds of the oceans, may also calm the tempests of the human hearts in battle and *give us peace in our days;* that peace which invites and calls the light and the darkness, the lightning and the storms, the sky and the winds, the earth and the mountains, the seas and the rivers, all to bless and offer thanks to the Lord, after the tempest has passed. — Amen.

HOMILY *In Tot Rerum Angustiis* IN HONOR OF THE NEWLY CANONIZED SAINTS, EUPHRASIA PELLETIER AND GEMMA GALGANI.[202]

> *Immoderate lust for human greatness and power is one of the causes of wars between nations.*

May 2, 1940

1554. . . . . . . How far removed, Venerable Brethren and Dear Sons, is our time from the radiant sanctity of these two virgins! How many men to-day seek, not eternal, but worldly joys; how many care not for redeeming their sins by penance, but seek instead with growing intensity the satisfaction of their guilty passions and desires, even at the cost of their eternal fatherland. Yet the immoderate lust for human greatness and power and the consequent rejection of God's law only blinds the mind, so that all canons of truth and rules of charity are broken in social relations, bonds between nations are severed and the barriers of justice thrown down. The consequence, as you know, is a war that for the last eight months has caused the blood of brothers to flow, dissipated immense wealth and laid to waste many countries. Numberless citizens driven into exile deplore the loss of their country, innocent children are crying over the loss of their parents, fathers and mothers are mourning the loss of their children. Averting Our eyes from these

---

[202] Translation from *The Tablet,* v. 175, p. 448 (May 11, 1940). Original Latin, *Discorsi e Radiomessaggi,* v. 2, pp. 93-94.

terrifying scenes, We turn them toward heaven on this morning of Our Lord's Ascension, imploring these virgins, who already enjoy His glory, to intercede for Us, that We may follow them to our heavenly home. . . .

SERMON *Ammirevole Spettacolo* ON ST. CATHERINE OF SIENA AND ST. FRANCIS OF ASSISI, THE PATRONS OF ITALY.[203]

The Italians are asked to pray to their special patrons, St. Catherine of Siena and St. Francis of Assisi, for the return of world peace.

May 5, 1940

1555. . . . . . . This hour, beloved children, is an hour of prayer for you, for all, great and small, fortunate and unfortunate, for the world, for Italy. It is an hour to pray and invoke the patronage and help of the saints. The tempest of war released from the depths of passions and human egoisms is sweeping noble nations into deplorable hostilities on land, on sea, and in the air. It rumbles dark and threatening beyond the barriers of the Alps. Meanwhile, God, Lord of the universe, on Whom empires depend, and Who alone lifts up and casts down thrones and makes the plans of peoples vain—He, the God of heaven, looks down to see if there be a man who meditates on such awful ruins and in pity sets his hand to that justice which brings back peace. With that God, Who chiefly shows His power by pardoning, We implore the intercession of our two great Protectors, Catherine and Francis, Guardians and Defenders of Italy. . . .

1556. Hear, O Jesus, our prayer which by their hands we present to Thee. Thou didst love them, Thou didst make them great and powerful; Thou also lovest us, who humbly pray to Thee; and Thy infinite love holds Thee present on this altar, as food and drink for us. . . . By the heavenly patronage of Thy glorious servants, let Thy grace, Thy pardon, Thy munificence, Thy peace triumph in us! Triumph, O great God, in us, in our families, in all the lands of Italy, in the plains and in the mountains, in palaces and cabins, in cloisters and in offices, in youth and in old age, in the dawns and

---

[203] Translation from *The Australasian Catholic Record*, v. 18, pp. 12-14 (January, 1941). Original Italian, *Discorsi e Radiomessaggi*, v. 2, pp. 104-105.

in the twilights of life. Triumph in the world, O God of armies, and make to return that peace which Thy Heart grants to Italy, that peace which Thou didst leave to Thy Apostles and which we invoke on all men—make that peace, O Lord, return in the midst of peoples and nations, which forgetfulness of Thy love separates, which rancor poisons, which passion for vengeance inflames. O Jesus, dispel the tempest of death which afflicts humanity redeemed by Thee; make one sole sheepfold of peace for all Thy lambs, faithful and straying. Thus may all hear Thee and follow Thy voice; may all the nations adore Thee and serve Thee, and may all in one same faith, hope and love mount up from the irrevocable passage of time to plunge themselves in the ineffable peace of a happy eternity! Amen.

ADDRESS *Nella Schiera* TO A GROUP OF NEWLY-WEDS ON THE FEAST OF THE APPARITION OF ST. MICHAEL.[204]

The paternal heart of Pius XII worries about young couples beginning their married life in these tragic times.

May 8, 1940

1557. . . . . . . The world, poisoned by lies and disloyalty, and wounded by excesses of violence, has lost its moral health and joy by losing its peace. If the earth after the original sin could no longer be an earthly paradise, it could and should at least be and remain a place of brotherly concord between men and nations. Instead the conflagration of war has burst over several nations and threatens to invade others. Our heart is worried about you, beloved sons and daughters, and about so many other young married couples of all nations, who are uniting their existences in this tragic springtime. Even from afar how can one contemplate without a feeling of horror the terrible spectre of war stretching over young homes smiling with hope? But if human efforts seem at present to fail in bringing back a just, loyal and enduring peace, it is always possible for men to implore God's intercession. Between God and men, the Lord has placed as mediatrix our most sweet Mother Mary. Invoke this

[204] Original Italian, *Discorsi e Radiomessaggi,* v. 2, p. 112.

"Mother Most Amiable," this "Virgin Most Powerful," this "Help of Christians" with more fervor and more eagerly in the present month of May—and to-day more specially under the title of Queen of the Most Holy Rosary of Pompei—that she may again unite under the mantle of her tenderness and in the peace of her smile her children now so cruelly divided. Invoke, as the Church does to-day in her sacred liturgy, "the angel of peace, St. Michael, to descend from heaven into our dwellings and, as a messenger of peace, to drive into hell these wars, cause of so many tears." [205]

MESSAGE *Au Moment* TO KING LEOPOLD OF BELGIUM.[206]

The Pope sends his sympathy to the Belgians.

May 10, 1940

1558. When, for the second time, against their will and rights, the Belgian people see their territory exposed to the cruelties of war, We, profoundly moved, send Your Majesty and all your beloved nation the assurances of Our paternal affection. Praying Almighty God that this hard trial results in the re-establishment of full liberty and the independence of Belgium, We accord with all Our heart to Your Majesty and to your people Our Apostolic Benediction.

MESSAGE *Apprenant* TO QUEEN WILHELMINA OF HOLLAND.[207]

The Holy Father sympathizes with the Dutch whose country has been unjustly invaded.

May 10, 1940

1559. We learn, with great emotion, that Your Majesty's efforts for peace have not been able to preserve your noble people from becoming, against their will and their rights, the theatre of war. We pray to God, the Supreme Arbiter of the destinies of nations, to hasten with His Almighty help the re-establishment of justice and liberty.

[205] Roman Breviary, May 8.
[206] Translation from *The Tablet,* v. 175, p. 514 (May 18, 1940). Original French, *L'Osservatore Romano,* May 12, 1940.
[207] Translation from *The Tablet,* v. 175, p. 514 (May 18, 1940). Original French, *L'Osservatore Romano,* May 12, 1940.

MESSAGE *En Ce Moment* TO THE GRAND DUCHESS CHARLOTTE OF LUXEMBOURG.[208]

The heart of the Holy Father is close to the people of Luxembourg in this tragic hour.

May 10, 1940

1560. In this sad moment, in which the people of Luxembourg, despite their love for peace, find themselves involved in a tempest of war, Our heart is close to them, and We implore from heaven aid and protection so that they may live in liberty and independence, and We accord to Your Royal Highness and to your faithful subjects Our Apostolic Benediction.

ADDRESS *Le Titre* TO THE RELIGIOUS OF THE SACRED HEART.[209]

The present world threatens to perish in violence, because too many men lack heart.

May 15, 1940

1561. . . . . . . The present world threatens to perish in violence, because too many men lack heart. This reproach, once addressed by St. Paul to the ancient pagan world,[210] may be repeated to the neo-pagans, worshippers of gold, pleasure and pride. The heart, no doubt, means courage and strength, but at the service of right and justice. The heart also means pity for the weak, tenderness towards pain and forbearance which forgives. The heart rebels against all evil but condescends to every good. You who have hearts, open them wide to God's great causes and man's great miseries. Act and pray; though you may not be able always to act, you can always pray. The last day of this month of Mary, when the Church asks for interior peace, the feast of Our Lady, Mediatrix of all graces, coincides with the feast of the Sacred Heart. A providential coincidence, so We hope, for here are two hearts, the purest, the strongest and the tenderest of all, that will restore some feelings to mankind. . . . . . .

---

[208] Translation from *The Tablet*, v. 175, p. 514 (May 18, 1940). Original French, *L'Osservatore Romano*, May 12, 1940.
[209] Translation from *The Tablet*, v. 175, p. 572 (June 8, 1940). Original French, *Discorsi e Radiomessaggi*, v. 2, p. 121.
[210] Cf. *Romans*, I, 31; II *Timothy*, III, 3.

ALLOCUTION *Sempre Dolce* TO THE COLLEGE OF CARDINALS ON
THE FEAST OF THE HOLY FATHER'S PATRON, ST. EUGENE.[211]

*Belligerent nations are asked to observe the principles
of humanity and of international law in their treatment
of non-combatants and occupied countries.*

June 2, 1940

1562. . . . . . . And would that, in His inscrutable and always
just councils for the government of the world, God had granted Us
the power of holding back in some manner the bloody course of
events! Now that the ninth month of the war has been completed
and the struggle is raging more violently on bloody fields, on treacherous seas, under the thundering fire of aeroplanes, and is spreading
even to peoples remote from the struggle, We recall those troubled
weeks during which We alternated between hope and fear. It was
then that, prompted still by a scant hope of peace, aware of the duties
of Our Apostolic Ministry, and following the impulses of Our heart,
We devoted Our every thought and effort to the well-being of all
peoples, exerting Ourselves to dissuade rulers from having recourse
to violence and trying to win them over to the idea of a settlement
at once peaceful, just and honorable and based on a sense of responsibility toward men and God.

1563. If to-day, Venerable Brethren and Beloved Sons, We turn
Our eyes and contemplate Europe, by divine vocation the land of
faith and of Christian civilization, tearing itself to pieces with sword
and fire; if We consider the vast destruction and the ruins and the
cruel suffering that are accumulating and spreading in so many
flourishing lands that at one time provided food and happiness to so
many peoples; if We ponder the sad economic, social, ideological,
religious and moral effects and the heavy repercussions which result
even beyond the oceans from the prolongation and cruel embitter-
ment of the conflict; if We consider and weigh all this, We see
before Us a vision that grieves Us deeply and weighs heavily upon
Our spirit, and makes Us raise Our eyes to heaven, invoking the
boundless mercy of God for the wretched sons of men divided
among themselves by conflicting ideas and interests, led astray by
enmity, by hatred, by rancor, by revenge into a sea of calamity and

[211] Original Italian, *Discorsi e Radiomessaggi*, v. 2, pp. 126-132.

sorrow. Is this perhaps the terrible hour in which God is weighing our merits and demerits? We bow Our head before the impenetrable divine judgment, and, communing with Ourself and Our conscience, We feel confident that, in Our efforts toward peace, We have followed the royal road which leads to interior serenity and to external peace, to respect for human feelings, to a sense of true justice and kindly fairness, to an objective attitude, and to a just esteem of the interests of all peoples.

1564. The present war has now reached all the intensity of pitched battles and destructive action, and its ruins are attaining gigantic proportions; but the external and material damages cannot compare with the interior collapse and destruction of man's moral and spiritual patrimony. What more eloquent and frightful sign of the progressive annihilation and subversion of spiritual values than the increasing dissolution of the norms of right, replaced by force which restrains, enchains and stifles ethical and juridical impulses? And is there not perhaps clear evidence of this in the fact that the hurricane of war has engulfed regions and peoples that were more than others traditional promoters of peace?

1565. Even under the weight of the hard necessities of the struggle, it is a rule of prudence to turn Our now beclouded eyes toward the dawn of a better and more ordered future, and not to forget the very illuminating words of St. Augustine: "For peace is not sought in order to kindle war, but war is waged in order that peace may be obtained. Therefore, even in waging war, cherish the spirit of a peacemaker, that, by conquering those whom you attack, you may lead them back to the advantages of peace."[212] If We, Venerable Brethren and Beloved Sons, moved by this wise maxim and likewise by what We explained under other circumstances, especially in Our Christmas Allocution, again insistently beseech all the hostile parties to remember always those duties of humanity that lose none of their value even in the face of the law and morality of war (wherefore the same great doctor exclaimed that "when faith is pledged, it is to be kept even with the enemy against whom the war is waged"[213]), it is not because Our words and Our work are partial; We are fulfilling a duty dictated to Us by truth and love, imposed upon Us by the good and the well-being of all,

[212] St. Augustine, *Epistolae,* in Migne, *P.L.,* v. 33, c. 856.
[213] St. Augustine, *Epistolae,* in Migne, *P.L.,* v. 33, c. 856.

being committed to it by the office of Common Father of those redeemed in Christ. And, for Our part, We shall, through the means furnished Us by Our Apostolic Ministry, contribute what We can to keep the world from losing sight of the ideal norms and essential prerequisites of a peace that must be just, honorable and lasting.

1566. Nor do We think it right on this occasion to refuse to express Our sorrow in seeing how the treatment of non-combatants in more than one region is far from being in conformity with humane standards. God is Our witness that, when We in duty bound affirm this truth, We are moved neither by a partisan spirit nor by partiality for any person. The moral judgment of an action cannot be determined by personal considerations. No people is free from the danger of seeing some of its children aroused by passions and sacrificing to the demon of hatred. What is important above all is the judgment passed by public authority upon such aberrations and degeneration resulting from the spirit of strife, and the rapidity with which they are stopped.

1567. Wherefore it belongs to the good name of the authorities themselves to see to it that, as the fields of war extend beyond one's own boundaries, the unperturbed dignity of reason shall not fail, for it is reason which dictates those sovereign principles for the promotion of good and the restraint of evil which strengthen and honor the legal dispositions of those who rule and conciliate those who are subjects, making them more willing and ready to bow their will and to work for the common good. And, therefore, the larger become the territories that the conflict subjects to foreign domination, the more urgent becomes the duty of bringing the juridical order which is applied to them into harmony with the provisions of international law and above all with the exigencies of humanity and equity. Nor is the fact to be disregarded that, along with the precautions of safety justified by the real necessities of war, the good of the peoples in occupied regions does not cease to be an obligatory norm for the exercise of public power. Justice and equity require that they be treated in the same manner as, under similar circumstances, the occupying power should wish to see its own citizens treated.

1568. From these elementary principles of sound reason, it is not difficult for those who wish to rise above human passions to draw the conclusion that they should draft regulations for settling special questions regarding occupied countries—regulations that should be as much in conformity with human and Christian conscience as with the true wisdom of the State: respect for the life, honor and property of citizens, respect for the family and its rights; and, on the religious side, freedom of private and public practice of divine worship and of spiritual assistance in a manner proper to each people and to its language, freedom of instruction and religious education, safety of ecclesiastical goods, and the right of bishops to communicate with their clergy and their faithful in matters concerning the care of souls.

1569. As for Us, *giving no offense to any man, that our ministry be not blamed,*[214] desirous at least of alleviating the consequences of war, We bestow Our paternal love on all Our sons and daughters, whether of the Germanic peoples always dear to Us among whom We spent long years of Our life, or of the Allied States to whom We are also bound by pleasant and holy memories, remembering also with constant solicitude the Polish nation so sorely tried and so dear to Us, or of other noble peoples whose tragic suffering We pray to the Highest may soon be propitiously relieved. For the rest, We place Our unshaken trust in God Who rules men and events as wisely as from heaven He rules His Church, to which He gave jurisdiction over souls and which He taught to proceed *with the armor of justice on the right hand and on the left, in honor and dishonor, in evil report and good report,*[215] on the irresistible way of truth and divine virtue assigned to it, benefiting those who calumniate it and those who praise it, loving those who love it and those who hate it, praying for those who persecute it and those who protect it, calling all people to the one Fold of Christ, beseeching heaven for kings and for those in power *that we may lead a quiet and a peaceable life in all piety and chastity,*[216] and pacifying on its voyage to eternity the discords and the conflicts of the world. . . . . . .'.

1570. But patience is indeed a great gift of God, and it becomes perseverance when it does not fall behind, but keeps abreast of the increase of suffering and misfortunes. Wherefore patience is joined to persevering prayer inculcated in us by the Divine Redeemer Himself. We cannot, therefore, desist from exhorting all who on earth are sons of the Church of Christ to offer with holy zeal their

---

[214] II *Corinthians,* VI, 3.
[215] II *Corinthians,* VI, 7-8.
[216] I *Timothy,* II, 2.

untiring prayers to the Heart of the Divine Saviour, King of Peace, that He may pour out the streams of mercy and humility on the people exasperated by the struggle, that He may restrain the massacres that are steeping the fields and the cities in blood, that He may inspire in the rulers of the nations those great thoughts of moderation and peace that come from the heart where God placed as its foundation goodness together with the divine likeness, so that the bloody struggle and the tragic destruction of the well-being of the peoples may cease and, through so many ruins and tears, there may be marked out and opened the way to the temple of a sound peace sealed not by hatred and revenge, but by the stamp of the noble majesty of justice. . . .

ADDRESS *Come Potremmo* TO A GROUP OF NEWLY-WEDS.[217]

> *Meekness and humility are the way to peace, both for individuals and for nations.*

June 5, 1940

1571. How could We, beloved newly-weds, omit talking to you of the Sacred Heart of Jesus in this month dedicated to Him and during the very octave of His Feast? How could We refrain from talking to you of the Sacred Heart, the inexhaustible Source of human and divine tenderness, at a time when your young love—palpitating now with hope at the dawning of the dreams that will brighten your future and now with fear because of the violence that has broken out to darken our present age—asks with anguish if there be still a corner of the earth where two human hearts can cherish each other in serenity and peace?

1572. Christ invites us to find peace in the loving submission to His Sacred Heart—at least that peace which can still exist in spite of the agitations of the external world. *Learn of Me*, He says, *because I am meek and humble of heart: and you shall find rest to your souls.*[218] To be in the school of Christ, to learn from His Heart meekness and humility—the divine remedies against pride and violence, the sources of all the ills of mankind[219]—this is the way to

[217] Original Italian, *Discorsi e Radiomessaggi,* v. 2, p. 135.
[218] *Matthew,* XI, 29.
[219] Cf. *Ecclesiasticus,* X, 15.

peace, both for individuals and for nations themselves. This will be for you the fountain of the happiness which you desire and which We wish for your domestic hearth. . . . . . .

REPLY *Les Paroles* TO THE HOMAGE OF THE NEW AMBASSADOR OF FRANCE, WLADIMIR D'ORMESSON.[220]

Passion, hatred, conscious or unconscious contempt for the ideas and opinions of others are among the unavoidable and deplorable consequences of war.

June 9, 1940

1573. The words which you have pronounced, Mr. Ambassador, while delivering to Us your credential letters, draw from the gravity of this hour, in which unspeakable sorrows lie on the sons and daughters of your country, a deeply pathetic accent. Going back in mind toward that French land which We admired three years ago during Our mission to Lisieux, in the gorgeous beauty of its summer fecundity, We see her to-day crimson with the blood of her sons, and covered with nameless ruins. Like Our Divine Model, the Good Shepherd, We feel Our heart touched with pity before these great devastations and sufferings, which give a concrete reality to the lamentations of the Psalmist: *Lord, You had Your people see hardships, You quenched its thirst with bitter wine.*[221]

1574. In this great disconcert you have recalled, Mr. Ambassador, the truths of general order that, beyond national and linguistic frontiers, represent the essential basis of the moral patrimony of humanity. Amidst these fundamental spiritual values you have given to the Christian faith, or as you say, "to the Christian conception of society and life," the place of honor to which she is entitled. Like lightning which flashes through heavy clouds, the devastating lights of war, whereof fires have again inflamed the ancient continent, have torn from the eyes of all careful observers that veil of prejudices which for half a century the voice of the Church and especially the reiterated warnings of the last Popes, Our venerated Predecessors, did not succeed in penetrating. The succession of causes and effects imposes itself even in certain minds

[220] Translation from *The Tablet*, v. 176, p. 150 (August 24, 1940). Original French, *A.A.S.*, v. 32, pp. 276-278 (July 6, 1940).
[221] *Psalms*, LIX, 5.

which, up to to-day, considered with indifference the rising de-Christianization of public and private life, and sometimes were induced to see in the recoiling of the Christian idea a progress of modern civilization. A good number of these begin to perceive and even sorrowfully take notice that the weakening of faith and the forgetfulness of the Gospel have, on the contrary, speeded up the internal decompositions and aggravated the external strains among social classes as well as among nations.

1575. May the lessons of this bitter experience result in acts which permit Us to hope in the future for a revival of the Christian spirit, particularly in the education of youth. France, who is legitimately proud of proclaiming herself the Eldest Daughter of the Church, will face with so much greater and energetic security the future trials, the more her sons, in all ranks, will appeal with determination to the resources of moral forces contained in her Christian tradition: opulent reserves stored for centuries and which await but to be freed from the bonds still enclosing their beneficial expansion, to have the governors and the people feel their full and total effect.

1576. In the present chaos of thought and sentiment We see, as the unavoidable and deplorable consequence of armed conflicts, open in increasingly wider manner between nations abysses of passion, of hatred and of conscious or unconscious contempt for the ideas and opinions of others. From all this comes upon Us, Father of Christianity, a double and urgent duty. Among Our sons and daughters of all countries and all peoples, We want on the one hand to revive the sentiments of responsibility which are necessary to Christian conscience; on the other hand, to prepare and to confirm in souls a determined inclination to be ready for any enterprise in order that the events which are changing the face of Europe and the external and social structure of humanity, may be succeeded by the creation of a new Christian order, in which those fundamental principles of equity and charity will be loyally and integrally applied, without which a real and lasting peace cannot be conceived. When will this desired hour arrive? God preserves the secret of it; but We beseech Him to hasten its advent. We implore also from Him light and wisdom for those to whom His Providence will entrust the task of architecture, full of responsibility, in the construction of the future City, based upon justice and sound freedom. Meanwhile, We recommend to the Lord's protection Our dear French sons.

ADDRESS *Noi Potremmo* TO A GROUP OF NEWLY-WEDS.[222]

To live in peace, the world needs the spirit of sacrifice.

June 26, 1940

1577. . . . . . . There is no doubt that if we wish to emerge from the present crisis permanently, society must be rebuilt on less fragile foundations, that is to say, more in harmony with Christian morality, the fundamental source of all true civilization. No less sure is it that if we are to achieve this end we must begin with the re-Christianization of the families, many of which have forgotten, together with the practice of the Gospel, the charity which it requires and the peace which it brings. . . . . . .

1578. What we need, what the whole world needs, in order to live happily and in peace, is the evangelical spirit of sacrifice. This spirit is lacking because with the turning away from faith egoism, which destroys and makes mutual happiness impossible, prevails. . . . Among men as among peoples, individual desires will never coincide with the common good. . . . To find peace again, men must learn again what Christ and His Church have been preaching for centuries: make the sacrifice of one's aspirations and desires when they appear incompatible with the rights of others or with the collective good. . . . . . .

LETTER *L'Expression de Dévouement* TO THE CARDINALS, ARCH-BISHOPS AND BISHOPS OF FRANCE.[223]

> *In Christian faith and charity, France will find the spiritual resources necessary to face adversity and to arouse its citizens to a consciousness of its Christian mission.*

June 29, 1940

1579. The expression of filial devotion which you sent to Us on the day after the unprecedented disaster which crossed your fatherland, and the prayer which you have uttered to have a word of comfort, correspond to Our deep desire to be at this moment in the midst of you, dear Sons and Venerable Brethren, and to ex-

---

[222] Original Italian, *Discorsi e Radiomessaggi,* v. 2, pp. 155-157.
[223] Translation from Rankin, *The Pope Speaks,* pp. 259-261. Original French, *A.A.S.,* v. 32, pp. 299-300 (August 6, 1940).

press to you the profound echo raised in Our fatherly heart by the calamity which has plunged France into mourning. Certainly these sentiments of paternal affection which have permitted Us so often, whether from near or far, to participate in the joys of your religious ceremonies do not permit Us to remain apart from your misfortunes while throughout France the tears flow as abundantly as the generous blood with which, in the course of this war, her valorous youth made such a great sacrifice.

1580.   Therefore, We are here among you, Pastors, priests and faithful, moved by your fate, but at the same time consoled again at finding anew in the day of trial, in all its dignity, the Catholic soul of this France whom misfortune has never crushed and has often brought nearer to God to make her more vigorous and faithful to her great spiritual and Christian mission. It is precisely toward this mission, which constitutes her greatest title to glory, that We desire to invite you to raise your eyes and your fondest hopes, to make yourself more perfectly realize that in so sad an hour in your history, your providential mission preserves all its value. Yes, these very misfortunes with which God to-day visited your people give assurance, We feel certain, through the adorable designs of His Providence, of the conditions for greater spiritual labor favorable to bring about a re-awakening of the entire nation.

1581.   Is not the true grandeur of a people, a spiritual grandeur like that of every man who is conscious of his dignity and of the value of life? Is it not through sorrow that it is given to all of us to open our eyes better to the eternal truth, to find again the path of wisdom which brings happiness?

1582.   We are not unaware of the spiritual resources with which France is prepared to enter upon this path and to take hold of herself once again, thus utilizing her misfortune as a lever of a new spiritual ascension, which will be for her a pledge of solid and lasting welfare. Her resources are so numerous and so powerful that We are sure she will not await the conclusion of peace to put them to work and will give to the world the spectacle of a great people, worthy of its secular traditions, who finds in its faith and infinite charity the strength to face adversity and to resume its march on the path of the future and of Christian justice.

1583.   Thus We like to believe that all of you dear Pastors and priests in Jesus Christ, after having given everything to your country during the horrors of war, will now hasten to return to your posts by taking up again the laborious life of the nation; that you will perform a duty like the Good Samaritan of the Gospels, in bending over the open wounds and solacing the sick, utilizing the numerous means of which the charity of your country has always had the secret. . . . . .

ADDRESS *La Pietà* TO A GROUP OF NEWLY-WEDS.[224]

> *When a Christian speaks of transmitting blood to his descendants he speaks not in a merely biological but in a spiritual and intellectual sense.*

July 3, 1940

1584. . . . . . . When, in a nation of baptized people, someone speaks of transmitting blood to his descendants, who should live and die, not like beasts without understanding, but as men and Christians, the words should not be limited to their simple biological or material sense. We must rather extend them to include the essence of intellectual and spiritual life—to that inheritance of faith, of nature, of honor, which is handed on from parents to their descendants and which is a thousand times more precious than the blood which flows through our veins. Members of a distinguished family pride themselves on being of noble blood: but all who receive the grace of baptism can call themselves, "Princes of the Blood"— of a Blood not only kingly, but Godly. With this there flows into your children a pride in their supernatural nobility, so that they will be ready to suffer rather than lose so precious a treasure. . . . . . .

ADDRESS *Nel Mese di Luglio* TO A GROUP OF NEWLY-WEDS.[225]

> *While defending his country faithfully and coura- geously, the Christian must abstain from hating those whom he is obliged to combat.*

July 10, 1940

1585. . . . . . . In the present hour there is danger that the noble and legitimate feeling of love for one's own country may degenerate

[224] Translation from *The Tablet*, v. 176, p. 252 (September 28, 1940). Original Italian, *Discorsi e Radiomessaggi*, v. 2, pp. 164-165.
[225] Translation from *The Tablet*, v. 176, p. 91 (August 3, 1940). Original Italian, *Discorsi e Radiomessaggi*, v. 2, pp. 173-174.

in the souls of many men into revengeful passion, an insatiable pride in some and an incurable rancor in others. While defending faithfully and courageously his country, a Christian must, however, abstain from hating those whom he is obliged to combat. One sees on the battlefields people assigned to the ambulance services, such as male and female nurses, who generously attend to the sick and wounded without distinction of nationality. But is it really necessary that men reach the threshold of death in order to discover that they are brothers? This belated charity is to be admired, but is not enough. The Christian peoples must become conscious of the brotherly ties that bind them to each other and their souls must find the strength, sometimes a truly heroic one, to pardon each other, without which it will never be possible to attain true and permanent concord. However, this pardon does not exclude the re-establishment of justice or of injured right. . . . . . .

LETTER *Septimo Labente Saeculo* TO THE VERY REV. A. SCOTTI, MASTER GENERAL OF THE ORDER OF MERCY.[226]

Rancor and hatred are the ruin of mankind.

July 15, 1940

1586. . . . We entertain a lively confidence that the illustrious example of such illustrious men may help not a little to restore the charity which has grown cold among peoples, so that, putting aside rancor and hatred which are the ruin of mankind, those who have been redeemed by the Precious Blood may return to mutual love for one another and in unity of will and effort, reach that real and solid glory which man derives from the virtues that preannounce happiness in heaven. . . .

---

[226] Translation from *The Tablet*, v. 176, p. 192 (September 7, 1940). Original Latin, *A.A.S.*, v. 32, p. 490 (November 19, 1940).

LETTER *Dans la Tristesse* TO CARDINAL VAN ROEY, ARCHBISHOP OF MALINES.[227]

Pius XII prays that God may prepare for Belgium a new future of peace and prosperity in justice.

July 31, 1940

1587. . . . . . . But in the midst of so many disasters it is very comforting for Us to learn from your letter that the sentiment of duty has not weakened in the pastors of souls and that all the bishops remain valiantly at their posts, doing honor to their mission and sharing with their flocks the sorrows of the present situation. Their conduct makes them particularly worthy of Our gratitude, and We would desire them to know with what tender affection We are united to them in sorrow, in prayer, and in firm trust in God.

1588. For the rest, it must be very sweet for you to have recourse to Divine Providence while accomplishing your arduous duties and in doing your best to sustain the courage and faith of your faithful. Place your hope in God and see to it that the religious soul of dear Belgium does not suffer from the storm that has broken loose, rather on the contrary, that it may draw from this storm a happy increase of Christian life and piety. It is with these sentiments that We ceaselessly raise Our prayers and supplications to God, beseeching Him to proportion His graces to the sufferings of all these dear children and to prepare for Belgium a new future of peace and prosperity in justice.

1589. Happy in the knowledge that you are united with Us in prayer to obtain from God the light and the strength which We need at this present hour, We ask you to continue to do violence to heaven, not forgetting, however, that for all of us our glory is in tribulations—*gloriamur in tribulationibus*[228]—and that it is by faith in the midst of trials that the Christian triumphs over the world. In the consoling vision of that spiritual victory, We entertain for your own person and for your whole diocese, for the episcopate of all Belgium, for your clergy and for your faithful, the most ardent good wishes, and We send to you all, as the pledge of Our paternal love, the Apostolic Blessing.

---

[227] Original French, *A.A.S.,* v. 32, pp. 549-550 (December 16, 1940).
[228] *Romans,* V, 3.

ADDRESS *L'Estate* TO AN AUDIENCE COMPOSED CHIEFLY OF NEWLY-WEDS.[229]

Peace will flourish only when fraternal love between men and nations returns.

July 31, 1940

1590. . . . . . . Peace—how many families to-day desire it! How many wives, mothers, betrothed—though strongly determined and ready to face even extreme sacrifice to fulfill their duty and obey the country they love—are heartbroken at seeing their loved ones depart for the most remote destinations, perhaps unknown and often dangerous! Others, with souls still more tortured because their agitated thoughts are lost in the night of painful uncertainty, plead with heaven and earth to learn at least with some certainty the fate, perhaps tragic, of the loved one concerning whom there is no news. Peace is a white dove which, unable to find a place to set down its feet on earth because the land is covered with corpses and submerged in a deluge of violence, seems to have returned to the ark of the new alliance, which is the Heart of Jesus . . . whence it will issue only when it is able to pluck from the tree of the Gospel a re-blossoming branch of fraternal love between men and nations. . . . . . .

DISCOURSE *Quando sotto il Sole* TO A GROUP OF NEWLY-WEDS.[230]

False propaganda can be just as deadly as armored cars and bombers.

August 7, 1940

1591. . . . . . . Together with writings propagating wickedness and bad customs, We cannot fail to mention other writings that spread falsehood provoking hatred. Falsehood is abominable in the eyes of God, and is detested by every just man.[231] It is much more detestable when it spreads calumny and the seed of discord among

---

[229] Translation partly from *The Tablet,* v. 176, p. 211 (September 14, 1940). Original Italian, *Discorsi e Radiomessaggi,* v. 2, p. 195.

[230] Translation from *The Tablet,* v. 176, p. 211 (September 14, 1940). Original Italian, *Discorsi e Radiomessaggi,* v. 2, p. 207.

[231] *Cf. Proverbs,* VI, 17 and XIII, 5.

brethren.[232] Anonymous letters written with rancor and detraction ruin the happiness of domestic life and the union of the family. And a certain Press appears to have proposed for itself the task of destroying, in the great family of peoples, fraternal relations between the children of the same Heavenly Father. This work of hatred is carried on sometimes by books, but still more often through newspapers. In the rush of urgent daily work, an error may slip by and be accepted by a badly managed source of information, and an unjust impression may be created. This may often be the result of lack of thought rather than deliberate. But a similar error committed through inadvertance may be sufficient, especially in periods of acute tension, to cause serious repercussions. Would to God that history showed no war provoked by a lie cleverly diffused.

1592. But a publicist aware of his mission and responsibility, who has published error, should feel himself obliged to re-establish truth. To the thousands of his readers upon whom his writings might make an impression, he is obliged not to destroy in them and around them the sacred patrimony of liberating truth and pacifying charity which nineteen centuries of Christianity have laboriously brought to mankind. It has been said that the tongue kills more people than the sword.[233] In the same manner lying literature can be just as deadly as armored cars and bombing airplanes. . . . . . .

REPLY *Después de Cosechar* TO THE HOMAGE OF THE NEW AMBASSADOR OF BOLIVIA, GENERAL CARLO QUINTANILLA.[234]

Divine Providence will draw moral and spiritual fruits from the war.

August 10, 1940

1593. . . . . . . While the convulsions of a tremendous war torment Europe, you come cordially wishing the consolation of success in Our efforts and Our most intense aspiration to peace. As a son and representative of a people who are proud of the Catholic culture received from Europe, you well know that in humanity redeemed

---

[232] *Cf. Proverbs,* VI, 19.
[233] *Cf. Ecclesiasticus,* XXVIII, 22.
[234] Translation from *N.C.W.C. News Service* (August 12, 1940). Original Spanish, *A.A.S.,* v. 32, p. 361 (September 25, 1940).

by Christ real peace is impossible outside the principles and rules of justice and charity promulgated by the Gospel. The See of St. Peter has always endeavored to bring it about that, without passion, men may find in these supreme principles of real human fraternity the noble solution of the problems which divide them. Conscious of the gravity of the burden of Our duty, We declare that We will not cease to admonish with paternal insistence all in the same way, especially those who shoulder the responsibility of the future of nations. We agree with St. Augustine that "it is God Who directs the beginning, the progress and the ends of the wars"[235]; and consequently We do not doubt that Divine Providence will draw spiritual and moral fruits even from this struggle; but at the same time We exhort men to listen to the voice of the Church, which with maternal love orders them to supplicate God and admonishes mankind to liberate men from the scourge of war. . . . . . .

ADDRESS *Se a Temperare* TO MEMBERS OF ITALIAN CATHOLIC ACTION.[236]

> *Members of Catholic Action are ready to give their lives every time the legitimate welfare of their country requires this supreme sacrifice.*

September 4, 1940

1594. . . . . . . The present hour is an hour of temptation for the soul. In the dizzy speed of material progress, in the conquests of human ingenuity over the secrets of nature and over the elemental powers of the earth, the seas and the skies, in the harassing contest to win supremacy over competitors, in the halls where daring researches are pursued, in the proud conquests of science, of industry, of factories and laboratories, in the lust for money and pleasure, in the struggle to gain a supereminent power more feared than coveted, more envied than enjoyed, in the din and confusion of modern life, where can the human soul, Christian by nature, find peace? Can it find it in being self-sufficient? Can it, perhaps, find it in the boast of being the lord of the universe because the soul, being so engulfed in the fog of delusion, confounds the material

---

[235] *De Civitate Dei*, bk. VII, ch. 30.
[236] Original Italian, *A.A.S.*, v. 32, pp. 364-367 (September 25, 1940).

with the spiritual, the human with the divine, the temporal with the
eternal? No, not in inebriating dreams can the tempest in the soul
and conscience be stilled, since they are agitated by the driving force
of the mind dominating matter and, conscious of its undeniable,
immortal destiny, pushing toward the Infinite and the attainment
of boundless desires. . . . . . .

1595.   To you, beloved sons and daughters of Catholic Action,
who have adopted the insignia of those laboring and suffering nobly
like Christians and like Romans, to you We extend Our paternal
congratulations, Our thanks and Our praise. You have deserved
well of the Church and of civil society; yes, of civil society, because,
diffusing and actuating in individual, family and social life the
Catholic principles of authority, of obedience, of order, of justice, of
equality and of charity, you have co-operated to make shine forth
again, to revive and to reinvigorate, those things which are the most
solid bases of society.

1596.   We repose in you Our hopes for the future. In this grave
hour in which human passions, dormant in peace, are aroused, burst
forth inflamed, and struggle in a duel of blood and injury that
makes Our heart shudder at the fierce conflict among sons dear to
Us, We fix Our glance on Catholic Action and We comfort Our
soul by being hopeful and trustful, finding in it devoted and ardent
collaborators in the great enterprise which above all weighs upon
Our spirit . . . the return of Christ into consciences and domestic
hearths, into the relations between social classes, into civil order and
into international relations. . . . . . .

1597.   Members of Catholic Action—which is not and never will
be a political organization, but a chosen band showing good example
and manifesting religious fervor—will demonstrate not only that
they are the most fervent Christians but also perfect citizens familiar
with the high obligations of a national and social character, loving
their country and ready to give even life for it every time the legitimate welfare of the country requires this supreme sacrifice.[237] . . . . . .

---

[237] See *supra Sapientiae Christianae* nn. 109-116.

ADDRESS *Mentre il Tumulto* TO THE MEMBERS OF THE SACRED
ROMAN ROTA.[238]

> *Men must pray that the tempest raging over poor humanity may be calmed.*

October 1, 1940

1598. . . . . . Let Our thoughts and Our heart return to the source of Our sorrow, contemplating Our sons armed and fighting one against the other, almost as though they were not brothers of one faith and one hope. History will pass judgment on this bloody and destructive struggle; but the thoughts and judgments of men are not those of God. At God's tribunal families of peoples, throughout the centuries, listen to the sentence that is infallibly fulfilled: *the counsel of the Lord standeth forever*[239]; and while the Lord *bringeth to naught the counsels of nations, rejecteth the devices of people and casteth away the counsels of princes,*[240] with justice and mercy He throws down and raises up, He raises and overthrows empires, He cancels and buries their names under heaps of ruins and under the sands of the desert, just as He has already dispersed to the four winds the remains of Israel upon the face of the earth.[241] To this God of mercy and of justice, Whose mercy is above all His works, We turn, invoking His pity. Before His Tribunal of justice nothing can prevail save prayer, supported by His mercy. Let us pray, dear sons, imploring the divine pity and clemency so that the tempest raging over poor humanity may be calmed, that the sky may be cleared and that the dawn of peace may return.

ADDRESS *Questo Vivace Spettacolo* TO THE MEMBERS OF FEMININE
CATHOLIC ACTION IN ITALY.[242]

> *Catholic Action must help in rebuilding society on a Christian basis.*

October 6, 1940

1599. . . . . . The present hour is an hour of devastation—but all the more it is for you an hour of confident and intense work in

[238] Original Italian, *Discorsi e Radiomessaggi*, v. 2, p. 236.
[239] *Psalms*, XXXII, 11.
[240] *Psalms*, XXXII, 10.
[241] Cf. *Ezechiel*, V, 1-4, 12; IX, 8-11.
[242] Original Italian, *A.A.S.*, v. 32, p. 411 (October 30, 1940).

behalf of your beloved country and of your neighbors, brothers and sisters in the charity of Christ. Tomorrow the world will have to strive to restore and rebuild its own ruins, if it does not want to remain buried forever in the shadows of death. Then the time will come, Catholic Youth, for your collaboration! How many beautiful works are awaiting your hand! The rebuilding of society on a Christian basis; the restoring to honor and dignity of the Gospel and its morality; the renovating of the family, giving back to marriage its aureola of sacramental dignity and to newly-weds the sense of their duties and the consciousness of their responsibilities; the reaffirming, among all classes of society, of the true notions of authority, of discipline, of respect for social laws and for the rights and duties that people owe one another. This is your tomorrow. . . . . . .

RADIO MESSAGE *Bendito Dios* TO THE THIRD NATIONAL EUCHARISTIC CONGRESS IN SANTA FE, ARGENTINA.[243]

In Christ alone is our hope for peace.

October 13, 1940

1600. *Blessed be the God and Father of our Lord Jesus Christ, the Father of mercies and the God of all comfort, Who comforts us in all our afflictions.*[244] This grateful praise, which the great Apostle places on Our lips in this grave hour of cruel conflicts in the world and of sorrow for Ourself, is the same which We raise to heaven in directing Our words to you who are Our consolation, walking as you do in the truth of love left by Christ as a mandate to men, and exalting Him on the throne of adoration from which He rules and reigns in the Church and over the whole world as a King of Peace. . . . . . .

1601. Seek justice and the Kingdom of God in yourselves and in your works. Let Christ always reign in your midst, in your people destined for great things. Let Him reign in the family . . . , among the children, in the State schools, in the Press, in the cinema . . . , in the radio, in your homes, in your social life, among the workers scattered in new farming and industrial regions. May the light of Christ and His justice, which raises up nations and like

[243] Original Spanish, *A.A.S.*, v. 32, pp. 418-421 (October 30, 1940).
[244] II *Corinthians*, I, 3.

a wall protects them from the snares and assaults of the wicked who would undermine their foundations, shine before the eyes of your rulers. . . .

1602. Pray, Venerable Brethren and Beloved Children, with Us and Our Legate, the Cardinal Archbishop of the capital of your illustrious Republic—pray with Us to the divine Prince of Peace, Who reconciled Heaven and earth with His blood and Who in the Mystical Banquet of His altar unites all believing people. Pray to Our Lord Jesus Christ, that He infuse the spirit of peace which subdues human passions in the souls of all people, so that it may overflow their hearts and quell the bitter strife which sows death on land, on the seas, and in the skies, and feeds the people with the bread of sorrow steeped in tears of blood. In Christ, the Saviour of the World, alone is our hope and trust, because in His Hands are the hearts of men, and He knows how to bring tranquillity to the stormy waves. . . .

RADIO BROADCAST *We Are on the Eve* TO THE UNITED STATES ON MISSION SUNDAY.[245]

The peace of the world is a missionary aim of the Church.

October 19, 1940

1603. . . . . . . Look, Venerable Brethren and beloved children, gaze on the world and on the harvest of souls everywhere so fair to see; but over it sweeps in thundering waves the tempest of battles, of destruction, of suffering, of countless human sorrows. Behold how many messengers of the Gospel, how many men and women, heroes of Christ, workers in His vineyard, are living and toiling and struggling and suffering amid dangers and obstacles, amid deprivations and destitution that chill the ardor of their zeal and put stumbling blocks in the path of their holy and charitable ambition. With eyes and hands upraised they look to you, and with them look the faithful of their flock, and those others, too, who have yet to hear the Shepherd's voice, while they wander and sit in the shadow of death, knowing nothing of Him Who has redeemed them and Who has promised them eternal life and peace. Pray

[245] Original English, *A.A.S.,* v. 32, pp. 425-426 (October 30, 1940).

that the Master of the vineyard send workers for these your brothers, too; for they also have been called to be born again in Christ. Prayer is the sword that pierces the Heart of God and lets flow His love and mercy; it is the offering made by your lips, by your heart's loving interest in the missioners of Christ, in those lambs that have strayed from the Fold, in those pathetic sufferers, who are bearing the burden and torments of our calamitous age.

1604. That offering of prayer, rising before the sacred tabernacles, where the Divine Shepherd of His redeemed flocks lives, encourages and associates Himself with His apostles in the fields and by-paths of their wearying toil, will not fail to be accompanied by the gift of your hand. You will offer it in this sad and distressing hour to help the Spouse of Christ in the propagation of the Faith. You will help her to push on the good work begun, to rebuild what has been damaged or destroyed; to reassure the faint-hearted and discouraged, to multiply the scant resources, to sustain, to increase and advance the whole missionary movement on toward the ultimate triumph of that Kingdom of God on earth, which is the subject of our daily petition to the Heavenly Father in that prayer taught us by Christ: Thy kingdom come. This is the kingdom of peace between our souls and God; it is the kingdom of peace between brothers founded on their mutual affection, of peace between the peoples and nations of the world based on the equitable adjustment of differences and on that union that comes with right order. At the present hour men are far, far removed from this peace; the intimate sense of common values, both in the natural and supernatural orders, threatens to abdicate in many hearts to opposing principles; so much the more comforting, then, and inspiring will be your efficacious fidelity to the Catholic missionary spirit. For after all, the peace of the world is also a missionary aim of the Church. On the tranquillity of order among men depend her life, the conquest and salvation of souls, the diffusion of the precious gift of faith, the triumph over evil—all leading to that goal of unchangeable peace in eternity. In these sublime and holy thoughts let your prayer and your generosity find their support. The money, which you give to help the poor missions, is a loan made to the Lord, and the Lord will recompense you for it; Christ, Who speaks and works in the champions of His Gospel, will grant you to share in their merits. . . . . . .

689

REPLY *Accreditée par une Lettre* TO THE HOMAGE OF THE NEW AMBASSADOR OF PORTUGAL, ANTONIO PACHECO.[246]

The work of peace requires continued loyal collaboration inspired by reciprocal confidence and mutual esteem.

October 20, 1940

1605. . . . . . . This year, 1940, the Portuguese Nation celebrates the eighth centenary of its independence and the third of its restoration; in a world shaken by the feverish agitations of the war, it has known how to give proof by its acts that its path was leading upwards toward a noble grandeur. In the sphere of religion itself this year has been a providential turning point—establishing relations between the Church and the State on a new basis, which justifies the most optimistic hopes, and constituting one of those great and symbolic acts of renovation, which are repeated in the history of the Church every time that a nation, after short-lived deviations, returns to the forgotten truths, to the abandoned ideals, to the deserted altars of a Faith from which their ancestors had drawn strength and support. . . . . . .

1606. The Lord has given to the Portuguese Nation a Minister in the Government who has been able to win not only the love of his people, and especially of the poorest classes, but also the respect and esteem of the world. To him belongs the merit of having been on the part of this Government, under the auspices of the eminent President of the Republic, the builder of a great work of peace between the State and the Church, that perfect and supreme society whose beneficent action, after the sad experiences of a troubled past, will now be able to be exercised with complete assurance among the dearly-beloved Portuguese people. . . .

1607. In truth, the accord between the two Powers is not accomplished, is not achieved in the simple conclusion of a diplomatic document, but in a kind of continued creation, by means of a loyal collaboration, inspired by a reciprocal confidence and a mutual esteem. The attentive care which has led the Portuguese Government to decide upon and to pursue this work of peace, is for Us a consoling pledge of the spirit in which it will continue it and favor its further development. . . . . . .

[246] Original French, *A.A.S.,* v. 32, pp. 416-418 (October 30, 1940).

Motu Proprio *Norunt Profecto* Appealing for Public Prayer
on November 24.[247]

To hasten the return of peace Pius XII calls for a crusade of prayer, accompanied by acts of penance and by the spiritual improvement of each one's life.

October 27, 1940

1608. All know that ever since a new and terrible war began to convulse Europe, We have left nothing undone which was called for by the responsibility attaching to the Office entrusted to Us by God, or suggested by Our paternal love for all peoples. We have done so, not only that by means of a more equitable and just order, the concord which is now, alas, lacking among so many nations should be re-established, but also that all those to whom the fury of the raging conflict has brought hurt and sorrow might have all possible divine comfort and human aid extended to them. But since this cruel struggle, instead of abating, continues to gather violence, and Our voice, pleading for peace, is drowned in the clash of arms, We turn Our mind in trepidation, but yet in confidence, to the *Father of mercies and the God of all comfort*,[248] and We implore for the human race times more peaceful from Him Who bends the wills of men and by His divine direction orders the course of events.

1609. Well do We know, however, that Our prayers will be more efficacious if, in perfect conformity of minds, the prayers of Our children are joined to Ours. As, therefore, at the approach of last May, We invited all the faithful and especially the children, to the altar of the Virgin Mother of God, to implore the aid of heaven,[249] so now We ordain that throughout the world, on November 24th next, public prayers be offered in union with Us; and We cherish the confidence that every child of the Church will willingly second Our desires, so as to form an immense chorus of prayer, which, rising aloft and penetrating the heavens, will win for Us the favors and mercy of God. We hope, too,—and this is something of graver importance—that the crusade of prayer will be accompanied by acts of penance and by the spiritual improvement of each one's life, brought into closer accord with the law of Christ. The

[247] Official English version, *A.A.S.*, v. 32, pp. 392-394 (October 30, 1940).
[248] II *Corinthians*, I, 3.
[249] *Cf. Superiore Anno*, April 15, 1940; *cf. supra* nn. 1548-1551.

present necessities and the possibilities of danger which the morrow may bring ask for this; the divine justice and divine mercy, which we must conciliate, demand it.

1610.   But since there is no more powerful means of placating and conciliating the Divine Majesty than the Holy Sacrifice of the Eucharist, through which the Redeemer of the human race Himself is offered *in every place . . . a clean oblation,*[250] We desire that on the day on which these sacred functions shall take place, all the ministers of the altar should in the due celebration of Holy Mass unite themselves spiritually to Us, who shall offer the Divine Sacrifice over the tomb of the Apostles in the Vatican Basilica. Accordingly by *Motu Proprio,* in virtue of Our Apostolic authority, We establish that on the 24th of November next, all those who are bound to say Mass for the people entrusted to them, apply it according to Our intention. We wish, moreover, that all other priests, whether secular or regular, should know that they will do something very pleasing to Us if on that Sunday, as they raise the Divine Host, they join in Our intention. And Our intention is this: that by the infinite worth of all these Sacrifices of the Eucharist to be offered that day to the Eternal Father at every moment and in every part of the world, all those who have died as a result of the war may obtain eternal rest; that exiles, refugees, the dispersed, prisoners, and all, in fine, who suffer or mourn through the calamity of the present conflict, may have the heaven-sent comforts of grace; that, finally, order being restored in justice and minds being appeased through Christian charity, a true peace may unite as brothers all peoples of the human family, giving them back tranquillity and prosperity. . . .

REPLY *L'Heure en Laquelle* TO THE NEW MINISTER OF RUMANIA, BASILIO GRIGORCEA.[251]

The cause of peace requires sacrifice from Governments and from their subjects.

November 15, 1940

1611.   The hour in which Your Excellency submits to Us the credentials from Your August Sovereign, His Majesty, King Michael

---

[250] *Malachias,* I, 11.
[251] Original French, *A.A.S.,* v. 32, p. 500 (November 19, 1940).

I, and thus inaugurates your honorable functions as Envoy Extraordinary and Minister Plenipotentiary of Rumania to the Holy See, is an hour overcast with shadows and controlled by the events which are transforming the exterior aspect and spiritual development of the European Continent, involving them in new ways and, at the same time, imposing upon the people sacrifices and trials which are daily increasing. The role of sacrifice which has fallen to the Rumanian people for the cause of peace, fills the heart of this noble nation with concerns and worries that are readily understandable. The discreet echo of these sentiments resounds in the words which Your Excellency has addressed to Us. By the material and spiritual repercussions of the recent events, Governments as well as their subjects are set face to face with duties which are arduous and heavy with responsibilities. . . . . . .

SERMON *Il Vangelo di Oggi* DURING THE MASS FOR PEACE IN ST. PETER'S BASILICA.[252]

> *The Pope prays for the return of an order of tranquillity, liberty and security for each nation.*

November 24, 1940

1612. . . . . . . *Behold I have told it to you beforehand . . . Heaven and earth shall pass, but My words shall not pass.*[253] Heaven and earth shall pass. This earth will pass which we tread under foot, which we till in the sweat of our brow, which we survey with our eyes; this earth torn up and tortured by our steel to expose the tombs of the dead past, of ancient monsters from the unknown shores, of vapors of extinct volcanoes, and of mineral veins and liquid fires that disturb the dreams of man and upset his peace. This old world of ours will pass, which seems no longer to suffice for men or to satisfy the roaring of their opposing aspirations which in our days have enkindled a conflagration of such gigantic dimensions that it surpasses and almost throws into obscurity the most grandiose events and upheavals in the history of the world. The earth will pass and we shall all have to appear before the judgment seat of

---

[252] Translation from *N.C.W.C. News Service* (November 24, 1940). Original Italian, *A.A.S.*, v. 32, pp. 531-536 (December 16, 1940).
[253] *Matthew*, XXIV, 25, 35.

Christ that everyone may receive reward or punishment according as he has done, whether it be good or evil,[254] but the Word of Christ shall not pass. It is He Who predicts and announces beforehand to the Apostles the story of His Church and of the world, and the vicissitudes through which they will pass in the course of ages. And there, in this same discourse on Mount Olivet in the sight of Jerusalem, He bids them beware that no one seduce them. For, He tells them, *You shall hear of wars and rumors of wars. See that ye be not troubled. For these things must come to pass, but the end is not yet.*[255]

1613. No! Consummation of the world is not yet come. Christ, even though He has ascended into heaven, is with us all the days, even in the midst of war and rumors of war. We must not be troubled, even as the Apostles were not troubled, in preaching the Gospel. But if the cataclysm does not depress our spirits, we feel nonetheless that the present hour is a phase in the solemn story of humanity foretold by Christ. And you, dear children, know how this new and fierce war which lies heavy on Europe and the world, by necessity weighs down Our heart through that paternal affection which derives from the office imposed on Us by God toward all peoples; for you well know that sorrow is a child of affection and love. Is not Christ's sorrowful passion the outcome of His love for us? *Sic Deus dilexit mundum: God so loved the world!*[256]

1614. During His triumphal entry into Jerusalem, which He so loved, nearing the city and contemplating it, did not the Divine Redeemer weep over it? And he said: *If thou also hadst known, and that in this thy day, the things that are to thy peace!*[257] This ineffable lament of Our Saviour over Jerusalem could not but find an echo in the heart of His humble Vicar as he beholds Europe and the world in brutal conflict. We have done everything for peace among nations, conscious as We are that it is Our duty to be a servant and a minister of peace, bringing the King on High Who makes peace not through the blood of battlefields, but through the blood of His Cross, both as to the things that are on earth, and the things that are in heaven.[258]

[254] *Cf.* II *Corinthians*, V, 10.
[255] *Matthew*, XXIV, 6.
[256] *John*, III, 16.
[257] *Luke*, XIX, 42.
[258] *Cf. Colossians*, I, 20.

1615. It was an impulse of Our heart that We followed, in striving to secure that concord might be re-established among nations—that concord which was for a long time upset and now is completely broken—and that there be set up an order of things more harmonious, based on that justice which soothes passions, allays hatreds, quenches rancor and bickerings; an order which would tend to give to every people in tranquillity, in liberty and in security that portion which belongs to each, of the earthly sources of prosperity and power, so as to make possible the fulfillment of the words of the Creator: *Increase and multiply, and fill the earth.*[259]

1616. From the outset of the conflict, Our attention and thoughts have never ceased to secure, insofar as We could, that divine purpose and human aid might be extended to those whom the clash of arms has caused loss and suffering. *For the charity of Christ presseth us.*[260] As the Common Father of all who believe in Christ, Shepherd of His immense Fold, We count among Our children, of Our flock, those near and far, the faithful, the lost or the strayed. To all are We debtor, to all do We owe love, comfort and help—to the weak and to the strong, to the miserable and to the unhappy, to the wise and to the unwise.[261] This vale of tears is now inundated with fresh tears to be dried on the faces of children, mothers, men and aged ones who feel a sense of cruel abandonment in their lives and souls, especially in this turbulent hour when the terrible conflict, instead of subsiding, goes on to gather new ferocity!

1617. But if the din of war seems to overcome and drown Our voice, We turn Our gaze away from earth to heaven, to the Father of Mercies and to the God of All Comfort,[262] Who contemplates all here below and commands the flow of the ocean: *Hitherto thou shalt come, and shalt go no further, and here thou shalt break thy swelling waves.*[263] To Him beneath Whose Hands in the universal order of events and things, the action of man is restless without being able to evade His provident and ineluctable counsel; to Him We raise the sorrowing cry of Our heart, imploring from Him better days for the human race, better dawns and better sunsets to our days. Grant us, O Lord, peace in our days!

[259] *Genesis*, IX, 1.
[260] II *Corinthians*, V, 14.
[261] *Cf. Romans*, I, 14.
[262] *Cf.* II *Corinthians*, I, 3.
[263] *Job*, XXXVIII, 11.

1618. No, Our God is not like the idols of the Gentiles that have ears and hear not, have hands and feel not, have hearts and love not.[264] Our God is love, is charity itself; and we have known and believed in the charity of God toward us: *We have known and believed the charity which God hath to us. God is charity.*[265] This is the mystery of the Heart of God, the great mystery of Christianity. God, with that infinite and tender mercy which is over all His works,[266] will hear us—at the moment and in the manner which He will have disposed—if we send up to the seat of His throne, with one voice, a trusting and fervent prayer enriched by the humiliation of penance; for it belongs to the Supreme Excellence of the goodness and charity of God, not only to bestow life and prosperity on all, but also to accede in His generosity to the pious wishes we express with prayer. Has not the Incarnate Son of God called us in His disciples, His friends? [267] And is it not a test of friendship that he who loves wishes to see the desire of the loved one satisfied?

1619. It was for this reason that on the Feast of Christ the King, under the protection of the glorious Queen of the Rosary, We called on all the children of the Church to offer public prayers together with Us to-day. We wished that there might be one immense choir of suppliants answering to Our voice—of every clime, of every tongue, dress, manner and rite, fired by one and the same faith, one and the same hope, one and the same love—to turn with Us their eyes beyond the stars and send their humble supplication for grace and mercy to the throne of the Most High. . . . . .

1620. O Jesus, our Saviour, speak to Thy Father for us, intercede with Him for us, for Thy Church, for all men who have been won by Thy blood, O Peace-bringing King, O Prince of Peace! Thou Who hast the keys of life and death, grant the peace of eternal rest to the souls of all the faithful who have been swept to their death in this whirlwind of war and have been known and unknown, wept and unwept, and buried beneath the ruins of cities and villages destroyed, or have met their deaths on gory plains, on war-torn hillsides, in gorges and valleys or in the depths of the sea. May Thy purifying Blood descend on them in their pains, to wash their mantles and render them worthy and bright in Thy blessed

---

[264] *Cf. Psalms,* CXIII, 5-7.
[265] I *John* IV, 16.
[266] *Cf. Psalms,* CXLIV, 9.
[267] *Cf. John,* XV, 15.

sight. Do Thou, O loving Comforter of the Afflicted, Who didst weep at the tears of Martha and Mary, desolate for their dead brother, grant peace and consolation, resignation and health to those poor people who are overcome by the sorrows and tribulations of war's calamities, to exiles, to refugees, to unknown wanderers, to prisoners and to the wounded, who trust in Thee.

1621. Dry the abundant tears of wives, mothers, orphans, of whole families, of so many left destitute; dry the heavy tears falling on the bread of sorrow eaten after long fast in cold hovels; bread divided between children who often have been brought to Thy altars in a little church to pray for father or elder brother, dead perhaps, or wounded, or missing. Console them all with divine gifts and with those helps and that effective charitable relief which is our task. Suggest to kindly souls that they recognize in the afflicted and unfortunate their brothers and love them as Thy image. Give to the combatants, together with heroism in full token of their duty even to the supreme sacrifice in defense of their native land, that noble sense of humanity by which they will not, no matter in what circumstances, do to others that which they would not have done to themselves or their country.[268]

1622. O Lord, may Thy Divine Spirit reign and triumph over the world. May the peace of concord and justice among nations be restored. May our prayers be acceptable and welcome to the Meek and Humble in Heart. May the numbers and devotion of Holy Sacrifices which Thy Church, on bended knee, offers to Thee, Priest and Victim eternally, through Thy Holy Mother, render Thee propitious toward us. Thou hast words which penetrate and overcome hearts, which enlighten intellects, which assuage anger and extinguish hates and revenge. Speak that word which will still the storm, which will heal the sick, which is light to the blind, hearing to the deaf and life to the dead.

1623. Peace among men, which Thou desirest, is dead. Bring it back to life, O Divine Conqueror of Death. Through Thee, at last may the land and sea be calmed. May whirlwinds, which in the light of day or in the dark of night scatter terror, fire, destruction and slaughter on humble folk, cease. May justice and charity on the one side and on the other be in perfect balance, so that all injustice may be repaired and the reign of right restored, all discord and

---

[268] *Cf. Matthew*, VII, 12.

rancor may be banished from men's minds. And may there arise, and gather strength in contemplation of a new and harmonious prosperity, true and well-ordered peace which will permanently unite as brothers, through the ages, in harmonious search of high good, all peoples of the human race in Thy sight. Amen.

MOTU PROPRIO *Cum Bellica Conflictio* IN WHICH THE POPE GRANTS THE PRIVILEGE OF CELEBRATING MIDNIGHT MASS ON THE AFTERNOON OF CHRISTMAS EVE.[269]

Pius XII wishes to bring every spiritual comfort to those suffering from the war.

December 1, 1940

1624. Since the present war is bringing ruin and carnage not only to combatant armies but sometimes even to peaceable citizens, We, inspired by the paternal affection which We cherish toward all peoples, are overlooking nothing which can bring at least spiritual comfort to those who are bearing sorrows and distress of all kinds because of war.

1625. With the approach, meanwhile, of the solemnities of Christmas Eve We are preoccupied with the thought, that in many places those sacred rites which are customarily celebrated at midnight Christmas Eve with such gentle emotion of Christian sentiment cannot be carried out without difficulty and danger. It has been established by the law in not a few nations, in fact, that for fear of reciprocal night air raids, lights must be put out or concealed in order that towns and villages will no longer be exposed to such attacks. Let Us hope and trust that, at least on that holy night and on that holy day, all belligerents will declare a truce, either spontaneously or by mutual accord, so that the clash of arms shall not surpass the angelic chorus of peace which will be repeated in the sacred temples and that there will be no new bloodshed to disturb or miserably extinguish the heavenly joy of that hour.

1626. In any event, however, moved by a desire that, as We said above, the faithful shall not lack heavenly blessings and comforts, after major deliberation, by virtue of Our Apostolic authority, We

[269] Translation from the *N.C.W.C. News Service.* Original Latin, *A.A.S.,* v. 32, pp. 529-530 (December 16, 1940).

decree and establish by *Motu Proprio* as follows: With the present very sad circumstances continuing, in those regions in which blackout laws are in force, it is permissible for individual Ordinaries to concede that in primatial, metropolitan, cathedral, collegiate and parochial churches, Mass, which usually is celebrated at Christmas midnight, be celebrated instead in the afternoon of Christmas Eve in such a way, however, that between the end of the sacred rite and the moment in which the above-mentioned laws are enforced there remain some intervals of time. . . . . . .

RESPONSE *Au Moment Où Votre Excellence* TO THE HOMAGE OF THE NEW AMBASSADOR OF FRANCE, LÉON BERARD.[270]

> *The Holy Father expresses his sorrow at the sad plight of France.*

December 9, 1940

1627. At the moment when Your Excellency, called by the confidence of the illustrious Marshal of France, head of the French State, to succeed to the well deserving Count d'Ormesson, inaugurates solemnly your important and honorable mission as Ambassador Extraordinary and Plenipotentiary, the words which you have addressed to Us reveal an emotion and a sadness before which any man who has a heart can only bow. The profundity of this sorrow, its reasons well known, the virile resolution to bring back, despite almost superhuman obstacles, your country and your people to better and serener days—where could these find readier understanding, deeper sympathy, more sincere encouragement than with the Common Father of all the faithful, that Father whose heart is with all nations in their joys and in their sorrows, and who cannot forget how mighty and how beneficent has been the contribution of thought and of action of a believing France in the history of humanity and of Christianity? . . . . . .

1628. To-day France is clothed in mourning. Stricken by a trial such as you will find seldom recorded in the annals of nations, the French people, conscious of its ancient glory, beholds in sadness its fields laid waste, its sons fallen, its citizens far removed from their homes, its children prisoners—sadness made greater by the uncer-

[270] Original French, *A.A.S.*, v. 32, pp. 550-551 (December 16, 1940).

tainties of the future. But howsoever profound this suffering of France may be, under her garb of mourning there beats a strong heart whose will to live will not pass away.

1629. It is Our wish and hope that all those to whom has fallen the task of ruling the present and of laying foundations, both spiritual and material, for the future, will know how to develop in order and concord the wealth of energy and of sentiment that lies deep-rooted in the souls of nations, and will know how to profit by the course of events in order to set before these nations a goal worthy of the devotion and the sacrifices of their citizens and thus capable of doing away with the shadows and inquietudes which are an obstacle to true harmony of thought and of wills. With all Our heart, We wish for your country—in the midst of its present trials— that moral strength which a profound phrase of ancient Roman wisdom defines as *scientia rerum perferendarum vel adfectio animi in patiendo ac perferendo summae legi parens sine timore.*[271]......

LETTER *Giungono da Ogni Parte* TO CARDINAL MAGLIONE, SECRETARY OF STATE.[272]

The generous contributions of the American hierarchy for the war victims are sincerely appreciated by the Holy Father.

December 21, 1940

1630. From every quarter, even in the great feast of peace— the Birthday of the Lord—come sorrowful echoes of a devastating war. They are the voices of Our children who struggle in great sufferings, imploring help. So great a measure of evil and suffer-ing, becoming more aggravated and more widespread every day, cannot but find the most sorrowful echo in Our heart of a father, which perceives the sorrows and the tears of all Our children with-out distinction. Therefore, We can desire nothing more in such a convulsion of things than to help the bodies and raise the spirits.

1631. We have always directed all Our energies to this end, and We have left nothing undone that, in such a great accumulation

---

[271] Cicero, *Tusculan Disputations*, IV, 24.
[272] Translation from *The Tablet*, v. 177, p. 149 (February 22, 1941). Original Italian, *A.A.S.*, v. 33, pp. 21-23 (January 21, 1941).

of miseries, the compassion of Jesus, Whose place on earth We unworthily take, may be unfolded, showing its good and gathering
its fruits. Alas, many of Our efforts have encountered difficulties
of every kind, still graver than in the last World War, some deriving
from the very nature of the scourge that rages, others (We may
also say it) created by the will of men. Unwilling to be an inert
witness of such a deplorable state of things, and armed only with
the weapons of truth and justice and Christian charity, what We
can still do once more is to invite all to propitiating prayer and
beneficent activity. Prayer is a force which, through mysterious
ways, storms heaven to act sweetly and irresistibly on the human
will, and reaches God with particular efficacy when it comes from
pure and innocent hearts.

1632. Beneficent activity is the duty of each and every one.
Diverse public initiatives are already dedicated to it, and thus, in
the grave hours through which Europe is presently passing, it has
the highest value of fraternal solidarity. From every quarter come
these pious and humane activities. We bless them with grateful
soul, and, encouraging and co-ordinating them in all possible forms
for their greater efficiency, We hope that all will persevere in them
without slackening, without distrust.

1633. Amongst all sufferers, We point out the children, who in
these days vividly recall the Infant of Bethlehem, Friend of the
little and innocent ones. He, Who defends them from harm, rising
severely against all forms of scandal that harm them, to-day, by Our
voice, is made their Defense against earthly evils, outstretching His
Hand to them and for them, who are the first among His least
brethren, repeating: *For I was hungry, and you gave Me to eat;
I was thirsty, and you gave Me to drink; I was a stranger, and you
took Me in; naked, and you covered Me.*[273] Our heart trembles
thinking over the misfortunes of these tender offspring who have
barely entered life, and are so soon condemned to taste only its
bitterness and to experience such hard hearts of men, whose glory
should be to procure their happiness. We embrace and bless these
little ones with all the greater affection as Our possibilities of aiding
them fall short of their needs. And still again We have confidence
that those in power will do honor to the good traditions of real
civilization by not permitting the children of belligerent nations,

[273] *Matthew*, XXV, 35-36.

or those in any way tormented by war, to undergo unmerited sufferings in so many calamitous vicissitudes.

1634. On Our part, as already We have invited Our good and Christian children to prayer, so to-day We wish to exhort them to remember their little brethren without bread, without clothes, without families. Hope flatters Us that Christmas, with its gifts to all, and the Feast of the Holy Innocents, with its remembrance of the first little flowers picked for Christ, will suggest thousands of good initiatives to the hearts of all Our children who still live in the peace and comfort of their well-ordered families, so that every derelict child—whether or not he is so through the cause of war—may through them have bread and help. If, because of multiple obstacles, it is not possible in the present circumstances to think of a real, proper and general organization to extend charity to the victims of war, and if, in not a few cases, it is also too difficult to make use of worthy institutions already in existence to send help where the need is most acutely felt, let everyone do what he can, where he can, how he can. . . .

1635. Meanwhile We will not silence Our eulogies and thanks to those who have helped Us in the work of charity which We have been enabled thus far to do. On this point Our thoughts of gratitude go especially to the American episcopacy, who, although far removed from the horrors of war, still wished to show again their full comprehension of the needs of the suffering Church, and, making an appeal to the traditional generosity of their Catholics—especially those who are kinsfolk of the peoples in countries stricken by the scourge—have so abundantly helped the beneficent charity of the Common Father. May Our gratitude go fully and entirely to them, and likewise Our blessing, and may it go no less affectionately to those who permit Us to dispense with a more generous hand that which the other hand receives. . . . . . .

SERMON *Grazie, Venerabili Fratelli* TO THE COLLEGE OF CAR-
DINALS.[274]

*Pius XII explains the victories that must be won as
conditions necessary for a new world order.*

December 24, 1940

1636. . . . . . . Millions of hearts are thinking to-day of the
Saviour's birth. So we express our gratefulness in the old words:
Venite adoremus.[275] The joy of mankind being redeemed from the
consequences of original sin is so strong that it has been asserting
itself continuously far beyond the turmoil which the world is experiencing. He who understands the message of the angels: *Peace to the
men of good-will,*[276] will not be overwhelmed by the events of the
disturbed present, but will keep aloof from pessimism. We thank God
that the Church is not without saintly and strong souls, priests and
laymen, who never waver in their strength or loyalty. We have to
live in a world which alienated itself from Christian principles, without which a sound life of the nations is unthinkable. Without a
living contact with the Church, the nations are apt to become victims
of ideologies which are alien or even hostile to Christianity. Many
of the faithful suffer when they have to watch how the Church of
Christ is misunderstood by the tribunal of Pilate, how the Church
stands there clad in the cloak of shame, and is even being nailed
to the Cross. But their reward is that in all their humiliation they
come near to Christ. If the secular power lays hands on spiritual
matters, as the soldiers did on our Lord, it may happen at any time
that they will flee in terror, as the soldiers did in the dark hour of
the Crucifixion. The vacillations and mistakes of others, Venerable
Brethren, should not surprise us. We are rewarded, on the other
hand, by the fact that countless sons and daughters are withstanding
all storms and dangers. In this connection We can say that faith
in Christ and the profession of His religion have been intensified,

[274] Translation from *The Tablet*, v. 177, pp. 7-8 (January 4, 1941). This is an excep-
tionally free translation of the Christmas sermon as published in the *Acta Apostolicae Sedis;* but it is better than the summary in *The Catholic Mind*, v. 39,
n. 913, pp. 1-6 (January 8, 1941). Because this version gives all the essential
parts of this document, we have used it here instead of trying to translate anew
the entire sermon. Original Italian, *A.A.S.*, v. 33, pp. 6-14 (January 21, 1941).
[275] Christmas matins in the Roman Breviary.
[276] *Luke*, II, 14.

especially when the profession of faith entails dangers and sacrifices for the individual. It is certain that the problems of the present time impose special demands on the care of souls.

1637.   This is true not only in the case of the dreadful war which is being fought at present, but also for the day on which the nations, after the conclusion of hostilities, will have to dedicate themselves to settling the economic and social legacies bequeathed to them. The war is being waged with awesome and almost inescapable tenacity. Venerable shrines, monuments and institutions of Christian charity are laid in ruins. The laws and morality of international warfare have been so callously ignored that future generations will look back on the present war as one of the gloomiest periods in history. Our thoughts anticipate with anxiety the moment when the complete chronicle of those who have been killed, maimed, injured, captured, those who have lost their homes and their relatives, will be known in all its details. What We know already, however, is enough to rend Our heart. Amid all the tribulations of the present time one group of men has Our special pity: the prisoners of war.

1638.   We had been allowed in the last war to do much on behalf of the prisoners, and, therefore, it is Our deep desire that now also We may be given the possibility of bringing them help and succor. This applies especially to the Polish prisoners, and to the Italian prisoners in Egypt, Australia and Canada. We do not want Christmas to pass without Our representatives visiting the British and French prisoners in Italy, the German prisoners in England, the Greek prisoners in Albania or the Italian prisoners in the different countries of the British Empire and giving them a sign of Our tender care, some encouragement, and Our blessing.

1639.   In the desire to share the troubles of the families who have lost touch with their relatives We have undertaken another responsible task; We have begun to transmit news for them as far as this is possible and permitted. This applies not only to a great number of prisoners of war, but also to refugees and to all those who, as a result of present vicissitudes, have been separated from their country and their families. It is a comfort to Us that We have been able, by the help of Our representatives and by Our own subsidy, to give support to a great number of refugees, homeless and emigrants—including also non-Aryans. Our task has been especially facilitated by the help given to Us by Our faithful sons in the United States of America.

1640. It is now one year since We made some fundamental declarations on the basic conditions of a peace built on justice, equity and honor, which could, therefore, be lasting. Although their realization has been put off to a later date by events, these principles have lost nothing of their truth and reality. We have to face to-day a fact of fundamental importance. Out of the passionate strife of the parties concerning peace and war aims, a common opinion emerges. It is that all Europe, as well as the separate nations, are in such a process of transformation that the beginning of a new period is clearly recognizable. Europe and the political order of its nations—it is emphasized—will cease to be what they have been heretofore. There will be something newer, something better, something more developed, organically sounder, freer and stronger than in the past. All the weaknesses revealed by the light of recent events are to be avoided. It is true that the different opinions and aims diverge; yet they agree in their wish to establish a new order and in their conviction that a return to the old order is neither possible nor desirable.

1641. This desire for renewal is dictated not only by the *rerum novarum cupido* but by the realization of deficiencies prevailing to-day, and by the firm determination to establish a new and just national and international order giving security. No one can be surprised that this desire should be especially strong in those strata of society which live by the work of their hands, and which are doomed to experience the hardships of national or international disturbances more than others. Still less could it be ignored by the Church, which, as the Common Mother of all, is bound to hear and to understand the outcries of suffering mankind.

1642. In such a strife of opinions the Church cannot be invoked to listen to one side more than to another. Within the divine laws given not only to the individual, but also to the nations, there is a wide sphere in which the most varied forms of political life have ample freedom of expression. The effects of one or other political system, however, depend on circumstances and reasons which, considered in themselves, are beyond the scope of the Church's activity. As protector and prophet of faith and morality the Church has only one interest and one desire, namely, to fulfill her educational mission and to carry religious teaching to all peoples without exception so that every nation may be enabled to avail itself of the principles laid down by Christianity in order to establish a dignified and spiritually ennobled life which is the source of real happiness. More than once the Church has had to preach to deaf ears. Times of adversity are more frequent than times of happiness; pain is sometimes better than cheap success. Let us hope that mankind and each single nation may grow more mature out of its present tribulations, with eyes able to distinguish between the genuine and the fallacious, with an ear alert for the voice of reason, be it pleasant or unpleasant, with a mind which, open to reality, is really determined to fulfill the demands of life and justice, not only when its own demands are met, but also when the equitable demands of others are heard.

1643. Only in such a state of mind does the tempting slogan of a new order acquire a beautiful, dignified and lasting conception based on moral principles. Only then can the danger be avoided that this slogan should come to be interpreted as a liberty-destroying mechanism enforced by violence, without sincerity, consent, joy, dignity or honor, oppressing souls. Only then can mankind be given a new hope, an aim which corresponds to the noble effort.

1644. The necessary premises for such a new order are as follows:

(1) Victory over the hatred which divides the nations to-day and the disappearance of systems and actions which breed this hatred. As a matter of fact, in some countries an unbridled propaganda is to be seen; it does not recoil from methodical distortion of the truth in order to show the enemy nations in a falsified and vilifying light. He who, however, really wants the good of the people and wants to contribute to the future co-operation of nations and to preserve this co-operation from incalculable damage, will consider it as his sacred duty to uphold the natural ideals of truth, justice and charity.

(2) Victory over distrust which exerts a paralyzing pressure on international law and makes all honest understanding impossible. Therefore, return to the principle of mutual trust. Return to the loyalty for treaties without which the secure co-operation of nations and especially, the living side by side of strong and weak nations, are inconceivable. The foundation of justice is loyalty, reliability

and truth of the pledged word, and of the understanding which has been reached.[277]

(3) Victory over the dismal principle that utility is the foundation and aim of law, and that might can create right. This principle is bound to upset all international relations and is inacceptable to all weaker nations. Therefore, return to honest, serious and moral international relations. This conception does not exclude the desire for the honorable improvement of conditions or the right to defend oneself if peaceful life has been attacked, or to repair the damage sustained thereby.

(4) Victory over those potential conflicts arising out of the unbalanced state of world economy. Therefore, a new economic order has to be gradually evolved which gives all nations the means to secure for their citizens an appropriate standard of life.

(5) Victory over the kind of egoism which, relying on its own power, aims at impairing the honor and sovereignty of nations, as well as the sound, just and ordered liberty of individuals. This egoism has to be replaced by a genuine Christian solidarity of a legal and economic character, and by a brotherly co-operation of the nations, the sovereignty of which has been duly secured.

1645. Venerable Brethren and Beloved Sons, We have a great longing for the moment when arms will be laid down and peace treaties signed, a deep desire that mankind should then have enough wisdom to prepare the foundations of a lasting and equitable order. We pray to God that it may be soon, and We admonish you to unite your prayers with Ours that the Almighty may preserve the world from the fate which would befall it if the mistakes and misunderstandings of the past were renewed in another form and the future of the nations were ruled not by genuine freedom, but by new and increased unhappiness. We pray that those on whom the realization of the future order will depend, may realize that the real victor is only he who conquers himself. With infinite faith, We put Our desires and Our hopes into the tiny Hands of the new-born Saviour; We pray with you, with all priests and laymen of the Holy Church, that mankind may be freed from discord. With this prayer on Our lips and with this thought in Our hearts, We give to you and to all Our sons throughout the world, and especially the war victims of all nations, Our Apostolic Blessing.

[277] Cf. Cicero, De Officiis, bk. I, ch. 7.

ADDRESS *Fonte* TO THE ROMAN NOBILITY IN RESPONSE TO THEIR NEW YEAR WISHES.[278]

The Pope ardently desires a just and lasting peace.

January 5, 1941

1646. . . . . . . What may be the course of this year just begun, is a secret and a counsel of God, wise and provident, Who governs and guides the path of His Church and of the human race toward that goal, where His mercy and His justice shall triumph. But Our ardent desire, Our prayer and Our wish is for a just and lasting peace, for an ordered tranquillity in the world; the peace which rejoices all peoples and nations; the peace which, recalling smiles on the faces of all, stirs in the heart a hymn of the highest praise and gratitude to the God of Peace Whom we adore in the crib of Bethlehem. . . . . . .

LETTER *It Is with Heartfelt Affection* TO FORDHAM UNIVERSITY ON THE CENTENARY OF ITS FOUNDATION.[279]

Students who graduate from Catholic schools must be prepared to advance Christian civilization and to live at peace with their fellow men.

February 24, 1941

1647. . . . . . . We are greatly consoled, in the midst of the sorrows which afflict Our Apostolic heart, by the thought of the many thousands of students who have gone forth from Fordham University, carefully trained in the secular sciences and arts, deeply imbued with the principles of the Faith, and ready and eager, both in mind and in heart, to defend the Kingdom of God, to contribute generously to the advancement of Christian civilization and to live at peace with their fellow men. And it is Our confident and prayerful hope that all those who in the future will partake of the rare privileges and bounteous advantages offered by your University, may be even more fully prepared to encounter with courage and conviction the difficulties and the perils which await them and which seem likely to be very greatly accentuated in the troublous times which may lie ahead. Thus your alumni will continue to be a very

[278] Original Italian, *Discorsi e Radiomessaggi*, v. 2, pp. 365-366.
[279] Original English, *A.A.S.*, v. 33, p. 329 (July 21, 1941).

definite asset to the great country to which they owe allegiance, and a source of joy and consolation to their Church and to their University. . . . . . .

DISCOURSE *Quale Santa Adunanza* TO THE LENTEN PREACHERS OF ROME.[280]

The war is a consequence of the denial of God and of the lack of religion in the contemporary world.

February 25, 1941

1648. . . . . . . People and society need to know God. The terrible events which we are witnessing to-day are mainly the consequence and almost the nemesis of the denial of God and of that want of religion which, like a plague, perturbs and corrupts the souls of the peoples and, like a fire, threatens to spread over all Europe and other entire continents; at the same time they are a trial, by means of which the Lord, with mighty voice, wishes to recall mankind to faith and to divine service. This is, Beloved Sons, the first great aim of your preaching: to recall men to the knowledge of the true, personal God: *that they may know Thee, the only true God,*[281] that they may walk again in His presence in fear and in love, and may learn once more to regulate all their actions, from their most secret thoughts to their very deeds, according to His holy law. . . . . . .

ADDRESS TO THE ARCHCONFRATERNITY OF THE MOST HOLY TRINITY.[282]

The Pope laments the cruel physical sufferings which result from modern warfare.

March 27, 1941

1649. . . . . . . To the mind of one who contemplates with the eyes of the soul the clash of terrible arms on the fields of battle, on the waves of the sea, amidst the storm winds of the sky, what tragic visions in the present hour are offered by the violence evidenced in

---

[280] Original Italian, *Discorsi e Radiomessaggi,* v. 2, pp. 406-407.
[281] *John,* XVII, 3.
[282] Original Italian, *Civiltà Cattolica,* 1941, v. 2, pp. 151-152 (April 12, 1941).

the broken and wounded bodies of men! How many young men, in full bloom, mature, thirsting for life, if not cut down, leave the struggle with mangled limbs and fractured bones! All humanity, with the cry of the blood gushing from its wounds, seems to make an anguished appeal to justice and to mercy. And to heal those wounds, how often the very work of human mercy and the hands of the surgeon must add wounds to wounds and blood to blood! Must the return of peace and harmony in the world and among peoples cost so much blood and so much pain when men of intellect, with good-will, with triumph over passions, with forgiveness of offenses, with conformity to justice and mutual equity might re-establish a peace that would restore tranquillity and contentment to the common life of the nations on the face of the earth? To heal a humanity so violently wounded there is needed the medicine of faith that makes brothers of all men; there is needed the balm of prayer to God, the Healer of the hearts of the strong and the weak. When peace on earth, in justice and in fraternity, is to be re-established and to triumph, is a secret of Divine Providence. We do not know the hour, the place, or the manner: but We are sure that Christ, the King of the Universe, Who warred only against unbelief and against the inordinate passions of men, will give back the true and good peace to men. For Our part, We shall never fail to work and to pray, in order to do all that seems possible to Us to hasten its advent.

RADIO ADDRESS *Di Cuore* TO THE WHOLE WORLD ON EASTER SUNDAY.[283]

The Holy Father pleads for a peace which will guarantee the honor of all nations, will satisfy their vital needs and will insure the legitimate rights of all.

April 13, 1941

1650. We most cordially greet you all, beloved sons and daughters of Rome and of the entire world, in the spirit of *Alleluia* of Easter morn, in the joyful spirit of the Resurrection and Peace in Christ, after the desolation of His divine Passion: but, unfortunately,

[283] Translation from *The Catholic Mind,* v. 39, n. 920, pp. 1-8 (April 22, 1941). Original Italian, *A.A.S.,* v. 33, pp. 112-117 (April 21, 1941).

there has been no resurrection, no restoration, of peace among nations, and in Our joyful greeting to you there must be intermingled that note of distress which was the cause of great sadness and continual sorrow to the heart of Paul, the Apostle, while he was preoccupied about his brethren who were his kinsmen according to the flesh.[284]

1651. In the lamentable spectacle of human conflict which We are now witnessing, We acknowledge the valor and loyalty of all those who, with a deep sense of duty, are fighting for the defense and prosperity of their homeland; We recognize, too, the prodigious and, in itself, efficacious development made in industrial and technical fields, nor do We overlook the many generous and praiseworthy gestures of magnanimity which have been made toward the enemy: but while We make these acknowledgments, We feel obliged nonetheless to state that the ruthless struggle has at times assumed forms which can be described only as atrocious. May all belligerents, who also have human hearts moulded by mothers' love, show some feeling of charity for the sufferings of civilian populations, for defenseless women and children, for the sick and aged, all of whom are often exposed to greater and more widespread perils of war than those faced by soldiers at the front!

1652. We beseech the belligerent powers to abstain until the very end from the use of still more homicidal instruments of warfare; for the introduction of such weapons inevitably results in their retaliatory use, often with greater violence and cruelty by the enemy. If already We must lament the fact that the limits of legitimate warfare have been repeatedly exceeded, would not the more widespread use of increasingly barbarous offensive weapons soon transform the war into an unspeakable horror?

1653. In this tempest of misfortunes and perils, of afflictions and fears, our most powerful and safest haven of trust and peace is found in prayer to God, in Whose Hands rests not only the destiny of men but also the outcome of their most obdurate dissensions. Wherefore We express Our gratitude to Catholics of the entire world for the fervor with which they responded to Our call to prayer and sacrifice for peace on November 24. To-day We repeat that invitation to you and to all those who raise their minds and hearts to God, and We beseech you not to relax your prayerful vigilance but

[284] Cf. Romans, IX, 2.

rather to reanimate and redouble it. Yes, let us pray for early peace. Let us pray for universal peace; not for peace based upon the oppression and destruction of peoples but peace which, while guaranteeing the honor of all nations, will satisfy their vital needs and insure the legitimate rights of all.

1654. We have constantly accompanied prayer with Our own endeavors. To the very limit of Our power and with a vigilant consciousness of impartiality in spirit and in Our Apostolic Office, We have left nothing undone or untried in order to forestall or shorten the conflict, to humanize the methods of war, to alleviate suffering and to bring assistance and comfort to the victims of war. We have not hesitated to indicate in unmistakably clear terms the necessary principles and sentiments which must constitute the determining basis of a future peace that will assure the sincere and loyal consent of all peoples. But We are saddened to note that there seems to be as yet little likelihood of an approximate realization of peace that will be just, in accordance with human and Christian norms.

1655. Thus Our supplications to heaven must be raised with ever increasing meaning and fervor, that a new spirit may take root and develop in all peoples, and especially among those whose greater power gives them wider influence and imposes upon them additional responsibility; the spirit of willingness, devoid of sham and artifice, that is ready to make mutual sacrifices in order to build, upon the accumulated ruins of war, a new edifice of fraternal solidarity among the nations of the world, an edifice built upon new and stronger foundations, with fixed and stable guarantees, and with a high sense of moral sincerity which would repudiate every double standard of morality and justice for the great and the small or for the strong and the weak.

1656. Truth, like man, has but a single face: and truth is Our weapon just as prayer is Our defense and strength, and the living, sincere and disinterested Apostolic word inspired by fraternal affection, Our entrée to the hearts of men. These are not offensive and bloody weapons but the arms of spirit, arms of Our mind and heart. Nothing can impede or restrain Us from using them to secure and safeguard just rights, true human brotherhood and genuine peace, wherever the sacred duty of Our office prompts Us and compassion for the multitude rekindles Our love.

1657. Nothing can restrain Us from repeatedly calling to the observance of the precept of love those who are children of the Church of Christ, and those who, because of their faith in the Divine Saviour, or at least in Our Father Who is in Heaven, are very near to Us. Nothing can impede or restrain Us from doing all in Our power in order that, in the tempest of surging waves of enmity among the peoples of the earth, the Divine Ark of the Church of Christ may be held firmly by the anchor of hope under the golden rays of peace—that blessed vision of peace which, in the midst of worldly conflicts, is the refuge and abode and sustenance of that fraternal spirit, founded in God and ennobled in the shadow of the Cross, with which the course must be set if we are to escape from the present tempest and reach the shore of a happier and more deserving future.

1658. However, under the vigilant Providence of God and armed only with prayer, exhortation and consolation, We shall persevere in Our battle for peace in behalf of suffering humanity. May the blessings and comforts of heaven descend on all victims of this war: upon you who are prisoners and upon your families from whom you are separated and who are anxious about you; and upon you refugees and dispossessed who have lost your homes and land, your life's support. We share with you your anguish and suffering. If it is not allowed Us—as We would honestly desire—to take upon Ourself the burden of your sorrows, may Our paternal and cordial sympathy serve as the balm which will temper the bitterness of your misfortune with to-day's greeting of the *Alleluia,* the hymn of Christ's triumph over earthly martyrdom, the blossom of the olive tree of Gethsemane flourishing in the precious hope of resurrection and of the new and eternal life in which there will be neither sorrows nor struggles. In this vale of tears there is no lasting city, no eternal homeland.[285]

1659. Here below we are all exiles and wanderers; our true citizenship, which is limitless, is in heaven, in eternity, in God. If worldly hopes have bitterly deluded you, remember that hope in God never fails or deceives. You must make one resolve—not to allow yourselves to be induced, either by your sad lot or by the malice of men, to waver in your allegiance to Christ.

1660. Prosperity and adversity are part and parcel of man's

[285] Cf. *Hebrews,* XIII, 14.

earthly existence; but what is of the utmost importance, and We say it with St. Augustine, is the use that is made of what is called prosperity or adversity. For the virtuous man is neither exalted by worldly well-being nor humbled by temporal misfortune; the evil man, on the other hand, being corrupted in prosperity, is made to suffer in adversity.[286]

1661. To the powers occupying territories during the war, We say with all due consideration: let your conscience guide you in dealing justly, humanely and providently with the peoples of occupied territories. Do not impose upon them burdens which you, in similar circumstances, have felt or would feel to be unjust. Prudent and helpful humanitarianism is the commendation and boast of wise generals; and the treatment of prisoners and civilians in occupied areas is the surest indication and proof of the civilization of individuals and nations. But, above all, remember that upon the manner in which you deal with those whom the fortunes of war put in your hands may depend the blessing or curse of God upon your own land.

1662. Contemplation of a war that is so cruel in all its aspects and the thought of the suffering children of the Church inspire in the heart of the Common Father and form upon Our lips words of comfort and encouragement for the pastors and faithful of those places where the Church, the Spouse of Christ, is suffering most; where fidelity to her, the public profession of her doctrines, the conscientious and practical observance of her laws, moral resistance to atheism and to de-Christianizing influences deliberately favored or tolerated, are being openly or insidiously opposed and daily in various ways made increasingly difficult.

1663. The records and artifices of this generally secret but at times even public martyrdom, which insidious or open impiety makes followers of the Crucified suffer, are multiplying daily and constitute, as it were, in an encyclopedia of many volumes, annals of heroic sacrifices, and furnish moving verification of the words of our Divine Saviour: *The servant is not greater than his Lord. If they have persecuted Me, they will also persecute you.*[287] Is this divine warning not a source of tender comfort on that sorrowful and bitter Way of the Cross which you are following because of

---

[286] Cf. *De Civitate Dei*, bk. 1, ch. 8, in Migne, *P.L.*, v. 41, c. 20.
[287] *John*, XV, 20.

your fidelity to Christ? To all of you who are walking so sadly along this way, priests and religious, men and women, and particularly you young men—pride and joy of your families—who are called upon to bear the burden of these merciless and bitter days— whatever be your origin, language, race, social condition or profession—all you upon whom the seal of suffering for Christ is stamped so clearly, a sign no less of suffering than of glory, as it was to the great Apostle, Paul; you are numbered among those privileged intimates who are nearest to the Cross of Calvary and by this very fact nearest also to the pierced Heart of Christ and to Our own.

1664. Oh, that We were able to make you appreciate how profoundly Our heart has been pierced by the cry of the Apostle of the Gentiles: *Who is weak, and I am not weak?*[288] The sacrifices you are called upon to make, your suffering in mind and body, your concern for your own faith and still more for the faith of your children, We are aware of them, We share them with you, We lament them before God. . . . . . . Beloved sons and daughters! To Jesus Christ, *Prince of Kings of the earth, Who hath washed us from our sins in His own blood,*[289] raise your eyes while, as pledge of that heavenly peace which He alone can give to us and which We implore of Him in superabundant measure for all humanity, We impart to you, to pastors and faithful, to your families, to your children, that Christ may protect and keep you in His grace and love; to those who, in the fulfillment of duty, are fighting on land and sea and in the sky, and especially to all those who have been so severely lashed by the scourge of war, with heart overflowing with love, Our paternal Apostolic Benediction.

LETTER *Quamvis Plane* TO CARDINAL MAGLIONE, SECRETARY OF STATE.[290]

Again the Pope summons all Catholics, and particularly the children, to pray for peace during the month of May.

April 20, 1941

1665. While We are fully confident that the faithful, and especially the children, under the guidance of their parents, will be mind-

---

[288] II *Corinthians,* XI, 29.
[289] *Apocalypse,* I, 5.
[290] Translation from *N.C.W.C. News Service,* April 28, 1941. Original Latin, *A.A.S.,* v. 33, pp. 110-112 (April 21, 1941).

ful of Our invitation of last year[291] and will gather before the altar of the Most Blessed Virgin Mother of God during the coming month of May to implore peace for anguished and afflicted humanity, We desire, nevertheless, through the medium of this Letter addressed to you, to repeat that exhortation to all as the bitterness of war increasingly distresses and crushes the hearts of men. And, as the dangers of every sort which threaten so many nations become ever more appalling, We confidently express the wish that the faithful raise their minds and hearts in prayer to heaven, whence alone, in the midst of such profound mental perplexity and material disorder, can come the hope of a better day.

1666. If our prayers and aspirations have not as yet had the result which we ardently desired, our trust in God must not be lessened on this account but we must all continue, with constant and persevering devotion, to be *patient in tribulation, instant in prayer.*[292] The designs of God are hidden from us, but we are certain that, although innumerable and grave offenses call down the avenging justice of heaven, the Lord is, nevertheless, *the Father of Mercies and the God of All Comfort.*[293] And we know that His love and benevolence for us is boundless. But there is still another reason for our trust and hope, for we have at the throne of Almighty God the most amiable Mother of God and our Mother, who, through her all-powerful intercession, can certainly obtain for us all favors that she asks of Him. Let us, then, place ourselves and our problems under her protection that she may make our prayers and aspirations her own and enhance the value of the works of expiation and charity which we must offer in generous measure to satisfy the Divine Majesty. May she dry all our tears, strengthen us in all our suffering, console us in all our sorrows and, in lightening these afflictions, enable us with the hope of eternal reward to bear them more easily.

1667. If in calling to mind our sinfulness we feel ourselves to be unworthy of her maternal affection, let us lead our children in ever-increasing numbers to her sacred shrine, especially during the coming month of May, that they may plead our cause—those little ones with innocent souls and lips unstained, who in their limpid

---

[291] *Cf. Superiore Anno,* April 15, 1940, *supra nn.* 1548-1551.
[292] *Romans,* XII, 12.
[293] II *Corinthians,* I, 3.

eyes seem to mirror and reflect something of the splendor of heaven. United with us in prayer, let them petition that wherever covetous greed now holds sway, there may the reign of love soon prevail; that where now the spirit of reprisal persists, forgiveness may be exercised so that instead of discord among men, there may be substituted the loving harmony which reconciles and unites them; and, finally, that where now deep enmities are aroused unhappily provoking widespread disorder there may be effected new ties of friendship which will calm the hearts of men and bring to the universe the tranquillity of an order founded on justice.

1668. Let these little ones implore of the most amiable Mother of God heavenly comforts for all those who are suffering, and particularly for exiled refugees and prisoners and for the wounded in the hospitals. Let them ask of her perseveringly with their innocent voices that the duration of this awful misfortune be brief, so that after having rightly suffered for our sins we may at last be relieved by the comforts of Divine Grace. And, therefore, may there soon return to the earth the resplendent rays of a universal, substantial and lasting peace which, in order to conform to the inviolable demands of justice and charity, will not conceal the germs of discord and rancor nor embody causes of future wars; but which by effecting a fraternal and harmonious union of nations bound together in friendship and by helping all peoples to enjoy the fruits of their labor in tranquil freedom, will accompany and lead them with hope and confidence along the path of their earthly pilgrimage toward their heavenly fatherland. . . . . . .

ALLOCUTION *Nei Tesori* TO THE ITALIAN UNIVERSITY STUDENTS IN CATHOLIC ACTION.[294]

A Catholic is forbidden to punish the guilty beyond the limits of justice.

April 20, 1941

1669. . . . . . . In your world overturned and torn asunder by struggles and wars, what lesson is more necessary than that of humility and charity inculcated by word and example with so much solicitude by the Divine Master, Meek and Humble of Heart . . . ?

[294] Original Italian, *A.A.S.*, v. 33, pp. 162-163 (May 10, 1941).

Teach not pride, which is weak, which puffs up but does not edify, which is a vain respecter of persons; but teach a sense of duty, the conquering of self, courage, heroism in trials and dangers, that virtue which does not become proud in victory and which renders the conqueror more amiable. . . .

1670. These virtues of humility and charity . . . are not enemies, nor are they out of keeping with human dignity. They do not lessen one's love of country. They do not diminish courage or impede a citizen who, in a truly just war, struggles for the defense, honor and salvation of his country, fights with full fortitude against an adversary armed to overcome him. But beneficent charity finds no pleasure in iniquity, not even on the battlefield nor in the most difficult vicissitudes; it forbids those who fight with cruelty against innocent persons or who punish the guilty beyond the limits of justice. . . . . . .

Address to the Ladies of Perpetual Adoration and to the Society for the Assistance of Poor Churches.[295]

The faithful must not cease to pray until peace and harmony return to the world.

May 1, 1941

1671. . . . . . . In this poor world, divided by burning passions, morally disoriented, lacerated by inexorable strife, indispensable beyond everything is an extraordinary effusion in souls, in all souls, of that spirit of charity that Christ came from the bosom of the Father to bring us as fire on earth and of which the brilliant center in the midst of us is His Heart really present on our altars. Now more than all exterior works, however beautiful and useful they may be, the need is imperious of a common effort, of an intense and continuous prayer of believing and loving souls to implore and obtain from the omnipotent mercy of God those victorious graces, which convince and conquer and also bend the most inflexible wills, which warm the coldest hearts, so that mutual charity and brotherly love of men among themselves may revive and flourish. Useless and vain palliatives will remain in any other remedy, until we have

---

295 Translation from *N.C.W.C. News Service,* June 30, 1941. It has been impossible to locate the original of this document.

obtained from the Infinite Goodness the profound and intimate renovation of souls. We ask you, all your associates, all the souls united with you in the different works of the Eucharistic Adoration to extend your prayers to the mercy of God. Cease not your prayers until the day when His mercy has heard them, and with the re-awakening of the fire of charity in the hearts of men, harmony may return among peoples and the world may be tranquilized in the order of peace.

TELEGRAM OF CARDINAL MAGLIONE, SECRETARY OF STATE, TO CARDINAL HINSLEY, ARCHBISHOP OF WESTMINSTER.[296]

A just and lasting peace will be founded on the Christian brotherhood of man.

May 3, 1941

1672. Holy Father appreciates expression of devotion of archbishops, bishops of England and Wales, and while thanking them for their prayers assures them that he continues to pray and work for a just, lasting peace founded on Christian brotherhood of man. His Holiness imparts from heart his Apostolic Blessing.

DISCOURSE *La Solennità della Pentecoste,* COMMEMORATING THE FIFTIETH ANNIVERSARY OF THE ENCYCLICAL *Rerum Novarum* OF POPE LEO XIII.[297]

Pius XII reaffirms the social teaching of the great Encyclicals, Rerum Novarum and Quadragesimo Anno, and applies their principles to current problems.

June 1, 1941

1673. The Feast of Pentecost, that glorious birthday of the Church of Christ, is to Our mind, dear children of the whole world, a welcome and auspicious occasion and one full of high import, on which to address to you, in the midst of the difficulties and strife of the present hour, a message of love, encouragement and comfort. We speak to you at a moment when every energy and force, physical

[296] Original English from *The Tablet,* v. 177, p. 351 (May 3, 1941).
[297] Official English version, *A.A.S.,* v. 33, pp. 216-227 (June 23, 1941).

and intellectual, of an ever-increasing section of mankind is being strained, to a degree and intensity never before known, beneath the iron, inexorable law of war; and when from other radio aerials are going forth words full of passion, bitterness, division and strife. . . . . . . In this hour, pregnant with events that are known only to the divine counsels which rule the story of nations and watch over the Church, it is for Us, beloved children, a source of sincere joy and gratification in letting you hear the voice of your Common Father, to call you together, so to speak, in a worldwide Catholic meeting, so that you may experience and enjoy in the bond of peace that *one heart* and *one soul*[298] which held together under the impulse of the Holy Spirit, the faithful of Jerusalem on Pentecost Day.

1674. As the circumstances created by the war make direct, living contact between the Supreme Pastor and His flock difficult in many cases, We greet with all the more gratitude this most expedite bridge which the inventive genius of our age throws across the ether in a flash, to unite across mountains, seas and continents every corner of the earth. And thus what for many is a weapon of war becomes for Us a heaven-sent means of patient, peaceful apostolate which realizes and gives new significance to the words of Holy Scripture: *Their sound hath gone forth unto all the earth; and their words unto the ends of the world.*[299] Thus does it seem as if were renewed the miracle of Pentecost, when the different peoples who had assembled in Jerusalem from regions speaking various languages, heard the voice of Peter and the Apostles in their own tongue. With genuine delight We to-day make use of so wonderful an instrument, in order to call to the attention of the Catholic world a memory worthy of being written in letters of gold on the Calendar of the Church: the fiftieth anniversary of the publication, on May 15, 1891, of the epoch-making social Encyclical of Leo XIII, *Rerum Novarum.*[300]

1675. It was in the profound conviction that the Church has not only the right but even the duty to make an authoritative pronouncement on the social question, that Leo XIII addressed his message to the world. He had no intention of laying down guiding principles on the purely practical, we might say technical side of

---

[298] *Cf. Acts,* IV, 32.
[299] *Psalms,* XVIII, 5; *Romans,* X, 18.
[300] *Cf. supra* nn. 118-175.

the social structure; for he was well aware of the fact—as Our immediate Predecessor of saintly memory, Pius XI, pointed out ten years
ago in his commemorative Encyclical, *Quadragesimo Anno*[301]—that
the Church does not claim such a mission. In the general framework
of labor, to stimulate the sane and responsible development of all
the energies, physical and spiritual, of individuals and their free
organization, there opens up a wide field of action where the public
authority comes in with its integrating and co-ordinating activity
exercised first through the local and professional corporations, and
finally in the activity of the State itself, whose higher moderating
social authority has the important duty of forestalling the disloca-
tions of economic balance arising from plurality and divergence of
clashing interests, individual and collective.

1676. It is, on the other hand, the indisputable competence of
the Church, on that side of the social order where it meets and
enters into contact with the moral order, to decide whether the
bases of a given social system are in accord with the unchangeable
order which God, our Creator and Redeemer, has shown us through
the natural law and Revelation, that twofold manifestation to
which Leo XIII appeals in his Encyclical. And with reason: for
the dictates of the natural law and the truths of Revelation spring
forth in a different manner, like two streams of water that do not
flow against one another but together, from the same divine Source;
and the Church, guardian of the supernatural Christian order in
which nature and grace converge, must form the consciences even
of those who are called upon to find solutions for the problems
and the duties imposed by social life. Upon the form given to
society, whether conforming or not to the divine law, depends and
emerges the good or ill of souls, depends the decision whether men,
all called to be revived by the grace of Christ, do actually in the
detailed course of their life breathe the healthy vivifying atmosphere
of truth and moral virtue or the disease-laden and often fatal air
of error and corruption. Before such a thought and such an anticipation, how could the Church, loving Mother that she is, solicitous
for the welfare of her children, remain an indifferent onlooker in
their danger, remain silent or feign not to see or take cognizance
of social conditions which, whether one wills it or not, make difficult
or practically impossible a Christian life? . . .

[301] *Cf. supra* nn. 924-1048.

1677. Conscious of such a grave responsibility, Leo XIII, addressing his Encyclical to the world, pointed out to the conscience of Christians the errors and danger of the conception of materialistic Socialism, the fatal consequences of economic Liberalism so often unaware, or forgetful, or contemptuous of social duties; and exposed with masterly clarity and wonderful precision the principles that were necessary and suitable for improving—gradually and peacefully—the material and spiritual lot of the worker.

1678. If, beloved children, you ask Us to-day, after fifty years from the date of publication of the Encyclical, to what extent the efficacy of his message corresponded to its noble intentions, to its thoughts so full of truth, to the beneficent directions understood and suggested by its wise author, We feel that We must answer thus: it is precisely to render to Almighty God from the bottom of Our heart, Our humble thanks for the gift which, fifty years ago, He bestowed on the Church in that Encyclical of His Vicar on earth, and to praise Him for the lifegiving breath of the Spirit which through it, in ever-growing measure from that time on, has blown on all mankind, that We on this Feast of Pentecost, have decided to address you.

1679. Our Predecessor, Pius XI, has already exalted, in the first part of his commemorative Encyclical, the splendid crop of good to which *Rerum Novarum,* like a fertile sowing, had given rise. From it sprang forth a Catholic social teaching which gave to the children of the Church, priests and laymen, an orientation and method for a social reconstruction which was overflowing with good effects; for through it there arose in the Catholic field numerous and diverse beneficent institutions that were flourishing centers of reciprocal help for themselves and others. What an amount of well-being, material and natural, what spiritual and supernatural profit have come to the workers and their families from the Catholic unions! How efficacious and suited to the need has been the help afforded by the syndicates and associations in favor of the agricultural and middle class to relieve their wants, defend them from injustice, and in this way, by soothing passion, to save social peace from disorder!

1680. Nor was this the whole benefit. The Encyclical, *Rerum Novarum,* coming down to the people and greeting them with esteem and love, went deep into the hearts and esteem of the working class, and inspired it with a sense of Christian sentiment and civil dignity; indeed its powerful influence came, with the passage of the years, to expand and spread to such an extent that its norms became almost the common property of all men. And, while the State in the nineteenth century, through excessive exaltation of liberty, considered as its exclusive scope the safeguarding of liberty by the law, Leo XIII admonished it that it had also the duty to interest itself in social welfare, taking care of the entire people and of all its members, especially the weak and the dispossessed, through a generous social program and the creation of a labor code. His call evoked a powerful response; and it is a clear duty of justice to recognize the progress which has been achieved in the lot of workers through the pains taken by civil authorities in many lands. Hence was it well said that *Rerum Novarum* became the "Magna Charta" of Christian social endeavor.

1681. Meanwhile, there was passing a half century which has left deep furrows and grievous disturbance in the domain of nations and society. The questions which social and especially economic changes and upheavals offered for moral consideration after *Rerum Novarum,* have been treated with penetrating acumen by Our immediate Predecessor in the Encyclical, *Quadragesimo Anno.* The ten years that have followed it have been no less fraught with surprises in social and economic life than the years before it, and have finally poured their dark and turbulent waters into the sea of a war whose unforeseen currents may affect our economy and society.

1682. What problems and what particular undertakings, some perhaps entirely novel, our social life will present to the care of the Church at the end of this conflict which sets so many peoples against one another, it is difficult at the moment to trace or foresee. If, however, the future has its roots in the past, if the experience of recent years is to be our guide for the future, We feel We may avail Ourself of this commemoration to give some further directive moral principles on three fundamental values of social and economic life; and We shall do this, animated by the very spirit of Leo XIII and unfolding his views which were more than prophetic, presaging the social evolution of the day. These three fundamental values, which are closely connected one with the other, mutually complementary and dependent, are: the use of material goods, labor and the family.

1683. The Encyclical, *Rerum Novarum,* expounds, on the ques-

tion of property and man's sustenance, principles which have lost
nothing of their inherent vigor with the passage of time, and to-day,
fifty years after, strike their roots deeper and retain their innate
vitality. In Our Encyclical, *Sertum Laetitiae*,[302] directed to the
bishops of the United States of America, We called the attention
of all to the basic idea of these principles which consists, as We said,
in the assertion of the unquestionable need "that the goods, which
were created by God for all men, should flow equally to all, according to the principles of justice and charity." Every man, as a living
being gifted with reason, has in fact from nature the fundamental
right to make use of the material goods of the earth, while it is left
to the will of man and to the juridical statutes of nations to regulate
in greater detail the actuation of this right. This individual right
cannot in any way be suppressed, even by other clear and undis-
puted rights over material goods. Undoubtedly the natural order,
deriving from God, demands also private property and the free
reciprocal commerce of goods by interchange and gift, as well as
the functioning of the State as a control over both these institutions.
But all this remains subordinated to the natural scope of material
goods and cannot emancipate itself from the first and fundamental
right which concedes their use to all men; but it should rather serve
to make possible the actuation of this right in conformity with its
scope. Only thus can we and must we secure that private property
and the use of material goods bring to society peace and prosperity
and long life, that they no longer set up precarious conditions which
will give rise to struggles and jealousies, and which are left to the
mercy of the blind interplay of force and weakness.

1684. The native right to the use of material goods, intimately
linked as it is to the dignity and other rights of the human person,
together with the statutes mentioned above, provides man with a
secure material basis of the highest import, on which to rise to the
fulfillment, with reasonable liberty, of his moral duties. The safe
guardianship of this right will ensure the personal dignity of man,
and will facilitate for him the attention to and fulfillment of that
sum of stable duties and decisions for which he is directly responsible
to his Creator. Man has in truth the entirely personal duty to preserve and order to perfection his material and spiritual life, so as to
secure the religious and moral scope which God has assigned to all

[302] November 1, 1939; *cf. supra* n. 1464.

men, and has given them as the supreme norm obliging always and everywhere, before all other duties.

1685. To safeguard the inviolable sphere of the rights of the human person and to facilitate the fulfillment of his duties should be the essential office of every public authority. Does not this flow from that genuine concept of the common good which the State is called upon to promote? Hence, it follows that the care of such a *common good* does not imply a power so extensive over the members of the community that in virtue of it the public authority can interfere with the evolution of that individual activity which We have just described, decide directly on the beginning or—excepting the case of legitimate capital punishment—the ending of human life, determine at will the manner of his physical, spiritual, religious and moral movements in opposition to the personal duties or rights of man, and to this end abolish or deprive of efficacy his natural rights to material goods. To deduce such extension of power from the care of the common good would be equivalent to overthrowing the very meaning of the word common good, and falling into the error that the proper scope of man on earth is society, that society is an end in itself, that man has no other life which awaits him beyond that which ends here below. Likewise the national economy, as it is the product of the men who work together in the community of the State, has no other end than to secure without interruption the material conditions in which the individual life of the citizens may fully develop. Where this is secured in a permanent way, a people will be, in a true sense, economically rich because the general well-being, and consequently the personal right of all to the use of worldly goods, is thus actuated in conformity with the purpose willed by the Creator.

1686. From this, beloved children, it will be easy for you to conclude that the economic riches of a people do not properly consist in the abundance of goods, measured according to a purely and solely material calculation of their worth, but in the fact that such an abundance represents and offers really and effectively the material basis sufficient for the proper personal development of its members. If such a just distribution of goods were not secured, or were effected only imperfectly, the real scope of national economy would not be attained; for, although there were at hand a lucky abundance of goods to dispose of, the people, in not being called upon to share them, would not be economically rich but poor. Suppose, on the other hand, that such a distribution is effected genuinely and permanently, and you will see a people, even if it disposes of less goods, making itself economically sound.

1687. These fundamental concepts regarding the riches and poverty of peoples, it seems to Us particularly opportune to set before you to-day, when there is a tendency to measure and judge such riches and poverty by balance sheets and by purely quantitative criteria of the need or the redundance of goods. If, instead, the scope of the national economy is correctly considered, then it will become a guide for the efforts of statesmen and peoples, and will enlighten them to walk spontaneously along a way which does not call for continual exactions in goods and blood, but will give fruits of peace and general welfare.

1688. With the use of material goods you yourselves, dear children, see how labor is connected. *Rerum Novarum* teaches that there are two essential characteristics of human labor: it is personal and it is necessary. It is personal, because it is achieved through the exercise of man's particular forces; it is necessary, because without it one cannot secure what is indispensable to life; and man has a natural, grave, individual obligation to maintain life. To the personal duty to labor imposed by nature corresponds and follows the natural right of each individual to make of labor the means to provide for his own life and that of his children; so profoundly is the empire of nature ordained for the preservation of man.

1689. But note that such a duty and the corresponding right to work is imposed on and conceded to the individual in the first instance by nature, and not by society, as if man were nothing more than a mere slave or official of the community. From that it follows that the duty and the right to organize the labor of the people belongs above all to the people immediately interested: the employers and the workers. If they do not fulfill their functions, or cannot because of special extraordinary contingencies fulfill them, then it falls back on the State to intervene in the field of labor and in the division and distribution of work according to the form and measure that the common good properly understood demands.

1690. In any case, every legitimate and beneficial interference of the State in the field of labor should be such as to safeguard and respect its personal character, both in the broad outlines and, as far as possible, in what concerns its execution; and this will happen, if the norms of the State do not abolish or render impossible the exercise of other rights and duties equally personal; such as the right to give God His due worship; the right to marry; the right of husband and wife, of father and mother to lead a married domestic life; the right to a reasonable liberty in the choice of a state of life and the fulfillment of a true vocation; a personal right, this last, if ever there was one, belonging to the spirit of man, and sublime when the higher imprescriptible rights of God and of the Church meet, as in the choice and fulfillment of the priestly and religious vocations.

1691. According to the teaching of *Rerum Novarum,* nature itself has closely joined private property with the existence of human society and its true civilization, and in a very special manner with the existence and development of the family. Such a link appears more than obvious. Should not private property secure for the father of a family the healthy liberty he needs in order to fulfill the duties assigned him by the Creator regarding the physical, spiritual and religious welfare of the family? In the family the nation finds the natural and fecund roots of its greatness and power. If private property has to conduce to the good of the family, all public standards, and especially those of the State which regulate its possession, must not only make possible and preserve such a function— a function in the natural order under certain aspects superior to all others—but must also perfect it ever more. A so-called civil progress, would, in fact, be unnatural, which—either through the excessive burdens imposed, or through exaggerated direct interference—were to render private property void of significance, practically taking from the family and its head the freedom to follow the scope set by God for the perfection of family life.

1692. Of all the goods that can be the object of private property, none is more conformable to nature, according to the teaching of *Rerum Novarum,* than the land, the holding on which the family lives, and from the products of which it draws all or part of its subsistence. And it is in the spirit of *Rerum Novarum* to state that, as a rule, only that stability which is rooted in one's own holding, makes of the family the vital and most perfect and fecund cell of society, joining up in a brilliant manner in its progressive cohesion the present and future generations. If to-day the concept and the creation of vital spaces is at the center of social and political aims, should not one, before all else, think of the vital space of the family and free it of the fetters of conditions which do not permit one even to formulate the idea of a homestead of one's own?

1693. Our planet, with all its extent of oceans and seas and lakes, with mountains and plains covered with eternal snows and ice, with great deserts and tractless lands is not, all the same, without habitable regions and vital spaces, now abandoned to wild natural vegetation, and well suited to be cultivated by man to satisfy his needs and civil activities; and more than once it is inevitable that some families, migrating from one spot or another, should go elsewhere in search of a new homeland. Then, according to the teaching of *Rerum Novarum,* the right of the family to a vital space is recognized. When this happens, emigration attains its natural scope, as experience often shows; We mean the more favorable distribution of men on the earth's surface, suitable to colonies of agricultural workers; that surface which God created and prepared for the use of all. If the two parties, those who agree to leave their native land, and those who agree to admit the newcomers, remain anxious to eliminate as far as possible all obstacles to the birth and growth of real confidence between the country of emigration and that of immigration, all those affected by such a transference of people and places will profit by the transaction: the families will receive a plot of ground which will be native land for them in the true sense of the word: the thickly inhabited countries will be relieved, and their peoples will acquire new friends in foreign countries; and the States which receive the emigrants will acquire industrious citizens. In this way the nations which give and those which receive will both contribute to the increased welfare of man and the progress of human culture.

1694. These are the principles, concepts and norms, beloved children, with which We should wish even now to share in the future organization of that new order which the world expects and hopes will arise from the seething ferment of the present struggle, to set the peoples at rest in peace and justice. What remains for Us but, in the spirit of Leo XIII and in accordance with his advice and purpose, to exhort you to continue to promote the work which the last generation of your brothers and sisters has begun with such stanch courage? Do not let die in your midst and fade away the insistent call of the two Pontiffs of the social Encyclicals, that voice which indicates to the faithful in the supernatural regeneration of mankind the moral obligation to co-operate in the arrangement of society, and especially of economic life, exhorting those who share in this life to action no less than the State itself. Is not this a sacred duty for every Christian? . . .

1695. If between the ideal and its realization there appears even now an evident lack of proportion; if there have been failures, common indeed to all human activity, if divergencies of view arose on the way followed or to be followed, all this should not make you depressed or slow up your step or give rise to lamentations or recriminations; nor can it make you forget the consoling fact that the inspired message of the Pope of *Rerum Novarum* sent forth a living and clear stream of strong social sense, sincere and disinterested; a stream which, if it be now partly perhaps covered by a landslide of divergent and overpowering events, tomorrow, when the ruin of this world hurricane is cleared, at the outset of that reconstruction of a new social order, which is a desire worthy of God and of man, will infuse new courage and a new wave of exuberance and growth in the garden of human culture. Keep burning the noble flame of a brotherly social spirit which fifty years ago was rekindled in the hearts of your fathers by the luminous and illuminating torch of the words of Leo XIII; do not allow or permit it to lack nourishment; let it flare up through your homage and not die, quenched by an unworthy, timid, cautious inaction in face of the needs of the poor among our brethren, or overcome by the dust and dirt carried by the whirlwind of the anti-Christian or non-Christian spirit. Nourish it, keep it alive, increase it; make this flame burn more brightly. . . .

ALLOCUTION *La Grandissima Solennità* TO THE COLLEGE OF CARDINALS ON THE POPE'S PATRONAL FEAST DAY.[303]

Pius XII prays that he may be able to continue his works of charity among the war victims.

June 2, 1941

1696. . . . . . . Although the Eternal City has until now been spared the horrors of war, yet the echoes of the murderous destruc-

---

[303] Original Italian, *A.A.S.*, v. 33, p. 192 (June 23, 1941).

tion, the mourning for the dead, the anxiety for the missing, the homesickness of prisoners, the tears of widows and orphans, the exile of the deported, the poverty and indigence of the homeless refugees are striving in their misery to find a way to Us, to Our attention and to Our heart. They speak to Us in every language with heartbreaking voices, and reveal and disclose every day and almost every hour, into what an immense and dark abyss of suffering and sorrow the present storm has driven and is still driving poor humanity, as well as destroying the Vineyard of God.

1697.   But even in such an anxious period of trial and sorrow, the Church does not cease to be "the field of those who hope." Before Our eyes appears, as a comforting and admonishing vision, the meek and compassionate image of the Holy Pontiff whose name was conferred upon Us in Baptism. In admiration of his example which serves as a guiding light to Our soul, We implore from the Eternal Priest of the sublime Altar of Golgotha, the focal point of the universe, a spark of that overwhelming flame of Apostolic love toward the poor and the miserable, which was one of the shining qualities of Saint Eugene I.[304] We ask him to obtain from the Lord that—thanks to the generous co-operation of so many elect souls who, inspired by the charity of Christ, make up for the scantiness of Our material means—We may continue to have the opportunity to convey to the victims of war and to the numberless other sufferers the most efficacious signs of Our tireless affection and paternal solicitude. . . . . . .

PRAYER FOR WORLD PEACE COMPOSED BY THE SUPREME PONTIFF ON HIS NAME DAY.[305]

The Pope ardently desires justice and peace, concord and forgiveness among nations.

June 2, 1941

1698.   O Jesus, Supreme Pontiff of the New and Eternal Testament, Who art seated at the right hand of God as a perpetual advocate for us, and art pleased to be, all days forever and ever, with

[304] *Cf. Liber Pontificalis,* n. 77.
[305] Translation from *Catholic Action,* v. 23, June, 1941, p. 5, where it stated that this prayer was "composed by the Supreme Pontiff on his name day in honor of St. Eugene." The original of this prayer is not given in the *A.A.S.*

Thy beloved spouse, the Church, and with Thy Vicar who governs her, Thou didst deign, Divine Prince of the pastors of Thy flock, to glorify on the throne of Peter Thy servant and Pontiff, Eugene, and to make him, in the midst of the iniquity of the time, mild amid hostile attacks, strong in the defense of the Faith, in the Pastoral Office a gentle father and watchful master. Deign through his merits, which are Your grace and glory, to give a kindly hearing to his prayer to Thee and hearken to Our prayers.

1699. May Thy kingdom come, O Immortal King of the Ages; may the truth which Thou didst bring from heaven reach even to the uttermost confines of the earth; may the fire which Thou didst will should be cast upon the earth inflame all hearts. This is the desire that is in the heart of Thy Vicar; a desire to reconcile men to Thee; a desire to give comfort in the grief of so many mothers and sons; a desire for concord and forgiveness among nations; a desire for justice and peace.

1700. Enlighten Thy Vicar, O Jesus. Strengthen him in his sorrows and in his universal cares; renew in him the spirit of the Holy Pontiff who intercedes for him in Thy presence; speak that potent word, O Lord, which shall change minds, turn hate into love, check the fury of human passions, temper the sufferings and dry the tears of those who are in sorrow. Increase the virtue and the resignation of families, pacify nations and peoples, so that the Church built by Thee on St. Peter to gather all peoples around Thy Altar of life and salvation, may invoke Thee, adore Thee and exalt Thee in tranquillity forever and ever. Amen.

RADIO ADDRESS *As We Send* TO THE NINTH NATIONAL EUCHARISTIC CONGRESS IN ST. PAUL, MINNESOTA, U.S.A.[306]

Unless it is protected by the bulwarks of morality and religion, no nation can aspire to prosperity and peace.

June 26, 1941

1701. . . . . . . You live in a country, where a tradition of human freedoms allows you to practice your Faith without let or hindrance. Your chief enemy is within you—that natural drag of our fallen humanity to self-seeking and sin. Self-sacrifice must com-

[306] Original English, *A.A.S.*, v. 33, pp. 353-354 (August 25, 1941).

bat it. Your parishes multiply, your schools and colleges and universities are thronged, your youth associations flourish, your organizations of social and civic service are reinforcing those bulwarks of morality and religion, without which no nation can aspire to prosperity and peace. But you must not forget that you belong to a Church, whose Founder and Head was scourged, mocked and crucified;[307] and that His Body, which is the Church, as it has always suffered persecution, so it is to-day being persecuted—persecuted in some of its members so artfully, that it is difficult to measure how far-reaching the effect may be. And—bitter tragedy of it all—loyal Catholic fathers and mothers, with sorrow gnawing at their hearts, must contemplate the danger, which every day looms more threatening, that their children and their children's children may be deprived of that precious heritage of faith, which they had hoped to safeguard for them.

1702. In Our discourse of last Easter,[308] as you well remember, Our paternal heart had a special word of comfort and encouragement for those whose fidelity to Christ is forcing them to walk the sorrowful Way of the Cross. These, Venerable Brothers and beloved children, are members of the same Body, Christ, as you. Through the Sacrament of our altars His same life-giving Spirit has nourished their souls and yours. If they are asked to suffer for our faith the physical pain and mental anguish of Christ's passion, have they not a special claim to the prayerful sympathy of Christ's other members? *Who is weak, and I am not weak?*[309] was the cry of the apostolic heart of St. Paul; it should find a clear echo in every truly Catholic heart—an echo which, like the Apostle's voice, is not broken against the narrow confines erected by man, but carries to every corner of the earth, where members of Christ's Body are suffering and in need. This burning, unquenchable zeal to defend and to spread God's Kingdom on earth, which made St. Paul's soul so truly Christ-like, has run through all the sessions of your Congress, We are sure, and has been fanned to steadier, purer flame by your love of the divine Victim of our Holy Sacrifice. Your lives will bear testimony to that zeal of an apostle. . . . . . .

---

[307] *Cf. Matthew*, XX, 19.
[308] April 13, 1941; *cf. supra* nn. 1650-1664.
[309] II *Corinthians*, XI, 29.

RADIO ADDRESS *In Questa Solennità* ON DIVINE PROVIDENCE IN HUMAN EVENTS.[310]

Pius XII explains how Divine Providence can permit the indescribable sufferings caused by the fury of the war.

June 29, 1941

1703. . . . . . . We, like you, feel Our heart grow faint at the thought of the tempest of evil, of suffering and of anguish that now rages over the world. There are not lacking, it is true, in the darkness of the storm, comforting sights which dilate our hearts with great and holy expectations; courage in defense of the fundamentals of Christian civilization and confident hope in their triumph; the most intrepid patriotism; heroic acts of virtue; chosen souls ready for every sacrifice; whole-hearted self-surrender; widespread reawakening of faith and of piety.

1704. But, on the other hand, sin and evil penetrate the lives of individuals, the sacred shrine of the family, the social organism. No longer merely tolerated through weakness or impotence, sin is excused, exalted, and enters as master into the most diverse phases of human life. There is a decadence of the spirit of justice and charity; peoples are overthrown or have fallen into an abyss of disasters; human bodies are torn by bombs or by machine-gun fire; wounded and sick fill hospitals and come out often with their health ruined, their limbs mutilated, invalids for the rest of their lives. Prisoners are far from those dear to them and often without news of them; individuals and families are deported, transported, separated, torn from their homes, wandering in misery without support, without means of earning their daily bread.

1705. All these evils affect not only the fighters but weigh on the whole population, old men, women and children; the most innocent, the most peace-loving, those bereft of all defense. Blockades and counter-blockades aggravate almost everywhere the difficulty of getting supplies of foodstuffs so that already, here and there, famine with all its horrors makes its presence felt. Added to this is the indescribable suffering, pain and persecution which so many of Our dear sons and daughters — priests, religious, lay

---

[310] Translation from *The Catholic Mind*, v. 39, n. 927, pp. 3-10 (August 8, 1941). Original Italian, *A.A.S.*, v. 33, pp. 320-325 (July 21, 1941).

folk—in some places endure for the name of Christ because of their religion, because of their fidelity to the Church, because of their Sacred Ministry—pains and bitterness which anxiety for those that suffer does not permit Us to reveal in all their sad and moving details.

1706. Before such an accumulation of evils, of obstacles to virtue, of disasters, of trials of every kind, it seems that man's mind and judgment go astray and become confused, and perhaps in the heart of more than one of you has arisen the terrible suggestion of doubt which perchance at the death of the two Apostles was a disturbing temptation for some of the less stanch Christians: how can God permit all this? Can an omnipotent God, infinitely wise and infinitely good, possibly allow so many evils which He might so easily prevent? And there arise to the lips the words of Peter, still imperfect when the Passion was foretold: *Far be it from Thee, O Lord.*[311] No, my God—they think—neither Your wisdom nor Your goodness nor Your honor itself can allow that evil and violence dominate to such an extent over the world, to deride You and triumph by Your silence. Where is Your power and providence? Must we, then, doubt either Your divine government or Your love for us? . . . . . .

1707. All men are as children before God; all, even the most profound thinkers and the most experienced leaders of peoples. They judge events with the foreshortened vision of time, which passes and flies past irreparably; God, on the other hand, sees events from on high, from the unmoved center of eternity. They have before their eyes the limited view of a few years; God has before Him the all-embracing panorama of the ages. They think of human events in relation to their proximate causes and immediate effects; God sees them in their remote causes and judges them in their remote effects. They stop to single out this or that particular responsible hand; God sees a whole hidden complicated convergence of responsibilities because His exalted Providence does not exclude the free choice of evil and good in human selection. They would have immediate justice and are scandalized at the ephemeral power of the enemies of God, the sufferings and humiliations of the innocent permitted by God; but our Heavenly Father, Who in the light of His eternity, embraces, penetrates and dominates the vicis-

[311] *Matthew*, XVI, 22.

situdes of time as much as the serene peace of the endless ages; God, Who is the Blessed Trinity, full of compassion for the weaknesses, ignorance and impatience of men, but Who loves men too much for their faults to turn Him from the ways of His wisdom and love, continues and will continue to make His sun to rise on the good and the evil, and to send rain on the just and the unjust,[312] to guide their childlike steps with firmness and kindness if only they will let themselves be led by Him and have trust in the power and the wisdom of His love for them.

1708. What does it mean to trust in God? Trust in God means the abandonment of oneself, with all the force of the will sustained by grace and love, in spite of all the doubts suggested by appearances to the contrary, to the wisdom, the infinite love of God. It means believing that nothing in this world escapes His Providence, whether in the universal or in the particular order; that nothing great or small happens which is not foreseen, willed or permitted, directed always by Providence to its exalted ends, which in this world are always inspired by love for men. It means believing that God can permit at times here below for some time pre-eminence of atheism and of impiety, the lamentable obscuring of a sense of justice, the violation of law, the tormenting of innocent, peaceful, undefended, helpless men. It means believing that God at times thus lets trials befall individuals and peoples, trials of which the malice of men is the instrument in a design of justice directed toward the punishment of sin, toward purifying persons and peoples through the expiations of this present life and bringing them back by this way to Himself; but it means believing at the same time that this justice always remains here below the justice of a Father inspired and dominated by love.

1709. However severe may seem the Hand of the Divine Surgeon when He cuts with the lancet into the live flesh, it is always an active love that guides and drives it in, and only the good of men and peoples makes Him interfere in such a painful way. It means believing finally that the fierce intensity of the trial, like the triumph of evil, will endure even here below only for a fixed time and not longer; that the hour of God will come, the hour of mercy, the hour of holy rejoicing, the hour of the new canticle of libera-

[312] *Cf. Matthew*, V, 45.

tion, the hour of exultation and of joy,[313] the hour in which, after having let the hurricane loose for a moment on humanity, the all-powerful Hand of the Heavenly Father with an imperceptible motion will detain it and disperse it, and, by ways little known to the mind or to the hopes of men, justice, calm and peace will be restored to the nations.

1710. We know well that the most serious difficulty for those who have not a correct sense of the divine comes from seeing so many innocent victims involved in suffering by the same tempest which overwhelms sinners. Men never remain indifferent when the hurricane which tears up the great trees also cuts down the lowly little flowers which opened at their feet only to lavish the grace of their beauty and fragrance on the air around them. And yet these flowers and their perfumes are the work of God and of His wonderful designing! If He has allowed any of these flowers to be swept away in the storm, can He not, do you think, have assigned a goal unseen by the human eye for the sacrifice of that most unoffending creature in the general arrangement of the law by which He prevails over and governs nature? How much more, then, will His omnipotence and love direct the lot of pure and innocent human beings to good?

1711. Through the languishing of faith in men's hearts, through the pleasure-seeking that molds and captivates their lives, men are driven to judge as evil, and as unmixed evil, all the physical mishaps of this earth. They have forgotten that suffering stands at the threshold of life as the way that leads to the smiles of the cradle; they have forgotten that it is more often than not the shadow of the Cross of Calvary thrown on the path of the Resurrection; they have forgotten that the cross is frequently a gift of God, a gift which is needed in order to offer to the Divine Justice our share of expiation; they have forgotten that the only real evil is the sin that offends God; they have forgotten what the Apostle says: *The sufferings of the present time are not worthy to be compared with the glory to come that will be revealed in us,*[314] that we ought to look on *the Author and Finisher of faith, Jesus, Who for the joy set before Him, endured a cross.*[315] . . .

[313] *Cf. Psalms,* XCVI.
[314] *Romans,* VIII, 18.
[315] *Hebrews,* XII, 2.

1712. Do you, too, dear children, look upon your sufferings thus; and you will find the strength not merely to accept them with resignation but to love them, to glory in them as the Apostles and Saints. Our fathers and elder brothers, who were formed of the same flesh as you and had the same power of suffering, loved them and gloried in them. Look on your sufferings and difficulties in the light of the sufferings of the Crucified, in the light of the sufferings of the Blessed Virgin, the most innocent of creatures and the most intimate sharer in the Passion of Our Lord, and you will be able to understand that to be like the Exemplar, the Son of God, King of Sufferings, is the noblest and safest way to heaven and victory. Do not look merely at the thorns which afflict you and cause you pain but think also of the merit which sprouts from your sufferings like the rose of heavenly garland; and you will find then, with the grace of God, the courage and strength of that Christian heroism which is at once sacrifice and victory, and peace surpassing all sense; heroism which your Faith has the right to exact from you. . . . . .

1713. To the whole world, finally, wherever We have children, all equally dear to Us, We extend Our blessing, while Our heart trembles within Us as We think of those people who suffer so much from the present disastrous calamities which have already filled the earth with such conflicts and such mourning. Nor would We exclude from Our prayer and good wishes those who as yet are far from the bosom of the Church, that they may feel her insistent invitation to return and that they, too, may seek in her salvation and peace. . . .

LETTER *Intimo Gaudio* TO THE SPANISH BISHOPS.[316]

It is the priest's duty to bring peace to souls.

June 29, 1941

1714. . . . . . . Among the alumni of the seminaries it is a pleasure to list those men who later, as bishops and priests of this our age, were the outstanding glory of the Church and the State, and who inspired the Spanish Catholics to such strength in their Faith that they were able to overcome the shocking attack launched

---

[316] Original Latin, *A.A.S.*, v. 34, pp. 225-226 (August 1, 1942).

against the most Holy Name of Christ—men who gave to the world a marvelous example of courage and meekness, even laying down their lives for the confession of the Faith because their love for their brethren impelled them. Their sacrifice offered from love of God has already brought most abundant fruit since their blood, not unlike the blood of the ancient martyrs, bringing innumerable souls to God, has become the seed of holy vocations to the ecclesiastical state. These vocations testify that the Faith, unsuccessfully harassed and troubled by the fearful attack, has become, with the restoration of the Christian name in your country, the leaven by which the life of all has been fashioned and directed to the work which Spain, under the direction of Divine Providence, has undertaken to fulfill in co-operation with other nations which will pool their resources in mutual peace and harmony. . . . . . .

1715. For if it is undoubtedly required of every priest that he appear, and actually be, *a perfect man of God, equipped for every good work*,[317] then even more must this be demanded of the priests of Spain—as they are your helpers not only in the administration of the Sacraments, but also and especially in performing works of charity, which the Church rightfully regards as her province, as her right and her duty, such as to relieve troubles by consolation through the instrumentality of her ministers, to assuage severe wounds and to compassionate crushing poverty and need. Consequently, she must show skill in bringing peace to souls, in comforting the faithful and finally in calling back to her maternal embrace all those who have abandoned her because they were tricked by false opinions or errors, or overcome by helplessness or weakness. . . . . . .

ADDRESS TO NEWLY-WEDS.[318]

The Holy Father asks the faithful to persevere in their prayers for peace.

July 3, 1941

1716. . . . . . . The whole Church and all peoples are multiplying their prayers for the early termination of the calamity which is affecting the human family. . . . That peace, with justice, which

---

[317] II *Timothy*, III, 17.
[318] Translation from *N.C.W.C. News Service*, July 7, 1941.

is longed for with such strong insistence and which seems so necessary for the good of all and for the good of souls is delayed; but
God does not deceive and cannot deceive. He will accomplish all
that was written. Perhaps that for which we ask is not received
because we ask badly. . . . . . .

LETTER *Nuper Agnovimus* TO THE PRESIDENT AND THE SUPREME
FEDERAL COUNCIL OF SWITZERLAND ON THE SIX HUNDRED
AND FIFTIETH ANNIVERSARY OF THE FOUNDING OF THEIR
FEDERATION.[319]

> *Switzerland is congratulated on its peaceful role in
> European history.*

July 12, 1941

1717. We have recently learned that the Swiss Federation will,
at the beginning of the month of August this year, joyfully celebrate the six hundred and fiftieth anniversary of its auspicious
founding. We Ourself most willingly share in the joy of beloved
Switzerland, from which a select body of men for so many centuries, not only with constant but at times even with heroic fidelity,
has been guarding the person of the Roman Pontiff. Illustrious
Gentlemen, your country, amid numerous differences of languages
and customs, presents indeed a most noble example of internal
domestic unity, which in God's Providence can strongly attract the
other nations also to mutual love and unity. Christian charity is
truly in highest esteem among your countrymen, and, as a result, a
nation like yours is hostile to no one and strives to help the citizens
of other countries, particularly those who feel most the sufferings
of abominable war. We, therefore, congratulate you again and
again, and together with you We are grateful and give thanks to
Divine Providence, which has so far watched over you in a special
manner. Illustrious Gentlemen, We also publicly congratulate you
on the peace and harmony which, because you are men of good-
will, reign in your cantons. We congratulate you on the prudence
and zeal with which in the midst of difficult circumstances you
govern your people and make every effort — which is particularly

---

[319] Original Latin, *A.A.S.*, v. 33, pp. 386-387 (September 12, 1941).

pleasing to Us—that the rights and obligations of religion be kept sacred and inviolate.

1718. Moreover, it is a pleasure for Us to call attention to the fact that the Swiss officials themselves do not fail to mention the name of God with confidence and respect in their public speeches, and that in observing this most praiseworthy custom, they always commend themselves and their countrymen to the divine Protection whenever they issue public orders. Thus you assuredly follow in the footsteps of your ancestors, who at the beginning of August in 1291 made a perpetual covenant "in the name of the Lord." Making this Our prayer, that your countrymen may have the same sentiments and strive for the same objectives as did Blessed Nicolas of Flue, who was renowned for the ardor of his Christian love and his devotedness to the Swiss Confederation, We fervently pray for your country that the Kingdom of Christ be more and more firmly established in its children and that, favored with every kind of prosperity, it may from day to day more perfectly carry out the mission divinely entrusted to it. Finally on this solemn anniversary of the founding of the Swiss Confederation We beseech God with unceasing prayer that He continue to guard noble Switzerland, turn away from her every evil and danger, and kindly enrich her rulers and all her people abundantly with heavenly blessings.

RESPONSE *Con la Mayor Satisfacción* TO THE HOMAGE OF THE NEW AMBASSADOR OF PERU, DIOMEDES ARIAS SCHREIBER.[320]

> *To all members of the great human family is rendered clearer each day their united destiny in happiness or misfortune.*

July 17, 1941

1719. . . . . . . To-day more imposing and vast than at other times, the problem of social justice which is the approach to social peace, rises before the responsibility of the Governments and the aspirations of the masses. . . . The spirit of *Rerum Novarum* is the spirit of peaceful, ordered and systematized evolution of social thought and social accomplishments. But it is also the spirit of resolute decision and initiative in favor of the poorest among poor. . . .

[320] Translation partly from the *English Catholic Newsletter*, n. 90, p. 3 (August 2, 1941). Original Spanish, *A.A.S.*, v. 33, pp. 357-358 (August 25, 1941).

1720. You, Mr. Ambassador, have alluded with special affection to the position of your country and your people with regard to international law, which, leaving the sovereignty of every State safe and perfect, imposes—as a postulate of the natural and Christian juridical conception—the recognition of the principle of peace with justice. With this you indicated the open wound whose healing tormented humanity implores with feverish ardor and anguished hearts. The tempestuous course of this warlike violence, of which the world to-day is both the witness and the unfortunate victim, the work of moral and material destruction which follows the sanguinary path made by the use of such violence, invite to reflection and deep thought those who before felt themselves inclined sometimes to prefer utilitarian and selfish considerations to moral principles.

1721. To-day, the question of the moralization of international law, of its preservation from egotistical deviations, of the necessity of replacing it on a morally sound and juridically protected basis appears as a vital problem of all nations, and especially for those peoples who are less provided with exterior means of force. And although at the present it is difficult to hope that these ideas— eminently humane, Christian and practical—may be applied in the heat of struggle, nevertheless, it brings comfort to observe that many authorized voices already speak in this vein, and let it be known that the result of military victory cannot prescind from respect for moral principles, which alone are capable of giving support and firmness to the fundamental pillars of the rights of peoples.

1722. Your high mission, Mr. Ambassador, begins in a moment when the soil of Europe, and not only of Europe, trembles under the iron shock of a war the economic and spiritual consequences of which are made more apparent every day even on the distant shores, in the fertile valleys and in the gigantic mountain chains of your distant country; in an hour when to all members of the great human family is rendered clearer each day their united destiny in happiness or misfortune. . . . Be assured, Mr. Ambassador, that in the fulfillment of your mission, you shall always find in Us that confidence and benevolent help which correspond to the importance of your charge and to your high ideals, no less than to the cordiality of the relations happily existing between the Holy See and the Republic of Peru. . . .

741

LETTER *Peramantes Litterae* TO BISHOP BIELER OF SION AND
TO THE OTHER SWISS BISHOPS.[321]

May Switzerland always remain an "island of peace!"

July 25, 1941

1723. . . . We clearly recognize your filial love in what you
have recalled concerning the works begun by Us and especially
concerning the paternal care with which We, embracing all regions
of the world, have surely tried and continue unceasingly to try in
every way to bring about a reconciliation of minds and a just peace
on earth. As regards Switzerland, a country especially dear to Us,
recently also, on the occasion of the six hundred and fiftieth anniversary of the foundation of your confederation, We gladly sent a
letter to the illustrious President and to the other members of the
Federal Council of Switzerland, and We congratulated them particularly on the peace and concord which your citizens enjoy in the
midst of such terrible tempests of war and on the special manner in
which the rights of religion, by the prudence and wisdom of the
rulers, are there held in honor. And We have no dearer thought than
that by the favor of God your "island of peace," as it were, in the
midst of a Europe seething in war may be preserved safe and sound
also for the future, so that it may be able to the best of its power to
alleviate the afflictions of this war and to perform the salutary
works of peace. . . .

REPLY *Les Circonstances* TO THE HOMAGE OF THE NEW MINISTER
OF RUMANIA, DANIEL PAPP.[322]

*Religion is indispensable in building up a sound life in
a nation.*

August 1, 1941

1724. . . . . . In the midst of the manifold preoccupations and
hopes of the present hour, and although stained with the blood of
numerous wounded, the Rumanian Nation has not forgotten to
render a conscious homage to spiritual and religious values and to

---

[321] Original Latin, *A.A.S.*, v. 33, p. 418 (October 25, 1941).
[322] Translation from the *N.C.W.C. News Service*, August 2, 1941. Original French,
  A.A.S., v. 33, p. 359 (August 25, 1941).

take care to give them that importance and consideration which are a measure of the real wisdom of the State and constitute the essential foundation of the sure and stable prosperity of the Government and of the people. It is from the conviction that religious forces are indispensable in building up a sound life in a nation, and from the desire of guaranteeing to Catholics of every rite in the whole Kingdom of Rumania the rights belonging to their religion, that the Concordat happily ratified in 1929 derives its origin. . . . . . .

ADDRESS TO NEWLY-WEDS.[323]

The Holy Father praises the newly-weds for founding homes despite these ominous times.

August 9, 1941

1725. . . . . . . In the midst of this formidable upheaval, you dear sons and daughters have not hesitated, in a great act of Christian faith, in proceeding with the foundation of new homes, knowing and believing that the infallible return of spring amid the tumult of human events is not a derision, not an act of cold indifference, not blindness of nature, not the mad vision of innocent dreamers, but the token of Dante's supreme and paternal "Love that moves sun and stars"; love, whose unceasing vigilance never relaxes for an instant its dominion and whose mercy dominates and tempers men's agitation. Your faith is indeed trust in the gentleness and strength of God's Hand, and its attentive and constant grip on things of this world, be they big or small, joyful or sad. . . . . .

ADDRESS *Già per la Terza Volta* TO THE MEMBERS OF THE SACRED ROMAN ROTA.[324]

The administration of justice is part of the care of souls.

October 3, 1941

1726. Again and for the third time, Our Beloved Sons, the solemn opening of the juridical year of the Sacred Roman Rota is

---

[323] Translation from *The Tablet,* v. 178, p. 87 (August 9, 1941). The date of this address is uncertain; therefore, it has been given the same date as the report in *The Tablet.*

[324] Original Italian, *A.A.S.,* v. 33, pp. 421-422 (October 25, 1941).

oppressed by the dark and violent atmosphere of war, that from month to month, from season to season, from year to year, like a storm, invades, violates and subverts everything, bursting out of all boundaries, overflowing all banks and continually bringing about new changes, new situations and renewed destruction.

1727. The tragic situation of the world, from both the human and the religious aspect, preys heavily upon Our soul and augments Our cares and sorrows, all the more painful and far-reaching inasmuch as Our pastoral love opens its bosom to embrace all peoples. As We gathered from the noble words of your worthy Dean, these Our feelings are fully understood by you who, by virtue of the office with which the Apostolic See has entrusted you, are ministers of the law in the spiritual center of Christianity, and chosen representatives of a judicial power which is steeped in a sacred sense of responsibility and dedicated to good administered with justice and equity in the Catholic world. Indeed, it is not new to you that the administering of justice in the Church is a part of the care of souls, an emanation of that power and pastoral solicitude, the fullness and universality of which find their source and origin in the entrusting of the keys to the first Peter. . . . At the present time, when respect for law is diminished by the regard being paid to such considerations as utility, interest, might and wealth, it is fitting that the law of the Church should shine forth as an example of a law that never changes its principles to suit the interests of the day, and ever advances faithfully in the fulfillment of its divine purpose. . . . . .

Radio Address *Es Siempre una Fecha* to the Eighth National Eucharistic Congress in Santiago, Chile.[325]

May the peace of South America, symbolized by the Christ of the Andes, spread over the entire world.

November 9, 1941

1728. . . . . . . May Christ the Redeemer, the Christ Who has been raised in your Andes, dominating the highest peaks, give you always the precious gift of peace as He generously gave it to you

---

[325] Translation from the *N.C.W.C. News Service,* November 11, 1941. Original Spanish, *A.A.S.,* v. 33, p. 443 (November 21, 1941).

once before. His presence on those mountains, the borderline between two great nations linked to-day by fraternal bonds, is a solemn memorial of this gift. May there flow from the Cross, which He presses against His heart, a torrent, a pacific waterfall which will inundate first your soil, then your entire continent, then all the seas, then all the lands, the entire world! And above this ocean, truly pacific, may His right Hand finish tracing the Sign of the Cross, which He has already begun, on the foreheads of all men, brothers at last. . . .

Letter *We Avail Ourselves* to the Bishops of the United States.[326]

American generosity has helped to relieve the sufferings of the war victims.

November 14, 1941

1729.   We avail Ourselves of the occasion afforded by the Annual Meeting of the Hierarchy of the United States to offer you, Beloved Sons and Venerable Brethren, Our cordial salutations and to assure you once again of Our paternal and grateful acknowledgment of your abiding and devoted interest in all the undertakings of the Holy See, an interest which has always been commensurate with the difficulties and needs of the times. In a very special way, We would assure you of Our heartfelt gratitude for the generous thoughtfulness which prompted the general collection taken up this year, and for the munificent assistance resulting therefrom. Saddened in heart by the terrible sufferings and misery about Us, it is Our ardent wish to offer the unfortunate and innocent victims every possible spiritual and material succor. In the fulfillment of that desire your gracious generosity and that of your devoted faithful has been of inestimable value, and We are confident that in Our prayerful remembrance We are joined by those countless thousands who in their awful need are comforted by that bountiful assistance. In loving testimony of Our grateful benevolence, We impart from Our heart to the members of the Hierarchy, to the clergy and to the faithful Our special Apostolic Benediction, that it may be to one and all a pledge of copious favors.

[326] Original English from *Catholic Action*, v. 23, December, 1941, p. 8.

ADDRESS TO THE PONTIFICAL ACADEMY OF SCIENCES.[327]

Science is a two-edged sword which heals and kills.

November 30, 1941

1730. . . . . . . In the hands of men, science can transform
itself into a two-edged sword which heals and kills. . . . May all
men become brothers again in love and concord in the victory of
good over evil, in justice and in peace! . . . . . .

ALLOCUTION *In Questa Sacra Vigilia* TO THE COLLEGE OF CAR-
DINALS.[328]

*No new order worthy of the name is possible unless the
peacemakers are enlightened with supernatural wisdom.*

December 24, 1941

1731. . . . . . . To-day the waves of the sea are more turbulent
and stormy than ever, and their terrible roaring seems little in
harmony with the sweet and tender eloquence of the infant's cry
of the Babe of Bethlehem, Who, with His first greeting, spreads
about Him the gleams of perfect joy and unites His smile to the
song of the angels who chant glory to God and peace to men.
How sharp is the contrast, Venerable Brothers and Beloved Sons,
between the divine manger in which there lies, in the dear guise
of a new-born babe, the Prince of Peace, and a whole world struck
and convulsed by the dire thunderbolt of a war whose like humanity
and the sun itself have never beheld; a war whose bloody front
is continually extended with iron-like implacability from the ice of
the Arctic to the desert, from continent to continent, from ocean
to ocean; a war which from external struggles and incidents passes
into the very hearts of men; from their hearts into their minds,
invading the field of culture and of public affairs, of society and
of the State, and producing there the germs of new attitudes of
spirit whose eventual development and interaction are fearful and
incalculable to estimate. Contributing to the deception of hearts
and minds, love and hate are confused or disguised, as are also
virtue and vice, praise and blame, justice and iniquity, peace and

[327] Translation from *The Tablet*, v. 178, p. 361 (December 6, 1941).
[328] Original Italian, *A.A.S.*, v. 34, pp. 7-10 (January 20, 1942).

war, friend and enemy, good and evil. A dark cloud seems to envelop in its folds human affections and judgments and to obscure the path of life already so deceitful and uncertain.

1732. When humanity suffers, the Church also suffers. The disagreements which disturb and break the harmony between nations, agitate the very air about us and beat also upon the door of the sanctuary. And although there, they are not and cannot be given an entrance, nevertheless, they frequently awaken an echo in the hearts of the faithful greater than that which, according to the law of God, should be allowed to such discords.

1733. You, Venerable Brothers and Beloved Sons, who are the most intimate and faithful co-operators in Our work, possess the judgment to appreciate and evaluate what tasks and duties, what preoccupations and troubles, what sorrows and trials in these tempestuous times weigh upon the shoulders and press upon the heart of him, who, according to the inscrutable plan of God, has been called to be the loving Father of all without exception, the universal comforter of the sorrows of others, the steadfast herald of truth, the watchful guardian of a unity of spirit desired by God above all that separates, the unwearying protagonist and promoter, amid the whirlwind of earthly strife, of that fraternal sentiment which is rooted in faith, in hope and in charity. Our soul, in the struggle for truth and for justice, for goodness and for holiness, for concord and for peace, does not and cannot refuse labor and toil, prayer and sacrifice. We are the Vicar of the Prince of Peace, Who pacified and reconciled heaven and earth by uniting them in Himself and Who from His crib inaugurated the Kingdom of Peace among men of good-will. For the tranquillity of the world We have learned from Christ, from Peter and from his Successors to join together consolations and tribulations, to pass from Bethlehem to Gethsemane, to listen to the angelic chant of the glory of God and to the sympathetic comfort of the angel of sorrow. And for Us as motives of confidence—and you can well judge with what gratitude Our heart makes response—are the good wishes, which count as a prayer, expressed with so much dignity and ardor by the Eminent Dean of the Sacred College, the interpreter of the affection and devotion of all of you.

1734. Yes; a real prayer are your Christmas wishes directed to heaven that they may descend upon Us as a help and blessing from God. Against the wiles of Satan, Our Lord, on behalf of Peter, set His own prayer, and said to him: *I have prayed for thee that thy faith may not fail,*[329] and the prayer of Christ was received by the Father Who always hears His beloved Son. From Him the primitive Church learned to pray for the first Pope when Peter lay in chains, separated from the flock of Christ and impeded in the exercise of his Pastoral Office: *Prayer was being made to God for him by the Church without ceasing.*[330]

1735. To-day when on the one hand the inevitable effects of war, and on the other various causes have raised, like a barrier of iron, obstacles which in some regions are almost insurmountable, against the direct, constant and living contact between the Shepherd and His flock, all Our most deep and tranquil comfort is based upon the hope of extraordinary assistance from the Lord and upon the prayers of the Church which implore it. Your promise of prayers to God, offered to Us in the spirit which animated the youthful Church, is for Us a pledge of that intimate and sublime union by which Head and members are joined, animated, comforted and helped in the Mystical Body of Christ; and at the same time, received with joy and exchanged with you in joy, it is the most longed-for Christmas gift which your love and devotion could have given to Us.

1736. In such an extraordinary condition of the Church and of the Christian people, We intend, as We have done before, to address to-day a radio message to all Our beloved sons and daughters of the world, particularly desirous on this solemn feast to hear the voice of their Common Father who is not ignorant of their needs, their sorrows, their anxieties and their longings; the voice of the Teacher who, amid the nebulous imaginings and dreams of the present hour, points out to them the true and brilliant paths which lead, in mind and in deed, to internal and external peace, to a new ordering of private and public life, rooted in the divine law; the voice of him, who, remaining aloof from all agitation and conflict while contemplating and studying them from afar, cannot and must not be considered swayed by any passion, prejudice, or partiality which may disturb the soul.

1737. In a little while, Our Christmas message will be broad-

[329] *Luke,* XXII, 32.
[330] *Acts,* XII, 5.

cast to a world torn asunder by discord, harassed by war, and bleeding from a thousand wounds. May He from Whose divine lips once came the cry: *Everyone who is of the truth hears My voice*,[331] deign to assist and accompany and strengthen by His grace Our feeble words, enliven them by His inspiration and illumine them with His light. May the Lord not permit that they dry up on the stony ground of hardened hearts, nor be choked by the pressure of blind and stupid egoism amid the briars of enmity, but may He prepare and grant to them the fruitful soil of minds and open hearts to which the calamity which has burst upon the world may be the teacher of a fortitude and prudence ready to dare all, with generous resolve and pure motives, in inaugurating and guiding along new paths the formidable undertaking of a new order which will look to and be able to secure for the human family and all of its members new possibilities and suitable conditions of life as well as the fresh joy of harmony.

1738. You and We know, Venerable Brothers and Beloved Sons, that the progress of the will and of action must be illuminated by the light of the intellect; and, hence, no new order worthy of the name is possible unless a ray of superhuman wisdom light up the way of those who enter upon the path of preparing for peoples and nations a new and better future. Whence will come to men this sublime wisdom? From what font will it be derived? It is written: *The Word of God on high is the fountain of wisdom*.[332] The Word of God to Whom glory in the highest is sung by the angels, He *Who has become for us God-given Wisdom*[333] deigned by His Incarnation to provide a remedy for the ignorance which man inherited from his first father who was deceived by the serpent that promised him the knowledge of good and evil. From the Word of God, the Idea of the Eternal Wisdom, through Whom all things were made and man was created to the divine image and likeness, comes all human wisdom. . . . . . .

[331] *John*, XVIII, 37.
[332] *Ecclesiasticus*, I, 5.
[333] I *Corinthians*, I, 30.

RADIO MESSAGE *Nell'Alba* TO THE WHOLE WORLD.[334]

The Holy Father expounds five fundamental conditions essential for an international order which will guarantee a just and lasting peace for all peoples.

December 24, 1941

1739. At the dawn of the light which rises in a hopeful and expectant joy out of the darkness of the holy night, the entire world prepares to bow its head and to go on its knees in adoration of the unspeakable mystery of the all-embracing mercy of God, Who, in His infinite love, gave the greatest gift to mankind embodied in His only Begotten Son. In this moment of sacred and joyful expectation, dear sons and daughters, Our heart turns toward you in all-embracing love: you, who are spread all over the world; and, although not forgetting our earth, soars into the realms of heaven. The star which brightly shone over the cradle of the newly-born Redeemer is still shining marvelously after twenty centuries in the heaven of Christianity.

1740. The Gentiles may rant and the nations may plot against God and His Messiah;[335] the star still shines through the dark clouds of mankind and will never set: as it was in the beginning, so it is now and so it ever will be. The past, the present and the future are His. The star's bright ray shines clearly down on the nations, albeit that storms rage over the world and dark clouds gather, harbingers of destruction and misery. Its light is comfort: it is hope, unshakable faith, living certainty of the Redeemer's final triumph, which will overflow on the world like a torrent of salvation, in the inward peace and the heavenly glory of all those who, thanks to their elevation into the supernatural order of grace, have received the power of becoming children of God, because they have been born in God.

1741. In the bitter travails of war, tormented by your torments, suffering from your pain, living like you under the heavy nightmare of an evil which is tearing humanity for the third year in succession, We, therefore, on the Eve of the Great Feast, want to address Our fatherly word to you from a heart full of emotion. We want

---

[334] Translation from *The Tablet*, v. 179, pp. 4-7 (January 3, 1942). Original Italian, *A.A.S.*, v. 34, pp. 10-21 (January 20, 1942).
[335] *Cf. Psalms*, II, 1-2.

to admonish you to remain strong in your Faith and We want to impart to you the comfort of that great and exuberant certainty and hope, which emanate from the cradle of the newly-born Saviour. Indeed, beloved sons, if Our vision were confined to this world of matter and flesh, Our eye would be unable to behold one ray of comfort. The bells are ringing out the Christmas message into the world; churches and chapels are bright with light; sweet melodies are resounding to pour joy into our hearts and the places of worship are festively decorated; yet men are tearing each other to pieces in a war of destruction.

1742. In the hour of sacred solemnity, the Church pronounces the wonderful message which heralds peace and the coming of its Prince. The entire world is anxious to behold His face, but the message remains unheard in the blatant contradiction of events, which in terrifying thunder take their way over valleys and mountains, destroy countries and houses in huge territories and drive millions of families into misery and death. It is true that everywhere the admirable spectacle of indomitable courage can be beheld in the defense of inherited rights and soil: the spectacle of equanimity amidst sorrow: the example of men who burn like fires of sacrifice for the triumph of truth and justice. Yet We feel deeply moved while We think of the terrible encounters in arms and fire, while We behold them in Our mind as they are happening as this year draws to its close: when We think of the terrible fate of the wounded and prisoners, of the mental and physical pain, death and destruction which the air warfare has inflicted upon cities, populations and industrial centers, when We think of the wealth of nations thrown away and all those millions of men, whom war and brutal force have driven into despair.

1743. The strength and health of the growing youth are threatened by the want created through war. The steadily increasing war expenses entail a curtailment of the social welfare work that is being carried out by the nations. It justifies sinister fears for the near future. Preponderance of might over right, the easy opportunity for individual or collective violation of the property and life of others, as well as all the other moral devastation, are creating a mental atmosphere in which the conceptions of good and evil, of right and wrong, are losing their clear-cut issues and are in danger of being completely obliterated.

1744. He who, as a priest, has opportunity of looking into hearts, is well aware what a mountain-like burden of pain and sorrow is heaped upon souls in many ways, he sees how working capacity and joy of living suffer, he beholds the stifling of the spirit by which men are turning silent, indifferent and suspicious: practically hopeless in the face of the events and of ever growing misery. These disturbances of the mental poise can leave nobody indifferent who cares for the welfare of the nations and for a speedy return to ordered life, who sees the present time in its intrinsic features: anybody aware of all these circumstances can only be the more sorrowful as no way of an understanding can as yet be discerned between the belligerents, and the war aims of either side are opposing each other without hope of reconciliation.

1745. When we investigate the reasons of that collapse with which mankind is hopelessly confronted nowadays, we sometimes hear the contention that Christianity has failed. Where have we to look for the origin and source of this accusation? Is it among those glorious Apostles of Christ, among the heroic fighters for truth and justice, among those many shepherds and priests of Christianity who, with their own blood, sealed their life's task to awake barbarous tribes to Christianity and civilization, who taught savages to kneel down in front of the Cross of Christ, who laid the foundation of Christian civilization and rescued the remnants of Roman and Greek scholarship, who united the nations in the name of Christ, who spread science and virtue, who crowned beautiful cathedrals with the Cross—those very cathedrals which still stand as symbols of faith, which still raise their lofty and venerated steeples in the midst of the ruins of Europe? Is it they who make that accusation? No, Christianity that arises from Him Who is the Way, the Truth and the Light, and Who is with us and shall remain with us to the consummation of the world, has not failed in its mission. But men have rebelled against Christianity which is true and faithful to Christ, and against its doctrines. In its place they have fashioned a Christianity to their liking: a new ideal which is not sane, which is not opposed to the passions of envy and desire, nor to the greed for gold and silver, nor to the pride of life. A new religion without a soul or a soul without religion. A mass of dead Christianity without the Spirit of Christ! And they have proclaimed that Christianity has failed!

1746. Let us look deeply into the conscience of modern society. Let us seek out the root of the evil. On the other hand, of course, We do not wish to withhold the praise due to the wisdom of those rulers, who either favored or desired and were capable of restoring to their place of honor, to the advantage of their people, the values of Christian civilization, by amicable relations between Church and State, by safeguarding the sanctity of marriage, and by the religious education of youth. However, We cannot close Our eyes in the face of an increasing de-Christianization which has come from the decay of morals and afterward spread to a full negation of the truths and forces which are meant to illuminate and clarify the conceptions of good and evil, and to strengthen family and private, political and public life.

1747. This religious anæmia can be compared with a contagious disease, and has infected many nations in Europe and in the world. It has created a moral vacuum, which no artificial substitute of religion, no national and no international myth are able to fill. For decades and centuries, men knew no better—or, rather, no worse—than to undermine in word and deed faith in God, the Creator and Father of all, the Rewarder of good, and the Punisher of evil, and to tear this faith out of men's hearts from their childhood to their old age. By misrepresenting religious education and upbringing, by suppressing the Religion and Church of Jesus Christ in all conceivable ways, by oral and printed propaganda, and by misuse of science and political authority, this war against Christianity has constantly been waged.

1748. For the human spirit, overwhelmed in the confusion of this moral abyss, by its alienation from God and Christian practices, no other course remained but that of turning all its thoughts, purposes and enterprises and every evaluation of men's possessions, actions and labor and directing them to the material world, striving and sweating with might and main to spread out in space, to surpass all previous accomplishments in the attainment of riches and power, to engage in a competition of speed, to produce in greater quantity and quality everything that material advancement and progress seemed to require. These very symptoms appear in politics as an unlimited demand for expansion and political influence without regard to moral standards. In economic life they are represented by the predominance of mammoth concerns and trusts. In the social sphere it is the agglomeration of huge populations in cities and in the districts dominated by industry and trade, an agglomeration that is accompanied by the complete uprooting of the masses who have lost their standards of life, home, work, love and hatred. By this new conception of thought and life, all ideas of social life have been impregnated with a purely mechanico-materialistic character.

1749. With the increasing lack of restraint, outward compulsion and domination founded purely on power seemed to prevail over the forces of order, which established the relations of law and charity in their natural and supernatural foundations as they had been laid down by God. To the detriment of human dignity and personality as well as society, the conception makes headway that it is might which creates right. Thus private property is being abused on the one hand as a means of exploitation; on the other hand, as a reason for envy, revolt and hatred. The situation ensuing therefrom is being exploited by a struggle of interests which is being waged without any restraint.

1750. In some countries a political conception which is godless and hostile to Christ has, through its many tentacles, achieved a complete absorption of the individual, so that it can hardly be said that there is any longer any independence either in private or political life. Can anyone be surprised if this far-reaching negation of all Christian principles leads to a clash of the inward and outward tensions arising from that way of thinking, resulting in the catastrophic annihilation of human lives and goods we are witnessing to-day with horror? The war, which is the sad result of the circumstances described, will never be able to stop this evil development. On the contrary, the war accelerates and accentuates this evolution the longer it lasts, and increases the greatness and incurability of the general collapse.

1751. Nobody should think that by indicting the materialism of the nineteenth and twentieth centuries We intend to blame technical progress. No, We do not indict what fundamentally is a gift of God; for, as the Lord God makes wheat to grow from earth and soil, thus, when He created the world, He hid for us in the depth of the earth treasures, metals and precious stones, so that they may be mined by man for his needs, for his works and for his progress. The Church, the mother of so many European universities, attracts to-day, as she always did, the most prominent scientists; but she is well aware that man can use every good entrusted to him, even the freedom of will, either for good or for evil. Thus the spirit and the direction in which technical progress has been used has now resulted in science having to expiate its own errors. Science has been misused for destruction, and, in fact, to-day it destroys the very buildings that it yesterday proudly erected.

1752. In view of the greatness of the disaster which has overtaken mankind as a consequence of the mistake described, there can be only one solution: back to the altars from which innumerable generations of our faithful ancestors received the moral power to master their life's task. Back to the faith in God in the light of which each individual and each community find their proper measure of right and duty. Back to the wise and unshakable norms of a social order which, in affairs of national as well as international import, erect an efficacious barrier against the abuse of liberty and against the misuse of power.

1753. But, an appeal for a return to these beneficent sources must be especially loud, persistent and universal, in that hour when the old order will be about to give way and cede its place to the new. The future reconstruction will present and offer very valuable opportunities to advance the forces of good, but it will also be fraught with the danger of a lapse into errors which will favor the forces of evil, and there will be demanded great sincerity and mature reflection, not only by reason of the gigantic difficulty of the task but also because of the grave consequences which, in the case of failure, will result in both material and spiritual ills. There will be required broad intellects and wills strong in their purposes, men of courage and enterprise; but, above and before all, there must be consciences which in their plannings, in their deliberations and in their actions are animated, moved and sustained by a lively sense of responsibility, and which do not shrink from submission to the holy laws of God. For if to the vigor which shapes the material order there be not united in a moral order the highest perfection and sincere purpose, then undoubtedly we will see verified the judgment of St. Augustine: "They run well but they have left the track. The farther they run the greater is their error, for they are going ever farther from their course."[336]

1754. Nor will it be the first time that men, in the expectation

[336] *Sermo* CXLI, c. 4, in Migne, *P.L.,* v. 38, c. 777.

of being crowned at war's end with the laurel wreath of victory, have dreamed of giving to the world a new order by pointing out new ways which, in their opinion, led to well-being, prosperity and progress. Yet whenever they yielded to the temptation of imposing their own interpretation contrary to the dictates of reason, moderation, justice and the nobility of man, they found themselves disheartened and stupefied in the contemplation of the ruins of deluded hopes and miscarried plans. Thus history teaches that treaties of peace formulated with a spirit and with conditions opposed to the dictates of morality and a genuine political wisdom have had but a wretched and short-lived existence, and so have revealed and testified to an error of calculation, human indeed, but fatal nonetheless.

1755. Now the destruction brought about by the present war is on so vast a scale that it is imperative that there be not added to it also the further ruins of a frustrated and deluded peace. In order to avoid so great a calamity, it is fitting that in the formulation of that peace there should be assured the co-operation, with sincerity of will and energy, with a purpose of a generous participation not only of this or that people, but of all peoples — yea, rather of all humanity. It is a universal undertaking for the common good which requires the collaboration of all Christendom in the religious and moral aspects of the new edifice which is to be constructed.

1756. We are, therefore, making use of Our right—or, better, We are fulfilling Our duty—as to-day, on this eve of the Holy Feast of Christmas, the divine dawn of hope and of peace to the world, with all the authority of Our Apostolic Ministry and with the fervid impulse of Our heart, We direct the attention and the consideration of the entire world to the dangers which lie in wait to threaten a peace which is to be the well-prepared basis for a truly new order and which is to fulfill the expectations and desires of all people for a more tranquil future.

1757. Such a new order, which all people desire to see brought into being, after the trials and ruins of this war, must be founded on that immovable and unshakable rock, the moral law which the Creator Himself manifested by means of a natural order and which He has engraved with indelible character on the hearts of men, that moral law whose observance must be inculcated and fostered by the public opinion of all nations and of all States, with such a unanimity of voice and energy that no one may dare to doubt it. Like a shining beacon this moral law must direct by the light of its principles the course of action of men and of States, and they must all follow its admonishing, salutary and profitable precepts if they do not wish to abandon to the tempests and to ultimate shipwreck every labor and every effort for the establishment of a new order. Consequently, recapitulating and integrating what We have expounded on other occasions, We insist once again on certain fundamental conditions essential for an international order which will guarantee for all peoples a just and lasting peace and which will be a bountiful source of well-being and prosperity.

1758. First: Within the limits of a new order founded on moral principles there is no room for violation of the freedom, integrity and security of other States, no matter what may be their territorial extension or their capacity for defense. If it is inevitable that the powerful States should, by reason of their greater potentialities and their power, play leading roles in the formation of economic groups, comprising not only themselves but smaller and weaker States as well, it is nevertheless indispensable that in the interests of the common good they, and all others, respect the rights of those smaller States to political freedom, to economic development, and to the adequate protection, in the case of conflicts between nations, of that neutrality which is theirs according to the natural as well as international law. In this way, and in this way only, shall they be able to obtain a fitting share of the common good and assure the material and spiritual welfare of the peoples concerned.

1759. Secondly: Within the limits of a new order founded on moral principles there is no place for open or secret oppression of the cultural and linguistic characteristics of national minorities, for the hindrance or restriction of their economic resources, for the limitation or abolition of their natural fertility. The more conscientiously the government of a State respects the rights of minorities, the more confidently and the more effectively can it demand from its subjects a loyal fulfillment of those civil obligations which are common to all citizens.

1760. Thirdly: Within the limits of a new order founded on moral principles there is no place for that cold and calculating egoism which tends to hoard economic resources and materials destined for the use of all, to such an extent that the nations less favored by nature are not permitted access to them. In this regard, it is a source of great consolation to see admitted the necessity of a participation of all in the natural riches of the earth even on the part of those nations which, in the fulfillment of this principle, belong to the category of givers and not to that of receivers. It is, however, in conformity with the principles of equity that a solution to a question so vital to the world economy should be arrived at methodically, and in easy stages, with a necessary guarantee, always drawing useful lessons from the omissions and mistakes of the past. If, in the future peace, this point were not to be courageously dealt with, there would remain in the relations between people a deep and far-reaching root blossoming forth into bitter dissensions and burning jealousies, which would lead eventually to new conflicts. It must, however, be noticed how closely the satisfactory solution to this problem is connected with another fundamental point of which We shall treat next.

1761. Fourthly: Within the limits of a new order, founded on moral principles, once the more dangerous principles of armed conflict have been eliminated, there is no place for a total warfare or for a mad rush to armaments. The calamity of a world war, with the economic and social ruin and the moral dissolution and breakdown which follow in its train, cannot be permitted to envelop the human race for a third time. In order that mankind may be preserved from such a misfortune, it is essential to proceed with sincerity and honesty to a progressive limitation of armaments. The lack of equilibrium between the exaggerated armaments of the powerful States and the limited armaments of the weaker ones is a menace to harmony and peace among nations, and demands that a peaceful and proportionate limit be placed upon production and possession of offensive weapons. In proportion to the degree in which disarmament is effected, means must be found which will be appropriate, honorable and efficacious in order that the principle, "pacts must be observed," may once again enjoy its vital and moral function in the juridical relations between States. Such a principle has undergone many serious crises and has suffered undeniable violations in the past, and has met with an incurable lack of trust among the various nations and among their respective rulers. To procure the re-birth of mutual trust, certain institutions must be established which will merit the respect of all, and which will dedicate themselves to the most noble office of guaranteeing the sincere observance

of treaties and of promoting, in accordance with the principles of
law and equity, necessary corrections and revisions of such treaties.
We are well aware of the tremendous difficulties to be overcome
and the almost superhuman strength and good-will required on
all sides if the double task We have outlined is to be brought to a
successful conclusion. But this work is so essential for a lasting peace
that nothing should prevent responsible statesmen from undertaking
it and co-operating in it with abundant good-will, so that, by bearing in mind the advantage to be gained in the future, they will be
able to triumph over the painful remembrances of similar efforts
doomed to failure in the past, and will not be daunted by the
knowledge of the gigantic strength required for the accomplishment
of their objective.

1762. Fifthly: Within the limits of a new order founded on
moral principles, there is no place for the persecution of religion
and of the Church. From a lively faith in a personal and tran-
scendent God there springs a sincere and unyielding moral strength
which informs the whole course of life, for faith is not only a virtue,
it is also the divine gift by which all the virtues enter the temple of
the soul, and it is the foundation of that strong and tenacious character which does not falter before the demands of reason and justice.
This fact always proves true, but it should be even more evident
when there is demanded of a statesman, as of the least of citizens,
the maximum of courage and moral strength for the reconstruction
of a new Europe and a new world on the ruins accumulated by the
violence of the world war and by the hatred and bitter disunity
amongst men.

1763. Regarding the social question which will be presented in
the post-war period in a form more acute than ever, Our Predecessors
and We Ourself have set forth principles for its solution. It is,
however, well to bear in mind that these principles can be followed
in their entirety and bear their fullest fruits only when statesmen
and people, employers and employees are animated by faith in a
personal God, the Legislator and Judge to Whom they must one
day give an account of their actions. For vile unbelief which arrays
itself against God, the Ruler of the Universe, is a most dangerous
enemy of a new order which would be just. On the other hand,
every man who believes in God is numbered among His champions
and knights. Those who have faith in Christ, in His Divinity, in

His love, in His work of love and brotherhood among men will make a particularly valuable contribution to the reconstruction of the social order. All the more priceless, therefore, will be the contribution of statesmen who show themselves ready to open the gates and smooth the path for the Church of Christ, so that, free and unhindered, it may bring its supernatural influence to bear in the conclusion of a peace amongst nations and may co-operate with its zeal and love in the immense task of finding remedies for the evils which the war will leave in its wake.

1764. For this reason We are unable to explain why it is that in some parts of the world countless deliberate obstacles bar the way to the message of the Christian faith while free and ample scope is given to a propaganda that opposes it. Youth is withdrawn from the beneficent influence of the Christian family, alienated from the Church, educated in a spirit contrary to the teachings of Christ, and imbued with ideas, maxims and practices which are anti-Christian. The work of the Church for the cure of souls and for charitable enterprises is rendered arduous and less efficacious, while its moral influence on individuals and on society is disregarded and rejected.

1765. All these forms of resolute opposition, far from being mitigated or eliminated in the course of the war, have, on the contrary, in many respects become even more marked. But that all this and even more should be continued in the midst of the sufferings of the present time is a sad commentary on the spirit that animates the enemies of the Church in imposing upon the faithful, already bearing many heavy sacrifices, the irksome and the troublesome burden of a bitter anxiety which weighs upon their consciences. We love—and in this We call upon God to be Our Witness—We love with equal affection all peoples without any exception whatsoever, and in order to avoid even the appearance of being moved by partisanship, We have maintained hitherto the greatest reserve. But the measures directed against the Church and their scope are of such a nature that We feel obliged in the name of truth to say a word about it, if only to eliminate the danger of unfortunate misunderstandings amongst the faithful.

1766. We behold to-day, beloved children, the God-Man, born in a manger to restore man to the greatness from which he had fallen through his own fault, and to place him once again on a

throne of liberty, of justice, and of honor which centuries of error
and untruth had denied him. The foundation of that throne shall
be Calvary; it shall be enriched not with gold or silver, but with
the Blood of Christ, the Divine Blood which has overflowed upon
the world for twenty centuries to give a reddening hue to the cheeks
of His spouse, the Church, and which in purifying, consecrating,
sanctifying and glorifying its children, takes on the brilliance of
heaven. Oh, Christian Rome, that Blood is your life. By reason
of that Blood you are great, and even the ancient ruins of your pagan
greatness are seen in a new light, and the heritages of the political
wisdom of the Cæsars are purified and consecrated. You are mother
of a higher and more human justice, which does honor to you, to
your See and to those who hear your voice. You are the beacon of
civilization, and civilized Europe and the world look to you for all
that is most sacred and most faithful, all that is most wise and most
honorable in the exalted traditions and proud history of their
peoples. You are the mother of charity, your splendor, your monuments, your hospices, your monasteries, your convents, your heroes
and your heroines, your voyages and your missions, your generations
and your centuries with their schools and universities, all their testimony is a triumph of your charity, that charity which embraces all,
suffers all, hopes for and accomplishes all, becoming all things to
all men, consoling and comforting all, curing all and restoring them
to that liberty given by Christ, uniting all peoples in a peace of
brotherly love; that charity which brings together all men, regardless
of country, language or custom, into one united family and makes
of the entire world one common fatherland.

1767. From this Rome, center, rock and teacher of Christianity,
from this city, called Eternal by reasons of its relations with the
living Christ rather than by reasons of its associations with the
passing glory of the Cæsars, from this Rome in Our ardent and
intense longing for the welfare of individual nations and of all
humanity, We direct Our appeal to all, beseeching and exhorting
that the day be not delayed in which, whatever hostility against God
and Christ is to-day driving men to temporal and eternal ruin, a
fuller religious consciousness and new and higher objective may
prevail, and that on that day there may shine resplendently over
the manger of a new order among peoples the guiding Star of
Bethlehem, herald of a new order which will rouse all mankind to

sing with the angels: *Glory to God in the Highest,* and to pro-claim as a gift restored at last by heaven upon the nations of the earth: *Peace to men of good-will.*[337] On the dawning of that day with what great joy will nations and rulers, freed in mind from the fear of the incipient dangers of future conflicts, transform the sword, nicked and jagged from constant use against their fellow men, into ploughs with which to furrow the fertile breast of the earth under the sun of heavenly benediction, and wrest from it their daily bread! . . .

1768. In expectation of that happy day, and with this longing prayer upon Our lips, We send Our greetings and Our blessing to all Our children of the entire universe; may Our benediction descend in more generous measure on those religious and lay persons who are suffering pain and anguish because of their Faith. May it also descend on those, who, although not members of the visible body of the Catholic Church, are near to Us in their faith in God and in Jesus Christ, and share with Us Our views with regard to the conditions for peace and its fundamental aims. May it descend with a quickened heart-beat of affection upon all those who are groaning under the weight of the sadness and the cruel anguish of the present hours. May it be a shield to the soldiers under arms, a healing remedy to the sick and wounded, a comfort to the prison-ers, to those expelled from their native land, to those who are far from their homes and loved ones, to those deported to foreign lands, to the millions of unhappy people who at every hour must bear up under the gnawing pangs of hunger. May it be a sweet balsam for all sorrows and misfortune, a support and consolation to all the suffering and needy as they wait in expectation of a friendly word that may instill into their hearts strength, courage and a comforting sense of compassion and fraternal assistance. Finally, may Our blessing rest upon those whose hands are being extended in mercy and in a spirit of generous and inexhaustible sacrifice to provide Us, above the limitations of Our Own, with the means which have enabled Us to assuage the tears and allay the poverty of many, especially of the most wretched and abandoned victims of the war, and in this way to make them realize how Divine Goodness and Loving Kindness achieved their highest and most surpassing revelation in the Infant in a manger. . . .

[337] *Luke,* II, 14.

MESSAGE OF PIUS XII TO THE BRITISH PRISONERS OF WAR IN ITALY.[338]

The Holy Father sympathizes with the prisoners of war.

December 25, 1941

1769. With ever greater paternal solicitude, We turn Our thoughts to each of you, who, in separation from distant homes at this Christmas season, feel very keenly the absence of your loved ones. May Our prayerful and affectionate good wishes sweeten the bitterness of that separation, and be to you all a source of divine comfort and Christian hope.

TELEGRAM TO THE PRESIDENT OF THE REPUBLIC OF POLAND, M. RACZKIEWICZ.[339]

The Holy Father sympathizes with the suffering Polish Nation.

January 1, 1942

1770. The greetings and good wishes which the President has expressed to Us in the name of the Polish Nation have found a strong echo in Our fatherly heart. In particular We feel the sorrow of those who are now suffering. We send Our Apostolic Blessing as a sign of God's comfort and help, which We ask both for the Polish Nation, so dear to Us, and for Your Excellency.

LETTER *Dum Saeculum* TO CARDINAL MAGLIONE, SECRETARY OF STATE.[340]

The Pope asks the Church to pray for peace during May.

April 15, 1942

1771. While the world, relying on the force of arms and the resources of all kinds which the age has introduced for waging war, pursues its way reddened with human blood, We, who grieve for this great destruction of men and have a paternal heart for all

[338] Original English, *English Catholic Newsletter*, January 3, 1942.
[339] Translation from *The Tablet*, v. 179, p. 47 (January 24, 1942).
[340] Original Latin, *A.A.S.*, v. 34, pp. 125-127 (May 1, 1942).

peoples, cannot but raise Our suppliant hands to God, relying chiefly on Him, while We try and commend all fitting means which may avail to win true peace and brotherly concord and to establish a new organization of affairs founded on right order and Christian principles; and We exhort all the sons in Christ whom We have everywhere on earth, again and again, to pour forth devout prayers. Therefore, as in previous years, so now with the approach of the month of May We wish through you, who are so closely associated with Us in governing the Universal Church, to invite all to a holy crusade of prayers, and in particular those who, flourishing in youth and innocence, are above all most dear to Us, as to the Divine Redeemer.

1772. And since we may hope for all things from Mary, We desire all to go to her especially during the coming month of May, dedicated to her in a special way: first of all, let the boys and girls, led by their parents, go to her altars as suppliants since their candid and trustful prayers cannot fail to be pleasing to the most gracious Mother of God and of us all. As indeed all know, just as Christ Jesus is King of All and Lord of Lords,[341] in Whose Hands are placed the fortunes of individual citizens and peoples, so His dear Mother Mary is honored as "Queen of the World" by all the faithful and has obtained so great a power of intercession with God. And if the first wonderful sign, performed by the Divine Redeemer in Cana of Galilee,[342] is due to her suppliant mercy; if her Only-Begotten Son, about to die hanging on the cross, gave to us what was still left to Him dearest on earth, giving us, namely, His Mother as Mother; if, lastly, through the lapse of centuries in every danger, public or private, our fathers fled to her in prayer and confidence, why, We ask, in the dreadful crisis of evils by which we are being tortured, should we not entrust ourselves and all our interests to her most powerful intercession? As all things obey and follow the eternal Will of God, so in some way it may be said that the kindness of her Only-Begotten always responds favorably to the prayers of the Virgin Mother of God; then especially when the same Blessed Virgin enjoys eternal happiness in heaven and, adorned with the triumphal crown, is hailed as the Queen of angels and of men.

1773. But if she has such power with God, she has no less love

341 Cf. I Timothy, VI, 15; Apocalypse, XVII, 14; XIX, 16.
342 Cf. John, II, 1-11.

for us since she is the most loving Mother of us all. With strong faith and fervent love, therefore, let all go to her, and let them bring not only suppliant prayers but also devout works of penance and charity by which the Divine Justice, violated by so many and such great sins, may be appeased. For prayer—We use the words of Our most wise Predecessor, Leo XIII—brings it about "that the soul is sustained, is strengthened for difficult tasks, and is raised to the divine; penance brings it about that we have control of ourselves, especially of our body, which is, on account of original sin, the most dangerous enemy of reason and the law of the Gospel. These virtues, it is clear, fit together most harmoniously, help each other, and work together to draw man, born for heaven, away from passing things and to raise him almost to heavenly union with God."[343]

1774. If there is no time when these virtues are not necessary for the faithful, yet beyond doubt the condition of most distressing affairs in which we are demands them more, since more readily through them may we, with the Blessed Virgin as our Patron, obtain from *the Father of mercies*[344] and God, the Giver of heavenly blessings, that true peace which we desire and await, real, enduring, conformed to and nourished by justice and charity.

1775. Doing penance, then, and supplicating with humble soul, let all—and especially the innocent boys and girls—ask of the Divine Redeemer and His most holy Mother that, while sky and sea are daily more convulsed with the flashing storm, light from on high may shine before Us who are sailing at the helm of the mystical ship, and that heavenly aid may be with Us; that to the wretched and starving, the needed food of soul and body may be supplied; that to exiles, their fatherland may be restored; to the wounded and sick, health; to prisoners, freedom; and that lastly to the whole human race, its evil desires being tamed by reason, and the right order of justice and charity toward God and neighbor being restored, Christian peace, which is true peace, both in the private life of each and in civil society, may at last be established. . . . . . .

---

[343] Encyclical *Octobri Mense* in *Acta Leonis XIII*, XI, p. 312.
[344] II *Corinthians*, I, 3.

Motu Proprio *Summo Solacio* GRANTING THE FACULTY OF A
PRIVILEGED ALTAR TO ALL PRIESTS FOR ONE YEAR.[345]

Nothing is more necessary to-day than divine help.

May 12, 1942

1776. With the greatest consolation We have noted that the
jubilee anniversary observance of Our Episcopate has inspired the
hearts of all Our children throughout the world to a marvelous
unison of prayers, by which they, during this terrible war by which
We are tormented, strive to obtain heavenly gifts from God for
their Common Father and for the Universal Church. This news
which has come to Us has been extremely gratifying; for We believe
that nothing to-day is more necessary than heavenly aid and divine
help—and after this proof of their loyalty, We know that to-day the
minds and the hearts of the faithful, as always in the past, are closely
united to Us by a wonderful union of mind and a burning love.
We desire to pay back in some measure for this very full expression
of love by bestowing some gift from the inexhaustible treasures of
the Church—something which We feel sure will be extremely pleasing to all, and especially to priests. By the plenitude of Our Apostolic Power We grant to each and every priest, in good standing, the
personal privilege, by reason of which he, in offering up the Holy
Sacrifice, can apply a plenary indulgence to some soul in Purgatory.
This privilege will endure from the 13th day of this month to the
13th day of May in the year 1943. . . .

Radio Address *Circondati dal Concorso* ON THE OCCASION OF
THE POPE'S EPISCOPAL SILVER JUBILEE.[346]

*The belligerents should not let pass any occasion that
may offer an opportunity for an honest peace of justice
and moderation, even if it should not correspond in all
particulars to their aspirations.*

• May 13, 1942

1777. . . . . . . This day, which should be one of pure and
serene joy for the Catholic world, comes at a time of the gravest

[345] Original Latin, *A.A.S.*, v. 34, p. 153 (June 1, 1942).
[346] Official English translation, *The Catholic Mind*, v. 40, n. 947, pp. 2-19 (June 8,
1942). Original Italian, *A.A.S.*, v. 34, pp. 154-167 (June 1, 1942).

anxieties and sufferings of which the words of our Saviour seem to be a vivid description: *For nation will rise against nation, and kingdom against kingdom; and there will be pestilences and famines and earthquakes in various places.*[347] In the midst of such widespread calamity, how could We hold those celebrations, even though strictly religious, that are proper to joyous and happy days? The infuriate tragedy of the events through which we are passing summons us not to joy but rather to penance and amendment, urges us on to self-examination and purification, warns us to reset the course and change the path of our thoughts, our aims and our conduct.

1778. It is for Us then, dear children, a source of joy, of deep satisfaction and of reassurance to know that Our jubilee is being celebrated throughout the Catholic world with prayers and sacrifices for the welfare of Holy Church and with generous almsgiving to the thousands and thousands of brethren, who, in their many grave needs, knock with confidence on the door of Christian charity, which suffers patiently along with them in the midst of strife and of the universally felt sorrows of the present moment. The impenetrable designs of God have disposed that it is We who should support the weight of pastoral anxiety which twenty-five years ago was borne by that great-souled one who imposed hands on Us at the altar of the Sistine Chapel and gave Us the plenitude of the priesthood.

1779. It is a holy heritage, but, oh, how heavy and full of sorrows the road by which the beloved Providence of God guided Us! It led back again to the Sistine, where on Our weak shoulders was laid the dignity of Supreme Pontiff, a dignity of which We feel deeply Our unworthiness. And with that dignity came a gigantic burden which, with the outbreak and extension of this second World War, has become so heavy as even to surpass that which the first World War brought with it in the days of Benedict XV. But for all that, dear sons, We should have passed in vain through the school of Leo XIII, with his brilliant wisdom; of Pius X, so outstanding for his piety; of Benedict XV, so gifted with far-seeing wisdom; of Pius XI, so full of holy courage and enterprise, if in the midst of this hurricane of universal grief We were to allow, even for a moment, to waver in Us the certainty founded on faith,

[347] *Matthew*, XXIV, 7.

strengthened by hope, ripened by charity; the certainty that our Lord is never more watchful, never nearer to His Church than in those hours when His children, under the stress of fear and tempest, might be driven to cry out: *Master, does it not concern Thee that we are perishing?*[348] *Lord, save us! we are perishing!*[349]. . . . . .

1780. With their minds tenaciously, perseveringly fixed on the Risen One and on their own resurrection; with their eyes ever intent with holy anticipation on the Glorified One sitting at the right hand of the Father and on the heavenly Jerusalem, everlasting abode of happiness for those who remain faithful to the end; with their souls filled with the certainty of the strengthening presence of the Holy Spirit promised and sent by Jesus, you can see the early Christians, when professing their faith in the midst of strife and suffering, rise to heroic stature, thanks to their noble thoughts, their vigorous action, the valiant rivalry they displayed in the arena of moral giants. They have left behind them an example whose conquering force expands and propagates down the centuries even to our own days, when, to have and keep the honor and the name of Christian, one must undergo struggles and face trials not unlike theirs. Before such athletes, on whose brows the victorious laurels of the militant Christian are often intertwined with the palm of martyrdom, all uncertainty and hesitation vanish. Does not the great lesson of their heroic life suffice to clear all mists from our minds, to put new life into our hearts, to raise aloft the heads of the Christians of to-day, making them conscious of their exalted dignity, eager to reach greater heights while they ponder the responsibility which their Christian profession stamps upon their souls?

1781. The spiritual profile of this primitive Christianity, whose beginnings are recalled for us by the coming Feasts of the Ascension and Pentecost, is refulgent with four unmistakable characteristics: (1) unshakable confidence in victory based on a profound faith; (2) serene and unlimited readiness for sacrifice and sufferings; (3) Eucharistic fervor and recollection arising from the deep conviction of the social efficiency of Eucharistic thought on all forms of social life; (4) a striving after an ever closer and more enduring unity of spirit and of hierarchy.

1782. This four-fold character of the Church's youth presents

[348] *Mark*, IV, 38.
[349] *Matthew*, VIII, 25.

in each of its dominant notes an appeal and, at the same time, a hope and a promise to the Christianity of our day, for the true Christianity of to-day is not different from that of the early ages. The youth of the Church is eternal, for the Church does not grow old, changing her age as she does according to the conditions of time while she marches on to eternity. The centuries that she has passed through are but a day as the centuries that lie before her are but as a day. Her youth in the days of the Caesars is the same that now speaks to us. The confidence in victory of the primitive Church drew its life, soundness and imperturbability from the words of the Master: *I have overcome the world.*[350] They are words which might well have been inscribed on the wood of His Cross, the standard of his victories.

1783. Let the Christianity of to-day be penetrated and inflamed by the burning and luminous fire of that watchword and you will feel in your hearts the peaceful, quiet confidence of victory that re-assures you with the passing of these dark days in which so many are living in terror and discouragement. There will come not the terrors which the timid dread but the brilliant fulfillment of the hopes of faithful and magnanimous souls. . . . . . . As at the out-set and more than in many other ages, the Divine Foundation of Christ, though never wavering before enemies, is struggling in more than one place to-day for its existence. Militant atheism, systematic anti-Christianity, cold indifference make war on it, making use of conceptions and thoughts which have nothing in common with the friendly usages of polite controversy but fre-quently descending to the crudity of violence.

1784. To-day again, as of old in some countries, those in au-thority, forgetful of moral ties and bent on replacing right by force, trump up against Christians the same infringements of the law which the Caesars of the first centuries pretended to have found in Peter and Paul, in Sixtus and Laurence, in Cecilia, Agnes, Perpetua and the countless line of those innocent victims who now are refulgent with the halo of martyrs—here below, in the sight of the Church, and in heaven, in the presence of the Lamb. And the crime which is cast up against Christians is always the same, their unfaltering loyalty to the King of Kings and the Lord of Lords.

1785. Nor is there any other explanation why to-day, too, prac-

[350] *John*, XVI, 33.

tical faith in the Son of God, submission to His law, spiritual union
with His Church, and loyalty to His representatives on earth have
meant in some places a continual succession of mistrust and abuse,
of degradations and disabilities, of personal and social discredit, of
shortened means and hard circumstances, of poverty and sufferings,
of misery and handicaps and injury, corporal as well as spiritual.
In such an atmosphere of terror and danger what remains, beloved
sons, in our time but the imperative need to refashion ourselves on
the model of the early Church and on the magnificent example
given by those Christians, on their burning faith, on their dauntless
spirit, on their conscious assurance of victory; to drink in, as from
a pure spring of courage and salvation, a new strength, a new drive,
a new constancy as we reflect that all that they believed in, hoped
for, loved, prayed for, worked for, suffered for and gloriously won
is also our life, our glory and the incorruptible treasure of the
Church?

1786. May the sight of the victories won by the early Church
strengthen and sublimate your hope and, in the midst of the present
storm, open up a horizon of new triumphs. Sooner or later, the
passing sequence of raging upheavals will serve only to put into
clearer light the consoling truth of these words of the beloved
Disciple: *This is the victory which overcomes the world, our faith.*[351]
If the seal of blood which beautified the Church's youth through
the centuries of trial, suffering and sacrifice appears to us now as the
brightest stone in her triumphal diadem, so, too, for Christendom
of to-day, the greatness of her future victory, won in the fire of
terrible tribulation, will correspond to the generosity of her sacrifice.
The stout, determined will of those heroes who went before us with
the standard of faith could not be broken by Nero's or Diocletian's
fury, or the insidious cunning of a Julian the Apostate. Calm and
ready, without counting the cost, in the face of every kind of torture
and martyrdom they did not tremble or waver before outrage piled
on outrage, blow on blow, before the violence or snares of the
enemies of Christ.

1787. A Christianity that has ever before its eyes the heroism
of the first centuries can never fail to be true to the spirit of those
words written by Peter while persecution raged, *but even if you*

---

[351] I *John*, V, 4.

suffer anything for justice' sake, blessed are you.[352] It will show itself worthy of the inheritance of its forefathers and, deeply conscious of its exalted mission, will secure in the hour prepared by God — through suffering indeed, but glorious suffering — a peace which will make it exclaim with the Apostle of the Gentiles, *thanks be to God Who has given us the victory.*[353]

1788. But whence did the courageous faith of the first Christians derive its life and its enthusiasm? From Eucharistic union with Christ, Who is the Inspiration of moral conduct that is pure and pleasing to God at the table of the Bread of the Strong. They felt enkindled in their hearts a zeal which gave and increased energy and peace. They felt themselves brothers and sisters of Christ, nourished by the same Food and the same Drink, united in fraternal union by one same love, one same unfailing hope, welded together by a mystic bond that makes of thousands of hearts and thousands of souls one great family, with but one heart and one soul. On the altar under the veil of bread and wine, there was present to them the God of their souls and of victories, Who would raise aloft His standards in the place of the Roman eagles for the conquest of the world—a world of which Rome would be the center not through her force, but through her faith. The thought of the Eucharist is the Center of the Faith, now as in the first centuries. Its increase in the Church and its spiritual vivifying radiation through mankind—tortured by egoism, envy, hate, contradictions, departures from the dogma of the Cenacle—must become more vital and more effective in bringing men to the Divine *agape* where the coldness of their hearts may be dispelled and those hearts may be touched by the fire that will warm them in anticipation of springtime harmony of united minds and brotherly co-operation which draws all together in unison and peace around the God of the Tabernacle. . . . . . .

1789. The divine mission of the Church, established immovably on the Rock of Peter, has no limits of space on earth and has no limit in its activity but the time limit of mankind; but, like every age that passes, the present moment presents to her and imposes on her new enterprises, duties, cares. The cries for help which each day brings to Us would tell Us, if We did not already know it, what the present moment in its onward rush asks and demands from the

---

[352] I *Peter*, III, 14.
[353] I *Corinthians*, XV, 57.

Church, namely, to use her authority to secure that the present terrible conflict may cease and the flood of tears and blood may issue forth into an equitable and lasting peace for all.

1790. Our conscience is Our witness that from the moment when the hidden designs of God entrusted to Our feeble strength the weight, now so heavy, of the Supreme Pontificate, We have labored both before the outbreak of war and during its course for peace, with all Our mind and strength and within the ambit of Our Apostolic Ministry. But now, when the nations are living in the painful suspense of waiting for new engagements to begin, We take the opportunity offered by this occasion to speak once again a word of peace; and We speak that word in the full consciousness of Our absolute impartiality toward all the belligerents and with equal affection for all peoples without exception. We know well how, in the present state of affairs, the formulation of specific proposals of a just and equitable peace would not have any well-founded probability of success—indeed every time that one speaks a word of peace, one runs the risk of offending one or other side. In fact, while one side bases its security on the results obtained, the other rests its hopes on future battles. If, however, the present lining up of forces, of gains and losses in the political and military sphere, does not show any immediate practical possibility of peace, the destruction wrought by the war among nations in the material and spiritual plane is all the time accumulating to such an extent that it calls for every effort to prevent its increase by bringing the conflict to a speedy end.

1791. Even prescinding from arbitrary acts of violence and cruelty—against which, on former occasions We raised Our voice in warning; and We repeat that warning now with insistent supplication—even in the face of threats of still more deadly warfare, the war of itself, through the perfect technical quality of its weapons, causes unheard-of pain, misery and suffering to the nations. Our thoughts are with the courageous combatants, with the multitudes that are living in the zones of operations, in occupied countries or within their own countries. We think—how could We not think— of the dead, of the millions of prisoners, of the mothers, wives, sons who for all their love of their country are prey to mortal anguish. We think of the separation of married people, of the breakdown of family life, of famine and economic penury. Does not each of these names of evil and ruin connote a numberless group of heart-rending cases in which is epitomized and condensed the most lamentable, bitter, excruciating phenomenon ever turned loose on humanity, thus to make us fearful of a near future full of terrible unknown economic and social hardships?

1792. For whole decades, a gigantic amount of study and the flower of intellect and good-will had been devoted to realizing a solution of the social question. And now, after all this, the peoples must behold how the public moneys, whose wise administration for the public good was one of the cardinal points in that solution, are being spent in hundreds of billions for the destruction of goods and life. But from the want and sufferings of home to which We have referred—and which now extend to the whole world—there arises behind the war front another huge front, the front of families injured and in anguish. Before the war, some peoples now in arms could not even balance their deaths with their births; and now the war, so far from remedying this, threatens to send new additions to the family of physical, economic and moral ruin.

1793. We should like, then, to address a fatherly word of warning to the rulers of nations. The family is sacred; it is the cradle not only of children but also of the nation—of its force and its glory. Do not let the family be alienated or diverted from the high purpose assigned to it by God. God wills that husband and wife, in loyal fulfillment of their duties to one another and to the family, should, in the home, transmit to the next generation the torch of corporal life and with it spiritual and moral life, Christian life; that within the family, under the care of their parents, there should grow up men of sincere character, of upright behavior, to become valuable, unspoiled members of the human race, manly in good or bad fortune, obedient to those who command them and to God. That is the will of the Creator. Do not let the family home, and with it the school, become merely an anteroom to the battlefields. Do not let the husband and wife become separated from one another in a permanent manner. Do not let the children be separated from the watchful care of their parents over their bodies and souls. Do not let the earnings and the savings of the family become void of all fruit.

1794. The cry that reaches Us from the family front is unanimous: "Give us back our peace-time occupations." If you have the future of mankind at heart, if your conscience before God ascribes some import to what the names of *father* and *mother* mean to men and to what makes for the real happiness of your children, send back the family to its peace-time occupation. As patron of this family front—from which may God keep far all open ways of unfortunate and disastrous upheaval—We make a warm, fatherly appeal to statesmen that they may not let any occasion pass that may open up to the nations, the road to an honest peace of justice and moderation, to a peace arising from a free and fruitful agreement, even if it should not correspond in all points to their aspirations.

1795. The world-wide family front which has at the war front so many hearts of fathers, husbands and children, which, amid the dangers and sufferings, hopes and desires, are beating with the double love of country and of home, will become tranquil in the prospect of a new horizon. The gratitude of mankind and the consent of their own nation will not be wanting to those generous leaders, who, inspired not by weakness but by a sense of responsibility, shall choose the road of moderation and the field of wisdom when they meet the other side, also guided by the same sentiments. Inspired as We are with this confidence, there remains only for Us, dear children, to lift up to the Father of Mercies and of the Light of Wisdom Our fervent prayers that He may hasten the dawning of that so much desired day. *Ask and you shall receive*[354] was the advice of our Divine Redeemer, Prince of Peace, Who, meek and humble of heart, calls us to give us rest from our labors and burdens. Let us rekindle in ourselves the spirit of love; let us hold ourselves ever ready to collaborate with our faith and our hands, after the most extensive, disastrous and bloody cataclysm of all history, to reconstruct from the pile of material and moral ruins, a world which the bonds of brotherly love will weld in peace, a world in which, with the help of the Almighty, "all may be new hearts, words and works."[355]

[354] *John*, XVI, 24.
[355] Matins hymn in the Feast of Corpus Christi.

SERMON *Lasciate* IN ST. PETER'S BASILICA ON THE FEAST OF THE ASCENSION.[356]

An intense desire for peace must be aroused not through fear of sacrifice but through moral re-awakening.

May 14, 1942

1796. . . . . . . Let us increase our faith now as the hurricane roars, rages and disrupts peoples and nations. It is not for us to know the times and the moments which the powerful Hand of our celestial Father regulates, shortening or lengthening them in accordance with that prudent and inscrutable counsel which ordains all events to the exalted and hidden end of His glory. He is *the Blessed and only Sovereign, King of Kings and Lord of Lords*:[357] He is unchangeable, but governs and controls all temporal changes with immutable design, giving and taking away power from whomsoever He wills, exalting the humble and humiliating the proud, in order that all men may acknowledge that all power comes from Him, and that they would have no power, were it not given them from above.[358] Our faith rises above this base world; the Kingdom of Christ is not of this world, though it is established here below: it is within us. Christ did not come, as the Apostles asked, to restore the Kingdom of Israel,[359] but to give testimony to the truth which so sublimates us, the truth which is justice, which is peace, which is respect for law, which is a holy and inviolable liberty of human conscience, which is comfort even in the midst of the present tribulations, sorrows and griefs, as it was comfort in the days of the martyrs, so it is for you, who make benign Divine Providence the foundation which sustains your hope. . . . . . .

1797. Through Thee, Illuminating Spirit, Spirit of counsel and fortitude, may Christian minds of every condition, humble or exalted, understand and feel not only the extraordinary gravity but also the heavy responsibility of the present hour, wherein an old world, which disappears in sorrow, is generating a new one. Make clear to all who bear on their foreheads the name of Christ the narrow path of virtue, which alone leads to salvation, so that they may

---

[356] Original Italian, *A.A.S.*, v. 34, pp. 168-171 (June 1, 1942).
[357] I *Timothy*, VI, 15.
[358] *Cf. John*, XIX, 11.
[359] *Cf. Acts*, I, 6.

arouse themselves from their sleep of indifference, lukewarmness and irresolution and undertake to free themselves from the disordered embroilments of earthly things.

1798. Through Thee, Consoling Spirit, may there return not only the solace of resignation but, above all, the vigor of trust to animate innumerable hearts that now groan and are about to break, crushed under the weight of anxieties and miseries, of sacrifices and injustices, of oppression and degradation. Be Thou our rest in labor, our calm in agitation, our warmth in coldness, our relief in lamentation. Be Thou the father of orphans, the defender of widows, food to the poor, support to the abandoned, roof to refugees, guardian of the persecuted, protection to the combatants, liberation to the prisoners, balm to the wounded, medicine to the sick, refuge of sinners, help to the dying. Console and reunite all those who with pure hearts love one another, whom present hard vicissitudes have separated. Grant that where the voice of human comforts is mute the smile and hand of Christian charity may speak, and before the eyes of their faith may shine, as a pledge of joy that never fails, the dawn of the day wherein the superabundance of Thy ineffable reward will fulfill the words of the Apocalypse: *God will wipe away every tear from their eyes, and death shall be no more; neither shall there be mourning, nor crying, nor pain any more, for the former things have passed away.*[360]

1799. O Spirit, Teacher of Truth, inspire and diffuse in the hearts and minds of men, not through fear of sacrifice but through moral re-awakening, an intense desire for peace, for a peace of justice, moderation and wisdom; a peace which, in its terms, in its basis, in its fulfillment, may not forget Thy warning words: *There is no wisdom, there is no prudence, there is no counsel against the Lord.*[361] And at the same time, infuse in them that deliberate will of such a peace which does not reject its indispensable presuppositions, its fundamental lines and the developments which follow from it. Grant that rulers of peoples may elevate and direct thought to the greatness, to the dignity, to the benefits, to the merits of such an auspicated peace, and may measure the rights of life of their nations not with the length of their sword, nor with the extension of coveted advantages, but according to the divine will and law. . . . . . .

[360] *Apocalypse,* XXI, 4.
[361] *Proverbs,* XXI, 30.

LETTER TO CARDINAL HLOND, PRIMATE OF POLAND.[362]

The Holy Father praises the heroism of the Polish people suffering from the war.

May 30, 1942

1800.   Among the many distinguished proofs of attachment We have received up to now on the occasion of the twenty-fifth anniversary of Our consecration as a bishop, We especially appreciate the congratulations which you have sent Us from Lourdes. For, as the worthy representative and protector of Our beloved Poland, you have conveyed to Us the sincere, heartfelt and filial congratulations of your nation, great by the nobility of its spirit and its glorious history. This beautiful message of veneration and love is cherished by Us all the more as We know precisely and are greatly pained by the present lamentable state of Poland, afflicted by so many terrible misfortunes and bearing indomitably all kinds of wrongs and persecutions. However, the history of the Polish nation shows irrefutably that even under the most painful trials the Poles do not give way. On the contrary, holding fast through the most stormy periods to the unimpeachable treasure of Catholic Faith, and by their lively attachment to the religion of their ancestors, the Poles are even now gathering more spiritual strength, thanks to which they have risen from the catastrophe to shine by yet more splendid heroism and memorable glory.

1801.   Thus, expressing to you, Our Beloved Son, to your venerable brothers of the episcopate and to all faithful the gratitude of Our heart for this proof of your attachment, in humble prayer We beseech Divine Providence, that, through the intercession of the Immaculate Mother of God, the passionate disputes between nations may cease and that after a happy ending of the war, which changes the life of humanity into sackcloth and ashes, Providence may offer Us the triumph of justice and brotherly reconciliation of minds and hearts, and that in this way also Poland and other nations may experience the benefits of a real and lasting peace. Accept as an earnest of those heavenly graces for Poland and as a proof of the great love We bear Our dear Poles, the Apostolic Blessing which

---

[362] Translation from *N.C.W.C. News Service*, August 31, 1942. Cardinal Hlond is now living in exile in Spain.

We grant to you, Our Beloved Son, and to all the Bishops of Poland
and to the entire Polish nation, from Our anguished heart.

ALLOCUTION *Le Parole* TO THE COLLEGE OF CARDINALS ON THE FEAST DAY OF POPE ST. EUGENE.[363]

*In the hour of confusion the misguided peoples will
turn to the Church for guidance.*

June 2, 1942

1802. . . . . . . In the extraordinary gravity of the present hour,
Our conscience feels the responsibility that binds Us before the
eternal High Priest as Pastor of the souls entrusted to Us in custody
by Him. But the more vividly We feel this responsibility, the more
We are consoled and joyful in the knowledge that the mysterious
force of Divine Grace cannot fail, even in the midst of the ferment
and fury of a world shaken by the fever of a crisis of life and death.
It is thus We know that now, more than ever, He is near His
Church, its defense and its comfort. In this tempestuous sea, amid
the waves of hate, the waves of love that transport and turn the
faithful to the Rock which is Peter's See become the oil that calms
the troubled waves and prevents shipwrecks and upheavals. These
are promising signs of victory over the tempest, of the dawn of
salvation and the returning murmur of that placid zephyr, to whose
appealing voice no ear can remain closed.

1803. What occult power, impossible for human hands to grasp,
inaccessible to human flattery, unassailable by whatever weapons of
war, teaches millions and millions of souls that the Church of Christ
is their joy, glory, health and happiness, the constancy of their faith
and their love, the goal of their fidelity and the light of their hope?
Who teaches them to remain faithful to her, when, in not a few
places, to share the sentiments of the Church means also to experience her sufferings? Who teaches them to love the Church, for
whom, as once for her Divine Founder, the modern Herods and
Pilates hold prepared the scoffer's garment and the crown of thorns,
to contemplate in her the Spouse of Christ, mystically imitating the
Redeemer's sorrows in her maternal passion and, therefore, the more

[363] Translation from *N.C.W.C. News Service,* June 8, 1942. Original Italian, *A.A.S.,*
v. 34, pp. 197-199 (July 14, 1942).

amiable and the more worthy of fervent and unconditioned love?

1804. *Many waters cannot quench charity*[364]: We can to-day with confidence, Venerable Brethren and Beloved Sons, thank God that in this violent storm on the human sea He walks upon and dominates the furious waves, watches and guides Peter's Ship in the darkness, performing with His grace this spiritual miracle of unshakable faith, of serene hope and of strong love day by day in millions of His elect. With gratitude toward God, We feel intensely also a gratitude toward all those who, co-operating with Divine Grace, are giving the world an example of generosity and greatness of soul which recalls the brave men and heroes of the most beautiful ages of the past. Perhaps never was the peaceful action of these strong, faithful souls for the preservation and the spread of the Kingdom of God so remarkable, so vital, so efficacious and bright with promises as it is to-day.

1805. To a Church which abounds in upright champions of truth, exemplary models of heroic virtue, luminous guides of the spirit, frank and wise moulders and teachers of noble humanity and of active charity, white lilies of innocence, purple roses of courage, ready to confess their faith even by the sacrifice of their lives; to such a Church has God made ready the time when innumerable minds and hearts, which have listened to other voices and followed other ideals, or rather false idols, will turn to her. That day must and will come—because not one of God's words will be unfulfilled— that day wherein humanity, torn by error and deceit, will be ready to listen with a new interest and a new hope to the Sermon on the Mount of love and true fraternity. Then this humanity, previously so proud of its riches and to-day more than ever aware of its poverty of spirit, talking nonsense in its confusion before the inevitable and decisive crossroads of its advancement, will turn to see in the bright horizon of a genuine Christianity, immutably deep and rich and immense, with useful and vast forms of family and social life, an inviting and engaging Christ shine forth as an Admonisher, Light of the World, true God and true Man, whilst the fatuous fires of false prophets will lie spent.

1806. Then, many people of good-will and clear sight will not fail to understand that the salutary mission of the Church is not a dream of the past, not a mere revival but is a prolongation of a

---

[364] *Canticle of Canticles*, VIII, 7.

present that lasts from centuries, that renews itself every day and with itself renews every civilization it accompanies and knows how to perfect; of a present which plants a future rich with promises, contributing anew seeds, producing wholesome fruits, admirable for their fecund maturity. Then, on the threshold of a new and real organization of the peoples, will sound the word of the Master, to Whose Heart, inflamed with love, the sign and source of grace, this month is dedicated: *Behold, I stand at the door and knock.*[365] What will be the reply of Christianity to this Divine Voice? What, that of the entire human family?

1807. Our duty, Venerable Brethren and Beloved Sons, co-operators in Our Apostolic Ministry, the duty of all members of the episcopate, of all priests, of all souls consecrated to God in the religious state, of all the laity who co-operate in the apostolate of the hierarchy, as well as all the faithful, is to prepare spiritually, with prayer and example, with purification and penance, with work and sacrifice, for this future meeting between Christ and a world more than ever needful of His light and grace, of His help and salvation, so that on such a meeting may finally shine a providential hour of new peaceful agreements and generous motives. . . . . . .

LETTER TO CARDINAL HINSLEY, ARCHBISHOP OF WESTMINSTER, AND TO THE ENGLISH BISHOPS.[366]

Pius XII stands horrified before the growing violence of the war.

June 29, 1942

1808. . . . . . . In the midst of this world war with all its human misery and widespread ruin, it was your good thought to bring balm to Our sorely anxious heart with your touching tribute of loving homage. Your letter has also proved a thing of which We were already convinced: that you highly prize and deeply take to heart any admonitions and recommendations which are sent forth from this Apostolic See for the benefit of Christendom and of humanity.

1809. As you truly observe, from the beginning of Our Pontificate We made every possible effort to avert this terrible conflict

---

[365] *Apocalypse,* III, 20.
[366] Translation from *N.C.W.C. News Service,* October 5, 1942.

when it was imminent, and since it has unhappily broken out We
have used all the means in Our power to alleviate the suffering and
distress which it is causing and to hasten the end of the deadly
conflagration. For We stand horrified before the spectacle of the
growing violence and fury of this war, which is everywhere spreading devastation and adding incessantly to the long tale of its miseries
and sorrows.

1810. All the more reason, therefore, why in your land, as in
every country throughout the world, all good men should be united
in will, so that God may at length be appeased by prayers and
supplications and the offerings of good works, and that, with the
establishment of those principles and solid foundations of true
peace which We have recently enumerated and described, waning
charity may thrive again and the broken harmony of mankind be
restored. Beseeching God earnestly that He may grant these our
common desires and prayers, as an augury of heaven's protection
and in token of Our special affection, We most lovingly grant the
Apostolic Benediction to you, Beloved Son, and to the other Archbishops and Bishops of England and Wales, and We extend the
same to the flocks committed to your care.

Radio address to the Fourth National Eucharistic Congress in Sao Paulo, Brazil.[367]

> The Holy Eucharist helps to unite States into one great
> family.

September 7, 1942

1811. . . . . . . The Eucharist is a mystery, a mystery of faith,
a mystery of love, revered by every Brazilian, as by his ancestors,
leading a sincere and essentially Catholic life. For was it not a living
faith that filled them when news of sacrilege against the Most Holy,
in the Royal Chapel of Lisbon, spread consternation among the
population, who rose as if a national calamity had occurred, organizing penitential processions and ceremonies of vindication and
atonement; and when, later, the unity of the country and the integrity of the Catholic Religion were threatened, was it not Jesus
in the Sacrament Who gave the men bearing arms courage to

[367] English translation, *English Catholic Newsletter,* n. 148, p. 1 (September 12, 1942).

fight and win, to abandon their own homes and possessions, and even to sacrifice their lives rather than deny their Faith? Let it be so with you, too, my dear children of Catholic Brazil. If at any time error or superstition should threaten your faith or attempt to rob you of Jesus in the Sacrament, unite with it still more closely and, armed with that strength—as your great and venerable apostle, Jose de Anchieta, sang—resist, fight and win. Keep intact that most precious of all heritages left to you by your ancestors: the Catholic, Apostolic, Roman Faith, mystery of love and unity.

1812. The Divine Host is the quintessence of love and purity manifested in the great hours preceding His victory. In the Eucharist the Bread and the Cup co-exist, extending in space up to the limits of the earth, and prolonged in time up to the end of the world. His infinite love is a union which takes us into mystic communion. *He who eats My Body and drinks My Blood abides in Me, and I in him. As I live in My Father and by My Father, he who eats Me shall live in Me and by Me.*[368] As Anchieta sang . . . it is the function of Communion, the Divine Eucharist, overflowing with charity and brotherly love, as the Heart of Jesus, ever to increase love and unity between workers and employers, between the faithful and the clergy, between the subjects and the authorities, between North and South, between the citizens of the same State and among the States themselves, for the general weal, in one great family which is the Brazilian Fatherland. The union which is strength is the family. Furthermore, the union of souls in God, when visited by the love of Jesus Christ, is bound together and strengthened. This union is not confined to promoting the temporal well-being of your country, but promotes the spiritual, eternal well-being extending to all souls united in the Blood of Christ. . . . . . . It was with satisfaction that We saw that one of the main points in the Agenda of the Eucharistic Congress was the study and solution of a problem vital for all the nations and chiefly for Brazil — the priestly vocation. We hope that a practical solution may be found and that this solution will be carried into effect without delay. . . . One can conceive of no position more exalted than that of a divine priest. No man in this world can be raised to a higher degree of eminence. . . . Beloved children of Catholic Brazil, do not neglect the call. . . .

[368] *John*, VI, 57-58.

ADDRESS TO MEMBERS OF ITALIAN CATHOLIC ACTION.[369]

Without the help of religion, that permanent, tranquil order, which is the definition of peace, cannot exist among men.

September 20, 1942

1813. . . . . . . To-day the whole world feels the need of a rebirth of order. Look at the statesmen. What is their ambition? Is it not to secure the common good in an atmosphere of temporal order, in harmony with the eternal and supernatural order? Look at the Church. She has a still higher mission—to restore, promote, propagate within society, the Kingdom of God without which there is not and cannot be, even from a purely natural point of view, that permanent, tranquil order which is the definition of peace. Certainly, not all can be statesmen or churchmen; but the ordinary citizens, the faithful . . . in their resolute devotion to the Church and to the State, can have great force in their labors—often humble and obscure, but diligent and efficacious—to sustain and to aid both societies, ecclesiastic and civil, in the furtherance of the end proper to each. . . . . . .

1814. The smallest act has its reaction for good or evil. No act of love, no aspiration, is without its effect on the whole Mystical Body of Christ. We appeal to you all, and not to a few privileged ones. You do not have to go outside the circles of your friends and your offices and workshops. Within your own circles you can help the apostolate. Remember that the Christian apostolate has various forms; there is an apostolate of silence and an apostolate of words; an apostolate of affection and of esteem and an apostolate of mercy and of succor; an apostolate of action and an apostolate of example. Especially in one who is professionally esteemed, the example of a holy life can do wonders. . . . . . .

---

[369] Translation partly from the *English Catholic Newsletter*, n. 150, p. 2 (September 26, 1942), and partly from the *N.C.W.C. News Service*, November 23, 1942.

ADDRESS TO THE DELEGATES OF THE ITALIAN SOCIETY FOR NATURAL
  SCIENCES.[370]

*The scientists must co-operate in the new world order
of justice and of peace.*

October 2, 1942

1815. . . . . . . We are fully confident that the present generation of natural scientists may still be able to employ all their intellectual powers and all their idealism to found a new world order
of justice and of peace, with the collaboration of all decent men
of all countries; an order which excludes everything extreme, evil
and unjust; an order which the Italian people, too, with their deep
faith, will be able to welcome with joy. The day on which scientists
can take up this gigantic task of reconstruction in the service of
mankind will be a day of pure and lasting joy. . . . . . .

RADIO MESSAGE ON THE PROPAGATION OF THE FAITH.[371]

*Despite the war, the missionaries continue their Apos-
tolic work.*

October 24, 1942

1816. . . . . . . We greatly esteem and follow with particular
solicitude both the missionaries, who in the tumult of this awful
conflict are striving to spread the Kingdom of Christ, and the faithful who assist the Missions through their ready charity, never sufficiently praised. For both We invoke from God perseverance in
good, increasing abundance in merits, and the comfort of peace
and joy, and We gladly impart to them from the heart Our Apostolic Blessing.

---

[370] Translation from *The Catholic Herald* (London), October 23, 1942, p. 6.
[371] Translation from *The Catholic Messenger* (Davenport), October 29, 1942.

RADIO ADDRESS TO PORTUGAL ON THE TWENTY-FIFTH ANNIVERSARY
OF THE APPARITION OF THE BLESSED VIRGIN AT FATIMA.[372]

*The Portuguese are urged to pray to the Blessed Virgin,
Queen of Peace.*

October 31, 1942

1817. . . . . . . Order emerged from chaos. The storm abated
and Portugal was able to find and to resume the lost thread of her
finest traditions as a devout nation, to continue, as in the early days
of Lusitania, her glorious crusading and missionary role. Honor to
those worthy men who were the instrument of Providence for such
a great enterprise! Their first glories earned the favors of the Virgin
Lady. She comes again to her land which she has so often saved,
and which always appealed to her in times of tragedy. Portugal,
despite everything and everybody, continues to enjoy a marvelous
peace, and to meet the sacrifices which are demanded by this war
of extermination that desolates the world. . . . . . .

1818. Queen of the Most Holy Rosary, Refuge of the human
race, Victress in all God's battles, we humbly prostrate ourselves
before thy throne, confident that we shall receive mercy, grace
and bountiful assistance and protection in the present calamity,
not through our own inadequate merits, but solely through the
great goodness of thy Maternal Heart. To thee, to thy Immaculate Heart in this, humanity's tragic hour, we consign and consecrate ourselves in union not only with the Mystical Body of thy
Son, Holy Mother Church, now in such suffering and agony in so
many places and sorely tried in so many ways, but also with the
entire world, torn by fierce strife, consumed in a fire of hate, victim
of its own wickedness. May the sight of the widespread material
and moral destruction, of the sorrows and anguish of countless
fathers and mothers, husbands and wives, brothers and sisters and
innocent children, of the great number of lives cut off in the
flower of youth, of the bodies mangled in horrible slaughter, and of
the tortured and agonized souls in danger of being lost eternally,
move thee to compassion!

1819. O Mother of Mercy, obtain peace for us from God and

[372] Translation partly from *The Tablet*, v. 180, p. 227 (November 7, 1942), and partly
from the *N.C.W.C. News Service*, December 7, 1942.

above all procure for us those graces which prepare, establish and assure the peace! Queen of Peace, pray for us and give to the world now at war the peace for which all peoples are longing, peace in the truth, justice and charity of Christ. Give peace to the warring nations and to the souls of men, that in the tranquillity of order the Kingdom of God may prevail. Extend thy protection to the infidels and to all those still in the shadow of death; give them peace and grant that on them, too, may shine the sun of truth, that they may unite with us in proclaiming before the one and only Saviour of the World, *Glory to God in the highest and peace to men of good-will.*[373] Give peace to the peoples separated by error or by discord, and especially to those who profess such singular devotion to thee and in whose homes an honored place was ever accorded thy venerated icon (to-day perhaps often kept hidden to await better days) : bring them back to the one Fold of Christ under the one true Shepherd. Obtain peace and complete freedom for the Holy Church of God; stay the spreading flood of modern paganism; enkindle in the faithful the love of purity, the practice of the Christian life and an Apostolic zeal, so that the servants of God may increase in merit and in number.

1820. Lastly, as the Church and the entire human race were consecrated to the Sacred Heart of Jesus, so that in reposing all hope in Him, He might become for them the sign and pledge of victory and salvation: so we in like manner consecrate ourselves forever also to thee and to thy Immaculate Heart, Our Mother and Queen, that thy love and patronage may hasten the triumph of the Kingdom of God and that all nations, at peace with one another and with God, may proclaim thee blessed and with thee may raise their voices to resound from pole to pole in the chant of the everlasting Magnificat of glory, love and gratitude to the Heart of Jesus, where alone they can find truth and peace.

[373] *Luke*, II, 14.

ADDRESS TO THE DELEGATES OF THE INTERNATIONAL CONGRESS ON
MATHEMATICAL SCIENCES.[374]

*Pius XII hopes that the just needs of the nations may be
recognized and satisfied in a just measure.*

November 20, 1942

1821. . . . . . . Mathematics is a science of peace and not of
conflicts. And it is for Us a lovely vision to contemplate the great
astronomers and mathematicians, in the quiet of the night in their
observatories, watching tranquilly the distant and peaceful constel-
lations and regions of the firmament, and measuring and calculating
the endless distances of the heavens; a sublime symbol and image
of that peace which nations hope to see return to the world. In
that vision Our hope and Our trust in peace are raised; so that also
in the progress, studies and proposals of your exacting science, so
resplendent in your Congress, We repose Our peaceful wish that the
number of peoples in agreement may be increased, that the just
needs of the nations may be recognized and satisfied in a just
measure. . . . . . .

RADIO BROADCAST TO THE FIRST NATIONAL EUCHARISTIC CON-
GRESS IN EL SALVADOR.[375]

*The world will find peace in a return to the super-
natural life.*

November 26, 1942

1822. . . . . . . Beloved faithful of El Salvador, and Venerable
Brethren to whom is entrusted the flock of the dioceses of Central
America and with whom so many illustrious prelates of the American continent have wished to unite on this solemn occasion, fervently We raise Our voice to-day with you, and from the depth
of Our heart as Common Father, anguished by a tragedy whose
burden becomes daily more difficult and sorrowful, We supplicate
the Spotless Lamb that He shorten the days of trial and hasten
to save us. . . . Behold Him, He seems to sleep behind the tabernacle veil. He reposes on the prow of His bark. But He is ever

[374] Translation from the *N.C.W.C. News Service*, November 23, 1942.
[375] Translation from the *N.C.W.C. News Service*, November 30, 1942.

awake. *Lord, save us! we are perishing.*[376] Lord, be in this hour, too, Our Saviour from Thy holy tabernacle, and grant that men, like thirsting deer, may run to the Spring of Life to satiate throats inflamed by feeding upon so much poisonous matter!

1823. Our Lord must save us now also at this turning point in history because to-day, as always, the salvation of the world is found only in the return to the supernatural life, to the Christian life which has its center and all its power in the Holy Eucharist. Woe to the world if this Divine Food were to fail to descend from heaven for a single day! Woe to us pilgrims if this Spring which issued forth at the striking of the rock, in order to quench the thirst of the people, were to run dry for even a moment at its life-giving source! . . . Lord, give us all those fruits which You have prepared for us, and among men, as a precious first fruit, the price-less gift of peace—peace with Thee, Redeemer of the World; peace among men, that peace which daily We invoke at the break of dawn, when, at the altar of sacrifice, We say: *Pax Domini sit semper vobiscum. Dona nobis pacem!* . . . . .

LETTER TO CARDINAL BOETTO, ARCHBISHOP OF GENOA.[377]

The Holy Father leaves nothing undone in his efforts to end or to alleviate the suffering caused by the war to the civilian populations.

December 4, 1942

1824. It is with great sorrow that We read the news in your letter. In this letter We see a proof of your confidence in Us and your fatherly devotion to your flock. For Our part, We can assure you that nothing will be left undone to end or alleviate the suf-fering caused by the war to the civilian populations. In the mean-while, We pray that the Grace of God may give the city spiritual fortitude. Charity rises from among the ruins; may this be a pre-sentiment for the future peaceful reconstruction and new brother-hood. May courage and penitence exterminate the evil and disorder in the world, which has provoked divine punishment.

[376] *Matthew,* VIII, 25.
[377] Translation from *The Catholic Herald* (London), December 4, 1942. The date of this letter is uncertain; hence, we have given it the date of the newspaper account.

ADDRESS TO RETREATANTS IN THE VATICAN.[378]

*To-day Christians must love their fellow men every-
where, unconditionally and unreservedly.*

December 5, 1942

1825. . . . . . . Supernatural charity is palpitating for the good
of souls, for their eternal salvation, for their sanctification here
below, but also for universal love which must embrace, for our
part, all our fellow men: all our fellow men means men everywhere, unconditionally and unreservedly. Is it not true that Christ
commanded us to love our brothers as ourselves,[379] and indeed to
love them as He Himself has loved us? . . . Apostolic charity and
charity with Apostolic zeal, that was the charity of the Doctor of
the Gentiles; charity embraces all peoples and all times; and this
particularly is the time for charity, this tragic time which is being
prolonged and extended and daily becomes more calamitous, imposing always a heavier burden on the face of the earth. . . . . . .

CHRISTMAS BROADCAST TO THE WHOLE WORLD.[380]

*The Holy Father explains the fundamental principles
concerning the internal order of States and peoples.*

December 24, 1942

1826. As the Holy Christmas Season comes round each year,
the message of Jesus, Who is Light in the midst of darkness, echoes
once more from the Crib of Bethlehem in the ears of Christians
and re-echoes in their hearts with an ever new freshness of joy and
piety. It is a message which lights up with heavenly truth a world
that is plunged in darkness by fatal errors. It infuses exuberant
and trustful joy into mankind, torn by the anxiety of deep, bitter
sorrow. It proclaims liberty to the sons of Adam, shackled with
the chains of sin and guilt. It promises mercy, love, peace to the
countless hosts of those in suffering and tribulation who see their
happiness shattered and their efforts broken in the tempestuous
strife and hate of our stormy days. The church bells, which announce

---

[378] Translation from the *N.C.W.C. News Service*, December 7, 1942.
[379] *Cf. Matthew*, XIX, 19.
[380] Translation from *The Catholic Mind*, v. 41, pp. 45-60 (January, 1943).

this message in every continent, not only recall the gift which God made to mankind at the dawn of the Christian Era; they also announce and proclaim a consoling reality of the present, a reality which is eternally young, living and lifegiving; it is the reality of the *True Light which enlighteneth every man that cometh into this world,*[381] and which knows no setting. The Eternal Word, Who is the Way, the Truth and the Life, began His mission of saving and redeeming the human race by being born in the squalor of a stable and by thus ennobling and hallowing poverty.

1827. He thus proclaimed and consecrated a message which is still, to-day, the Word of Eternal Life. That message can solve the most tortuous questions, unsolved and insoluble for those who bring to their investigations a mentality and an apparatus which are ephemeral and merely human; and those questions stand up, bleeding, imperiously demanding an answer, before the thought and the feelings of embittered and exasperated mankind. The watchword, *I have compassion on the multitude,*[382] is for Us a sacred trust which may not be abused; it remains strong, and impelling in all times and in all human situations, as it was the distinguishing mark of Jesus. The Church would be untrue to herself, ceasing to be a mother, if she turned a deaf ear to her children's anguished cries, which reach her from every class of the human family. She does not intend to take sides for any of the particular forms in which the several peoples and States strive to solve the gigantic problems of domestic order or international collaborations, as long as these forms conform to the law of God. But, on the other hand, as the "Pillar and Ground of Truth" and guardian, by the Will of God and the mandate of Christ, of the natural and supernatural order, the Church cannot renounce her right to proclaim to her sons and to the whole world the unchanging basic laws, saving them from every perversion, frustration, corruption, false interpretation and error. This is all the more necessary for the fact that upon the exact maintenance of these laws, and not merely by the effort of noble and courageous wills, depends in the last analysis the solidity of any national and international order, so fervently desired by all peoples. We know the qualities of courage and sacrifice of those peoples, and We also know their straitened conditions and

[381] *John,* I, 9.
[382] *Mark,* VIII, 2.

their sorrow; and in this hour of unspeakable trial and strife We feel Ourself bound to each and every one of them without exception, by a deep, all-embracing, unmovable affection, and by an immense desire to bring them every solace and help which is in any way at Our command.

1828. In Our last Christmas message, We expounded the principles which Christian thought suggests for the establishment of an international order of friendly relations and collaboration such as to conform to the demands of God's law. To-day We shall with the consent, We feel, and the interested attention of all upright men, pause to consider very carefully and with equal impartiality, the fundamental laws of the internal order of States and peoples. International relations and internal order are intimately related. International equilibrium and harmony depend on the internal equilibrium and development of the individual States in the material, social and intellectual spheres. A firm and steady peace policy toward other nations is, in fact, impossible without a spirit of peace within the nation which inspires trust. It is only, then, by striving for an integral peace, a peace in both fields, that people will be freed from the cruel nightmare of war, and the material and psychological causes of further discord and disorder will be diminished and gradually eliminated. Every society, worthy of the name, has originated in a desire for peace, and hence aims at attaining peace, that "tranquil living together in order"[383] in which St. Thomas finds the essence of peace. Two primary elements, then, regulate social life: a living together in order and a living together in tranquillity.

1829. Order, which is fundamental in an association of men (of beings, that is, who strive to attain an end appropriate to their nature) is not a merely external linking up of parts which are numerically distinct. It is rather, and must be, a tendency and an ever more perfect approach to an internal union; and this does not exclude differences founded in fact and sanctioned by the Will of God or by supernatural standards. A clear understanding of the genuine fundamentals of all social life has a capital importance to-day as never before, when mankind, impregnated by the poison of error and social aberrations, tormented by the fever of discordant desires, doctrines and aims, is excitedly tossing about in the dis-

---

[383] *Summa Theologica*, 2a 2ae, q. 29, a.1, ad 1um.

order which it has itself created, and is experiencing the destructive force of false ideas, that disregard the Law of God or are opposed to it. And since disorder can only be overcome by an order which is not merely superimposed and fictitious (just as darkness with its fearful and depressing effects can only be driven away by light and not by will-o'-the-wisps); so security, reorganization, progressive improvement cannot be expected and cannot be brought about unless by a return of large and influential sections to correct notions about society. It is a return which calls for the Grace of God in large measure, and for a resolute will, ready and prepared for sacrifice on the part of good and farseeing men. From these influential circles which are more capable of penetrating and appreciating the beauty of just social norms, there will pass on and infiltrate into the masses the clear knowledge of the true, divine, spiritual origin of social life. Thus the way will be cleared for the reawakening, the growth and the fixing of those moral principles without which even the proudest achievements create but a babel in which the citizens, though they live inside the same walls, speak different and incoherent languages.

1830. From individual and social life we should rise to God, the First Cause and Ultimate Foundation, as He is the Creator of the first conjugal society, from which we have the society which is the family, and the society of peoples and of nations. As an image, albeit imperfect, of its Exemplar, the One and Triune God, Who, through the Mystery of the Incarnation, redeemed and raised human nature, life in society, in its ideals and in its end, possesses by the light of reason and of Revelation a moral authority and an absoluteness which transcend every temporal change. It has a power of attraction that, far from being weakened or lessened by delusions, errors, failures, draws irresistibly the noblest and most faithful souls to the Lord, to take up with renewed energy, with added knowledge, with new studies, methods and means, the enterprises which in other times and circumstances were tried in vain.

1831. The origin and the primary scope of social life is the conservation, development and perfection of the human person, helping him to realize accurately the demands and values of religion and culture set by the Creator for every man and for all mankind, both as a whole and in its natural ramifications. A social teaching or a social reconstruction program which denies or prescinds from this internal essential relation to God of everything that regards man, is on a false course; and while it builds up with one hand, it prepares with the other the materials which sooner or later will undermine and destroy the whole fabric. And when it disregards the respect due to the human person and to the life which is proper to that person, and gives no thought to it in its organization, in legislative and executive activity, then instead of serving society, it harms it; instead of encouraging and stimulating social thought, instead of realizing its hopes and expectations, it strips it of all real value and reduces it to an utilitarian formula which is openly rejected by constantly increasing groups.

1832.   If social life implies intrinsic unity, it does not, at the same time, exclude differences which are founded in fact and nature. When we hold fast to God, the Supreme Controller of all that relates to man, then the similarities no less than the differences of men find their allotted place in the fixed order of being, of values, and hence also of morality. When, however, this foundation is removed, there is a dangerous lack of cohesion in the various spheres of culture; the frontier of true values becomes uncertain and shifting, even to the point where mere external factors, and often blind instincts, come to determine, according to the prevalent fashion of the day, who is to have control of this or that direction. After the fatal economy of the past decades, during which the lives of all citizens were subordinated to the stimulus of gain, there now succeeds another and no less fatal policy which, while it considers everybody and everything with reference to the State, excludes all thought of ethics or religion. This is a fatal travesty, a fatal error. It is calculated to bring about far-reaching consequences for social life, which is never nearer to losing its noblest prerogatives than when it thinks it can deny or forget with impunity the eternal Source of its own dignity: God.

1833.   Reason, enlightened by faith, assigns to individuals and to particular societies in the social organization a definite and exalted place. It knows, to mention only the most important, that the whole political and economic activity of the State is directed to the permanent realization of the common good. . . . In a conception of society which is pervaded and sanctioned by religious thought, the influence of economics and of every other sphere of cultural activity represents a universal and most exalted center of activity, very rich in its variety and coherent in its harmony, in which men's intellectual equality and diversity of occupation come into their own and secure adequate expression. When this is not so, work is depreciated, and the worker is belittled.

1834. That social life, such as God willed it, may attain its scope, it needs a juridical order to support it from without, to defend and protect it. The function of this juridical order is not to dominate but to serve, to help the development and the increase of society's vitality in the rich multiplicity of its ends, leading all the individual energies to their perfection in peaceful competition, and defending them with appropriate and honest means against all that may militate against their full evolution. Such an order, that it may safeguard the equilibrium, the safety and the harmony of society, has also the power of coercion against those, who only by this means can be held within the noble discipline of social life. But in the just fulfillment of this right, an authority which is truly worthy of the name will always be painfully conscious of its responsibility in the sight of the Eternal Judge, before Whose tribunal every wrong judgment, and especially every revolt against the order established by God, will receive, without fail, its sanction and its condemnation.

1835. The precise, bedrock, basic rules that govern society cannot be prejudiced by the intervention of human agency. They can be denied, overlooked, despised, transgressed, but they can never be overthrown with legal validity. It is true indeed that, as time goes on, conditions of life change. But there is never a complete break or a complete discontinuity between the law of yesterday and that of to-day, between the disappearance of old powers and constitutions and the appearance of a new order. In any case, whatever be the change or transformation, the scope of every social life remains identical, sacred, obligatory; it is the development of the personal values of man as the image of God; and the obligation remains with every member of the human family to realize his unchangeable destiny, whosoever be the legislator and the authority whom he obeys. In consequence, there always remains, too, his inalienable right, which no opposition can nullify—a right which must be respected by friend and foe—to a legal order and practice which appreciate and understand that it is their essential duty to serve the common good.

1836. The juridical order has, besides, the high and difficult scope of insuring harmonious relations both between individuals and between societies, and within these. This scope will be reached if legislators will abstain from following those perilous theories and practices, so harmful to communities and to their spirit of union, which derive their origin and promulgation from false postulates. Among such postulates We must count the juridical positivism which attributes a deceptive majesty to the setting up of purely human laws, and which leaves the way open for a fatal divorce of law from morality; there is, besides, the conception which claims for particular nations, or races, or classes, the juridical instinct as the final imperative and the norm from which there is no appeal; finally, there are those various theories which, differing among themselves, and deriving from opposite ideologies, agree in considering the State, or a group which represents it, as an absolute and supreme entity, exempt from control and from criticism even when its theoretical and practical postulates result in, and offend by, their open denial of essential tenets of the human and Christian conscience.

1837. Anyone who considers with an open and penetrating mind the vital connection between social order and a genuine juridical order, and who is conscious of the fact that internal order in all its complexity depends on the predominance of spiritual forces, on the respect of human dignity in oneself and in others, on the love of society and of its God-given ends, cannot wonder at the sad effects of juridical conceptions which, far from the royal road of truth, proceed on the insecure ground of materialist postulates. But he will realize at once the urgent need of a return to a conception of law which is spiritual and ethical, serious and profound, vivified by the warmth of true humanity and illumined by the splendor of the Christian Faith, which bids us seek in the juridical order an outward reflection of the social order willed by God, a luminous product of the spirit of man which is in turn the image of the Spirit of God. On this organic conception which alone is living, in which the noblest humanity and the most genuine Christian spirit flourish in harmony, there is marked the Scriptural thought, expounded by the great Aquinas: *Opus Justitiæ Pax*—The work of justice shall be peace,[384] a thought which is as applicable to

---

[384] *Summa Theologica,* 2a 2ae, q. 29, a.3, ad 3um.

the internal as to the external aspect of social life. It admits of neither
contrast nor alternative such as expressed in the disjunction, love or
right, but the fruitful synthesis, love and right. In the one as in
the other, since both radiate from the same Spirit of God, We read
the program and the seal of the human spirit; they complement
one another, give each other life and support, walk hand in hand
along the road of concord and pacification, while right clears the
way for love and love makes right less stern, and gives it a higher
meaning. Both elevate human life to that social atmosphere where,
even amid the failings, the obstacles and the difficulties of this earth,
a fraternal community of life is made possible. But once let the
baneful spirit of materialist ideas predominate; let the urge for
power and for predominance take in its rough hands the direction
of affairs; you shall then find its disruptive effects appearing daily
in greater measure; you shall see love and justice disappear; all
this as the sad foretaste of the catastrophes that menace society
when it abandons God.

1838. The second fundamental element of peace, toward which
every human society tends almost instinctively, is tranquillity. Oh,
blessed tranquillity, thou hast nothing in common with the spirit
of holding fixedly and obstinately, unrelentingly and with childish
stubbornness, to things as they are; nor yet with the reluctance—
child of cowardice and selfishness—to put one's mind to the solution
of problems and questions which the passage of time and the
succession of generations, with their different needs and progress,
make actual, and bring up as burning questions of the day. But,
for a Christian who is conscious of his responsibilities even toward
the least of his brethren, there is no such thing as slothful tranquillity; nor is there question of flight, but of struggle, of action against
every inaction and desertion in the great spiritual combat where
the stakes are the construction, nay the very soul, of the society of
tomorrow. In the mind of Aquinas, tranquillity and feverish activity are not opposed, but rather form a well-balanced pair for him
who is inspired by the beauty and the urgency of the spiritual foundations of society, and by the nobility of its ideals. To you, young
people, who are wont to turn your backs on the past, and to rely
on the future for your aspirations and your hopes, We address Ourself with ardent love and fatherly anxiety; enthusiasm and courage
do not of themselves suffice, if they be not, as they should be, placed

in the service of a good and of a spotless cause. It is vain to agitate, to weary yourselves, to bustle about without ever resting in God and His eternal law. You must be inspired with the conviction that you are fighting for truth, that you are sacrificing in the cause of truth your own tastes and energies, wishes and sympathies; that you are fighting for the eternal laws of God, for the dignity of the human person, and for the attainment of its destiny. When mature men and young men, while remaining always at anchor in the sea of the eternally active tranquillity of God, co-ordinate their differences of temperament and activity in a genuine Christian spirit, then if the propelling element is joined to the refraining element, the natural differences between the generations will never become dangerous, and will even conduce vigorously to the enforcement of the eternal laws of God in the changing course of times and of conditions of life.

1839. In one field of social life, where for a whole century there was agitation and bitter conflict, there is to-day a calm, at least on the surface. We speak of the vast and ever-growing world of labor, of the immense army of workers, of breadwinners and dependents. If we consider the present with its wartime exigencies, as an admitted fact, then this calm may be called a necessary and reasonable demand; but if we look at the present situation in the light of justice, and with reference to a legitimately regulated labor movement, then the tranquillity will remain only apparent, until the scope of such a movement be attained. Always moved by religious motives, the Church has condemned the various forms of Marxist Socialism; and she condemns them to-day, because it is her permanent right and duty to safeguard men from currents of thought and influences that jeopardize their eternal salvation. But the Church cannot ignore or overlook the fact that the worker, in his efforts to better his lot, is opposed by a machinery which is not only not in accordance with nature, but is at variance with God's plan and with the purpose He had in creating the goods of earth. In spite of the fact that the ways they followed were and are false and to be condemned, what man, and especially what priest or Christian, could remain deaf to the cries that rise from the depths and call for justice and a spirit of brotherly collaboration in a world ruled by a just God? Such silence would be culpable and unjustifiable before God, and contrary to the inspired teaching of the

Apostle, who, while he inculcates the need of resolution in the fight against error, also knows that we must be full of sympathy for those who err, and open-minded in our understanding of their aspirations, hopes and motives.

1840. When He blessed our first parents, God said: *Increase and multiply and fill the earth, and subdue it.*[385] And to the first father of a family, He said later: *In the sweat of thy face shalt thou eat bread.*[386] The dignity of the human person, then, requires normally as a natural foundation of life, the right to the use of the goods of the earth. To this right corresponds the fundamental obligation to grant private ownership of property, if possible, to all. Positive legislation regulating private ownership may change and more or less restrict its use. But if legislation is to play its part in the pacification of the community, it must prevent the worker, who is or will be a father of a family, from being condemned to an economic dependence and slavery which is irreconcilable with his rights as a person. Whether this slavery arises from the exploitation of private capital or from the power of the State, the result is the same. Indeed, under the pressure of a State which dominates all and controls the whole field of public and private life, even going into the realm of ideas and beliefs and of conscience, this lack of liberty can have more serious consequences, as experience shows and proves. . . . . . .

1841. To-day, as never before, the hour has come for reparation, for rousing the conscience of the world from the heavy torpor into which the drugs of false ideas, widely diffused, have sunk it. This is all the more so because in this hour of material and moral disintegration the appreciation of the emptiness and inconsistency of every purely human order is beginning to disillusion even those who, in days of apparent happiness, were not conscious of the need of contact with the eternal in themselves or in society, and did not look upon its absence as an essential defect in their constitutions. What was clear to the Christian, who in his deeply founded faith was pained by the ignorance of others, is now presented to us in dazzling clearness by the din of appalling catastrophe which the present upheaval brings to man and which portrays all the terrifying lineaments of a general judgment even for the tepid, the indif-

[385] *Genesis*, I, 28.
[386] *Genesis*, III, 19.

ferent, the frivolous. It is indeed an old truth which comes out in ever new forms and thunders through the ages and through the nations from the mouth of the Prophet: *All that forsake Thee shall be confounded; they who depart from Thee, shall be written in the earth: because they have forsaken the Lord, the Vein of Living Waters.*[387]

1842. The call of the moment is not lamentation but action: not lamentation over what has been, but reconstruction of what is to arise and must arise for the good of society. It is for the best and most distinguished members of the Christian family, filled with the enthusiasm of Crusaders, to unite in the spirit of truth, justice and love to the call: "God wills it," ready to serve, to sacrifice themselves, like the Crusaders of old. If the issue was then the liberation of the land hallowed by the life of the Incarnate Word of God, the call to-day is, if We may so express Ourself, to traverse the sea of errors of our day and to march on to free the holy land of the spirit, which is destined to sustain in its foundations the unchangeable norms and laws on which will arise a social construction of solid internal consistency.

1843. With this lofty purpose before Us, We turn from the crib of the Prince of Peace, confident that His grace is diffused in all hearts, to you, beloved children, who recognize and adore in Christ your Saviour; We turn to all those who are united with Us at least by the bond of faith in God; We turn, finally, to all those who would be free of doubt and error, and who desire light and guidance; and We exhort you with suppliant, paternal insistence not only to realize fully the dreadful gravity of this hour, but also to meditate upon the vistas of good and supernatural benefit which it opens up, and to unite and collaborate toward the renewal of society in spirit and truth. The essential aim of this necessary and holy crusade is that the Star of Peace, the Star of Bethlehem, may shine out again over the whole of mankind in all its brilliant splendor and reassuring consolation as a pledge and augury of a future, better, more fruitful and happier. It is true that the road from night to full day will be long; but of decisive importance are the first steps on the path, the first five milestones of which bear chiseled on them the following maxims:

1844. First: He who would have the star of peace shine out

[387] *Jeremias*, XVII, 13.

799

and stand over society should cooperate, for his part, in giving back to the human person the dignity given to it by God from the very beginning; should oppose the excessive herding of men, as if they were a mass without a soul; their economic, social, political, intellectual and moral inconsistency; their dearth of solid principles and strong convictions, their surfeit of instinctive sensible excitement and their fickleness.

1845.   He should favor, by every lawful means, in every sphere of life, social institutions in which a full personal responsibility is assured and guaranteed both in the earthly and the eternal order of things.

1846.   He should uphold respect for, and the practical realization of, the following fundamental personal rights: the right to maintain and develop one's corporal, intellectual and moral life and especially the right to religious formation and education; the right to worship God in private and public and to carry on religious works of charity; the right to marry and to achieve the aim of married life; the right to conjugal and domestic society; the right to work, as the indispensable means toward the maintenance of family life; the right to free choice of a state of life, and hence, too, of the priesthood or religious life; the right to the use of material goods, in keeping with his duties and social limitations.

1847.   Second: He who would have the star of peace shine out and stand over society should reject every form of materialism which sees in the people only a herd of individuals who, divided and without any internal cohesion, are considered as a mass to be lorded over and treated arbitrarily; he should strive to understand society as an intrinsic unity, which has grown up and matured under the guidance of Providence, a unity which — within the bounds assigned to it and according to its own peculiar gifts— tends, with the collaboration of the various classes and professions, toward the eternal and ever new aims of culture and religion.

1848.   He should defend the indissolubility of matrimony; he should give to the family—that unique cell of the people—space, light and air so that it may attend to its mission of perpetuating new life, and of educating children in a spirit corresponding to its own true religious convictions, and that it may preserve, fortify and reconstitute, according to its powers, its proper economic, spiritual, moral and juridic unity.

1849. He should take care that the material and spiritual advantages of the family be shared by the domestic servants; he should strive to secure for every family a dwelling where a materially and morally healthy family life may·be seen in all its vigor and worth; he should take care that the place of work be not so separated from the home as to make the head of the family and educator of the children a virtual stranger to his own household; he should take care above all that the bond of trust and mutual help should be re-established between the family and the school, that bond which in other times gave such happy results, but which now has been replaced by mistrust where the school, influenced and controlled by the spirit of materialism, corrupts and destroys what the parents have instilled into the minds of the children.

1850. Third: He who would have the star of peace shine out and stand over society should give to work the place assigned to it by God from the beginning. As an indispensable means toward gaining over the world that mastery which God wishes for His glory, all work has an inherent dignity and at the same time a close connection with the perfection of the person; this is the noble dignity and privilege of work which is not in any way cheapened by the fatigue and the burden, which have to be borne as the effect of original sin, in obedience and submission to the Will of God.

1851. Those who are familiar with the great Encyclicals of Our Predecessors and Our Own previous messages knew well that the Church does not hesitate to draw the practical conclusions which are derived from the moral nobility of work, and to give them all the support of her authority. These exigencies include, besides a just wage which covers the needs of the worker and his family, the conservation and perfection of a social order which will make possible an assured, even if modest, private property for all classes of society, which will promote higher education for the children of the working class who are especially endowed with intelligence and good-will, will promote the care and the practice of the social spirit in one's immediate neighborhood, in the district, the province, the people and the nation, a spirit which, by smoothing over friction arising from privileges or class interests, removes from the workers the sense of isolation through the assuring experience of a genuinely human, and fraternally Christian, solidarity.

1852. The progress and the extent of urgent social reforms

depend on the economic possibilities of single nations. It is only through an intelligent and generous sharing of forces between the strong and the weak that it will be possible to effect a universal pacification in such.wise as not to leave behind centers of conflagration and infection from which new disasters may come. There are evident signs which go to show that, in the ferment of all the prejudices and feelings of hate, those inevitable but lamentable offspring of the war psychosis, there is still aflame in the peoples the consciousness of their intimate mutual dependence for good or for evil, nay, that this consciousness is more alive and active. Is it not true that deep thinkers see ever more clearly in the renunciation of egoism and national isolation, the way to general salvation, ready as they are to demand of their peoples a heavy participation in the sacrifices necessary for social well-being in other peoples? May this Christmas Message of Ours, addressed to all those who are animated by a good-will and a generous heart, encourage and increase the legions of these social crusades in every nation. And may God deign to give to their peaceful cause the victory of which their noble enterprise is worthy.

1853. Fourth: He who would have the star of peace shine out and stand over social life should collaborate toward a complete rehabilitation of the juridical order. The juridic sense of to-day is often altered and overturned by the profession and the practice of a positivism and a utilitarianism which are subjected and bound to the service of determined groups, classes and movements, whose programs direct and determine the course of legislation and the practices of the courts. The cure for this situation becomes feasible when we awaken again the consciousness of a juridical order resting on the supreme dominion of God, and safeguarded from all human whims; a consciousness of an order which stretches forth its arm, in protection or punishment, over the unforgettable rights of man and protects them against attacks.

1854. From the juridic order, as willed by God, flows man's inalienable right to juridical security, and by this very fact to a definite sphere of rights, immune from all arbitrary attack. The relations of man to man, of the individual to society, to authority, to civil duties; the relations of society and of authority to the individual, should be placed on a firm juridic footing and be guarded, when the need arises, by the authority of the courts.

1855. This supposes: (a) A tribunal and a judge who take their directions from a clearly formulated and defined right; (b) Clear juridical norms which may not be overturned by unwarranted appeals to a supposed popular sentiment or by merely utilitarian considerations; (c) The recognition of the principle that even the State and the functionaries and organizations dependent on it are obliged to repair and to withdraw measures which are harmful to the liberty, property, honor, progress or health of the individuals.

1856. Fifth: He who would have the star of peace shine out and stand over human society should co-operate toward the setting up of a State conception and practice founded on reasonable discipline, exalted kindliness and a responsible Christian spirit.

1857. He should help to restore the State and its power to the service of human society, to the full recognition of the respect due to the human person and his efforts to attain his eternal destiny.

1858. He should apply and devote himself to dispelling the errors which aim at causing the State and its authority to deviate from the path of morality, at severing them from the eminently ethical bond which links them to individual and social life, and at making them deny or in practice ignore their essential dependence on the Will of the Creator. He should work for the recognition and diffusion of the truth which teaches, even in matters of this world, that the deepest meaning, the ultimate moral basis and the universal validity of "reigning," lies in "serving."

1859. Beloved children, may God grant that while you listen to Our voice your hearts may be profoundly stirred and moved by the deeply felt seriousness, the loving solicitude, the unremitting insistence, with which We drive home these thoughts, which are meant as an appeal to the conscience of the world, and a rallying-cry to all those who are ready to ponder and weigh the grandeur of their mission and responsibility by the vastness of this universal disaster. A great part of mankind, and let Us not shrink from saying it, not a few who call themselves Christians, have to some extent their share in the collective responsibility for the growth of error and for the harm and the lack of moral fibre in the society of to-day. What is this world war, with all its attendant circumstances, whether they be remote or proximate causes, its progress and material, legal and moral effects? What is it but the crumbling process, not expected, perhaps, by the thoughtless but seen and deprecated by those whose gaze penetrated into the realities of a social order which—behind a deceptive exterior or the mask of conventional shibboleths—hid its mortal weakness and its unbridled lust for gain and power?

1860. That which in peacetime lay coiled up, broke loose at the outbreak of war in a sad succession of acts at variance with the human and Christian sense. International agreements to make war less inhuman by confining it to the combatants, to regulate the procedure of occupation and the imprisonment of the conquered remained in various places a dead letter. And who can see the end of this progressive demoralization of the people, who can wish to watch impotently this disastrous progress? Should they not rather, over the ruins of a social order which has given such tragic proof of its ineptitude as a factor for the good of the people, gather together the hearts of all those who are magnanimous and upright in the solemn vow not to rest until in all peoples and all nations of the earth a vast legion shall be formed of those handfuls of men who, bent on bringing back society to its center of gravity, which is the law of God, aspire to the service of the human person and of his common life ennobled in God?

1861. Mankind owes that vow to the countless dead who lie buried on the field of battle: the sacrifice of their lives in the fulfillment of their duty is a holocaust offered for a new and better social order. Mankind owes that vow to the innumerable host of sorrowing mothers, widows and orphans who have seen the light, the solace and the support of their lives wrenched from them. Mankind owes that vow to those numberless exiles whom the hurricane of war has torn from their native land and scattered in the land of the stranger; who can make their own the lament of the Prophet: *Our inheritance is turned to aliens: our houses to strangers.*[388] Mankind owes that vow to the hundreds of thousands of persons who, without any fault on their part, sometimes only because of their nationality or race, have been consigned to death or to a slow decline. Mankind owes that vow to the many thousands of noncombatants, women, children, sick and aged, from whom aerial warfare—whose horrors We have from the beginning frequently denounced—has, without discrimination or through inadequate pre-

[388] *Lamentations*, V, 2.

cautions, taken life, goods, health, home, charitable refuge, or house of prayer. Mankind owes that vow to the flood of tears and bitterness, to the accumulation of sorrow and suffering, emanating from the murderous ruin of the dreadful conflict and crying to heaven to send down the Holy Spirit to liberate the world from the inundation of violence and terror. And where could you with greater assurance and trust and with more efficacious faith place this vow for the renewal of society than at the Feet of the *Desired of all Nations*,[389] Who lies before us in the crib with all the charm of His sweet humanity as a babe, but also in the dynamic attraction of His incipient mission as Redeemer?

1862.   Where could this noble and holy crusade for the cleansing and renewal of society have a more significant consecration or find a more potent inspiration than at Bethlehem, where the new Adam appears in the adorable mystery of the Incarnation? For it is at His fountains of truth and grace that mankind should find the water of life if it is not to perish in the desert of this life; *of His fullness we all have received.*[390] His fullness of grace and truth flows as freely to-day as it has for twenty centuries on the world. His light can overcome the darkness, the rays of His love can conquer the icy egoism which holds so many back from becoming great and conspicuous in their higher life.

1863.   Do you, crusader-volunteers of a distinguished new society, lift up the new call for moral and Christian rebirth, declare war on the darkness which comes from deserting God, on the coldness that comes from strife between brothers. It is a fight for the human race, which is gravely ill and must be healed in the name of conscience ennobled by Christianity. May Our blessing and Our paternal good wishes and encouragement go with your generous enterprise, and may they remain with all those who do not shirk hard sacrifices—those weapons which are more potent than any steel to combat the evil from which society suffers. Over your crusade for a social, human and Christian ideal may there shine out as a consolation and an inspiration the star that stands over the Grotto of Bethlehem, the first and the perennial star of the Christian Era. From the sign of it every faithful heart drew, draws and ever will draw strength: *If armies in camp should stand together against me,*

[389] *Aggeus*, II, 8.
[390] *John*, I, 16.

my heart shall not fear.[391] Where that star shines, there is Christ. "With Him for leader we shall not wander; through Him let us go to Him, that with the Child that is born to-day we may rejoice forever."

[391] *Psalms,* XXVI, 3.

LIST OF DOCUMENTS

LEO XIII

* Newly translated.

PIUS X

BENEDICT XV

* Newly translated.

* Newly translated.

* Newly translated.

* Newly translated.

* Newly translated.

* Newly translated.

* Newly translated.

* Newly translated.

* Newly translated.

* Newly translated.

* Newly translated.

* Newly translated.

* Newly translated.

BIBLIOGRAPHY

OFFICIAL SOURCES

Acta Apostolicae Sedis. Rome, Typis polyglottis Vaticanis, 1909–
(*A.A.S.*)

Acta Sanctae Sedis. Rome, Ex typographia polyglotta S.C. de propaganda fide, 1878–1908. (*A.S.S.*)

Leonis XIII Pontificis Maximi Acta. 23v. Romae, Ex typographia Vaticana, 1881–1905.

L'Osservatore Romano. Rome, 1861–

BOOKS

Actes de Benoît XV; encycliques, motu proprio, brefs, allocutions, actes des dicastères, etc. Texte latin avec traduction française, précédés d'une notice biographique suivis d'une table générale analytique. 3v. Paris, Bonne Presse, 1926–1934.

Actes de Léon XIII; encycliques, motu proprio, brefs, allocutions, actes de dicastères, etc. Texte latin et traduction française. 7v. Paris, Bonne Presse, 1931–1937.

Actes de S.S. Pie XI; encycliques, motu proprio, brefs, allocutions, actes de dicastères, etc. Texte latin avec traduction française. 7v. Paris, Bonne Presse, 1932–1936.

Appeals for Peace of Pope Benedict XV and Pope Pius XI. Washington, Catholic Association for International Peace, [1931?].

Arnaud d'Agnel, G. *Benoît XV et le Conflit Européen.* 2v. Paris, P. Lethielleux, [1916].

Atheistic Communism. Washington, National Catholic Welfare Conference, 1937.

Beales, A. C. F. *The Catholic Church and International Order.* New York, Allen Lane, 1941.

Benkert, Gerald F. *The Catholic Conception of an International Society.* Washington, Catholic University of America Press, 1942.

Binchy, Daniel A. *Church and State in Fascist Italy.* London, New York, Oxford University Press, 1941.

Bouscaren, Timothy Lincoln. *The Canon Law Digest; officially published documents affecting the Code of Canon Law.* Milwaukee, Bruce Publishing Co., 1934–

Brennan, Anthony. *Pope Benedict XV and the War.* 2nd ed. London, P. S. King & Son, 1918.

Carlen, Sister Mary Claudia. *A Guide to the Encyclicals of the Roman Pontiffs from Leo XIII to the Present Day, 1878–1937.* New York, H. W. Wilson Co., 1939.

Catholic Action. Encyclical Letter of His Holiness, Pope Pius XI. Washington, National Catholic Welfare Conference, 1931.

The Catholic Priesthood. (Ad Catholici Sacerdotii.) New York, America Press, [1936].

Catholicism in Mexico. (The Encyclical Firmissimam Constantiam.) London, Catholic Truth Society, 1938.

The Church in Germany. Encyclical Letter of His Holiness, Pope Pius XI. Washington, National Catholic Welfare Conference, 1937.

Clonmore, Lord. *Pope Pius XI and World Peace — an authentic biography.* . . . London, The Catholic Book Club, [1938].

Colleción de Encíclicas y Otras Cartas de los Papas Gregorio XVI, León XIII, Pío X, Benedicto XV y Pío XI, con otros documentos episcopales y de máxima autoridad sobre doctrina política, social, educación-familia y acción católica, compiladas, anotadas y ordenados sus conceptos en un índice alfabético. Madrid, Imp. "Sáes hermanos," 1935.

Discorsi e Radiomessaggi di Sua Santità Pio XII. 2v. Milano, Società editrice "Vita e Pensiero," 1941.

Eckhardt, Carl Conrad. *The Papacy and World Affairs, as Reflected in the Secularization of Politics.* Chicago, University of Chicago Press, [1937].

The Encyclicals of Pius XI; introduction and translation by James H. Ryan. St. Louis, B. Herder, 1927.

Encyclical on Spain, (Dilectissima Nobis); and, To the Spanish Refugees, (Discourse of Sept. 14, 1936). New York, America Press, [1937].

Eppstein, John. *The Catholic Tradition of the Law of Nations.* Washington, Catholic Association for International Peace, 1935.

Foundations for Peace. Letters of Pope Pius XII and President Roosevelt. London, Catholic Truth Society, [1940].

Fülöp-Miller, René. *Leo XIII and Our Times.* . . . London, Longmans, Green & Co., 1937.

Furey, Francis T. *Life of Leo XIII and History of His Pontificate.* New York, Catholic Educational Company, 1903.

Gasparri, Petrus, cardinal, ed. *Codicis iuris canonici fontes.* vol. 3. Romae, Typis polyglottis Vaticanis, 1932–1933.

The Great Encyclical Letters of Pope Leo XIII. With preface by Rev. John J. Wynne, S.J. New York, Benziger Brothers, 1903.

Gwynn, Denis. *The Vatican and War in Europe.* London, Burns, Oates and Washbourne, [1940].

Hayes, Carlton J. H. *Political and Cultural History of Modern Europe.* 2v. New York, Macmillan, 1932–1936.

La Hiérarchie Catholique et le Problème Social depuis l'Encyclique "Rerum Novarum," 1891–1931. Ed. "Union Internationale d'Etudes Sociales fondée à Malines." Paris, Ed. Spes, 1931.

Holls, Frederick W. *The Peace Conference at the Hague and Its Bearings on International Law and Policy.* New York, Macmillan, 1900.

The Holy Ghost and the Sacred Heart. The Encyclicals "Divinum Illud" and "Annum Sacrum." London, Catholic Truth Society, [1938].

How the Roman Question Was Settled. London, Catholic Truth Society, [1929?].

Hughes, Philip. *Pope Pius the Eleventh.* New York, Sheed & Ward, 1938.

Husslein, Joseph C. *Social Wellsprings.* 2v. Milwaukee, Bruce Publishing Co., 1940–1942.

Jarlot, Georges, ed. *De principiis ethicae socialis; documenta ultimorum Romanorum Pontificum.* Romae, Pontificia universitas Gregoriana, 1932. vol. 1. (Textus et documenta; series philosophica, n.3.)

Keller, Joseph E. *The Life and Acts of Pope Leo XIII. Preceded by a sketch of the last days of Pius IX and the origin and laws of the Conclave.* New and enlarged edition with supplementary chapters containing the latest and most interesting events of the Holy Father's pontificate up to the end of July, 1887. New York, Benziger Brothers, 1889.

The Kingship of Christ. The Encyclical "Quas Primas." London, Catholic Truth Society, [1938].

La Brière, Yves de. *La Patrie et la Paix; textes pontificaux traduits*

823

et commentés par Yves de la Brière, S.J. et P. M. Colbach, S.J.
Paris, Desclée de Brouwer, 1938.

Lama, Friedrich von. *Papst und Kurie in ihrer Politik nach dem Weltkrieg, dargestellt unter besonderer Berücksichtigung des Verhältnisses zwischen dem Vatikan und Deutschland.* Illertissen (Bayern), Martinusbuchhandlung, 1925.

Lettres Apostoliques de S.S. Pie X; encycliques, motu proprio, brefs, allocutions, etc. Texte latin avec française en regard, précédées d'une notice biographique, suivies d'une table générale alphabétique. 8v. Paris, Bonne Presse, 1930–1936.

The Light of Truth. Concerning the Celebration of the Fifteenth Centenary of the Oecumenical Council of Ephesus. Washington, National Catholic Welfare Conference, 1932.

Loeffler, James D. *Directives for Catholic Action, expounded by Pope Pius XI.* St. Louis, Central Bureau Press, 1938.

Lo Grasso, Giovanni B. *Ecclesia et Status. De mutuis officiis et juribus fontes selecti.* Romae, Apud aedes universitatis Gregorianae, 1939.

McCarthy, Justin. *Pope Leo XIII.* New York, Frederick Warne & Co., [1896].

The Mexican Persecution. The Encyclical "Acerba Animi." London, Catholic Truth Society, [1932].

Migne, Jacques Paul. *Patrologiae cursus completus. Series Graeca.* 162v. Parisiis, J. P. Migne, 1857–1866. *(P.G.)*

Migne, Jacques Paul. *Patrologiae cursus completus. Series Latina.* 217v. Parisiis, J. P. Migne, 1844–1855. *(P.L.)*

Miscellanea Agostiniana; testi e studi, pubblicati a cura dell'Ordine Eremitano di S. Agostino nel xv centenario dalla morte del santo dottore. . . . 2v. Roma, Tipografia poliglotta Vaticana, 1930–1931.

Müller, Joseph. *Das Friedenswerk der Kirche in den letzten drei Jahrhunderten. v.1: Die Friedensvermittlungen und Schiedssprüche des Vatikans bis zum Weltkriege, 1917. Sammlung ausgewählter Aktenstücke über die Friedenstätigkeit des Heiligen Stuhles.* Berlin, Deutsche Verlagsgesellschaft für Politik und Geschichte, 1927.

Oakeshott, Michael. *Social and Political Doctrines of Contemporary Europe.* Cambridge, University Press, 1939.

On the Economic Crisis, Unemployment and Increase of Arma-

ments. The Encyclical "Nova Impendet." London, Catholic Truth Society, [1938].

On the Recitation of the Rosary to Combat Modern World Evils. Washington, National Catholic Welfare Conference, 1937.

L'Opera della Santa Sede nella Guerra Europea. Raccolta di documenti (Agosto, 1914–Luglio, 1916). Roma, Tipografia poliglotta Vaticana, 1916.

O'Reilly, Bernard. *Life of Leo XIII. From an Authentic Memoir Furnished by His Order. Written with the encouragement and approbation and blessing of His Holiness the Pope. The complete life of the Venerable Father.* London, Sampson, Low, Marston & Co., 1903.

Pacelli, Eugenio. *Discorsi e Panegirici. Seconda ed. con l'aggiunta di nuovi discorsi e panegirici (1931–1938).* Milano, Società editrice "Vita e Pensiero," 1939.

Packard, Reynolds. *Balcony Empire. Fascist Italy at war.* New York, Oxford University Press, 1942.

The Persecution of the Catholic Church in the Third Reich; facts and documents translated from the German. New York, Longmans, Green & Co., 1940.

Pius XII and Peace, 1939–1940. Washington, National Catholic Welfare Conference, 1940.

The Pope and the People; select letters and addresses on social questions by Pope Leo XIII, Pope Pius X, Pope Benedict XV, and Pope Pius XI. London, Catholic Truth Society, 1932.

The Pope on the Spanish Terror. The speech delivered by Pope Pius XI to bishops, priests, nuns and laity, refugees from Spain . . . on Monday, September 14, 1936. London, Catholic Truth Society, [1936].

The Pope Speaks: the words of Pius XII, with a biography by Charles Rankin. New York, Harcourt, Brace & Co., [1940].

The Pope's Five Peace-points. Allocution to the College of Cardinals by His Holiness, Pope Pius XII, on December 24, 1939. London, Catholic Truth Society, [1940].

Premoli, Orazio M. *Contemporary Church History (1900–1925).* London, Burns, Oates & Washbourne, 1932.

The Promotion of True Religious Unity. Washington, National Catholic Welfare Conference, 1928.

Rome Hath Spoken: papal pronouncements on the Third Order Secular of St. Francis. Chicago, Franciscan Herald Press, 1932.

Rope, Henry E. G. *Benedict XV, the Pope of Peace.* London, John Figgord, [1941].

Rouët de Journel, M. J. *Enchiridion patristicum.* Ed. quarta et quinta. St. Louis, B. Herder, 1922.

Ryan, John A. *The State and the Church.* New York, Macmillan, 1922.

The Sacred Heart and World Distress. . . . Encyclical Letter (Caritate Christi Compulsi). Washington, National Catholic Welfare Conference, 1932.

Schaefer, Mary C. *A Papal Peace Mosaic, 1878–1936. Excerpts from the messages of Popes Leo XIII, Pius X, Benedict XV and Pius XI.* Washington, Catholic Association for International Peace, 1936.

Schmitz, E. *Life of Pius X.* New York, American Catholic Publication Society, [1907].

Selected Papal Encyclicals and Letters, 1928–1931. London, Catholic Truth Society, 1932.

Sixteen Encyclicals of His Holiness Pope Pius XI, 1926–1937. Washington, National Catholic Welfare Conference, 1937. (Without general title-page; title taken from cover).

Talbot, James F. *Pope Leo XIII. His Life and Letters.* Boston, etc., Gately & Co., [1886].

Thomas Aquinas, Saint. *Summa theologica.* 6v. Taurini (Italy), Marietti, 1928.

Treaty and Concordat between the Holy See and Italy. Official documents. Washington, National Catholic Welfare Conference, [1929?].

Two Basic Social Encyclicals: On the Condition of Workers, Leo XIII; and Forty Years After, On Reconstructing the Social Order, Pius XI. Latin text and English translation. New York, Benziger Bros., 1943.

Van den Heuvel, J. *The Statesmanship of Benedict XV.* Translated by J. C. Burns. New York, Benziger Bros., 1923.

Vistalli, Francesco. *Benedetto XV.* Roma, Tipografia poliglotta Vaticana, 1928.

Wright, John J. *National Patriotism in Papal Teaching.* Boston, The Stratford Co., [1942].

Wright, Quincy. *A Study of War.* 2v. Chicago, University of Chicago Press, [1942].

PERIODICALS, NEWSPAPERS, ETC.

Acta Ordinis Fratrum Minorum. Claras Aquas (Quaracchi, Italy), 1882–

America; a Catholic Review of the Week. New York, 1909–

The American Catholic Quarterly Review. Philadelphia, 1876–1924.

American Ecclesiastical Review. Philadelphia, 1889–

Annuario Pontificio. Roma, Tipografia poliglotta Vaticana, 1912–

Australasian Catholic Record. Springwood, Australia, St. Columba's College, 1924–

Catholic Action . . . a National Monthly; official organ of the National Catholic Welfare Conference. Washington, 1919–

Catholic Herald. London.

The Catholic Messenger. Davenport, Ia., 1882–

The Catholic Mind. New York, 1903–

The Catholic University Bulletin. Washington, 1895–

La Civiltà Cattolica. Rome, 1850–

Documentation Catholique. Paris, 1919–

Dublin Review. London, 1836–

L'École Sociale Populaire. Publication Mensuelle. Montreal, 1911–

English Catholic Newsletter. London, 1939–

International Conciliation. New York, Carnegie Endowment for International Peace, 1935–

International Correspondence. An interpretative news service for clarification of spiritual issues. New York, Center of Information pro Deo, 1942–

Irish Ecclesiastical Record. Dublin, 1864–

Il Monitore Ecclesiastico. Rome, 1876–

National Catholic Welfare Conference News Service. Washington.

The New World; Chicago's official Catholic paper. Chicago, 1893–

Revue des Deux Mondes. Paris, 1829–

Rome. A weekly record of everything worth knowing about the Eternal City. Rome, Palazzo Taverna, 1907–1917.

The Sword of the Spirit. Bulletin. London, 1940–

The Tablet. London, 1840–

INDEX OF SUBJECTS AND NAMES

[Numbers refer to Paragraphs]

Associations *(continued)*
for farmers, 942, 955, 1253, 1467, 1679
for the middle class, 1679
for workers, 947, 948, 950-52, 1000, 1041, 1253, 1467, 1675
for workers and employers, 947, 1001
freedom in, 997, 1000
interest of clergy in workers', 951
natural right to form, 948, 955
professional and interprofessional, 1243, 1675
relations of small and large, 991
State interference in, 1002
See also Corporative order, Guilds, Trade-unions

Atheism
and economic crisis, 1080
and peace, 1082
Church opposed by militant, 1282, 1783
moral resistance of Catholics to, 1662
reason for Spanish Civil War, 1330
source of many evils, 1276
spread of, 1079, 1199, 1708

Athleticism, opposed to true physical training, 906
Au Milieu des Sollicitudes, 176, 654
Au Milieu de Vos Angoisses, 393
Au Moment, 1558
Au Moment Ou Votre Excellence, 1627
Audistis, Venerabiles Fratres, 1460
Augurio, 1364
Auguste Pontife, 1115

Augustine, St.
on apostolate of laity, 1442
on brotherly love, 795
on charity, 469
on the Church, 673, 1455, 1521
on error, 1753
on material possessions, 779
on music, 1545, 1547
on peace, 662, 679, 1316, 1321, 1365, 1459, 1521, 1565
on the teachings of Christ, 7
on use of prosperity, 1660
on wars, 1593

Augustus Caesar, peace of, 1500
Auspicandae Celebritatis, 221

Australia
congratulations upon Lateran Treaty from, 892
papal help for Italian prisoners in, 1638

Austria
grave troubles in postwar, 694, 706
intolerable condition of postwar, 706
letters of Benedict XV to bishops of, 564, 694
Papal Peace Note approved by bishops of, 564
persecution of Church in, 1301
sympathy of Benedict XV for postwar, 694, 706

Austria-Hungary
confiscation of *Palazzo di Venezia* belonging to, 462
consequences of the collapse of, 597, 624
in favor of a peace without indemnities, 546
letter of Cardinal Gasparri to Ambassador of, 315
papal solicitude for captured soldiers of, 447
plea of Benedict XV to Emperor of, 383
telegram of Benedict to Emperor of, 312
territorial questions with Italy, 529, 597
See also Austria, Hungary

Authority
and liberty, 861, 1112, 1227
Catholic principles of taught by Catholic Action, 1595
Church as supporter of, 861
civil, 1414, 1415
coercive powers of, 1223
Communistic idea of, 1204
disregard for, cause of war, 282, 286
duties of public, 1685
duty to resist unjust, 115
false basis of, 781
fear of God as foundation of, 908
God as author of, 52, 114, 246, 792, 863, 1022, 1414, 1449
lack of respect for, 781, 792, 1463
limitations of power in public, 1685

[Numbers refer to Paragraphs]

Bolshevism
strict interpretation of dialectical materialism, 1203
worst manifestation of Communism, 1201
See also Communism
Bombardment of open cities condemned, 383, 436, 450, 1539
Boniface, St., encyclical on twelfth centenary of, 630
Bonum Sane, 685
Borromeo, Charles, St., 907
Boundaries
charity not restricted by national, 1147
controversies concerning, 241
moral patrimony of humanity not restricted by, 1574
recognition by Church of legitimate revision of, 597
See also Territorial disputes
Bourne, Francis Cardinal, Archbishop of Westminster
letter of Pius XI to, 751
letters of Cardinal Gasparri to, 299, 646
Boycott as a sanction against violated agreements, 541, 549
Brazil
abolition of slavery in, 88
address of Pius XII to Eucharistic Congress in, 1811
letter of Leo XIII to bishops of, 88
letter of Pius XI to bishops of, 1143
papal arbitration in, 241, 260
Brotherhood of man
doctrine of the Church, 92, 206, 224, 234, 280, 283, 435, 475, 503, 520, 634, 644, 679, 719, 751, 875, 913, 1077, 1101, 1145, 1228, 1229, 1376, 1412, 1413, 1493, 1515, 1516, 1585, 1649, 1656, 1728, 1730, 1763
exaggerated nationalism opposed to, 1105
necessary for peace, 640, 749, 1672
new, 1824
nourished by Christian charity, 1105
See also Fraternity
Brussels, economic conference in, 757
Bucovina, care of Holy See for refugees from, 434

Buenos Aires
address of Pius XI to Eucharistic Congress in, 1119
letter of Pius XI to Archbishop of, 923
Business, evil practices of corporate, 1033
Byzantine clergy, address of Pius XII to Rumanian, 1528

Canada
address of Pius XI to Eucharistic Congress in, 1292
desire of Pius XI for continued peace in, 1292
duty of bishops to restore harmony in, 468, 584
duty of priests to learn two languages in, 472, 584
language disputes among Catholics in, 465, 583
letter of Cardinal Maglione to Social Week of, 1370
letters of Benedict XV to bishops of, 464, 583
papal help for Italian prisoners in, 1638
papal peace efforts supported by Catholics of, 593
Capital
and labor, 135, 811, 919, 970, 1006, 1522
exorbitant claims of, 971, 1006
exploitation of private, 1840
individual and social character of, 1014
Capitalism
changes in, 1009
spread of, 1008
Captives. *See* Prisoners
Cardinals, College of
allocutions, addresses of Benedict XV to, 308, 321, 412, 418, 494, 495, 554, 603, 615, 635, 655, 700, 701, 711, 715, 725
allocutions, addresses of Leo XIII to, 71, 103, 186, 210, 221, 223
allocutions, addresses of Pius X to, 240, 271
allocutions, addresses of Pius XI to, 757, 826, 854, 856, 860, 866, 884, 913, 1059, 1100, 1105, 1116, 1120, 1124, 1144, 1148, 1278, 1302

[Numbers refer to Paragraphs]

Cardinals, College of *(continued)*
  allocutions, addresses of Pius XII to, 1313, 1342, 1489, 1529, 1562, 1636, 1696, 1731, 1802
Cari Combattenti, 1138
Caritate Christi Compulsi, 1074, 1098, 1199, 1256, 1258
Caritatis, 190
Carnegie Endowment for International Peace, praise of Pius X for, 265
Caroline Islands
  adjustment by Leo XIII of dispute concerning, 68, 78
  civilized by Spaniards, 75
  Leo XIII as arbitrator in question of, 48, 72
  proposal of Leo XIII concerning, 48
Castel Gandolfo, address of Pius XII to an audience from, 1459
Catherine of Siena, St., sermon of Pius XII on, 1555
Catholic Action
  address of Pius XI to 400 teachers in, 1294
  address of Pius XII to feminine Italian, 1599
  address of Pius XII to Italian, 1594, 1813
  address of Pius XII to Italian university students in, 1669
  allocution of Pius XI to Italian, 967n.
  and economic question, 868, 1003, 1039
  and love of country, 1597
  and peace, 451, 880, 881, 915, 923, 1143, 1270, 1271
  attacks upon, 1050, 1306, 1307
  deep interest of Pius XI in, 807, 880, 1251, 1306
  duties of, 248
  encyclical of Pius X on Italian, 242
  encyclical of Pius XI on, 1049
  exhortation of Pius XII for more, 1474
  field of, 614, 881, 1270
  hope of Pius XII for future, 1596
  in China, 880
  in Italy, 1306
  in Mexico, 1270, 1271
  letter of Pius XI to bishops of Brazil on, 1143

Catholic Action *(continued)*
  militant leaders of, 1252
  nature of, 247
  politics excluded from, 1003, 1143, 1270, 1306, 1597
  praised by Pius XII, 1440, 1595
  purpose of, 923, 1270
  social apostolate, 1251
  welfare of State fostered by, 881
Catholic Central Verein of America, letter of Cardinal Gasparri to, 638
Catholic Church. *See* Church, Catholic
Catholic social doctrine
  aid to internal peace of a nation, 1528
  enemies of, 1212
  further developed by clergy and laity, 937
  held suspect by some Catholics, 933
  influence of outside the Church, 939, 946
  inspired by *Rerum Novarum,* 1679
  means of propagating, 938
  necessity of practicing, 451, 1014, 1232
  necessity of teaching, 291
  on guilds, industries, and professions, 997
  on problem of classes, 1360
  opponent of Communistic ideology, 1232
  promotion of a wider study of, 1244
  superiority of, 1228
  a true science, 938
  value of, 1228
Catholic University of America, fiftieth anniversary of, 1471
Catholics
  Catholic social doctrine held suspect by some, 933, 948
  concord among, 584
  duties of as citizens, 109, 249
  good citizenship common among, 13, 907
  interest of in social question, 926
  necessity for unity among, 1084, 1255
  of all nations bound by mutual love, 404
  persecuted in Germany, 12
  persecuted in Russia, 20
  strongest supporters of order, 201
Causa Nobis Quidem, 715

[*Numbers refer to Paragraphs*]

Cecil, Robert, and conscription, 550

Cecilia, St., address of Pius XII to Royal Academy of, 1545

Celeberrima Evenisse Sollemnia, 654

Cenacle, address of Pius XII to Religious of, 1541

Central Europe

collection for starving children in, 652

difficulties in, 834, 854

famine in, 646, 650, 854

papal relief for starving children in, 653

Central Lithuanian Committee, message of to Benedict XV, 499

Central Verein. *See* Catholic Central Verein of America

Certiores Quotidie, 337

C'Est avec Couleurs Bien Sombres, 338

C'Est avec la Plus Vive Complaisance, 626

C'Est avec un Intérêt, 277

C'Est avec un Vif Sentiment, 1326

C'Est une Vive Satisfaction, 1382

Chaplains

apostolate of, 1481, 1482, 1485

courage of, 1483

efforts of to bring tranquillity to souls, 1486

exhortation of Pius XII to, 1479

extraordinary faculties for, 360, 1480

good example as duty of, 1483

models of obedience to authority, 1482

sacrifices of, 1480, 1482, 1484, 1486

Charity

all men everywhere embraced by, 1825

and justice, foundation of peace, 105, 268, 734, 757, 758, 876, 1338, 1390, 1498, 1549, 1593, 1774

basis of peace, 283, 285, 404, 612, 662, 674, 852, 1237, 1383, 1413, 1533, 1576

brotherhood of man nourished by, 1105

Catholic principles of taught by Catholic Action, 1595

Christian faith as foundation of, 1474

Church as depository of, 1161

compendium of Christian ideal, 1497

decadence of spirit of, 1704

different from state benevolence, 143

Charity *(continued)*

distinctive note of Benedict XV, 1056

during World War II, 1634

duty of, 279

duty of private to relieve public poverty, 47

duty of public to relieve private poverty, 47

early Christians' example of, 142, 667, 1236

equal distribution of goods demanded by, 1464, 1683

essence of Christian life, 665

false, 1238

forgotten by modern world, 237, 1533

German bishops distinguished by works of, 475

in the Gospel, 1438

individuals and nations obliged by same law of, 675

infusion of into socio-economic order, 1225

inspiration of governments, 858

justice and social, 834, 838, 1238, 1243

law of universal, 1528

left by Christ as mandate, 1600

mission of the popes, 317, 383, 385, 437, 719, 729, 738, 746, 753

motive of papal peace action, 664

natural ideal of, 1644

nature of, 1236

no distinction of religion, nationality, or language made by, 307, 490, 519, 615, 695, 751, 1766

not a veil for injustice, 926, 1238

obligations of during war, 730, 1454, 1528, 1671

obligations of towards the poor, 137, 1532

of St. Boniface embraced all nations, 631

peace conferences in vain without, 635, 637, 662

perfect balance between justice and, 1623

proper to the Church, 673

remedy for envy, 1413

remedy for hatred, 632, 662, 1147, 1191, 1413

remedy for war, 496, 632

[Numbers refer to Paragraphs]

Charity *(continued)*

right order based on justice and, 1775

solution of problems of race and nationality, 469, 1147

soul of social order, 998

special duty of Catholics, 641

special duty of clergy, 1494

universal law of, 519, 636

works of, 1773

world reconstruction based on justice and, 1453

See also Love

Charlotte, Grand Duchess of Luxembourg, message of Pius XII to, 1560

Chesnelong, Charles, letter of Leo XIII to, 117

Chesnelong, Jean, Archbishop of Sens, letter of Cardinal Gasparri to, 543

Child labor condemned, 155

Children

appeals of Benedict XV for starving, 650, 661, 695

appeals of Pius XII for starving, 1634

as workers, 155, 946, 984

asked by Pius XII to pray for peace, 1334, 1340, 1348, 1551, 1634, 1667, 1772

asked to receive Holy Communion for Holy Father, 457, 459, 479

atheism among, 1078

encyclical on the, victims of the war, 695

not mere creatures of the State, 900

papal alms for starving, 653, 699, 912

plight of after war, 671, 695, 703, 763

plight of in war, 440, 486, 1387, 1493, 1539, 1554, 1616, 1621, 1633, 1651, 1705, 1818, 1861

relief for starving Belgian children from American, 488

Socialistic propaganda for, 1024

starvation of Belgian, 486

starvation of in Central Europe, 646, 650, 661, 695

Chile

address of Pius XII to Eucharistic Congress in, 1728

address of Pius XII to new Ambassador of, 1506

dear to the heart of Pius XII, 1507

China

Catholic Action in, 880

Communism in, 1152

congratulations on Lateran Treaty from, 892

contribution of missions to peace of, 879

deep interest of Pius XI in, 877

letter of Pius XI to Vicars Apostolic of, 870

restoration of peace in, 877

Christ

and politics, 862

as King, 863, 887

author of peace, 425, 824, 1339, 1649

cross of, source of peace, 271

encyclical of Pius XI on kingship of, 862

the Gift of Peace, 310

the King, 1453, 1455, 1460, 1649

King of Peace, 107, 314, 413, 423, 474, 602, 623, 705, 864, 1059, 1320, 1501, 1570, 1600, 1620

Lord of Peace, 1316, 1500

mediator of peace, 1407, 1501

the Mystical Body of, 641, 999, 1038, 1151, 1221, 1362, 1413, 1701, 1702, 1735, 1814, 1818

of Andes as symbol of peace, 1525, 1728

our peace, 755, 787, 1316

peace in, 1650

peace of, 329, 559, 705, 786, 787, 789, 790, 791, 793, 797, 800, 803, 850, 887, 914-17, 1058, 1132, 1165, 1166, 1320, 1397, 1410, 1517, 1521, 1522, 1544

Peacemaker, 1520

Prince of Peace, 267, 274, 297, 308, 320, 413, 533, 556, 743, 757, 822, 859, 1138, 1165, 1315, 1339, 1384, 1445, 1493, 1499, 1500, 1511, 1602, 1620, 1731, 1733, 1795, 1843

restoration of mankind through, 1536, 1539

return of society to, 742, 748

sovereignty of, 214, 216, 226, 802

Christianity

so-called failure of, 1745

war against, 1747

[*Numbers refer to Paragraphs*]

[*Numbers refer to Paragraphs*]

[Numbers refer to Paragraphs]

[*Numbers refer to Paragraphs*]

Concordats *(continued)*
  willingness of Holy See to make, 725,
    1112, 1167
  with France, 46, 256
  with Germany, 1167, 1169, 1188
  with Italy, 1307, 1308
  with Rumania, 1724
Condonation of war costs and damages,
  527, 537, 546
Confederacy of mankind, 1539
Confidence. *See* Trust
Congregation of Extraordinary Ecclesiastical Affairs, decree of concerning
  treatment of war prisoners, 305
Congrès Démocratique International, telegram of Cardinal Gasparri to, 728
Congress of nations, 589
Conquered. *See* Vanquished
Conquerors. *See* Victors
Conquest
  instinct of curbed by Church, 212
  war of, 1134
Conscience
  freedom of. *See* Freedom of conscience
  rights of, 1425
Conscription
  boycott as penalty for reestablishment
    of, 549
  cause of many evils, 542, 551
  disarmament as a result of abandoning,
    550
  suppression of, 541, 549
Conspiracy
  abhorred by the Church, 26
  avoided by Catholics, 201
Conspirantibus Adversus, 564
Constantinople, disorder in, 756
Consultation. *See* Negotiation
Convocare Vos, 321
Corporations. *See* Associations,
  Corporative order
Corporative order
  description of, 1243
  in society, 1253
  not of itself sufficient for peace, 1370
  property restored by same, 1225
Corriere d'Italia, neutrality of, 311
Costantini, Celso, Archbishop, Apostolic
  Delegate to China, telegram of Car-
  dinal Gasparri to, 877

Country (fatherland)
  approval of Church for defense of, 98,
    110, 906, 1597, 1621, 1670
  approval of Church for independence
    of, 99
  love of, 111, 117, 263, 1077, 1098,
    1412, 1585, 1597, 1670, 1795
  neglect of duty towards one's, 1463
  promotion of temporal well-being of
    one's, 1812
Courage
  in defense of Christian civilization,
    1703
  not same as violence, 906
  obligation of chaplains to be models of,
    1483
Courts
  authority of, 1854
  practices of, 1853
Creditor nations
  duties of, 834
  guarantees for, 834, 843
  rights of, 834, 840
Crisis
  armed force no solution for, 82
  before World War II, 1375
  causes of the economic, 1057, 1074,
    1100
  duties of clergy in, 1250
  encyclical of Pius XI on economic, 1056
  Europe in, 587
  miseries of, 1104
  no merely human solution for, 1071
  of unemployment, 1318
  of World War II, 1577, 1772, 1803
  responsibility of State in, 1260
  spiritual, 1402
  universal extent of economic, 1075,
    1121
  war no solution for, 1750
Croatia, address of Pius XII to national
  pilgrimage from, 1474
Cruelties in war deplored by Benedict
  XV, 596
Crusade, new, 1842, 1863
Cruz-Ocampo, Luis, address of Pius XII
  to, 1506
Csernoch, Johann Cardinal, Archbishop of
  Strigonia, letters of Benedict XV to,
  403, 417, 552, 624

[*Numbers refer to Paragraphs*]

[Numbers refer to Paragraphs]

[*Numbers refer to Paragraphs*]

[Numbers refer to Paragraphs]

[Numbers refer to Paragraphs]

God *(continued)*

  and juridical order, 1853

  author of true peace, 574, 824, 916, 1049, 1090, 1140, 1332, 1365, 1500, 1527

  condemnation of German "believers" in, 1172

  foundation of peace, 1322

  hatred of, 1283

  heresy of a "national," 1173

  just wrath of, 439, 575, 1064, 1083

  man's absolute need of, 1083

  no peace without, 239, 561, 858, 1064, 1365

  of peace, 1132, 1316, 1331, 1446, 1646

  return to as basis of peace, 516, 557, 748

  right of man to worship, 1690

  source of law, 1463

  sovereign rights of, 1174, 1175, 1475

  Spirit of Peace, 584, 729, 828, 915

  war caused by denial of, 1648

  war on, 1107, 1109

Good will

  bond between nations, 675, 738

  Church teacher of, 795

  condition of peace, 281, 310, 596

  necessary for disarmament, 549

  necessary for solution of social question, 1792

Goods

  created by God for all men, 1464, 1683

  distribution of. *See* Distribution of goods

  peace and use of material, 1683

  right of man to use material, 1683-85, 1840, 1846

  unequal distribution of earthly, 292

Gosálvez, Gabriele, address of Pius XII to, 1350

Gospel, liberty in, 1463

Government

  and problem of social justice, 1719

  and refusal to recognize God, 781

  and unemployment, 1466

  Christian civilization results in good, 244

  Church indifferent to any just form of, 24, 53, 64, 92, 179, 597, 654, 766, 997, 1112, 1827

Government *(continued)*

  common good aim of, 54, 148, 179

  cooperation with Church duty of, 7

  divine basis of human, 794

  duty of obedience to, 22, 39, 47, 54, 112, 654, 879

  necessary for public order, 181

  not mere guardian of law, 943

  See also Civil Society, Nations, State

Grande Pensiero, 1372

Grandi, Diletti Figli, 1526

Grandissima Solennità, 1696

Gratias Vobis, 553

Gratissimum Hibernis, 585

Gratum Equidem, 278

Gratum Nobis, 826

Gratum Vehementer, 711

Graves de Communi, 937n.

Graves Equidem, 1144

Graves inter Amaritudines, 535

Gravissimo Officii Munere, 258

Grazie, Venerabili Fratelli, 1636

Greece, papal help for war prisoners from, 1638

Greed

  and class warfare, 1147

  cause of economic crisis, 1076, 1088

  cause of revolutions and war, 227

  evil results of, 1076

  prayer as cure for, 1088, 1667

  result of materialism, 1235

  under pretence of patriotism, 865

Gregory XVI and Poland, 588

Grigorcea, Basilio, address of Pius XII to, 1611

Guarantees

  difference between juridical and moral, 890, 891

  for creditor nations, 834, 843

  for Holy See, 889-92

  for new edifice among nations, 1655

  of conscience, 1091, 1258

Guibert, Joseph Cardinal, Archbishop of Paris, letter to, 22

Guilds

  benefits of medieval, 163

  destruction of medieval, 121

  free right of association in, 997

  influence of Church in, 1230

  modern revival of, 1230

Guilds *(continued)*
  natural to civil society, 994
  ridiculed by Liberalism, 1230
  See also Associations, Trade-unions
Guilty, punishment of limited by justice,
  1670
Guiñazú, Enrico, address of Pius XII to,
  1337
Gusmini, Giorgio Cardinal, Archbishop
  of Bologna
  letter of Benedict XV to, 561
  letter of Cardinal Gasparri to, 479

Hac Sollemni Hora, 1292
Haerent Animo, 403
Hague, International Peace Conference at
  The, 208, 210, 217, 221
Haiti
  boundary disputes of with Santo
  Domingo, 218
  letter of Benedict XV to bishops of, 458
Happiness, peace as source of true, 1365,
  1367
Harding, Warren, President of the United
  States, telegram of Benedict XV to,
  724
Harmony
  among nations, 1547, 1649, 1671,
  1732, 1761
  and the new order, 1737
  fraternal, 1545, 1667
  restoration of, 1810
Hartmann, Felix Cardinal von, Archbishop of Cologne
  and French priest war prisoners, 278,
  298, 302, 348
  letter of Cardinal Gasparri to, 594
  letters of Benedict XV to, 278, 404,
  535, 619
Hatred
  allayed by justice, 1615
  bitter fruits of, 1453
  bred by Communism, 1214, 1226
  cause of war, 389, 718, 1395, 1563
  charity as remedy for, 632, 662, 1147,
  1191, 1413
  Christians obliged to abstain from,
  1585
  common today, 1286
  confused ideas concerning, 1731

Hatred *(continued)*
  consequence of materialism, 783
  elimination of necessary for peace, 453,
  559, 634, 637, 640, 674, 1081, 1487,
  1552
  extinguished by Christ, 1622
  gigantic walls of, 1495
  mankind tortured by, 1788
  men blinded by, 1539
  nations divided by, 1644
  of Church, 1152, 1156, 1158, 1569
  of God, 1156, 1283
  of race common, 284
  product of selfish nationalism, 920,
  1077
  provoked by false propaganda, 1591,
  1644
  result of war, 407, 425, 509, 563, 607,
  640, 747, 764, 774, 784, 1576, 1762,
  1852
  ruin of mankind, 1586
  unsolved social question a cause of,
  1464
  victory over as condition for new
  order, 1644
  world consumed by, 1818
Hertling, Georg von, letter of to Archbishop Aversa, 504
Heure en Laquelle, 1611
Heureux Est pour Nous, 1391
Heylen, Thomas, Bishop of Namur, letter
  of Benedict XV to, 332, 376
Hinsley, Arthur Cardinal, Archbishop of
  Westminster
  letter of Pius XII to, 1808
  telegram of Cardinal Maglione to,
  1672
Hirohito, Emperor of Japan, message of
  Pius XII to, 1518
Hlond, August Cardinal, Archbishop of
  Gnesen
  address of Pius XII to, 1386
  letter of Pius XII to, 1800
Holland
  condemnation of invasion of, 1559
  desire of Pius XII for reestablishment
  of liberty in, 1559
  See also Wilhelmina, Queen of Holland
Holy Eucharist. *See* Eucharist

[*Numbers refer to Paragraphs*]

[Numbers refer to Paragraphs]

Justice *(continued)*

order impossible without, 1165, 1323
peace the work of, 403, 787, 876, 918, 1322, 1837
perfect balance between charity and, 1623
poor observance of, 1236
popes as defenders of, 578, 1198
promoted by Church, 27, 193, 199, 221, 624, 830, 1445
punishment of guilty limited by, 1670
re-establishment of, 1585
religious persecution a threat to, 1330
reparations determined by equity and, 1497
requirements of, 1323
restoration of, 1709
restriction of Holy See's liberty harmful to, 80
sense of, 1563, 1708
social. *See* Social justice
tempered by charity, 238, 734, 757, 758, 787, 876, 918, 1370, 1456, 1540
triumph of, 1742, 1801
violations of in business, 926
violence opposed to, 35, 1323
unchanging principles of, 607
wages an obligation in, 135, 158, 1238
world reconstruction based on charity and, 1453

Kakowski, Aleksander, Archbishop of Warsaw, letters of Benedict XV to, 568, 587, 716
Karevic, Francis, Bishop of Samogizia, letter of Cardinal Gasparri to, 498
Knights of Malta, address of Pius XII to, 1514
Koppes, Johann, Bishop of Luxembourg, letter of Cardinal Gasparri to, 397

Labor
and capital, 135, 811, 919, 970, 1006, 1522
and Liberalism, 1358
and management, 919
and ownership, 969
and production, 1088
as a right of workers, 1689, 1846

Labor *(continued)*

Christ's example of, 136
class warfare detrimental to, 765
code for, 1680
dignity of, 1224, 1229, 1850, 1851
economic system founded on ownership and, 1014
external calm in world of, 1839
freedom of organization for, 1675
limited right of State to interfere in, 1689, 1690
not a commodity, 994
proper conditions for, 154
purpose of, 1318
relation of property to, 970
rights of, 1224
social and personal nature of, 983, 1014
two essential characteristics of, 1688
Labor movement, scope of, 1839
Laborers. *See* Workers
Ladies of Charity of St. Vincent de Paul, address of Pius XII to, 1532
Ladies of Perpetual Adoration, address of Pius XII to, 1671
La Fontaine, Pietro, Archbishop of Venice
letter of Pius XI to, 848
letters of Benedict XV to, 478, 683
Laicism
false doctrine of, 1231
in Spain, 1331
Laity
collaboration of in apostolate of hierarchy, 1441-43
cooperation with clergy, 810
duty of obedience of to their bishops, 848
Land
flight from, 1463
life of family supported by, 1692
most proper object of private property, 1692
Language problem
and national minorities, 1759
cause of dissension, 708
Christian solution for, 283
duties of clergy in, 233, 472, 584, 710
duty of clergy to use vernacular, 710
in Belgium, 708
in Bohemia, 230

[Numbers refer to Paragraphs]

[*Numbers refer to Paragraphs*]

[Numbers refer to Paragraphs]

Military service
  compulsory. *See* Conscription
  legitimate schools for, 906
  public order maintained by voluntary,
    542, 550
  See also Armed force
Minorities
  no oppression of national, 1759
  real needs and just demands of racial,
    1497
Mirae Caritatis, 236
Miserentissimus Redemptor, 1199
Missioni e il Nazionalismo, 1293
Missions
  address of Pius XII at consecration of
    native bishops for, 1460
  alms for, 1604
  Catholic social doctrine in, 1039
  dispersal of in the Near East, 616
  effect of war on, 772, 1133, 1603
  exaggerated nationalism a curse to,
    1293
  in great peril, 700
  intervention in behalf of at Versailles,
    635
  liberty for, 879
  not in service of foreign nations, 870
  peace contributions of, 879, 1604
  proper regard for native civilization in,
    1409
  restoration of in the Near East, 618
  spread of despite war, 1816
  true apostolic nature of, 751
Mit Brennender Sorge, 1167
Modernism, condemned by Church, 812,
  964
Molti e Segnalati, 186
Mondragone, address of Pius XI to
  students from, 896
Money
  control of, 1010
  ownership of distinct from use of, 137
  squandering of public, 1057
  wasted in World War II, 1792
  See also Wealth
Montenegro, urged by Benedict XV to
  treat prisoners fairly, 298
Mora y del Rio, Joseph, Archbishop, telegram of Cardinal Merry del Val to,
  270

Morality
  and Christian reform, 934
  and economics, 960, 1034, 1093, 1217
  and peace treaties, 1754
  and politics, 1748
  and prosperity, 141
  and religion, 1083, 1182, 1183
  and social order, 1676
  and solution of current problems, 1369
  and State, 1858
  and Utilitarianism, 1720
  basis of, 1470
  Church as teacher of, 91, 1003
  definition of, 178
  divorce of law from, 1836
  double standard of, 1655
  necessity of for public welfare, 149
  necessity of returning to Christian, 1475
  new order based on, 1643, 1758-62
  no national peace without, 1701
  of war, 1565, 1637
  popes as guardians of, 452, 849
  reform of, 989, 1004, 1005
  rejection of universal norm of, 1398
  restoration of Christian, 1599
  tranquillity dependent on, 1183
  true civilization founded on Christian,
    1577
  undermined by materialism, 28
  utilitarian, 1416
  victory and principles of, 1721
Moravia. *See* Bohemia
Morganti, Pasquale, Archbishop of
  Ravenna, letter of Cardinal
  Gasparri to, 436
Mortalium Animos, 875
Mortification. *See* Penance
Mossa dal Pio Desiderio, 341
Mouraviev, Count of Russia
  first note of Cardinal Rampolla to, 202
  second note of Cardinal Rampolla to,
    207
Movies
  Communistic propaganda in, 1211
  means of spreading atheism, 1079
  reign of Christ over, 1601
Multiplices Quidem, 624
Mundelein, George, Archbishop of Chi-
  cago, letter of Cardinal Gasparri to,
  638

[Numbers refer to Paragraphs]

Nations *(continued)*

new organization of, 1806

obligated by divine law, 1642

obligation of mutual justice and charity among, 1098

one Church for all, 1177

origin of new, 725

peace among, 862, 869, 1104, 1105, 1228, 1319, 1331, 1332, 1340, 1353, 1368, 1371, 1413, 1431, 1498, 1539, 1546, 1548, 1556, 1557, 1604, 1622, 1650, 1699, 1714, 1761, 1763, 1767, 1794, 1819, 1820

perpetual state of war between, 1183

problems of at conclusion of World War II, 1637

proper concept of economic riches of, 1686, 1687

real needs and just demands of, 1497, 1653, 1821

reconciliation between, 675, 676

relations between. *See* International relations

religion indispensable for sound life of, 1724

respect for rights of small, 1758

restoration of by Christian social order, 200

restoration of justice and peace to, 1709

return of to Christian principles, 1067

rights of, 390, 1497, 1653, 1721

rivalries between, 763, 865

security of, 1384

sense of responsibility among, 1497

social peace and, 873

society of, 1830

solidarity among, 1655

sovereignty of, 1644

suspicion between, 1286

tranquillity of, 712, 1384

transformation of by World War II, 1640

union of, 1668

united destiny of, 1722

united in league, 597

united in name of Christ, 1745

unjust desires of, 858

utilitarianism not acceptable to weaker, 1644

Nations *(continued)*

value of emigration and immigration for, 1693

victims of false ideologies, 1636

See also Civil society, Creditor nations, Debtor nations, Government, State

Native tongue. *See* Language problem

Naturalism

as a cause of World War II, 1471

cause of public unrest, 200, 685

greatest plague in world, 685

Natural law

and education, 900, 1185

and neutrality of small nations, 1758

certain acts in World War II violation of, 1493

Church as guardian of, 1186

Communism contrary to, 1198

origin of, 89, 1183, 1215

necessary for individuals and for nations, 435

persecution of religion in contradiction to, 1184

relation of positive law to, 1183

Near East

disorder in, 756, 826, 855

famine in, 763, 855

missions in, 616, 618

new threats of war in, 763

papal solicitude for Christians of, 616

restoration of peace in, 756

See also Asia

Negotiation

honorable peace never precluded from sincere, 1377

necessary preparation for peace, 390, 413, 437, 1298, 1377, 1383

trust of Holy See in, 890

war upon abandoning principle of, 1382

Nei Tesori, 1669

Nel Grave Periodo, 587

Nel Mese di Luglio, 1585

Nell'Alba, 1739

Nella Schiera, 1557

Neutral nations, effects of war upon, 764

Neutrality

of Holy See, 311, 323, 414, 519, 580, 592, 713, 717, 885, 1382, 1642

of small nations, 1758

Newly-weds, addresses of Pius XII to,
1364, 1541, 1557, 1571, 1577, 1584,
1585, 1590, 1591, 1716, 1725
Newspapers. *See* Press
New Zealand
address of Pius XII to Eucharistic
Congress in, 1517
congratulations from on Lateran
Treaty, 892
Nicholas II, Czar of Russia, suggests
peace conference, 217, 221
Nicholas of Flue, Blessed, 1718
Nieuwenhuys, Adrian, address of Pius
XII to, 1382
Nina, Lorenzo Cardinal, letter of Leo
XIII to, 8
Nobilissima Gallorum Gens, 45, 898
Nobility of Rome. *See* Roman nobility
Nobis Quidem, 635, 700
Noi Potremmo, 1577
Non Abbiamo Bisogno, 1049
Non È Piccolo, 825
Non-Aryans, solicitude of Pius XII for,
1639
See also Jews
Noncombatants. *See* Civilians
Norunt Profecto, 1608
Nos Es Muy Conocida, 1266n.
Nostis Errorem, 103
Nostis Profecto, 412
Nostis Qua Praecipue, 860, 1199n.
Nostro, 886
Notizie, 719
Notizie Che, 883
Nous Ne Pouvons, 217
Nous Vous Remercions, 262
Nova Impendet, 1056, 1074
Nuovi Motivi, 478
Nuper Agnovimus, 1717
Nurses
and war, 1131
discourse of Pius XI to International
Congress of Catholic, 1131

O Dio di Bontà, 718
Obedience
Catholic principles of taught by
Catholic Action, 1595
Christian duty of, 863
duty of to bishops, 40

Obedience *(continued)*
duty of to government, 22, 39, 47, 54,
112, 654, 879
duty of to law, 16, 658, 881, 1323
obligation of bishops to teach, 26
taught by the family, 1793
unlawful when law is unjust, 93
Occupation
and sovereignty, 77
as guarantee for reparations, 834, 843
bitterness caused by postwar, 835
elimination of postwar, 834, 844
international agreements concerning,
1860
Occupational groups
associations for, 1243
unity of, 1225
See also Associations, Corporative
order, Guilds, Trade-unions
Occupied territories
and international law, 1567
duties of army in, 325, 1384
duties of authorities in, 1567, 1661
duties of inhabitants in, 325, 847
evacuation of, 528
norm for exercise of public power in,
1567
special questions concerning, 1568
October devotions, prayers for peace
during, 407
Octobri Mense, 1067n., 1773n.
Officiosissimis Litteris, 395
Opinionem Quam Habebamus, 330
Or È Più, 1516
Ora Grave, 1375
Ora Sono Pochi Mesi, 752
Order
and peace foundation of all good, 1139
basis of, 783
Catholic principles of taught by
Catholic Action, 1595
Catholics strongest supporters of, 201,
253, 601, 1113
Church as guardian of natural and
supernatural, 1827
corporative. *See* Corporative order
defense of public, 979
definition of, 995, 1829
disorder overcome only by, 1829
domestic, 1827

[*Numbers refer to Paragraphs*]

[Numbers refer to Paragraphs]

Peace (in general) *(continued)*

efforts of Pius XII to restore, 1313, 1345, 1349, 1368, 1373, 1380, 1383, 1477, 1478, 1511, 1549, 1563, 1608, 1614, 1615, 1649, 1654, 1658, 1672, 1723, 1733, 1790, 1809

elimination of hatred necessary for, 453, 559, 634, 637, 640

encyclical of Benedict XV on, 662

endowment of Christianity, 1514

equitable, 1547, 1789, 1790

essence of, 769, 921, 1828

external compared with internal, 1103, 1321, 1371

extreme nationalism dangerous to, 906, 920

factor in progress, 1413

factors of, 1355

failure of human efforts to restore, 1557

false, 792

firm and steady policy of, 1828

five points for, 1497, 1644, 1758, 1844

for Church, 1819

formulation of a new, 1755

foundation of public prosperity, 739

founded on justice and charity, 105, 187, 272, 404, 452, 494, 574, 787, 876, 877, 1310, 1325, 1332, 1338, 1383, 1390, 1498, 1499, 1549, 1593, 1774

friendly relations between Church and State a contribution to, 1474

friends of, 1511, 1513

fruits of, 692, 713, 876

frustrated and deluded, 1755

future, 1760

gift of, 308, 561, 662, 736, 742, 853, 1089, 1128, 1292, 1310, 1321, 1329, 1332, 1728, 1823

God as author of true, 574, 824, 916, 1049, 1090, 1140, 1332, 1365, 1500, 1527, 1540

God as foundation of, 1322

good will as condition of, 106, 281, 310, 596

Gospel of, 665, 1103, 1315, 1577

guarantees of, 731, 1121

harmony among men necessary for, 1546

Peace (in general) *(continued)*

help of friendly alliances to, 1310

honest, 1794

honorable, 521, 596, 663, 1368, 1384, 1385, 1488, 1497, 1503, 1562, 1565, 1640, 1653

hope for, 1562

hope of nations for return of, 1821

hunger and thirst for, 1446

impossible without Christianity, 227

impossible without social justice, 1331

in danger, 1344

in different nations. *See* nation in question

indispensable condition of social reconstruction, 742

indispensable presuppositions for, 1799

inestimable treasure, 893

institutions for establishment of, 1038

integral, 1828

intention of 1925 Holy Year, 857-60, 866, 869

intention of 1933 Holy Year, 1102-04, 1115, 1122

in liturgy, 836, 1090, 1557, 1823

in *Summa Theologica,* 788, 845, 918, 1828, 1837

in truth, justice, and charity of Christ, 1819

invitation of Pius XII to, 1310

joy of Benedict XV at return of, 662

just, 413, 495, 508, 519, 525, 535, 536, 543, 580, 587, 596, 600, 610, 612, 663, 1497, 1498, 1503, 1513, 1557, 1562, 1565, 1640, 1646, 1654, 1672, 1723, 1757, 1790

a kind of continued creation, 1607

lasting, 413, 476, 495, 519, 525, 529, 535, 536, 542, 543, 580, 596, 600, 610, 612, 662, 663, 711, 713, 788, 803, 858, 862, 876, 877, 886, 917, 1093, 1101, 1119, 1160, 1323, 1331, 1473, 1488, 1557, 1565, 1576, 1640, 1646, 1668, 1672, 1757, 1761, 1789, 1801

Lateran Treaty as contribution to, 887

liberty for Church condition of, 1444, 1445

little immediate hope for, 1511, 1654, 1790

Peace (religious) *(continued)*
  of God, 793, 916, 1068
  of hearts, 1334, 1528
  of soul, 786, 858, 1060, 1117, 1309
    1321, 1340, 1715
  of supernatural order of grace, 1740
  opposed to hatred and vengeance, 559,
    1081
  penance and mystery of, 1093
  possible in most difficult circumstances,
    561, 1049, 1572
  practice of charity necessary for, 1237
  prayer haven of, 1653
  prelude to eternal life, 718
  promised by Christ, 1603, 1826
  promoted by kindness, 658
  result of zeal, 1788
  sacrament of penance as fount of, 1321
  source of true happiness, 1365, 1367
  spiritual peace more important than
    political, 893
  through suffering, 1787
  value of penance for, 658
  vision of, 1657
  with Christ, 1823
  with God, 1367
  worldly possessions not source of, 776
Peace (social)
  aspiration of all nations, 873
  between capital and labor, 1522
  between social classes, 937, 1002
  by social reforms, 979
  desire of all men for, 1018
  desire of Pius XI for, 744
  destroyed by unequal distribution, 919
  destruction of, 1288
  family as sanctuary of, 767
  impossible without reform of minds,
    1288
  legislation and, 1840
  necessity of friendly collaboration among
    capital, management, and labor for,
    919
  of Christian society threatened, 196
  priests as ministers of, 1147
  private property as aid to, 1683
  restoration of, 1085
  saved from disorder, 1679
  social justice approach to, 1719
  unemployment as threat to, 987, 1318

Peace conference
  and Holy Places, 617
  at Brussels, 757
  at Genoa, 729, 733, 741, 757
  at Lausanne, 756, 1069
  difficult problems of, 600
  encyclical of Benedict XV on future,
    598
  intervention of Holy See in, 634
  papal support for just deliberations of,
    610
  prayers for, 601, 609
  wishes of Benedict XV for success of,
    608
Peace Note of Benedict XV. *See* Papal
    Peace Note of 1917
Peace treaties
  animated by justice and equity, 1434
  continuation of war spirit despite, 721
  maintained inviolate by justice, 193
  not real foundation of peace, 705, 711,
    721, 725, 774, 1093
  obtained by popes, 212, 218
  short-lived existence of, 1754
  sometimes founded on false principles,
    1754
  See also Treaties
Peacemakers
  bishops as, 750
  called blessed, 390
  Christ as greatest of, 1520
  St. Ambrose as one of, 1524
  spirit of, 1565
Pelletier, St. Euphrasia, homily of Pius
    XII in honor of, 1554
Pellizzo, Luigi, Bishop of Padua, telegram
    of Cardinal Gasparri to, 491
Penance
  and peace, 1093, 1094
  as cure for modern evils, 1248, 1824
  necessary to appease divine justice, 1773
  necessity of, 384, 386, 439, 460, 476,
    496, 534, 535, 658, 1086, 1385, 1609,
    1777, 1807
  sacrament of, 1321
  value of, 1092, 1773
Pentecost, discourse of Pius XII on, 1673
Peoples. *See* Nations
Peramantes Litterae, 1723
Pergratus Nobis, 1124

[*Numbers refer to Paragraphs*]

[*Numbers refer to Paragraphs*]

[Numbers refer to Paragraphs]

Race *(continued)*
   enfeeblement of, 1463
   individual character of each, 1409
   inspirations of blood and, 1181
   Italian propaganda on, 1294
   law of, 1120
   myth of blood and, 1176
   no distinction of in Christianity, 223,
     283, 751, 1147, 1462
   pagan worship of, 1172
   persecution because of, 1861
   problems of solved by charity, 469, 583
   unity of human, 1098, 1406, 1408,
     1409
Raczkiewicz, M., telegram of Pius XII to,
   1770
Radio
   Communistic use of, 1211
   means of attacking Church in
     Germany, 1187
   means of spreading atheism, 1079
   reign of Christ over, 1601
Rampolla del Tindaro, Mariano Cardinal
   first note of to Count Mouraviev, 202
   letter of Leo XIII to, 82
   letter of to Seventh World Peace
     Congress, 198
   second note of to Count Mouraviev,
     207
Rappresentanti in Terra, 897, 1025, 1221
Rationalism, influence of on economic life,
   1034
Ratti, Achille, Apostolic Visitor to Poland,
   571
Ravenna, sympathy of Benedict XV for,
   436
Reason, force of arms opposed by force of,
   1377
Rebellion
   avoided by Catholics, 201
   by violence, 54
   condemnation by Church of unjust,
     1269
   consequence of neglect of moral law,
     1463
   envy of wealth as cause of, 88
   ethics of, 18
   provoked by atheism, 1276
Reconciliation
   apostolate of, 825

Reconciliation *(continued)*
   as yet no hope of in World War II,
     1744
   between men, 733, 761, 1312
   between nations, 675, 676, 689, 714
   of minds, 1723, 1801
   with God as preparation for peace, 866
Reconstruction
   based on justice and charity, 1453
   charity and peaceful, 1824
   need for natural scientists in, 1815
   need of the moment, 1842
   of a new Europe, 1762
   of social order, 1695, 1763
   opportunities for, 1753
   program for social, 1831
   See also Economic reconstruction
Red Cross
   motto of, 730
   praised by Benedict XV, 333
Redditae Sunt Nobis, 539
Referendum, right of peace or war
   reserved to people by, 551
Reform
   Christianity as inspiration of true, 1178
   of morality, 989, 1004, 1005
   of social conditions, 940
Refugees
   charitable work of Pius XII for, 1639
   Holy Mass and prayers for, 1610
   interventions of Benedict XV in behalf
     of, 279, 434
   plight of, 1387, 1554, 1704, 1768, 1861
   prayers for, 1610, 1620, 1668, 1773,
     1798
   sympathy of Pius XII for, 1658, 1768
   unjust attacks upon, 1493
   Vatican Information Bureau concerning,
     1639
Religion
   and aid to State, 95, 199
   and morality, 1083, 1182, 1183
   and solution of current problems, 1369
   artificial substitute for, 1747
   bond of peace, 177, 257
   Catholic Church as guardian of, 81
   comforts of in war, 360
   Communistic idea of, 1216
   defense of, 178, 1085
   duty of good journalism to promote, 65

[Numbers refer to Paragraphs]

[Numbers refer to Paragraphs]

[*Numbers refer to Paragraphs*]

[*Numbers refer to Paragraphs*]

[Numbers refer to Paragraphs]

[Numbers refer to Paragraphs]

[*Numbers refer to Paragraphs*]

[*Numbers refer to Paragraphs*]

[*Numbers refer to Paragraphs*]

[*Numbers refer to Paragraphs*]

[Numbers refer to Paragraphs]

[*Numbers refer to Paragraphs*]